MODERN CANADIAN PLAYS

Other Books by Jerry Wasserman

Spectacle of Empire:
Marc Lescarbot's Theatre of Neptune in New France

Theatre and AutoBiography:
Writing and Performing Lives in Theory and Practice
  (with Sherrill Grace)

Twenty Years at Play: A New Play Centre Anthology

All available from Talonbooks

Modern
Canadian Plays

VOLUME 2
5th EDITION

Edited by
Jerry Wasserman

TALONBOOKS

Talonbooks

9259 Shaughnessy Street, Vancouver, British Columbia, Canada V6P 6R4

www.talonbooks.com

Third printing: 2021

Typeset in Frutiger and printed and bound in Canada
Printed on 30% post-consumer recycled paper
Typeset and cover design by Typesmith

Talonbooks acknowledges the financial support of the Canada Council for the Arts, the Government of Canada through the Canada Book Fund, and the Province of British Columbia through the British Columbia Arts Council and the Book Publishing Tax Credit.

LIBRARY AND ARCHIVES CANADA CATALOGUING IN PUBLICATION

Modern Canadian plays / edited by Jerry Wasserman. — 5th edition.

Includes bibliographical references. Issued in print and electronic formats.
ISBN 978-0-88922-679-1 (pbk. : v. 2).—ISBN 978-0-88922-739-2 (epub : v. 2)

1. Canadian drama (English)—20th century. 2. Canadian drama (English)—21st century. I. Wasserman, Jerry, 1945–, editor of compilation

PS8315.M63 2012   C812'.5408   C2012-903922-5
                                             C2012-903923-3

PREFACE

When Volume One of this fifth edition was published in 2012, I began by noting the significance of certain events and phenomena affecting Canada and the world since the fourth edition of *Modern Canadian Plays* appeared in 2000: the 9/11 attacks and their aftermath; the legalization of same-sex marriage in Canada; the nation's rapidly and radically changing demographics; the economic meltdown of 2008; the climate change crisis; the ascension of a Conservative federal government; the digital revolution. Plays emerge from within specific socio-historical milieus, and recent history is one of the primary filters through which we see the world – and see and read plays. We need to be aware of our filters and those of our artists. I argued that live performance was paradoxically more important than ever in the age of iPhones, Twitter, and YouTube, as a means of keeping us in touch – sometimes literally – with our culture, its stories, and each other. I also asserted the value of the traditional printed book in the form taken by *Modern Canadian Plays*. Our aim is to offer an efficient, functional toolkit for learning and teaching, reasonably priced, easily accessible, providing historical, biographical, and critical contexts, with wide, empty margins that allow for interactivity between reader and text that requires only a pencil or pen.

Nothing that has occurred in the year since Volume One appeared has made me think otherwise about any of these matters. The same fundamental principles apply here in Volume Two. The sixteen compelling plays in this volume, dating from 1988 to 2011, record a wide range of the theatrical stories that Canadian playwrights have told during the past quarter-century. The major difference between this volume and all its previous incarnations is that the broad swath of life, history, and experience it dramatizes can no longer accurately be said to come from the Great *White* North.

Anthologies are always only a particular selection of the genre being anthologized. An almost infinite number of Canadian play collections is possible, each based on a different set of purposes, tastes, and assumptions, all shaped by strong doses of the anthologist's subjectivity. Following the same criteria that have guided every previous version of this text, I have chosen plays that I believe work effectively on the stage, on the page, and in the classroom; intelligent, provocative works that have made an impact on audiences and critics in Canada and often abroad; plays worth reading and rereading, staging and restaging. I have also looked for gender balance, some regional distribution, and variation in subjects, styles, themes, and tones. Ethnic diversity was the key additional factor that kept asserting itself as I sought the combination of texts for this volume that met all those other criteria and most excited me. So many of the finest

Canadian plays of the past quarter-century tell intercultural stories generated from the multiplicity of backgrounds that make up what Guillermo Verdecchia, in his 1993 play *Fronteras Americanas*, eloquently calls "this Noah's ark of a nation."

One of the hardest things about putting together an anthology is deciding what *not* to include, and the wealth of recent Canadian drama made that task particularly onerous this time around. I could easily have contrived a second volume of twenty or twenty-five plays if the contingencies of publishing had allowed it. Still, I am thrilled to have been able to expand Volume Two from twelve plays in the previous edition to sixteen here, making a total of thirty-one plays in this fifth edition, up from twenty-four in the fourth. And I absolutely love the material in this book.

Five plays in this volume return from the fourth edition while eleven are entirely new to *Modern Canadian Plays*. Returning are Robert Lepage and Marie Brassard's *Polygraph*, a play that marked the fall of the Berlin Wall – one of the originary moments of our age – and the global ascension of Robert Lepage; Morris Panych's existential breakout comedy, *7 Stories*; Daniel MacIvor's classic examination of masculinity, *Never Swim Alone*; George F. Walker's bleakly hilarious *Problem Child*, the play that kicked off the triumphant second phase of his career; and Djanet Sears' *Harlem Duet*, her revisioning of *Othello* that has generated more scholarly responses than anything else in this volume. Here for the first time are Wendy Lill's Cape Breton love story, *The Glace Bay Miners' Museum*, which became a Genie Award–winning film; Rahul Varma's Montreal murder mystery of clashing ethnicities, *Counter Offence*; Ronnie Burkett's astonishing puppet play about AIDS, vampires, and Jesus on the Alberta prairie, *Street of Blood*; Joan MacLeod's powerful portrayal of female bullying, *The Shape of a Girl*; Robert Chafe's *Tempting Providence*, an elegant Newfoundland history play; Wajdi Mouawad's remarkable Lebanese-Québécois journey through civil war and family mysteries, *Scorched*, also an Oscar-nominated film (*Incendies*); Marcus Youssef, Guillermo Verdecchia, and Camyar Chai's scathing post-9/11 political satire, *The Adventures of Ali & Ali and the aXes of Evil*; Linda Griffiths's suffragist comedy, *Age of Arousal*; Theatre Replacement's unique reconceptualization of the audience-stage relationship, *BIOBOXES: Artifacting Human Experience*; Marie Clements's examination of history and photography through an Aboriginal lens, *The Edward Curtis Project*; and Ins Choi's phenomenally popular immigrant family play, *Kim's Convenience*. If these plays comprised a single theatrical season, it would be the most extraordinary season ever mounted in a Canadian theatre. Prepare yourself for a banquet – a delicious, enthralling smorgasbord of plays. Read them with your imagination wide open.

Once again this volume begins with a general introduction tracing my particular selective history of Canadian theatre over the past century or so to more or less the present day. This history presents a linear, evolutionary, nationalist-oriented genealogy – "regimented," in Alan Filewod's term – a schema that many of my fellow Canadian theatre historians reject.[1] Feel free to use parts of it, argue with it, or ignore it. Deregiment it as much as you like. I believe it represents a useful *version* of Canadian theatre history, one of the only such versions in print. Consider the introductions to each of the playwrights and plays in both this volume and Volume One as addenda to the general introduction and correctives to some of its omissions. Once again we include a lengthy bibliography of books on modern Canadian drama, plus critical material and a range of reviews specific to each playwright and play; many of the newspapers and reviewers cited in the bibliographies recur multiple times and invite critical examination of their own logic and aesthetics. New to this volume are production photos for two plays. Because of the unique ways in which the scripts of *Street of Blood* and *BIOBOXES* are tied to their original productions, we include illustrative photos to help readers understand the staging of these two plays. Production photos and YouTube video snippets of most of the other plays are available online.

This new edition of *Modern Canadian Plays*, vol. 2, would not have been possible without the provocation and inspiration of my students and colleagues in the Department of Theatre and Film and the Department of English at the University of British Columbia; my superb research assistants, Sarah Banting, Martha Herrera-Lasso Gonzalez, and Petra Klupkova; the UBC Dean of Arts office, which helped fund their research and mine; my excellent editor, Ann-Marie Metten; Greg Gibson, Les Smith, Erik Johnson, Chloë Filson, and all the Talon staff who helped with this book; Talonbooks' astute publishers, Kevin and Vicki Williams; and the love of my life, Sue Wasserman. Canadian theatre is made possible by thousands of men and women who are criminally underpaid and whose artistry and hard work often go unrecognized. This book is dedicated to them: the writers, actors, directors, designers, dramaturgs, stage managers, carpenters, publicists, and all their colleagues who toil for the love of theatre in Canada.

Jerry Wasserman
VANCOUVER, BRITISH COLUMBIA
JULY 2013

1   Alan Filewod, "Named in Passing: Deregimenting Canadian Theatre History." *Writing and Rewriting: National Theatre Histories*, ed. S.E. Wilmer (Iowa City: U of Iowa P, 2004): 106–26.

Running continually through the long and fascinating theatrical history and pre-history of Canada, Aboriginal performances reach back millennia. Canadian plays by European settlers date from as early as 1606 when Marc Lescarbot wrote *Le Théâtre de Neptune en la Nouvelle-France* and staged it in Mi'kmaq war canoes to honour the arrival of a French ship at Port Royal in the future Nova Scotia. Playwriting in Canada in English dates back to the late 1700s, and nineteenth-century Canadian playhouses sprang up in substantial numbers, mostly to accommodate American and British touring companies.[1] The first half of the twentieth century saw the development of a thriving amateur-theatre movement, the best radio drama on the continent, and the emergence of a handful of noteworthy playwrights. But as late as 1945, there were no Canadian professional theatre companies. In 1959, the foremost theatre critic in the country wrote, "there is not in Canada a single person who earns a living as a playwright, or who has any practical hope of doing so."[2] A 1965 report on "Trends in Canadian Theatre" omits any mention of the role of Canadian plays or playwrights.[3]

Canadian theatre as an indigenous professional institution dates only as far back as the end of World War Two. English-Canadian drama, as a body of dramatic work by Canadian playwrights written for performance in professional theatres, is a more recent development still. Modern drama in Quebec had its inception with Gratien Gélinas's *Tit-Coq* in 1948. For English Canada, the key date was 1967: Centennial Year, the year of Expo 67, and of the first (and last) all-Canadian Dominion Drama Festival (DDF). Over the course of that year, amateur companies presented sixty-two Canadian plays in French and English in the DDF competitions, twenty-nine performed for the first time. A play from Quebec, Robert Gurik's *Le Pendu*, took all the major awards.[4] More important was the success of the new plays given professional productions from coast to coast as part of the Centennial celebrations: Gélinas's *Yesterday the Children Were Dancing* in English translation at Prince Edward Island's Charlottetown Festival, James Reaney's *Colours in the Dark* at the Stratford Festival in Ontario, Ann Henry's *Lulu Street* in Winnipeg, John Coulter's *The Trial of Louis Riel* in Regina, George Ryga's *The Ecstasy of Rita Joe* in Vancouver. All across the country, audiences and critics, buoyed by a new national self-consciousness, were taking note of this latest cultural phenomenon – plays by Canadian playwrights, performed by Canadian actors in Canadian theatres. A Canadian play, John Herbert's *Fortune and Men's Eyes*, was even a major hit in New York.

These events and the subsequent explosion of Canadian drama over the next decade seem in retrospect products of a particular historical moment, like the new European theatre that appeared in the 1870s, the new American theatre of the 1920s, and the British theatrical renaissance of the mid-1950s. Yet all these movements were culminations of social and cultural forces that had been gathering momentum for many years. In the case of Canadian theatre, the revolution of 1967 was rooted in an evolutionary process that had begun much earlier but accelerated significantly around the time of World War One.[5]

The Canadian stage at the turn of the century was, in Alan Filewod's words, "a branch-plant extension of the novel American discovery that if theatre was business, then it could be big business ... By 1910 almost every playhouse in Canada was owned directly [by] or contractually locked into the American theatrical syndicates ..."[6] Those syndicates offered Canadian playgoers a predictable commercial product delivered by imported talent – American plays with American players. As an alternative, and an antidote to the Americanism with which many Canadians still attached to the British Empire felt uncomfortable, Canada's theatrical pioneers turned to trans-Atlantic models. In the first decade of the century, Toronto's Arts and Letters Club Players presented contemporary works from the world repertoire. They were inspired by the vogue of European art theatres, especially the Irish Abbey Theatre, which would be cited time and again as a positive model for Canadians. Another paradigm was the British model of high art infused with the ideal of a National Theatre. As the notion of an indigenous Canadian theatre began to come into focus, one thing was clear: it would need its own dramatists. "There are no signs as yet upon our literary horizon of the arrival of our dramatist," a writer for the *Canadian Magazine* declared poignantly in 1914, "but we are waiting expectantly, for we feel that he should soon come now."[7] Cultural mandarin Vincent Massey was more assertive: "if we are to have a Canadian drama we must have a Canadian theatre in which to produce it."[8]

Canadian theatres gradually began to appear: the Ottawa Drama League and University of Toronto Players Club (both 1913), the University of British Columbia Players Club (1915). With the end of the Great War in 1918, an enhanced sense of national confidence carried over into theatrical development. In 1919, Vincent Massey opened Hart House Theatre, a state-of-the-art facility meant to accommodate Toronto's most talented actors, designers, and directors, dedicated to doing plays which would otherwise have gone unproduced in that city, including plays written by Canadians. Encouraged by this policy, enough dramatists did arrive to fill two modest volumes of *Canadian Plays from Hart House Theatre* (1926–27), edited by Massey. Foremost among them was Merrill Denison. His Hart House successes, especially the satirical comedy "Brothers in Arms," along with his published collections of stage plays, *The Unheroic North* (1923), and radio dramas, *Henry Hudson and Other Plays* (1931), established him as Canada's first major dramatist. Unable to make a living as a playwright in Canada, Denison moved to the United States in 1931 to write for American radio, although he also continued writing about Canada and Canadian institutions for the next four decades.

Included in Massey's collection along with Denison's plays were plays by Isabel Ecclestone Mackay, Canada's major female playwright of the 1920s, and Carroll Aikins, who took over running Hart House Theatre later in the decade. Aikins's own experimental Home Theatre, built in the middle of an apple orchard in British Columbia's Okanagan Valley, lasted from 1920–22. Another notable Hart House participant was Roy Mitchell, its first artistic director, a guru of creative, non-commercial theatre and a seminal figure in both Toronto and New York's Little Theatres.[9]

Throughout the 1920s and into the '30s, amateur theatre flourished under the umbrella of the Little Theatre movement, a burgeoning of homegrown playmaking in communities on both sides of the Canada-U.S. border. Little theatres sprouted in dozens of cities and towns across Canada. Some commentators saw them as a harbinger, "because they build the foundation for more mature creative theatres and develop an audience for the Ultimate National Canadian theatre."[10] That lofty goal seemed to move a step closer to realization with the establishment in 1932 of the Dominion Drama Festival, a nationwide competition organized by the new Governor General, Lord Bessborough, and chaired by the ubiquitous Vincent Massey. The festival would consist of an annual series of regional playoffs climaxing in a final (held in a different city each year) at which awards would be given for production and performance. Community theatres, school and university drama groups, and established companies like Hart House would all be eligible, and adjudicators would provide feedback as well as award trophies. The DDF aimed to showcase theatre in Canada and at the same time upgrade the quality of Canada's theatrical arts and crafts through competition and cross-fertilization.

During the years of its existence (1933–70, with a wartime hiatus from 1940–46), the Dominion Drama Festival helped institutionalize amateur theatre in Canada. Whether it accomplished much more than that has been hotly debated. It provided a proving ground for Canadian talent which often went on to New York, London, Hollywood, or by the 1950s to Stratford or other areas of the nascent Canadian professional theatre. Through trophies and cash prizes, the DDF also encouraged the writing and production of Canadian plays, an encouragement that proved statistically impressive. In 1934, festival organizers could suggest just nine Canadian titles for its participating groups; by 1966, the list contained 240 Canadian titles in English alone. But the quality and adventurousness of the work the festival inspired were often questionable. As late as 1967, the DDF would refuse to allow Michel Tremblay's *Les Belles-Soeurs* to be produced as part of its all-Canadian celebrations.[11]

An earlier indictment of the DDF's limitations was its inability to contend with the multimedia expressionism of Herman Voaden's plays, which consistently failed to advance beyond regional competitions in the 1930s. Ironically, Voaden had been a vocal advocate of a national drama league like the DDF to help encourage Canada's theatrical development and serve as a bulwark against the dangerous "pressure of American influence" threatening to "override our national and British character." An ardent cultural nationalist and theatrical innovator, he advocated a Canadian dramatic art as distinctive as the paintings of the Group of Seven. To that end, he sponsored a 1929 playwriting competition requiring that each play be set in the Canadian North with its subject or mood based on the writer's favourite Canadian painting. Voaden's own plays combined a mystical vision of the Canadian landscape with modern dance, Wagnerian opera, and symbolist dramatic techniques, resulting in a synaesthetic form he called "symphonic expressionism," with titles like *Rocks*, *Earth Song*, and *Hill-Land*. Voaden's Play Workshop in Toronto produced twenty-five new Canadian plays from 1934–36. But for all his extensive work as playwright, producer, director, and educator, Voaden's most significant contribution to the development of Canadian theatre may have been his persistent lobbying for government support for the arts. In 1945, he was elected first president of the new Canadian Arts Council.[12]

The Play Workshop and Hart House were not the only centres of Canadian playwriting activity. A group of women journalists organized the Playwrights' Studio Group in Toronto in 1932 and by the end of the decade had produced more than fifty new plays, mainly society comedies. At the other end of the spectrum were the Progressive Arts Clubs in Toronto, Montreal, Winnipeg, and Vancouver, leftist workers' theatre groups that created and performed agitprop and social protest plays throughout the Depression years. In Alberta, the Banff School of the Theatre was founded in 1933, evolving into the Banff School of Fine Arts, still an important centre for theatre training and workshop production. Alberta's Elsie Park Gowan and Gwen Pharis Ringwood wrote some of the strongest Canadian plays of the period. Ringwood, who would later teach playwriting at Banff to George Ryga among others, created stark prairie tragedies such as "Still Stands the House" and *Dark Harvest*. Gowan's *The Last Caveman* (1946) would be one of the first Canadian plays produced professionally in postwar Canada.[13]

Perhaps the most significant development for English-Canadian drama in the 1930s and '40s was the rise of radio. The Canadian Broadcasting Corporation (CBC) had been established in 1932, in part to resist the powerful tide of American commercial radio flowing across the border. In 1936, it began broadcasting radio plays for which it paid writers, producers, actors, musicians, and technicians. What came to be known as "The Golden Age" of Canadian radio – Canada's equivalent of a national professional theatre – began with Andrew Allan's appointment as supervisor of drama for CBC and producer of its weekly *Stage* series. Under Allan from 1944 to 1955, hundreds of original scripts and adaptations by house writers such as Lister Sinclair and Len Peterson were produced for live broadcast on *Stage* and *Wednesday Night*: consistently bold and imaginative drama that maintained high standards of excellence while proving broadly popular. At one time only *Hockey Night in Canada* drew more listeners than *Stage*. The stable of writers and actors that Allan assembled, including performers like John Drainie, Don Harron, and Frances Hyland, who would become mainstays of the new professional theatre, was "far and away the most exciting repertory group that can be heard," the *New York Times* radio critic wrote in 1946.[14] Although radio's golden age faded with the coming of television in the 1950s, radio drama continued to provide an important source of work and income for Canadian actors and playwrights until 2012, when the budget cuts that have steadily eviscerated CBC since the 1980s finally resulted in the cancellation of all original radio drama creation on Canada's national network.

Despite the varied successes of the DDF and the CBC, neither amateur theatricals nor radio drama could satisfy the need for a vibrant, professional domestic stage culture. John Coulter, who became an award-winning DDF playwright and a frequently produced CBC dramatist soon after emigrating from Ireland to Canada in 1936, was a vocal critic of the Canadian theatre scene. In a magazine article published in 1938, he proposed Dublin's Abbey Theatre as a model for Canadians, a theatre "showing the Irish to themselves ... Irish mugs in Irish mirrors."[15] Canadian audiences, too, he argued, could see their lives reflected in the work of their playwrights if the writers would find their subject matter in Canadian stories. After a series of plays set in Ireland, Coulter took his own advice and turned to writing radio plays about Canadian history. He achieved his greatest success with a trilogy of stage plays about Louis Riel. First produced in 1950, Coulter's *Riel* would serve as a paradigm for the history plays of James Reaney and the Theatre Passe Muraille dramatists of the 1970s: revisionist Canadian history with the rebel or underdog as hero, presented as a synthesis of documentary and myth.

Coulter had the good fortune to see *Riel* produced by the New Play Society (NPS), founded by Dora Mavor Moore in 1946. Moore had been the first Canadian to attend London's Royal Academy of Dramatic Arts, and she had directed extensively at Hart House and other Toronto amateur theatres. When World War Two ended, she established the New Play Society as a professional company, paying actors fifteen dollars per production. The NPS opened with a classic of the Abbey Theatre, Synge's *Playboy of the Western World*, but it also produced new Canadian work by writers like Coulter, Lister Sinclair, Harry Boyle, and Dora's son Mavor, who played the title role in *Riel* and would become a major figure in Canadian arts. Mavor Moore created the company's most substantial success, *Spring Thaw*, a satirical musical revue on Canadian topics, first staged in 1948 and remounted with increased popularity annually for the next twenty years. The NPS remained active until 1971, but its prime years were 1946–50 when its full seasons of plays in the Royal Ontario Museum Theatre (a basement auditorium) proved to many skeptics the viability of a professional Canadian stage.[16]

Other professional companies followed, among them Sydney Risk's Everyman Theatre in Vancouver (1946–53), which toured across western Canada, and Ottawa's Canadian Repertory Theatre (1948–56), whose casts featured future Canadian stars Christopher Plummer, William Shatner, Amelia Hall, and William Hutt, among others. The co-founders of Toronto's Jupiter Theatre (1951–54) included Lorne Greene and John Drainie. In 1954, brothers Donald and Murray Davis founded Toronto's Crest Theatre, which presented quality work in continuous repertory for thirteen seasons. The major Canadian playwright associated with the

Crest was Robertson Davies, whose *A Jig for the Gypsy* and *Hunting Stuart* premiered there in 1954–55. Davies was already English Canada's foremost playwright on the amateur circuit with "Eros at Breakfast," "Overlaid," and *Fortune, My Foe* in 1948–49, satires of Canadian philistinism and "emotional understimulation," which he considered the national disease. Davies remained a significant force in Canadian theatre until the mid-1960s when his playwriting career gave way to his work as a novelist.[17]

Aside from playwriting, Davies's journalism made a strong contribution to the developing Canadian theatre in the postwar era. Under both his own name and the pseudonym Samuel Marchbanks, he railed in protest like Voaden and Coulter against the conditions under which would-be Canadian theatre artists had to labour – what he called in 1952 "the seedy amateurism which has afflicted the arts here for so long."[18]

With fond reminiscences of his experience as a young actor in England, Davies reacted with enthusiasm to the idea of a world-class Shakespearean festival theatre in Stratford, Ontario. Along with Dora Mavor Moore and festival organizer Tom Patterson, he was instrumental in arranging for innovative British producer-director Tyrone Guthrie to head the venture, which held its first season of two plays under a tent in the summer of 1953. Guthrie imported stars Alec Guinness and Irene Worth to play the leads and fleshed out the rest of the company with Canadian actors, a policy that by and large remained standard for Stratford well into the 1980s.

Reviewing that first season, Davies concluded that it had given Canadians "a new vision of the theatre": "This cannot help but have its effect on work everywhere in the country. For one thing, many of our best Canadian actors are working at Stratford ... Are these actors, who have tasted the wine of true theatre, ever again to be satisfied with the sour slops of under-rehearsed, under-dressed, under-mounted, under-paid, and frequently ill-considered and ill-financed theatre projects? ... The Stratford Festival is an artistic bombshell, exploded just at the time when Canadian theatre is most ready for a break with the dead past and a leap into the future."[19]

The Stratford Festival had an enormous impact on theatre and the idea of theatre in Canada. It became an event of international importance and influence: its new non-proscenium thrust stage designed by Guthrie and Tanya Moiseiwitsch made waves in theatres worldwide. It raised the profile of theatre in Canada as nothing else had been able to do and served as a focus of national cultural pride. The festival also became a training ground for many of the best actors to emerge in Canada over the next three decades.

But Stratford initially did little to support the development of Canadian playwriting. Writers like John Herbert and James Reaney would receive workshop and small-scale public performances of their plays there in the late 1960s. In 1971 a Third Stage was added, in part to produce Canadian work. But by that time, with its huge financial operation, Stratford had become in many eyes a cultural dinosaur, devouring large subsidies at the expense of the smaller theatres whose productions of Canadian plays, often on shoestring budgets, were more central to an emerging national drama than was a theatre run by British artistic directors and devoted to Shakespeare. Ironically, while Stratford feasted, Canadian drama came of age in the early 1970s as a kind of poor theatre nourished on just those "sour slops" that Davies had complained of in 1953. By the 1980s Stratford began regularly commissioning Canadian plays and hiring Canadian artistic directors. Now, six decades after its creation, with four stages, the Stratford Festival remains a central element of Canada's theatrical ecology, with a significant commitment to Canadian plays. A full 50 per cent of its fourteen productions in 2012 were written by Canadians.[20]

In 1956, Mavor Moore wrote, "the Canadian theatre ... like the stock market, is bullish these days ..."[21] The success of Stratford and the other new professional theatres was augmented by the inception of CBC television in 1952, giving starts to a number of important dramatists who would later go on to write for the stage, including George Ryga, David French, and Michel Tremblay. The Canadian economy was booming. And on the horizon was the Canada Council, whose founding in 1957 would change the nature of theatre in Canada more than any other single development, providing a massive influx of government funding for buildings, companies, and individuals engaged in the arts.

The Canada Council was the most concrete manifestation of the Royal Commission on National Development in the Arts, Letters, and Sciences appointed by Prime Minister Louis St. Laurent in 1949 with Vincent Massey as chair. While Canada had established its economic and military bona fides in both war and peace, it remained seriously underdeveloped culturally and artistically. Why had Canada so few creative artists of note compared to other major nations, and so relatively little in the way of arts, including theatre? The Massey Commission, as it came to be called, aimed to find out.

The Commission concluded that "the forces of geography" had conspired to put a nation of fourteen million (at the time) alongside a behemoth ten times as populous and many times more culturally aggressive. As the Cold War had replaced the postwar peace, the growing threat of nuclear conflict between the United States and the Soviet Union, the outbreak of the Korean War, and the military and economic weakness of postwar Britain had all drawn Canada increasingly into the American orbit. Canada and the United States were partners in NATO (the North Atlantic Treaty Organization) and NORAD (the North American Air Defense Agreement). They fought together in Korea and shared in the Red scare. Despite continued discomfort among some Canadian artists, politicians, and educators about the overwhelming influence of American culture, the two nations had become increasingly integrated since the United States had replaced Britain as Canada's leading trading partner in 1921. Between 1948 and 1953, Canada's military expenditures grew from 7 per cent of its federal budget to 43 per cent. Yet, the Commission's 1951 *Report* argued, Canadians lacked "the advantages of what soldiers call defense in depth" against the "American invasion by film, radio, and periodical." Continuing the metaphor, the *Report* asserted, "Our military defences must be made secure, but our cultural defences equally demand national attention ..."[22]

Even if, as some have argued, the Massey Commission proceeded from British-imported, elitist cultural biases, it proved a game-changer. Because it found that Canadian culture was being stifled not just by the omnipresence of American influences but also by the lack of support and facilities for artists in Canada, it concluded that the nation's cultural defences could only be secured through significant government financial aid for artists and infrastructure. Modelled along the lines of the British Arts Council, the Canada Council for the Encouragement of the Arts, Letters, Humanities, and Social Sciences would support Canadian culture at home and abroad. From an initial outlay of $2.6 million in arts grants in 1957, the Canada Council's investment in individuals and groups grew to more than $60 million by 1970, a quantum leap in the funds available to fuel the engine of Canadian cultural nationalism.

Money wasn't the only catalyst for change. In 1958 in Winnipeg, Tom Hendry and John Hirsch merged their amateur Theatre 77 with the Winnipeg Little Theatre to create a regional professional theatre, the Manitoba Theatre Centre (MTC), with Hirsch as its first artistic director. From the start, the MTC "was meant to be more than a theatre, something that could in fact become a focus for all theatrical energy and resources in one community."[23] Combining mainstage productions in Winnipeg with a touring company, children's theatre, and school, the MTC succeeded so well in galvanizing the support and resources of its constituency that it became the basis for a new concept: a decentralized, regional Canadian version of a national theatre. With support and encouragement from the Canada Council a network of regional theatres spread across the country: Vancouver's Playhouse and Halifax's Neptune in 1963, Edmonton's Citadel in 1965, and Regina's Globe in 1966. By 1970 Montreal, Calgary, Fredericton, and Toronto also had theatres catering to regional communities.

Canada, it seemed, had indeed become bullish on theatre. To train and supply actors for the new national theatre network, the National Theatre School was opened in Montreal in 1960 with separate French and English programs. At Niagara-on-the-Lake, Ontario, the Shaw Festival began operation in 1962, and Prince Edward Island's Charlottetown Festival was inaugurated in 1964, specializing in Canadian musical theatre. St. John's got its Arts and Culture Centre in 1967. And in 1969–70, the completion of three major Centennial construction projects – Ottawa's National Arts Centre, Toronto's St. Lawrence Centre, and a new building for the MTC – rounded out a decade of extraordinary growth for the Canadian theatre.

With the superstructure essentially intact, the missing link now was the plays. Where were the plays that might crystallize the new drama in English Canada the way John Osborne's *Look Back in Anger* had done in Britain and Gélinas's *Tit-Coq* in Quebec (and the way Tremblay's *Les Belles-Soeurs* would do again in Quebec, in a different way, in 1968). Those plays had in common vernacular speech, anti-establishment anger, and characters, settings, and situations definitively of their own time and place.

So too had the play that finally touched the nerve of English Canada. *The Ecstasy of Rita Joe* premiered at the Vancouver Playhouse on November 23, 1967, in a landmark production remounted for the opening of the National Arts Centre in 1969. That year the play was also broadcast on CBC-TV and produced in a French translation by Gratien Gélinas in Montreal. In 1971 choreographer Norbert Vesak adapted the play for the Royal Winnipeg Ballet. *Rita Joe* reverberated through the nation's collective consciousness. In a review of a later production, critic Jamie Portman recalled, "*Rita Joe* happened during Centennial year when Canadians were anxious to look at themselves. But the look that this play provided was an unsettling one. It punctured the euphoria and the smug complacency of Canada's birthday celebrations and declared unequivocally that all was not well with this country and its institutions." Its implications for Canadian playwriting were equally dramatic:

> This was an indigenous Canadian drama that surfaced and succeeded at a time when indigenous Canadian drama was generally considered to be an aberration. It was a play of merit, worthy of production in any Canadian theatre. It prompted an awareness of the existence of other plays potentially worthy of production. It provided resounding evidence that it was not necessary for any Canadian theatre to rely solely on imported fare. With the arrival of *The Ecstasy of Rita Joe*, Canadian plays ceased to be a rarity in English-speaking Canada. Companies dedicated to the production of new Canadian drama sprang up, and in so doing nurtured the further growth of playwriting activity. Canada's regional theatres – some of them grudgingly – found themselves forced to take the Canadian playwright seriously for the first time.[24]

Yet the battle for credibility was not so easily won. Just how grudgingly the theatrical establishment received the Canadian playwright was vividly registered by statistics from 1970, during which the seven major regional theatres produced the work of only two Canadian dramatists and paid them less than $5,000 out of combined budgets of more than $2 million.[25] Consider the case of the Manitoba Theatre Centre. Despite its success with Winnipeg writer Ann Henry's *Lulu Street* in 1967, more than a decade would pass before the MTC presented another new play by a local playwright. The flurry of Canadian play production in 1967 had been in some respects no more than Centennial Year tokenism.

The stage history of John Herbert's *Fortune and Men's Eyes* reveals the challenges faced by Canadian playwrights. *Fortune* had been workshopped at Stratford in 1965. Denied a full production there or anywhere else in Canada, the play opened in New York in 1967 and ran for a year off-Broadway. In 1968, it had a long run in London and became a full-scale international hit. By 1969, it was already being revived in New York. The play's impact on other Canadian dramatists was immediate and inspirational: "the ice-breaker in the channel," George Ryga called it.[26] But for all that, professional productions of *Fortune and Men's Eyes* in Canada to

1970 consisted of a week at the Vancouver Playhouse's Stage 2 and a brief run in the MTC's Studio Theatre. There was not a mainstage production to be seen. Herbert's hometown of Toronto would have to wait until 1975 to see the play at all.

What had gone wrong? The expectations and struggles of more than a half-century had resulted in a Canadian theatre that by the late 1960s had already become entrenched and conservative. Rather than living up to the original promise of the regionals to create new models adapted to the distinctive needs of their communities, which should have meant presenting plays written about those communities from within them, the large subsidized theatres tried to emulate Broadway and London's West End. When artistic directors were asked about Canadian plays and playwrights, their responses were often remarkably similar:

> I don't see how a play can be Canadian.
>
> I don't think there are any plays that you could call strictly Canadian.
>
> But if you start to define what is a Canadian and what is a Canadian playwright, what do you end up with?
>
> What does the phrase mean?[27]

With few exceptions, the regionals served up homogenized theatre: safe, commercial seasons of British and American hits plus a smattering of world classics. Moreover, it was theatre as Cultural Event, like the opera or the symphony, the kind of thing you got dressed up for.

But the late 1960s was the Age of Aquarius and the Generation Gap. Theatre artists – many of them in the first wave of Baby Boomers graduating from university – and much of their potential audience were evolving in a different direction. The Canadian Centennial and the emergence of a Canadian professional theatre community just happened to coincide with the most radical cultural upheaval of the century in the Western world. There was a sexual revolution, a musical revolution, a drug revolution; long hair, peace marches, and a Summer of Love. By 1968 in Chicago, Paris, and Prague, the revolution would spill over into the streets. Canada wasn't immune to these forces nor could its theatre be, no matter how stubbornly middle-aged and middle-class it tried to remain.

That the most significant Canadian plays of the decade should have appeared in 1967–68 was not coincidental. *The Ecstasy of Rita Joe*, *Fortune and Men's Eyes*, and *Les Belles-Soeurs* are plays very much of their age, marked by strong social consciousness and anti-establishment anger. Alienated from the mainstream themselves, the playwrights were in sync with the temper of the times. Herbert and Tremblay were gay men, and Tremblay a Québécois nationalist. Ryga and Herbert were outspoken and uncompromising in their social and political views. Characteristic of their outsider status, neither was initially allowed entry into the United States to see his own play in production; characteristically, Herbert refused the Dominion Drama Festival's Massey Award (and its $1,000 prize) for Best Play for *Fortune and Men's Eyes* in 1968; characteristically, Ryga's 1970 play

Captives of the Faceless Drummer so upset the Vancouver Playhouse board, which had commissioned it, that they refused its production. It was ironic but perhaps inevitable that the two writers whose plays brought modern English-Canadian drama into existence would eventually find themselves virtually unproduced by the major Canadian theatres.[28]

Modern Canadian drama was born out of an amalgam of the new consciousness of the age – social, political, and aesthetic – with the new Canadian self-consciousness. Since the larger theatres were generally unsympathetic and unaccommodating to both these forces, an even newer Canadian theatre had to be invented, an alternate theatre. One of its prime movers in Toronto was Martin Kinch, who claimed that those first heady days had little to do with nationalism:

> The real influences were Fritz Perls and Timothy Leary, Peter Brook and Jerzy Grotowski, Tom O'Horgan, Café La Mama, Julian Beck, Judith Malina, and the ensemble of the Living Theatre; in short, a host of European and American artists, most of them primarily dedicated to the ethic and the aesthetic of "doing your own thing" ... It was an exciting time, a time of experiment and exploration ... expressionism, hallucination, confrontation, and audience participation flourished. Perhaps most important, however, there existed a definite bond between the theatres and their audience; an audience that was characterized by long hair, beards, bells, and babies in the front rows of the most outrageous plays. Its concerns were the concerns of "the sixties": the breaking of sexual taboo, the problems of individual freedom, and the yearning for community.[29]

In 1969, Kinch became a co-director of Toronto's Theatre Passe Muraille, founded the previous year by Jim Garrard. As its name suggests, Passe Muraille was to be a theatre without walls: neither the traditional fourth wall between actors and audience nor necessarily even the walls of a theatre building. Garrard envisioned "a guerrilla theatre": "Theatre in the subways, get a truck and do theatre in small towns, real circuses, grab people in the streets ... I'd like to make theatre as popular as bowling."[30] A milestone for the new alternate theatre movement was Passe Muraille's production of American playwright Rochelle Owens's *Futz* in 1969. A play about a man in love with a pig, in both style and content it established the parameters of the alternate theatre's self-conscious anti-conventionality. The sex, obscenity, and nudity it featured would become almost obligatory. When the show was shut down by the morality squad, and the company charged and subsequently acquitted, the new movement had its red badge of courage.

Nationalism soon joined, and to some extent eclipsed, sensationalism in Toronto's new alternate theatre scene, largely through the efforts of Ken Gass and Paul Thompson. Gass set out to prove that Canadian playwrights indeed existed, and were just waiting to be discovered and encouraged. His Factory Theatre Lab was both a factory and a laboratory, presenting polished new plays as well as experimental works-in-progress. Most importantly, he would call it "The Home of the Canadian Playwright." Gass's concept paid off with a string of notable new plays: David Freeman's *Creeps*, Herschel Hardin's *Esker Mike and His Wife, Agiluk*, and George Walker's *Prince of Naples* all in 1971; most of Walker's other plays over the next dozen years; and exciting (though not necessarily enduring) work by Hrant Alianak, Larry Fineberg, Bryan Wade, and Gass himself. Gass remained artistic director of Factory Lab until 1979, then returned to the post again in 1996 and, with the help of George F. Walker's *Suburban Motel* plays, saved the company, now called Factory Theatre, from imminent demise. Gass retained the post until his controversial dismissal by the Factory's board in 2012.

Paul Thompson became artistic director of Theatre Passe Muraille after working in France with Roger Planchon, whose process-oriented, political brand of theatre contrasted dramatically with Thompson's experiences during a brief apprenticeship at Stratford. Rejecting the Stratford model, Thompson focused his company on local subject matter and collective creation, involving his actors in first-hand research, improvisation, and continual revision, utilizing their individual skills as key elements in the play wherever possible. When Thompson took over Passe Muraille, he already had a precedent for this kind of theatre in Toronto. George Luscombe had worked with Joan Littlewood's Theatre Workshop in England in the mid-1950s and had founded Toronto Workshop Productions in 1959 based on Littlewood's political and stylistic principles: left-wing politics and an eclectic style integrating improvisation, documentary, commedia dell'arte, and often collective scripting. In the late 1960s and early '70s, TWP produced potent socio-political theatre with its agitprop pieces, *Mister Bones* and *Chicago '70* on race and politics in America, and its bittersweet evocation of the Canadian Depression, *Ten Lost Years*. The partnership of Luscombe and Toronto Workshop Productions lasted for thirty years until the company folded in 1989 and its building passed on to Sky Gilbert's Buddies in Bad Times Theatre.[31]

Under Thompson's stewardship (co-artistic director 1969–72; sole artistic director 1972–81), Theatre Passe Muraille became the most important Canadian theatre of the 1970s. Creations like *Doukhobors*, *The Farm Show* (first staged in a Clinton, Ontario barn), and *The Adventures of an Immigrant* (performed in Toronto streetcars) made often stirring theatrical poetry out of material that was sometimes mundane and always local. Docudrama with a high degree of theatricality became the Passe Muraille trademark: a small company of actors using little but their own bodies and voices to create ingenious stage metaphors.

They inspired countless imitators across the country, although in less-talented hands the deceptively rigorous demands of collective scripting and a presentational style sometimes had unfortunate results. Among the best of their offshoots were Newfoundland's CODCO and Saskatoon's Twenty-Fifth Street House Theatre (now Twenty-Fifth Street Theatre), whose play about the founding of the co-op movement on the prairies, *Paper Wheat*, was in the finest Passe Muraille tradition. Theatre Passe

Muraille also specialized in resurrecting, popularizing, dramatizing, and often mythicizing Canadian history in collective scripts or in conjunction with a writer. *Buffalo Jump* with Carol Bolt, *1837: The Farmers' Revolt* with Rick Salutin, *Them Donnellys* with Frank MacEnany, and *Far as the Eye Can See* with Rudy Wiebe were some of the best of the collaborations. Later in the decade, Passe Muraille company members John Gray (now John MacLachlan Gray) and Eric Peterson would write and perform *Billy Bishop Goes to War*, and Linda Griffiths would do the same with *Maggie & Pierre*. Perhaps the most exciting Canadian playwright to emerge in the 1980s, Judith Thompson, also came out of Passe Muraille with her extraordinary first play, *The Crackwalker*. Theatre Passe Muraille and Factory Theatre remain to the present day two of the primary loci of Canadian theatrical production and development.

Not everything was happening in Toronto. In Vancouver, where Sidney Risk had pioneered postwar professional touring with his Everyman Theatre, and where John Juliani's experimental Savage God project had been operating since 1966, John MacLachlan Gray, Larry Lillo, and a group of other University of British Columbia graduates formed Tamahnous Theatre in 1971, a collective that would remain Vancouver's most original and progressive company for the next ten years. Among its most important productions were the small-cast musicals *Billy Bishop Goes to War* and Morris Panych's "post-nuclear cabaret," *Last Call!* Vancouver's New Play Centre had come into being in 1970 dedicated to developing new scripts by local writers. Under the direction of Pamela Hawthorn from 1972 until 1989, the New Play Centre (NPC) had a hand in most of the drama to come out of British Columbia, including the work of Margaret Hollingsworth, Tom Walmsley, Ted Galay, John Lazarus, Sheldon Rosen, Betty Lambert, Eric Nicol, and Sherman Snukal. In the late 1990s, the NPC metamorphosed into Playwrights Theatre Centre, which continues its predecessor's work.

Seeded by government grants from Local Initiatives Programs (LIP) and Opportunities for Youth (OFY), new companies doing indigenous theatre sprouted everywhere in 1971–72: Edmonton's Theatre 3, Calgary's Alberta Theatre Projects, Pier One in Halifax, the Mummers Troupe in St. John's. Festival Lennoxville in Quebec presented all-Canadian summer seasons of plays by the likes of Michael Cook, Herschel Hardin, and Sharon Pollock from 1972 until its demise in 1982.

Most of the action, though, was in Toronto, and nothing did more to cement its position at the centre of the new movement than Tarragon Theatre. Founded in 1971 by Bill Glassco, who had directed David Freeman's powerful *Creeps* at Factory Lab earlier in the year, Tarragon opened with a revised *Creeps* that proved even more successful than the original. The first Tarragon season ended with a new work that became the single most influential Canadian play of the 1970s, David French's *Leaving Home*. Its story of generational conflict and a singularly Canadian form of immigrant alienation (ex-Newfoundlanders spiritually adrift in Toronto) elicited strong audience identification, and its straightforward, accessible style had broad appeal. *Leaving Home* created a vogue for domestic realism that some saw as a debilitating counterforce to the more adventurous directions Canadian drama seemed to be taking at the time. Tarragon soon became identified with that style, especially in light of Glassco's subsequent productions of other realist plays by Freeman and French. But Tarragon also introduced English Canada to the plays of Michel Tremblay with Glassco as director and co-translator – plays domestic in setting but hardly realistic in style. Moreover, from 1973–75 Tarragon produced James Reaney's Donnelly trilogy, plays far removed from stylistic realism or naturalism. Unlike most companies devoted to Canadian plays, Tarragon managed to combine artistic and commercial success and to sustain it over many years. More than any other theatre, it succeeded in bringing Canadian drama into the mainstream. After Glassco left Tarragon in 1985, its status was maintained under the artistic director-ship of former theatre critic Urjo Kareda, followed by Richard Rose. The many playwrights in *Modern Canadian Plays* whose work is associated with Tarragon – James Reaney, Michel Tremblay, David French, Joan MacLeod, Ann-Marie MacDonald, Judith Thompson, Morris Panych, and Wajdi Mouawad – testify to the continued influence, importance, and adventurousness of the company.

The wave of new alternate theatres in Toronto crested in 1972 with the founding of Toronto Free Theatre by Tom Hendry, Martin Kinch, and John Palmer. Subsidized by LIP grants, performances were literally free until 1974 when the impossible economics of that policy led to gradually increasing admissions. Toronto Free's reputation rested on its excellent ensemble of actors and a distinctive taste for the psychologically bizarre. Many of its early successes were plays by its in-house triumvirate – espe-cially Hendry and Palmer – or by Carol Bolt. George F. Walker and Erika Ritter were among the most noteworthy later additions to Toronto Free's playwriting corps.

Despite the dynamism of the alternate companies, Canadian theatre in the early 1970s was in danger of falling victim to an insidious form of ghettoization. Canadian plays were relegated to small, low-budget the-atres lacking the financial and technical resources available to the heavily subsidized festivals and regionals. While non-Canadian works had access to lush productions, large casts, and relatively well paid actors, Canadian plays were doomed to what George Ryga called "beggars theatre"[32] – the same conditions about which Robertson Davies had complained in 1953 – and Canadian playwrights were denied opportunities to make a living by their craft. In an attempt to remedy this situation, a group of playwrights met in the summer of 1971 to consider "The Dilemma of the Playwright in Canada." Their most contentious recommendation called for a 50 per cent Canadian content quota for all theatres receiving government funding. Most artistic directors and editorialists were predictably outraged. "If it ever happened, then critics should also get Canada Council grants for sitting through the plays," was one wit's response.[33] Though no formal quota system was adopted, the controversy led to an informal policy deci-sion by the Canada Council to "appeal" to its client theatres to do more Canadian plays. The results were startling. By the 1972–73 season, nearly

50 per cent of the plays produced by subsidized theatres in both English and French were Canadian.

Among the most tangible consequences of this new policy was a return to one of the original precepts of the regional ideal, the commissioning by regional theatres of new plays from local playwrights. These arrangements proved mutually fruitful to Sharon Pollock with the Vancouver Playhouse and Theatre Calgary, John Murrell and W.O. Mitchell with Theatre Calgary, Ken Mitchell and Rex Deverell with Regina's Globe, and David Fennario with the Centaur in Montreal. The Blyth Festival, in cultivating playwrights like Anne Chislett, proved the value of a homegrown product even in the traditionally more commercial milieu of small-town summer theatre. (The motto of Blyth, still going strong in 2013, is "Stories from Where We Live.") In each of these cases, plays written with specific associations for local audiences made their way into theatres across the country. Canadian writers and producers may have finally learned what John Coulter had called, back in 1938, "the paradoxical truth that the most effective way to keep an eye on Broadway is to keep on looking attentively at the life passing under your own nose in your own home town."[34]

Another way to keep an eye on both Broadway and London was to strengthen the organizational infrastructure of Canadian theatre. As Americans celebrated their bi-centennial in 1976, Canadians founded the Professional Association of Canadian Theatres (PACT) and the Association for Canadian Theatre History, a national academic organization (now called the Canadian Association for Theatre Research / Association Canadienne de la Recherche Théâtrale). Actors' Equity Association, which had come to Canada in 1955 to represent professional actors at Stratford, officially became Canadian Actors' Equity Association in 1976, declaring its independence from American Equity.

Given the tremendous expansion Canadian theatre had undergone since 1967, a certain amount of retrenchment was inevitable by the 1980s. Theatres as widely divergent as Saskatoon's Twenty-Fifth Street and the Stratford Festival had to weather financial and artistic crises that threatened their survival. Some went under: Vancouver's Westcoast Actors, Edmonton's Theatre 3, Montreal's Saidye Bronfman. Facing new audience expectations and a changing ideological climate, Toronto and Vancouver's most significant smaller companies underwent structural reorganization and found new artistic directors. Toronto Free would soon disappear in a merger and Tamahnous would disappear altogether. But Passe Muraille, Tarragon, and Factory, along with the resurgent regionals and successful middle-of-the-road theatres like Vancouver's Arts Club, continued to provide a springboard for Canadian plays. And across the country a new generation arose: the Vancouver East Cultural Centre and Touchstone Theatre in Vancouver, Prairie Theatre Exchange in Winnipeg, Ottawa's Great Canadian Theatre Company, Nova Scotia's Mulgrave Road Theatre and Ship's Company, and Rising Tide Theatre in St. John's. Nakai Theatre Ensemble in Whitehorse and Tununiq Arsarniit Theatre Group in what is now Nunavut ensured the exposure of lively theatrical voices in the Canadian North. Vancouver's Green Thumb set the pattern for hard-hitting young people's theatre.

Edmonton was particularly fertile ground. Theatre Network, Northern Light, Catalyst, Workshop West, and Phoenix Theatre all came on stream before 1982, the year the Edmonton Fringe Festival was born. Modelled on the Edinburgh Fringe, Edmonton's festival soon became a hugely successful affair with annual attendance in the quarter-million range, and a prototype for the many other Canadian Fringes that sprang up in its wake.

Meanwhile, Toronto's theatrical expansion continued to the point where it could claim second-place to New York as a mecca for theatre in North America. Among its important new companies were Necessary Angel, Buddies in Bad Times (soon the country's most important queer theatre company as well as a centre for new play development with its spinoff Rhubarb Festival), Nightwood (which became Canada's foremost feminist theatre), clown-based Theatre Columbus, multicultural Cahoots, and Native Earth Performing Arts, which, along with De-ba-jeh-mu-jig Theatre on Manitoulin Island in Lake Huron, led the 1980s renaissance of First Nations theatre in Canada. Initially under Tomson Highway's artistic directorship and subsequently under the direction of Floyd Favel, Drew Hayden Taylor, Yvette Nolan, and Tara Beagan, Native Earth has fostered the work of a whole generation of Aboriginal Canadian theatre artists.[35] The Toronto International Theatre Festival, and its successor, Harbourfront, showcased Canadian plays and productions alongside some of the best theatre companies in the world.

Canadian theatre's growing cultural prominence was signified by a series of new awards and textbooks. Joining the prestigious Chalmers Award, given by the Toronto Drama Bench since 1972 for best Canadian play produced each year in Toronto, were the Canadian Authors' Association Award for Drama (1975) and, in 1981, the Governor General's Award in Drama for the best new Canadian plays in French and English publication. The Doras in Toronto (after Dora Mavor Moore), the Jessies in Vancouver (after Jessie Richardson), the Sterlings in Edmonton (after Elizabeth Sterling Haynes), and the Bettys in Calgary (after Betty Mitchell) celebrate the best work done on those cities' stages in the name of a local theatrical pioneer. The MECCAs (Montreal English Critics Circle Awards) were established in 1998, and the METAs (Montreal English Theatre Awards) in 2012. The Nathan Cohen Award for excellence in theatre criticism commemorated a legendary theatre critic. The publication of three Canadian drama anthologies in 1984–85, including the first version of this one, made Canadian plays more accessible to students, more entrenched in curricula, more academically respectable.

By the mid-1980s, the nationalism that had largely inspired and in some ways kick-started the new Canadian theatre had pretty much gone out of vogue. "Free trade" and "globalism" were soon to become the new keywords. Even the old keywords had new meanings. As Alan Filewod points out, "in 1974 the terms 'native' and 'indigenous' meant 'Canadian' as opposed to British or American; by 1984 they had acquired a much more specific value (pertaining to aboriginal peoples) which challenged the very meaning of 'Canadian' as it was understood only a decade earlier."[36]

Nevertheless, the next few years were marked by an unprecedented series of theatrical coups led by what John MacLachlan Gray has called the Old Warriors of Canadian Nationalism. Tarragon pioneer Bill Glassco became artistic director of southern Ontario's major regional theatre, CentreStage, in 1985, then engineered a merger with Guy Sprung and Toronto Free Theatre to create the Canadian Stage Company in 1988. That year Tamahnous co-founder and West Coast alternate-theatre icon Larry Lillo made a triumphant return to Vancouver to run British Columbia's flagship regional theatre, the Playhouse; Martin Kinch became artistic director of Theatre Calgary; and Sharon Pollock took over her hometown regional, Theatre New Brunswick. The Stratford Festival's controversial attempt to hire a non-Canadian artistic director in 1980 was resolved with the appointment of John Hirsch, who had co-founded Manitoba Theatre Centre back in 1958. Canadian actor Richard Monette, who had performed cross-dressed and naked in Michel Tremblay's *Hosanna* at Tarragon two decades earlier, took over the festival's reins in 1992. With such apparent victories the nationalist agenda receded in importance. In relative terms this was the case even in Quebec.

But as economic issues superseded nationalism in the larger political landscape, economics also had greater political and artistic impact in the theatre. Canada's non-profit, publicly subsidized theatre system had to deal with shrinking government support in the face of growing deficits and an unsympathetic federal regime under Conservative Prime Minister Brian Mulroney. Theatre was increasingly perceived as just another commodity, forced to find its niche in a competitive and fragmented cultural marketplace battered by recessions and dominated by home video. Theatre boards run by businessmen assumed more and more power, and corporate sponsors stepped in to replace lost government funding. Conflicts between the artistic and corporate agendas led to a series of crises. If 1988 had seen the apparent victory of the cultural nationalists, 1989 showed how fragile the new theatrical order really was. First, Canada's longest-running alternate theatre, Toronto Workshop Productions, shut down in a struggle between its artists and its board. Then Canadian Stage Company's board forcibly removed artistic director Guy Sprung, and Sharon Pollock resigned in frustration from Theatre New Brunswick. *Canadian Theatre Review* titled its Summer 1990 issue, "Surviving the Nineties." A 1996 issue would be titled "Survivors of the Ice Age."

For a few playwrights, the commercialization of Canadian theatre meant not just surviving but thriving, as hit plays from small non-profit stages got remounted in large, long-run commercial venues. Toronto led the way with George F. Walker's *Love and Anger* and Brad Fraser's *Unidentified Human Remains and the True Nature of Love* crossing over into commercial production in 1990, and Tomson Highway's *Dry Lips Oughta Move to Kapuskasing* in 1991.

Despite the challenges, new festivals and companies continued to emerge. Montreal's Festival de théâtre des Amériques (now Festival

TransAmériques) (1985), Toronto's du Maurier World Stage (1986), and SummerWorks Festival (1991) became important showcases for innovative theatre from Canada and around the world. Two Calgary festivals, Alberta Theatre Projects' New PlayRites (now the Enbridge playRites Festival of New Canadian Plays) (1986) and One Yellow Rabbit's experimental High Performance Rodeo (1987), as well as Native Earth's Weesageechak Begins to Dance festival in Toronto (1988), joined established new play development organizations like the Banff Centre, Playwrights' Workshop Montreal, Vancouver's New Play Centre, and the Rhubarb Festival. Women in View (1988–97) in Vancouver, Festival Antigonish (1988) and Wolfville's Atlantic Theatre Festival (1995) in Nova Scotia, as well as a number of new summer Shakespeare festivals set up shop – Montreal's Repercussion Theatre (1988), Calgary's Shakespeare in the Park (1988), Edmonton's Free-will Shakespeare Festival (1988), Vancouver's Bard on the Beach (1990), Shakespeare by the Sea in St. John's (1993), Winnipeg's Shakespeare in the Ruins (1993), and Halifax's Shakespeare by the Sea (1994) – joining Toronto's Shakespeare in High Park (1983) and Saskatoon's Shakespeare on the Saskatchewan (1985). All these Shakespeare companies remain in production in 2013. Playwright Wendy Lill and director Mary Vingoe co-founded Eastern Front Theatre (1993) in Dartmouth, Nova Scotia, while a dozen Toronto actors, many of whom had worked together at Stratford, established Soulpepper (1998) as a repertory company for modern classics. Under the direction of Albert Schultz, Soulpepper has become Toronto's largest company, with a season of sixteen plays in 2012.

The most significant commercial development of late twentieth-century Canadian theatre was the arrival of the mega-musical. In 1985, to accommodate Andrew Lloyd Webber's *Cats*, Toronto's old Elgin Theatre–Winter Garden complex was restored to its former glory and *Cats* ran for two years. In 1989, entertainment mogul Garth Drabinsky renovated another magnificent old Toronto vaudeville house, the Pantages, for Lloyd Webber's *Phantom of the Opera*, which then ran for ten years, selling more than seven million tickets. Producers Ed and David Mirvish opened *Les Misérables* at their historic Royal Alexandra Theatre. The extraordinary success of these huge imported shows, not just in Toronto but in their spin-off tours across Canada, led to more of the same. In the early 1990s, the Mirvishes built the Princess of Wales Theatre to house *Miss Saigon*, and Drabinsky's Livent became North America's largest theatrical production company. Livent opened the North York Performing Arts Centre, then in a corporate deal renamed it the Ford Centre for the Performing Arts. While still importing productions, Canadian mega-musical producers also began creating their own versions of musical theatre classics for export (*Show Boat, Joseph and His Amazing Technicolor Dreamcoat*), as well as commissioning new shows like Drabinsky's *Kiss of the Spider Woman* and *Ragtime*.

The mega-musical boom had the virtue of fueling the theatrical economy, creating international stars of Canadian actors like Brent Carver and Jeff Hyslop, and spin-off opportunities for a few Canadian non-musical plays. Drabinsky was responsible for the commercial remount of Walker's *Love and Anger*, and the Mirvishes for Highway's *Dry Lips*. But on the whole it posed severe challenges for Canadian non-profit theatres. Rather than benefitting from a trickle-down of the new audiences created and abetted by the megas, low-budget companies found themselves in difficult competition for the theatre-going dollar. The success of these shows also shaped audience expectation and demand, and fostered pressures, subtle and unsubtle, from boards, funding agencies, and others to conform to the mega-musical aesthetic: high on spectacle, low on content, lacking in Canadian reference, and empty of political challenge. "Megamusicals can kill intelligent theatre," Sky Gilbert complained. "Megamusicals actually make you stupid."[37]

Intelligence eventually triumphed. With the novelty of the genre waning, his overextended empire straining, and Drabinsky himself accused of cooking the books, Livent collapsed in 1998. Drabinsky would go to prison for fraud. Toronto's Ford Centre was taken over by the city and renamed Toronto Centre for the Arts. In 2009, Toronto Centre partnered with Dancap Productions to present large-scale musicals, but in 2012 Dancap shut down. Vancouver's Ford Centre, another Livent creation, was sold to private interests in 2001 and renamed The Centre for Performing Arts in Vancouver, then resold in 2013 to an American evangelical church. Mirvish Productions continued to thrive; in 2013–14, now Canada's largest producer of commercial theatre, Mirvish was staging high-quality musicals in four large Toronto venues, along with edgier work like George F. Walker's *Dead Metaphor*. The spectacle musical retained its popularity in Canada. Disney's *The Lion King* played to over three million people during its two lengthy runs in Toronto (2000–04, 2011–12), with another remount scheduled for 2014.

While the non-profit theatres, where most Canadian plays are born and performed, survived the mega-musical challenge, theatrical economics remained a significant issue for Canadian theatre as the new millennium dawned. The news wasn't all bad. A series of rich cash prizes became available to artists and producers: the $100,000 Siminovitch Prize for a Canadian theatre artist in mid-career, a $25,000 playwriting prize offered by the University of British Columbia, and the $50,000 Alcan Arts Award to a producing company in B.C. (By 2013 all but the last were gone, the Alcan now called the Rio Tinto Alcan Performing Arts Award and worth $60,000.) But when deficit-cutting federal and provincial governments reduced their grants, and the prohibition of tobacco advertising in 2003 caused the loss of du Maurier arts sponsorships, the result was a funding crisis. Calgary's Alberta Theatre Projects nearly folded. Toronto's Theatre Plus did. Many in the Canadian theatre community echoed the sentiments of the *Los Angeles Times* critic who lamented how the economic squeeze of the 1990s created a "survival mentality" in the United States, whereby artistic directors tended to minimize risk and opt for safe programming. In Canada, critic Kate Taylor complained, "the poorly funded non-profits embrace facile populism."[38]

Despite such claims, Canadian theatre entered the twenty-first century on the strength of complex new visual vocabularies, from the neo-baroque *mise en scène* favoured by many Québécois playwrights and directors to image-based physical theatre, clown, mime, movement, dance, and puppetry. Artistic Fraud of Newfoundland, Montreal's The Other Theatre and Carbone 14 (dissolved in 2005), Toronto's Theatre Smith-Gilmour, Winnipeg's Primus (until its demise in 1998), and Calgary's One Yellow Rabbit were some of the leading companies that subordinated the spoken word to sharply detailed, carefully choreographed visual effects. Mump and Smoot, Toronto's "clowns of horror," became Fringe favourites, vocalizing only in gibberish. The brilliant marionette shows of Calgary's Ronnie Burkett, represented here by *Street of Blood*, began to be seen and honoured around the world. The first national success of the new millennium, Morris Panych's Vancouver Playhouse production and subsequent Canadian tour of Gogol's *The Overcoat*, was performed and choreographed to a score by Shostakovich with no dialogue. Robert Lepage's stunning designs, as much as his writing, direction, and performances, have made him an international phenomenon. Canada's greatest economic success on the world stage, and one of its artistic triumphs, is the spectacle theatre of Cirque du Soleil. Since its founding in 1984, the Montreal-based company has redefined the circus and established a global empire. In 2013, eight different Cirque shows were running in Las Vegas alone.

"Canada on the World Stage" became an increasingly meaningful phrase. It headlined *Canadian Theatre Review*'s Winter 2001 issue examining the export of Canadian drama to the United States, Europe, India, and Australia. That issue appeared around the time that plays by Tremblay, Panych, Walker, and Daniel MacIvor, as well as the latest Cirque du Soleil show, were appearing on Washington, D.C. stages, leading the *Washington Post* to declare, "Suddenly ... Canada is hot."[39] Canada remains a net theatrical importer, but Canadian work is now frequently performed outside the country – the case for nearly all the plays in this volume. Postcolonial studies have also brought attention to Canadian theatre at international conferences and in collections of plays and essays published abroad.

Canada's internal theatrical borders remain a challenge, although the divide between Quebec's French culture and the theatre of English Canada has become more permeable in the new century. Only a handful of francophone playwrights have had substantial success in English Canada: Gélinas, Tremblay, Lepage, Michel Marc Bouchard, and more recently, Carole Fréchette and Wajdi Mouawad. But ninety-one additional playwrights whose work has been translated into English are listed along with those six on the website of Montreal's Centre des auteurs dramatiques (CEAD) in 2013, up from a total of sixty-two in 1998. Many of their translations have been produced in English-Canadian theatres. As well, the Association des théâtres francophone du Canada (ATFC) lists fourteen French-language theatres operating outside Quebec, from New Brunswick to British Columbia. The bridging of the solitudes from the English side to the French has been less dramatic. Major anglophone playwrights including Walker, Thompson, MacIvor, Brad Fraser, Sally Clark, Colleen Wagner, and Wendy Lill have been produced in Quebec. Montreal's Théâtre de Quat'Sous, the theatre most closely associated with Tremblay's cultural nationalism in the 1960s and '70s, staged four of Walker's *Suburban Motel* plays in translation in its 1998–99 season, as well as MacIvor's *Monster*, its first play ever in English.[40]

Canadian theatre has also become increasingly diverse in the twenty-first century, following well behind but starting slowly to catch up to the changing Canadian demographic. Colour-blind and gender-blind casting has become widely discussed and at least somewhat more widely practised. Multiple companies dedicated to African Canadian, Asian Canadian, South Asian Canadian, Latino/a Canadian, and disability theatre have joined Aboriginal, queer, and feminist theatre companies within the richer, more complex Canadian theatrical ecology. Many other companies have declared intercultural mandates. A marked diversity in style and theatrical approach has also resulted from companies practising devised theatre and site-specific production. The introductions to a number of plays in this volume detail the development and distribution of some of these myriad practices across Canada.[41]

If the first dozen years or so of Canadian theatre in the twenty-first century has a theme, it might be continuity and renewal. Théâtre du Rideau Vert, Théâtre du Nouveau Monde, and the Stratford Festival all celebrated sixtieth anniversaries; Théâtre de Quat'Sous, Manitoba Theatre Centre, the Shaw Festival, Halifax's Neptune, Vancouver's Arts Club, and the National Theatre School hit the half-century mark. Forty years after having made "Canadian theatre" a meaningful term in the 1970s, most of the companies responsible, "alternate" or not, were still around, still developing, producing, and staging Canadian plays. Some of the great actors of the Canadian stage were still around, too: William Hutt played lead roles at Stratford and Soulpepper until a couple of years before his death at age eighty-seven in 2007; Christopher Plummer, also in his mid-eighties, starred at Stratford, won an Academy Award, and wrote a lively, informative memoir.[42]

Even renewal has been marked by continuity, especially in central Canada, where new artistic directors have included some of the best-known builders of modern Canadian theatre. When Urjo Kareda died in 2001, Richard Rose replaced him at Tarragon, and director Daniel Brooks took over from Rose at Necessary Angel. Jackie Maxwell succeeded Christopher Newton at Shaw in 2002 when he stepped down after twenty-three seasons. Des McAnuff assumed the mantle at the Stratford Festival, after a brief transitional period, when Richard Monette died in 2008. Other changes of the guard included new artistic directors at Theatre Calgary (Dennis Garnhum), Passe Muraille (Andy McKim), the Vancouver Playhouse (Max Reimer), the Centaur (Roy Surette), Alberta Theatre Productions (Vanessa Porteous), Persephone (Del Surjik), Buddies in Bad Times (Brendan Healy), Canadian Stage (Matthew Jocelyn), Neptune (George Pothitos), and Stratford again in 2012 (Antoni Cimolino) when McAnuff left.

Maybe the most exciting changes happened at Ottawa's National Arts Centre. Peter Hinton took over the English Theatre section in 2005 and instituted a major revival, producing an all-Canadian season (2006), championing Aboriginal work (Marie Clements's plays, *Death of a Chief*, an all-Aboriginal *King Lear*), and restoring the NAC's resident acting company. Developments on the NAC's French Theatre side were just as dramatic with Wajdi Mouawad becoming artistic director in 2008 and, like Hinton, programming controversial seasons with significant Canadian content. Mouawad was succeeded in 2011 by Brigitte Haentjens, the first woman to run the French Theatre. And in 2012 (the year Jean Roberts died, Roberts having established and run the NAC's theatre section in the 1970s), Siminovitch Prize–winning director Jillian Keiley left Newfoundland's Artistic Fraud to take over from Hinton as artistic director of the English Theatre. Keiley brought in Nathan Medd from Vancouver's dynamic Electric Company Theatre as managing director, completing a bi-coastal renewal of what should be and looks to be – but for decades was not – one of Canada's flagship companies.

Renewal took place in the infrastructure as well: renovations at St. John's LSPU Hall (once the home of the Longshoremen's Protective Union), Montreal's Segal Centre, and the Vancouver East Cultural Centre (rechristened The Cultch); new buildings for Soulpepper (Young Centre for the Performing Arts) in Toronto's Distillery District, Crow's Theatre in east end Toronto, and Persephone in Saskatoon; major new festivals in Edmonton (Nextfest), Vancouver (PuSh), Toronto (Luminato), and Ottawa (Magnetic North). Established in 2003 under founding artistic director Mary Vingoe, the Magnetic North Festival showcases Canadian work from across the country, alternating between Ottawa and another city every year. Vancouver's Brenda Leadlay took over in 2012. Bright new names on the marquee included Toronto playwright Hannah Moscovitch and director Weyni Mengesha; Jacob Richmond, playwright and director for Victoria's exciting Atomic Vaudeville company; Vancouver director Kim Collier; Edmonton playwright / performer Chris Craddock and designer Bretta Gerecke.

Pioneering playwrights David French and David Freeman passed away, but other Toronto writers kept the flame burning bright. Michael Healey's *The Drawer Boy* (1999), a play based on Theatre Passe Muraille's 1972 classic, *The Farm Show*, and John Mighton's *Half Life* (2005), set in a home for the aged, became international hits. Trey Anthony's *'da Kink in my Hair* went from the Toronto Fringe to Passe Muraille to the Mirvishes' Princess of Wales Theatre, becoming the most commercially successful play in Toronto history and a TV series. *The Drowsy Chaperone*, with music and lyrics by Lisa Lambert and Greg Morrison, book by Bob Martin and Don McKellar, travelled from the Toronto Fringe to Passe Muraille to a Mirvish production at the Winter Garden to Broadway in 2006, where it ran for over a year, winning two Tony and four Drama Desk awards, including Outstanding Musical. Multiple national and international tours followed.

Some of the most dramatic and traumatic developments occurred in Vancouver. In 2012, just a year short of its fiftieth anniversary, the Playhouse Theatre Company permanently shut its doors. With a declining audience and growing debt, and without a building of its own, the Playhouse had been just hanging on. But its demise sent shock waves through the community. Was this a sign that the regional theatre model was no longer relevant? Possibly, though the Arts Club, with a larger subscriber base and three theatre buildings, had effectively assumed that role in Metro Vancouver. Did it signal a death knell for theatrical culture in the city? Hardly. Despite the loss of the Playhouse and severe provincial funding cuts in 2009, the Greater Vancouver Professional Theatre Alliance counted seventy member companies. Small, adventurous outfits like Neworld, Theatre Replacement, Electric Company, Boca del Lupo, Radix, The Only Animal, and Leaky Heaven Circus were among Canada's leading proponents of innovative, site-specific work, many of them getting national exposure at the NAC's BC Scene in 2009. The PuSh Festival grew in size and importance every year, and The Cultch would get a third stage in 2013, the newly renovated 1913-vintage York Theatre. Things could have been a lot worse.[43]

Politics provided a good deal of drama in an era scarred by 9/11 and the wars in Iraq and Afghanistan. Director Ross Manson and playwright Jason Sherman created the Wrecking Ball in 2004, an annual protest-oriented showcase in Toronto based on the American Living Newspapers of the 1930s, inviting Canadian playwrights to respond to current political events. During the federal election campaigns of 2008 and 2011, the Wrecking Ball was held in cities across Canada, aimed at Prime Minister Stephen Harper and the federal Conservatives for their cuts to arts funding and general hostility to Canadian culture. During the 2008 campaign, in response to criticism of the cuts, Harper infamously remarked that "ordinary working people" didn't want to see artists at "a rich gala all subsidized by taxpayers claiming their subsidies aren't high enough."[44] The furious response from the arts community, especially in Quebec (led in part by Wajdi Mouawad), was credited by many as having prevented the Conservatives from winning a majority in that election. But they got their majority in 2011 and continued their cuts and ideological attacks on the arts. When Justin Trudeau became leader of the federal Liberal Party in 2013, Conservative TV ads belittled him for having been a drama teacher.

Among the casualties of Conservative government cuts between 2008 and 2012 was Prom Arts, a program that funded artists' travel abroad to promote Canadian culture; the Canadian Conference of the Arts, the national network of arts organizations founded in 1945 as the Canadian Arts Council; and CBC's radio drama department, eliminated after eighty years of commissioning, producing, and airing Canadian radio plays. Another kind of attack was launched in 2010, when the Prime Minister's Office complained that Catherine Frid's play *Homegrown* at Toronto's SummerWorks Festival "glorified terrorism" – though none of the complainers actually saw the play. In a mysterious coincidence SummerWorks lost its funding for 2011. Seventy theatre companies across the country subsequently held readings of *Homegrown* in protest and sympathy, with proceeds going to help SummerWorks make up its lost revenue. The festival just as mysteriously had funding restored the following year.[45]

Michael Healey's play *Proud*, a political satire centred on a Canadian prime minister closely resembling Stephen Harper, was dropped from its scheduled slot in the 2012 Tarragon season, an apparent victim of libel chill. In protest Healey quit his post as Tarragon's playwright-in-residence. The same year, in an event unrelated except insofar as it occurred at another of Toronto's iconic original alternate theatres, long-time artistic director Ken Gass was fired by the Factory Theatre board. The "Factory fiasco," as *Toronto Star* critic Richard Ouzounian called it, led to angry protests from the theatre community. Judith Thompson and George Walker both pulled their new plays from the Factory season. But neither theatre backed down.[46]

Life and art, of course, in their resiliency, go on. *Proud* was staged instead at the Berkeley Street Theatre to great reviews, with Healey in the central role. Gass revived his dormant Canadian Rep Theatre, a company he founded in the 1980s, and Thompson and Walker gave him the plays they pulled from Tarragon (*Watching Glory Die* and *Dead Metaphor*) to premiere in his 2013–14 season, along with the English-language premiere of Wajdi Mouawad's *Pacamambo*. Not bad consolation prizes. Tarragon continues to be a flagship company for the production of Canadian plays: seven in 2013–14, including work by Daniel MacIvor and Joan MacLeod. Ditto for Factory. New co-artistic directors Nina Lee Aquino and Nigel Shawn Williams announced a four-play, all-Canadian season for 2013–14, comprising three premieres and MacIvor's *Bingo!*

The Canadian theatre story awaits its next dramatic chapter.

NOTES

1   The story of pre-twentieth century Canadian theatre has been told only in bits and pieces. For a general overview, see Eugene Benson and L.W. Conolly, *English-Canadian Theatre* (Toronto: Oxford UP, 1987). Anton Wagner and Richard Plant, ed., *Canada's Lost Plays* (Toronto: CTR, 1978–81) is an excellent anthology in four volumes presenting plays from the nineteenth through the mid-twentieth century with extensive historical introductions. See also, among others, Jerry Wasserman, *Spectacle of Empire: Marc Lescarbot's Theatre of Neptune in New France* (Vancouver: Talonbooks, 2006); Leonard E. Doucette, *Theatre in French Canada: Laying the Foundations, 1606–1867* (Toronto: U of Toronto P, 1984); Yashdip S. Bains, *English Canadian Theatre, 1765–1826* (NY: Peter Lang, 1998); Mary Elizabeth Smith, *Too Soon the Curtain Fell: A History of Theatre in Saint John, 1789–1900* (Fredericton: Brunswick, 1981); Murray D. Edwards, *A Stage in Our Past: English-Language Theatre in Eastern Canada from the 1790s to 1914* (Toronto: U of Toronto P, 1968); Franklin Graham, *Histrionic Montreal: Annals of the Montreal Stage, with Biographical and Critical Notices of the Plays and Players of a Century*, 2nd ed. (Montreal: John Lovell & Son, 1902); Chad Evans, *Frontier Theatre: A History of Nineteenth-Century Theatrical Entertainment in the Canadian Far West and Alaska* (Victoria: Sono Nis, 1983); E. Ross Stuart, *The History of Prairie Theatre: The Development of Theatre in Alberta, Manitoba, and Saskatchewan, 1833–1982* (Toronto: Simon & Pierre, 1984); John Orrell, *Fallen Empires: Lost Theatres of Edmonton, 1881–1914* (Edmonton: NeWest, 1981); Ann Saddlemyer, ed., *Early Stages: Theatre in Ontario, 1800–1914* (Toronto: U of Toronto P, 1990); Kym Bird, *Redressing the Past: The Politics of Early English-Canadian Women's Drama, 1880–1920* (Montreal: McGill-Queen's UP, 2004).

2   Nathan Cohen, "Theatre Today: English Canada," *Tamarack Review* 13 (Autumn 1959): 28.

3   Thomas B. Hendry, "Trends in Canadian Theatre," *Tulane Drama Review* 10:1 (Fall 1965): 62–70. That same year Michael Tait concluded his survey of "the grey wastes of Canadian drama," 1920–60, by noting "perhaps the most depressing feature of theatre in Canada: the lack of any vital and continuing relationship between theatrical activity and the work of the Canadian playwright." "Drama and Theatre," *Literary History of Canada*, ed. Carl F. Klinck, 2nd ed. (Toronto: U of Toronto P, 1976), ii, 159, 167.

4   Betty Lee, *Love and Whisky: The Story of the Dominion Drama Festival* (Toronto: McClelland & Stewart, 1973), 296.

5   For an important collection of articles documenting twentieth-century Canadian theatre, see Don Rubin, ed., *Canadian Theatre History: Selected Readings* (Toronto: Playwrights Canada, 2004). See also Jerry Wasserman, "Early English-Canadian Theater and Drama, 1918–1967," *History of Literature in Canada: English-Canadian and French-Canadian*, ed. Reingard M. Nischik (Rochester: Camden House, 2008), 207–21.

6   Alan Filewod, "National Theatre / National Obsession," *Canadian Theatre Review* 62 (Spring 1990): 6; rpt. Rubin, ed., *Canadian Theatre History*, 410. Cf. Patrick B. O'Neill, "The British Canadian Theatrical Organization Society and the Trans-Canada Theatre Society," *Journal of Canadian Studies* 15:1 (Spring 1980): 56–67; Anthony Vickery, "Two Patterns of Touring Canada: 1896 to 1914," *Theatre Research in Canada* 31 (Spring 2010): 1–19; and Robertson Davies, "Mixed Grill: Touring Fare in Canada, 1920–1935," *Theatrical Touring and Founding in North America*, ed. L.W. Conolly (Westport, CT: Greenwood, 1982), 41–56.

7   Fred Jacobs, "Waiting for a Dramatist," *Canadian Magazine* 43 (June 1914): 146. On the relationship between Canada's theatre critics and Canadian theatrical development, see Anton Wagner, ed., *Establishing Our Boundaries: English-Canadian Theatre Criticism* (Toronto: U of Toronto P, 1999).

8   Vincent Massey, "The Prospects of a Canadian Drama," *Queen's Quarterly* 30 (Oct. 1922): 200; rpt. Rubin, ed., *Canadian Theatre History*, 55.

9   See Dick MacDonald, *Mugwump Canadian: The Merrill Denison Story* (Montreal: Content, 1973); Barbara Godard, "MacPherson, Isabel Ecclestone (Mackay)." *Dictionary of Canadian Biography*, ed. George W. Brown, vol. XV (1921–30) (Toronto: U of Toronto P, 2005); James Hoffman, "Carroll Aikins and the Home Theatre," *Theatre Research in Canada* 7.1 (Spring 1986): 50–70; Patrick O'Neill, "Carroll Aikins's Experiments in Playwriting," *BC Studies* 137 (Spring 2003): 65–91; Roy Mitchell, *Creative Theatre* (NY: John Day, 1929); Renata Usmiani, "Roy Mitchell: Prophet in Our Past," *Theatre Research in Canada* 8.2 (Fall 1987): 147–68; and Scott Duchesne, "The Impossible Theatre: Roy Mitchell and the Chester Mysteries: Experience, Initiation, and Brotherhood," *Theatre Research in Canada* 27.2 (2006): 227–44.

10   Rupert Caplan, "The Ultimate National Theatre," *Canadian Forum* 9 (Jan. 1929): 143–44; rpt. Rubin, ed., *Canadian Theatre History*, 78.

11   Lee, 287–98; Gaetan Charlebois, "*Les Belles-Soeurs*," *Canadian Theatre Encyclopedia*. www.canadiantheatre.com. Betty Lee's *Love and Whisky*, the primary source for information on the DDF and the only book on the subject, is packed with information but lacks footnotes and often quotes inaccurately. Cf. Herbert Whittaker, "Dominion Drama Festival," *Oxford*

Companion to Canadian Theatre, ed. Eugene Benson and L.W. Conolly (Toronto: Oxford UP, 1989), 144–45.

12 H.A. Voaden, "A National Drama League," *Canadian Forum* 9 (Dec. 1928): 105; rpt. Rubin, ed., *Canadian Theatre History*, 76. See Anton Wagner, ed., *A Vision of Canada: Herman Voaden's Dramatic Works, 1928–1945* (Toronto: Simon & Pierre, 1993). Wagner's website, *The Worlds of Herman Voaden*, contains twenty-two of Voaden's plays, nearly thirty of his articles, and numerous articles about him. http://www.lib.unb.ca/texts/theatre/voaden/index.htm

13 See Anton Wagner, ed., *Canada's Lost Plays, Volume Three: The Developing Mosaic: English-Canadian Drama to Mid-Century* (Toronto: CTR, 1980); Benson and Conolly, *English-Canadian Theatre*, ch. 2; Rubin, ed., *Canadian Theatre History*, sec. 3; Alan Filewod, *Committing Theatre: Theatre Radicalism and Political Intervention in Canada* (Toronto: Between the Lines, 2011), ch. 4; Susan McNicoll, *The Opening Act: Canadian Theatre History 1945–1953* (Vancouver: Ronsdale, 2012); Geraldine Anthony, *Gwen Pharis Ringwood* (Boston: Twayne, 1981); Moira Day, ed., *The Hungry Spirit: Selected Plays and Prose by Elsie Park Gowan* (Edmonton: NeWest, 1992).

14 Jack Gould, "Canada Shows Us How," *New York Times* (1 Sept. 1946): Sec. II: 7. Cf. Howard Fink and John Jackson, ed., *All the Bright Company: Radio Drama Produced by Andrew Allan* (Kingston & Toronto: Quarry / CBC, 1987); N. Alice Frick, *Image in the Mind: CBC Radio Drama, 1944 to 1954* (Toronto: Canadian Stage & Arts, 1987); and Knowlton Nash, *The Microphone Wars: A History of Triumph and Betrayal at the CBC* (Toronto: McClelland & Stewart, 1994).

15 John Coulter, "The Canadian Theatre and the Irish Exemplar," *Theatre Arts Monthly* 22 (July 1938): 503; rpt. Rubin, ed., *Canadian Theatre History*, 119.

16 See Paula Sperdakos, *Dora Mavor Moore: Pioneer of the Canadian Theatre* (Toronto: ECW, 1995); Mavor Moore, *Reinventing Myself: Memoirs* (Toronto: Stoddart, 1994); Allan Boss, *Identifying Mavor Moore: A Historical and Literary Study* (Toronto: Playwrights Canada, 2011).

17 See McNicoll, *The Opening Act*; James Hoffman, "Sydney Risk and the Everyman Theatre," *BC Studies* 76 (Winter 1987–88): 33–57; Amelia Hall, *Life before Stratford: The Memoirs of Amelia Hall* (Toronto: Dundurn, 1989); Paul Illidge, *Glass Cage: The Crest Theatre Story* (Toronto: Creber Monde, 2005); Susan Stone-Blackburn, *Robertson Davies, Playwright: A Search for the Self on the Canadian Stage* (Vancouver: UBC Press, 1985).

18 Robertson Davies, *The Well-Tempered Critic: One Man's View of Theatre and Letters in Canada*, ed. Judith Skelton Grant (Toronto: McClelland & Stewart, 1981), 66.

19 Davies, 74.

20 See Tom Patterson and Allan Gould, *First Stage: The Making of the Stratford Festival* (Toronto: McClelland & Stewart, 1987); John Pettigrew and Jamie Portman, *Stratford: The First Thirty Years* (Toronto: Macmillan, 1985); Martin Hunter, *Romancing the Bard: Stratford at Fifty* (Toronto: Dundurn, 2001); Robert Cushman, *Fifty Seasons at Stratford* (Toronto: Madison, 2002).

21 Mavor Moore, "A Theatre for Canada," *University of Toronto Quarterly* 26 (Oct. 1956): 2; rpt. Rubin, ed., *Canadian Theatre History*, 233.

22 *Report of the Royal Commission on National Development in the Arts, Letters, and Sciences* (Ottawa: Edmond Cloutier, 1951), 13, 18, 275. On Massey, cf. Alan Filewod, *Performing Canada: The Nation Enacted in the Imagined Theatre* (Kamloops, BC: Textual Studies in Canada, 2002), ch. 3; and Karen A. Finlay, *The Force of Culture: Vincent Massey and Canadian Sovereignty* (Toronto: U of Toronto P, 2004).

23 Tom Hendry, "MTC: A View from the Beginning," *Canadian Theatre Review* 4 (Fall 1974): 16. See Fraidie Martz and Andrew Wilson, *A Fiery Soul: The Life and Theatrical Times of John Hirsch* (Montreal: Véhicule, 2011).

24 Jamie Portman, "*Ecstasy of Rita Joe* Still Manages to Shock and Scourge," *Vancouver Province* (12 April 1976): 10. Cf. Neil Carson, "Towards a Popular Theatre in English Canada," *Canadian Literature* 85 (Summer 1980): 64–65.

25 David Gustafson, "Let's Really Hear It for Canadian Theatre," *Maclean's* 84 (Oct. 1971): 84.

26 George Ryga, "Contemporary Theatre and Its Language," *Canadian Theatre Review* 14 (Spring 1977): 8.

27 Quoted verbatim from a series of interviews with artistic directors of regional theatres in *The Stage in Canada*: Edward Gilbert (Manitoba Theatre Centre), 3 (May 1967), 14; Robert Glenn (Citadel [Edmonton]), 3 (June 1967), 7; Joy Coghill (Vancouver Playhouse), 3 (Sept. 1967), 10; Kurt Reis (MTC), 5 (Nov. 1969), 13.

28 See Bryan D. Palmer, *Canada's 1960s: The Ironies of Identity in a Rebellious Era* (Toronto: U of Toronto P, 2009); Benson & Conolly, *English-Canadian Theatre*, ch. 3; James Hoffman, *The Ecstasy of Resistance: A Biography of George Ryga* (Toronto: ECW, 1995); Erin Hurley, *National Performance: Representing Quebec from Expo 67 to Céline Dion* (Toronto: U of Toronto P, 2011), ch. 3–4.

29 Martin Kinch, "The Canadian Theatre: In for the Long Haul," *This Magazine* 10 (Nov.–Dec. 1976): 4–5.

30 Qtd in Robert Wallace, "Growing Pains: Toronto Theatre in the 1970s," *Canadian Literature* 85 (Summer 1980): 77. Cf. Johnston, *Up the Mainstream*.

31 See Neil Carson, *Harlequin in Hogtown: George Lus-combe and Toronto Workshop Productions* (Toronto: U of Toronto P, 1995). For Thompson and Theatre Passe Muraille, see Alan Filewod, *Collective Encounters: Documentary Theatre in English Canada* (Toronto: U of Toronto P, 1987), ch. 1–2; Denis Johnston, *Up the Mainstream: The Rise of Toronto's Alternative Theatres, 1968–1975* (Toronto: U of Toronto P, 1991); Diane Bessai, *Playwrights of Collective Creation* (Toronto: Simon & Pierre, 1992); Judith Rudakoff, ed., *Dangerous Traditions: A Passe Muraille Anthology* (Winnipeg: Blizzard, 1992).

32 George Ryga, "Theatre in Canada: A Viewpoint on Its Development and Future," *Canadian Theatre Review* 1 (Winter 1974): 30; rpt. Rubin, ed., *Canadian Theatre History*, 339.

33 Bill Thomas in the *Times Colonist* (Victoria), quoted in "Playwrights," *The Stage in Canada* 6 (Jan. 1972): 17. See "A Strange Enterprise: The Dilemma of the Playwright in Canada" [The Gaspe Manifesto, 1971], Rubin, ed., *Canadian Theatre History*, 292–96.

34 Coulter, 123.

35 See Sky Gilbert, *Ejaculations from the Charm Factory* (Toronto: ECW, 2000); Shelley Scott, *Nightwood Theatre: A Woman's Work Is Always Done* (Edmonton: AU Press, 2010); Jennifer Preston, "Weesageechak Begins to Dance: Native Earth Performing Arts, Inc.," *TDR / The Drama Review* 36 (Spring 1992): 135–59; Shannon Hengen, *Where Stories Meet: An Oral History of De-ba-jeh-mu-jig Theatre* (Toronto: Playwrights Canada, 2007).

36 Alan Filewod, "Between Empires: Post-Imperialism and Canadian Theatre," *Essays in Theatre* 11 (Nov. 1992): 11.

37 Sky Gilbert, "Gotta Sing, Gotta Dance, Gotta Cry," *Globe and Mail* (3 Nov. 1997): C1.

38 Michael Phillips, "21st Century Theater: Calling All Risk Takers," *Los Angeles Times* (28 Nov. 1999): Calendar 46–47; and Kate Taylor, "The Play's the Thing," *Globe and Mail* (26 Dec. 2000): R1. See also Jason Sherman, "S.O.S: A Message in a Bottleneck," *Globe and Mail* (17 Aug. 1998): C1.

39 Lloyd Rose, "Onstage, Works with a Distinct Canadian Accent," *Washington Post* (10 Sept. 2000): G24. Cf. Pat Donnelly, "Canadians Are Invading Washington with Great Success," *Montreal Gazette* (23 Sept. 2000): D1–2.

40 See Annie Brisset, *A Sociocritique of Translation: Theatre and Alterity in Quebec, 1968-1988*, trans. Rosalind Gill and Roger Gannon (Toronto: U of Toronto P, 1996); Louise Ladouceur, *Dramatic Licence: Translating Theatre from One Official Language to the Other in Canada*, trans. Richard Lebeau (Edmonton: U of Alberta P, 2012); and Louise H. Forsyth, ed., *Anthology of Québec Women's Plays in English Translation*, vol. I (1966-1986) & vol. II (1987-2003) (Toronto: Playwrights Canada, 2006).

41 Numerous anthologies published over the past decade collect plays representative of these various cultural communities. Thanks largely to Ric Knowles's editorial work with Playwrights Canada Press, collections of scholarly and critical essays devoted to these specific areas have also proliferated. See Rob Appleford, ed., *Aboriginal Drama and Theatre*, 2005; Natalie Alvarez, ed., *Latina/o Canadian Theatre and Performance*, 2013; Nina Lee Aquino and Ric Knowles, eds., *Asian Canadian Theatre*, 2011; Susan Bennett, ed., *Feminist Theatre and Performance*, 2006; Rosalind Kerr, ed., *Queer Theatre in Canada*, 2007; Ric Knowles and Ingrid Mündel, eds., *"Ethnic," Multicultural, and Intercultural Theatre*, 2009; Maureen Moynagh, ed., *African-Canadian Theatre*, 2005; Bruce Barton, ed., *Collective Creation, Collaboration, and Devising*, 2008; and Andrew Houston, ed., *Environmental and Site-Specific Theatre*, 2007. See also Kirsty Johnston, *Stage Turns: Canadian Disability Theatre* (Montreal: McGill-Queen's UP, 2012); and Jerry Wasserman et al, "All White All Right? Vancouver Theatre Artists Talk about Vancouver's Monochrome Stages," *alt.theatre* 7.1 (Sept. 2009): 8–19.

42 Christopher Plummer, *In Spite of Myself: A Memoir* (NY: Knopf, 2008); Keith Garebian, ed., *William Hutt: Masks and Faces* (Oakville, ON: Mosaic, 1995). See also Richard Monette (as told to David Prosser), *This Rough Magic: The Making of an Artistic Director* (Stratford: Stratford Festival of Canada, 2007).

43 See Janet Smith, "Theatre Takes Centre Stage," *Georgia Straight* (21 June 2012): 31–32; J. Kelly Nestruck, "Annus Mirabilis, Annus Horribilis," *Globe and Mail* (25 June 2012): R1–2; and Nestruck, "Superstar Showdowns, Touring Triumphs, Aboriginal Firsts," *Globe and Mail* (28 Dec. 2009): R1–2.

44 Robert Benzie, Bruce Campion-Smith, and Les Whittington, "Arts Uproar? Ordinary Folks Just Don't Care, Harper Says," *Toronto Star* (24 Sept. 2008): A1. Cf. Sherry Simon, "When Artists Carry the Torch," *English Studies in Canada* 33 (Sept. 2007): 6–9.

45 David Akin, "Conservatives Set to Cancel Program Promoting Culture," *Vancouver Sun* (8 Aug. 2008): A6; Angela Hickman, "SummerWorks Gets Homegrown Support," *National Post* (7 July 2011): AL3.

46 Ian Brown, "The Play's the Thing," *Globe and Mail* (17 Mar. 2012): R7; J. Kelly Nestruck, "Gass's Dismissal from Factory Shocks Toronto Theatre World," *Globe and Mail* (22 June 2012): R1; Richard Ouzounian, "Offstage Events Rival Onstage," *Toronto Star* (26 Dec. 2012): E1.

ROBERT LEPAGE

(b. 1957)

MARIE BRASSARD

(b. 1961)

"Using dialogue, mime, dance, music, and lighting as means of frustrating and then illuminating the linear, the narrative, and the rational, it captures the greatness of what theatre – and only theatre – can do." *Globe and Mail* critic Stephen Godfrey's comment on *Polygraph* typifies the extravagant praise gleaned by the work of Robert Lepage in the 1980s when he exploded onto the international stage. It also points to the complex theatricality that remains the essence of Lepage's dramatic art. In much the same way that Michel Tremblay's concern with language helped define Québécois theatre a generation earlier, Lepage's vivid baroque style with its emphasis on the visual, physical, and sonic elements of the stage captures the shape of that theatre since the mid-1980s. At the same time, Lepage has not shied away from the theatre of words, or words and music, establishing himself as a director of world stature with his productions of Shakespeare, opera, rock concerts, and film. The transnational scope and sensibility of his work, along with its brilliant theatricality, has made Lepage Canada's first international theatrical superstar.

As writer, director, performer, and often designer of his own plays, movies, and operas, Lepage has pushed the boundaries of the performance text further than nearly any other Canadian dramatist writing in English or French. "I find myself more than ever returning to the idea of the theatre as a meeting place for architecture, music, dance, literature, acrobatics, play, and so on," Lepage told Rémy Charest in interviews published as *Connecting Flights* (1998). All Lepage's plays are resolutely theatrical and multilingual, incorporating English, French, and other tongues as well as the non-verbal languages of scenography and performance. In *Polygraph*, he collaborated with actress Marie Brassard to create what its title etymologically suggests: a kind of multiple writing. In the guise of a murder mystery, the play explores questions of truth and falsehood, examining the nature of technology and art, criminology, politics, and the human heart.

Lepage was born into a bicultural home in Quebec City: his adopted older brother and sister spoke English and continued attending English-language schools while Robert and another sister were raised francophone.

His early theatrical influences included the elaborate rock concerts of the band Genesis with lead singer Peter Gabriel, whose 1993 and 2002 solo world tours Lepage would eventually stage. After graduating in 1978 from the Conservatoire de musique et d'art dramatique du Québec (also attended by Marie Brassard), he studied in Paris with Swiss director Alain Knapp, who taught actors to become *acteurs-créateurs* by combining writing and directing with their performance skills. Returning to Quebec, Lepage played improvisational theatresports with the Ligue nationale d'improvisation, winning its Most Popular Player award one year. In 1981, he joined Théâtre Repère, a Quebec company that based its work on the *RSVP Cycles* of the San Francisco Dancers' Workshop. Beginning with a *Resource* (a concrete object or image rather than a theme), they arrange a *Score*, which is then analyzed (*Value* action), and ultimately *Performed*. (In French, *REssources, Partition, Evaluation*, and *REpresentation* = REPÈRE.)

Most of Lepage's shows in the 1980s were devised and produced under the auspices of Théâtre Repère, with Lepage serving as co-artistic director from 1986 to 1989. Marie Brassard joined the company in 1985 and has been an important collaborator in Lepage's work ever since, as well as an independent film and theatre actor. She formed her own company, Infrarouge, in Montreal in 2001, and has toured internationally with it, writing, directing, and performing in *Jimmy* (2001), *The Darkness* (2003), *Peepshow* (2005), *The Invisible* (2008), *Me Talking to Myself in the Future* (2010), and *Trieste* (2013). Lepage has compiled an extraordinary international resumé since his first two plays, *Vinci* and *Le trilogie des dragons* (*The Dragons' Trilogy*), premiered in 1985–86. A one-man show based on the attempted suicide of an artist friend and on Leonardo da Vinci's paintings, *Vinci* features Lepage as a cathedral, the *Mona Lisa*, and a blind Italian tour guide. *The Dragons' Trilogy* grew from a ninety-minute piece in Quebec City in 1985, to a three-hour Toronto production in 1986, to a six-hour epic for Montreal's Festival de théâtre des Amériques in 1987. An archeological tour (and tour de force) through three Canadian Chinatowns during three different eras in three different languages, the trilogy has played across North America, Europe, and Australia to enormous critical praise, and was rewritten and remounted for another world tour in 2003.

His next two major works, *Le polygraphe* (*Polygraph*) and *Les plaques tectonique* (*Tectonic Plates*), appeared in 1988, the latter a vision of shifting continents and cultures colliding and metamorphosing across centuries on a stage dominated by two grand pianos suspended over a pool of water. After premiering in Toronto, *Tectonic Plates* played to great acclaim in England, Scotland, and the United States, and in French and English versions at the National Arts Centre, where Lepage served as artistic director of French theatre from 1989 to 1993. His second one-man show, *Les aiguilles et l'opium* (*Needles and Opium*, 1991), a theatrical meditation on Miles Davis, Jean Cocteau, drugs, and art, consolidated Lepage's reputation at home and abroad. *Alanienouidet* (1992), written (partly in Mohawk) with Marianne Ackerman, continued Lepage's exploration of colliding cultures in its examination of English actor Edmund Kean's fascination with the Hurons during his Canadian tours in the early nineteenth century.

Even as his career became increasingly international, Lepage insisted to Charest that his work "remains profoundly Québécois ... It's from Quebec that I want to make contact with the rest of the world." When he founded the multidisciplinary company Ex Machina in 1994 to develop and produce his work, he based it in Quebec City, where he also built an elaborate multimedia production centre, La Caserne, to house the company. Ex Machina's first production was *Les sept branches de la rivière Ota* (*The Seven Streams of the River Ota*), a seven-hour epic about Hiroshima, the Holocaust, and their aftermaths that evolved in three parts from 1994 to 1996. The first part premiered in Edinburgh, the second in Vienna, and the third in Quebec City, with subsequent tours of the United Kingdom, Europe, Japan, and North America. Also touring internationally after its Montreal debut was *Elsinore* (1995), Lepage's adaptation of *Hamlet* in which he played all the roles himself, except Rosencrantz and Guildenstern, who were represented by surveillance cameras. Co-produced by Ex Machina and Austria's Salzburg Festival, *La géométrie des miracles* (*The Geometry of Miracles*, 1998) chronicles the life of architect Frank Lloyd Wright, though Wright himself is only seen from behind in a play that incorporates French, English, Russian, and Serbo-Croatian. *Zulu Time* (1999), which premiered in Zurich, is a meditation on air travel featuring dance, mime, electronic music, and robots.

La face cachée de la lune (*The Far Side of the Moon*, 2000) premiered in Quebec City and has since appeared in four dozen cities around the world. A solo show performed by Lepage, or sometimes Yves Jacques, about a Russian cosmonaut, two Quebec brothers, and their dead mother is one of his most moving and visually exciting plays to date, winning Best Play awards in Montreal, London, and Moscow. Lepage and Jacques also took turns performing *The Andersen Project* (2005), a solo show about Hans Christian Andersen, a rock singer, an arts administrator, and a janitor, which took home Best Play awards in four Canadian cities, Moscow, Milan, and Boston. Lepage adapted John Gay's *The Beggar's Opera* as *The Busker's Opera* (2004), opening in Montreal and playing Paris and Melbourne.

Lipsynch (2007), a nine-hour epic exploring the human voice through nine different characters, was co-produced by Ex Machina and London's Théâtre sans frontières, and toured worldwide. Quebec meets Shanghai in *The Blue Dragon* (2008), a sequel to *The Dragons' Trilogy*, co-written with Marie Michaud. Lepage created *Eonnagata* (2009) with choreographers Sylvie Guillem and Russell Maliphant, exploring the sexual ambiguity of the eighteenth-century Chevalier d'Éon via ballet, contemporary dance, and Kabuki theatre. In 2012, he debuted *Playing Cards 1: Spades*, and in 2013 *Playing Cards 2: Hearts*, the first two of a four-part theatre piece structured around the symbolism and numerology of playing cards and the tarot deck.

In addition to directing all his own plays, Lepage has exercised his multifaceted talents in a variety of other arenas. Beginning with a bilingual *Romeo et Juliette* (1989) in Saskatoon, co-directed by Gordon McCall and set on the Trans-Canada Highway, he rapidly became one of the world's foremost directors of Shakespeare. His productions of *Coriolanus, Macbeth,* and *The Tempest* (with Marie Brassard as Ariel) in Paris and Montreal (1992–93) were "the first really imaginative Shakespeare we've seen in Canada," according to critic Ray Conlogue. His 1992 *A Midsummer Night's Dream* at London's Royal National Theatre – set in a pool of mud – elicited comparisons to the great Peter Brook's touchstone production of twenty years earlier. In 1994, Lepage directed adaptations of *The Tempest* and *Macbeth* in Tokyo with Japanese actors and, in 2011, he created a Native *Tempest* set on a Huron reserve near Quebec City. At the invitation of Ingmar Bergman, he directed a production of Strindberg's *A Dream Play* in Stockholm in 1994.

Lepage has also joined the first rank of opera directors since his 1993 production of the Canadian Opera Company's double bill of Bartók and Schönberg (*Bluebeard's Castle / Erwartung*) won the $100,000 Scotsman's Hamada Festival Prize at the Edinburgh International Festival. His operatic highlights include *The Damnation of Faust* (1999) in Japan and Paris, revived in 2008 at New York's Metropolitan Opera; *1984* (2005) in Covent Garden; *The Rake's Progress* (2007) and *The Nightingale and Other Short Fables* (2009) with Toronto's Canadian Opera Company; and Wagner's *Ring Cycle* (2010–12) at New York's Met. The latter production was hugely controversial, reportedly costing $45 million to design and build. A full-length documentary on the project, by filmmaker Susan Froemke, is titled *Wagner's Dream* (2013).

As a film actor, Lepage made notable appearances in Denys Arcand's *Jesus of Montreal* (1988) and *Stardom* (2000). As screenwriter and film director, he made *Le confessional* in 1995, a byzantine family drama set against the backdrop of an Alfred Hitchcock film shoot in Quebec City. Marie Brassard wrote and stars in the film adaptation of *Le polygraphe* (1996), which Lepage directed. *Nô* (1998) is Lepage's own adaptation of *The Seven Streams of the River Ota*, and *Possible Worlds* (2000) is his first feature film in English, adapted from the play by Toronto's John Mighton. *The Far Side of the Moon* (2003) has been his most honoured film to date.

If all that wasn't enough, Lepage has directed and designed two Cirque du Soleil shows, *Kà* (2004) and *Totem* (2010), and for Quebec City's four hundredth anniversary in 2008, he created, with Ex Machina, *The Image Mill*, the world's largest projection design, an outdoor chronicle of the city's history.

Lepage's many individual honours include Toronto's Herbert Whittaker Drama Bench Award, Quebec's Prix Denise-Pelletier, the Queen's Golden Jubilee Medal, France's Chevalier de la Légion d'honneur and Prix Samuel-de-Champlain, Moscow's Stanislavsky Award, the Europe Theatre Prize, and the Governor General's Performing Arts Award. He has honorary degrees from the universities of Laval, McGill, Toronto, and Concordia.

Le polygraphe was first produced by Théâtre Repère in French in Quebec City in 1988, developed through improvisation by Lepage, Brassard, and Pierre Phillipe Guay, with contributions from Gyllian Raby. A revised version, co-produced by Montreal's Théâtre de Quat'Sous later that year, was translated into English for a 1989 production in London, which won Lepage the *Time Out* award for his direction. The script continued to evolve in both languages between 1990 and 1992 as it played Toronto (winning the 1991 Chalmers Award) and six European summer festivals (including Barcelona, where Marie Brassard won the Best Foreign Actress award), as well as New York, Ottawa, Edmonton, and Vancouver (the first place any Lepage play was directed by someone other than himself). In 1996, a Japanese version was performed in Tokyo and Osaka. In 2000, *Le polygraphe* toured Spain and Italy in a co-production involving Lepage's Ex Machina and three Spanish and Italian theatre companies. It had major productions in English in Nottingham and Melbourne (2001), in Belgrade (2011), and in Calgary (2013). Always a work in progress, the script of the play has continued to evolve. The version printed here is the English-language production script from 1993, substantially different from the script first published in *Canadian Theatre Review* in 1990, and no doubt different from the scripts developed for subsequent productions.

Lepage and Brassard have called *Polygraph* "a metaphysical detective story." A London critic called it "a play disguised as a film." Loosely based on the actual murder of a friend for which Lepage was interrogated by the police, the play invokes the cinematic traditions of the murder mystery with its use of film-style titles, credits, stage directions, and music, as well as various *film noir* devices, at the same time as it questions the ability of cinema to embody artistic truth. Structurally, we are presented with a film and play within a play. Lucie acts the part of the murdered woman for the exploitative film version of the "real" story in which she, her neighbour François, and her lover, David, find their lives still inextricably bound together. As an actress, she is also involved in another murder plot, playing the title role in a stage production of *Hamlet*. Does theatrical art approach truth more closely than the cinematic? Is Yorick's prop skull any less a contrivance than the movie's fake tears or the three takes of Lucie's nude death scene? Are the multiple deceptions and manufactured emotions of the characters' lives any more or less authentic than the representations of screen or stage? In a more complicated way than the Russian doll that David gives Lucie, which stands, as he says, for "one truth that is hiding another truth and another one and another one ...," *Polygraph* presents a reality in which truths are layered within lies, mirroring and distorting one another in the deceptions that make up life, art, and the technologies we use to help structure them both.

Along with the movie camera, the polygraph machine is the play's primary technology, a device intended to distinguish truth from falsehood by recording physiological responses to questions. Yet the polygraph itself is subject to manipulation and falsification. François's test established his innocence in the murder of Marie-Claude Légaré, but David and the police have kept this information from him, driving him eventually to suicide. In an earlier draft of the play, David says: "The body never lies." In fact, the play is full of lying bodies: that of Lucie, whose body lies for the movie camera; of David, who checks his watch while making love to Lucie at the end of scene 11, betraying her no less than he has his girlfriend in Berlin; of François, in his "soul-weary," masochistic sexual encounters, whose body lies to itself that pain is pleasure.

Physically and metaphorically, the wall dominates the stage. It stands variously for the wall in François's garden, the wall between his and Lucie's apartments, the ramparts of Quebec City, and the "fourth wall" of naturalistic theatre itself, smashed to pieces by the raw presence of the actor in Lepage's metatheatrical dramaturgy – literally when François's naked body crashes through it in the play's spectacular climax. Characters clamber over the wall and slide down it. At one point, the wall bleeds. The opening scene equates it to both the Berlin Wall and the septum bisecting the human heart. If the heart is indeed divided, if wall building as a tactic to defend an ideology of lies merely reflects some kind of biological imperative, then the lies with which we practise our art, politics, crime, criminology, and love should come as no surprise. But the constant theatrical surprises of Lepage and Brassard's script continue to jolt us into fresh experiences of the world and whatever truths there are in it.

Polygraph

Robert Lepage and Marie Brassard
Translated by Gyllian Raby

Polygraph was first performed in French as *Le Polygraphe*, produced by Théâtre Repère, at Implantheatre in Quebec City on May 6, 1988, with the following cast:

LUCIE CHAMPAGNE	Marie Brassard
DAVID HAUSSMANN	Robert Lepage
FRANÇOIS	Pierre Phillipe Guay

Directed and Designed by Robert Lepage

Polygraph was first performed in English, translated by Gyllian Raby, at the Almeida Theatre in London, England, on February 21, 1989, with the same cast, director, and designer.

CHARACTERS

LUCIE CHAMPAGNE, *an actress*
DAVID HAUSSMANN, *a criminologist*
FRANÇOIS, *a waiter*

SETTING

Montreal, Quebec City, and Berlin, 1992.

TRANSLATOR'S NOTE

I first translated *Polygraph* as it was being created, with the odd result that an English text existed before the authors considered their French production to be complete. Through the major revisions since then, I have been more distant from the creation process, but it seems to me that the ideas under exploration have mostly remained the same (along with the majority of the words), even though characters, time frame, and situations have altered – and in our separate reality the Berlin Wall has fallen. The living performance script has been allowed to metamorphose to reflect the authors' deepening perception of and relationship with their material; while the present version has been stable for eighteen months now, if the world continues to change while the authors are engaged with this work, it will also continue to regenerate.

Punctuation in the fast-moving dialogue section is coded as follows: where speeches intersect, as in The Filter, " – " indicates that the speech is suspended in mid-breath; "..." indicates that the breath is trailing away.

– Gyllian Raby, 1993

PROLOGUE

A brick wall runs right across the playing area, behind a shallow platform forestage. Music plays in a film-style opening title sequence, during which projections in a format large enough to completely cover the wall flash the play title and actors' credits. Then, stage right, a projection titles the first scene. The film-style introduction of each scene continues in this way throughout the play. Dialogue and action begin during the projection of the credits and scene title.

PROJECTION:

1. THE FILTER

Stage left, in a "flashback" performance at an inquest six years prior to the action of the play, DAVID reads a pathologist's report about a murder victim. He demonstrates by pointing at the anatomy of a skeleton that lies on the stage floor near his feet. Stage right, behind and above the wall, FRANÇOIS is in a political science class at the university, delivering a presentation on the Berlin Wall.

DAVID: The autopsy has revealed that the stab wounds were caused by a sharp, pointed instrument that penetrated the skin and underlying tissues –

FRANÇOIS: After the fall of the Third Reich, little remained of its capital, Berlin, except a pile of ruins and a demoralized people –

DAVID: The body wounds are extremely large considering the small size of the inflicting instrument:

I would surmise that the shape, depth, and width of the wounds were enlarged during the struggle –

FRANÇOIS: The triumphant Allies enforced a new statute –

DAVID: – by the slicing action of the knife –

FRANÇOIS: – which split the city into international sectors: American, French, British –

DAVID: – as the victim attempted to defend herself.

FRANÇOIS: – and to define their sector, the Soviets built a wall more than forty kilometres in length, cutting the city in two.

DAVID: The victim received cuts to the left hand, the right upper arm, and was pierced through the rib cage and the right lung, to the stomach. We have determined that the fatal cut was given here –

DAVID & FRANÇOIS: – Right through the heart –

FRANÇOIS: – of the city.

DAVID: – between the fifth and sixth ribs.

FRANÇOIS: The "Wall of Shame," as the West Germans called it, was built to stop the human –

DAVID & FRANÇOIS: Hemorrhage –

FRANÇOIS: – of Berliners leaving the East for the West –

DAVID: – was caused by the laceration of the septum.

FRANÇOIS: – symbolic of the division between the communist and capitalist worlds.

DAVID: The septum functions like a wall bisecting the heart; it controls the filtration of blood –

FRANÇOIS: For almost three decades, visitors from the West have been permitted to enter the Eastern bloc –

DAVID: – from the right ventricle to the left –

DAVID & FRANÇOIS: – but the passage is one way only. A sophisticated system of alternating doors open and close to allow the flow of –

FRANÇOIS: – visitors from the West –

DAVID: – deoxygenated blood –

DAVID & FRANÇOIS: – and to impede –

FRANÇOIS: – inhabitants of the East –

DAVID: – oxygenated blood –

DAVID & FRANÇOIS: – from circulating the "wrong" way.

As if a continuous loop, the tempo of the dialogue increases with the volume and drive of the music.

*As it is repeated, the naked body of **LUCIE** rises stage left behind the wall, lit by anatomical slide projections: muscles, veins, organs, and bones superimposed on her flesh, so that she seems transparent. The scene ends on a musical crescendo and a brief blackout. During the blackout, meditative music plays.*

PROJECTION:

2. INSTITUT MÉDICO-LÉGAL, PARTHENAIS,[1] MONTREAL
INTERIOR, NIGHT.

*Lights reveal first the skeleton, which slowly rises to its feet, and then the rest of the scene. Stage right, **DAVID** is at work, taking notes as he intently watches the bleeping, whirring polygraph machine. He turns off the polygraph, puts on his coat, and takes a letter from the pocket. He reads a few lines to himself, then replaces it. Thoughtfully, he lights a cigarette. He approaches the skeleton and slowly takes its head in his hand, assuming the clichéd pose of Hamlet with Yorick's skull. Lights cross-fade to the next scene as **LUCIE**'s voice is heard.*

PROJECTION:

3. HAMLET
EXTERIOR, NIGHT.

***LUCIE** appears in profile stage left, above and behind the wall, reciting Hamlet's speech to Yorick (Act V, Scene i). She wears black and holds a skull.*

LUCIE: Hélas, pauvre Yorick.

Je l'ai connu, Horatio …

Un amuseur infatigable, d'une fantaisie
    extraordinaire:

Il m'a mille fois porté sur son dos.

Et maintenant, que de dégout ne m'inspire-
    t-il pas …

J'en ai des haut-le-cœur …

Ici étaient attachées les lèvres où j'ai déposé
    je ne sais combien de baisers …

Où sont vos malices maintenant, vos pirou-
    ettes, vos chansons, vos éclats de joie?

Nul maintenant n'imite vos grimaces …

---

1   "Parthenais" – the colloquial name for Le centre de prévention de Montréal, a remand centre located on the Parthenais. For the purposes of this play, it is to be understood as a medico-legal forensic institute.

Vous avez comme perdu la face, non?

Tenez, allez dire cela à ma belle dans sa chambre:

Qu'elle peut s'enduire de fards, mais que c'est à cela qu'elle doit en arriver ...

Lights cross-fade into the next scene. A change in soundscape now suggests the hubbub of a busy restaurant.

PROJECTION:

4. FRANÇOIS
INTERIOR, NIGHT.

FRANÇOIS enters stage left with a table for two over his shoulder. This he swings down in an easy movement. Quickly setting it with plates and cutlery, he then positions two chairs either side. When the table is "set," he immediately unmakes it, swings it over his shoulder, and repeats the whole sequence in a different space, all the while talking rapidly to invisible customers. During the course of the scene, he covers the entire stage, suggesting a room full of tables, and he never stops talking.

FRANÇOIS: Vous avez bien mangé? Je vous apporte la facture monsieur. Par ici s'il vous plaît. Vous avez regardé le menu du jour sur le tableau? Oui. C'est pour combien de personnes? Par ici s'il vous plaît. Prendriez-vous un digestif? Deux cafés cognac ... toute de suite ... Ça sera pas long monsieur ... Oui bonjour. Non, malheureusement, on a plus de rôti à l'échalote. À la place, le chef vous suggère son poulet rôti, un poulet au citron, c'est délicieux. Alors deux fois. Allez-vous prendre un dessert? Aujourd'hui, c'est la tarte à l'orange maison. C'est excellent, je vous le recommande ... Oui. Une personne. Par ici s'il vous plaît. For two? ... I'm sorry we don't 'ave any English menu ... I'll translate for you. Deux places? Par ici s'il vous plaît. Pardon? Vous auriez dû me le dire, je vous l'aurait changé sans problèmes. Oui, la prochaine fois, d'accord. Par ici s'il vous plaît.

[The food was good? I'll bring you the bill, sir. Would you please follow me? Have you noticed today's specials on the board? Yes. You'd like a table for ...? Please, follow me. Something to drink, perhaps? You would like to see the wine list? Two coffees with cognac ... It's coming in a minute, sir! Good evening. No, unfortunately we're all out of rôti à l'échalote. The chef suggests the roast chicken in lemon as a substitute; it's really delicious. So ... two chickens. Would you care for dessert? Today's special is homemade orange pie; it's excellent ... So, a place for one ... Would you please follow me? ... For two? ... I'm sorry, we don't have any English menu ... I'll be happy to translate for you. For two ... I have one table over there ... Sorry? Oh ... You should have told me before, I could have changed it, no problem ... Okay ... Next time ... This way, please; a table for ...?]

LUCIE: (*entering and sitting at the table, while talking rapidly to keep pace with his non-stop work*) Salut, François! Aie, ça a l'air que toé pis ton chum, vous êtes venus voir mon show hier ... Vous êtes pas venus me voir après, c'est tu parce que vous avez pas aimé ça?

[Hi François! How're you doing? ... Hey, I heard that you and your boyfriend came to see my show yesterday? How come you didn't come backstage to see me – didn't you like it?]

FRANÇOIS: Ah non! C'était magnifique ... On a beaucoup aimé l'idée de faire jouer Hamlet par une femme ... De nos jours, c'est beaucoup plus percutant que ce soit une femme que tienne ces propos-là plutôt qu'un homme.

[Oh no! It was great! We really liked the idea of a woman playing Hamlet. Especially these days, it's more appropriate to have a woman say all that stuff – much more than a man.]

LUCIE: Ben en fait à l'origine, c'tait pas prévu. Parce que moi je faisais le régie du show mais le gars qui jouait Hamlet y'é tombé malade pis vu qu'y avait juste moi qui savait le texte par cœur, y m'ont coupé les cheveux pis asteur, c'est moi qui le fait ... Aie, François, j'ai entendu dire ... ça d'l'air qu'à CKRL, y cherchent un annonceur pour lire le bulletin de nouvelle le soir ... t'as une belle voix ... y m'semble que tu serais bon là d'dans.

[In fact, it wasn't exactly planned ... I was stage-managing the show, but the guy playing Hamlet got sick, and so, me being the only one who knew the script by heart, they cut my hair, and now I do it! Hey François, I heard that radio station CKRL is looking for a guy to read the late-night news. You've got such a nice voice, you should apply. You'd be great!]

FRANÇOIS: C'est gentil d'avoir pensé à moi, mais ces temps-ci c'est pas possible, j'ai trop d'ouvrage au restaurant.

[It's very nice of you to think of me, but right now it wouldn't be possible. There's too much work at the restaurant.]

LUCIE: Aie, j'ai croisé Alain dans l'escalier tantôt, y m'a même pas dit bonjour ... c'tu parce qu'yé choqué contre moi?

[François, is Alain angry at me? I met him going down the stairs at home, and he didn't even say hello ... Is there a problem?]

FRANÇOIS: Fais-toi en avec ça ... c'est à moi qu'y en veut. [Don't worry. It's me he's mad at. We had a fight ...]

LUCIE: En tout cas, j'te remercie beaucoup, c'était très bon. [Well ... Thank you very much. It was very good.]

LUCIE exits; FRANÇOIS continues at the same pace.

FRANÇOIS: A bientôt, Lucie. [See you soon!]

FRANÇOIS goes out with the table settings, returns, and sits at the table. Changes in lights and music indicate that it is now the end of the day, and he is exhausted. He taps out three lines of coke and snorts them. DAVID enters the restaurant over the wall, sliding down with his back to it, his arms and his suit jacket spread like a giant, ominous spider. DAVID lands smoothly in the empty seat across the table from FRANÇOIS.

DAVID: François, can you hear me properly?

But you can't actually see me, can you?

François, we are going to conduct a little test.

Are we in Canada?

Is it summertime?

Was it you who killed Marie-Claude Légaré?

FRANÇOIS shakes his head, as if to dislodge these disturbing thoughts. DAVID leaves in a slow reversal of the way he came. Lights cross-fade to a bright spotlight stage right.

PROJECTION:

5. THE AUDITION /
6. SAUVÉ METRO STATION
INTERIOR, DAY.

LUCIE walks diffidently into the bright spotlight. She squints nervously at the light as she begins her audition, talking to unseen interviewers positioned in the audience. Her English is good, but sometimes hesitant and a bit convoluted.

LUCIE: Hi. My name is Lucie Champagne ... My hair is shorter than in the photograph because I'm doing a show right now where I play a guy and so,

they cut them a bit ... First, I should tell you right off – I've never ... What? To the camera! ... Okay ...

She turns slightly to face the camera.

Yes, I've never worked on a movie but I've done lots of videos ... mainly comedies, but I like doing drama just as much ... I did lots of videos for the government social services ... Let's see ... What would be an example ...? Oh yes! They gave me the part of this woman whose money was stolen by her brother-in-law ... Between you and I, that might seem a pretty tame crisis but for this woman it is something very dramatic and completely devastating because ... it's her money ... and ... it's her brother-in-law ... And so I had to play this part with as much emotion as I possibly could.

Oh yes! One thing I loved to work on while I was still at the theatre school was this play by Tennessee Williams called *Talk to Me Like the Rain and Let Me Listen*. The title is very long but the play is actually very short. It is the story of a couple, and I played the woman, and my character, she was anorexic. But not by choice – I mean, she was anorexic because she hadn't eaten for four days, because she didn't have any money, because her boyfriend took off with the welfare cheque ... I just loved playing that role ...

My first experience? Well, I'll tell you, you are going to laugh!

It was for the priest's birthday when I was in grade one. Everyone in my class was in it, the other kids all lined up in front of the wall behind me, and they sang: "Where are you going, little Bo-Peep, where are you going, Bo-Peep ...?" And there I was, out in front and wearing this little white dress, and I sang back: "I am following this beauteous star and all my sheeps are saying baaa ...!" My God, I loved it! I was a kid who liked telling lies you know – I was not a liar but ... I used to be fascinated that I could say things that weren't true but do it so convincingly that people would believe me. So I used to make up all these stories ... Maybe the fact I always wanted to be an actress comes from there ...

Oh yes! ... For my audition, I brought a soliloquy from Shakespeare's *Hamlet* ... No, no, not the part of Ophelia, the part of Hamlet.

Oh ... you would prefer an improv. Euh ...

She looks around.

Should I improvise here? … What would you like me to improvise? … To imagine myself in a tragic situation … Is that so you can see if I can cry? Because, I mean … I can't cry just like that … Well, no, I mean … Put me in a movie that has a sad scene where I have to cry, I'd concentrate to the point where tears would well up, but I can't cry just like that …

To imagine myself in an absolute state of panic … Don't you think I'm panicking enough here?

Okay, okay, I'll do it.

> *Projection of a Montreal Metro logo and the sign for Sauvé metro station. The soundscape evokes a large, hollow-echoing underground. LUCIE focuses on the front edge of the stage, an expression of absolute horror on her face; she backs up to lean against the wall with an inarticulate scream. DAVID enters. He kneels solemnly beside the "tracks" at the edge of the stage. In his hand he holds a bloody T-shirt, which he places in a zip-lock plastic bag. He takes out a notebook and writes. LUCIE, meantime, is going into shock, shouting and crying in semi-hysteria. DAVID assesses her state, contemplates his notes, carefully puts away his notebook, then goes to her. As she sobs for breath, he pulls her away from the wall to lean against him and rhythmically rubs her shoulders. Gradually, she is able to control her breathing. He checks her pulse, her heartbeat, and takes some pills from a bottle in his pocket, which he offers to her. When he speaks, it is with a German accent.*

DAVID: Take this, it's a mild tranquilizer.

LUCIE: The guy … was he killed on impact?

DAVID: Yes. Can I give you a lift somewhere?

LUCIE: Yes.

DAVID: Where do you live?

LUCIE: In Quebec City.

> *DAVID is alarmed momentarily as it is three hours' drive to Quebec City from Montreal.*

LUCIE: I was on my way to get the bus.

DAVID: I'll walk you to the bus terminal then.

> *DAVID puts his arm around her shoulders and they move off toward stage left. LUCIE breaks away, runs back to look at the tracks, and then returns to her original position against the wall in the audition spotlight. As DAVID exits, this is now the only light onstage.*

LUCIE: (*back in her audition*) Was that enough?

> *Blackout. A metallic, driving music accompanies a red light that shines from behind the wall.*

PROJECTION:

7. THE FLESH
INTERIOR, NIGHT.

> *FRANÇOIS enters over the top of the wall into a gay bar. He drinks a beer, watching bodies on the dance floor. Soon he realizes that he's been assessed by one of the crowd, and he agrees to follow the man stage right to a backroom for sex. A change in light and baffle of sound indicates they are now private. In a very sensual scene, FRANÇOIS takes off his shirt, and then his belt, which he gives to his companion. Their relationship is one where they "play" at coercion. FRANÇOIS unzips his pants and kneels facing the wall, supported by the wall. We hear the sound of whiplashes; FRANÇOIS's body physically recoils against the wall with each blow. As he comes, as his body shudders, the wall bleeds, gushing blood. FRANÇOIS meets the eyes of his lover. He gives a cursory wave as the other man leaves. With an air of soul-weary satisfaction, FRANÇOIS gathers his clothes and returns to the bar. As lights fade to black, he drinks another beer and watches the dance floor.*

> *In the blackout, a two-way mirror drops from the ceiling to hang above the wall stage right. It is the makeup mirror of LUCIE's dressing room at the theatre. The audience watches the scene through the mirror.*

PROJECTION:

8. THE TEARS
INTERIOR, NIGHT.

> *DAVID is waiting in the dressing room with a bunch of carnations, a flower associated with funerals and said by Québécois actors to bring bad luck to a show. LUCIE enters, having finished her performance of Hamlet; she holds the skull of Yorick.*

DAVID: Good evening.

LUCIE: David, my God, it's you! Did you come all the way from Montreal just to see the show?

DAVID: Well, in fact, I had some business this week in Quebec City, and I promised myself I was going to see you act one day, so here I am!

LUCIE: We were not exactly sold out tonight …

DAVID: Well, that just makes it more intimate theatre.

LUCIE: So, what did you think? Did you like it?

DAVID: Well, I thought it was quite interesting. Oh ... here!

He presents her with the carnations.

LUCIE: Oh my God! Carnations! – Thank you ...

DAVID: (*examining the skull on the dressing-room table*) Is this Yorick?

LUCIE: You recognize him?

DAVID: Of course ... He is the only character who isn't killed at the end of the play!

LUCIE: I like the way you call him by his name. Everyone around here just calls him "the skull." But he was more than that once ... whoever he was ...

DAVID: What is written on his forehead? (*reading*) ... "Hélas pauvre Yorick ..."

LUCIE: My lines! Since I didn't have time to learn them properly, I just wrote them down ... Would you mind waiting for me, just a second? I have to get changed and I'll come back. (*exits*)

DAVID: "To be or not to be, that is the question ..." It must be very difficult for an actress to say things like "To be or not to be" and to deal with the fundamental things in life like love, honour ...

DAVID & LUCIE: (*simultaneously, as she re-enters*) Death ...

LUCIE: It's on my mind ... more than ever now, after seeing that guy throw himself under the train in Montreal. You know ... I want to thank you for driving me all the way back to Quebec City ... you didn't have to do that!

DAVID: Let's just say I was not acting purely out of duty; it also gave me the opportunity to get to know you a little better and to make a new friend! So ... What about the movie? Did you get the part?

LUCIE: Not yet ... In fact, next week, we are going to do some screen tests. It makes me very nervous because they want to shoot a scene where I will have to cry and it's not so easy to do ... They gave me this. (*taking a tube from the dressing-room table*) You'll never guess what this is made for. It is a special product they use in movies to help actors cry.

DAVID: Really! Why?

LUCIE: Well ... Imagine redoing the same sad scene twelve times? It's hard to cry every time, right? So, they put it into the actor's eyes and the tears flow all by themselves.

DAVID: Wait a minute. Are you trying to tell me that when an actress like, let's see ... Jane Fonda ... when she cries ... it's all fake?

LUCIE: Sometimes, yes.

DAVID: What a deception! I truly believed that, for an actor at least, tears were the ultimate proof of true emotion!

LUCIE: This is another of the misconceptions people have about acting! D'you want to try it?

DAVID: Surely, you don't want to make me cry!

LUCIE: Yes! You'll see, it won't hurt ... It will be funny!

DAVID: Well ... All right then! What should I do here?

LUCIE: First ... I'll ask you to take off your glasses. And now, since we are making a movie, I'll ask you to think about something sad, so the scene will be truthful.

DAVID: Something sad ... Something recent?

LUCIE: Whatever you want! And now I say: "Quiet on the set ... sound ... camera ... action!"

As DAVID remembers, a musical theme plays that is reminiscent of his past in East Berlin. LUCIE freezes, still holding his glasses. Like a statue, she slowly recedes from the playing area, as if flying away. The set of the dressing room disappears simultaneously, and a projection of the Brandenburg Gate fills the cyclorama above the wall. DAVID, in another time, pulls a letter from his pocket. We hear the sound of a woman's voice, reading the letter in German. In slow motion, DAVID acts out his fearful escape and crossing of the Berlin Wall. He swings his upper body over, out, and down, head first, holding his legs vertical above him. Gripping the wall, he swivels his legs down into a standing position, but remains suspended against the wall. English subtitles, projected on the wall, translate the letter.

DAVID: Ich weiss, dass man niemanden zur Liebe zwingen kann. Aber ich möchte, dass Sie wissen, das ich das Gefühl habe, Sie sind ein Stück von mir. An dem Morgen, als Sie Ostberlin verliessen, zitterte ich am ganzen Körper. Sie sagen: "Ich bin bald wieder zurück," aber ich wuste sofort, obwohl ich es nicht sagte. Was nicht von Herzen kommt, geht nicht zu Herzen. Ich kann in Ihren Augen lesen. Wenn ich hier nicht gefangen wäre, wäre ich nah bei Ihnen. Sie fehlen mir. Anna.

[I know that it is impossible to force someone into loving ... But I want you to know that I feel you are a part of me. The morning you left East Berlin, I was quite shaken. When I asked, "When will you return?" you replied, "Soon." I did not let on, but at that instant, I knew you were lying. What does not come from the heart is not taken to heart ... I can see it in your eyes. If I could leave this city, I would be with you. I miss you deeply. Anna.]

As the letter ends, DAVID reverses his movement, until he is standing where he was when the memory began, in the dressing room, behind the mirror, talking to LUCIE. But now DAVID is crying. He wipes his eyes.

DAVID: This stuff really burns ... It's like getting soap in your eyes.

LUCIE: It won't hurt for long ... I guess that sometimes you have to suffer if you want it to look like you are suffering ...

Gently, she wipes his eyes. The lights fade as they start to kiss.

PROJECTION:

9. APARTMENT #7
INTERIOR, NIGHT.

Stage left, a wash basin set into the wall, with a mirror above it, indicates the bathroom in FRANÇOIS's apartment. FRANÇOIS enters, drunk, limping, and sore. He puts his ear against the wall to hear if anyone is home next door. He calls through the wall.

FRANÇOIS: Lucie! ... Lucie ...

FRANÇOIS puts a glass against the wall to listen for any sounds from next door. Silence; there is no one home. He drops his leather jacket on the floor and peels off his T-shirt. His back is marked with whiplash weals. He soaks the shirt in water and lays it across his back with a sigh of relief.

LUCIE: (*entering his apartment suddenly*) François?

FRANÇOIS: Oui ... entre. [Come in.]

LUCIE: Qu'est-ce qu't'as ... Es-tu malade? [What is the matter ... Are you sick?]

FRANÇOIS: Oui ... J'me sens pas bien ... J'pense que j'ai trop bu ... Ça te tentes-tu de rester prendre un café?

[Yes ... I don't feel very good ... I think I drank too much ... Would you like to stay and have a coffee with me?]

LUCIE: Ben ... J'aimerais ça mais ... (*pointing at the silhouette of a man waiting at the door*) c'est parce que j'suis pas toute seule ...

[Well ... I'd like to but ... I am not alone.]

FRANÇOIS: Ah ... Y a quelqu'un qui t'attend ... [Ah ... Someone's waiting for you ...]

LUCIE: Oui. On se reprendra ... Excuses-moi de te déranger à cette heure-là ... C'est parce que je viens d'arriver chez nous pis j'peux pas rentrer, j'ai pas mes clés.

[Yes ... well ... I'll take a rain check ... Sorry to bug you so late, but I only just got home, and I can't get in. I must have lost my keys.]

FRANÇOIS: Ah ...

He digs for LUCIE's key inside his jeans pocket and gives it to her.

LUCIE: Merci ... Prends soin de toi là ... [Thank you. Well, take care ...]

As she goes to kiss him on both cheeks, she inadvertently touches his back; FRANÇOIS winces. LUCIE tries to look at his back.

LUCIE: Qu'est-ce que t'as, j't'ai-tu fait mal? [What's the matter, did I hurt you?]

DAVID: (*his voice coming from behind the wall*) Lucie? ...

FRANÇOIS: Non, non ... Laisse faire. [No, no ... It's nothing.]

LUCIE: (*trying again to see his back*) Ben voyons ... Qu'est-ce que t'as? [Come on ... What's the matter?]

FRANÇOIS: Laisse faire j'te dis ... c'est rien. [Leave me – I said it's nothing!]

LUCIE: Okay, okay! ...

DAVID: Lucie, are you all right?

LUCIE: Yeah, yeah ... (*awkwardly, as she exits*) Merci.

FRANÇOIS is now very much alone. Lights crossfade to fill the expanse of the cyclorama above the wall.

PROJECTION:

10. THE SNOW
EXTERIOR, NIGHT.

Above the wall, the moonlit night sky glows and snow falls gently. Music accompanies this action. FRANÇOIS appears, as if walking on the ramparts of Quebec City. He wears no shirt, only his leather jacket, which he holds together against the cold. At one point, he stops, climbs onto the edge of the wall, and stares down as if he's considering a suicide jump. He cries silently.

PROJECTION:

11. APARTMENT #8
INTERIOR, DAY.

Stage right, a wash basin full of water is set into the wall, with a mirror above it to indicate the bathroom of LUCIE's apartment. DAVID is shaving when he hears violent and lamenting cries from the other side of the wall. The voice belongs to FRANÇOIS. He checks to see if LUCIE is still sleeping, then puts his ear against the wall to listen. The cries get louder. DAVID knocks on the wall a couple of times. The lamentation stops. LUCIE enters, surprising him. She is still sleepy and goes to embrace him, but he politely fends her off.

LUCIE: David, what are you doing?

DAVID: Good morning! ... Lucie, listen ... I really have to go! I promised my secretary I'd be in Montreal at ten o'clock ... It's now eight thirty and I haven't even left Quebec City yet ... So, you can imagine how impossibly behind I am!

LUCIE: That's too bad, I thought we would have breakfast together. I could put some coffee on –

DAVID: That's very nice of you, but I really must go ...

LUCIE: Will we see each other again?

DAVID: Soon.

LUCIE: When?

DAVID: In fact, next week I have some business in Quebec City. Perhaps we could arrange a rendezvous? I'll be at the morgue.

LUCIE: At the morgue? I would prefer a restaurant!

She walks toward him, allowing her robe to slide from her shoulders to the ground.

DAVID: That's what I meant ...

As they move into a kiss, the cries from FRANÇOIS's apartment begin again. LUCIE stops and turns her head to listen, but DAVID pulls her passionately against him. As they embrace, DAVID checks his watch behind her back and, figuring he has enough time, he gives in to the love scene. He lifts her up on him, turning so that she stretches out her arms to grip the wall for support as he caresses her body with his lips, and lights fade ...

PROJECTION:

12. TRAVELLING BACKWARD[2]
INTERIOR, DAY.

Thriller music begins in the blackout. Stage right, in shadow, FRANÇOIS prepares the restaurant table for the following scene. Stage left, LUCIE stands naked, her back to the wall. Suddenly, she contracts as though she has been stabbed. She staggers forward and to the left, clawing at the air, then swivels as she falls: her back is covered with blood from the wall. Her movement is closely tracked by a camera on a Panasonic PeeWee dolly that zooms maniacally in and out on her face and body with the tension-rhythm of the music. LUCIE falls, dead, to the floor. The music stops abruptly and she gets to her feet, appearing to listen to instructions from a director. She performs three "takes" of the death scene. After the last one, she receives the thumbs-up signal. She speaks to the director.

LUCIE: Can I go now?

LUCIE covers herself with a towel and exits.

PROJECTION:

13. THE WOUND
INTERIOR, NIGHT.

At FRANÇOIS's restaurant. DAVID enters.

FRANÇOIS: Bonsoir, monsieur. Ce sera pour combien de personnes?

DAVID: *(failing to understand because he doesn't speak French)* I'm sorry, euh ...

FRANÇOIS: Excuse me. You would like a table for how many?

DAVID: For two, please.

FRANÇOIS: Does this one suits you?

DAVID: Yes, that's fine ... oh ... excuse me ... could you take my coat, please?

FRANÇOIS: Sure.

FRANÇOIS leaves with the coat. As he waits, DAVID hides a small gift bag under his chair.

LUCIE: *(entering in a rush)* Oh ... David, I'm sorry, I'm late ...

DAVID: That's all right.

LUCIE: I hope you haven't been waiting too long ...

---

2   "Travelling" is Québécois film parlance for a "dolly": smooth lateral movement of a film camera.

DAVID: I just walked in this minute ... It's nice to see you.

LUCIE: It was longer than I expected ... We were supposed to finish shooting at three o'clock, but we had a very complicated technical scene.

DAVID: You look tired ...

LUCIE: Playing a victim is tiring!

FRANÇOIS: (*entering to serve them*) Bonjour Lucie.

LUCIE: Ah. Bonjour, François ... Tiens, je te présente un ami [Let me introduce you to a friend], David Haussmann, François Tremblay ... He's my next-door neighbour ...

DAVID: Oh ... you're the one in apartment number eight!

FRANÇOIS: Yes.

DAVID: (*shaking his hand*) I heard ... so much about you!

LUCIE: David is the one who drove me back to Quebec City after I saw the guy throw himself in front of the train in Montreal.

FRANÇOIS: Strange circumstances to meet someone.

DAVID: Yes, indeed ... Metro stations in Montreal seem to be used more often now to commit suicide than for commuting ...

LUCIE: Why's that?

FRANÇOIS: C'est la façon la plus cheap de se suicider ... [It's the cheapest way to kill yourself.]

DAVID: What?

FRANÇOIS: ... Do you want to order something to drink before your meal?

DAVID: Well ... I think I'll avoid hard liquor –

LUCIE: – Me too –

DAVID: – But ... would you like to drink some wine with the meal?

LUCIE: Yes ... sure.

FRANÇOIS: I'll leave you to look at the wine list.

He gives it to LUCIE, who passes it to DAVID.

DAVID: What kind of wine do you prefer?

LUCIE: Well ... red or white.

DAVID: That's what I meant ... Red or white?

LUCIE: I like both.

DAVID: How about red?

LUCIE: Red! Perfect!

DAVID: What kind of red do you like ... Bourgogne, Bordeaux, Beaujolais ...

LUCIE: I like all of them.

DAVID: Beaujolais?

LUCIE: Beaujolais ... great!

DAVID: What kind of Beaujolais would you prefer?

LUCIE: Euh ... It's up to you!

DAVID: How about a bottle of Brouilly?

LUCIE: Good idea!

DAVID: Do you like Brouilly?

LUCIE: I love it! You know ... it's a very good restaurant here. They serve a kind of "mixed-genre" cuisine ... A little of this ... a little of that ... French, Hindu, vegetarian ...

FRANÇOIS: (*re-entering for their order*) Have you decided on the wine?

LUCIE: (*scanning the wine list*) Yes, we will have a bottle of ... Brouilly.

FRANÇOIS: Brouilly ... Okay. (*exiting with their order*)

DAVID: So! How does it feel to be a movie star?

LUCIE: My God, give me a chance! ... It's my first day of filming! I think I felt a bit ... silly ...! I found the director quite aggressive with his camera ... He wanted to shoot a scene from above, you know, as if you're looking through the eyes of a murderer who's watching his victim through a skylight. But during the shooting, I felt more observed by the crew, and the director himself, than by the voyeur in the scenario.

DAVID: But aren't you used to being watched?

LUCIE: In theatre it's very different. When you perform, the audience is watching the whole you ... But today, I felt that they were taking me apart.

DAVID: Taking you apart ...

LUCIE: Yes ... Close-up of one eye, middle shot of the knife in the back, my right hand scratching at the floor.

FRANÇOIS comes back with the bottle and shows it to LUCIE, who simply reads the label.

LUCIE: Brouilly.

DAVID: What were you filming exactly? Indoor scenes, outdoor scenes?

LUCIE: We were taking the interiors first, because the film is set in spring ... So we have to wait for the end of winter.

DAVID: What will you do if it rains all the time?

LUCIE: It's a thriller! They want it to rain, because all the scenes happen in the rain!

DAVID: What if it never rains?

LUCIE: Well ... I suppose they'll make it rain!

DAVID: Of course ... It's like for tears ... As far as they are concerned, making it is not the problem, it's just a question of water quantity!

LUCIE: (*trying to make a pun, just as FRANÇOIS appears with the wine*) Well, in fact, yeah. For "making it," it's the size of the equipment that counts!

She laughs, joined by FRANÇOIS, who pours a little wine into her glass so she can taste it. LUCIE is surprised not to get more.

LUCIE: Merci!

FRANÇOIS: Ben ... Goûtes-y.

DAVID: Taste it.

LUCIE: Oh ... yes, sure. Hum ... it's very good ... (*as FRANÇOIS pours the rest*) It's even a little bouchonné!

FRANÇOIS: Oh – I'll get you another bottle ...

LUCIE: No, no, it's very good ... It is *bouchonné* ... Bouchonné.

FRANÇOIS: Yes, but ... if it's bouchonné –

DAVID: Isn't that supposed to mean that it tastes like cork?

LUCIE: Well ... in this case, it can't possibly be bouchonné because it tastes great!

DAVID: Maybe I should double-check ... It's a very good bottle!

DAVID does so, religiously. As he looks at FRANÇOIS, he seems to recognize him.

FRANÇOIS: Something wrong?

DAVID: No, no ... It's an excellent wine!

LUCIE: Like I said.

FRANÇOIS: Are you ready to order?

DAVID: Go for it, Lucie.

LUCIE: No, no ... You go first, David. You are the guest!

DAVID: What do you mean, I am the guest? I thought I was the one inviting you to dinner!

LUCIE: No, no ... I mean ... you are the foreigner!

DAVID does not respond.

DAVID: (*to FRANÇOIS*) Is this soup?

FRANÇOIS: Yes ... Potage Crécy.

DAVID: Well. I'll have that, please, and the filet de boeuf Brisanne. I'd like that done rare but please in the French understanding of the word "rare" ... not the Canadian.[3]

LUCIE: I'll have the same as him, but with the Canadian rare!

FRANÇOIS leaves with the order.

DAVID: Well ... Here's to your film!

They toast.

DAVID: (*taking the package from under his chair*) I'm not very good at this ... but here! (*putting it on the table and offering it to her*) This is for you.

LUCIE: What is it?

DAVID: What do you think it is? ... It's a present!

LUCIE: But it's not my birthday.

DAVID: It's a present just the same.

LUCIE: No ... I mean ... there is no need for you to be buying me presents, David.

DAVID: Well ... I'm sorry then.

A very awkward pause, which LUCIE breaks.

LUCIE: No ... No ... I'm sorry ... I'm the one acting weird here ... Let me open it! Oh! ... a Russian doll!

DAVID: Yes ... the real thing.

LUCIE: These come in all different sizes, and people collect them!

DAVID: In fact ... you won't have to collect them ... They are all there, included one inside the other.

LUCIE: What do you mean?

DAVID: Open it!

LUCIE: Oh ... it's beautiful ...

DAVID: It's called a matryoshka.

LUCIE: A matryoshka.

LUCIE opens up the dolls and lines them up on the tabletop so that they form a wall between her and DAVID.

DAVID: I bought them in Eastern Europe but you find them everywhere now. It's a traditional doll. Representing generations ... So, this big one here is the mother of this one and also the grandmother of this one because she is the mother of this one and this one is the mother of that one and that one ... and ... to infinity, I suppose! But ... I like to

_____

3   In France, the expression "à point" means quite red and bloody meat.

think it may stand for other things like ... hidden feelings ... One truth that is hiding another truth and another one and another one ...

LUCIE: I'm very moved ... Thank you.

DAVID: I'm glad you like it.

A marked "slow" change in sound and lights indicates a time warp: time is rapidly passing. LUCIE and DAVID reach for their coffee cups in slow motion, their eyes locked together. FRANÇOIS glides in to take away the empty dishes and glasses. As he takes the bottle of wine, he slowly lays it across the middle of the table, tipping its contents so that the red wine stains the white tablecloth and drops to the floor.

DAVID: (*back to real time*) ... And at one point in the film, the angel turns to him and says: "Beware death ... She comes and goes through mirrors ... Gaze upon yourself all your life in the looking glass and you will see death at work."

LUCIE: That's beautiful.

DAVID: That's Cocteau.

Another time warp, marked in the same way with sound, lights, and slow motion as LUCIE and DAVID stir their coffee, the sounds of the spoons making an evocative late-night rhythm on their china cups. FRANÇOIS comes in, looking at his watch. The meal has been over for a long time.

FRANÇOIS: I'm sorry but I am going to have to close now.

DAVID: What time is it?

FRANÇOIS: A quarter past three.

DAVID: A quarter past three!

LUCIE: My God! ... We didn't notice the time pass!

DAVID: I'm very sorry ... We were completely engrossed in our conversation while digesting this excellent meal!

LUCIE: Oui. Merci beaucoup ... C'était très bon.

DAVID: Can you tell me where I could find my coat, please!

FRANÇOIS: It's in the cloakroom ... I'll get it for you.

DAVID: Lucie ... You are forgetting your matryoshka!

LUCIE: Oh ... my matryoshka ... (*showing it to FRANÇOIS*) Regarde François ce que David m'a donné ... C't'une poupée Russe ... un matryoshka. Y l'a acheté à l'Est. [Look at what David gave me.

It's a Russian doll; a matryoshka. He bought it in the East.]

FRANÇOIS: C'est beau. [It's nice.]

They move towards the exit of the restaurant. LUCIE stands against the wall with one man on either side. FRANÇOIS addresses DAVID.

FRANÇOIS: You're from Europe?

DAVID: Yes. I'm from East Berlin. But I have been a Canadian citizen for many years now.

FRANÇOIS: And what do you do here?

DAVID: I am a criminologist. I work for a criminal institute in Montreal.

FRANÇOIS: Parthenais?

DAVID: Yes, Parthenais.

LUCIE: Tu connais ça? [You know this place?]

FRANÇOIS: Oui ... J'ai déjà eu affaire-là. [Yes, I had to go there once.]

LUCIE: Comment ça? [Why?]

FRANÇOIS: Pas en prison ... [Not to prison ...] I went there to undergo a polygraph test.

LUCIE: A what?

FRANÇOIS: Un test de polygraphe.

DAVID: A lie detector ... For what?

FRANÇOIS: Because six years ago one of my best friends was murdered here in Quebec City. I was the last one to see her alive, so I was a suspect. In fact, it was me who found her dead in her apartment. She had been tied up, raped, and stabbed many times.

DAVID: Did they find the murderer?

FRANÇOIS: No. They never tracked him down.

DAVID: What was your friend's name?

FRANÇOIS: Marie-Claude Légaré.

LUCIE reacts to the name. As if "flashing back" to the previous film shoot scene, she turns to face the wall, as though she's been stabbed. Her back is covered with blood. She falls to the ground between the two men who, without acknowledging her fall, continue to face each other in conversation.

DAVID: Yes ... I think I remember ... Don't worry, they'll track him down. Nobody is able to go through life with a murder on their conscience ...

As DAVID continues to talk to the place where FRANÇOIS was standing, FRANÇOIS "relives" finding his friend's corpse, kneels down by her, and silently enacts his grief.

DAVID: Well, thank you once again and my compliments to the chef; the food was indeed excellent. And the service, impeccable! Have you been a waiter for long?

FRANÇOIS stands again to continue the conversation normally. He speaks to DAVID's original position as DAVID in turn kneels by LUCIE and performs an "autopsy" on her, ripping her shirt with a scalpel.

FRANÇOIS: Long enough ... three years now. Before this, I was at school, university, studying political science – and I worked part-time in a Yugoslavian restaurant.

DAVID: Yugoslavian ...

FRANÇOIS: Yes. I like it better here, though; it's more friendly.

DAVID: Do you intend to do this for long? I mean ... waiting tables! I know how transient things are in the restaurant business.

FRANÇOIS: I don't know. If I could find work related to my studies, I'd move on for sure.

DAVID: Well ... it's better than no work at all. You know, when I lived in East Berlin, I thought the West was full of "golden opportunities" – but I see now how hard it is to succeed here. Over there, the jobs are trivial sometimes, but at least everybody has the right to work.

LUCIE uncoils from the floor to take her original position against the wall; simultaneously, the two men each put one foot on the wall, turning their bodies horizontally so they appear to be in the classic cinematic "top shot" of a corpse. FRANÇOIS and DAVID shake hands "over" her body.

DAVID: Sure was a pleasure meeting you, François.

The scene returns to "real" time and space.

DAVID: Well ... if we want to exercise our own right to work tomorrow, maybe we should be moving along.

LUCIE: (*kissing him*) Salut, François.

FRANÇOIS: À bientôt, Lucie.

LUCIE walks slowly toward DAVID, looking at her hand.

DAVID: What's the matter, Lucie? (*taking her hand*) You're bleeding!

LUCIE: It's nothing ... I must have cut myself with a knife.

DAVID: Come ... we'll take care of it.

As soon as they are gone, FRANÇOIS pulls out a bag of coke and prepares himself a few lines.

PROJECTION:

14. THE RAMPARTS
EXTERIOR, NIGHT.

A projection of the Quebec City skyscape fills the cyclorama above the wall. LUCIE and DAVID enter. She is withdrawn and quiet.

DAVID: What an exquisite city.

LUCIE: I come walking here very often but in summer generally, not winter.

DAVID: I greatly prefer the winter. I don't know why really, but I find I like the cold ... anything cold. Perhaps it's because I was born in December. You know, usually, when people talk about the cold, it's always in pejorative terms. But for me, the cold evokes a kind of objective calm, wisdom, and above all, a great gentleness ... like these snowflakes slowly falling ... Leaning against the ramparts like that, you remind me of someone I once knew ...

LUCIE: Really? Who was she?

DAVID: Someone whom I loved deeply and to whom I did a great wrong ... A German woman.

LUCIE: I am too nosy, aren't I?

DAVID: It was a long time ago ... What's wrong, Lucie? ... Since we've left the restaurant you seem preoccupied somehow.

LUCIE: Well ... I am. It is because – you know the story François just told us in the restaurant? The story of the film in which I'm playing is identical. It's based on the real murder – but I didn't know François was connected to it. It gave me a shock ... And now, I feel uneasy about being a part of it, and I'm wondering if there's still time for them to find someone else.

DAVID: They have lousy taste ... to base a film script on an unresolved murder case ... How do they end the movie?

LUCIE: Well ... after the girl's been killed, they set everything up to look as if it was one of her close friends who did it, and at the end ... we discover ...

DAVID: At the end, we discover that it was the police who did it.

LUCIE: How did you know?

DAVID: It's a classic. When you don't know how to end a whodunit, you always blame it on the cops. It's easy ... When I was a student of criminology, I feared that the people developing investigative techniques were violent brutes: a product of their line of work. But I needn't have worried about becoming a brute. No, they are much more dangerous than that. The men leading the field of criminal research are very, very intelligent; a fact you will never see in a thriller. It's too frightening perhaps. Poor François ... At Parthenais they know he is innocent, but he'll probably never be told.

LUCIE: Why?

DAVID: In a police inquiry where the guilty party hasn't been identified, it's strategy to keep everyone in ignorance.

LUCIE: How do you know François is innocent?

DAVID: ... François does not know, but I was the one who conducted his polygraph test. This must remain between us, Lucie; it's a confidence.

LUCIE: But – how can I meet his eyes and not tell him?

DAVID: Stop seeing him for a while.

He tries to hold her, but she gently pushes him away and continues walking along the ramparts. He follows her offstage.

PROJECTION:

15. THE CALL
EXTERIOR, NIGHT.

FRANÇOIS enters, stage right, takes change from his pocket and crosses to stand at a phone booth in the stage-left wing. We hear the sound of dialing a pay phone. FRANÇOIS is lit so that his shadow is a huge projection across the entire wall, in such a way that every movement of his dialing and speaking on the phone registers. Over the phone line, we hear LUCIE's answering machine.

LUCIE: Bonjour, vous êtes bien chez Lucie Champagne ... Malheureusement, je ne peux pas vous répondre pour le moment mais si vous voulez bien laisser votre nom et votre numéro de téléphone, je vous rappelle dans les plus bref délais.

FRANÇOIS lets the phone drop as the message continues. He comes back onstage, kicks the wall, then leans against it, pressing his face and body

into it. As lights fade to black, we hear the tone of the answering machine.

PROJECTION:

16. THE LINEUP
INTERIOR, NIGHT.

The lineup is a recap scene that shows the most telling moments in the play so far. It begins with a matrix projected on the wall, reminiscent of the "Man in Motion" photographs by Eadweard Muybridge. The scene is played nude by the actors. Choreographic images of FRANÇOIS working in the restaurant, LUCIE in shock in the subway, FRANÇOIS being whipped, DAVID's meeting with LUCIE, DAVID and LUCIE embracing against the wall, the "film-noir top shot" of the handshake in the restaurant. The scene and movement fragments are repeated, overlaid, dissected, and recombined at a pace of increasing frenzy. Blackout.

PROJECTION:

17. THE SPRING
EXTERIOR, DAY.

FRANÇOIS has a bucket of water with which he sluices the wall. With a brush, he starts to scrub it. DAVID enters, with sunglasses and a travel bag.

DAVID: Hello, François. Have you seen Lucie?

FRANÇOIS: Not for a month, at least. She must be busy shooting her movie.

DAVID: I came to say goodbye, but if she is off on location ...

FRANÇOIS: You're going away?

DAVID: I'm going back to East Berlin. The government is sending me there for a series of conferences in investigative techniques. Now that the Wall has disappeared, there's this sudden demand for up-to-date technologies. But to tell the truth, my motivation is more personal than professional.

FRANÇOIS: But what's the government's motivation: to share knowledge or sell free enterprise?

DAVID: To share knowledge. Well ... if you see Lucie, tell her I was here ... (*making as if to leave, then stopping*) What the hell are you doing, François?

FRANÇOIS: I'm washing the wall.

DAVID: Yes, I can see, but why?

FRANÇOIS: The landlord told me to strip my graffiti off the garden wall before I move out, or else he'll prosecute.

DAVID: Prosecute ... for graffiti! ... What did it say?

FRANÇOIS: L'histoire s'écrit avec le sang.

DAVID: Which means?

FRANÇOIS: History is written with blood. It means that we write history through war, fascism, and murder.

DAVID: Murder ... you mean political assassinations.

FRANÇOIS: No. I mean murders. The smallest little killing, of some totally unimportant person ... In a way that's still a political act, don't you think?

DAVID: Is that what you learned in political science?

FRANÇOIS: (*losing his temper*) Why do you ask me so many questions? You sound like an interrogator in a bad detective movie!

Defiantly, FRANÇOIS gathers up his bucket and brush, and exits.

PROJECTION:

18. TRAVELLING FORWARDS[4]
EXTERIOR, NIGHT.

LUCIE appears in profile, stage left, behind and above the wall. She's lit from behind by the beam of a movie projector positioned in the stage-left wing. The rushes of the movie are projected onto the stage-right wall, but are not visible to the audience while she is watching. The projector stops.

LUCIE: (*addressing the director offstage*) Were these shot yesterday? And what we will shoot tomorrow will be linked with it –? (*starting to cry silently*) Excuse me ... (*pulling herself together*) May I see it again please?

Blackout.

PROJECTION:

19. APARTMENT #8
INTERIOR, DAY.

FRANÇOIS is packing boxes in the bathroom of his apartment. The wash basin is set into the wall as before. LUCIE enters with books. English subtitles are projected on the wall.

LUCIE: Salut, François, je t'ai rapporté les livres que tu m'avais prêté ... *L'orgasme au masculin*, j'ai trouvé ça ben intéressant.

---

4   "Travelling forwards" – a film term: dollying in, or tracking forwards.

[Hi François ... I brought back the books you loaned me ... I found *The Male Orgasm* pretty interesting.]

FRANÇOIS: Tu peux les garder encore si t'en a pas fini. [You can keep them if you're not finished.]

LUCIE: Non non ... j'sais c'que j'voulais savoir ... [No, no. I found out everything I wanted to know!]

LUCIE examines the cosmetics strewn in the wash basin.

Ouan ... t'en a des affaires pour un gars ... [You got a lot of stuff for a guy ...]

She starts to poke around in one of the boxes as he adds the books to it.

LUCIE: Tu marques pas ce que tu mets dans tes boites? [You don't write what you put into the boxes?]

FRANÇOIS: C'est pas nécessaire ... Pour ce que j'ai ... [It's not necessary. I don't have so many things.]

LUCIE: Marque où c'est que ça va toujours, sinon tu vas être mêlé quand tu vas arriver. [You should at least write where it goes, so you won't be mixed up when you move to your new place.]

She points to a box.

Ça c'est quoi? Des cosmétiques? J'vas écrire pharmacie dessus. Pis celle-là? [What is in there? Cosmetics? I'll write "personal things" on the side. And what's in this one?]

FRANÇOIS: Là-dedans ... des couvertures, serviettes des débarbouillettes, des livres, des vieux journaux ... [... blankets, face cloths, books, old newspapers ...]

LUCIE: J'pourrais écrire divers ... [I could write ... "miscellaneous."]

Inside the box, LUCIE finds a long leather strap with a strange fastening at the end.

LUCIE: Ça ... ça sert à quoi? [And ... what is this used for?]

FRANÇOIS: (*putting the strap around his neck and demonstrating*) Quand je me masturbe, j'me sers de ça. J'tire – pis j'lâche, j'tire – pis j'lâche. Pis juste avant de venir, j'tire de plus en plus fort ... Mais un moment donné, y faut qu'tu lâches, si tu veux pas venir pour la dernière fois ... [When I masturbate, I use it. I pull then release, pull and release, and just before I come, I pull harder and harder ... But at a certain point, you have to stop unless you want it to be the last time you come.]

LUCIE: Ça sert-tu juste à ça? [Is that all you use it for?]

FRANÇOIS takes the strap from around his neck and goes to the wash basin.

FRANÇOIS: Viens ici. [Come here.]

She hesitates.

FRANÇOIS: Viens ici!

She goes.

FRANÇOIS: Assis-toi, donnes-moi ta main. [Sit down ... give me your hand.]

He ties the belt around LUCIE's hand, passes it through the U-bend pipe on the wash basin, and wraps it round her neck before tying it up.

In a simultaneous scene, DAVID gives a lecture about the polygraph machine in East Berlin. He stands upstage of the wall, but not above it. He is visible to the audience only as a reflection in the two-way mirror that is positioned at an angle so as to reveal him.

DAVID: ... Firstly, the lie registers on the *cardiograph*, with an accelerated heartbeat. At the *temple*, we monitor for an increase or, in the case of some subjects, a decrease of arterial pressure –

FRANÇOIS: Là m'a serrer un peu ... [I'm going to tighten it a bit ...]

DAVID: *Respiration* has a direct effect on the person responding to questions: this contributes yet another reading of the physical response. Lastly, we measure the subject's *perspiration*. The polygraph machine detects the most minute psychophysical variations occurring during interrogation.

FRANÇOIS: (*putting a blindfold over her eyes and rendering her completely helpless*) Comme ça, t'as vraiment l'impression d'être vulnérable ... [This gets you feeling really vulnerable ...]

DAVID: The fear and mystique that surrounds the polygraph machine makes it a useful pressure tactic in obtaining a confession. But such strategies, I believe, should be used only with great care and compassion. Sometimes, the psychological response we trigger is so violent as to effect a lasting disorder in the mind of a totally innocent suspect.

LUCIE: Pis après? [And then?]

DAVID: Let me tell you about a polygraph test undertaken in the context of an unresolved murder case. The questioning of a particular suspect went something like this:

FRANÇOIS: Des fois, quand on se ramasse une gang de gars ... [Sometimes, when I get together with a gang of friends ...]

DAVID: François, we are going to conduct a little test.

FRANÇOIS: Y'en a un qui se fait attacher comme ça ... [One of us gets tied up like this ...]

DAVID: Can you hear me properly?

FRANÇOIS: ... Pis au hasard y'en a un qui est choisi pour aller le rejoindre ... [... then someone is picked at random to go in and join him ...]

DAVID: But you cannot actually see me, can you?

FRANÇOIS: ... celui qui est attaché, y peut rien faire ... [... the one who's all tied up can't do anything ...]

DAVID: François, are we in Canada?

FRANÇOIS: ... Y peut rien voir ... [... he can't see anything ...]

DAVID: Is it summertime?

FRANÇOIS: ... pis l'autre y fait ce qui veut avec ... [... and the other one does whatever he wants with him.]

DAVID: Was it you who killed Marie-Claude Légaré?

FRANÇOIS: (*reliving, in his memory, the polygraph test*) Non.

DAVID: Is it 1986?

FRANÇOIS: Oui.

DAVID: Are we in the month of August?

FRANÇOIS: Non.

DAVID: Are we in the month of July?

FRANÇOIS: Oui.

DAVID: Are you responsible for the death of Marie-Claude Légaré?

FRANÇOIS: Non.

DAVID: Now, the result of this polygraph test gave evidence that this witness was actually telling the truth. But the person conducting the test told him afterwards that the machine had established that he was lying. The spontaneous reaction of the witness could be considered the ultimate proof of his innocence ...

FRANÇOIS: (*a complete emotional breakdown*) Allez-vous me lâcher tabarnak! C'est pas moé qui l'a tuée!! C'est pas moé!! Vous voulez me rendre fou, c'est ça!! Y vont me rendre fou 'ostie ...

[Let me fucking go! I didn't kill her!! It wasn't me! It wasn't me! You want to drive me crazy, is that it? You're driving me out of my goddamn mind ...]

LUCIE is frozen, blindfolded, and terrified.

LUCIE: François ...? François ...? François ...?

FRANÇOIS gives her no response.

DAVID: But the police never told him he was released from suspicion ... He was never let off the hook.

He slowly recovers, goes to her, and removes the blindfold.

FRANÇOIS: Tu veux-tu que je te détache? [Do you want me to untie you?]

He does so, then silently puts the belt and blindfold in a box.

LUCIE: C'est tu toi que l'a tuée? [Was it you who killed her?]

FRANÇOIS: ... J'pense pas non ... [I don't think so ...]

LUCIE: Pourquoi tu dis "J'pense" pas? [Why do you say ... you don't "think" so?]

FRANÇOIS: Parce que des fois ... je l'sais ... pu ... [Because sometimes ... I don't know ... anymore.]

He starts to cry, releasing an emotion from deep inside. LUCIE goes to him, takes him in her arms.

LUCIE: Moi, je l'sais ... que tu serais pas capable de faire mal à une mouche. [Listen ... I know that you couldn't hurt a fly.]

She holds him, fiercely comforting and reassuring him. She touches his face, and the comfort becomes passion. Lights fade as they start to embrace.

PROJECTION:

20. THE RAIN
EXTERIOR, DAY.

Rain falls from the ceiling behind the wall. Above the wall, the camera appears, covered with an umbrella. There is just the camera; no one else is around.

PROJECTION:

21. APARTMENT #7
INTERIOR, NIGHT.

An eerie dream sequence. LUCIE leans against the wall with a hidden light strapped to her back. It shines on the wall, creating a strange halo around her body and placing her in silhouette. She walks slowly to the front of the stage.

DAVID: (*entering stage left*) Lucie! I'm back!

FRANÇOIS enters from LUCIE's bedroom, without a shirt. DAVID is shocked. He appears not to see LUCIE downstage and speaks only to FRANÇOIS.

DAVID: What are you doing here? Where's Lucie?

FRANÇOIS: She's in the room.

DAVID goes into the room, then comes back in anger.

DAVID: (*pointing to the exit*) Get out!

FRANÇOIS: Maybe we could talk ...

DAVID: Get out!

FRANÇOIS: Wait ...

DAVID seizes FRANÇOIS to throw him out, and they fight violently. FRANÇOIS's head is knocked against the wall. Slowly, LUCIE walks backwards to her original place, and the lighting changes. She leans against the wall, lost in thought. FRANÇOIS enters from the bedroom. He stands against the wall beside LUCIE. He is restless and anxious. They smile gently at one another, and FRANÇOIS takes her hand, as if unable to speak the things in his heart. He holds her like a frightened child – which then becomes a passionate kiss. As in the previous scene, DAVID's voice is heard offstage. FRANÇOIS immediately bids farewell to LUCIE.

DAVID: Lucie! I'm back!

As FRANÇOIS goes out, he and DAVID meet.

DAVID: Hi!

FRANÇOIS: Hi! (*exits*)

DAVID: How are you?

LUCIE: I'm fine ...

DAVID takes his bag into the bedroom, then comes back and starts to wash his face in the wash basin.

DAVID: Weren't you supposed to be shooting today?

LUCIE: Yes ... I was scheduled, but I decided not to go ...

DAVID: Why?

LUCIE: Because we were supposed to shoot the death sequence, and I think that I don't have the right to do that.

DAVID: That is very courageous of you.

LUCIE: François just left for Montreal ... David ... While you were away – I slept with François.

DAVID stops washing, abruptly. He holds very still.

LUCIE: I've spent the whole week with him because he needed someone. And I told him everything you told me on the ramparts ... He told you the truth, but you lied to him.

LUCIE looks at DAVID, who has straightened to look at her, without expression.

LUCIE: David, react! Feel something!

DAVID: (*calmly turning to her*) What do you want me to "feel"? You want me to be jealous of a fucking homosexual?

LUCIE: If that's the truth, yes! If you want to cry, cry!

The lights fade on them.

PROJECTION:

22. DEATH
INTERIOR, NIGHT.

In silhouette projected on the cyclorama above the wall, FRANÇOIS arrives at the metro station and paces impatiently, waiting for the train. We hear the sound of a train approaching. FRANÇOIS takes off his leather jacket and lets it fall to the floor behind him; without hesitation, he throws himself in front of the oncoming train. As his silhouette dives out of sight, the brick wall suddenly falls and a piercing light shines through as FRANÇOIS's naked body comes hurtling along with the falling bricks to land on a hospital gurney. There he lies, amidst the broken bricks, dead and awaiting an autopsy. DAVID pushes the gurney stage right, until it is positioned beneath the mirror, which is hung at an angle to reflect FRANÇOIS's body.

LUCIE appears stage left, above and behind the wall. She holds a knife, as she recites the famous Hamlet soliloquy.

LUCIE: Être ou ne pas être. C'est la question.

Est-il plus noble pour une âme de souffrir

les flèches et les coups d'un sort atroce,

ou de s'armer contre le flot qui monte,

et de lui faire face, et de l'arrêter?

Mourir, dormir ... rien de plus.

Terminer par du sommeil la souffrance

du cœur et les mille blessures qui sont le lot
de la chair.

C'est bien le dénouement que l'on voud-
rait ... et de quelle ardeur!

Mourir, dormir ...

Dormir ... peut-être rêver.

C'est l'obstacle ...

Car l'anxiété des rêves qui viendront dans
ce sommeil des morts,

Quand nous aurons chassé de nous le
tumulte de vivre,

Est là pour nous retenir ...

Et c'est la pensée qui fait que le malheur à si
longue vie.

The lights on LUCIE fade slowly until FRANÇOIS's corpse is all that is illuminated. But now the reflection in the mirror changes so that we no longer see his body, but a skeleton that lies in the same position, as if the mirror sees through his flesh. Across the cyclorama above the wall, clouds run in a vast sky.

END

MORRIS
PANYCH

(b. 1952)

With its roots firmly fixed in the cultural nationalism of the 1965–75 era, and with an implicit mandate to hold up the theatrical mirror to reflect Canadians as they have been, late twentieth-century English-Canadian drama generally tended to favour the social problem play, the family play, the history play: theatre grounded in the particularities of Canadian experience. Morris Panych's work was a rare exception in the 1980s and '90s. Perhaps because he came of age, theatrically speaking, at the tail end of the nationalist period; perhaps because he cut his teeth on introspective West Coast experimentalism rather than the naturalistic, socially committed alternate theatre more common in the era; certainly for personal reasons of temperament and philosophy, Panych has gone his own way. As a prolific triple-threat writer, director, and actor – not unlike Robert Lepage – Panych has built a substantial body of work that draws on an array of cosmopolitan influences from literature, music, philosophy, and the stage, but rests heavily on the mid-twentieth-century paradigms of existentialism and the absurd. His 7 *Stories* is an existential parable and absurdist fantasy that Pat Donnelly, reviewing a Montreal production, called "a revelation of intelligent theatricality ... guaranteed to change one's perception of Canadian playwriting forever."

Born in Calgary and raised in Edmonton, Panych got a diploma in radio and television from the Northern Alberta Institute of Technology. He worked briefly at CBC Radio before enrolling at the University of British Columbia to study creative writing and theatre (BFA, 1977). After two years at East 15 Acting School in London, he returned to Vancouver, where he quickly established himself as the city's most dynamic and versatile actor, beginning with his own sensational playwriting debut.

Last Call, subtitled *A Post-Nuclear Cabaret*, was first produced by Tamahnous Theatre in 1982, then toured Canada, and was filmed for CBC-TV. A two-man musical structurally similar to *Billy Bishop Goes to War*, which Tamahnous had also premiered, and with distinct echoes of Samuel Beckett's *Endgame*, *Last Call* is set amid the rubble of a nuked Vancouver. The only survivors are a couple of vaudevillians who sing and dance their way through the apocalypse. The play introduced Panych's characteristic dramatic theme and strategy: the meaning of life in the face of death explored through witty metatheatricality. Panych's partner, Ken MacDonald, who also wrote and played the music, was the other actor in the show. His creative collaborations – especially his imaginative set designs – have been a key element in virtually all Panych's subsequent successes.

As artistic director of Tamahnous from 1984–86, Panych co-wrote two more musicals with MacDonald, *Contagious* (1985) and *Cheap Sentiment* (1985), and Panych and MacDonald both performed in Panych's *Simple Folk, Songs of a Generation* (1987), a lovely play about coming of age during the folk music era that toured Russia. *7 Stories* opened at Vancouver's Arts Club in 1989, directed by Panych with a startlingly effective set by MacDonald. It swept the city's Jessie awards, then had a successful run at Toronto's Tarragon. The Arts Club–Tarragon connection has proven productive for Panych, the two theatres having premiered many of his subsequent plays. *7 Stories* had major remounts at the Arts Club in 2004, off-Broadway in 2008, and at Toronto's Canadian Stage in 2009, plus more than a hundred productions across Canada and the United States, Europe, Australia, and the United Kingdom.

7 Stories also kicked off a series of existential comedies written and directed by Panych, variations on the theme of "this little nothing of a man" (who, he told critic Barbara Crook, "is me"), struggling to make sense of it all. *The Necessary Steps* (1990) and *The Ends of the Earth* (1992), the latter a Governor General's Award winner, tell relatively epic versions of this story, with casts of four and five taking on multiple roles. In *The Story of a Sinking Man* (1993), Panych himself played the Beckettian solo character literally sinking into the muck. *Lawrence & Holloman* (1998) is a darkly comic two-hander, and *Earshot* (2001) Panych describes as a one-character play about "a man who hears too much."

The 1990s also saw two of Panych's most acclaimed forays into the fate of the little man. In *Vigil* (1995), his most widely produced play, a misanthropic man sits at the bedside of a dying old woman. The *Washington Post* called it "delectably weird" and "a morbid masterpiece." Retitled *Auntie and Me*, it had a major production in 2003 in London's West End. *Vigil* played Paris in 2005 and New York in 2009, and Panych directed Olympia Dukakis in productions at San Francisco's ACT and Los Angeles' Mark Taper Forum in 2010–11. Panych's *The Overcoat* (1997), adapted from Gogol's classic tale, is theatre without words, every movement of the twenty-two-member cast carefully choreographed to the music of Shostakovich. Co-creator Wendy Gorling and rubber-limbed lead actor Peter Anderson both played in the original cast of *7 Stories*. *The Overcoat* opened at the Vancouver Playhouse, toured worldwide to great acclaim, and Panych directed a film version for CBC-TV.

Back at the Arts Club, Panych won his second Governor General's Award for *Girl in the Goldfish Bowl* (2002), an excellent Cold War comedy about a young girl in an eccentric, dysfunctional family. *The Dishwashers* (2005), set in a restaurant basement, takes a turn towards the naturalistic – unusual for Panych. *What Lies Before Us* (2007), a nineteenth-century Canadian western, and *Benevolence* (2007), a dark comedy about a man who tries to help the homeless, both premiered in Toronto.

Between 2006 and 2008, Panych wrote and directed four major adaptations: a version of Gogol's *The Government Inspector* (2006) for

Toronto's Soulpepper; a Feydeau farce titled *Hotel Peccadillo* (2007) for the Shaw Festival; Arthur Schnitzler's *The Amorous Adventures of Anatol* (2008) for the Vancouver Playhouse (all three published in a collection titled *Still Laughing*); and he made his Stratford debut directing his own adaptation of *Moby Dick* (2008).

Stratford also premiered *The Trespassers* (2009), a family play about a teen and his grandfather, and *Wanderlust* (2012), a musical about Robert Service with script, lyrics, and direction by Panych. Montreal was the site of the premieres of *Gordon* (2010), which finds Panych in Sam Shepard territory, and *In Absentia* (2012), a play about love and loss in which a woman must deal with her husband's abduction.

Panych has had success in a wide range of theatrical endeavours. His plays for young audiences – *Co$t of Living* (1990), *2B WUT UR* (1992), and *Life Science* (1993) – have toured nationally and internationally, produced by Vancouver's Green Thumb Theatre and published under the title *Other Schools of Thought*. In addition to his many playwriting awards, he has frequently been honoured for his acting and directing, including his direction of other playwrights' work in Toronto, Vancouver, and at the Shaw Festival. He has directed operas for the Banff Centre and Vancouver Opera, and music videos for the band Spirit of the West. His film and TV credits include a recurring role on *The X-Files*.

"There is but one truly serious philosophical problem, and that is suicide," Albert Camus wrote in *The Myth of Sisyphus*. "Judging whether life is or is not worth living amounts to answering the fundamental question of philosophy." The meaning and value of life, and the particular choices we humans make to give our lives meaning and value (or the illusions thereof), are heady themes that Panych treats with the profound seriousness of comedy. The (every)Man on the ledge in *7 Stories* is clearly in crisis. Costumed in the original production like a silent-movie Buster Keaton, he seems to be undergoing an existential crisis or nervous breakdown. As he explains to Lillian, the routine terms of existence that allowed him to cruise thoughtlessly through his daily life have mysteriously dissolved. His "faith in the days of the week has been seriously undermined"; his hands look strange; his shoes and hat and car seem to contain him like prisons. He has confronted the fact of mortality that makes life in a godless universe absurd: "I saw in the mirror a condemned man, serving a life sentence inside his body." So he climbed out on the ledge "to get a better perspective on my exact situation." Perhaps in the hope of a last-minute reprieve, an answer to the ultimate question, he asks Lillian, "There really is no reason to live, is there?" When she answers, "Not really," he is left in the fundamental existential quandary: without help from outside himself, confronting "the dizziness of freedom" (in Kierkegaard's phrase), having to choose whether to be or not to be.

The Man is not alone in this predicament. Standing precariously on the seventh-storey ledge – a privileged position, both inside and outside the social systems he observes – he serves as a lens through which we see other people in the building trying frantically to make sense of their lives. Totally immersed in their own personal fictions, in the "stories" they tell themselves to give their existence some semblance of meaning, no one even notices until near the end of the play that the Man might be thinking of jumping. Charlotte the poet and Rodney the lawyer find a superficial antidote to their boredom in the sado-masochistic game of trying to kill each other. Leonard the psychiatrist derives meaning from his own paranoia. For Marshall, acting is so perfect a metaphor for life that he literally transforms himself into his character "for a long run." Rachel plays God, while Michael and Joan decide, "style is absolute," and embrace the lifetime challenge of continuous interior decoration. Percy, Jennifer, and Al find ultimate value in the social whirl (Percy, with his 940 friends, anticipating Facebook many years before its inception). As Nurse Wilson observes, no one is interested in other people's problems because everyone is too busy "finding reasons not to jump themselves."

Only Lillian seems to have really figured things out. With the benefit of a century's wisdom, she calmly acknowledges that nothing has any intrinsic meaning, that each experience she recounts is "just a story," that "when you're a hundred years old you'll understand. And then you'll die." But through exploring her own rich internal life, she has realized the immense possibilities of transcendence in the free play of the creative imagination. In what Camus calls "a blind act of human confidence" ("nothing logically prepares this reasoning"), she gives the Man the courage to take the existential leap of faith that leads to the play's exhilarating conclusion.

Morris Panych

7 Stories

7 *Stories* was first produced at the Arts Club Theatre in Vancouver, British Columbia, in May 1989 with the following cast:

MAN	Peter Anderson
CHARLOTTE, JOAN, NURSE WILSON	Sherry Bie
RODNEY, MARSHALL, PERCY	David King
JENNIFER, LILLIAN (MRS. WRIGHT), RACHEL	Wendy Gorling
LEONARD, AL, MICHAEL	Norman Browning

Directed by Morris Panych
Set Design by Ken MacDonald
Lighting Design by Marsha Sibthorpe
Costume Design by Nancy Tait
Original Music by Jeff Corness
Stage Management by Marion Anderson

CHARACTERS

MAN
CHARLOTTE
RODNEY
JENNIFER
LEONARD
MARSHALL
JOAN
MICHAEL
RACHEL
PERCY
AL
NURSE WILSON
LILLIAN (MRS. WRIGHT)
POLICE (*megaphone voice*)
FOUR NEIGHBOURS
EFFIE (*offstage voice*)

ACT ONE

The action of the play takes place outside an apartment building – on the ledge, outside various windows of the seventh storey. As the play progresses, the lights emphasize the time elapsed between early evening and late night.

As the play opens, we hear a party in progress from one of the windows. **MAN** *stands on the ledge, in a state of perplexity, contemplating the depths below. He seems disturbed, confused. Then he comes to what seems to be a resolution. He prepares to jump. As he is about to leap, the window next to him flies open.* **CHARLOTTE** *appears. She holds a man's wallet, which she attempts to throw out the window.* **RODNEY,** *charging up from behind, grabs her hand. A window-ledge struggle ensues.*

CHARLOTTE: Let GO of me!!! Let GO!!

RODNEY: (*threatening*) So-help-me-GOD, Charlotte ...!!

CHARLOTTE: (*daring him*) What?? WHAT??!!

RODNEY: Give me back my wallet!

She tries to throw it again. They struggle.

RODNEY: What's WRONG with you? Are you CRAZY?!

CHARLOTTE: YES! YES, I AM!!!

RODNEY: MY GOLD CARD is in there!!

CHARLOTTE: Oh? Is it? Is your GOLD CARD in here ...

She searches through his wallet as he tries to retrieve it.

Oh my goodness! So it is!! And your RACQUET CLUB membership!! Oooo! And a LOVELY picture of your LOVELY wife! We mustn't drop THAT, must we? We wouldn't want someone picking HER up off the street!!

RODNEY: Give it here!

CHARLOTTE: Leave me alone, or I'll call the police!

RODNEY: You wouldn't dare.

CHARLOTTE: HELP! POLICE!

RODNEY: SHUT UP!!

CHARLOTTE: You STRUCK me!!

RODNEY: I did not!

CHARLOTTE: Yes, you did! He STRUCK me! HELP!

RODNEY: I did not!! SHUT UP!

CHARLOTTE: Yes you did! You bastard!

CHARLOTTE goes to strike him. They struggle violently out the window, as MAN watches in terror. RODNEY manages to grab CHARLOTTE by the throat and starts to strangle her.

CHARLOTTE: HELP! Helgpjhhgghp!

RODNEY: (*strangling her*) You're quite unattractive when you're dying. Did you know that, Charlotte?

CHARLOTTE: Gddldjkiqk!!!

RODNEY: (*calmly*) You lose all your CHARM! You lose all your SPARKLE! Charlotte! I believe you're turning blue! It's most unbecoming!

CHARLOTTE: Gahhghh!

RODNEY: Is that all you've got to say, Charlotte? Ordinarily you're so outspoken. One might even say LOUD and CONSPICUOUS! What's that you say, Charlotte?

CHARLOTTE: Grrghaah!

RODNEY: Yes, the view from here is BREATHTAKING, isn't it!

MAN: Excuse me.

RODNEY and CHARLOTTE are stopped cold.

MAN: Would you mind letting go of her. You're hurting her.

RODNEY: (*with feigned surprise*) Hurting her!?

He looks at CHARLOTTE.

Am I hurting you, Charlotte?

CHARLOTTE: Yeghhgg!

RODNEY: (*letting go*) What's that, Charlotte?

CHARLOTTE: (*hoarsely*) Yes!

RODNEY: I am sorry! (*to MAN*) You were right. I was hurting her. And thank you for pointing that out. Why don't we go inside, Charlotte? We seem to be attracting a crowd.

CHARLOTTE: I am not going anywhere with you! You tried to KILL me!

RODNEY: Kill you! Really, Charlotte! Now why would I do that? (*to MAN*) She has an overactive imagination, you know. Dabbles in the creative arts.

MAN: Oh.

CHARLOTTE: Dabbles!

RODNEY: You're misinterpreting the facts once again, Charlotte. (*to MAN*) Apparently she misunderstood my intentions. Come inside, Charlotte.

CHARLOTTE: Misunderstood, nothing! You tried to kill me, Rodney. He saw the whole thing. Didn't you?

MAN: I –

CHARLOTTE: He's a key witness. And we know all about key witnesses, don't we? (*to MAN*) Rodney's a lawyer.

MAN: Oh.

RODNEY: Charlotte! I'm warning you –

CHARLOTTE: And of course we know all about lawyers, don't we?

MAN: Actually, he's the only one I've ever met.

CHARLOTTE: Really?!

RODNEY: Oh for heaven's sake!

CHARLOTTE: Well, in that case, let me fill you in. Lawyers are the people who BORE you to death with the facts. (*to RODNEY*) By the way, Rodney. Why would you go to all the trouble of strangling me, when you simply could have BORED me to death?

RODNEY: You're making a public spectacle!

CHARLOTTE: My goodness, that would have been the perfect crime. I would have died, slowly, over the course of one of our romantic evenings together. Hanging, as it were, on his every word –

RODNEY: I need a drink.

CHARLOTTE: Would you like a drink? (*to RODNEY*) Fix us a drink, would you, Rodney?

RODNEY goes.

MAN: I –

CHARLOTTE: Yes ... I suppose you're wondering why I don't just leave him.

MAN: Well, I –

CHARLOTTE: That's a very good question. (*to RODNEY*) Rodney! What the gentleman wants to know is why I don't just leave you.

RODNEY: Does he?

MAN: I don't really –

CHARLOTTE: Shall I tell him?

No answer.

CHARLOTTE: He's not answering. He's standing there, giving me that LOOK again. (*to RODNEY*) Don't just stand there giving me that stupid LOOK. I'm not threatened by you in the least. (*to MAN*) He thinks I'm threatened. (*to RODNEY*) In case you forgot, I have a key witness here who fully intends to testify at your attempted murder trial.

MAN: I don't think I'll be around, I –

CHARLOTTE: You won't? Why not?

RODNEY: (*now at the window*) What a pity, Charlotte. Your KEY WITNESS won't be here. (*to MAN*) I can quite understand your reservations. Considering her history. (*to CHARLOTTE*) Get in here!!

CHARLOTTE: Don't listen to him. He'll say anything. He spins a web of lies, like a spider.

RODNEY: Really, Charlotte. I'm surprised at your use of such a tired metaphor. And you call yourself a poet.

CHARLOTTE: You see! He tries to make you lose your train of thought.

RODNEY: I shouldn't think you'd need any help with that.

CHARLOTTE: Where's my drink?

RODNEY: Haven't you had enough. (*to MAN*) She loses count after ten cocktails. (*to CHARLOTTE*) Anyway, I'm leaving.

CHARLOTTE: (*to MAN*) Ha!

RODNEY: Where are my Italian brogues?

CHARLOTTE: (*to MAN*) Most people wear shoes. (*to RODNEY*) I have no idea. Perhaps I threw them out the window.

They all look down.

RODNEY: Did you?

CHARLOTTE: I honestly can't remember.

RODNEY: You've hidden them. Where are they? (*to MAN*) What's she done with my shoes?

MAN: I –

CHARLOTTE: I TOLD you – I can't remember. Besides – you happen to be interrupting our conversation.

RODNEY: Oh really? I'm sorry.

He goes.

MAN: It's quite all right!

CHARLOTTE: Don't pay any attention to him. As I was saying … the reason I don't leave here is because Rodney and I are inseparable. The question of leaving, although it arises constantly, is – dare I say – moot. (*to RODNEY*) MOOT? Is that right, Rodney?

RODNEY: WHAT!!?

CHARLOTTE: Can I say "the question of my leaving is MOOT"?

RODNEY: You can say whatever you like.

CHARLOTTE: He's not usually so generous with my word usage. He finds himself correcting just about everything I say.

RODNEY: (*correcting her*) Irrelevant!

CHARLOTTE: What?

RODNEY: The question of your leaving is irrelevant.

CHARLOTTE: Thank you. (*to MAN*) You see.

MAN: Yes, I see.

CHARLOTTE: But I suppose you don't think the question is irrelevant? Since he just tried to kill me.

MAN: Well –

CHARLOTTE: Rodney!

RODNEY: WHAT, for heaven's sake?!

CHARLOTTE: He doesn't think the question of my leaving is irrelevant.

RODNEY: Who doesn't?

CHARLOTTE: He doesn't.

RODNEY: Well, he doesn't know the facts.

CHARLOTTE: Oh. Apparently you don't know the facts. Only Rodney, of course, knows the facts. "The World According to Rodney." My God. Where would we be without all those specific details? Life would be so – vague. Perhaps even meaningless.

MAN: Yes.

CHARLOTTE: When you come to think of it, the Rodneys of this world are man's salvation in a way. They build us the ramparts, stone by stone, each one another absolute little certainty. Another "fact." All piled high against the onslaught of the absurd truth!

RODNEY: (*appearing with two drinks*) Really, Charlotte. You sound like a cheap novelist.

CHARLOTTE: IT'S POETRY!! (*taking drinks*) Thank you. (*giving MAN one of the drinks*) Naturally, he despises poetry. He despises all art. Because art is the act of climbing to the top of that ridiculous wall of his – and standing on the ledge – to look out into a cruel and pointless world – devoid of meaning – where fact is merely fiction. And anybody with any courage would simply leap off the edge and be done with it.

RODNEY: I could give you a little push if you'd like.

CHARLOTTE: Go ahead and push me!

RODNEY goes.

MAN: I wouldn't provoke him.

CHARLOTTE: Oh good heavens. That would be much too quick for him. He'd rather kill me little by little than all at once.

RODNEY approaches from behind and points what seems to be a gun at the back of CHARLOTTE's head.

RODNEY: One more word and I'll blow your head off.

CHARLOTTE: I do hope that's a gun, Rodney, and not just your finger.

RODNEY: That's our little secret. Now come inside. I don't want any witnesses this time.

CHARLOTTE: Will you excuse us?

CHARLOTTE slowly closes the window. After a brief moment, a shot rings out.

As MAN stands, martini glass in hand, JENNIFER appears from the party window.

JENNIFER: Was that gunfire?

MAN: Uh – I don't …

JENNIFER: (*looking down*) Was somebody gunned down, or what?

MAN: I'm not sure.

JENNIFER: I just LOVE your neighbourhood. It's so … third world!

LEONARD appears from his window, dressed in pajamas.

LEONARD: SHUT UP!! SHUT UP for GOD'S SAKE!! SHUT UP!! I'm TRYING to get some SLEEP!!

JENNIFER: Oh, I know! I tried that once. Scary isn't it?

LEONARD: What's she talking about?

JENNIFER: I was just lying there … and I could hear myself breathing? You know? I thought "Oh God! I can hear myself breathing!!" I'll never try THAT again!

LEONARD quietly closes his window.

JENNIFER: Wow! Your friend is so intense!

MAN: He's not –

JENNIFER: (*looking down*) Do you ever feel like throwing yourself out of a building?

MAN: (*pause*) …

JENNIFER: Whenever I get too close to the edge, I just feel like jumping. Isn't that wild?!

MAN: (*pause*) …

JENNIFER: It's probably symbolic.

MAN: (*pause*) …

JENNIFER: Will you excuse me. It's not that I don't like you or anything – 'cause I really do – it's just that there's too many pauses in this conversation.

She disappears, closing the window. After a moment, LEONARD opens his window.

LEONARD: Listen, lady … where did she go? She wasn't even there. Oh my God! (*to MAN*) She wasn't even there!

He closes his window again. After a brief moment, he opens it again.

LEONARD: What do you want?

MAN: Uh …

LEONARD: A likely story! What?

MAN: I think there might have been a murder committed.

LEONARD: A murder! So THAT's where she went.

MAN: No. Your neighbours.

LEONARD: My neighbours murdered her!?

MAN: No.

LEONARD: She murdered my neighbours?

MAN: It's got nothing to do with her. I think there's been a murder committed. I think you should call the police.

LEONARD: Let me get this straight. You murdered the neighbours?

MAN: I didn't say that!

LEONARD: Yes, you did. Are you trying to tell me I'm hearing things? Is that what you're saying? I distinctly heard you say you murdered my neighbours. That it had nothing to do with her!

MAN: All I said was: "I think there's been a murder committed." There was an argument. Didn't you hear the gunshot?

LEONARD: Gunshot! I didn't hear any gunshot! Are you sure it was a gunshot?

MAN: Positive.

LEONARD: Oh dear. This is a new twist. Usually I'm hearing things. Now, I'm *not* hearing things. Oh dear. I've gone deaf.

MAN: Hadn't we better call the police?

LEONARD: Did you say something just now?

MAN: Yes.

LEONARD: Are you sure?

MAN: Of course I am. I said, "We'd better call the police."

LEONARD: Oh good. Well, I heard that quite distinctly. Every word of it.

MAN: Look – this could be serious.

LEONARD: Do you think so? I'm only a little tense. That's all. If I had some sleep I'd be just fine. Maybe it's just a little wax buildup.

MAN: What are you talking about?

LEONARD: What are you talking about? Aren't we both talking about the same thing?

MAN: I was talking about your neighbours. About the gunshot.

LEONARD: The gunshot! Yes! About whether I heard it or not.

MAN: Look – that doesn't matter.

LEONARD: It matters to me!

MAN: There was a gunshot. That's all that matters. Just call the police!

LEONARD: Now how can you expect me to do that? I didn't even hear a gunshot. What am I supposed to tell them – when and if they answer? Am I supposed to *admit* that I didn't even hear a gunshot from twenty feet away? Or am I supposed to pretend that I'm hearing things. They'll think I'm insane!

MAN: What difference does it make?

LEONARD: They ask for your name. Am I supposed to lie about that as well? They'll just find out anyway. Because they'll trace the call back to me. Why did I have to get dragged into this?

MAN: Why are you taking it so personally? It's got nothing to do with you.

LEONARD: Oh, that's right! Accuse me of being one of those!

MAN: One of what?

LEONARD: Those people who shut themselves off from the rest of the world.

MAN: Good God! I wasn't accusing you of anything.

LEONARD: Yes you were!

MAN: No I wasn't!

LEONARD: Are you positive about that?

MAN: Of course I am. I don't even know you.

LEONARD: There was a tone of accusation in your voice. You have to admit it.

MAN: I think you're just being paranoid.

LEONARD: Why would you say that? (*pause*) You don't know anything about paranoia. What experience do you have in that field – if any?

MAN: None.

LEONARD: A likely story! (*pause*) What did you say?

MAN: I said I don't have any experience in the field.

LEONARD: What's that supposed to mean?

MAN: I mean I don't know anything about paranoia.

LEONARD: Implying that I'm paranoid.

MAN: Not at all.

LEONARD: By inference. Saying that you don't know anything about it. Inferring that I know a great deal.

MAN: You said so yourself.

LEONARD: I did not.

MAN: You indicated as much.

LEONARD: This is a trap! You're trying to trap me into something. Aren't you? You think I'm insane! That I've completely lost my grip on reality. And that's where you're wrong. I happen to be painfully cognizant of the world around me. I might be going deaf, but I'm not blind. I'm a qualified professional, and I'm trained to keep my eyes wide open.

LEONARD instantly falls asleep. MAN studies LEONARD for a moment, then looking at his martini glass, goes back over to CHARLOTTE's window. He raps on the pane. RODNEY opens the window.

RODNEY: What do YOU want?

MAN: Is everything all right?

RODNEY: Couldn't be better.

MAN: I heard a gunshot. I thought maybe there'd been an accident.

RODNEY: Charlotte!?

CHARLOTTE: (*inside*) What?!

RODNEY: The gentleman heard a gunshot. He thought there'd been an accident. Isn't that amusing?

CHARLOTTE: Ha! Ha!

RODNEY: As a matter of fact there was a bit of an accident. I aimed for her head and accidentally hit the wall. But thank you for your concern.

RODNEY slams the window shut, waking LEONARD.

LEONARD: Ah! What happened?

MAN: I don't know. You fell asleep.

LEONARD: No I didn't. What?

MAN: You – fell – asleep.

LEONARD: I did? Well, of course I did! What did you expect?

MAN: I don't know.

LEONARD: That's right, you don't. I haven't slept more than two hours in the past month. I never sleep. I work nights.

MAN: So why don't you sleep during the day?

LEONARD: Why do you want me to go to sleep?

MAN: I don't. It makes no difference to me.

LEONARD: Just what are you planning?

MAN: Me? I'm not planning anything. I was only thinking ... for your well-being ...

LEONARD: My well-being? You think I'm not well.

MAN: I never said that.

LEONARD: Somebody told you something, didn't they?

MAN: No. Nobody told me anything.

LEONARD: Why didn't they? Why would they want to keep YOU in the dark?

MAN: Who?

LEONARD: I don't know!! Has it occurred to you yet that you could be an innocent pawn in all this? A dupe?

MAN: No.

LEONARD: Well, you see! You're naive. You're the perfect candidate for them to carry out their insane plan.

MAN: What insane plan?

LEONARD: Well, they didn't tell you of course. They wouldn't want YOU to know!!

MAN: Know what? Who's they?

LEONARD: You said you heard a gunshot. Right?

MAN: Yes. I did. But ...

LEONARD: Coming from where?

MAN: Your neighbours, but ...

LEONARD: Well, they're in on it too. Don't you see?

MAN: No. It's all been a mix-up. I mean, I heard a gunshot, but it turns out it was nothing.

LEONARD: Nothing? You don't know what's going on in the world, do you?

MAN: I used to think I did. I don't know. No ... I don't.

LEONARD: I suppose you think all these things happen by chance? Just one GREAT BIG HAPPY coincidence. Gunshots are fired. Then they're not fired. A woman appears who was never there. That light in that apartment over there. I guess you didn't notice that either. Because you don't think these things are important.

MAN: Light?

LEONARD: Over there. It just went on. Don't look.

A slight pause as MAN considers this.

MAN: And?

LEONARD: And!? And WHAT?!

MAN: I don't get it.

LEONARD: Of course you don't get it. You don't know the code. Fortunately – I do. I have deciphered the code. I know EXACTLY what's going on. Ah. There goes that other light. Don't look.

MAN: There are lights going on and off all over the place. You don't think everybody's in on it.

LEONARD: In on WHAT? There IS something, isn't there?

MAN: I'm not really sure anymore.

LEONARD: And you think I'm confused!

MAN: I never said you were.

LEONARD: Well, who said I was, then?

MAN: Nobody.

LEONARD: Well, where did you get the information?

MAN: I have no information. I don't know anything.

LEONARD: Oh. (*pause*) Well, I don't know anything either. In fact, I don't even know what we were talking about.

MAN: That makes two of us.

LEONARD: Two of us?

MAN: I don't know what you're talking about either.

LEONARD: Oh. (*pause*) You don't?

MAN: No.

LEONARD: Was I being incoherent?

MAN: I don't know what to say.

LEONARD: What does that mean?

MAN: You're bound to take it the wrong way.

LEONARD: What?

MAN: Whatever I say.

LEONARD: What are you going to say?

MAN: Nothing.

LEONARD: You can tell me. What is it? Is there something I should know about myself?

MAN: Look – it's none of my business.

LEONARD: What? What's none of your business?

MAN: You asked if you were being incoherent. I don't know what to say. If I tell you you were, you'll fly into a panic. If I tell you you weren't, you'll think I'm trying to hide something from you. You take everything I say the wrong way.

LEONARD: You think I'm insane.

MAN: Now, there's a case in point. I don't think you're insane. I don't think anything. The word "insane" didn't even enter into it.

LEONARD: Yes, it did.

MAN: Well, you said it. I didn't say it. I'm in no position to judge the state of your mind. I'm not a psychiatrist.

LEONARD: A psychiatrist? Why did you mention a psychiatrist? I never said anything about a psychiatrist.

MAN: I was only making a point.

LEONARD: Well, you can make a point without mentioning a psychiatrist, can't you? You could have mentioned a proctologist.

MAN: Why would I do that?

LEONARD: Precisely!

MAN: Very well, then. Have it your way. Let me correct myself. What I meant to say is, I'm in no position to judge the state of your mind. I'm not a proctologist. Is that better?

LEONARD: Why are you making fun of me?

MAN: I'm sorry.

LEONARD: Do you find psychiatry amusing? Well, let me tell you – it's no joke.

MAN: I didn't say it was.

LEONARD: Oh, I realize it's an easy target for satire. One might even say an obvious one. But it's serious work, involving a lot of time and dedication. And we don't get paid nearly as much as you'd like to think.

MAN: You're a psychiatrist?

LEONARD: Why do you say it like that? What are you implying?

MAN: I'm not implying anything. I'm a little surprised. That's all.

LEONARD: Why should you be? Do you think there's something strange about it? Why are you looking at me like that?

MAN: I'm not even looking at you.

LEONARD: Why aren't you looking at me? Are you afraid of me? Are you afraid I'll find something out about you? Some dark, terrible secret? You can tell me – I'm a psychiatrist. Here – why don't you take my card. You can set up an appointment with my secretary. I work nights at the loony bin. But I have a private practice in the mornings. I've got to run now. It's time to get up and go to work. I haven't slept in three years, but what difference does that make to them? They're all on drugs. They sleep all the time. I hate insane people. They drive me crazy. I don't mean literally crazy. You didn't take that literally, did you?

MAN: No.

LEONARD: Are you patronizing me?

MAN: No.

LEONARD: In the future, don't patronize me. I'm the doctor, and I'll do all the patronizing. You'll find, once we've begun to develop a professional relationship, that you'll come to rely on me for emotional support. I'll be carrying the weight of all your problems, so that you can feel free to let go. You won't have to hang onto your sanity. I'll be the one who's hanging on. That's my job.

> *LEONARD closes the window. The MAN studies the card. As he is pocketing the card, MARSHALL, wearing a tuxedo, opens another window and climbs out onto the ledge. Without noticing the MAN, he takes out a cigarette and lights it. For a moment, he luxuriates in this obviously great pleasure. As he exhales, he notices the MAN looking at him. MARSHALL speaks with a very "theatrical" accent.*

MARSHALL: Oh pardon me. I hope you don't mind my smoking. It's my last cigarette.

MAN: That's all right.

MARSHALL: Would you like one?

MAN: I don't know. I've never tried one before.

MARSHALL: Here. Be my guest. You can take them all.

MAN: (*making his way a little along the ledge*) I guess it can't do any harm now.

MARSHALL: And I certainly won't be smoking them.

> *He hands the MAN his cigarettes.*

> *Suddenly, LEONARD's window opens once again, behind him.*

LEONARD: I have a question I forgot to ask you. (*not noticing that he has moved*) My God! He wasn't even there!

MAN: I'm over here. I'm having a cigarette.

LEONARD: Who's that?

MAN: A gentleman. I don't know his name. We only just met.

MARSHALL: It's Marshall. Actually, it's Mike.

LEONARD: Well who is he?

MAN: I don't know. We only just met.

> *He moves along the ledge, a little way back to LEONARD's window.*

MAN: What was your question?

LEONARD: What question?

MAN: You have a question you forgot to ask me.

LEONARD: What sort of question?

MAN: I don't know.

LEONARD: Well what? Was it a personal question?

MAN: You were the one who wanted to ask it.

LEONARD: Then it was personal.

MAN: I really don't know.

LEONARD: Could I have a word with you for a moment?

MAN: What is it?

LEONARD: (*sotto voce*) What does he want?

MAN: I don't think he wants anything. I think he's just having a cigarette.

LEONARD: Does he know about our conversation?

MAN: No. I don't think so.

LEONARD: Well, don't say a word to him. Keep it private.

MAN: All right.

LEONARD: We must pretend that we never spoke.

MAN: We're speaking now.

LEONARD: Act like you don't know me.

MAN: I don't.

LEONARD: Otherwise he might get the wrong idea. He'll think that just because you're seeing a psychiatrist that you're insane. And that kind of information can get into the wrong hands.

> *Without saying another word, LEONARD slowly closes the window, putting his finger to his lips in a secret gesture.*

MARSHALL: (*who has been watching*) Friend of yours?

MAN: No. I don't know him.

MARSHALL: Best to keep it that way. People know far too much about each other these days. I much prefer to form my own false impressions. Don't you?

MAN: I really don't like to speculate.

MARSHALL: What difference does it make? The truth is irrelevant. One's own opinion on the other hand is far more appealing. One should always form a strong opinion, one way or the other. Regardless of the facts.

MAN: That seems to be a popular theme around here.

MARSHALL: After all, it's about the only thing people are entitled to. Except for me. I've completely relinquished my personality. I've even relinquished my hair colour. Can you believe it?

MAN: That's not your real hair colour?

MARSHALL: Oh, there's no need to pretend you didn't know.

MAN: I didn't.

MARSHALL: I won't be offended if you don't like it. I'm not that sort of person. But you can decide what sort of person I am for yourself. And anyway – it's got nothing to do with me. It's my wife's decision really. Well, it's not really a decision. But then, she's not really my wife, is she? Not yet. But almost.

MAN: You're getting married.

MARSHALL: Yes. In a little more than half an hour, my life, as you and I know it, will be over. Finished. Butted out. Extinguished.

MAN: I suppose congratulations are in order.

MARSHALL: Don't be absurd. Congratulations aren't in order at all. On the other hand, I don't expect any sympathy. You wouldn't feel the least bit sorry for me if you knew the whole story. (*suddenly switching to another, more natural voice*) Is my moustache on straight?

MAN: It looks fine.

MARSHALL: (*returning to accent*) Of course it doesn't look fine. Don't be ridiculous. I'm only asking if it's straight. This damn glue doesn't stick properly.

MAN: You mean it's false?

MARSHALL: (*normal voice*) Couldn't you tell?

MAN: No.

MARSHALL: (*accent*) Oh good. Of course I suppose it'll fall off in the middle of the ceremony, and that'll be the end of it. I really ought to have grown one. But I can't stand moustaches. The itching drives me mad. Oh God. I've only got half a cigarette left! It seems to be burning awfully fast. Isn't that always the way? You're not smoking yours.

MAN: I'm sorry. I don't find it very pleasant.

MARSHALL: (*normal voice*) Well, don't waste it, for God's sake. Here. I'll finish it.

MARSHALL now has two cigarettes, which he smokes alternately.

MARSHALL: (*as he continues to speak, he gradually loses his accent*) If I had the time, I'd smoke the whole pack. But the best man is waiting for me. He thinks I'm in the bathroom. Thank God for bathrooms. Where would we be without them, eh? Those little private oases in the desert of eternal wedlock. Wedlock! There's a good name for it. Sounds like "padlock," doesn't it? What a perfect description for marriage. Wed – *Lock*. The penitentiary of betrothal! I imagine I'll be spending the rest of my life locked in a bathroom somewhere. Oh, there's no need to be concerned about it. The house has seven different bathrooms. Excluding the ensuites.

MAN: No. It's not that.

MARSHALL: What is it then? You look troubled.

MAN: I'm sorry. It's no business of mine, but why are you wearing a false moustache?

MARSHALL: Well, it's part of my character, isn't it?

MAN: It is?

MARSHALL: He wears a moustache. His hair is auburn. And he doesn't smoke, among other things. And his name is Marshall. And I keep losing my accent.

MAN: You mean to say that's not your real accent?

MARSHALL: (*accent*) Well, it is now. Now that I've fully adopted this character.

MAN: You had *me* fooled.

MARSHALL: That's the idea.

MAN: It's so realistic.

MARSHALL: (*changes to normal voice*) Well, there's a lot at stake, isn't there?

MAN: There is?

MARSHALL: About a hundred and fifty million, I'd say. Give or take a million. But who's counting?

MAN: Dollars?

MARSHALL: Dollars. Debentures. Stocks. Bonds. Futures. Securities. You name it.

MAN: Yours?

MARSHALL: If I play my part well enough. If the moustache doesn't fall off at the altar.

MAN: And what if it does?

MARSHALL: Then they'll wonder, won't they? Wouldn't you?

MAN: Well, yes. I'm wondering now.

CHARLOTTE bursts forth.

CHARLOTTE: Help!

MARSHALL: (*assuming accent again*) Are you in some sort of trouble, madam?

CHARLOTTE: Help me.

MARSHALL: Should I call the police this time?

CHARLOTTE: He tried to kill me!

MARSHALL: Oh dear. Again?

MAN: Again?

Offstage, we hear a little girl's voice.

EFFIE: Marshall!! Marshall!!

MARSHALL: (*own voice, to MAN*) It's that horrible little flower girl. Will you excuse me? (*He goes.*)

MAN: Again?

CHARLOTTE: What?

MAN: You mean to say he's tried to kill you before.

CHARLOTTE: On several occasions. Not the least of which was my BIRTHDAY!!

RODNEY: (*from off*) Oh for heaven's sake ... get in here!!

CHARLOTTE: Don't you think that's insensitive?

MAN: Well yes, I ...

CHARLOTTE: Rodney!

RODNEY: What!?

CHARLOTTE: This gentleman thinks it's incredibly insensitive that you tried to kill me on my birthday.

RODNEY: Oh, does he?

MAN: I –

RODNEY: He doesn't know the whole story.

CHARLOTTE: Oh. You don't know the whole story.

RODNEY: And what's more, it wasn't your birthday.

CHARLOTTE: It was MY BIRTHDAY!! He has a tremendous sense of occasion.

RODNEY: You're distorting the facts once again.

MAN: Why do you treat each other this way?

CHARLOTTE: It's all words and gestures. Pomp. There's absolutely no substance to it.

MAN: He was choking you to death.

CHARLOTTE: Oh, that. It gives him a tremendous sense of power to hear me gasping helplessly for air.

MAN: And the gun?

CHARLOTTE: Blanks.

MAN: You were both just pretending?

CHARLOTTE: Oh, I don't know. There's such a fine line between truth and fiction, isn't there? It's the subject of a number of foreign films. (to RODNEY) Oh for God's sake, Rodney. What are you doing now?

RODNEY: I'm killing all your goldfish.

CHARLOTTE: Did you hear that? He's killing all my goldfish.

MAN: Yes. I heard.

CHARLOTTE: The neighbours can hear you, Rodney.

RODNEY: What? Killing a fish?

CHARLOTTE: He's not really doing anything. He's standing there looking at my goldfish. Giving them that LOOK. That DEADLY LOOK. Yes. I was only acting.

MAN: Pardon?

CHARLOTTE: I was pretending to die. He finds it amusing.

MAN: Oh. Well, I don't.

CHARLOTTE: Then why were you watching us?

MAN: I happened to be here. That's all.

CHARLOTTE: I see.

RODNEY: (inside) Come inside, Charlotte. I've got a knife and I want to cut your head off.

CHARLOTTE: (to RODNEY) That knife isn't even sharp. You'd have to poke my head off with that!

RODNEY: Now there's an idea!

CHARLOTTE: He's threatening to cut my head off with a butter knife. Can you imagine?!

MAN: No, not really.

CHARLOTTE: Well, at least it's something. I suppose there's a certain affection in it. It keeps the relationship alive anyway. It used to be one of those dreary, mindless little affairs that start with a bang and end with a whimper. We weren't even lovers anymore. Just zombies. You can't imagine. He started reading the paper at dinner. I started having another affair. You can't believe how complicated that is. Cheating on the man you're cheating with. Anyway – it had all the trappings of a marriage. Which is precisely what both of us were trying to escape. We began to dread seeing one another. Finally, I suppose out of sheer exasperation, dear Rodney, the boring lawyer, tried to run me down with his car. It's hard to explain, but as I lay on the curb, half-conscious, I felt – revitalized. We both did. And we've been trying to kill each other ever since.

RODNEY: Charlotte ...?

CHARLOTTE: (to MAN) It's not entirely an act. We really do hate each other. But there's something to be said for that, isn't there? There's a certain zeal to it.

CHARLOTTE leaves.

MARSHALL returns, now speaking in his normal voice.

MARSHALL: They're quite an item, those two.

MAN: You know them?

MARSHALL: I've seen them around. She tried to stab him to death in the hallway last week. It's really an incredible love story.

MAN: Love?

MARSHALL: What would you call it?

MAN: I –

MARSHALL: Oh. I forgot. You don't like to speculate on these things.

MAN: No.

MARSHALL: I do. I think they're deeply and passionately in love, and I think that one day soon, quite by accident, there will be casualties. It's not my kind of love, mind you. I'm much more inclined toward the romantic. The sentimental. The sort of love that brings a tear to the eye. Like a good television commercial. Counterfeit emotion is really my style. Counterfeit everything.

MAN: Like your moustache?

MARSHALL: It is perfect when you think about it.

MAN: What is?

MARSHALL: This masquerade.

MAN: Wouldn't it be easier just to be who you are?

MARSHALL: I wonder what that would be? Anyway – it wouldn't be what she wants. This is what she wants, so this is what she gets. After all, I'm being well compensated for it. So what do I care? It's no worse than what I was doing. Just a little more involved.

MAN: What were you doing?

MARSHALL: Acting. I was acting for a living.

MAN: Oh. You're an actor.

MARSHALL: Well, not anymore. I've forfeited that as well. Along with my name. It used to be Mike. Michael Merchant. I take it you've never heard of me.

MAN: I, uh …

MARSHALL: But then, why would you have? I was never really very good. Quite second-rate, in fact. I've played all the great roles, but I've played them all very badly. Acting is such a desperately futile profession anyway. Playing out the lives of other men. Knowing of their failures and successes long before they ever do. Living, suffering, murdering, dying … all in the space of three hours. Sometimes only two. And in such a confined little area. And over and over again every night. Can you imagine anything more perfectly stupid? Squeezing a whole existence into a measly evening's entertainment on the stage? And not only that – in the middle of it all – pausing for an intermission. It makes one's own life seem unbearably preposterous, doesn't it?

MAN: Yes. I suppose it does.

MARSHALL: So I'm more than happy to give it up.

MAN: But you're acting now.

MARSHALL: Well yes but this is different, isn't it?

MAN: Is it?

MARSHALL: Most certainly and definitely. This is one play where the curtain never goes down. I will play this character until I die. Or until she does. But that's another story.

JOAN and MICHAEL burst forth from another window, struggling with an antique vase.

JOAN: No. No, Michael. Please!

MICHAEL: Pull yourself together, Joan. Be a little more objective.

JOAN: Michael … Michael …

MICHAEL: Joan!

In their struggle, the vase breaks.

JOAN: Oh no. It was family!

MICHAEL: Yes, but it was completely out of fashion.

JOAN: It meant a great deal to me, Michael.

MICHAEL: My mother meant a great deal to me, Joan, but she didn't go with anything either.

They go.

MAN: I don't get it. I just can't understand why your fiancée would want you to be someone else.

MARSHALL: She doesn't want me to be someone else. As far as she's concerned, I am someone else. I'm Marshall. She doesn't know anything about Michael Merchant, and she never will. In about five minutes from now, Michael Merchant will disappear from the face of the earth. He'll be nothing but a fleeting memory.

MAN: Where will he go?

MARSHALL: That's probably a very interesting philosophical question. But I'm not a philosopher. I'm Marshall.

MAN: So you said.

MARSHALL: Yes. Well, it doesn't hurt to remind myself. (*normal voice*) She first met me, that is, she first met him one night about a year ago. I was playing Horatio and, as usual, playing it very badly. Not only that – but on this particular evening, I was also playing it very fast. The flights of angels had never so quickly sung poor Hamlet to his rest. I had a date with destiny, you see. Actually, I had a date with a sailor.

MAN: A sailor? A *male* sailor?

MARSHALL: Yes. It's funny, now that I think about it. Well, it's all an act anyway. Isn't it? The whole stupid dumb show. Life, I mean. His name was

Marshall. And it was him I was thinking about, as I dashed from the theatre, still in makeup and in this ridiculous hair colour, and moustache, when this sleek, red Mercedes came roaring around the corner …

MAN: So she hit you.

MARSHALL: Almost hit me. But she'll never know. I must say – it was a much better performance than the one I'd just given. And I thought – well, a Mercedes … there's got to be a little money here somewhere. And as it turns out, there was. Quite a little.

MAN: A hundred and fifty million.

MARSHALL: It does come trippingly off the tongue, doesn't it? Like the name Marshall. It seemed to suit the scenario. More like the name of the sort of person who might be worth her while. Anyway, it worked. She loved the name, she loved the hair colour, and she adored the moustache. And the rest of the character just slowly fell into place, until it was exactly what she wanted. She couldn't have done better if she'd ordered me from a catalogue, which is just the sort of thing she usually does. Who'd believe it, eh?

MAN: I would think she's bound to find out the truth.

MARSHALL: Well, as I say. Who'd believe it?

MAN: But what about family and friends?

MARSHALL: They go with the forfeit. Vanish into thin air.

MAN: They'll see you in the street.

MARSHALL: We'll hardly be travelling in the same circles. And if they ever do see me, I'll simply remind them of someone they used to know.

MAN: But what about records of birth, that sort of thing? Don't you have to prove who you are? Even to get a marriage licence?

MARSHALL: I have a friend in props. He's very good.

MAN: Well, you can't just appear out of nowhere. What about parents?

MARSHALL: Yes. Those were difficult parts to cast.

MAN: You mean there are others in on this?

MARSHALL: Oh, just a couple of old actors, in need of a steady job. I have to admit she's a bit of a ham. Calls me "son" too much. But I've passed it off as eccentricity. The in-laws find them terribly charming. And there's an uncle. He's an old friend of mine. I owe him a few favours, so he's part of the family now. It's quite a collection. Between them, they've come up with more than a few fond memories of my childhood.

MAN: This is total fraud!

MARSHALL: Well, we're looking at it more like a long run.

MAN: What's more, it's immoral!

MARSHALL: Don't be ridiculous. It's nothing of the kind. It's simply patronage of the arts. It all depends on your point of view. And anyway, no one's doing anyone any harm.

MAN: But you've given up your family. Your friends. You're making a complete mockery out of your existence. A joke. Doesn't your life mean anything?

MARSHALL: Well, I've lived so many, haven't I? Lives are just short little episodes. You're on and then you're off. Just like that. Which reminds me. I'm off.

Just as MARSHALL is leaving, RACHEL opens her window.

RACHEL: Oh, excuse me.

LEONARD reappears as RACHEL closes her window.

LEONARD: Oh good. You're still here. (*producing pills*) Here take a couple of these.

MAN: What are they?

LEONARD: Oh, you know. The usual.

MAN: There's nothing wrong with me. Nothing – psychiatric. I don't really have any of the necessary symptoms.

LEONARD: (*another bottle*) Then you'll want to take a couple of these first before you take a couple of those. Otherwise, there's no reason to take any of those. These ones pick you up and those ones bring you down. So it's really better if you take them both at the same time. That'll keep you more or less balanced until I get back from the booby hatch.

He goes. MAN studies the pills. RACHEL opens her window.

RACHEL: How long are you going to be out there? Roughly speaking?

MAN: Huh?

RACHEL: Are you going to be out there for long?

MAN: I have no idea.

RACHEL: Oh. Well, don't rush. I can wait.

Pause.

RACHEL: Will it be more than ten minutes?

MAN: What?

RACHEL: Will it be more than ten minutes, or less than ten minutes?

MAN: I don't really know.

RACHEL: Oh.

A pause. She watches, as he contemplates the depths.

RACHEL: So you really don't know how long you'll be.

MAN: Does it make any difference?

RACHEL: No. I suppose not. Not if you're preoccupied.

MAN: Preoccupied?

RACHEL: With your thoughts.

MAN: Oh. Yes. I am.

RACHEL: You have your thoughts and you need somewhere to think them. Someplace private. I understand.

MAN: You do?

RACHEL: Well, of course. I value my privacy, too. A person needs to be alone with God.

MAN: God.

RACHEL: So go ahead. I'm not going to bother you anymore.

As he contemplates, she lowers money on a string.

MAN: (*muttering to himself*) Monday, Tuesday, Thursday, Friday … (*noticing the money*) What are you doing?

RACHEL: (*retrieving money*) Oh, it's nothing. Really.

MAN: What is that?

RACHEL: What?

MAN: In your hand?

RACHEL: Are you asking me what I've got in my hand? Is that what you want to know?

MAN: Yes. Well, no. Well, I know what you've got. You've got some money.

RACHEL: Well, then you don't need to ask.

MAN: On a string?

RACHEL: I thought you had some thinking to do?

MAN: I do. But I just couldn't help noticing. That's all.

RACHEL: I'm sorry if I was distracting you.

MAN: Well, it's not my place, really. I mean – I don't belong here. It's your business what you do with your money. If you want to lower it on a string, that's your business.

RACHEL: It does seem odd from this perspective, I'll admit; when you see it from above. You're getting the seventh-storey perspective. If you were on the sixth storey, this would look quite different.

MAN: Yes. I'm sure it would.

RACHEL: But please don't let me interrupt. You were in the middle of prayer.

MAN: No, I wasn't. In fact, I'm not even sure I believe in God.

RACHEL: Sometimes in a person's life, they're not really sure. They lose their faith. They become pragmatic about things. They need hard evidence of God's existence. But the evidence of God is everywhere.

MAN: Where?

RACHEL: Well, since you asked about the money, I'll tell you. There's a man here. Just below us. On the sixth floor? Last night, he turned to God for help. He's in a great deal of trouble. He drinks quite heavily, you see. His wife left him three years ago. Then he lost his job. He was a carpet wholesaler, or a carp-fish processor. I'm not really sure. He slurs his words quite a bit. Last year, his son was killed on a motorbike. Or murdered with a knife. And six months ago, a close friend of his was killed in what sounds like a freak accident, involving either a stray piece of glass, or the spraying of some gas, or a suspension bridge collapse. And now, they're evicting him. He's asked for money. And God is answering. Could the evidence be clearer?

MAN: It's not clear to me.

RACHEL: Unfortunately, you're on the wrong floor. I can't help people up here on the seventh storey. But the people on the sixth and fifth are well looked after.

MAN: You're answering all their prayers?

RACHEL: Not all. I try to spread things around a little. A toaster here, an electric heater there. Besides, they can't have everything they ask for. I've only got so much. And I wouldn't want them taking it for granted. Miracles don't just happen, you know. They require a great deal of prayer. Even little miracles.

MAN: But you can't expect people to believe that this is God's work. They might as well believe in Santa Claus! And what's the procedure if they don't believe? Do you lower down overdue electric bills and eviction notices?

A pause.

MAN: You didn't!

RACHEL: What difference does it make?

MAN: You sent him that eviction notice?

RACHEL: I'm giving him the rent money. Everything will be fine now. He was lost and now he's found.

MAN: Lost! The poor man lost his wife, his job, his son, his best friend. Isn't that punishment enough? You weren't involved with any of that, were you?

RACHEL: That's so typical.

MAN: What is?

RACHEL: It's just so easy to be cynical, isn't it?

MAN: Under the circumstances.

RACHEL: These people's lives have changed! You've never heard so many prayers as the ones that rise up from directly below this window.

MAN: No. I don't doubt it.

RACHEL: And that is the power of faith!

MAN: What is? Hoping for a toaster? How do you know it isn't the power of greed?

RACHEL: I don't know who you are, and I don't know who sent you, but I have a pretty good idea. And you're not going to alter my relationship with God.

MAN: I have no interest in your relationship with God.

RACHEL: You want to make me say something, but I won't.

MAN: I don't want to make you say anything. Don't be ridiculous. What on earth would I want you to say?

RACHEL: Oh, you know perfectly well.

MAN: No I don't.

RACHEL: Yes you do.

PERCY appears from the party window.

PERCY: Say – where did you get that drink? I've been looking everywhere. Nobody's drinking anything. Is this a new trend or what? First nobody was smoking, so I had to give up smoking. I never really liked smoking, you know, but everybody was smoking, so I started smoking, and then I got hooked. Then everybody was quitting so I had to quit. And now it looks like nobody's drinking. Everybody's walking. Everybody used to run. I'm glad that's over. Now everybody is walking. Nobody's running anymore. Well, I guess because everybody's getting older. Well – nobody's getting younger, that's for sure! Yeah – everybody's in the same boat, and nobody's rocking it anymore. Everybody used to rock the boat. Everybody used to be different from everybody else, so nobody would be the same. But that didn't work, because everybody was the same, because everybody was different. Now everybody is just plain "the same." Except for you. You're drinking. I wish I was.

RACHEL: You've got your priorities all wrong, mister. You don't need a drink. You need God.

PERCY: God? Nobody's doing God! Okay – some people were doing God, but not everybody. And that was before everybody was doing sex and hardly anybody's doing sex anymore. Everybody's doing children. Children – and walking – and gas ranges. Not God!

He goes.

RACHEL: He's the devil.

MAN: No, he's not.

RACHEL: Well, he's not actually the devil. The devil doesn't make personal appearances. He acts through people.

MAN: What? You don't think that people are capable of acting on their own? You think the devil sent me?

RACHEL: Can you think of any other explanation?

MAN: Yes. I can.

RACHEL: Well, of course you can. You could probably come up with at least a dozen reasons why you're standing on the ledge outside my window. He's very good at making even the most perverse things seem perfectly reasonable.

MAN: Well, if you must know the truth …

RACHEL: The truth! How clever! Go ahead. Try and seduce me.

MAN: Seduce you. I haven't got the slightest interest in you.

RACHEL: You know what I mean.

MAN: No. I don't.

RACHEL: Try and convince me that God doesn't exist.

MAN: Why would I do that? No. Really. Why would I try and convince you that God doesn't exist? In the first place, I don't care whether you believe in him or not. In the second place, I'm not really sure myself.

RACHEL: This is amazing! You are so devious. Pretending that you don't care. Even pretending that you sort of believe in God yourself.

MAN: But I'm not pretending.

RACHEL: And even pretending that you're not pretending.

MAN: This is hopeless.

RACHEL: Yes. It's hopeless. You won't make me say it.

MAN: Say *what?*

RACHEL: Well, I'm not going to say it, am I?

MAN: How do I know if I don't even know what you're going to say?

RACHEL: I have to admit that you're very shrewd. You think that if you act stupid enough, that somehow I'll confess to my doubts. But you'll never make me.

MAN: If I'm not mistaken, you already have.

RACHEL: I have not.

MAN: You said that you'll confess to your doubts.

RACHEL: You've turned this whole thing inside out.

MAN: Well, I won't argue the point. I really don't care. I was merely concerned about the effects of your faith on other people. Especially poor, desperate people.

RACHEL: What do you know about desperate people? When have you ever been desperate? Ask *me* about desperation. I'll tell you all about it. God has tested my faith in many horrible ways! He has sent me almost every disease imaginable. He has crippled me, and bruised me, and pushed me around. And, as if that isn't enough, he shoved my mother down a flight of stairs, and turned her into a human vegetable. I had to care for her. I had to change her dirty clothes and feed her like a baby. She was my daily torment for sixteen years until finally, out of sheer divine mercy, he gave her an overdose of two thousand milligrams of diazepam!

RACHEL cries. The MAN is in shock at what RACHEL has just told him. Another window opens. JOAN, holding two bolts of cloth, leans out the window.

JOAN: It's even worse in the street light, darling. There's red in it!

MICHAEL: (*from inside*) Oh please! Are you blind?

JOAN: It's not beige at all. It's pink! Look!

MICHAEL: (*appearing*) Why do I even argue with you? It's pointless!

JOAN: But can't you see the red?

MICHAEL: It's the reflection of the neon, dear. There's too much bounce out here from the lights. Where's your sense of colour?

JOAN: Well, what's wrong with this other shade?

MICHAEL: It's not a *shade!* It's a tint for heaven's sake! Please!

JOAN: What's wrong with it?

RACHEL cries.

MAN: (*to RACHEL*) Stop crying for heaven's sake!

MICHAEL and JOAN stop and notice the MAN, who smiles back.

JOAN: Are we interrupting something?

MAN: No. Nothing. Sorry. Carry on.

RACHEL: No one will ever destroy my faith! Not you – not even God!

JOAN: At least let her have her faith, for heaven's sake.

MAN: She can have it. I'm not stopping her.

JOAN: What sort of faith are we talking about anyway?

RACHEL: My faith in God.

JOAN: Oh. How interesting. Well, I know what it's like.

MICHAEL: Yes. She has absolutely no faith in me!

JOAN: Don't be ridiculous, Michael. Of course I do!

MICHAEL: Then why don't you believe me when I tell you this has absolutely no pink tones?!

JOAN: Because it does! (*to RACHEL and the MAN*) Would you mind giving us your opinion?

MICHAEL: Really, Joan! You're not serious. You can't be!

JOAN: I'm only asking.

MICHAEL: This is an outrage!

He leaves the window.

JOAN: Oh dear. I've upset him. Excuse me. (*she leaves*) Michael!

MAN: That's murder, you know.

RACHEL: What is?!

MAN: Giving your mother an overdose of diazepam. That's cold-blooded murder.

RACHEL: I didn't give her an overdose. She took the pills.

MAN: Oh!

RACHEL: She wanted to die, so God gave her the strength to do it.

MAN: Suicide is not an act of God.

RACHEL: How do you know?

MAN: Because it's a human act. It's the one act that defies all pre-destiny. And it's got nothing to do with anybody else. It stands alone. Complete and of itself. What are you doing?

RACHEL: I'm praying.

MAN: Well, please don't. You're wasting your time. Unless there's somebody just like you up on the eighth floor. Look. Please. Don't bother.

RACHEL: Do you want to go to hell someday?

MICHAEL returns, leaning out of the window, sulking.

JOAN: (*from behind*) Michael. Please. I'm sorry.

RACHEL: Well, I can't help you if you want to go to hell.

JOAN: I'm sorry, darling.

MICHAEL: Go ahead and make a fool out of me. See if I care.

JOAN: Nobody's trying to make a fool out of you.

MICHAEL: (*referring to the MAN*) What does he know about hue? About value, or intensity? About pair interpretation, for that matter? It's all subjective with him. Low and common. Is that what you want? The lowest common denominator? Consensus? A thousand people all shouting, "Beige! Beige!" And who asks the all-important question, "Which beige?" Someone's got to ask that question, Joan. Or the world becomes nothing. Just an ugly great wash!

RACHEL: (*to MAN*) If you change your mind and decide to go to heaven, let me know.

RACHEL closes her window

MICHAEL: Heaven? My goodness – she has a very high opinion of herself.

MAN: She was speaking theologically.

JOAN: (*to MICHAEL*) Am I forgiven, then?

MICHAEL: You must stop questioning my stylistic perceptions.

JOAN: I don't.

MICHAEL: You can't just go out and buy an ashtray – or a vase.

JOAN: I can't help it.

MICHAEL: You've got to learn to disassociate yourself with your emotions a little and finally come to terms with style.

JOAN: I'm trying, Michael. I'm really trying.

MICHAEL: And you can't just go asking any idiot off the street what he thinks.

JOAN: Well, he looked like he might be objective.

MICHAEL: But what does he know about the physiological capacities? What does he know about black, about white? About anything at all, for that matter? He's nothing but an animal, in an animal world.

They both study the MAN.

MICHAEL: Look at the way he's dressed. Can you seriously take his word for anything?

MAN: What's wrong with the way I'm dressed?

JOAN: Nothing darling. You look perfectly charming.

MICHAEL: There's no thought. There's no justification. It's all mood. Stream of consciousness.

MAN: I beg your pardon …

MICHAEL: He's a walking fatality. A casualty of function!

MAN: Excuse me …

JOAN: Yes?

MAN: Well, I couldn't help overhearing you.

MICHAEL: I'm sorry. I was just being emphatic.

JOAN: Michael is very emphatic.

MAN: If I'm not mistaken, you called me an idiot.

JOAN: Try not to take it personally, darling.

MICHAEL: I wasn't referring to you. You're no more idiotic than the next person.

MAN: I don't mind being called an idiot. It's not that. It's just that you don't know me.

MICHAEL: Well, no. I don't. Why on earth would I?

MAN: Well, if you don't know me, how do you know I'm an idiot? What if I said you were an idiot?

MICHAEL: You'd be an idiot for saying it. (*back to JOAN*) Now, let's discuss this green thing for a moment. I'm not entirely averse, but you must remember that unlike nature, where it's so pervasively vital, green can take on a role of defensiveness and obstinacy. It has its devious side.

JOAN: But don't you think it reflects my character?

MICHAEL: The character of a colour depends entirely on the colours around it. You can't take a colour out of context.

MAN: Just how is it that you can call me an idiot, but if I call you an idiot, then I'm an idiot for saying it?

MICHAEL: (*to MAN*) Do you mind? (*to JOAN*) Who is this man?

JOAN: I suppose he's a neighbour. Are you a neighbour?

MAN: No. And there's nothing wrong with the way I'm dressed, either.

MICHAEL: Nobody said there was. I don't make value judgments. I'm not a fascist.

JOAN: Michael never makes value judgments.

MAN: I didn't say you were a fascist.

JOAN: He's just being sensitive, aren't you Michael?

MICHAEL: I'm not *being* sensitive. I *am* sensitive.

JOAN: Of course you are.

MAN: I merely took exception to your sweeping generalizations. About me – and about the world at large. After all, you said I was nothing but an animal, in an animal world.

MICHAEL: I can't deal with this, Joan.

JOAN: Of course you can't. You go inside for a moment, darling, while I send the gentleman away.

MICHAEL goes.

MICHAEL: I just can't deal with it.

MAN: What's he so upset about? I'm the one who's been insulted.

JOAN: Of course you have. Can I write you a cheque or do you want cash?

MAN: Why would I want cash?

JOAN: Good. I'll write you a cheque, then.

MAN: I don't want a cheque either.

JOAN: No? Well, what do you want?

MAN: Nothing.

JOAN: Oh. How interesting.

MAN: I certainly don't want money.

JOAN: I'm sorry if my offer offended you. It's just that ... so often, in situations involving Michael, it's much more expedient to simply buy one's way out.

MAN: Does he always go around insulting people?

JOAN: Michael is an artist. People don't understand him. He's intensely visual. The sight of red with yellow gives him heart palpitations. Certain shades of magenta make him physically nauseous. He can feel the space around him so much that he becomes the space. The presence of Dacron gives him the flu. So you can imagine how difficult he is. Very hard to keep up with. He's cost me a fortune but it's worth it. Left on my own, I couldn't decorate a closet. I have absolutely no imagination. But I admire a perfect work of art. Although it's something we've yet to achieve. Since I've known him, Michael and I have redecorated my apartment eighteen times. Including this one. Eighteen times. Top to bottom. We're only halfway through this one and already I know we'll have to start again. So I hope you can understand the frustration. And if Michael insulted you, I – we – apologize.

MAN: Well, thank you for explaining the situation. Although as situations go, I have to admit, I don't really get it. Why would you go to all the trouble?

JOAN: It is a lot of trouble, of course, yes. There are times when I've felt like giving up. Michael gives me the inspiration to keep searching for that perfect constellation of form, texture, and colour. We look on it as a lifetime challenge.

MAN: A lifetime is a lot of time.

JOAN: There are a lot of choices. Probably too many.

MAN: It sounds to me like you'll never be satisfied.

JOAN: Yes. It does, doesn't it? But one day we'll find what we're looking for.

MAN: And then what?

JOAN: Oh. What an interesting question. Perhaps it's a little too interesting. (*calling*) Michael!

MICHAEL: I won't be compromised!

JOAN: Nobody's compromising anybody. (*to MAN*) He thinks you're putting in your two cents' worth about the apartment. People usually do. They think they know how to decorate because they think they know what they like. I used to be the same. But I'm trying not to have any opinions now. Sometimes it's difficult to be objective though, isn't it? But one has to be. Especially if you live in it. After all, on a purely subjective level, my apartment looks ridiculous. And I don't even have a decent, comfortable bed to sleep in. So you can understand why it's necessary for us to disassociate ourselves from our personal feelings. Personal feelings are so difficult anyway. Whereas style is absolute. Whether it's absolutely this, or absolutely that.

Another window opens, and PERCY leans out. He emits an audible sigh. Inside, behind him, a party is in full swing.

PERCY: Dreary, isn't it?

MAN: Sorry?

PERCY: My God I feel like jumping. Right here and now. I'd rather splatter my guts all over the pavement than go back in there.

JOAN: Oh, don't do that, darling. You leave too much up to chance. If you want to convey the right message, you may want to slash your wrists over a simple, pale cotton print, for instance. It has a stronger impact. More clarity.

MAN: You don't really want to jump, do you?

JOAN: Of course he doesn't. People don't jump from buildings anymore.

MAN: Why not?

JOAN: The trend is much lighter. More whimsical.

MAN: He's talking about suicide.

PERCY: No I'm not. I'm talking about dying of boredom.

JOAN: Well, if you'll excuse me ...

She starts to go.

PERCY: I wonder if you could do me a favour?

JOAN: Yes?

PERCY: I wonder if you could call next door here in about five minutes, asking for me and sounding quite urgent. Say your name is Rhonda. I'll give you the number.

JOAN: I'd love to oblige you, darling, but I no longer have a telephone. It didn't fit in with the decor.

JOAN leaves and closes her window. The MAN and PERCY are left alone.

PERCY: Everybody has a telephone. Nobody doesn't have a telephone. How on earth does she survive?

MAN: It wouldn't be so bad.

PERCY: I'd be lost. I wouldn't have a single friend. As it is now, I have 940.

MAN: Friends?

PERCY: Yes.

MAN: You have that many friends?

PERCY: Yes. Isn't it fabulous? People are always saying, "I can't count the number of friends I have!" When what they actually mean is that they only have a handful. Maybe two, three hundred. But I can, and I've got 940.

MAN: I didn't think it was possible to be intimate with that many people.

PERCY: Who said anything about being intimate? I couldn't care less about most of them.

MAN: Well, then they're not really your friends, are they?

PERCY: Why not?

MAN: The whole idea of friendship is that you like someone.

PERCY: Why would I like them? They're awful. What an odd notion!

MAN: You don't like any of them.

PERCY: "Like" is a big word. If we're counting friends that I *like*, I've actually got more sweaters. I've got 268 sweaters, but actually sort of *like* three of them. Of the friends I have – uh ... let's see ... (*thinks*) No. I don't really like her, but I *love* her work. Uh ... can I count you?

MAN: What? As a friend?

PERCY: No. As a friend I *like*. I already count you as a friend.

MAN: But I'm not.

PERCY: I beg your pardon.

MAN: I'm not your friend.

PERCY: Oh. Well, I guess I'll have to put you in the "don't like" column, then.

MAN: Don't put me in *any* column.

PERCY: What?

MAN: I don't want to be in one of your columns.

PERCY: Well, where would you suggest I put you?

MAN: Don't put me anywhere. You don't own me. I'm not a sweater.

PERCY: What are you taking about? Of course you're not a sweater. You're not even wearing a sweater.

JENNIFER pokes her head through the same window.

PERCY: Jennifer. I want you to meet a friend of mine.

MAN: I'm not his friend.

JENNIFER: Well, any friend of Jack's is a friend of mine.

MAN: I'm – not – his – friend!

PERCY: That's all right. I'm not Jack.

JENNIFER: You're not? Why aren't you?

PERCY: Because I'm Percy.

JENNIFER: Yes – well … It's the details that start to ruin a perfectly good relationship. I like to know as little about a person as possible. Preferably nothing at all.

Now AL leans out the same window.

AL: I hope you guys don't think this is the way out.

PERCY: Not unless you want to jump.

All laugh.

MAN: What's so funny about that?

AL: (*to MAN*) Hi! Don't I know you?

MAN: No.

AL: Are you sure?

MAN: Of course I'm sure.

JENNIFER: I don't know a soul.

PERCY: Well, I can introduce you. They're all my friends.

AL: Are they? Well, they're certainly not mine.

JENNIFER: I don't even know which one is the host.

AL: I am.

JENNIFER: Oh! Well, it's a fabulous party. I wasn't invited. That's the only reason I'm here.

PERCY: It's the best party I've been to in a long time. I've been to 111 parties this year, and this is one of the best. Oh! Look! I think I see a friend of mine. Excuse me, will you?

PERCY leaves.

AL: Who's he?

JENNIFER: (*referring to MAN*) A friend of his.

AL: Oh!

MAN: No. He's not.

AL: Well, whoever he is, I hope he leaves and takes everybody else with him. Except for you two, of course.

JENNIFER: I'm afraid I can't stay. As much as I'm enjoying this one, I'm due at another party any minute now.

AL: Oh? Whose party?

JENNIFER: I'm sure you know her.

AL: Probably.

JENNIFER: But I can't remember her name. I'm not sure I even know her address. It's … somewhere.

AL: I'd love to come.

JENNIFER: Why don't you? Why don't you both come?

MAN: I wasn't invited. I don't even know what you're talking about.

JENNIFER: (*to AL, referring to MAN*) I just love your friend. (*as she goes*) He's so specific.

AL: Isn't he!

She's gone.

AL: Who's *she?*

MAN: I haven't got any idea.

AL: You meet the worst people at your own party.

MAN: Then why give a party?

AL: Well, I don't want to be anti-social. Don't get me wrong. I love parties. If only it wasn't for the people at them. But this is really the worst part, isn't it?

MAN: What is?

AL: The actual event. It's always such a crushing disappointment. From the minute the first guests arrive, I just want to evaporate into thin air. At my last party, I had to start a fire in the kitchen to get rid of them.

MAN: You started a fire!?

AL: Just a small one. But there was a lot of smoke. It cleared the place out quite nicely. It wasn't fifteen minutes before I was finally alone again.

MAN: Someone could have been seriously hurt.

AL: Oh, the fire department was there instantaneously. I called them ahead of time. But I'll never try that one again. There was a hell of a mess. This time I'm taking a more subtle approach. There's no food, no drinks, and the music is far too loud. Lots of people have already left.

Another window opens. NURSE WILSON pokes her head out.

NURSE WILSON: Turn that godawful music down!

AL: I was actually planning on turning it up!

NURSE WILSON: Oh, were you? Well, we'll just see about that!

AL: Why don't you call the police, if you don't like it?

NURSE WILSON: That's exactly what I intend to do!

AL: If you do call, though – please don't tell them about all the drugs.

NURSE WILSON: Drugs!

She goes inside.

AL: Well, thank God for the neighbours. This thing might have gone on forever, and we've got that other party to go to. You don't happen to remember the address, do you?

MAN: No.

AL: Well, someone else is bound to know. That's where all these people will be going after they've been herded out of here.

MAN: Why would you bother getting rid of them, just to follow them to another party?

AL: I'm always hearing about parties I didn't go to. How great they were. What a fabulous time everybody had. The ones I miss are always the good ones. So I never miss one now. Are you coming?

MAN: I don't like parties.

AL: Why did you come to this one, then?

MAN: I didn't.

AL: Well, what are you doing here?

MAN: Actually –

AL: You're not thinking about jumping, are you? It's seven storeys.

MAN: Yes. I know.

AL: A guy could kill himself.

MAN: Well ... yes ... he could, but ...

The next window opens.

NURSE WILSON: I called the police!

AL: This guy's gonna jump, lady.

NURSE WILSON: Really!

AL: You sure you wouldn't rather go to this party?

NURSE WILSON: If he wants to jump, why don't you let him?

MAN: Look – I didn't say I wanted to. I don't know what I'm doing. I really –

NURSE WILSON: Would you like us to convince you?

LILLIAN: (*a voice from inside*) Is that Albert?

NURSE WILSON: (*to LILLIAN*) No. It isn't Albert. It's a man. He's thinking about jumping off the side of the building.

LILLIAN: (*inside*) Why doesn't he then?

NURSE WILSON: (*to LILLIAN*) That's what I asked him.

MAN: Look – this has nothing to do with either of you. Why don't you both go inside and just carry on with your lives?

AL: You don't mind if I go to this party, then?

MAN: No. Of course I don't mind.

AL: It's not that I don't care about your plight or anything. It's just such a downer – that's all. Anyway, this lady looks pretty serious. Maybe she can talk you out of it.

NURSE WILSON: I am serious and I'm not talking him out of anything.

AL: Look – the police'll be here any minute. Just hang on until they get here. I gotta go. I don't even know where I'm going so who knows how long it'll take to get there.

AL goes, closing his window.

NURSE WILSON: Some friend.

MAN: He's not a friend.

LILLIAN: (*inside*) Albert?

NURSE WILSON: (*to LILLIAN*) It's not Albert, Mrs. Wright. Albert's gone! He FLEW AWAY!!

LILLIAN: Why?

NURSE WILSON: You know why. Because he's a bird. (*to MAN*) God, I hate old people.

LILLIAN: (*inside*) Who's a bird?

NURSE WILSON: Albert! Albert's a bird. We let him go, remember? We let him go because he was unhappy.

LILLIAN: (*inside*) Oh!

NURSE WILSON: She remembers the whole thing.

LILLIAN: (*inside*) No I don't!

NURSE WILSON: She's supposed to be deaf but she can hear the grass growing. So what's stopping you?

MAN: Huh?

NURSE WILSON: What's stopping you from jumping? Wait – let me guess. You're afraid of heights. Now that's a pity. Letting a little thing like that stand in the way of your suicide, when really it's such a perfectly logical thing to do.

MAN: Logical?

NURSE WILSON: I started out my career thinking I wanted to save people's lives. Imagine!

MAN: I think that's very noble.

NURSE WILSON: A lot you know. Where's the nobility in watching people hang on to the last shred of a meagre existence? Hooked up to every imaginable medical apparatus. Jumping is the only way to go these days, otherwise you run the serious risk of a protracted survival. My! Doesn't the sidewalk look inviting from here!

MAN: I'd rather not look down if you don't mind.

NURSE WILSON: Aren't you even the least bit curious?

MAN: I can imagine what it's like.

NURSE WILSON: I suppose you expect me to ask you what your reasons are for jumping.

MAN: You're probably not interested.

NURSE WILSON: You're probably right.

MAN: Nobody seems terribly interested.

NURSE WILSON: Why should they be? Death isn't terribly interesting. I work in a hospital when I'm not here cleaning up after this thing and I can tell you first hand, death isn't the least bit interesting. In fact – it's very routine. Besides, people are too busy to be interested in other people's problems. These days you have to pay someone to be interested.

MAN: Busy doing what?

NURSE WILSON: Finding reasons not to jump themselves.

MAN: So what's your reason?

NURSE WILSON: Me? I'm a humanitarian.

MAN: You don't seem the type.

NURSE WILSON: Oh? What type is that?

MAN: You don't seem very – well – very friendly.

NURSE WILSON: Why should I be friendly? I despise almost everyone I meet.

MAN: I thought humanitarians were supposed to like people.

NURSE WILSON: I like people on the whole. It's individuals I can't stand.

LILLIAN: (*from inside*) Has he jumped yet?

NURSE WILSON: No. He's vacillating.

LILLIAN: (*inside*) What?

NURSE WILSON: He hasn't made up his mind yet – one way or the other.

LILLIAN: He shouldn't be so tentative.

MAN: I have made up my mind.

NURSE WILSON: Oh. (*to LILLIAN*) He has made up his mind. The police will be here soon. You'd better go now or they'll definitely talk you out of it. They're experts. They listen to all your problems. They sympathize with every one of them. Eventually, they convince you that life has some meaning. That there's some little thread to hang on to. So you hang on, as they slowly reel you in. But you never let go again, not for the rest of your life. The next thing you know, you're old, and by that time you've been hanging on so long and so tightly to that little thread that it practically has to be pried loose.

MAN: You know something – you're astonishingly morbid.

LILLIAN: (*close to the window*) What seems to be the problem?

NURSE WILSON: I already told you, Mrs. Wright. I'm not going to tell you again.

LILLIAN: (*appearing now in window*) Well, get out of my way then.

NURSE WILSON: You're not supposed to be up and around.

LILLIAN: Where is this man?

NURSE WILSON: Die of heart failure. See if I care.

LILLIAN: She doesn't really want me to die, because then she'd have to fill out a form.

NURSE WILSON: I've already filled it out!

LILLIAN: I'm a hundred years old. Does that impress you?

MAN: That's very old.

LILLIAN: Yes. They send people like her to look after me.

MAN: She's not very nice.

LILLIAN: She doesn't have a very nice job. Looking after sick people. Waiting for them to die. So she thinks that she has to pretend she has no feelings.

NURSE WILSON: I haven't!

LILLIAN: But she's afraid.

NURSE WILSON goes.

LILLIAN: Don't pay any attention to her. (*pause*) Oh my, what a lovely evening.

MAN: I never noticed.

LILLIAN: I haven't looked out this window in years. I used to go out on evenings like this. I walked down to the end of that street and took the streetcar as far as it went. Up where there weren't any houses. That's where we stopped. That's where the streetcar turned around. As though the world was flat, and that was the end of it, where you fell off. That was about seventy years ago, so I imagine the houses go quite a bit farther now. But not far enough, of course. I imagine the streetcar eventually stops somewhere and turns around.

MAN: There isn't any streetcar.

LILLIAN: There isn't?

MAN: There hasn't been one for about thirty years.

LILLIAN: Well, that just goes to show you what I know. I haven't gone out since ... well, in about fifty years.

MAN: Fifty years?

LILLIAN: Well, as I said – you can really only go out so far, and then you've got to turn around and come back. I find that somewhat limiting. I prefer to go nowhere at all. As it turns out, my apartment is much larger than I thought. In fact, it's enormous.

MAN: It can't be more than a few hundred square feet at the most.

LILLIAN: Yes. It's almost too much to grasp, isn't it? Of course it looks a lot smaller now. Since she came to look after me. She cleaned it all up. Put everything in order. Kicked Albert out. She has a very sanitary point of view. Doesn't like pigeons. I imagine he'll come back though. When he's had enough of flying.

NURSE WILSON: (*inside*) He's not coming back in here.

LILLIAN: I used to have all kinds of things piled up against this window. Until *they* came and took everything away. And once Albert saw the window, there was just no keeping him. After all those years, his little head was suddenly filled with big ideas.

MAN: All what years?

LILLIAN: Those years.

MAN: Pigeons don't live that long.

LILLIAN: How long?

MAN: How many years are we talking about exactly?

LILLIAN: Oh, I don't know. About fifty.

MAN: That doesn't make any sense.

LILLIAN: No. It doesn't. (*pause*) Must be a riddle.

> *Pause.*

MAN: I don't get it.

LILLIAN: Neither do I. Well – it's just a story. It's not important. People attach too much importance to these things. That reminds me of another story.

> *MAN waits as she loses her train of thought. Finally, he coughs, which rouses her.*

LILLIAN: Oh my! What a lovely evening.

MAN: You were going to tell me something?

LILLIAN: What about?

MAN: I don't know. Something reminded you of a story.

LILLIAN: A story? – Let's see ...

> *A long pause.*

MAN: I guess you don't remember. It's not important. Really. I thought – I thought it might be – well – important, somehow.

LILLIAN: You're looking for something important.

MAN: No. Well, I – I need – I'm looking for something, yes.

LILLIAN: I don't have anything. Just an empty room. It'll be coming up for rent soon, if you're interested.

MAN: No. I'm not looking for a room.

LILLIAN: It's a place to hang your hat. To sort out all your shoes.

MAN: I don't need to sort out my shoes. All my shoes are the same. Every pair identical. All seven pairs. I have seven hats also. All like this one. I have one for every day of the week. Only I can't remember what day it is.

LILLIAN: Oh.

MAN: I've lost track, you see. I went to sleep and I had a dream. I – I think it was a dream. I dreamt that I got up, and made my way to work, and when work was over I came home and went to bed. And then I woke up. I think I woke up.

LILLIAN: It's Wednesday.

MAN: It is?

LILLIAN: I don't know, but I thought it would make you feel better.

MAN: (*now he speaks slowly and deliberately, in an attempt to understand his own words*) Not really. You see – my faith in the days of the week has been seriously undermined. When I woke up this morning, I wasn't exactly sure what day it was. And for that brief moment – it was only a matter of seconds – I think it was seconds – I stood – or I should say I "lay" – on very shaky ground. After all – how could I act with assuredness? How could I rise up and plunge headlong into Friday's world, if it was actually Saturday? And so I lay completely still for a moment, pondering this question. That's when I noticed my hands. I'd never noticed them before. How they moved with amazing dexterity. But this flexibility, this movement of hands, can never extend beyond the boundaries of its own flesh – can only reach as far as the fingertips and no farther, much as the movement of time is restricted by the days of the week. So I got up and tried to erase these things from my mind. I tried to get dressed. But then I began to understand other things; for example, the meaning of shoes. They were little prisons for my feet. Absolute definitions of space. I could run a million miles, in any direction, and still not escape them. And my hat – forming a firm idea around my head, as if to say, "Well, that's about the size of it." My mind could expand into infinite space, and still never change the shape of my head. I saw in the mirror a condemned man, serving a life sentence inside his body. Even the car – I drove – to work. My car. This thing. This instrument of liberation. It wasn't freedom. It was merely the idea of freedom, bound in metal. A kind of hope, but with a speed limit attached to it. Now I was travelling an unknown route along a familiar road. It led in exactly the direction I was going, but not by coincidence. The asphalt was not laying itself a path in front of me. I was merely following a prearranged course and then something happened, something that had never happened before. When I finally arrived in town at my usual space it was taken. I was late for work you see and there was another car in my space. Someone had taken my space, you see. I sat in my car for a moment, not knowing where to go. Just staring straight ahead. And then I put my car into gear and drove into it. Drove right into this other car. There didn't seem to be any other choice. No place else to go, you see. So I put my car in reverse, backed up, and rammed into this car again. And then again, and again and again, until

finally this other car – this intruder of my space – was smashed up against the side of the building like an accordion. So now I had my space back, and I parked. I got out of the car, and turned to head for my office. That's when I realized. It wasn't my space at all. Somehow I got completely turned around. This wasn't anywhere near where I work. I didn't know where I was. I hadn't any idea. I had always depended on the road which led there. The way I've always believed that one thing leads to another. Then I saw this building. I thought I'd come up here to get a better perspective on my exact situation. And from here the view is quite clear. There are no spaces left, you see. I have no place to park my car.

LILLIAN: Have you tried The Bay?

MAN: Don't you understand?

LILLIAN: Of course I understand. You didn't need to make such a long speech. When you're a hundred years old you'll understand everything. And then you'll die.

MAN: Why wait?

LILLIAN: Something interesting might happen. But then again, it might not. I think you should jump now.

MAN: You do?

LILLIAN: If that's what you want to do, I think you should do it.

MAN: There really is no reason to live, is there?

LILLIAN: Not really.

MAN: (*as he prepares to jump*) It's sort of disappointing. I wonder where they'll tow my car.

LILLIAN: Oh. Now I remember!

MAN: (*stopping*) What?

LILLIAN: That story. Some years ago, I went to Paris to see the *Mona Lisa*. It's in the Louvre, the largest building in the world, probably. But the *Mona Lisa*, as it turns out, is very small. So naturally I couldn't find it. I kept looking for something – big. Then I saw a huge crowd of people all standing around – looking disappointed. And there she was – smiling as if she knew.

MAN: That's it? That's the whole story?

LILLIAN: You do like a long story, don't you? Let's see. There was a young Frenchman standing next to me, in a terrible state of despair. He began talking to me as if he'd known me all his life. I didn't understand a word he was saying, but he didn't seem to take any notice. I thought I'd lose him in the crowd, but he followed me right out of the museum. He told me a very long and involved story, often punctuating the words with his fists. Occasionally, he would sink into a sadness the like of which I'd never seen. And then he would start raving again. The farther we walked, the more distressed he became – the more enraged. By the time we reached the Pont Neuf he was sobbing uncontrollably. It seemed very clear that he wanted me to say something. We hadn't walked halfway across, when he started to climb over the side of the bridge. I didn't know what to say. So I blurted out the only thing in French that I'd ever learned. "La pamplemousse est sur la table." I don't even know what it means. But he responded very positively. He thought about it for a moment, and then smiled. After that his mood changed considerably. In fact, he was delighted. Whatever it was I said, it seemed to be something for him to hang his hat on. And he walked away a new man. Determined, it seemed, to live by this philosophy the rest of his life.

MAN: It doesn't mean anything

LILLIAN: It must mean something. I learned it in school.

MAN: "The grapefruit is on the table"?

LILLIAN: Oh. Is that what it means? (*pause*) Well, that's not a bad philosophy to live by. As philosophies go. It has a certain – preciseness.

MAN: How have you managed to stay alive so long?

LILLIAN: I forget.

MAN: Shut up in your room like that? Never going out?

LILLIAN: There are other places to go besides *out*. There's *in*. There's *around*. There's *under*. *Over*. *Between*.

MAN: Down.

LILLIAN: Well, you might go down. But you might go up. If you're going to go to all the trouble of jumping, you might as well try going up and see what happens. Albert went up. Straight up.

MAN: Albert was a pigeon.

LILLIAN: He didn't know that. Not for sure. He'd never flown a day in his whole life, not until the day we let him go. You could be the first of a kind. Imagine what a story that would make! You'd be interviewed by just about every newspaper in the world. You'd travel around giving lectures. You'd be an inspiration to others. There'd be people flying all over the place. That sort of thing has to start somewhere. It might as well start with you. If you're going to give your life up anyway, you may as well give it up to something. The principle is very simple. You just have to let go and let the wind currents do the rest. You know about airflow, don't you?

MAN: I really don't think …

LILLIAN: No. Don't think. The important thing is to just let it happen. Let it take you where it wants. Don't try to go anyplace special this first time. Just do a circle once around the building, and come back. Once you get a better feel for it, you can go a little farther.

Suddenly, a huge spotlight shines on MAN.

POLICE MEGAPHONE: Stop! This is the police!

LILLIAN: Go!

MAN: I don't know what to do – I can't – fly –

POLICE MEGAPHONE: Just stay calm. Don't move.

LILLIAN: Don't listen to them. They're all trying to put the world in order. They don't want people flying around all over the place. They'd have to make up a whole bunch of new regulations. That's just bullshit. Just go.

MAN: Are you sure?

LILLIAN: Just up and away.

POLICE MEGAPHONE: Stop!

MAN: Just like that?

POLICE MEGAPHONE: Stay right where you are!

MAN: I'm supposed to stay right where I am.

LILLIAN: Go!

MAN: All right – I'm going.

LILLIAN: Then go!

MAN: Goodbye!

A blackout.

MAN: Ahhhhhhhhhhhhhhhhhhhhhhhhh!

As the lights come up, the MAN flies with the aid of his umbrella. He then lands on the ledge of another building. Four people open their windows.

ONE: We saw that.

MAN: What?

TWO: We saw you fly over here from that building across the street.

MAN: You did?

THREE: We've been watching the whole thing.

MAN: You have?

FOUR: Yes. We have.

TWO: We saw you talk to that old lady.

FOUR: To all those people.

TWO: We saw the whole thing from beginning to end.

THREE: And then we saw you fly over here and land!

FOUR: There's just one thing ...

TWO: We don't get it.

ONE: What's the flying supposed to represent? Is it an existential statement or what?

TWO: It's a Jungian thing, isn't it?

THREE: I don't agree. I think it's political.

ONE: Is it about enlightenment?

THREE: There's a suggestion of mass revolt.

TWO: There's an archetypal quality about it.

ONE: I detect strong religious overtones.

THREE: It's a struggle against tyranny, isn't it?

FOUR: I think it's just weird.

MAN: Will you excuse me?

Suddenly the MAN is airborne, and he flies through the stars. He then returns to the original window ledge. LILLIAN is gone. Below, an ambulance light flashes. The MAN knocks at the window.

MAN: Hello! HELLO – O!!

NURSE WILSON appears.

NURSE WILSON: Yes?

MAN: The old lady. I'd like to speak to her. I have to tell her about – something – something quite incredible!!

NURSE WILSON: Yeah ... well, she's gone.

MAN: Gone?

They look down.

MAN: So sudden? She was here just a few minutes ago.

NURSE WILSON: Yeah, well ... that's the way it always happens. So – what's this "something incredible"? As if I really want to know.

MAN: It was ... it was nothing.

NURSE WILSON: I thought you were going to jump off the ledge.

MAN: I did.

NURSE WILSON: Oh. You did, did you?

MAN: Yes, I did. I flew across the street to that building and back.

NURSE WILSON: I suppose you want to come inside now.

MAN: I'm just fine where I am.

NURSE WILSON: You can't stay perched out there forever.

MAN: Why not?

NURSE WILSON: Because it's abnormal behaviour.

MAN: Not for a pigeon.

NURSE WILSON: You're not a PIGEON!!

MAN: Yes ... I know that now.

She goes.

MAN: But for a moment ... for a brief ... moment ... I didn't know. And the wind carried me up and took me along for a ride. And I forgot. I forgot my own story ... and I flew ... flew on the wings of someone else's.

POLICE MEGAPHONE: This is the police.

MAN: I have to forget ... try ... to forget everything. Forget everything that has ever happened to me ... everything that ever *will* happen ... everything ... and wait ... just wait for the wind again ... and do nothing ... nothing ... and ... wait ... just ...

The sound of the wind and the music increases as the lights fade. In the blackout we hear the police megaphone.

POLICE MEGAPHONE: All right, ladies and gentlemen – break it up. Just break it up now and go home. Come on, move along – move along now, ladies and gentlemen. Everything will be fine. Everything's under control, so let's just disperse with this little gathering and go home. The show's over.

END

DANIEL MACIVOR

(b. 1962)

The year 1988 marked a turning point in Daniel MacIvor's playwriting career. Sandwiched between his first two successes – the hard-hitting female mono- logue *See Bob Run*, co-produced by his da da kamera company in 1987, and the bleakly comic, wildly surreal one-man show *Wild Abandon* in 1988, his first performance of his own work – came an invitation to write for Tarragon Theatre. MacIvor's project for Tarragon was a memory play about growing up in Cape Breton called *Somewhere I Have Never Travelled* (1988). It proved, in his own words, "a disaster." Writing discursively in a conventional mode and letting a major producer stage his work was not to be his path to initial suc- cess. Creating offbeat plays that intimately connect performer and audience and maintaining firm artistic control as well as personal involvement as actor and/or director – these would become this artist's hallmarks. Eventually, as MacIvor's career gained international scope, he expanded his repertoire to include a broader range of styles and cast sizes. But his best early work involves the simplicity of a single actor or two or three on a nearly bare stage spinning a bizarre but compelling narrative with precisely choreographed theatricality. *Never Swim Alone* is classic MacIvor: "a beautiful piece," said *Books in Canada*, "spare, evocative, funny, and sad."

Born to a working-class family in Sydney, Nova Scotia, MacIvor stud- ied theatre at Dalhousie University before leaving to work as an actor with Newfoundland's Stephenville Theatre Festival. He moved to Toronto in 1984, completed the theatre program at George Brown College, and founded da da kamera in 1986. After some early experimental work with Sky Gilbert's Buddies in Bad Times Theatre and the debacle of *Somewhere I Have Never Travelled*, MacIvor developed da da kamera into one of Toronto's premier cutting-edge companies. He surrounded himself with a group of like-minded artists with whom he collaborated on many subsequent projects: actress Caroline Gillis, actor-director Ken McDougall (until his death in 1992), pro- ducer Sherrie Johnson, composer Richard Feren, and eventually writer- director Daniel Brooks.

The 1990s proved extraordinarily productive for MacIvor, whose first four plays of the decade all received Chalmers Best New Canadian Play Award nominations, as had that first success, *See Bob Run*. MacIvor co-wrote, co-directed, and performed in *White Trash Blue Eyes* (1990), a large-cast barroom play about neighbourhood gentrification. He also wrote and per- formed in *Never Swim Alone* (1991), which reunited actress Gillis and director McDougall from *See Bob Run*, and in *2-2-Tango* (1991), a choreographed duet about gay mating rituals, directed by McDougall. *House* (1991) took the form and surreal flavour of the earlier *Wild Abandon*. It inaugurated MacIvor's relationship with Daniel Brooks, who directed him in this remarkable solo piece in which a dyspeptic character named Victor regales and abuses the audience with details of his life and family, his experiences in group therapy, and other bizarre misadventures. *House* won the Chalmers Award, received the first of MacIvor's five Governor General's Award nominations, and has been one of his most widely produced plays. In 1995, he reprised his role as Victor in a film version. Also in the early 1990s, MacIvor wrote *This Is a Play* (1992), directed by McDougall with MacIvor and Gillis in the cast, which hilariously exposes what actors *really* think when onstage. It was published with *Never Swim Alone* in 1993 and the two are regularly produced together as a double bill. MacIvor directed McDougall and Gillis in *Jump* (1992), a wordless play about weddings, co-produced with Theatre Passe Muraille, which revived it to strong reviews in 2001.

He performed in the otherwise all-female *The Lorca Play* (1992), deconstructing the Spanish playwright's *House of Bernardo Alba*. MacIvor co-wrote and co-directed the play with Brooks, the two sharing the Dora Mavor Moore Award for best director. They collaborated again on the movement piece *Excerpts from the Emo Project* (1994) and co-created *Here Lies Henry* (1995), a sound-and-light show in which MacIvor, directed by Brooks, assaults the audience in the guise of a pathological character much like Victor in *House*. The play won MacIvor his second Chalmers and initiated an innovative program that had da da kamera touring each new show, before and after its official opening, to "development partners" in different cities while the work continued to evolve. Regular partners included Festival Antigonish in Nova Scotia, the Vancouver East Cultural Centre, Calgary's High Performance Rodeo, and Edinburgh's Traverse Theatre, and on the basis of this new approach to play development da da kamera won a Chalmers Award for Innovation in Theatre in 1998.

With *The Soldier Dreams* (1997) and *Marion Bridge* (1998), MacIvor re-entered more conventional territory: the deathbed vigil play. In *The Soldier Dreams*, for which he and Brooks once again shared a Dora Award for best director, a family gathers around a young man dying of AIDS. In *Marion Bridge*, co-produced by Nova Scotia's Mulgrave Road Theatre, three sisters await their mother's death in Cape Breton. *Marion Bridge* earned MacIvor his second Governor General's Award nomination in 1999, and premiered off-Broadway in 2005. He also wrote the Genie Award–winning screenplay for the feature film version, directed by Wiebke von Carolsfeld in 2002. Talonbooks has published the stage script and screenplay in a single volume.

Monster (1998) got MacIvor, with Brooks, his third Governor General's Award nomination. It presents his character, here called Adam, engaging the audience in an outrageous psychodrama involving Oedipal revenge fantasies. After opening in Toronto, *Monster* toured the United States, Ireland, Australia, Norway, and Israel, and became the first English-language play staged at Montreal's Théâtre de Quat'Sous. *In On It* (2001), a two-hander about playmaking and memory, was directed by and featured MacIvor along with the unlikely musical combination of Maria Callas and Leslie Gore. It premiered in Vancouver and went on to New York, where it won a GLAAD

Award and a *Village Voice* OBIE Award. MacIvor directed an unusually large cast of eight in *You Are Here* (2001) to delineate a woman's emotionally painful life. Another Governor General's Award nomination came for *Cul-de-sac* (2002), his fifth monologue and the fourth directed by Daniel Brooks, in which MacIvor's character narrates the events leading up to his own murder. Opening in Montreal, it played from St. John's to New Orleans with another successful stop in New York.

A Beautiful View (2006), chronicling an intense relationship between two women, garnered some of MacIvor's best reviews: "great art" (Toronto); "a remarkable achievement" (New York); "you will rarely see a better contemporary play" (North Carolina). MacIvor dissolved da da kamera in 2007 but his prolific work rate didn't slow. That season (2006–07), he performed *House*, *Here Lies Henry*, and *Monster* in a da da kamera retrospective at Buddies in Bad Times. He finally made a successful return to Tarragon, directing *How It Works* (2007), a funny, compassionate play about an estranged couple and their drug-addicted adolescent daughter. *His Greatness* (2007), MacIvor's take on Tennessee Williams's time in Vancouver in 1980, opened in Vancouver, where it won the Jessie Richardson Award for best new play, went on to New York, then Toronto (with MacIvor in the cast), and in 2012 had a highly praised London production.

Communion (2010), a three-hander about a mother, daughter, and therapist, played across Canada after its Tarragon premiere, and *Was Spring* (2012), a play about three women of different generations, also opened at Tarragon. *This Is What Happens Next* (2010) saw MacIvor reunite as playwright and actor with director Daniel Brooks for yet another solo performance, this time about gay divorce and addiction, Schopenhauer and John Denver. MacIvor returned to his Nova Scotia roots for the Mulgrave Road production and tour of *Bingo!* (2011), a comedy about five friends at a high-school reunion. He performed in his sibling rival comedy *The Best Brothers* at Stratford in 2012. *Arigato, Tokyo* (2013), a play about a Canadian writer's visit to Japan, received eight Dora Award nominations, including Outstanding New Play, for its Buddies in Bad Times première.

In addition to his work on and in his own plays, MacIvor has made notable appearances as an actor in other people's plays, in Canadian films (among them *Justice Denied: The Donald Marshall Story*, *I Love a Man in Uniform*, and *The Five Senses*, for which he received a Genie Award nomination), and on series television (CBC's *Twitch City* and *Republic of Doyle*). He has also written, directed, and performed in his own films, including the features *Past Perfect* and *Wilby Wonderful*, and he wrote the screenplays for *Whole New Thing* and Bruce McDonald's *Trigger*. In 2000, he was writer-in-residence at the National Theatre School in Montreal. His 2006 collection *I Still Love You: Five Plays by Daniel MacIvor*, which includes *Never Swim Alone*, was nominated for and this time won the Governor General's Literary Award for Drama. In 2008, he was awarded Canada's richest and most prestigious playwriting prize, the Siminovitch.

Never Swim Alone remains one of MacIvor's most often produced plays. It had four New York City productions alone between 1999 and 2007, and in 2006–07 it also played in Australia, New Zealand, Cincinnati, and Seattle.

The *Seattle Times* critic wrote: "What seemed at first like bombastic but pathetic machismo turns into combat most dangerous and haunting."

The play sprang from a variety of sources. The gender wars were at their fiercest at the time MacIvor was writing *Never Swim Alone*. The massacre of fourteen women by Marc Lépine at Montreal's l'École polytechnique had occurred in December 1989. The Christian men's organization Promise Keepers was founded in 1990 and Robert Bly's influential (and much parodied) *Iron John: A Book About Men*, a New Age celebration of ritual masculinity, was published the same year. MacIvor has said that his own competitive relationship with Ken McDougall provided a thematic framework, while the sophisticated, rapid-fire word games in a show he saw by Montreal's Théâtre Ubu offered a stylistic template. His Cape Breton heritage gave him both a love of storytelling and "a suspicion of language, a distance from words," he told R.M. Vaughan. "[I'm] not making poetry out of the way people speak but manipulating the way people speak into poetry. Cutting it up, rearranging it ..." Hence the lyrical, almost incantatory quality of the language in parts of the play and the self-consciously rote, mechanical quality in others.

Words are weapons for these testosterone-fuelled combatants, from eloquent rhetoric to crude insult. They stand back and watch the effects of their comments on each other and on the Referee, who is also the girl on the beach they want to impress, the female swimmer who claims that she can beat them to the point. "It's like a *Nature* documentary of rutting stags who can talk," *Toronto Star* critic Geoff Chapman wrote, straining metaphors to find a way to describe this curious piece. With its overt engagement of the audience whose sympathies the men attempt to enlist even before stepping onstage, *Never Swim Alone* seems more like a WWE wrestling match, sharing as well that spectacle's crafted artificiality and parodic (de)constructions of masculinity. Though the Referee officially scores the rounds, in performance the play's audience actively keeps its own score with laughter, cheers, and boos. The only thing missing in Round Eleven is a tag team.

As an old-fashioned pissing contest, the play offers a transparently exaggerated comic portrait of white-collar machismo. The briefcase-toting men whip out penises, cellphones, and cigars, and "cock their guns." They insult each other's fathers and impugn each other's wives. Bill even invokes his MASSIVE STAIRCASE. The rutting-stags metaphor hits closest to home when Frank invokes the guilt-free Darwinian ethic of winning at all costs: "Compassion will lose the race ... And being first, my friends, is the point."

Yet ironically, what makes the play so effective onstage is precisely the cooperation and harmony of the two actors working in concert, in vocal and often physical lockstep. At the level of performance, being first is specifically not the point. As another counterpoint, the play juxtaposes the bravado of adult maledom with the bittersweet memory of boys and a girl enacting one of the proto-sexual rituals of adolescence. Its disastrous outcome may be a lesson, as the title suggests. But the lessons the men think they learn seem to be something altogether different. The enigmatic final tableau leaves them and the audience suspended in the pure theatrical ether that remains a favourite Daniel MacIvor milieu.

Daniel MacIvor

Never Swim Alone

Never Swim Alone was first produced by Platform 9 Theatre in association with da da kamera at the Theatre Centre, Toronto, on February 26, 1991, with the following cast:

REFEREE   Caroline Gillis
ALPHONSE FRANCIS (FRANK) DELORENZO
                         Robert Dodds
WILLIAM (BILL) WADE   Daniel MacIvor

Directed by Ken McDougall
Designed by Steve Lucas

CHARACTERS

> FRANK
> BILL
> REFEREE

SET

> Up centre a tall referee's chair. Stage left a small table and chair for *BILL*. Stage right a small table and chair for *FRANK*. A scoreboard.

> As the audience enters, the *REFEREE* lies onstage under a sheet. 1970s beach music plays. *FRANK*, a man in a blue suit, and *BILL*, an almost imperceptibly shorter man in a blue suit, enter through the house, greeting the audience individually. Before stepping onstage, they turn and greet the audience.

FRANK & BILL: (*in unison*) Hello. Good to see you. Glad you could come.

> They step onto the stage and slowly lift the sheet from the *REFEREE*. She rises. She wears a blue bathing suit. She looks out and steps down centre.

REFEREE: A beach.

A bay.

The point.

Two boys on a beach. Late afternoon. They have been here all day and all day every day all summer.

It is the last day of summer before school begins. Nearby is a girl. She as well has been here all day and all day every day all summer. She lies on her green beach towel in her blue bathing suit with her yellow transistor. The boys have been watching the girl from a distance but now that the summer is nearly over, from very close by. She reminds one boy of his sister, she reminds the other of a picture of a woman he once saw in a magazine. She turns her head a little over her shoulder and speaks to the boys: "Race you to the point?"

This is the beach.

Here is the bay.

There is the point.

> *REFEREE* climbs the steps to her chair and takes her place. She blows her whistle. The men exit.

REFEREE: Round One: Stature.

> *REFEREE* begins Round One. We hear footsteps.

FRANK & BILL: (*offstage*) Two. Two. Two. Two. Two. Two. Two. Two. Men.

Enter a

room.

> *FRANK* and *BILL* enter.

FRANK: Good to see you Bill.

BILL: Good to see you Frank.

FRANK: How long's it been?

BILL: Too long Frank.

FRANK: Too long indeed Bill.

FRANK & BILL: (*in unison*)

How's things?

Can't complain.

How's the family?

Just great.

How's business?

Well a whole heck of a lot better than it was this time last year let me tell you.

Ha ha ha.

How's the blood pressure.

(*aside and snide*) Ha ha ha.

FRANK: Two men.

BILL: Two men.

FRANK & BILL: (*in unison*) Two men enter a (*They step downstage.*) room. A taller man and –

> *They stop. They laugh. FRANK gestures toward BILL as he speaks the line, and vice versa. They continue.*

A taller man and –
A taller man and –
A taller man and –
A taller man and –
A taller man and –
A taller man and –

> *REFEREE ends the round. The men stand side by side facing her. She inspects them carefully. She gives the victory to FRANK. BILL takes his seat. FRANK steps front and centre and addresses the audience.*

FRANK: A. Francis DeLorenzo. My friends call me Frank. The "A" is for Alphonse and not even my enemies call me Alphonse. Alphonse Francis DeLorenzo: French, English, Italian. Behold before you a square of the Canadian Quilt. To those of you I didn't have a chance to greet as I entered, I'd like to welcome you and thank you for coming. I'm sure you all have busy schedules and many other concerns in these troubled times and your presence here tonight is greatly appreciated. A hand for the audience! And if I might I would like to start off with a favourite quote of mine: "We do not place especial value on the possession of a virtue until we notice its total absence in our opponent." Friedrich Nietzsche. Once again, thanks for coming.

> *FRANK resumes his seat.*

REFEREE: Round Two: Uniform.

> *REFEREE begins Round Two. FRANK and BILL step forward.*

FRANK & BILL: Two men enter a room.

FRANK: A taller man and

BILL: an almost imperceptibly shorter man.

FRANK: They both wear

FRANK & BILL: white shirts. Blue suits. Silk ties. Black shoes. Black socks. White shirts, blue suits, silk ties, black shoes, black socks. White shirts, blue suits, silk ties, black shoes, black socks. White shirts blue suits silk ties black shoes black socks.

White shirts blue suits silk ties black shoes black socks. White shirts blue suits silk ties black shoes black socks. White shirts:

BILL: a hundred and ten twenty-five at Cyrus K.

FRANK & BILL: Blue suits:

FRANK: six twenty two twenty two

BILL: on sale

FRANK: at Brogue.

FRANK & BILL: Silk ties:

BILL: came with the suit?

FRANK: Present.

BILL: From Donna?

FRANK: Ah … no.

BILL: Oh. It's nice.

FRANK: How's Sally?

BILL: Oh good good. How's Donna?

FRANK: Oh good good.

BILL: How's the house?

FRANK: Very good.

FRANK & BILL:

How's the boy?

Just fine.

Now there's an investment, eh?

FRANK: Three?

BILL: Four? Five?

FRANK: Four.

FRANK & BILL:

Right right.

Good kid?

Great kid.

Smart kid?

A little genius.

Must get it from his mother.

Ha ha ha ha ha ha ha.

Black shoes:

FRANK: two twenty-five even, David's Uptown.

FRANK & BILL: Black socks:

BILL: (*excitedly noting FRANK's socks*) BLUE SOCKS!

> *REFEREE ends the round. She inspects the men's socks. She gives the victory to BILL. FRANK takes his seat. BILL steps forward and addresses the audience.*

BILL: Hello to all the familiar faces in the audience tonight and a very extra-special hello to all the friends I haven't met yet. William (Bill) Wade: Canadian, Canadian, Canadian. That's what's beautiful about this country: doesn't matter where you came from, once you're here you're a Canadian, and that makes me proud. And I'd also like to add a bit of a quote myself, as my old man always used to say: "If bullshit had a brain, it would quote Nietzsche." Thank you.

BILL resumes his seat.

REFEREE: Round Three: Who Falls Dead the Best.

REFEREE begins Round Three.

FRANK & BILL: Two men enter a room

BILL: and each man carries

FRANK & BILL: a briefcase.

FRANK: The first man seems very much like the second man and

BILL: the first man seems very much like the second man.

FRANK & BILL: Yes.

FRANK: But

BILL: they

FRANK: are

FRANK & BILL: not.

FRANK: For two reasons.

BILL: Two.

FRANK: One:

FRANK & BILL: one man is the first man, and

BILL: two:

FRANK & BILL: one man, in his briefcase has

FRANK: a gun

BILL: a gun.

FRANK & BILL: A gun.

BILL: Which man is

FRANK: the first man and

BILL: which man has

FRANK & BILL: the gun?

FRANK and BILL mime shooting one another in slow motion. They die elaborately also in slow motion. REFEREE ends the round. The men face the REFEREE. She calls a tie. FRANK and BILL step forward and address the audience.

FRANK & BILL: I've known this guy for years.

BILL: Years.

FRANK: And this is sad

FRANK & BILL: but it's true …

BILL: And when I say "years"

FRANK: I mean *years*.

FRANK & BILL: I mean

FRANK: I saw the look of another woman in his father's eyes.

BILL: I smelled the bourbon on his mother's breath.

FRANK: I kept it a secret his aunt was his sister.

BILL: I knew his brother was gay before he did.

FRANK & BILL: I mean *years*.

FRANK: I mean

BILL: we spent summers together.

FRANK & BILL: Real summers

BILL: when you're a kid.

FRANK: Remember real summers

FRANK & BILL: when you were a kid?

FRANK: It stayed bright 'til nine o'clock, and when it did get dark it got so dark you never wanted to go home.

BILL: Smoking Sweet Caps in the woods with a *Playboy* magazine and warm beer from somebody's father's basement.

FRANK & BILL: No school and Kool-Aid and baseball and hide-and-seek late at night and hot dogs and full moons and overnights outside and swimming.

FRANK: And when they said not to swim alone

BILL: this

FRANK: here

FRANK & BILL: this is the guy I swam with!

BILL: I know this guy better than he knows himself.

FRANK: And that's what makes it sad

BILL: but sad as it is it's true

FRANK & BILL: and the truth of it is:

FRANK: and this is much

BILL: much

FRANK & BILL: much more

FRANK: than something as simple as

BILL: his bum leg

FRANK: his trick knee

BILL: his weak wrist

FRANK: his slipped disc

BILL: his bad nerves

FRANK: his trouble sleeping

BILL: his dizzy spells

FRANK: his heart

FRANK & BILL: pa- pa- pa- pa- pa- pa- pa- pa- pa- pa- palpitations

FRANK: this is

BILL: much

FRANK: much

FRANK & BILL: much sadder than that.

FRANK: He's not happy.

FRANK & BILL: He's not happy at all.

BILL: He feels cornered.

FRANK: He feels stuck.

BILL: He feels tied.

FRANK: He feels bound.

FRANK & BILL: He feels trapped.

BILL: And he's a young man

FRANK: he's still a young man.

FRANK & BILL: And that's sad.

BILL: And I'm just saying that

FRANK & BILL: that's really sad.

FRANK and BILL resume their seats.

REFEREE: Round Four: Friendly Advice, Part One.

FRANK and BILL bring their chairs centre and sit. REFEREE begins Round Four.

BILL: Okay, here's the story, these are the facts, this is where I stand, this is the point from which I view the situation.

FRANK: Go on.

BILL: Your situation.

FRANK: Yes.

BILL: I'm not going to pull any punches, I'm not going to cut any corners, I'm not going to give you the short shrift, I'm not going to shovel the shit.

FRANK: The only way to be.

BILL: The only way to be.

FRANK & BILL: Straight up!

BILL: Can I get personal?

FRANK: Personal?

BILL: We're friends.

FRANK: And?

BILL: Well Frank ... I've got two good eyes I can't help but see, I've got two good ears I can't help but hear what's being said, and what's being said, around, is ... Frank, I'm not saying I've got the goods on what makes a marriage work, God knows me and Sally, the honeymoon was over long ago but Frank ... it works! And maybe that's just communication, and maybe that's just luck but Frank ... All I'm trying to say here buddy is if you ever need an outside eye, if you ever need a friendly ear, then hey, I'm here.

FRANK: Are you thinner?

BILL: Wha?

FRANK: Are you thinner?

BILL: No.

FRANK: You're not thinner?

BILL: No I'm just the same.

FRANK: Really?

BILL: Same as always.

FRANK: It must just be your hair.

REFEREE ends the round. She gives the victory to FRANK. BILL takes his seat. FRANK steps forward.

FRANK: Last Saturday night I'm on the street after before-dinner cocktails on my way uptown. I flag a cab, I tell him where I'm going, he says, "Okay."

All right. Driving lights cars thinking so on, and he says something about the night and I say something about the moon and he says something about the weather and I say "Yeah."

The radio on and I say something about the music and he says something about the singer and we both say

"Yeah."

All right. Driving lights cars thinking so on.

Now, on the radio a commercial. "Butter Butter Eat Butter" or something. "Milk Milk Drink Milk" or whatever, and he says something about cows and I say something about horses and he says, "Do you like horses?" and I think about it ... and I think about it ... and I realize ... Dammit yes! Yes I do! I had never thought about it before but I am the kind of guy who likes horses. The kind of guy who likes John Wayne and Wild Turkey and carpentry and fishing on lazy August afternoons and horses. Then he says something about the moon and I say something about the night. But you see ... I like horses.

Thank you.

FRANK resumes his seat.

BILL: You're a real cowboy.

REFEREE calls a foul on BILL.

REFEREE: Round Five: Friendly Advice, Part Two.

FRANK and BILL bring their chairs centre and sit. REFEREE begins Round Five.

FRANK: Seen Phil lately?

BILL: Oh yeah sure.

FRANK: Phil's a good guy, eh?

BILL: The best.

FRANK: The best yes. The kind of guy a guy admires. A guy who's got it all together. A guy who picks his friends carefully because he understands a friend is a mirror and a mirror is a reflection of the thing before it.

BILL: So.

FRANK: I mean ... look, I'm not going to pull any punches and I don't want you to take this the wrong way but Phil mentioned it and Phil knows we're tight and I'm sure he wouldn't have mentioned it to me if he didn't think I would mention it to you. I mean he likes you. I'm almost sure he does. He thinks you're a fine guy, a good guy, he does, but he mentioned that maybe lately you ... and I don't ... I'm only saying this out of concern, as I'm sure Phil was as well ... but he mentioned that, maybe lately, you've been a little on the ... well ... a bit ... how did he put it? A bit too "palpably desperate" I think was his phrase. And Bill you can't hold yourself responsible for the fact that business is bad, it's not your fault, and tomorrow is another day no matter how bad things seem right now. And Phil is worried, he wouldn't have mentioned it otherwise, and hey, I'm worried, too. And I think you should be complimented ... You should take it as a compliment to your character that a good guy like Phil is concerned about you.

BILL: That's funny.

FRANK: Funny?

BILL: Yeah. He didn't mention it last night.

FRANK: Last night?

BILL: We saw a movie.

REFEREE moves to end the round. FRANK stops her.

FRANK: Which movie?

BILL: *High Noon.*

FRANK: What time?

BILL: Seven forty.

FRANK: We're going to the game on Thursday.

BILL: We're going to Montreal for the weekend.

FRANK: We're driving to Arizona for Christmas.

BILL: I'm taking his son camping.

FRANK: He asked me to lend him fifty bucks.

BILL: He wants me to help him build his house.

FRANK: His wife made a pass at me.

BILL: That dog?

REFEREE ends the round. She gives the victory to BILL. FRANK takes his seat. BILL steps forward.

BILL: Not only do I like horses I love horses, I have ridden horses, I have ridden horses bareback, I have owned a horse, I have seen my horse break its leg and I have shot my horse. And not only have I shot my horse I have made love in a stable.

BILL resumes his seat.

FRANK: With who, the horse?

REFEREE calls a foul on FRANK.

REFEREE: Round Six: Members Only.

REFEREE begins the round. Slowly the men approach one another at centre. They face one another and make the sound of a telephone. They return to their briefcases, open them, pull out cellphones.

FRANK & BILL: Yeah? Oh hello, sir! Yes sir.

FRANK: Thank you sir.

BILL: I'm sorry sir.

FRANK: Thank you sir.

BILL: I'm sorry sir.

FRANK: Thank you sir.

BILL: I'm sorry sir.

FRANK: Ha ha ha!

BILL: Hee hee hee.

FRANK: Thank you –

BILL: I'm sorry –

FRANK: Bobby.

BILL: Sir.

Good –

FRANK and BILL hang up. Slowly they approach one another at centre. They face one another and make the sound of a telephone. They return to their phones once again.

FRANK & BILL: Yeah?

Hi. I'm in the middle of something right now. Can I – Can I – Can I –

Can I call you back?

I don't know.

I told you that. Yes I'd – Yes I did this morning.

Well it's not my fault if you don't listen.

Is it!

That's right. When I get there.

They hang up.

BILL: Sally says "Hi."

FRANK: Donna says "Hi."

FRANK & BILL: Hi.

FRANK and BILL slowly approach centre. They meet and turn to face the REFEREE, their backs to the audience. They take out their penises for her inspection. After some deliberation she calls a tie. Relieved, FRANK and BILL step forward.

FRANK & BILL: No One Is Perfect.

BILL: By William (Bill) Wade

FRANK: and A. Francis DeLorenzo. No one is perfect.

BILL: No one. Were our fathers perfect?

Certainly not.

FRANK: Were our mothers perfect?

FRANK & BILL: Perhaps.

BILL: But I am not my mother.

FRANK & BILL: No.

FRANK: Nor is my wife my mother.

BILL: No.

FRANK: Nor will she ever be as much as I might wish she were as hard as she might try.

BILL: Frank?

FRANK: I digress.

Am I perfect?

BILL: Am I perfect?

FRANK & BILL: No.

FRANK: Yet, let us consider a moment,

BILL: a moment,

FRANK: that I am not myself

BILL: myself

FRANK: but rather

FRANK & BILL: someone else.

FRANK: Then as this person

BILL: I could

FRANK: watch me

BILL: take note

FRANK: take note

FRANK & BILL: of all the things I do

BILL: the small selfishnesses

FRANK: the minor idiosyncrasies

FRANK & BILL: the tiny spaces

BILL: between me

FRANK & BILL: and perfection.

FRANK: Perhaps then it would

FRANK & BILL: be e- be e- be easier

BILL: to see

FRANK: to look at me

BILL: and see

FRANK & BILL: be e- be e- be easier

FRANK: to change.

FRANK & BILL: But of course if I was someone else I would have my own problems to deal with.

FRANK: So what is perfect?

BILL: What?

FRANK: Besides tomorrow.

FRANK & BILL: Ah tomorrow!

BILL: Because tomorrow is an endless possibility

FRANK & BILL: and an endless possibility is the second-best thing to wake up next to.

FRANK: But what?

Let us consider a moment,

BILL: a note.

FRANK & BILL: A note.

BILL:	**FRANK:**
Laaaaaaa	At first faltering and self-conscious
aaaaaaaa	then building up then pushed forward
aaaaaaaa	then gaining commitment then losing
aaaaaaa.	breath and trailing off near the end.

BILL: But in it there was something

FRANK & BILL: perfect.

FRANK: A happy accident?

BILL: A fluke?

FRANK: Mere chance?

FRANK & BILL: Perhaps. But back to me.

FRANK: And me

BILL: for all my weaknesses

FRANK: as a note

FRANK & BILL: let's say

BILL: a note stretched out from birth

FRANK & BILL: to death,

FRANK: I will allow

BILL: that here and there

FRANK: from time to time

BILL: there is a sound

FRANK: a thought

BILL: a word

FRANK & BILL: that touches on perfection.

BILL: But overall

FRANK: and wholly, no

FRANK & BILL: I know

FRANK: I am not perfect

FRANK & BILL: I know

BILL: I am not perfect.

FRANK & BILL: And neither is he!

FRANK and BILL resume their seats.

REFEREE: Half-time.

REFEREE comes down centre.

REFEREE: This is the beach. Here is the bay. There is the point.

FRANK and BILL come down and join her on either side.

REFEREE:
This is the beach.
Here is the bay.
There is the point.

REFEREE:	**FRANK & BILL:**
This is the beach.	On the beach.
Here is the bay.	At the bay.
There is the point.	On the beach.
This is the beach.	At the bay.
Here is the bay.	On the beach.
There is the point.	At the bay.
This is the beach.	On the beach at the bay.
Here is the bay.	On the beach at the bay.
There is the point.	On the beach at the bay.
This is the beach.	On the beach at the bay.
Here is the bay.	On the beach at the bay.
There is the point.	On the beach at the bay.

REFEREE:
Race you to the point?

Sun.

Boys.

Sand.

Water.

Summer.

FRANK: On the beach at the bay.

BILL: Every day that summer.

FRANK: On the beach at the bay.

BILL: All day every day.

FRANK: On the beach at the bay.

BILL: Every day that summer.

FRANK: On the beach at the bay.

BILL: All summer long.

REFEREE: It is the last day of summer before school begins. Two boys and the girl. She lies in the sun in her blue bathing suit on her green beach towel with her yellow transistor. Turning front. Turning back. And I could tell you little things about her. Turning front turning back. I could tell you that her name was Lisa. Turning front turning back. I could tell you that she had a big brother. Turning front turning back. I could tell you that she loved going to movies. Turning front. Turning back. But that doesn't matter now, all that matters is she is here on the beach with the two boys.

Turning front.

Turning back.

The boys watch the girl. She stares out past the point to where the sea makes a line on the sky. The boys are silent and shy. She can hear them blush. She reminds one boy of his sister, she reminds the other of a picture of a woman he once saw in a magazine. The boys simply watch the girl.

FRANK and BILL sing a verse of a summer song.

The sun hangs about there, just over the point. She is a little drowsy. She gets up and wanders to the edge of the water. She looks out. She feels a breeze. She turns her head a little over her shoulder and speaks to the boys:

"Race you to the point?"

This is the beach.

Here is the bay.

There is the point.

REFEREE:	FRANK & BILL:
This is the beach.	On the beach.
Here is the bay.	At the bay.
There is the point.	On the beach.
This is the beach.	At the bay.
Here is the bay.	On the beach.
There is the point.	At the bay.
There is	On the beach at the bay.
There is	On the beach at the bay.
There is	On the beach at the bay.
There is	On the beach at the bay.
There is	On the beach at the bay.
There is	On the beach at the bay.
There is	On the beach at the bay.
There is	On the beach at the bay.
There is	On the beach at the bay.
There is the point.	

FRANK: And we sat

BILL: on the sand

FRANK: at the edge

BILL: of the point

FRANK: and we waited

BILL: and we waited.

REFEREE: Race you to the point?

Do you remember?

FRANK: One.

REFEREE: Do you remember?

BILL: Two.

REFEREE: I remember too.

I remember. Three!

REFEREE resumes her position on chair. She ends half-time. The men return to their chairs.

REFEREE: Recap: two men enter a room. A taller man and a shorter man. They both wear white shirts, blue suits, silk ties, black shoes, black socks –

BILL: Blue socks!

REFEREE: and blue socks. And each man carries a briefcase. The first man seems very much like the second man and the second man seems very much like the first man but they are not

FRANK & BILL: No.

REFEREE: They are not for two reasons. One: one man is the first man, and two: one man in his briefcase has a gun.

BILL: A gun.

FRANK: A gun.

REFEREE: Which man is the first man and which man has the gun? Round Seven: Dad.

REFEREE begins the round. FRANK and BILL approach one another at centre. FRANK does the "what's-on-your-tie" gag to BILL. BILL shoves FRANK. FRANK shoves BILL. BILL shoves FRANK, knocking him down. REFEREE calls a foul on BILL. FRANK and BILL circle one another.

FRANK: How's your dad?

BILL: Why?

FRANK: I always liked your dad.

BILL: Really?

FRANK: Yeah.

BILL: Well, I always liked your dad.

FRANK: Really?

BILL: Yeah.

FRANK & BILL: Gee.

FRANK: Your dad was a real easygoing guy.

BILL: Your dad was a real card.

FRANK: Your dad was a real dreamer.

BILL: Your dad was a real character.

FRANK: Your dad was a real nice guy.

BILL: He was a real maniac.

FRANK: He was a real boozer.

BILL: Ha. He was a real wild man.

FRANK: A real cuckold.

BILL: A real wiener.

FRANK: A real dick.

BILL: A real prick.

FRANK: A lemming.

BILL: A fascist.

FRANK: An ass.

BILL: A pig!

How's your mom?

REFEREE ends the round. She calls a tie.

FRANK:
Please be warned
that if you think
I'm going to stand
here and start dishing
dirt and airing
laundry about
HIS FATHER,
I won't. But let's just
say the desperation
he displays
comes from
HIS FATHER.
Not that I'm sure
he wasn't a
well-intentioned if
ill-educated man
but, and education
isn't everything, but
FOR EXAMPLE:
Rather than
face criminal
charges
HIS FATHER
said he could not
multiply eight times
nine when
HIS FATHER's
company was missing
some seventy-two
thousand dollars
at the year-end audit.
HIS FATHER
claimed he had marked
down twenty-four.
Twenty-four? Give me
a break.
AND THAT'S JUST ONE
EXAMPLE.
Dishonest?
Well he did admit to
an ignorance in
arithmetic and
WELL I'M SURE YOU
KNOW WHAT THEY
SAY ABOUT FATHERS
AND SONS
and far be it, far be
it indeed for me to
say that
HE IS THE PERFECT
EXAMPLE.
Thank you.

BILL:
Now this is more
than name-calling
here although
that of course
is the temptation
but
HIS FATHER
drove his mother crazy,
I mean she did have
a drinking
problem but
HIS FATHER
didn't help at all.
She spent the last
fifteen years
in and out of detox
as a result of
his antics.
FOR EXAMPLE:
At the Girl Guide
Boy Scout
banquet in grade eight
HIS FATHER
was supposed
to make a presentation,
but when the time came
HIS FATHER
was nowhere to be
found. Twenty minutes
later five guys from the
Sixth Pack found
HIS FATHER
in the boiler room
with Suzie Walsh
a sixteen-year-old
Girl Guide.
AND THAT'S JUST ONE
EXAMPLE.
Is he like that?
Well they say
a guy and his
father are
WELL I'M SURE YOU
KNOW WHAT THEY
SAY ABOUT FATHERS
AND SONS
and I'm not saying
they're right all the
time, but in this case,
HE IS THE PERFECT
EXAMPLE.
Thank you.

REFEREE: Pardon me?

FRANK and BILL repeat the lines above at twice the speed.

REFEREE: Thank you.

FRANK & BILL: You're welcome.

REFEREE: Round Eight: All in the Palm of His Hand.

REFEREE begins the round. FRANK and BILL come to centre. FRANK takes out two cigars. He gives one to BILL. FRANK lights them. They face one another.

FRANK: You've got auction preferreds yielding 70 per cent of prime and 50/51 up either side what do you want to do? Convert with three-year hard call protection, two-year pay back, the hedge is a layup? I don't think so. I say capitalize the loss by rolling it into goodwill and amortizing over forty years. Of course profits will be decreased by the switch from FIFO to LIFO. And then remember Bethlehem! Where application of FASB 87 meant balance sheet quality went way down because of the unfunded pension liability. I mean if we were in the States I could offer at one-half and give up an eighth to the market-maker for three-eighths net fill, but unfortunately we're not. Are you with me?

BILL stubs out the cigar in the palm of his hand. REFEREE ends the round. She gives the victory to BILL. FRANK resumes his seat. BILL steps forward.

BILL: Let's go to my place everybody. Okay. Ready?

This is the back door.

We always use the back door.

Here is the rec room. There is the bar. There is the laundry room.

Hallway, stairs.

Going up stairs, going up stairs.

Out that window that's the yard.

Here's a hallway. There's the kitchen.

Microwave butcher's block breakfast nook.

Hallway.

Turn.

Dining room.

Oak table, eight chairs, hallway, French doors, living room.

It's sunken!

Big window.

Big skylight.

Grand

piano

(white).

Through the hallway into the foyer.

Front –

We never use the front door.

Window window powder room.

MASSIVE STAIRCASE!

One. Two. Three. Four. Five bedrooms (Can in two.)

Long hallway.

Smaller staircase.

Going up stairs. Going up stairs. Going up stairs.

Door. Locked. Key. Open the door. And this

is my

secret room.

FRANK: I heard you rent.

> *REFEREE calls a foul on FRANK. BILL approaches FRANK.*

BILL: Where'd you hear that?

FRANK: Around.

BILL: Yeah?

FRANK: Yeah.

BILL: Around where?

FRANK: Just around.

BILL: Phil?

FRANK: Might've been Phil.

BILL: Phil's full of shit.

> *BILL returns to centre.*

BILL: As I was saying.

This is my place.

Back door rec room bar laundry out that window that's the yard

kitchen hallway turn dining room turn living room turn hallway

MASSIVE STAIRCASE

one two three four five bedrooms hallway staircase.

Going up stairs going up stairs going up stairs

Door locked key open the door

and this is my

secret room.

And this is my secret room. And it's empty except for a great big window right here, and when I look out of it I see the tops of trees, and hills, black roads with white lines, and a whole lake, and two kinds of earth: dark wet earth and clay, and big green fields and sky that's only ever blue.

And all of it.

Everything.

Theskythefieldsthetreesthelakethehillstheroad-theclay.

Everything I see, and farther where you can't see, all of it, everything, is mine.

It's all mine.

> *BILL resumes his seat.*

REFEREE: Round Nine: Power Lunch.

> *FRANK and BILL bring their chairs centre. They sit facing one another with their briefcases on their laps. REFEREE begins the round.*

FRANK: Been here before?

BILL: Oh yeah.

FRANK: How's the steak?

BILL: Very good.

FRANK: How's the swordfish?

BILL: Very good.

FRANK: How's the shark?

BILL: Greasy.

FRANK & BILL: Excuse me a second.

> *FRANK and BILL reach into their briefcases and take out their cellphones. They dial and both make a ringing sound. As BILL speaks, FRANK continues to ring.*

BILL: Hi doll!

Listen sorry I was short with you before.

Did you go ahead and have dinner anyway?

Ahhh ... Well how 'bout I pick up a pizza on my way home?

And a movie?

Something funny?

Something romantic! That sounds nice!

Okay "Turnip."

I do you too.

Bye bye.

> *FRANK and BILL hang up.*

BILL: How's Donna? (*pause*) How's –

FRANK: I heard you.

She's very good.

BILL: Really?

FRANK: Yes.

How's the spaghettini?

BILL: Oily. I saw Donna at the Fullers' party.

FRANK: Oh yes.

BILL: You weren't there.

FRANK: No I wasn't.

BILL: Phil was there.

FRANK: Was he?

BILL: He was having a good time.

FRANK: Good.

BILL: So was Donna.

FRANK: Donna likes a good –

BILL: Party?

FRANK: Yes.

BILL: I've heard that.

FRANK: How's the squid?

BILL: Sneaky.

FRANK: Sneaky?

BILL: Sneaks up on you. Nice tie.

FRANK: Yes you mentioned –

BILL: Somebody has good taste.

FRANK: How's Sally?

BILL: Very good.

FRANK: Really?

BILL: She was at the Fullers'.

Strange you weren't there.

FRANK: Well I wasn't.

BILL: Working late?

FRANK: I don't believe you've ever had the steak or the swordfish or the shark or the spaghettini or the squid here.

BILL: No I haven't. But it was a good party.

REFEREE ends the round. She gives the victory to FRANK.

BILL: Bullshit call!

REFEREE calls a foul on BILL. BILL resumes his seat. FRANK steps forward.

FRANK: Let's not use the word "class." Class being such a nebulous word. Let's instead use the word "mountain." Mountain. And many men are born without a mountain. It is not a birthright. This is not to say that a mountain is particularly better than a valley – just as we may find from time to time that knowledge is not particularly better than ignorance. And even being second has its benefits. For example … less income tax? But some men live on mountains and some men live in valleys and if only those men standing small and insignificant in the valley would stop their futile fight to stake a claim at the crest of a hill they can never hope to own. If only they would not be so blind and for a moment consider the privilege of living in the benevolent shadow of a mountain. But to be brave enough to see that truth and face it, that takes balls, and like mountains many men are born without them.

FRANK resumes his seat.

BILL: Fuck you Alphonse.

REFEREE calls a foul on BILL.

FRANK: I beg your pardon?

REFEREE calls a foul on FRANK.

REFEREE: Round Ten: Business Ties.

REFEREE begins the round. FRANK and BILL step centre. FRANK faces the audience. BILL faces FRANK and stands at an uncomfortably close distance.

FRANK: Now I don't want to harp on business Bill but I happen to be pretty tight with Bobby and Bobby runs everything and I know how things are with you and there's a chance that there might be a place opening up in accounting and from what I've heard –

BILL: Frank I really like that tie.

FRANK: And from what I've heard about business Bill –

BILL: Silk?

Of course.

How could I imagine Donna would buy a tie like that?

FRANK: I'm offering you a break here Bill I'm –

BILL: That's not Donna's taste.

Very flashy.

Yet tasteful.

Where would a person buy a tie like that?

What kind of store?

FRANK: Bill ...

BILL: What kind of person would go into that kind of store and buy a tie like that?

FRANK: Don't Bill.

BILL: A very young tie!

FRANK: Shut up about the goddamn tie!

FRANK resumes his seat. REFEREE ends the round. She gives the victory to BILL. BILL steps forward.

BILL: Two stories.

The first story is a very familiar story because everybody knows it. And it's a story about a little temp, eighteen years old, who is, by the way, knocked up and who happens to have not bad taste in ties don't you think?

And the second story is a secret so just keep it to yourselves.

We're at the Fullers' party. Me and Sally. Huge spread, packed bar, beautiful house, the works. Tons of people, people everywhere. There's Donna! Where's Frank? Frank's not there. Donna's there though. She looks great! Who's that she's talking to? It's Phil. I wander over. They're talking about politics. I wander off. Have a drink, have a chat, check out the pool, come back in, poke around some more at the buffet, shoot the shit ... Phil and Donna still talking! I cruise over. Now they're talking about poetry. I cruise off. Time comes to go Sally's pulling on my arm I'm talking to Mister Fuller. Look around for Donna to say goodbye ... No Donna. Look around for Phil ... No Phil. I gotta take a pee before we leave, walk in the can. There's Donna. In the shower. With Phil. And when she sees me she smiles and she says: "Shh! Close the door Bill." Now the first story you can repeat but the second story, that's a secret.

BILL resumes his seat.

REFEREE: Round Eleven: My Boy.

REFEREE begins the round. FRANK and BILL step to centre.

FRANK & BILL: Let me tell you something about my boy ...

FRANK does the wrong physical choreography.

FRANK: Sorry.

FRANK & BILL: Let me tell you something about my boy.

He's a good boy, my boy.

A good boy, a smart boy.

He's the best boy, my boy.

No question, he's the best –

FRANK makes another error.

BILL: (*to FRANK*) Are you with us?

FRANK & BILL: Let me tell you something about my boy ...

FRANK again makes an error. FRANK steps away. REFEREE moves to end the round. BILL stops her.

BILL: What's your problem?

Hey.

Hey.

What's your problem?

BILL looks to the audience, shrugging.

FRANK: Password.

BILL does not respond.

FRANK: Password!

BILL does not respond.

FRANK: Winner rules.

BILL: That's not in the game.

FRANK: (*steps to centre*) Password.

BILL: (*joins him at centre*) Winner rules.

FRANK & BILL:

Cut!

Spit!

Mix!

Brothers brothers never part

through broken vows or covered hearts

in all our weakness, all our woes

we stick together, highs and lows.

FRANK: Pledge?

BILL: Made.

FRANK: Promise?

BILL: Kept.

FRANK: To what end?

FRANK & BILL: Never end. Transit! Transport!

FRANK and BILL join hands and raise arms overhead to form an arch. REFEREE walks through the arch and down centre.

BILL: One.

FRANK: Two.

REFEREE: Three.

> *FRANK, BILL, and REFEREE begin a "swimming" action.*

FRANK, BILL & REFEREE:

Cut through the water to the point. Cut through the water to the point.

Cut through the water to the point. Cut through the water to the point.

Cut through the water to the point. Cut through the water to the point.

Cut through the water to the point. Cut through the water to the point.

> *The three continue the swimming action and the men continue to repeat the lines through the following.*

REFEREE: I'll beat you.

I'm a good swimmer.

You guys think you're so hot.

My brother taught me to swim and he's on a team.

What's your names anyway?

My name's Lisa.

My mom calls me Rosie but I hate that.

What's your names anyway?

You guys got a cottage here?

You brothers?

We've got a cottage up by the store, on the hill, you know where I mean? It used to be a farm but we don't have any animals. I wish we had a horse; I love horses. I go to the movie on Sunday. I go every Sunday even if it's one I saw already. Hey slow down it's far. Slow down.

REFEREE:	**FRANK & BILL:**
What's your names?	And I feel her fall back.
Hey.	And I feel her fall back.
Wait.	And I feel her fall back.
Let's not race.	And I feel her fall back.
Wait.	And I feel her fall back.
We're too far.	And I feel her fall back.
Slow down.	And I feel her fall back.
Hey.	And I feel her fall back.
Wait.	And I feel her fall back.

REFEREE: Hey ...

REFEREE:	**FRANK:**	**BILL:**
His decision.	Cut through the water to the point.	And I feel her I feel her fall back.
His compassion.	Cut through the water to the point.	And I feel her I feel her fall back.
His desire.	Cut through the water to the point.	And I feel her I feel her fall back.
His jealousy.	Cut through the water to the point.	And I feel her I feel her fall back.
His guilt.	Cut through the water to the point.	And I feel her I feel her fall back.
His self-image.	Cut through the water to the point.	And I feel her I feel her fall back.
His self-knowledge.	Cut through the water to the point.	And I feel her I feel her fall back.
His self-loathing.	Cut through the water to the point.	And I feel her I feel her fall back.
His fear of death.	Cut through the water to the point.	And I feel her I feel her fall back.
His weakness.	Cut through the water to the point.	And I feel her I feel her fall back.
His pride.	Cut through the water to the point.	And I feel her I feel her fall back.
His pleasure.	Cut through the water to the point.	And I feel her I feel her fall back.
His body.	Cut through the water to the point.	And I feel her I feel her fall back.
His politics.	Cut through the water to the point.	And I feel her I feel her fall back.
His will to power.	Cut through the water to the point.	And I feel her I feel her fall back.

REFEREE:	**FRANK & BILL:**
His concept of God.	Cut through the water to the point.
His warrior instinct.	Cut through the water to the point.
His dreams.	Cut through the water to the point.
His memory.	Cut through the water to the point.
And first there is panic.	Cut through the water to the point.
And so much sound.	Cut through the water to the point.
Rushing.	Cut through the water to the point.
Swirling.	Cut through the water to the point.
Pulsing.	Cut through the water to the point.

FRANK *slowly raises his arms in victory. BILL continues the swimming action.*

REFEREE: And then no sound. And then peace. And then you will float or you will sink. And if you float you will be as if flying and if you sink, when you hit bottom, you will bounce like a man on the moon.

REFEREE returns to her chair. FRANK walks toward BILL. BILL continues to the swimming action.

BILL:

Cut through the water to the point. Cut through the water to the point.

Cut through the water to the point. Cut through the water to the point.

Cut through the water to the point. Cut through the water to the point.

BILL rises as he continues to speak. FRANK places his hand on BILL's shoulder.

BILL:

Cut through the water to the point. Cut through the water to the point.

Cut through the water to the point. Cut through the water to the point.

FRANK and BILL are now standing face to face. With his other hand FRANK punches BILL in the stomach. BILL goes down. REFEREE ends the round. She gives the victory to FRANK. BILL struggles to his feet and approaches FRANK. FRANK addresses the audience.

FRANK: I'd like to make a few things clear.

These are my ears, these are my eyes, this is the back of my hand.

FRANK strikes BILL with the back of his hand. BILL goes down.

And the winner has, and will always, rule.

That is the way of the world. Like battle, like business, like love. A few may fall along the way but compared to the prize what are a few. And the prize is what you want and what you want is what you hear in every mouth, every buzz, every bell, every crack, every whisper.

Don't be afraid.

The thing we must learn is how to balance compassion and desire.

For example:

Bill? You like this tie?

FRANK *takes his tie off and puts it around BILL's neck.*

FRANK: Have it. (*yanks on the tie*)

Say thank you.

Say thank you!

BILL: Thank you.

FRANK: No thanks necessary Bill. I've got a dozen just like it at home.

You see.

Don't be fooled.

FRANK lifts BILL and supports him.

FRANK: Beware compassion. Compassion will lose the race. Compassion is illogical. If you let it compassion will kill desire. Especially the desire to be first. And being first my friends is the point.

FRANK throws BILL across the room.

Compassion is the brother of guilt

FRANK lifts BILL by his tie.

and guilt is the mother of stomach cancer.

FRANK knees BILL in the stomach.

The first man is the man

FRANK knees BILL in the chest. BILL goes down.

who is guiltless beyond all circumstance

FRANK kicks BILL.

and sure of his right

FRANK kicks BILL.

to be first.

FRANK kicks BILL.

The first man is the man

FRANK kicks BILL.

who can recognize

the second man.

BILL lies motionless. FRANK steps forward.

FRANK: And we sat on the sand at the edge of the point and we waited and we waited and you got scared and you ran home and all night long I waited and in the morning when her body washed up on the shore I tried to comfort her but she did not respond, then to evoke some reaction I slapped her so hard my hand still hurts. And then learning my lesson I declared myself first to the point.

FRANK resumes his seat.

REFEREE: Round Twelve: Rumours of Glory.

FRANK steps to centre. BILL tries to struggle to his feet. REFEREE calls a foul on BILL. BILL continues to struggle. REFEREE calls a foul on BILL. BILL continues to struggle. REFEREE ends the round. She gives the victory to FRANK. FRANK steps forward. BILL manages to get to his feet. He approaches his briefcase.

FRANK: I have always been, will always be, the first.

FRANK resumes his seat. BILL opens his briefcase, takes out a gun, aims it at FRANK.

BILL: And I learned my lesson Frank, I won't be second again.

FRANK opens his briefcase. BILL laughs. FRANK takes out a gun and aims it at BILL.

FRANK: The game isn't over yet Bill.

REFEREE: The two men will stand here just like this for a long time to come with one thought, one thought racing through each man's mind:

FRANK & BILL:

Somebody lied.

Somebody lied.

Somebody lied.

REFEREE steps down and to centre carrying a yellow transistor radio. The men continue to repeat "somebody lied" through the following.

REFEREE: Two boys on a beach. The last day of summer before school begins. Nearby is a girl. She lies in the sun in her blue bathing suit on her green beach towel listening to her yellow transistor. She reminds one boy of his sister, she reminds the other of a picture of a woman he once saw in a magazine. The sun hangs about there. Just over the point. She turns her head a little over her shoulder and speaks to the boys: "Race you to the point?"

The men stop speaking.

REFEREE: And they do.

One two three.

The boys are afraid.

The boys are still afraid.

REFEREE: Round Thirteen:

The men cock their guns.

REFEREE: Only One Gun Is Loaded.

She begins the round. The men look at her in disbelief, still keeping aim. She places the transistor radio on the stage and turns it on. She exits the way the men came in. The radio plays a happy beach song. The men look at one another, still keeping aim. Lights fade.

END

WENDY LILL

(b. 1950)

Wendy Lill has been one of modern Canadian theatre's strongest voices against social injustice, both in her plays and her political life. Born in Vancouver, Lill grew up in London, Ontario, graduating from York University in 1971 with a B.A. in political science. After working in Toronto as a community organizer and in Northern Ontario as a consultant for the Canadian Mental Health Association, she moved to Winnipeg in 1979 and began writing full-time for CBC radio, winning two ACTRA awards in 1981 for the documentary *Who Is George Forest?* and the radio drama *Shorthanded*. Her first stage play, *On the Line* (1982), was produced by Winnipeg's Agassiz Theatre. Though more heavily rhetorical and politically one-sided than her subsequent plays, this sympathetic account of a strike by immigrant women garment workers in Winnipeg established the primary subject matter of Lill's dramatic world, including *The Glace Bay Miners' Museum* – the lives of women in crisis, isolated from mainstream society and its values.

With *The Fighting Days* (1983), Lill began a productive association with Winnipeg's Prairie Theatre Exchange and its artistic director, Kim McCaw. Another treatment of Manitoba history, the play deals with the women's suffrage movement in the early part of the century. But instead of the well-known Nellie McClung, its focus is the more obscure, more radical Francis Beynon, who opposed McClung's support of the Great War and her failure to champion the rights of foreign-born women. *The Fighting Days* has been revived three times in Winnipeg, most recently in 2012, and has had productions across Ontario and the prairies.

Directed by Kim McCaw, *The Occupation of Heather Rose* premiered at Prairie Theatre Exchange in 1986, a powerful solo drama in which a young, naive, well-meaning white nurse recounts her terrible loss of innocence on an Aboriginal reserve in the Canadian North. Nominated for the Governor General's Award, the play has been produced across Canada, from Vancouver Island to the Yukon to Newfoundland, as well as in Copenhagen, Edinburgh, and Düsseldorf. In 1987, Lill moved to Dartmouth, Nova Scotia, where she still lives, although she remained for a while, as Doug Smith wrote in 1989, "Winnipeg's most popular writer in non-residence."

Her next play, *Memories of You* (1988), also opened at Prairie Theatre Exchange. It examines Canadian writer Elizabeth Smart's lifelong obsession with her lover, British poet George Barker, in a memory play in which the elderly Elizabeth conjures up her past in response to accusations of neglect by her adult daughter. Strongly influenced by Sharon Pollock's *Doc*, the play was directed by Pollock at Theatre New Brunswick, and performed in Ottawa, Halifax, Victoria, and Toronto, where it received a Chalmers Award nomination, and in French translation in Montreal as *Les traverses du coeur*.

Sisters (1989) had its second production at Prairie Theatre Exchange, but premiered in Parrsboro, Nova Scotia, commissioned by Ship's Company Theatre artistic director Mary Vingoe, another important collaborator in Lill's theatrical career. A study of the Catholic nuns who ran a Native residential school, this memory play exposes the horrors of that system while at the same time attempting to understand the forces that (mis-)shaped the white women charged with administering it. Like *The Occupation of Heather Rose*, *Sisters* does not bring any Native characters directly onstage nor attempt to tell the Native children's story. Lill did, however, dramatize Aboriginal experience directly in her screenplay *Ikwe* (1986), part of the National Film Board series *Daughters of the Country*, about Métis women. *Ikwe* won a Golden Sheaf Award in 1986, and Lill's television adaptation of *Sisters* received a Gemini nomination as Best Performing Arts Program in 1991. In 1993, *All Fall Down* premiered at Calgary's Alberta Theatre Projects, earning a Governor General's Award nomination for its powerful portrayal of hysteria in a community where a female daycare worker is accused of sexual abuse.

After moving to Nova Scotia, Lill held the posts of writer-in-residence at Mulgrave Road (Co-op) Theatre (1984) and Neptune Theatre (1991), and in 1993 she co-founded the Eastern Front Theatre Company in Dartmouth. Eastern Front opened with *The Occupation of Heather Rose*, then premiered *The Glace Bay Miners' Museum* (1995) at Ship's Company Theatre in Parrsboro, directed by Mary Vingoe. In 2011, Lill received the Merritt Legacy Award for her contributions to theatre in Nova Scotia.

Elected New Democratic Party Member of Parliament for Dartmouth in 1997, Lill served as the party's spokesperson for media and communications, human rights, persons with disabilities, and Canadian heritage. She remained an MP through two terms until 2004, when she chose not to run again. In 1999, the National Film Board produced a documentary about her first year in office, titled *Wendy Lill: Playwright in Parliament*. While in Parliament, she wrote *Corker* (1998), receiving her fourth Governor General's Award nomination. Halifax's Neptune Theatre premiered this study of a neo-conservative provincial politician whose life is invaded by a mentally handicapped man. Also influenced by her time in Ottawa, *Chimera* (2007), directed by Mary Vingoe at Toronto's Tarragon, explores the ethics of stem-cell research and related legislation. Lill drew on her parliamentary experiences again to write a twenty-one-episode radio drama series, *Backbencher*, produced by CBC in 2010–11.

The Glace Bay Miners' Museum began life as a short story by Cape Breton writer Sheldon Currie, published in the *Antigonish Review* in 1976 and developed from a song he had written, "The Ballad of Charlie Dave."

Currie says he was inspired to write the story after visiting the newly built Cape Breton Miners' Museum in Glace Bay, Nova Scotia, and feeling that it didn't properly commemorate the difficult lives those miners had lived. Lill first adapted Currie's story as a ninety-minute radio drama for CBC in 1991, then further expanded it for her stage play. Following its premiere, the play had multiple productions across Canada, received a Governor General's Award nomination for its published text, and had a major remount in 2012–13, co-produced by Ottawa's National Arts Centre and Halifax's Neptune Theatre. The feature film version, *Margaret's Museum,* was released in 1995. It won six Genie Awards, including best screenplay for director Mort Ransen and co-writer Gerry Wexler, best actress for Helena Bonham Carter as Margaret, and supporting actress and actor awards for Kate Nelligan and Kenneth Welsh. In 1995, Sheldon Currie published *The Glace Bay Miners' Museum* as a novel.

Lill sets her memory-play treatment of love and loss in Cape Breton's hardscrabble coal-mining community just after World War Two, a time when Maritime coal production was declining as the war effort wound down; new open-pit mines were coming on stream out west; and diesel, nuclear, and hydroelectric power began replacing coal as a primary fuel. Working conditions in the pits and living conditions in the company towns of Cape Breton may have been particularly bad then, but they had been brutal since the mines first came into operation more than a century before. Grandpa, with what is likely black-lung disease, is a (barely) living symbol of those conditions. Although Lill insists in an interview with Karen Gilodo that the play is above all a love story, she and Currie both place that story in a context of severe personal, social, and economic challenge.

"It's time everybody woke up," announces Neil Currie, the disruptive outsider who loves a fight and whose role is to bring the MacNeil family and the Glace Bay community "out of hibernation" with his energy and skepticism, his sense of cultural history, and his pride. But Neil experiences his own awakening as he embraces Ian's union politics and the solidarity that the strike is briefly able to bring about. He broadens his understanding of what it means to be a man.

The play concerns itself as least as much with the role of women in this poor mining town and their strategies for dealing with both the everyday difficulties of life and more acute situations. These women have grown used to burying their men before their time. In Margaret and her mother, we see very different ways of dealing with the stresses and tragedies. Catherine is more pragmatic and probably less sympathetic than young, romantic Margaret. Of course, we see the story through Margaret's eyes, so we tend to share her perspective. Her hero worship of dead brother Charlie Dave and taunting of living brother Ian, her love and admiration for Neil, and her shifting sense of optimism and pessimism in the face of the evolving plot carry us along with her. Nevertheless, nothing really prepares us for the shock of the ending and the new understanding that it brings to the play's title.

Lill leavens the play's darkness with comedy and music. Margaret's wry, stoic narrative humour complements Neil's extroversion, which manifests itself through his bagpipes as well as his comic view of life. The bagpipes are a lot more evident in production than they are on the page. Their sonic power, the bittersweet songs they convey, and the culture they symbolize represent the strength of this Gaelic-Canadian community. They remind the people, as does Margaret's memorial museum and the theatrical tale she retells, that "it's important to remember."

The Glace Bay Miners' Museum

Wendy Lill
Based on the novel by
Sheldon Currie

The Glace Bay Miners' Museum was co-produced
by Eastern Front Theatre and Ship's Company
Theatre in August 1995 at Ship's Company
Theatre in Parrsboro, Nova Scotia, and
subsequently at the Sir James Dunn Theatre in
Halifax in September, with the following cast:

MARGARET	Mary-Colin Chisholm
GRANDPA	Peter Elliott
CATHERINE	Niki Lipman
IAN	Ross Manson
NEIL	Hugh Thompson

Directed by Mary Vingoe
Set Design by Stephen Britton Osler
Lighting Design by Michael Fuller
Costume Design by Gay Hauser
Music Composed by Paul Cram
Stage Managed by Johanne Pomrenski

"Margaret, are you grieving?"
 – Gerard Manley Hopkins, *Spring and Fall*

CHARACTERS

MARGARET MACNEIL
CATHERINE MACNEIL
IAN MACNEIL
GRANDPA
NEIL CURRIE
WAITRESS (*offstage voice*)
OWNER (*offstage voice*)

SETTING

Glace Bay, Cape Breton, Nova Scotia; 1947 and
later.

The Glace Bay Miners' Museum is a memory
play.

ACT ONE

SCENE 1

*A house on the ocean near Glace Bay, Cape Breton
Island. The sound of waves slapping softly at the
shore. MARGARET is looking out the window and
over the ocean. She begins singing a Gaelic air.*

MARGARET:

> Suilean dubha dubha dubh
> Suilean dubh aig m'eudail
> Suilean dubha dubha dubh
> Cuin' a thig thu cheilidh

She switches to a bawdy Cape Breton ditty.

> Balls to yer partner back against the wall
> If you can't get shagged on Saturday night
> You'll never get shagged at all!

*She stops singing, goes over to a table, and picks
up a teapot.*

Here is the teapot from the house at Reserve. Here
is the teapot that steeped the tea that went down
the hatch and warmed the guts of all the poor
buggers that went down the hole at the Glace Bay
mines. God bless them all. And over there are their
cans and their lamps, their boots and the likes ...
More in the other room. And while you're in there,
take a minute to stop at the window and look
out – If it weren't for that little stretch of water
out there, you could see right clear over to the Isle
of Skye. That's what Neil used to say. Just take a
look around. Don't be shy. There's lots to see. Look
and ye shall see.

MARGARET sings a bit more.

The first time I ever saw the bugger, I thought to myself, him as big as he is, me as small as I felt, if he was astraddle on the road, naked, I could walk under him without a hair touching. That's what I thought. I was sitting alone at the White Rose Café wishing my girlfriend Marie would come by but knowing she wouldn't. None of the boys would sit with me, and none of the girls either 'cause the boys wouldn't. For one thing, I had a runny nose. If a boy walked home with me, they'd say things like, "I see you're taking out snot face these days. Don't forget to kiss her on the back of her head." The other reason no one would sit with me was because I screwed a couple of boys when I was little. I didn't know you weren't supposed to, and I didn't REALLY screw either of them 'cause they didn't know how to do it, and it was too late before I could tell them, although, God knows, I knew little enough myself of the little there is to know. They didn't walk home with me after. Neither one. But they told everybody I was a whore. So I was not only a whore, but a snot-nosed whore. Marie was the only one who didn't care about any of that stuff, and when she wasn't around to talk to, I spent a lot of time staring at my little hands.

The sounds of the White Rose Café begin. Dishes clacking, voices, silverware. MARGARET is now twenty-one. It is 1947.

WAITRESS: (*offstage*) Two chips and eggs, over easy ... coffee ...

MARGARET: So, I was sitting alone in the last booth at the White Rose Café right by the kitchen and the washroom when this giant of a man with a box in his hand came bearing down the aisle looking left and right and he kept on coming 'til he got to my booth and saw there was nobody there but me with my lovely long hair. When he stood there holding his box, before he said anything, I thought to myself: I wish he'd pick me up and put me in his shirt pocket.

NEIL: Can I put this here on your table?

MARGARET: Suit yourself.

NEIL: Can I sit down then?

MARGARET: Suit yourself again.

NEIL: All right, I will.

NEIL places the box on the table and eases himself into the booth. He lays his hands out in front of him.

MARGARET squirms about, trying to avoid his gaze and his knees beneath the table.

NEIL: That your knee?

MARGARET: Yeah. Where d'you think I keep them when I'm sitting down?

NEIL: (*laughs*) Do you want something?

MARGARET: I already had something.

NEIL: Would you like something else?

MARGARET: I don't have any more money.

NEIL: I'd like to buy you a bite to eat, if you don't mind.

MARGARET: Why?

NEIL: You still look like you're a bit hungry. What do you want?

MARGARET: I'll have a cup of tea and an order of chips.

NEIL: I'll have the same.

NEIL looks around.

MARGARET: She's over there having a smoke.

When NEIL turns to get the attention of the waitress, MARGARET grabs the metal napkin dispenser and inspects her face, wipes some dirt from her cheek and tries to tidy her hair.

NEIL: (*calling*) Two orders of chips and tea, please.

Then he turns back and looks at MARGARET.

WAITRESS: (*hollering order offstage*) Two orders of chips and tea for snot nose and her friend.

MARGARET, embarrassed, coughs to mask the waitress's remark. NEIL has had a few to drink. He begins singing low a Gaelic song, then breaks off.

NEIL: You like that song?

MARGARET: (*offhand*) It's all right.

MARGARET jumps up and comes back with the food. She lays out the plates and the tea, nervously. NEIL watches her.

MARGARET: Pass me that ketchup. Please.

NEIL passes it.

MARGARET: Thank you. Will you pass the sugar, too. Please.

NEIL passes it, still watching her. MARGARET stirs her tea.

MARGARET: So why are you looking at me? Haven't you ever seen a girl with a runny nose before?

NEIL: Not since my sister. Makes me feel right at home.

MARGARET: Is that so?

MARGARET watches in wonder as he throws back his head and laughs. Then he looks back at her.

NEIL: Yeah. That's so. So what do you think?

MARGARET: I think you're the biggest son of a bitch I ever saw.

NEIL: Know what I think?

MARGARET: What?

NEIL: I think you're the smallest son of a bitch I ever saw. And all of this rain, what do you think of that?

MARGARET: I don't mind it. Kind of like it.

NEIL: And the fog?

MARGARET: That too. It's kind of cozy.

NEIL: Yes it is. Do you come here often?

MARGARET: Every week at this same exact time. After I finish cleaning MacDonald's house.

NEIL: And what's your name?

MARGARET: Margaret MacNeil.

NEIL: Well now, Miss MacNeil, it's been a pleasure meeting you. Perhaps we'll meet again.

MARGARET: Suit yourself.

NEIL: Okay, I will. My name is Neil Currie.

NEIL gets up to leave. MARGARET doesn't want him to.

MARGARET: So what have you got in that big ugly box?

NEIL: Let me show you.

NEIL opens the box and proudly inspects the parts of a set of bagpipes. MARGARET stares at them.

MARGARET: What in God's earth is that?

NEIL: (*amazed*) You've never seen bagpipes before!

MARGARET: Sure I have.

NEIL: Then what are these? (*holding up the bagpipes*)

MARGARET: A bunch of brown sticks.

NEIL: And this?

MARGARET: It's a stupid-looking plaid bag!

NEIL: You've never clapped your eyes on bagpipes! I can tell by that stunned look on your face!

MARGARET: Drop dead!

NEIL: Your name's Margaret MacNeil and you've never seen a set of pipes!

MARGARET: And I sure haven't missed them ... so get out of here and leave me alone!

NEIL: I will not.

NEIL begins to assemble his bagpipes.

MARGARET: What the hell are you doing?

NEIL: I'm putting it all together, and then I'm going to play you a tune.

MARGARET: (*looking around uneasily*) I don't know about that, mister.

NEIL starts up the beginning snarls and squeals of the bagpipes. MARGARET covers her ears. NEIL starts to play.

OWNER: (*offstage*) Get that goddamn fiddle out of here!

NEIL: (*protesting*) Just a minute!

OWNER: (*offstage*) No minute! Get out of here! Get out! Get out! Get out!

NEIL puts down the pipes and rolls up his sleeves to get ready to fight. MARGARET jumps up.

MARGARET: I wouldn't do it. He's big.

NEIL: I'm ready!

NEIL bounds off in the direction of the kitchen. The sound of a struggle ensues.

OWNER: (*offstage*) And don't come back!

NEIL comes hurtling through the air towards MARGARET and lands in front of her.

MARGARET: You silly bugger. Are you hurt?

NEIL: My ears hurt and my pride's hurt. (*hollering towards the kitchen*) That's no way to treat a war hero!

MARGARET: (*helping him up*) Some hero.

NEIL: (*muttering*) One thing I thought a China-man would never have the nerve to do is criticize another man's music!

MARGARET: That's not music. That's what a cat sounds like when he gets his tail caught in the screen door.

NEIL: That's no way for a MacNeil to be talking.

MARGARET: Serves you right. Try standing up.

NEIL: If I wasn't drunk, I'd give you my pipes to hold and I'd go back in there and get the shit kicked out of me again.

MARGARET: Where do you live?

NEIL: I have a room down on Brookside.

MARGARET: Want me to walk you down?

NEIL: Where do you live?

MARGARET: Reserve.

NEIL: You live with your father and mother?

MARGARET: I live with my mother and grandfather. My father got killed in the pit. I gotta go. I need to get home before bingo. And my brother Ian, too.

NEIL: In a company house?

MARGARET: In a two-room shack my father built that you can't even turn around in. He said he had to work in the goddamn company mine but he didn't have to live in a goddamn company house with God only knows who in the next half.

NEIL: Your father was right.

MARGARET: My mom said he was too mean to pay the rent. But only when he wasn't around to hear it. Then he got killed.

NEIL: I'll see you home. Sober me up. Perhaps you could make us some tea.

MARGARET: Well, if you promise to keep that thing in the box.

MARGARET and NEIL exit.

SCENE 2

Lights up on the shack. IAN sits at the kitchen table reading the Glace Bay Gazette Steel Worker and Miner's News, *his boots and can (lunch box) in front of him. GRANDPA is playing darts, just missing CATHERINE as she walks by. CATHERINE is always straightening, always cleaning, obviously bothered by the presence of these two other beings in her space.*

CATHERINE: Where is that girl? Probably in a fight with somebody. I asked her to get me some thread and buttons. Where in the hell is she? Move your boots. Move your can. I'm trying to make tea for your grandpa before I get out of here.

IAN moves his boots but not his can.

CATHERINE: And move that, too! Why doesn't your grand and glorious union get you lockers to put all your stuff in?

IAN: We have more important things to think about.

CATHERINE: Is that so?

GRANDPA scribbles something in his notebook, bangs his slipper on the table, and shoves the notebook out into the air to no one in particular.

CATHERINE: See what your grandfather wants.

IAN gets up, takes the scribbler and reads.

IAN: "Where is my tea?"

CATHERINE: Don't get your shirt in a knot. I'm doing my best. Your father told me he'd build me a pantry but he never got around to it. "Too busy talking to the demerara." And Charlie Dave would've done it, but before he could put his mind to it, Maggie June came along and had him building shelves in their own little square yard of space. So I never got my pantry. It would have been nice to have it in time for the wake. I remember every woman there trying to cram in here to see what my kitchen looked like. It was their big chance to finally get a look at one of the shacks. Straining like a bunch of piglets to get past their men and into my kitchen to see what I could possibly have in here. But I held my head high. It was clean. It served the purpose. The wife of the mine manager, Mrs. MacDougall herself, said you should have had it at the hall dear, as if to say, to spare you the embarrassment – but I wasn't embarrassed. I shot right back at her: "It does the job. It was good enough for him to live in and it's good enough for him to be dead in."

GRANDPA waves his scribbler about.

CATHERINE: What now?

IAN takes the notebook and reads.

IAN: "Did you pay the light bill?"

CATHERINE: Yes, I paid it. I took my little pot of gold down to the office and paid it. And then their men ... I'm convinced not one of them went to the toilet before he came. They had to use the outhouses of all our neighbours. They said they didn't mind, but those that didn't have them sitting over old bootleg pits were worried they were going to get overfull. The honey man must have had quite the week of work after that wake.

GRANDPA writes something else and hands it to IAN.

IAN: (*reading*) "Then turn on some lights."

CATHERINE turns on a light.

CATHERINE: Is there anything else I can do for Your Highness?

GRANDPA scribbles something and hands it to IAN.

IAN: "Your dress is ripped under the arm."

CATHERINE: Well! Thank you for telling me. I'm waiting for Margaret to bring me some thread so I can fix it. Where is she? I'm going to miss the first card.

IAN: She probably went into the movie to get out of the rain.

CATHERINE: Well, why don't you go see if you can find her?

IAN: And what if I do? She won't come home with me. Probably make a big scene in the movie theatre. I don't need that.

CATHERINE: He doesn't need that. I'll fix it when I can.

GRANDPA hands CATHERINE his notebook. She reads.

CATHERINE: (*reading*) "You don't have to holler at me. I'm not deaf." I know you're not deaf. (*throwing up her hands in exasperation*) How do I live in this place with the lot of you – him scribbling at me, her sliding around out there like a stray cat. And then there's you ... with your head screwed on backward.

IAN: What do you mean?

CATHERINE: I cleaned the MacDougall's house yesterday. Minnie was sick so I did it for her as well as my own. Well, it's quite the place. Were you ever in it? I bet the kitchen's as big as your union hall. With an electric stove and an electric fridge and an electric toaster and an electric clock humming away – everything hums. And shiny. Everything is so shiny. How in God's name can you keep anything shiny?

IAN: It's upwind from the pit.

CATHERINE: I guess so. Everything matches everything else. The kitchen curtains are made of the same material as the oven mitts and the tea cozy. And while I was taking all of that in, in walked your heartthrob Peggy and, wouldn't you know,

she was wearing a dress of the same stuff. What do you make of it?

IAN: I don't know. Maybe they got a big bolt of the stuff from the co-op.

CATHERINE: That stuff didn't come from any co-op store. The colours are too bright. Minnie says it came from Montreal and that it costs a fortune.

IAN: (*getting up*) I gotta go, Mom.

CATHERINE: And do you think you would be able to afford the likes of that for Her Highness Peggy with what you make in the pit? Well, you can't. Even if your union gets the raise – which it won't.

IAN: We'll get the raise.

CATHERINE: Even so, it wouldn't be enough to buy what she's got.

IAN: (*irritated*) For the love of Jesus, who's talking about buying bolts of cloth?

CATHERINE: Who's taking out the mine manager's daughter?

IAN: I walked her home from the dance. That's all.

CATHERINE: You were down at Dominion Beach with her all day Saturday. Margaret told me.

IAN: Margaret's a snitch.

CATHERINE: You're either taking out the manager's daughter or you're thick with the union. You're either one or the other. Where is your head?

MARGARET and NEIL enter, soaking wet. CATHERINE is visibly impressed with NEIL's size and stature.

CATHERINE: (*sarcastic*) Well, thank you for coming!

MARGARET: I'm not late. It's only two minutes to eight.

CATHERINE: You got my thread?

MARGARET: Oh God! I knew I forgot something!

CATHERINE: What did I expect?

MARGARET: I'm sorry.

CATHERINE: Well, sure you're sorry. And who have you dragged in from the rain?

MARGARET: This is Neil, Neil Currie.

NEIL: How do you do?

CATHERINE: Where'd you find him?

MARGARET: In the Bay.

CATHERINE: He looks a bit rough.

MARGARET: He got in a fight. I'm gonna clean him up.

CATHERINE: You from the Bay?

NEIL: No, I just came.

CATHERINE: Where from?

NEIL: St. Andrew's Channel.

CATHERINE: Never heard of it. You working in the pit? You look like you could use a shovel.

NEIL: I was. I started but they fired me.

IAN: Why'd they fire you?

NEIL: Well, I wouldn't talk English to the foreman.

CATHERINE: You an Eyetalian?

NEIL: No, I was using the Gaelic. Like our ancestors.

IAN: I heard about that.

NEIL: What did you hear?

IAN: Just yesterday, up at No. 10. I heard there was a guy down in Lingan bellowing at the top of his lungs. The word was he'd snapped ...

NEIL: I was the sanest one there.

IAN: (*studying him*) Well, I don't imagine you need to talk English to dig coal. If that's all it was about, I'll bring it up at the union meeting tonight.

NEIL: Don't bother. I was going to quit anyway.

IAN: How come?

NEIL: I got no use for it.

IAN: Is that so?

NEIL: That's so. Burrowing underground is a good job for worms.

IAN: Is that so?

NEIL: And unions just trick poor suckers into thinking they got some say in things.

IAN: Then why'd you bother going down to begin with?

NEIL: Why'd you take your first drink? All your buddies were doing it. And I needed the money. I just got back from overseas.

CATHERINE: (*new respect*) You're a vet.

NEIL: That's right.

CATHERINE: Well, it's a bloody disgrace. We sent you off to fight for a new world, a new heaven, a new earth, and you're back and your choice is the pit or relief.

NEIL: I won't take relief.

CATHERINE: Get this man some tea, Margie. And get him a pair of your father's pants.

MARGARET: You might as well keep them. They don't fit anyone else around here.

CATHERINE: Well, I'm going to bingo. Come on, Ian, or you'll be late for your meeting.

CATHERINE gestures towards GRANDPA who has fallen asleep.

CATHERINE: Don't forget your ancestor over there, Margie. I hit him about an hour ago.

MARGARET: Okay, Mom. Hope you win it.

CATHERINE: Me too.

CATHERINE and IAN leave. MARGARET gets a wet cloth and starts wiping NEIL's face.

NEIL: Ouch!

MARGARET: Serves you right.

NEIL tries to pull her close to him. She pulls away.

MARGARET: If you kept your hands to yourself, you wouldn't get in so much trouble.

NEIL: I know that. Wouldn't have as much fun either.

NEIL looks over at the sleeping GRANDPA.

NEIL: What's the matter with him? Why do you have to thump him?

MARGARET: He's got something wrong with his lungs. Every hour or two he can't breathe and we have to pound him on the chest.

NEIL picks up one of GRANDPA's scribblers from the table and opens it.

NEIL: (*reading*) "Thump my chest. Dinner. Beer. Water. Piss-pot. Ask the priest to come. Time to go now, Father. I have to get me thump. No, Ian'll do it."

MARGARET: He doesn't talk. He used to talk but it hurt him to talk after he came home from the hospital with his lung problem so he just quit doing it. I don't know if it got better or not because he never tried again; same as he quit walking after he got out of breath once from it. He took to writing notes. I gotta go change my clothes.

MARGARET exits. Lights up on the tiny room next to the kitchen, which MARGARET shares with her mother. She goes to the mirror, slaps on some of her mother's powder and lipstick, drags a brush through her hair

NEIL: So does the poor old fellow just sit here all day?

MARGARET: No, he chases the girls down on Dominion Beach. Of course he just sits there!

NEIL: Does he ever go out?

MARGARET: No. He hates sun. That's why the curtains are closed. After working in the pit so long, it hurt his eyes. He mostly just sleeps like the old tomcat.

NEIL: (*softly, looking at the sleeping old man*) No wonder. Look at this place.

NEIL goes and opens up the windows. Light pours in. GRANDPA snorts, then goes back to sleep.

NEIL: Well, old man, I guess you're it, eh? This is where we got to.

MARGARET: (*calling out*) What are you talking about?

NEIL: Oh nothing. I'm just talking to myself.

NEIL looks closely at GRANDPA's scribblers.

NEIL: Do you know that under all his scribbles are ... it looks like someone's written a diary ... some of it's in Gaelic. Looks like he's just written right over them.

MARGARET: (*calling out*) That's probably what he did. They must have been his mother's. When he stopped talking, he probably just hauled them out.

NEIL: I wouldn't mind reading them sometime.

MARGARET: (*calling out*) Help yourself. We use them for hot plates and for fly swatters.

NEIL opens his bagpipe case and starts assembling his bagpipes. MARGARET yanks off her dress and begins digging around in a drawer for something prettier. She picks out a dress, shakes out the wrinkles. NEIL begins to play. GRANDPA startles and starts to wake. MARGARET, with her dress half on, comes running out.

MARGARET: Are you out of your brain? I told you to leave that thing in the box.

She sticks her fingers over the bagpipe holes.

NEIL: What are you doing?

MARGARET: I'm plugging up the holes. You're making too much noise.

NEIL: Your dress is falling off.

MARGARET, embarrassed, finishes doing up her dress. She notices that GRANDPA is awake. His breathing is heavy, laboured.

MARGARET: You woke him up!

NEIL: So? It's time everybody woke up!

MARGARET goes over to GRANDPA and rearranges his blanket.

MARGARET: Grandpa? You all right? Want your thump?

GRANDPA shakes his head and scribbles in the notebook.

NEIL: What does he want?

MARGARET: Probably wants you to clear right out.

MARGARET looks at the notebook.

MARGARET: Well, Christ in harness!

NEIL: What did he write?

MARGARET: (*reading*) "Tell him to play some more."

NEIL laughs, goes over to GRANDPA, and bows.

NEIL: I would be honoured to, sir.

NEIL plays a short, happy tune. GRANDPA's head bobs along with it.

NEIL: So what does that sound like?

MARGARET: Two happy hens fighting over a bean.

NEIL: (*to GRANDPA*) Do you like that?

GRANDPA nods.

NEIL: Do you know that tune?

GRANDPA hesitates, then nods again.

NEIL: I thought you would.

NEIL starts to play again, this time a gentle soothing tune. GRANDPA slowly falls asleep again. MARGARET relaxes in a chair against the wall, her toes tapping. She closes her eyes, her body relaxing, her knees falling open. NEIL stops playing, comes over, leans down, and kisses her. MARGARET puts her two feet up on his chest and tries to push him away but nothing happens. They remain there, his chest against her feet, NEIL looking up her leg.

NEIL: Did you know you got a hole in your underwear?

MARGARET: Frig off.

NEIL: What's the matter with you?

MARGARET: With me? Just because you play that thing doesn't mean you can jump me.

NEIL: Well, why not? You looked like you were ready.

NEIL runs his hand down MARGARET's leg. MARGARET jumps up and away from him.

MARGARET: Frig off!

NEIL: Fair enough. I won't jump you 'til we're married.

MARGARET: Married? Who'd marry you? You're nothing but a goddamn Currie.

NEIL: (*laughs*) And why wouldn't you marry a goddamn Currie?

MARGARET: Because they come into your house, play a few snarls on their pipes, and they think you'll marry them for that.

NEIL: I'll tell you what. I'll play for you every night until you think you're ready. I'll even make you a song of your own.

MARGARET: What kind of song?

NEIL: I don't know. We'll wait and see what I can make. I got to know more about you first.

MARGARET: I want a song a person can understand so I'll be sure what it's saying.

NEIL: Fair enough. I'll make you two. One to sing and one to guess at. What would you like for the singing one?

MARGARET: How should I know?

NEIL: Well, what's the happiest thing in your life or the saddest?

MARGARET: They're both the same. My brother. Not the one living here now. He's just someone to put up with along with everything else. I mean my older brother, Charlie Dave.

NEIL: What do you like about him?

MARGARET: He used to fight for me, wouldn't let anybody call me names. He could clean anybody's clock in Reserve.

NEIL: Where's he now?

MARGARET: He got killed in the pit with my father.

NEIL: How old was he?

MARGARET: Sixteen.

NEIL: Jesus! He couldn't have been in the pit very long.

MARGARET: Not even a year. He started working with my grandfather just before he quit for his lungs. Then he started with my father. Then he got killed.

NEIL: Tell me more about him.

MARGARET: Why should I?

NEIL: 'Cause I'm gonna write a song about him.

MARGARET: He was good in school but he got married so he had to go to work. They didn't even have the chance to have their baby.

NEIL: What happened to his wife?

MARGARET: What do you think happened to her? Nothing! She had the baby. A sweet baby. He's eight now. They live up in the Rows. In a company house. With her mother and her sister. (*her voice breaking with emotion*) Now look what you've made me do. It's time for you to clear out. I'm tired of your questions and your racket. (*blowing her nose*) My mother knew it was going to happen.

NEIL: How did she know?

MARGARET: Women know! They just know. Now pack up your sticks and leave.

NEIL: Okay, I'll go. But I'll be back again and I'll play to you every night 'til you're ready.

MARGARET: I won't hold my breath.

> *NEIL kisses MARGARET lightly on the lips. Then leaves.*

MARGARET: (*to audience*) But I did hold my breath and I near died of happiness!

SCENE 3

> *The next morning. Dawn. A rooster calls. The sound of bagpipes begins in the distance, coming closer. CATHERINE and MARGARET are asleep in the bedroom. IAN is in a bedroom offstage. GRANDPA is asleep in his chair. They all begin to stir.*

CATHERINE: What in hell ...

> *IAN comes stumbling out of his room.*

IAN: (*semi-asleep*) What's happening? Has the roof caved in?

> *CATHERINE gets up and opens the curtain. First light shines in.*

CATHERINE: For the love of God. Will you look at that?

> *IAN grabs his pants.*

IAN: What is it? What time is it? (*joining her at the window*) Jesus Christ!

CATHERINE: Even the chickens are diving for cover. And he's got a string of kids running after him like he was the Pied Piper.

MARGARET: And he's heading this way!

CATHERINE: He must be nuts.

IAN: Well, he's not coming in here at this hour or any hour.

MARGARET: And who are you to say?

IAN: I pay the bills here.

MARGARET: Oh yeah? Big deal, big talk, big head. You don't pay all the bills.

IAN: That's right – you two pay for the tea.

CATHERINE: Will you listen to that thing? He's making enough noise to raise the dead. I haven't heard those things since … (*turning, she looks around*) Will you look at this place!

GRANDPA starts to bang his slipper in excitement. CATHERINE starts straightening things.

IAN: What's the matter with it?

MARGARET: Where's my hairbrush?

IAN: Why do you want your hairbrush?

MARGARET: You never know. (*jokingly*) He might ask me to get married.

IAN: (*snorts derisively*) Why would he want to marry a dog?

MARGARET: Well, I'd rather be a dog than a dog's arsehole, which is what you are.

CATHERINE: Stop it you two.

MARGARET: Where is my hairbrush?

IAN: A total stranger arrives at six in the morning playing the bagpipes and you're all …

GRANDPA bangs his slipper and points in the direction of her hairbrush. MARGARET goes over and kisses him, and grabs her hairbrush. IAN sees the excitement in his grandfather's eyes.

IAN: Oh for the love of God. You'd think the Messiah himself was about to arrive.

The sound of the bagpipes arrives at the door, then stops. There's a knock. They all stand looking at it.

MARGARET: He's here.

CATHERINE: Well, open it.

MARGARET opens it.

MARGARET: Hello.

NEIL: Good morning, Margaret. I've come for a visit.

NEIL pulls a bouquet of flowers from his pack and hands them to CATHERINE.

NEIL: Some flowers for you, Mrs. MacNeil.

CATHERINE takes the flowers, speechless.

NEIL: You look lovely this morning, Margaret.

MARGARET: Thank you.

NEIL: And good morning to you too, Ian.

Then NEIL takes off his cap to GRANDPA and shakes his hand.

NEIL: And to you, sir. A good morning.

GRANDPA waves his scribbler about eagerly.

NEIL: (*reading*) "Do you know 'Guma slan to na ferriv chy harish achun'?" Yes, I do, and I'll be glad to play that for you … if you'll pay me back with a story.

GRANDPA hesitates, then nods.

IAN: So what do your parents do up there in that place … St. Andrew's Channel?

NEIL: They're farmers.

IAN: Is that so? What kind of farm?

NEIL: They grow vegetables. They raise cattle.

MARGARET: Sounds like something you'd like, Ian. You're so fond of animals. He's been dragging poor animals home since he was this high. The weirder, the better. Salamanders, turtles, snakes, bugs. I came in once and caught him kissing a mouse. Charlie Dave was out playing hockey and he was in here kissing mice.

IAN: Oh, stop your yapping.

MARGARET: Mr. Kiss-a-Mouse.

IAN: Yap, yap, yap!

MARGARET: The next time I see Peggy, I'm going to tell her you like kissing mice, too.

CATHERINE: Tea, Margaret, tea!

IAN: So why didn't you go back there when the war ended?

NEIL: I wanted to but there wasn't any land left. I had seven brothers and two sisters.

IAN: The boys all farmers?

NEIL: Nope. One of them's a teacher. One of them's a doctor.

IAN: A doctor?

IAN would have loved to have been a doctor.

NEIL: Three of us were mucking about in the war.

IAN: Three of you fought in the war?

NEIL: Two of us didn't come back.

MARGARET: Jesus!

CATHERINE: Your poor mother. War is worse than the mines.

MARGARET: The war'd be over before Ian ever got to it. He's got to know everything first.

CATHERINE: Stop it, Margie.

MARGARET: And he's not a fighter anyways.

IAN: Would you shut your mouth?

MARGARET: Charlie Dave jumped at the chance of a fight. He woulda been there in a second if he could.

CATHERINE: Oh for the love of God.

MARGARET: Charlie Dave loved it when someone stole my mitts. Then he'd wade in and beat the shit right out of them. But not our Ian. He's a mouse-kissing mama's boy.

IAN: And you're a snot-nosed whore!

NEIL: Wait a minute! You can't call her that!

IAN: And you can get out of my house!

IAN's and NEIL's fists go up, and they start circling each other.

CATHERINE: Now look what you've done.

MARGARET: Isn't it exciting?

CATHERINE: You nitwit.

MARGARET: Come on, Mom. When was the last excitement we had around here?

CATHERINE: I guess the wake.

GRANDPA bangs his shoe on the table and shoves a notebook at MARGARET.

MARGARET: What?

She reads, then grudgingly steps between IAN and NEIL.

MARGARET: Grandpa's got a story for you.

GRANDPA bangs his slipper again.

MARGARET: (reluctantly) Do you want to hear it?

NEIL: Yes, I do.

MARGARET: There was this fellow worked in the pit named Spider MacDougall who only wanted to do two things in life – work in the pit and snare rabbits. Until one day, Madeline Boyd caught up with him on his trapline and taught him how to do something else. After they'd done it, he told her that he'd never heard of it before except with rabbits and dogs. They had fifteen kids after that.

NEIL: What happened to him?

MARGARET: Spider got so sick of the pit he went funny one night and burned down the company store. They threw him in jail, where he died.

NEIL: That's a sad story.

MARGARET: That's a true story.

NEIL puts down his fists. He nods to GRANDPA.

NEIL: Thank you. (turning to IAN) Look, I don't want to fight either, Ian. Not with you. You seem like a smart fella. You obviously think a lot. I just want to visit here. I want to hear your grandfather's stories. I want to read his scribblers. Let's not use our fists on each other. It's a waste of energy. Is it a deal?

IAN: (putting down his fists) It's a deal.

NEIL: D'you play cards?

IAN: Yeah.

NEIL: Do you drink rum?

IAN: Sure.

NEIL pulls out a flask and passes it to IAN.

IAN: It's only six o'clock.

NEIL: D'you care?

IAN: No.

They clear the table, sit down, and start playing cards.

MARGARET: (to audience) Then after that, he came back and came back and came back and there was nothing but noise. My mother took to going out every night as soon as she saw the sight of his hat coming over the hill. He'd play songs and I'd tell stories from Grandpa, and if Ian was around, I'd razz him about Peggy, and Ian and Neil would argue the leg off an iron pot, then we'd walk Ian to the pit, then go over to the wharf and watch the seagulls swooping and screeching like little airplanes. That was what I liked. The water. The sound of the waves. Neil would laugh and say to me, "There's hope for you yet."

Sounds of the sea.

NEIL: Why are you so hard on your brother?

MARGARET: Dunno. 'Cause he just stands there and takes it. It's none of your business.

NEIL: And why does your mom play bingo all the time?

MARGARET: I guess she likes it, eh? Why do you drink rum all the time?

NEIL: (*laughs*) I guess I like it, eh? How do women know that their men are going to die?

MARGARET: Jesus! Will you ease up? We've come to enjoy the evening.

NEIL: You're right. Let's just skip rocks and smell the fishy air.

MARGARET: The dogs were howling three nights in a row at the full moon. Those goddamn dogs, once one starts, they all start. That was the first thing that tipped her off.

NEIL: (*scornful*) She knew because of the dogs barking?

MARGARET: That's not all. It was in the cards ...

NEIL: (*snorts derisively*) In the cards?

MARGARET: I was up at the underground manager's house helping Mom with the housework the night it happened, and I had a game of Auction Forty-Five with the girls – me and Mary against Morag and Peggy.

NEIL: (*sarcastic*) And you saw it in the cards!

MARGARET: I didn't see it right away. First, I thought I was lucky. All them shovels. The five, the king, the queen, the jack, and the ten of spades, but then I remembered what my mother always said.

NEIL: What was that?

MARGARET: Spades mean death. Shovels dig the hole. The only thing can save you is a heart. A heart can block four shovels. Only heart's desire can conquer, even death. I needed the ace of hearts. So I threw in my ten and dealt myself the card off the top – I couldn't believe my eyes.

NEIL: What?

MARGARET: It was the ace of spades. And then the sirens started to wail.

NEIL: Oh come on!

MARGARET: It was in the cards!

NEIL: That's just a bunch of malarkey!

MARGARET: Then why are your eyes popping out like a scared rabbit's?

NEIL: Let's not talk about it anymore.

MARGARET: (*miffed*) Fine. We'll just lie down here in the grass and look at the stars.

They lie silently for a while.

MARGARET: What was it like over there in France?

NEIL: Lots of pretty girls. Lots of cheap wine. I had the time of my life.

MARGARET: How come you went berserk that day down in the shaft?

NEIL: (*sitting up*) I don't want to talk about that.

MARGARET: What about your brothers who didn't make it back? Were you together?

NEIL: Yeah. One minute they were smelling the air beside me and the next minute they weren't. I don't want to talk about that either.

MARGARET: (*after a pause*) My mother even told him not to go down that day. It was the last day of work before vacation. She told him, if he spent that day in the garden and the next two weeks in the garden, instead of that day in the pit and the next two weeks drinking, then he'd have more money at the end of it, and vegetables to boot. And not rum sick at the end of it, if not dead.

NEIL: Sounds like a man after my own heart.

MARGARET: I could hear the tears coming up in her throat. "If you don't go to the pit today, you won't get kilt in it, and I'll buy you the moonshine myself." That's what she said. "I'd rather have you dead drunk than dead." And he just stood there beside Charlie Dave. He'd come to pick him up. Just stood there with his lunch can under his arm and a smirk on his face. And he said, "You're my sweet little gyroch."

NEIL: (*laughs*) His sweet little pain in the ass.

MARGARET: Is that what that means? She thought it was a pet name.

NEIL: It is in a way. It's like a cow that gives a whole bucketful of beautiful creamy milk morning and night, but every time with the last spurt, she puts her shitty hoof in it. What happened then?

MARGARET: Then the two of them pursed their lips and lifted their hands like in a little wave ... and they went out the door, and out the world altogether.

NEIL: Go on.

MARGARET: What do you mean, go on. They are dead! D-E-A-D! Dead. There isn't anymore. She changed after that. All she does now is talk about the wake and go to bingo. I hate talking about the dead.

NEIL: Then why do you do it all the time?

MARGARET: Because you keep asking me! Why do you want to know all of this?

NEIL: 'Cause I'm going to marry you. I'm going to be part of the family.

MARGARET: That'll be the day! I'll be living in that shack with my mom 'til the end of time!

NEIL: You'll be living with me.

MARGARET: Don't talk nonsense.

NEIL starts kissing her neck.

NEIL: All right. We won't talk at all.

NEIL pushes MARGARET down on the grass and they start necking.

SCENE 4

The shack. GRANDPA is slumped over, spluttering and gasping for air. CATHERINE rushes into the room.

CATHERINE: Omigod!

CATHERINE pulls GRANDPA upright and positions herself so she can give him a sound thump on the chest.

CATHERINE: Christ in harness. That was a close one.

GRANDPA's breathing begins to return to normal. CATHERINE rubs his back.

CATHERINE: I was just at the head of the road looking for her. It's way past midnight! How are you now? Is that better?

GRANDPA nods.

CATHERINE: Good. (*walking to the window and looking out*) What am I going to do with that girl? She's crazy for him. Mr. Neil Currie. He's a bit too sure of himself but he's got a fresh way about him and he's gentler then most of the scrappers she knocks about with. But she's so … unprotected. What's going to become of her? She's got about as much sense as a turnip.

GRANDPA hands her a scribbler. CATHERINE smiles and reads.

CATHERINE: "And you had more?"

CATHERINE picks up a dishtowel and swats his shoulder.

SCENE 5

Outside the shack. NEIL is reading the diaries. MARGARET is around and about. CATHERINE walks out carrying a basket of laundry.

NEIL: Listen to this. "1745, hardly half of them left alive. Nineteen hundred ten and four, half in the pit and half in the war." Your great-grandmother Morag MacNeil was a bit of a poet.

CATHERINE: She was a snarly old woman who never liked anybody, especially me.

NEIL: And why was that?

CATHERINE: 'Cause I snatched her favourite grandson out from under her nose. She used to sit in the window of her house spying on my every move.

NEIL: It says here, "Catherine Chisholm …" (*looking up*) I guess that was you, eh? "Catherine Chisholm was the liveliest, spunkiest creature to ever grace our house. She was like May after March. She was a jewel of a girl for our Angus."

CATHERINE: (*astounded*) Where does it say that?

NEIL: Right here.

CATHERINE: Let me see that!

CATHERINE takes the scribbler, looks.

CATHERINE: Well, I'll be damned. (*reading*) "A jewel of a girl for our Angus." Well, I'll be damned! Who would have thought? (*reading*) "That lively lass was out there any minute she could grab, riding around on her bike, playing Peggy with those three dear children …"

Peggy is a stickball game played by people of French and Scottish descent in Eastern Canada.

MARGARET: I remember that. You used to be a lot of fun.

CATHERINE: Well, I was hardly more than a kid myself. I wasn't about to sit around in the house all day listening to the old women. I hated being cooped up inside. So when did she write that?

NEIL: (*reading*) "July 8, 1931. Sunny."

MARGARET: Ian couldn't hold the bat without smacking someone.

CATHERINE: Sports was not one of Ian's strengths. Isn't that incredible? And all those years, I thought that she thought … (*shaking her head*) Well, I'd better get going or I'll miss my bingo.

NEIL: I thought you hated being cooped up inside.

CATHERINE: I do.

NEIL: Then why are you going off to sit in a smoky bingo hall? Why don't we have a game?

CATHERINE: Of what?

NEIL: Peggy.

CATHERINE: I'm too old for that.

NEIL: That "lively lass," "that spunky creature."

CATHERINE: That was nearly twenty years ago. I'm an old bag now.

NEIL: Tell that to the men downtown on Water Street. Don't tell me you don't catch them looking at you.

CATHERINE: Well, they're all blind and half-dead. They got pretty low standards.

NEIL: I bet Morag must have liked your sense of humour, too.

CATHERINE: I'm too old to play Peggy.

NEIL: No, you're not.

MARGARET: C'mon, Mom.

CATHERINE: I don't play games.

NEIL: (to MARGARET) Go get your brother.

CATHERINE: This is foolish!

> NEIL marks out a circle in the dirt with his boot. MARGARET goes into the shack and interrupts IAN, who is reading the newspaper.

IAN: What? What do you want?

MARGARET: We're going to play a game, egghead. C'mon.

IAN: What do you mean? A game?

MARGARET: A game. We're going to have some fun.

IAN: Jesus.

> GRANDPA grabs IAN's sleeve as he walks by.

MARGARET: He wants to come. (calling out to NEIL) We need help with Grandpa.

> NEIL comes in.

IAN: What's going on?

NEIL: We're going to play a game of Peggy. (to GRANDPA) You can be the cheering section.

MARGARET: Some cheering section.

> NEIL and IAN carry GRANDPA in his chair and put him down outside. NEIL pulls a picket from the fence.

MARGARET: Give it to me, I'll start. Pitch it to me.

IAN: I don't want to play.

MARGARET: You're pitiful, Ian.

IAN: Oh, give me the goddamn thing.

> IAN pitches it. MARGARET bats it. IAN tries to catch it and misses.

MARGARET: Butterfingers.

IAN: Snot nose.

CATHERINE: Stop it, you two.

MARGARET: Hope you know how to hold your own Peggy better than that.

CATHERINE: (trying to stifle a laugh) You stop that. It's none of your business, Margie. My turn.

> CATHERINE gets up to bat and she blossoms. The years fall away. She hits it. GRANDPA claps, maybe even whistles.

CATHERINE: I hit it! I hit it!

NEIL: Jeez, you are good!

MARGARET: Way to go, Mom!

NEIL: It's your turn now, Ian.

IAN: I don't wanna play this.

CATHERINE: Come on. Take a shot.

> Reluctantly, IAN takes the picket.

MARGARET: This'll be a laugh.

NEIL: Let him concentrate.

MARGARET: Look at him. Pitiful. He can't fight. He can't sing. He can't hardly even hold a picket!

IAN: Trap up.

MARGARET: Charlie Dave used to hit it clear over the outhouse.

> IAN is getting more agitated.

MARGARET: What in the name of God does Peggy MacDougall see in you?

NEIL: Maybe she likes him for who he is and not for who he is not.

MARGARET: Well, I guess that makes some sense, but what the hell does it mean?

NEIL: It means that it's not his fault that he's alive and someone else is dead.

> NEIL pitches the Peggy to IAN. He hits it. MARGARET tries to catch it but fumbles it.

IAN: (surprised) I hit it!

MARGARET: Well, so you did. (a new recognition here) Good shot, Ian.

SCENE 6

> A half-hour later. IAN and NEIL carry GRANDPA back into the shack. CATHERINE sinks into her chair, exhausted.

CATHERINE: I'll pay for this in the morning.

NEIL: It'll be worth it.

CATHERINE: I'm going to bed.

MARGARET: Don't go yet. Stay and have a hot one.

CATHERINE: Just a little one. Might do some good.

MARGARET gets up and pours some rum and hot water into a cup for her mother. GRANDPA bangs his slipper and hands her a notebook on the way by.

MARGARET: (*reading*) "Tell him about George Stepenak and Fergus MacLeod."

NEIL: Let's hear it.

MARGARET: Do you think you could handle that, Ian? You worked with those guys.

IAN: Oh, that was years ago …

MARGARET: So?

IAN: Well, I don't remember.

MARGARET: Well, Grandpa wants Neil to hear it.

IAN: Well, God, let me see … all right. There was this fella named George Stepenak, and he was a Pole as you can tell by the name. I'm no good at telling stories.

NEIL: Go on.

IAN: Okay, so, he used to bring garlic in his can, and his can would stink and his breath would stink.

NEIL: Go on.

IAN: So, the men used to tease him all the time, which made him cross, and then one day Fergus said, "George, what in the name of Jesus have you got in that can?" "Shit," George said. And then I hear Fergus say, "I know that, but what did you put on it to make it smell so bad."

They all laugh. IAN is surprised and pleased with himself.

MARGARET: (*turning to CATHERINE*) Why don't you tell us about when you met Dad.

CATHERINE: That's ancient history. No one wants to hear that.

GRANDPA bangs his slipper on the table and nods his head.

NEIL: You're wrong, Catherine.

CATHERINE: Well, it was kind of … well, I was … and he was … well, it's not really very …

IAN: Well, spit it out!

CATHERINE: (*finally diving in*) I met your father at the wake of Minnie's Uncle Joe Archie in the Bay. I was sneaking a smoke behind the outhouse. Your father knew I was there. He was two sheets to the wind, showing off for me, playing horseshoes, and when the priest came up to tell him to stop, he said, "I'll stop playing horseshoes if you'll stop squeezing the girls as they go by Joe Archie to pay their last respects. That probably offends him more than what I'm doing!" And when we were married two weeks later, you can bet it wasn't that priest who tied the knot. We were in too much of a hurry for priests anyway. We went to a Justice of the Peace in Sydney. Can you imagine it? Nobody ever did the likes of that. When we came out of his office after the ceremony, there was a parade going by with a band of pipers. That was the last time I heard the bagpipes played – 'til now. When we got home, somebody told Angus the priest was going to excommunicate him for what he'd done. And you know what Angus did? He marched right down to the glebe house and when the Father opened the door, Angus said, "You're too late. I excommunicated myself last week." And he did. Never went back there 'til the funeral. (*holding up her glass*) Cheers, Angus. I think I'll have another one of those hot ones. (*laughs*)

NEIL: You've got a beautiful laugh, Catherine MacNeil.

NEIL begins to play a reel on his bagpipes.

MARGARET: (*to audience*) It was like the whole family was coming out of hibernation after a long sleep. The music was sweetening us up and firing us up. The rum would come out and the cards would come out and every Sunday afternoon we'd take the world apart and put it back together. Or fall over trying!

IAN clears the table and brings out a deck of cards. The flask of rum comes out.

IAN: The only hope, Neil-Know-It-All-Currie, for the miners in Cape Breton is to get a strong union.

NEIL: Bullshit!

IAN: If my father and brother had a strong union, they wouldn't have died in that death trap.

NEIL: Your father and brother should have stayed on the surface of the world to begin with.

IAN: Well, they didn't and it's too late for that talk and it's STILL a death trap 'cause the company doesn't think they have to pay any attention to us. We need a strong union to fight against those bullies.

NEIL: Good men don't burrow in the ground like worms!

IAN: That's what men here do. Good men!

NEIL: Good men till the earth.

IAN: Women have gardens here. Lots of women have gardens.

NEIL: Good men stand tall. They're king of their own hills. They don't crawl around tunnels for a company or a country that doesn't give a damn about them.

IAN: You're full of shit.

CATHERINE: You're both full of shit. The last man who had any sense left here thirty years ago and went to Boston, and he's at least got buckles on his shoes.

NEIL: The pit is death.

IAN: Why do you say that? Look at me. I'm not dead.

NEIL: I could feel it in my bones, the one time I went down there. It was the wrong place to be. I felt the same thing when I had my nose in the dirt staring through the sights of a gun over there in France. I saw death there and that's the truth.

IAN: You got your head up your arse and you're facing backward and that's the truth.

NEIL: There is no future down there.

IAN: There has to be a future.

NEIL: See your grandfather? That's the future.

IAN: Well, he's there, isn't he? Don't knock my grandfather.

NEIL: I'm not knocking your grandfather. I love your grandfather. But he can't breathe, he can't talk, he can't walk. You know the only thing he's got? Some old songs in his head that he can hardly remember, that your father hardly knew and you don't know at all. Came here and lost their tongues, their music, their songs. Everything but their shovels.

IAN: Too bad you wouldn't lose yours. (*throwing him the flask*) Have a drink and shut up.

NEIL: I will not shut up. However, I will have a drink.

IAN: The only way to be strong is to be organized. We have to be strong as they are and then they'll negotiate. Now, Neil, is that right or wrong?

NEIL: They'll send in the army.

IAN: Who?

NEIL: The government. They'll turn the boys against each other, the bastards. That's what they always do.

IAN: How do you know that's what they always do. You only been here two months.

NEIL: We've been here for a long, long time, John.

IAN: My name's not John.

NEIL: Well now, John is English for Ian. I thought you might like it better. A union leader maybe should have a good English name.

IAN: I don't think I need you to tell me my name. I can remember my own name.

NEIL: Well, what else do you remember, John? Do you remember 1745?

IAN: I guess nobody remembers 1745, eh?

NEIL: Go and read your grandfather's scribblers, John. He remembers. His blood was spilled there, on the ground, and our blood was spilled there, spilled on the ground. He remembers. (*opening up a scribbler and pounding on it*) Look at this! (*reading*) "1745, hardly half of them alive. Nineteen hundred ten and four, half in the pit, half in the war." Look, it's all there! Read it.

IAN: I don't have time to read ancient history. I'm working my ass off right here and now, and that is hellish hard enough.

NEIL: Well, if you don't have time to read it then go and put your ear on your grandpa's chest, and listen to his lungs singing, and maybe it will tickle your memory. (*to MARGARET*) And what do you think, little mouse?

MARGARET: (*taking the bottle from him*) I think that the square on the long side of a triangle is equal to the sum of the squares on the other two sides.

NEIL laughs with delight. MARGARET leaves the room. NEIL reaches over and retrieves the bottle.

NEIL: I don't think anybody could have put it any better. So why don't we just play cards and have another drink.

SCENE 7

Bedroom. CATHERINE is lying in bed. MARGARET enters. CATHERINE watches her brush her hair and undress.

CATHERINE: That man'll never live in a company house. You'll be moving out of one shack and into another.

MARGARET: I can stand it.

CATHERINE: You can stand it. You can stand it. And is he going to work? Maybe Ian can get him on up at No. 10. He can work with Ian. Is that what you want? He's a rebel. He's a troublemaker.

MARGARET: I can stand it.

CATHERINE: You'll end up in another place just like this 'cause he's the way he is. And you're going to be the one who suffers.

MARGARET: I can stand it, Mom.

CATHERINE: Oh you can, can you? They can die together, and you can stand it. And you can live in your shack alone. Stand it then.

MARGARET climbs into bed.

MARGARET: We're different.

CATHERINE: Sure.

MARGARET: I'm not you, Mom!

CATHERINE: Then who are you?

MARGARET: (*fiercely*) Well, I won't be you.

CATHERINE: You're young and stupid.

MARGARET: I'm glad of it.

CATHERINE: Don't ever say I didn't warn you.

MARGARET: I'll never say it!

CATHERINE: If you let love in, you'll get hurt. That's what happens.

MARGARET: You said a heart could block four shovels.

CATHERINE: I was wrong. The spades overtake the hearts, Margie. They always do. Think about it, Margie! I'm warning you.

MARGARET rolls over in bed, her back to her mother.

MARGARET: I'll think about it.

SCENE 8

Time passes. The men are into hard drinking.

NEIL: Nothing left. Nothing. Only thing you can do different from a pit pony is drink rum and play Forty-Five. 'Course you got your ...

IAN is embarrassed.

NEIL: Come on. I've seen you down there in the sand dunes necking with Peggy. Nothing to be ashamed of.

IAN: (*drunk*) You go to hell. Why don't you get the hell out of here and go to mass.

NEIL: I might just do that. I'd rather listen to the music than your drunken ramblings ... and pray for your soul at the same time.

IAN: My soul's all right. It's got a union card.

NEIL spits out his drink.

NEIL: And you think that'll protect you, you idiot.

IAN: I'll put more faith in it than your bloody bagpipes. You're nothing but a freak, Neil Currie. You're not a farmer, you're not a miner. You can't do nothing but make a whole lot of noise.

NEIL: Unless you know your history and your music, you don't know that the way things are is not necessarily the way things have to be.

IAN: That's why we need a union.

NEIL: That's why you need to know where ya came from. You got roots deeper that those pits; you weren't born into them, you were born to beautiful rolling fields. We were farmers and we were sailors ...

IAN: And you're a pain in the arse.

NEIL: You don't understand what I'm talking about.

IAN: And that's the God's truth for you, Neil. Now why don't you go on the couch and have a lay down.

NEIL stumbles to the couch and lies down.

NEIL: I have one final question for you, John.

IAN: What is it?

NEIL: Why were you kissing that mouse?

IAN: I wasn't kissing it. I was counting its teeth and that's the God's truth.

NEIL: That's a good story, John. You stick to it.

SCENE 9

NEIL is standing looking out at the ocean. The sound of seagulls screaming, wind, water. MARGARET joins him.

NEIL: I have your song for you, Mairead. The song about your brother. Would you like to hear it?

MARGARET: Is it in English? Will I understand it?

NEIL: I think so.

MARGARET: All right then. Sing it.

NEIL: (*singing*)

> My brother was a miner.
> His name was Charlie David,
> He spent his young life laughing,
> And digging out his grave.

Chorus:

Charlie Dave was big
Charlie Dave was strong,
Charlie Dave was two feet wide
And almost six feet long.

When Charlie David was sixteen
He learned to chew and spit,
And went one day with Grandpa
To work down in the pit.

> *Chorus*

When Charlie David was sixteen
He met his Maggie June,
One day shift week they met at eight
On back shift week at noon.

> *Chorus*

When Charlie David was sixteen
He said to June, "Let's wed."
Maggie June was so surprised
She fell right out of bed.

> *Chorus*

When Charlie David was sixteen
They had a little boy,
Maggie June was not surprised,
Charlie danced for joy.

> *Chorus*

When Charlie David was sixteen
The roof fell on his head.
His laughing mouth is full of coal,
Charlie Dave is dead.

> *Chorus*

Silence.

NEIL: Margaret?

MARGARET: (*sniffling*) It's lovely. It's almost as lovely as Charlie Dave himself.

NEIL: Good. Then it's settled. Let's lay him to rest. We've talked enough about death. Let's get on with our life.

MARGARET: All right.

NEIL: Do you like it here?

MARGARET: I love it. I could stay here forever.

NEIL: Then you will.

MARGARET: What?

NEIL: This land right here that we're standing on, I bought this yesterday with the pittance I got when I left the army. I'm going to build you a house, right here on the cliff, with the ocean boiling and spuming below. What do you think?

MARGARET: I think that I'm ready, Neil Currie!

> *NEIL lets out a shriek of happiness. He grabs her and twirls her around, then they kiss. Then he lets go of her and stamps his feet on the ground.*

NEIL: Right here, Margaret! We're going to make our stand right here!

> *The light changes on MARGARET. NEIL moves away and she is back in the present.*

MARGARET: Right here.

> *Blackout.*

ACT TWO

SCENE 1

> *MARGARET is standing in her house, among her artifacts. She holds up a handful of notebooks.*

MARGARET: (*reading*) "This won't be written great, for I am written it most in English for fear none will be able to read it in the Gallick, for I can see how things are going." These are my great-grandmother's scribblers. I finally found the time to read them … the ones I used for hot plates and fly swatters. Morag MacKinnon. Mabou born and raised. Left with her Donald and the fiddlers and the pipers and the dancers, any that could walk at all and sober. Took the music with them and went to take jobs in the mines. It sounds like she was an awful terror. One day, when she came into the kitchen, the men were drinking and talking about giving up the only land they had left so they could make more money in the mines. So she grabbed the bottle and poured it into the slop pail with the morning piss. And they just sat there like gawks watching as she slapped the whole thing down on the table, piss splashing all over: "If you want to make pigs of yourself, here's the clear thing for it." Guts I'd say that took. Delicious guts. Morag. My mother's father's mother. Always raging. I vowed if I could even be half as lively as her …

> *Lights up on the shack. NEIL is poring over a pile of scribblers. CATHERINE is stepping around him, cleaning. GRANDPA is napping. MARGARET walks in with*

a basket of vegetables from the garden and throws it all over the area that CATHERINE just cleared.

MARGARET: Turnips for dinner!

CATHERINE: I just wiped that!

MARGARET: Why'd you bother?

CATHERINE: Because I don't like living in a pigsty.

MARGARET: There are no pigs here, Mother. I wish there were. We could use a ham right now.

NEIL: (*holding up a notebook*) Read this, Margaret.

MARGARET: I don't have time. I've got to make dinner … for my husband!

CATHERINE: Why don't you take some of your husband's clutter into your husband's bedroom.

MARGARET: Sure!

NEIL: Then listen to this. (*reading*) "The silly arses, they think the job is like the land, that it just stays there. They're all too stunned to know that the job is like the music – it's like water in the woods. It's only there 'til it's gone. Show up one day for work and the washhouse door is locked." Now that's the truth. The truth lies there.

CATHERINE: Well, move it please, 'cause I want to set the table.

NEIL: Seventy years ago your great-grandmother knew that. And it's still the truth today.

CATHERINE: It may be the truth but it's the job that puts the food on the table, not that pitiful excuse for a garden out there, nor that pile of scribblers that you pore over all day.

NEIL: That's short thinking, Catherine.

CATHERINE: That's realistic thinking. Just one turnip each, Margie. Those have to stretch a long way now that we've got one more mouth to feed – and a large one at that!

MARGARET comes over and kisses NEIL.

MARGARET: There's more where that one came from.

NEIL: (*to CATHERINE*) Morag MacNeil had ten children living in a space not much bigger than this.

CATHERINE: And I should get comfort from that?

NEIL: Well, maybe encouragement and maybe even courage.

CATHERINE: Well, I don't.

MARGARET: Sit down, Mom, and take a load off your feet.

CATHERINE picks up the newspaper and scans the front page.

CATHERINE: There are no jobs on the entire island, it says here. Why put that in that paper? That's not news. We all know that. And I see we've just elected a CCFer to Parliament. A socialist. Where are our heads? (*throwing the paper aside*) The papers just put me in a foul mood.

MARGARET: Well, we don't want that.

CATHERINE takes a letter from her apron pocket.

CATHERINE: The time has finally come to read my letter from your father's second cousin Roddie in Boston. I've let it age a couple of months. I guess I might as well get to it. See if there's any pressing news.

CATHERINE opens the letter and reads.

CATHERINE: "Dear Catherine, Has it really been a year since last we corresponded?"

MARGARET: That's how he starts every letter.

CATHERINE: Thank heavens it has. (*reading*) "I trust you are all as well as can be expected." Given what he considers the pitiful state of our lives, but instead … "Given the uncertain nature of modern life."

MARGARET: What in God's earth is uncertain about putting buckles on patent-leather shoes all day?

CATHERINE: "And that you are managing as well as can be expected since your terrible loss."

MARGARET: Why doesn't he ever say their names?

CATHERINE: "We've been blessed with another good year." Here they come … all their biggers and brand-news. "We bought a brand-new car to replace our old one, which you may remember was the Ford Ambassador that we drove up to the funeral."

MARGARET: We crammed every kid in the village into it while he wasn't looking.

CATHERINE: I remember him turning up his nose at every car that came up the road. "Now how old is that 'ka' anyways?"

MARGARET: And old Sadie Gillis would answer with a smirk, "Oh well, she's old enough now, isn't she? She certainly isssss." That's the way the old Scotchy people talked.

CATHERINE: She sort of hissed like a tiny snake. (*reading on*) "This one has a bigger engine and a bigger wheelbase and a bigger glove compartment and a bigger steering wheel ..."

NEIL: Sounds to me like he wishes he had a bigger ...

MARGARET slaps him with a dishtowel. He grabs her, pulls her down.

CATHERINE: "... and a bigger seating capacity to meet the needs of our growing family."

CATHERINE looks over at MARGARET and NEIL horsing around.

CATHERINE: Well, bully for you, Roddie.

MARGARET: What else does he say?

CATHERINE: (*reading on*) "And although I resisted as long as I could, Betty finally got her way with a brand-new bathroom, brand-new sink, brand-new flooring, brand-new bathtub and, most important of all, a spanking bright brand-new toilet, which sits on what can only be described as a bit of a pedestal in the middle of the room."

NEIL: God's teeth.

MARGARET giggles.

CATHERINE: "Betty absolutely loves it."

MARGARET: She's in love with a toilet.

NEIL: Maybe she's never sat on anything else.

MARGARET giggles.

CATHERINE: Don't knock a toilet, Margie. It's nothing to snicker at.

CATHERINE throws the letter aside.

CATHERINE: I'm not even going to finish it. It just makes me ... sour. I don't want to hear another word.

MARGARET: Oh come on, Mom.

NEIL: There have always been people like that – they're little inside so they have to talk big.

CATHERINE: Still.

MARGARET: Finish it. He went to the trouble to write it. The least you can do is finish it.

CATHERINE: I don't want to.

MARGARET: Then I'll finish it. (*taking the letter from CATHERINE and continuing to read*) "We were delighted to hear that your sweet young daughter Margaret finally found a man to marry and regret that we could not make it to the wedding."

CATHERINE: Not that anyone asked you.

MARGARET: "We know how you have struggled and suffered over the years and hope that things will now look up for you with another bread-winner in the family. That's all for now. I'll write again soon."

MARGARET puts the letter down. The mood has changed. She, too, looks subdued.

MARGARET: What an arse.

CATHERINE: What does he know about struggling and suffering?

NEIL starts tuning his bagpipes.

MARGARET: Do you have to do that now?

NEIL: Yes, I do.

MARGARET: (*short*) Well, do it in the shed or the outhouse.

NEIL: I will not.

MARGARET: Sometimes I feel I married the both of you.

NEIL: Well, better than me and a toilet.

MARGARET: I don't know. I'm sure a toilet brings some joy.

IAN walks in, stooped, exhausted, silent. He sits down, exhausted, stunned, black. They all watch him.

NEIL: Up from the deep for another whiff of air.

NEIL hands him the flask of rum. IAN takes a swig, closes his eyes.

NEIL: Can't your union do anything about all that soot, John, that lands on your clothes?

IAN: I'm not in the mood for your cracks tonight.

NEIL: Why not?

MARGARET: (*teasing*) Did Peggy stand you up before your shift?

IAN doesn't answer.

CATHERINE: What is it?

IAN: We're all getting cut back two shifts a week.

CATHERINE: They can't do that.

NEIL lets out another loud discordant blast on the pipes.

IAN: They're doing it.

CATHERINE: We can't pay the bills now.

MARGARET reaches into the pot and takes out two potatoes.

MARGARET: We'll manage.

IAN: MacDougall says they don't need as much coal now that the war is over. Factories aren't producing.

NEIL: That's the truth. Don't need to make as many bombs to kill people.

IAN: So they're squeezing the wages down.

NEIL: The bastards! "Show up for work one day and the washhouse door is locked."

IAN: I've got a union meeting tonight. We have to talk about strategy.

MARGARET: (repeating) We'll manage. We always do. I've got a story. Did you hear about Johnny and Angie loading in twenty-four, the roof so low they had to take pancakes in their cans?

NEIL continues to tune his bagpipes.

CATHERINE: Outside with that.

NEIL: I'm tuning it for the ceilidh tonight.

CATHERINE: Well, that'll do us a lot of good. More money for rum.

MARGARET: Mother!

CATHERINE: Well?

NEIL: It will bring in a little. As much as they can pay.

CATHERINE: Milk money. Maybe. What's the value in that?

NEIL: It will bring a smile and a tear and a memory to the people listening, Catherine, and I can only hope there is value to that in heaven.

CATHERINE: Oh for God's sake! What's that worth?

MARGARET: He works whenever he can. He's travelled from one end of this island to the other to find work. But there is none. Even the paper says it. Half the island is on relief!

CATHERINE: Well, why isn't he on relief? He's fought for it. That's the least they can do for him. If it wasn't for his goddamn pride ...

NEIL: I won't take relief.

MARGARET: (jumping in) Why don't you play that tune about the two hens fighting over a bean. Cheer us up.

CATHERINE: I don't want to hear any more of that noise in this house. It gets in the way. We can't afford to be singing and dancing.

GRANDPA thumps his shoe in disapproval.

CATHERINE: Don't try to shut me up. Someone's got to say what needs to be said. You've all gone off half-cocked. Look at poor Ian sitting there, half-dead from exhaustion. He's been working underground since he was fifteen years old. He's already stooped over from feeding us. And he doesn't have his own room anymore. Look at him. He never talks, he never says what's on his mind unless he's got two sheets to the wind, and then it's all just union nonsense.

MARGARET: Stop it, Mom.

CATHERINE: Speak up, Ian. What have you got to say about that?

IAN: How about some peace and quiet?

CATHERINE: Speak up for yourself, Ian. How can you not mind? Three men in the house, one can't talk or won't, the other can't stop talking or squawking. Three men, one pay. What do you think of that?

They all look to IAN. MARGARET holds her breath.

IAN: I don't mind, Mom.

CATHERINE: Why not?

IAN: Because that's the way he sees it. You've got to believe in something. I believe in the union but I gotta admit we're not making much headway right now. I'm not sure what he believes in but he sure as hell believes it hard. (turning to NEIL) Hey, I forgot to tell you. I saw a truck pull up at the co-op. They might be looking for a hand.

NEIL gets up quickly and leaves. MARGARET looks over at her brother with love in her eyes.

SCENE 2

Night. NEIL comes stumbling in, good and drunk, singing. MARGARET is sleeping. She hears him stumbling in, gets up and helps him.

MARGARET: Shh ... You drunken fool! Shh ...

NEIL: Don't shush me up, Margaret.

MARGARET: I will. Or you'll wake everyone.

NEIL: Well, wake 'em all and let's have a party.

MARGARET: Get your boots off. Get to bed.

NEIL: Do you love me, Mairead?

MARGARET: A little. Get your boots off.

NEIL: D'you wish you had a toilet to sit on and a great big car?

MARGARET: Don't be foolish.

NEIL: I can't give you those things.

MARGARET: That's not what I want.

NEIL: I want to give you a house by the ocean cause you're a little sea dog ... I can tell. That's where you want your nose ... sniffing the salt air.

MARGARET: And you will. We'll build that house.

NEIL: Where's the pride, Mairead?

MARGARET: What?

NEIL: Where's the pride?

MARGARET: Shut your yap and go to sleep.

NEIL: Know what I did tonight from one 'til four in the morning?

MARGARET: No, but I guess I'm gonna hear about it.

NEIL: I unpacked a whole truck to get the six boxes of supplies going to the Glace Bay Co-op, then I loaded it up again. Then 'cause some goddamn idiot had forgotten about two pitiful boxes of toilet paper at the very back I unloaded it all again. And I got yelled at for that by a mean-mouthed excuse of a man 'cause I wasn't working fast enough. And I wanted to pound him but I didn't 'cause I needed the two dollars. Where's the pride? There's got to be pride in the work just like there's pride in the music. That's one thing you can say about Ian. He's got a man's job. He knows he's not a worm even though he is worming around in the ground. The money is in the pit.

MARGARET: Oh shut up. You made two bucks. That'll buy food and shingles. Stop feeling sorry for yourself.

NEIL: Maybe he's right. Maybe I am some kind of a freak who just makes noise.

MARGARET: (*stroking his hair*) Go to sleep.

NEIL starts to snore. MARGARET pulls herself out from under NEIL's weight, then stands up.

MARGARET: (*to audience*) But it wasn't always like that. There were times away from the shack when we'd get down to the water. We'd start at one end of the beach the Dominion side, and walk along the breaking waves in our bare feet across to the Lingan side and cross the bridge there and sometimes we'd find Ian and Peggy sneaking some time together and we'd throw sand on top of them then haul them along with us but more often it would just be Ian who'd come so they could get in a bit more squabbling time, and if lobster was in season, we'd buy some and borrow

a pot from a fisherman and cook 'em up and eat them right there and drink beer ... God, you talk about good.

NEIL: Your union's got about as much clout as a wet mop in a rainstorm.

IAN: I got an idea. How 'bout we start a farm in the backyard. We got at least fifty square feet, we'll grow all our own vegetables, and keep a cow and a pig and a couple of beef cattle and some chickens, and for money to buy beer and pay the light bill, we'll rent you and your pipes out to concerts!

NEIL: I like the sound of that!

The sound of people yelling. They all stop and look at something ahead, their eyes wide.

NEIL: There's something happening up ahead.

MARGARET: (*to audience*) There was a whale stranded half onshore and half in the water and there were two fishing boats straining with all their might to tug it out to sea with ropes. And there was a bunch of drunken galoots on top of the poor brute, dancing on it, trying to punch holes in its sides.

IAN: Look what those bastards are doing!

NEIL holds on to IAN's arm.

NEIL: It's too late to help. The whale's dead.

IAN: You don't know that.

NEIL: Look at it!

IAN: Let me go!

NEIL: There's gotta be ten of them, you silly bugger! You can't beat your way through that bunch.

IAN: Well, I'm gonna try.

IAN breaks free. NEIL has no choice but to follow.

MARGARET: (*to audience*) I watched them run down the beach and then wade into the middle of those bloody brawling fools. I don't think even Charlie Dave could of made a dent in that bunch. There were arms and fists and feet and oaths flying 'til the air was black and blue but maybe it satisfied the bullies' bloodlust, because after they finished beating the pulp out of Ian and Neil, they gave up on the poor stranded beast and left it alone. Then the Mounties came – too late as usual – and everyone hurried off so they wouldn't be part of a police report. That is, everyone but the whale, which was still waiting for high tide.

NEIL and IAN enter, bloody but walking.

IAN: You all right?

NEIL: Yeah. You?

IAN: Yeah.

NEIL: You goddamn idiot. I should have let you kill yourself.

IAN: Well then, why didn't you?

NEIL: I got my pride, eh.

IAN: Well Jesus, Neil, didn't you see what they were doing?

NEIL: I'm not blind. I saw what was going on but it wasn't our business.

IAN: How would you like someone spittin' in your face?

NEIL: For Chrissake Ian, it's only a goddamn whale.

IAN: Sure it's only a goddamn whale and I'm only a goddamn coal miner.

NEIL: What's that supposed to mean?

IAN: It was just trying to save its life, and when it needed a bit of help, a bunch of bullies come along and try punching holes in it, spit on it, and piss all over it. You gotta help out. We knocked them off at least, didn't we?

NEIL: Just about killed ourselves.

IAN: But we didn't, did we?

NEIL: The friggin' thing's had it. Look at him. He's not going anywhere.

IAN: You don't know that for sure. You don't know what it's made of, what kind of will it's got to live ... or how strong those fishermen's lines are. If the fishermen can pull him off with their ropes when the tide comes in, who knows, it might have a chance yet. Those bastards spit in its face but that whale's still got pride.

NEIL: A friggin' whale's pride.

IAN: Yeah. A friggin' whale's pride. It's struggling along too, eh, just like the rest of us. You just can't give up. You can't just sit by. We helped him out and maybe now he's got a chance.

NEIL: Maybe he does and maybe he doesn't.

IAN: Well, one thing I know for sure – if you don't work at it, if you don't fight for it, it ain't gonna happen. That's what the union's all about.

NEIL: Well, maybe you're right about the union ... but the best thing would be if you didn't work in the pit at all.

IAN: The thing of it, Mr. Neil-Know-It-All-Currie ... what did you say? Did you say that I'm right about union?

NEIL: Yes, I did say that, Ian.

IAN: Well, wonder of wonders. And you called me Ian.

NEIL: Yes, I did.

IAN: Well, God Almighty.

NEIL: I guess you spent so much time nosing through the earth, you wore your nose down short and now you can see beyond the end of it.

IAN: I can?

NEIL: Yep. You got a good head, you got a brave heart, and you got a short nose, and your great-grandmother Morag would've been proud of you. She was all in favour of people whose eyes are longer than their noses.

IAN seems to grow taller as NEIL talks.

IAN: Say that again – about being right about the union.

NEIL: But she wasn't crazy about the rum bottle. She'd a thought piss would've been a better drink for the likes of us!

IAN: Come on, say it again.

NEIL: Oh for God's sakes.

IAN: Just say that part about me being right about the union.

NEIL: Give it up.

IAN: Just say it. Slowly.

NEIL: You're right about the union.

IAN lets out a yip of delight and the two of them walk off wrestling.

SCENE 3

The shack. A month later. GRANDPA is methodically lifting a pair of soup cans up and down, trying to build his muscles. He starts to wheeze and cough. NEIL enters, comes over, and gives him his thump. GRANDPA's breathing improves.

NEIL: Better not overdo it, Gramps.

NEIL sits down heavily and starts carving a piece of wood. GRANDPA scribbles something in his note-book and hands it to NEIL.

NEIL: (*reading*) "Call the undertaker. Neil Currie's passed away." (*laughs*) Do I look that bad?

GRANDPA nods.

NEIL: I'm sorry. I'm not very good company for you.

GRANDPA writes something.

NEIL: (*reading*) "I'm no hell either."

NEIL looks at GRANDPA and laughs.

NEIL: At least I don't have to fight to get a word in edgewise. (*studying the old man*) Why did you stop talking?

GRANDPA stares off.

NEIL: Would you like me to sing you something?

GRANDPA nods. NEIL starts singing "The Isle of Skye." While he sings, GRANDPA writes something in his notebook. By the time NEIL finishes, GRANDPA has nodded off to sleep. NEIL takes the notebook and reads it.

NEIL: (*reading*) "The doctor said there was nothing wrong with my lungs. He was a liar. But no one wanted to hear what I had to say." (*to the sleeping man*) So you stopped talking. Nobody wants to hear what I have to say either. I sleep in my wife's mother's shack and I hardly make enough to buy the tea.

NEIL puts a blanket over GRANDPA's chest.

NEIL: Well, at least I take care of you. I give you your thump every hour.

NEIL gets out his flask, takes a drink, and goes back to woodworking. MARGARET, CATHERINE, and IAN enter. The women are tired. They drop their bags. MARGARET looks over at NEIL, who keeps his head down. Two pillows lie on a kitchen chair. CATHERINE stares at them, then moves them out of the way.

CATHERINE: Well, it's good to be home. To the things I'm used to. When I work up at the Mac-Dougall's or the MacGregor's, I miss the pillows on the kitchen chairs. I miss the underwear draped over my one decent sitting chair.

MARGARET tries to find a place for the pillows and her underwear. She is sick of her mother's wisecracks. She looks over at NEIL, who is ignoring her.

CATHERINE: I see we've got a new leak in the roof. Oh well, I guess I should be glad I've got a roof over my head at all these days. Wipe your nose, Margie, it's dripping like a tap.

MARGARET takes out a handkerchief and wipes it.

CATHERINE: You peel the potatoes. And try not to whittle them down to nothing like you did last night. And don't boil the daylights out of them either. I'll try to squeeze another meal out of this scrawny little chicken for the five of us.

MARGARET gets out some potatoes and starts slamming them into the pot. IAN drops his stuff. He opens a little bag and pulls out a new tie. He examines it proudly. Then he pulls out some paper, sits down at the kitchen table, and starts writing.

CATHERINE: And what's all this?

IAN: I'm working on a talk I'm gonna give at the union hall tonight. I'm the new secretary treasurer for District 26.

CATHERINE: Will that bring more money into the house?

IAN: It's not a paying position, Mom. It's an honour.

CATHERINE: Oh. (*to MARGARET*) Don't leave the lid off the oil. I can never find it.

IAN: Did you know that the old Sydney and Dominion collieries pay two completely different wage scales for exactly the same kind of operation?

CATHERINE: Which is lower?

IAN: Ours.

CATHERINE: Figures.

IAN: And that the contract mining rates are seven per cent lower than they were in '26 in terms of real money.

CATHERINE: There was no money anywhere in '26. Just turnips and weak tea. Don't talk to me about '26.

CATHERINE takes exception to the new location where MARGARET has put the pillows and blanket.

CATHERINE: And don't leave them there! I'll just trip over them on my way to the outhouse.

MARGARET: Well, where should I put them? Should I hang them from the roof?

CATHERINE: Could you? That might help.

MARGARET: (*short-tempered*) No, I cannot!

IAN: We want a pension plan for all miners over sixty-five. Only a quarter of them get any kind of pension at all and that just depends on whether you sucked up to the company enough.

CATHERINE: (*looking over at GRANDPA*) He sure didn't and look what he got. Nothing! They didn't even give him the time of day.

IAN: And we want to get rid of the company doctors 'cause they just say what the company wants to hear.

NEIL looks up and over at the sleeping old man, then back down at his carving. He takes another drink from his flask. MARGARET watches him, steaming.

CATHERINE: Speaking of the doctor, I cleaned over there today. She's got shelves for this and shelves for that ... If Charlie Dave were here –

MARGARET: (*sharply*) Well, he's not.

CATHERINE: (*taken aback*) Well, I know he's not. I was just going to say that if he were, he'd be able to rig up some kind of shelves to put all that stuff on. I don't know where he got so handy. He sure didn't get it from his father and he sure didn't pass it along to his brother. Now if I had a kitchen like that –

MARGARET: Well, you don't!

CATHERINE: I know I don't. What's wrong with you today?

MARGARET shakes her head.

IAN: Now all I need to do is get everyone talking about this stuff. There's a lot of them have their noses so close to the rock face, they can't see for nothing.

MARGARET tries to stuff the pillows into a drawer. CATHERINE picks up some clothes.

CATHERINE: And while you're at it, could you get these out of sight?

MARGARET: No, I cannot! There is nowhere to put it.

CATHERINE: Don't pout. You're not ten years old.

MARGARET: That's right. I am not ten years old. I am a grown woman. A married woman. I don't have to listen to my mother bossing me around from dawn 'til dusk!

NEIL: (*looking up*) Steady, Margaret.

MARGARET: No, I won't be steady! All you do is sit around and drink all day and play those damn things. I'm sick of it! I don't want to live here anymore. I want to be on our own land. I want to live with my husband in my own place. Where's my house?

MARGARET storms out. CATHERINE goes into the other room. GRANDPA nods off to sleep. NEIL and IAN start playing cards.

IAN: There's a job opened up in No. 10. I could get you in.

NEIL says nothing.

IAN: Whaddya say?

NEIL says nothing.

IAN: What happened to you that day down there when you were roaring around like a stuck bull?

NEIL: I've told you what I think about the pit and it's the God's truth.

IAN: I know it is ... but I wanna know about that day.

NEIL: (*after a pause*) I was down there a mile below the earth digging away at the coal face trying not to think about where I was and what I was doing ... and then all of a sudden my light went out. Ever happen to you?

IAN: Yeah.

NEIL: I was scared shitless. I never be so scared in my life – not over there in the war, not anywhere. And then this song came into my head, something I'd heard the old people sing, in Gaelic, and it started pouring out of me, and it kept getting louder and louder. And the foreman came roaring up and told me to shut up but I wouldn't, I couldn't. And maybe everyone thought I was crazy but it helped me. It was like a light guiding me. As soon as we got back up top, I quit, just a second before he fired me. (*long pause*) You ever get scared down there?

IAN: Christ, all the time.

NEIL: You do?

IAN: Margaret used to have to walk me to work back shift when I started 'cause I was so scared of the dark. (*laughs*) That was one of the reasons I started going with girls ... I couldn't have my sister walking me to work forever.

NEIL: Well, I'll be damned.

IAN: I don't know this for sure, but maybe everyone feels the same way. I could use some help for a while, Neil. You could work right beside me. The union needs good men.

NEIL throws the cards down on the table. The lights go down.

SCENE 4

The ocean. MARGARET is on their land. NEIL joins her.

MARGARET: I'm sorry I said those things.

NEIL: What you said cleared the air. (*looking out*) You know, Mairead, if it weren't for that bit of water out there, you could walk right up on the shore of the Isle of Skye. (*after a pause*) I'm going to go underground and help Ian. I'll be a miner until I can put a roof over our head and a down payment on ten sheep.

He kisses her.

SCENE 5

The shack. MARGARET is reading the paper. CATHERINE is cleaning. GRANDPA is napping with a couple of soup cans lying in his lap. CATHERINE looks at GRANDPA.

CATHERINE: Well, I think I'll take these back, Mr. Charles Atlas, if you don't mind.

CATHERINE tries to ease the soup cans out of GRANDPA's lap and he wakes up, grabs hold of the soup cans, and starts lifting them up and down. CATHERINE watches him, smiles, and rubs his shoulder affectionately.

CATHERINE: Maybe I'll get my shelves built yet!

MARGARET: (*reading from newspaper*) "This is the first time since 1917 the miners have entered wage negotiations armed with a strike mandate." (*looking up*) I wish I was at that strike meeting.

CATHERINE: I wish I was at bingo. At least there I have a hope in hell of winning.

IAN and NEIL enter. MARGARET, CATHERINE, and GRANDPA all look expectant.

MARGARET: Well?

NEIL: Well, I thought the union head made pretty good sense. We could sure use $2.50 more a day. It would get me out of that hole faster. I think it's time to bust their asses.

MARGARET: That's 'cause you love a fight!

NEIL: (*turning to IAN*) What do you think? You've been pretty quiet all the way home. Cat got your tongue?

IAN: (*cautious*) We'd need somebody to talk to the women, to explain how much better off we'd be if we stick together.

NEIL: Margaret can do that. Maybe get Peggy to help you. (*laughs*) That would be a sight, wouldn't it? The mine manager's daughter organizing the miners' wives!

MARGARET: You think I'm gonna talk to every coal miner's wife in Reserve?

IAN: No, it would have to be all the collieries. We'd have to get the wives from every colliery backing their men.

MARGARET: I'd do it, but I don't know how.

CATHERINE: You're all talking like it's a picnic you're organizing. It's not. A strike is hell. I know. (*nodding to GRANDPA*) So does he.

NEIL: Do you think we can get all the collieries?

IAN: I think we can. All of them in District 26.

NEIL: But you're nervous, aren't ya? What is it?

IAN: I asked Peggy to sound out her father on a strike.

NEIL: Well, I guess we know what he'd say.

IAN: He used to be a miner. He's not a bad guy. He might be telling the truth.

NEIL: So what did he tell her?

IAN: That hell would freeze over before the company would touch its profits ... and in the meantime, the miners' families could starve ...

CATHERINE: And they will.

NEIL: But the UMW will back us up. They said so.

IAN: MacDougall says they say they will – but they won't.

NEIL: How the hell does he know that?

IAN: In the last election the miners elected a socialist to the federal government. The UMW is an American union. To an American, a socialist is a communist. The union can't be seen in the States as supporting communism. As soon as word gets out that the Glace Bay miners are a bunch of communists, the American union leaders will drop us like a hot potato.

CATHERINE: Well, that settles it. Forget the whole thing.

NEIL: Is that all?

IAN: MacDougall said there are some good jobs coming up. Jobs he thought the two of us would be just right for. Surface jobs. The pay's good and good chance for advancement. But if we were seen as instigators of the strike, we wouldn't have a hope in hell of getting them after the dust settled.

NEIL: The bastard's trying to buy us off.

CATHERINE: Take them. For God's sake, take the jobs. Forget the strike. MacDougall's already said that the deck's stacked against you.

NEIL: We don't know if he's right. He may be just trying to spook us.

IAN: Is that what you think, Neil?

CATHERINE: Why don't you ask what I think? If you're so interested in stories, why don't you ask what *I* think?!

NEIL: What *do* you think, Catherine?

CATHERINE: I remember standing on the hill above Lingan beach with my three children – Margaret was in my arms, watching my own grandfather and my father and my husband and three thousand miners take a strike vote in front of a bonfire. They were so full of themselves, so sure that they were right, that they would win. But they didn't.

IAN: But they were right.

CATHERINE: I remember no food and filthy water and children dying of disease 'cause our water was filthy. I remember company thugs setting fires to our houses and police running over people with their horses ... and in the end, they only got back a fraction of what they'd lost. And now, I have one less son and a dead husband and an old man who's lost his voice. You can't win against them.

They are all silent.

IAN: There's another thing.

NEIL: What's that?

IAN: Peggy said if we go on strike, I shouldn't count on her being there when it's over.

MARGARET: That's low.

NEIL turns to GRANDPA.

NEIL: What do you think, Grandpa? If you were still in the pit what would you do?

Everyone waits. GRANDPA finally scribbles a note and pushes it towards NEIL.

NEIL: (*reading*) "I'd fight again. If you don't fight for what you believe, you are a worm!"

MARGARET: (*to audience*) I helped out during the strike. People who wouldn't even give me the time of day when I walked by welcomed me into their homes 'cause I was Ian's sister or I was Neil Currie's wife. And a lot of the older ones even remembered the role my great-grandmother

Morag played in the last great strike, hauling endless stores of vegetables which she'd wrapped in paper in her cellar and giving them to the children in exchange for their learning some Gaelic. Being Morag MacNeil's great-granddaughter, I had about as much roots as a scraggly little bush could have in this godforsaken windy place.

MARGARET is remembering music.

MARGARET: And 'cause nobody was working, all the singers and fiddlers and dancers had time on their hands and they'd go around giving free concerts, or they'd charge a little and give the money to the relief fund. Neil was in seventh heaven. This was what life was supposed to be. But the best thing of all about the strike was that it gave Neil time to finish the house.

NEIL: Here it is, Mairead. Your house on the ocean. This is where we'll make our stand.

NEIL watches MARGARET take a deep breath, then let out a triumphant whoop.

NEIL: You're like a perfectly tuned set of pipes. You always make the right sound. It comes from deep inside you. You'll be all right, Mairead. You'll always do the right thing. I love you, Margaret MacNeil.

MARGARET: I love you, Neil Currie.

He kisses her. NEIL moves off.

MARGARET: (*to audience*) Of course, everything MacDougall said came true. Once the strike got going, it seemed to drop out of the hands of the miners completely. The big meetings all took place in Montreal. Nobody knew what was going on, but when it finally ended, we were no better off than before. Instead of the $2.50 that we asked for, the union made a deal for a dollar a day, I think it was, but even that didn't amount to anything because they only got the raise if they put out more coal than before the strike, which was nearly impossible. But the worst of it was, if there hadn't been a strike and MacDougall kept his word, Ian and Neil might have been working on the surface instead of in the pit. As it were, they were both killed the same minute.

The sound of a mine whistle.

MARGARET: I was up to Reserve keeping house for my mother when I heard the whistle. I heard the dogs howling for two nights before so soon's I heard the whistle, I took off for the pit. They were both just being taken up when I got there. They had them in the half-ton truck with blankets over them. I told them to take them to my mother's, where they lay one of them on Mama's bed and one on the couch in the kitchen. Then I told them to get out. I knew what to get. I helped Charlie Dave keep a dead frog for two years when he was going to school. I went to the medical hall and got two gallons of the stuff. Cost me a lot. I got back as fast as I could, but it wasn't quick enough. I locked the house before I left so nobody could get in. Mama was visiting her sister in Bras d'Or and I didn't know when she'd be back. When I got back, there was a bunch around the door. I told them to fuck off. I was busy. To make matters worse my grandfather was left alone all that time. He died. He choked. But before he did, he wrote this –

MARGARET picks up a notebook.

MARGARET: (*reading*) "It's kind of comical if it wasn't so sad, there's our Margaret married to the only one you'd think wouldn't work in the pit but there he is working in it anyway and him working with Ian, if the two of them get killed ... what will the poor girl do?"

MARGARET looks up from the notebook.

MARGARET: I took his lungs. It wasn't so much the lungs themselves, though I think they were a good thing to take, though they don't keep too well, especially the condition he was in, as just something to remind me of the doctor who told him he couldn't get compensation because he was fit to work. Then I took Neil's lungs because I thought of them connected to his pipes and they show, compared to Grandfather's, what lungs should look like. And I took his tongue since he always said he was the only one around still had one. I took his fingers, too, because he played the pipes with them. I didn't know what to take from Ian so I took his dick, since Neil always said that was Ian's substitute for religion to keep him from being a pit pony when he wasn't drinking rum or playing Forty-Five. I had each thing in its own pickle jar. I put them all in the tin suitcase with the scribblers and the deck of cards and the half-empty quart of Black Death they left after last Sunday's drinking and arguing, got Neil's bagpipes, and took it all over to my friend Marie's next door for safekeeping. They came in a police car and I didn't give them a chance to even get out of the car. I jumped right into the back seat like it was a taxi I was waiting for. I just sat right in and said,

"Sydney River, please." Sydney River, if you're not from around here, is the cookie jar where they put rotten tomatoes so they won't spoil the barrel. So they put me in 'til they forgot about me; then when they remembered me, they forgot what they put me in for. So they let me go.

SCENE 6

MARGARET's house by the ocean. MARGARET is standing looking out the window, suitcase on the floor beside her. CATHERINE enters. They look at each other.

MARGARET: Hello, Mom.

CATHERINE: (*guarded*) Hello, Margie.

MARGARET takes a deep breath.

MARGARET: Oh, the air smells like heaven here, doesn't it?

CATHERINE: I guess.

MARGARET: You look good. The house looks good. Thank you for keeping it so nice for me 'til I got back.

CATHERINE: I didn't mind. It's a bit big for me, though. Alone.

MARGARET: You can stay here and live with me, Mother, if you like.

CATHERINE: Thanks anyway. But I'm not feeling too good. I think I'll go back to Reserve.

MARGARET: So stay. I'll look after you.

CATHERINE: Yes, you'll look after me. You'll look after me. And what if I drop dead during the night?

MARGARET: If you drop dead during the night, you're dead. Dead in Glace Bay is the same as being dead in Reserve.

CATHERINE: Yes. And you'll look after me dead, too, I imagine. You'll look after me. What'll you do? Cut off my tits and put them in bottles.

MARGARET: Mother, your tits don't mean a thing to me.

CATHERINE picks up her suitcase, opens the door, and leaves.

MARGARET: (*calling after her*) Have you got everything?

CATHERINE: (*calling back*) If I've forgotten anything, pickle it.

MARGARET: Okay.

CATHERINE: Keep it for a souvenir!

MARGARET: Okay!

MARGARET shuts the door.

MARGARET: (*to audience*) I was sorry after that I said what I said. I wouldn't have minded having one of her tits. After all, if it wasn't for them, we'd have all died of thirst before we had our chance to get killed.

The strains of "MacPherson's Lament" begin and grow louder throughout the rest of MARGARET's memories.

MARGARET: Marie came over with the suitcase and we had a cup of tea and she helped me set things up. We had to make shelves for the jars. Everything else can go on tables and chairs or hang on the wall or from the ceiling, as you can see. Marie is very artistic, she knows how to put things around. I'm the cook. We give tea and scones free to anyone who comes. You're the first. I guess not too many people know about it yet. But it will pick up. These things take time.

A light comes up on NEIL in memory.

NEIL: I think you're the smallest son of a bitch I ever seen. I love you, Margaret MacNeil.

A light comes up on CATHERINE.

CATHERINE: That man will never live in a company house. And he can work with Ian. They can die together. And you can live in your shack alone. Stand it then.

Another light comes up on IAN.

IAN: It's only a goddamn whale and I'm only a goddamn coal miner. But one thing I know for sure, if you don't work at it, if you don't fight for it, it ain't gonna happen.

MARGARET continues humming. Another light.

NEIL: Go and read your grandfather's scribblers. He remembers. His blood was spilled there, on the ground, and our blood was spilled there, on the ground. He remembers.

MARGARET: It's important to remember. Because we sort of are what we remember. And when you leave, take a walk out to the cliff. Take a good look.

Light on NEIL.

NEIL: You know, Mairead, if it wasn't for that bit of water out there, you could walk right up on the shore of the Isle of Skye. That's where we come from.

Bagpipes swell at the end.

MARGARET: Just an ocean away. Just one good spit away.

END

RAHUL VARMA

(b. 1952)

"There was a time when politically conscious theatre in Montreal – French or English – was represented by the silence of the dead," *Montreal Gazette* critic Gaëtan Charlebois wrote in 2005. "Then along came a small company, Teesri Duniya Theatre, with a mandate to provide work for South Asian artists." *Teesri Duniya*, meaning "Third World" in Hindustani, was co-founded in 1981 by Rahul Varma and Rana Bose, immigrants from India living in Montreal. Varma became the company's artistic director in 1986 and soon its major playwright, writing his plays first in Hindi, then later in English, and producing plays in Hindi about India and then later about South Asian immigrants in Canada.

Before long, Varma expanded the company's mandate to include stories and communities, voices and performers from across the diverse Canadian cultural landscape, while always retaining Teesri Duniya's political edge. "Change the world, one play at a time" is the company's motto. The Teesri Duniya website in 2013 describes the company as "dedicated to producing, developing, and presenting socially and politically relevant theatre, based on the cultural experiences of diverse communities. Multicultural diversity, intercultural relations, relevance, and compelling stories are defining features of our work. We are committed to multiethnic (as opposed to color-blind) casting." Varma's *Counter Offence* powerfully expresses this vision of diversity in a murder mystery about complex, overlapping personal, social, and political agendas in a contemporary Montreal defined and divided by more than just English and French language.

Rahul Varma was born in the village of Narion in north-central India, trained as a research technician, and earned a B.Sc. from the University of Lucknow before immigrating to Canada in 1976. Neither he nor Rana Bose had much formal theatre experience from their time in India. But they saw a need to give theatrical voice to the South Asian community in Montreal at a time when, Varma says in an interview with Jolene Owen, "there was [a] complete absence of cultural diversity in Canadian theatre." Indo-Canadian theatre would soon find other outlets when Sadhu Binning founded the Punjabi-oriented Vancouver Sath company in 1983 and Bose left Teesri Duniya in 1986 to establish Montreal Serai.

In its early years, Teesri Duniya produced a series of contemporary Indian plays and some original plays by Varma, all in Hindi. The success of the company's first English-language play, Sue Townsend's *The Great Celestial Cow* in 1984, led Varma to begin writing in English and directing his own work. Typically, his new plays involved collaborations across ethnic borders. *Job Stealer* (1987), co-written with Helen Vlachos and Ian Lloyd-George, *Isolated Incident* (1988) with Stephen Orlov, and *Equal Wages* (1989) with Vlachos were essentially agitprop pieces, according to Varma. In *Job Stealer* and *Equal Wages,* multi-ethnic casts played immigrants and refugees from the developing world – immigrant women in *Equal Wages* – who are blamed for stealing Canadian jobs and end up in Canadian sweatshops. *Isolated Incident* revisited the 1987 shooting death of an unarmed black man, Anthony Griffin, by Montreal police – an incident that continues to resonate strongly in the background of *Counter Offence*.

Varma tackled First Nations issues involving the James Bay hydro megaproject in northern Quebec in his first full-length play, *Land Where the Trees Talk* (1990), introducing a female Indo-Canadian doctor character, he says, to "emphasize the need for solidarity between new cultural minorities and First Nations people" ("Teesri Duniya Theatre"). The play was directed by Jack Langedijk, who would direct both the English and French premieres of *Counter Offence*. In *No Man's Land* (1992), written with Ken McDonough, a family of Indian refugees living in Montreal is shaken by the threat of Quebec separatism. *No Man's Land* generated controversy when the Strathearn Intercultural Centre refused to let Varma stage it in their theatre on the grounds that the play "failed to promote intercultural dialogue."

Teesri Duniya received its first Canada Council grant in 1995, having been supported until then only by Department of Multiculturalism funding. Canada Council support resulted in more fully developed professional productions, including *Counter Offence,* which premiered at the Strathearn Centre in 1996 to excellent reviews. It was remounted the following year at the Monument Nationale in a co-production with Montreal's Black Theatre Workshop, followed by a highly praised French-language version called *L'affaire Farhadi,* staged at La Licorne in 1999. *Counter Offence* subsequently played at Vancouver's Firehall Arts Centre in 2000, and in Venice in Italian translation (*Il caso Farhadi*), directed by Bill Glassco.

Varma followed *Counter Offence* with another very successful project: *Bhopal* (2001), a play about the 1984 Union Carbide pesticide factory explosion that killed or disabled tens of thousands of people in that Indian city. *Bhopal* was remounted in 2003 in a co-production with Toronto's Cahoots Theatre, directed by Guillermo Verdecchia; translated into Hindi and toured to six Indian cities by acclaimed Indian director Habib Tanvir in 2003–04; and produced in Montreal and Quebec City in French translation in 2005–06. The play has subsequently enjoyed multiple productions across the United States and India, including a 2013 Punjabi translation. Varma's *Truth and Treason* (2009) tells a complex story about the American invasion of Iraq, involving a Canadian mother and her Iraqi daughter. In *State of Denial* (2012), a Rwandan-Canadian documentary filmmaker investigates the Armenian massacres of World War One and finds a connection, through Canada, to the Rwandan genocide of the 1990s.

As well as Teesri Duniya's productions of Varma's own plays, his company has mounted other major Canadian plays about complex socio-political issues that cross many ethnic and cultural boundaries, including *The Adventures of Ali & Ali and the aXes of Evil* by Camyar Chai, Guillermo Verdecchia, and Marcus Youssef; Nina Aquino and Nadine Villasin's *Miss Orient(ed)*; MT Space Theatre's *The Last 15 Seconds*; Daniel David Moses's *Almighty Voice and His Wife*; and Jason Sherman's *Reading Hebron*, directed by Wajdi Mouawad. The *Globe and Mail*'s Philip Fine described the latter production as "an English work by a Toronto Jewish playwright on a Mideast topic ... being put on by an East Indian artistic director's company employing a French-speaking Lebanese director" – in other words, typical Teesri Duniya fare. In 1998, Varma and Kapil Bawa founded the journal *alt.theatre: cultural diversity and the stage*, published by Teesri Duniya as a forum for discussion and analysis of the kind of theatre the company continues to practice. In 1999, Varma was honoured with a MECCA Award from the Montreal English Critics Circle for his body of work.

In his playwright's foreword to the first edition (1997) of *Counter Offence*, Varma states, "Violence against women in its various forms is the most serious problem in our country ... But 'cultural differences' are often invoked to justify abusive behaviour." The police, he asserts, also use cultural differences as "an excuse for misconduct perpetrated against ethnic minorities." So what happens when a white policeman tries to arrest an ethnic-minority wife beater, especially "if the battered woman is of the same colour and culture as the batterer"? These are some of the complexities Varma explores in *Counter Offence*.

The wife, Shazia, an Indo-Canadian with traditional Muslim parents, and Shapoor, the husband, an Iranian with immigration issues and parental problems of his own, are in fact not of the same culture. Galliard, the white arresting officer, is both racist and dedicated to preventing and punishing violence against women. And Mr. Moolchand, the Indo-Canadian political activist who defends Shapoor, has a variety of mixed motives (and accents to go with them). All this is played out against the background of the 1995 referendum on Quebec sovereignty. The Yes side had just barely lost, a loss that then-Quebec Premier Jacques Parizeau infamously blamed on "money and the ethnic vote," referring to "us" (*nous*), the francophones of Quebec, as opposed to the "ethnics." In the play, we learn that the police chief has gotten a call from the new Parti Québécois premier, Lucien Bouchard, doing "damage control after Parizeau's ethnic remark." Multiple forces are at work here.

Among the most interesting of the complications is the conflict between Clarinda, the black social worker who runs the centre for battered women, and Moolchand. They, too, argue over the meaning of "we" and "us" – whether those pronouns should signify identification based primarily on race, political orientation, or gender. Moolchand appeals to Clarinda to join with him on racial grounds: "us, the East Indians, the Africans, the Chinese ... you know – people like you and me." She should help him defend Shapoor, he says, because "He's one of us, see?" Clarinda responds, "Isn't *she* also one of us?" Clarinda's notion of solidarity is based more on gender than on race or ethnicity. When Moolchand angrily says to her, "there is something wrong with a person who doesn't stand by her own community," Clarinda shoots back, "Shazia's my community."

In her book *Irony's Edge*, Canadian literary theorist Linda Hutcheon argues that irony often derives from conflicts among the multiple, overlapping "discursive communities" to which we all belong: race, ethnicity, national origin, gender, sexual orientation, political affiliation, class, profession, and so on. *Counter Offence* theatricalizes these ironic clashes in important, compelling ways. "There are no heroes in this play," Varma has written, in an article for the journal *South Asian Popular Culture*, "only compromised characters with competing agendas ... For every social offence there is a counter offence, for every cultural truth there is a competing truth."

Counter Offence

Rahul Varma

Counter Offence was first produced by Teesri Duniya Theatre at the Strathearn Intercultural Centre in Montreal on March 14, 1996, with the following cast:

SHAZIA RIZVI	Raminder Singh
SHAPOOR FARHADI	Cas Anvar
CLARINDA KEITH	Judy Rudd
GUY GALLIARD	Stephen Orlov
GILLES PROUGAULT	Mark Walker
MOOLCHAND MISRA	Prasun (Raja) Lala
MOHAMMAD MURAD RIZVI	Kapil Bawa
SHAFIQA RIZVI	Ranjana Jha

Directed by Jack Langedijk
Set and Lighting Design by J. David Gutman
Music by Raiomond Mirza
Costume Design by Rosanna Higgins
Stage Managed by James Douglas

CHARACTERS

SHAZIA RIZVI, *a twenty-six-year-old Muslim woman brought up in Canada*

SHAPOOR FARHADI, *her Iranian husband who came to Canada as a student*

CLARINDA KEITH, *a black woman who runs a centre for battered women*

GUY GALLIARD, *a white police sergeant who works in the domestic violence unit*

GILLES PROUGAULT, *a white police lieutenant who is Galliard's boss and president of the Police Brotherhood (union)*

MOOLCHAND MISRA, *an Indo-Canadian anti-racism activist*

MOHAMMED MURAD RIZVI, *Shazia's father, retired, from India*

SHAFIQA RIZVI, *Shazia's mother, a good woman who speaks frankly and without fear*

SETTING

A multiple-location set consisting of a family home, a women's shelter, a police station, a room at the YMCA, and an imaginary courtroom. The location of the courtroom keeps changing throughout the play. The sense of different locations in the court-room is created by an illuminated area from where the characters talk to an unseen judge. When the stage directions say that the character addresses an unseen judge, the actor could simply step into the illuminated area and speak as if from a witness stand. However, he or she could speak from any location onstage.

ACT ONE

SCENE 1

The actors walk in and place themselves at various locations onstage. MOOLCHAND enters.

MOOLCHAND: (*to audience*) I speak to you for a just cause, not because a young Muslim is being thrown out of the country, but because I'm driven by a social justice that thrives in this city. God knows, I'm doing something that our ancestors could not do when they stepped on the soil of Canada. *Komagata Maru*, the Chinese head tax, Native babies being taken away from their families, spouses kept apart right after their marriages because of the so-called immigration backlog. History that can't be rewritten, but we can learn from the past and it can guide us to a more hopeful future. I'm not fighting against racism, I'm fighting for equality. Where police identify people by their acts and not by their skin. I'm fighting for a Canada that accepts what it is: a multi-ethnic society. I heard somebody say the other day that just like all people of colour, I am in the habit of putting down Canada. No sir, I chose Canada – this very city – to be my home and all I'm trying to do is make my home better for my children, where I hope that someday we will focus on values rather than the colour of one's skin.

PROUGAULT: Will the defendant please rise. Guy Galliard, you stand accused of the murder of Shapoor Farhadi.

ALL ACTORS: (*repeating*) I swear to tell the truth, the whole truth, and nothing but the truth. I swear to tell the truth, the whole truth, and nothing but the truth. I swear to tell the truth, the whole truth, and nothing ...

From some location onstage, GALLIARD addresses an unseen judge.

GALLIARD: No, it's the goddamn truth. Excuse me, Your Honour, but I have said the same thing every time. What, sir? Shapoor called me – at my home ... We talked for a short time. I don't know ... five minutes ... no, not even, three. I went to his room at the YMCA. I remember the door was slightly open.

Flashback to the YMCA room where SHAPOOR is seen lying (dead) on the bed. GALLIARD walks across the room.

Shapoor? ... Shapoor?

He comes close to the dead body and shakes SHAPOOR – the body falls on the floor. He looks around the room nervously, then shakes the dead body.

Oh shit. Oh, oh ... What the ... Come on, you can't be ...

In walks SHAZIA. She gasps, seeing her husband's dead body lying on the floor and GALLIARD standing over him.

SHAZIA: What are you doing here?

GALLIARD: He called ... I ... I ... I don't know ... He is dead.

SHAZIA: What? ... What? ... My God ... Shapoor ...

She runs to him and holds SHAPOOR's body in her arms.

Shapoor, Shapoor ... Oh please, no ... no ... Oh my God. Please, Shapoor, look at me, please, I'm sorry, too. Shapoor, come on ...

GALLIARD: It's all right ...

SHAZIA: (*screaming*) Get away, don't touch us ... Oh my Shapoor ... (*to GALLIARD*) Get out, get out ...

Transition to the present as GALLIARD continues his testimony.

GALLIARD: (*to the unseen judge*) Yes, I did, I did, Your Honour, I called 9-1-1 but he was gone ... I mean dead when I got there. (*pause as he listens*) No ... Yes, I did arrest Mr. Shapoor, seven months ago. But that doesn't mean that I ... Your Honour, he won't even let me finish. Fine ... yes, seven months ago, that was the first time I ever met him.

Flashback to the police station. GALLIARD is interrogating SHAPOOR.

SHAPOOR: Please, let me go ... Why have you brought me here? Please, let me go home.

GALLIARD: Home?

SHAPOOR: I want to know how she is doing.

GALLIARD: Shut up.

SHAPOOR moves.

GALLIARD: Don't turn around.

SHAPOOR: Sir, you can't keep me here. Please, I need to get back home.

GALLIARD: To Aiiran? No! No, you're going to sit here and you are going to tell me exactly what you did.

SHAPOOR: What more can I tell, I have told you everything. I need to call my friend. Please just let me ...

SHAPOOR takes a step.

GALLIARD: Stop right there!

SHAPOOR is shocked to stillness.

GALLIARD: 'N don't bloody shine your eyes on me ... Now very slowly, turn around ... don't even blink, boy. Are you sure you don't have anything more to say? That's it? Put your hands behind your head.

SHAPOOR turns toward him.

GALLIARD: (*shouting*) I said don't come near me! Walk out that door, head back to the cell, nice and slow ...

SHAPOOR: This is insulting.

GALLIARD: Shut up.

GALLIARD pushes SHAPOOR away and walks up to PROUGAULT, who is busy writing a report.

GALLIARD: Guys like him are scum, no better than pimps and child molesters.

PROUGAULT: (*holding up the report*) What does this say?

GALLIARD: (*spelling out the word*) A-I-I-R-A-fuck-ing-*N* – born in Aiiran.

PROUGAULT: Okay, so what's it gonna be? Disorderly conduct?

GALLIARD: Assault.

PROUGAULT: Oh yeah? (*taking a photo from the file*) I am looking at the photo. I don't see any bruise 'n blood 'n broken bone. Where is the doctor's report?

GALLIARD: (*snatching the photo from him*) He's already confessed!

PROUGAULT: Guy, don't waste your time on minor matters.

GALLIARD: You need a damned seminar on wife assault.

PROUGAULT: You need a seminar on how things work around here. You can't lock him up on this.

GALLIARD: Sir, this is not his first time. Check the ...

PROUGAULT: There is a thing called a restraining order.

GALLIARD: How many ladies have been saved by a restraining order? Come on, he will be out gunning for her and he damn well knows where she lives.

PROUGAULT: That's when you lock him up.

GALLIARD: When she's dead?

PROUGAULT: Sergeant, if you put him away for a little thing like this, he will come out even madder than before he went in.

GALLIARD: Oh, you give me a black eye but I can't lock you up, even though I know you'll whack me again.

PROUGAULT: Okay, Guy, I guess you know your job better than I do. Where is the wife?

SCENE 2

From some location onstage, CLARINDA addresses the unseen judge.

CLARINDA: It's impossible, I can't believe Shazia could or would kill him. She was no different than any other woman in her situation. The man did beat her ... Mad? Of course she was mad. But I really believe she was willing to forgive.

Flashback to CLARINDA's office. She is counselling SHAZIA. GALLIARD is also present.

SHAZIA: I had to call the police.

CLARINDA: You might have waited until it was too late.

SHAZIA: I can't believe he hit me again.

CLARINDA: Again?

GALLIARD: Yes, in the report ...

CLARINDA: Thank you, Sergeant. I am sorry, Shazia – please ...

SHAZIA: Well, not like this ... A month ago he threw hot coffee on my face.

GALLIARD: (*under his breath*) Shit ...

CLARINDA: Sergeant ...

SHAZIA: I was so insulted ... so embarrassed.

CLARINDA: Didn't you tell anyone?

SHAZIA: No. I feel so little ...

GALLIARD: You don't have to, sweetheart. (*to CLARINDA*) It's okay. (*to SHAZIA*) You don't have anything to feel ashamed about. You haven't done anything wrong, he has.

SHAZIA: What will happen to him?

CLARINDA: Don't worry.

SHAZIA: Where is he?

GALLIARD: He's locked up.

CLARINDA: Please, Sergeant, will you excuse us now? Don't worry, Shazia. Sergeant Galliard will make sure ...

SHAZIA runs up to the door as GALLIARD starts to exit.

SHAZIA: (*to GALLIARD*) Don't let him out. Please don't let him. (*to CLARINDA*) They won't let him out, will they? Don't let –

CLARINDA: They won't. Not this time.

MURAD and SHAFIQA enter. They meet GALLIARD in the hallway.

SHAFIQA: Thank you, sir, thank you for saving our daughter.

MURAD: Thank you, sir.

GALLIARD: It's all right, she is safe.

MURAD: I never approved of that man.

GALLIARD: Don't worry, he won't hurt her again.

SHAFIQA: Thank you.

GALLIARD: Don't worry, he will never –

MURAD: Where is he?

GALLIARD: He's locked up. Your daughter is down the hall in that room.

SHAFIQA: Do you have him?

GALLIARD nods.

SHAFIQA: Don't let him out!

SCENE 3

From some location onstage, MURAD addresses the unseen judge.

MURAD: He deserved to die. I am sorry, Your Honour, but Sergeant Galliard, he had saved her once. He probably was doing the same. What? I don't care if he did call him Camel Breath. He could call me a Paki a thousand times if it would save my daughter …

Flashback to CLARINDA's office. She is counselling SHAZIA as in Scene 2. MURAD and SHAFIQA are present.

SHAZIA: Options?

CLARINDA: None of us are ever prepared for a thing like this. (*looking at file*) Now, you're the breadwinner in the family?

SHAZIA: He just graduated.

SHAFIQA: To his fist!

MURAD: He sits home doing nothing while you pay the bills …

SHAFIQA: While he moans about his carpet business.

SHAZIA: Ma! … (*to CLARINDA*) His father sent him carpets from Iran. But he needed a loan to start a business. (*spilling her hidden anger*) If his father tells him to sell carpets, he will sell carpets, whether he wants to or not. The carpets are lying on some dock right now. Fool of a son of a fool of a father. If his father says go jump in a well, he will bloody well go jump in a well. He is cooking up a business like a fool in an Iranian folk tale … pot hanging from the tree and candlelight on the ground.

MURAD: And she's left to fix the screw-ups!

CLARINDA: Thank you. Shazia, do you want your parents here?

SHAZIA: Yeah, it's okay. (*to her parents, in Hindi*) *Thodi dayre kay liye jaban par tala laga sakte hain?* [Can you stop talking for some time?] Please!!

SHAFIQA: Sorry, go on, doctor.

CLARINDA: So you refused to co-sign a loan for him?

SHAZIA: He can't get a loan on his own until his immigration is complete. Only God knows how long that will take. And he has already … He has already added his father and mother to the list.

MURAD: Mobsters.

SHAFIQA: They want a visa in dowry.

MURAD: Bloody criminals.

CLARINDA: What list?

SHAZIA: He went ahead and sponsored his parents even before his own visa was final. I'm broke, and he added two more dependents. I just can't. I have my parents here already. I can't.

CLARINDA: He didn't ask you first?

SHAZIA: No! He never does. It pisses me off. I'm sorry.

SHAFIQA: No, don't worry, it's okay.

CLARINDA: I understand.

SHAZIA: I just can't handle any more … I have my parents here …

MURAD: Are we a burden?

SHAFIQA: She's not saying that.

MURAD: Are we a burden? (*to CLARINDA*) Doctor, we are waiting 'til our son – he lives in Vancouver –

SHAZIA: Abbu, please, I am only saying –

MURAD: That we are a burden?

SHAFIQA: She is not saying that. And if you think you are, shut up and don't burden any more.

SHAZIA: *Ummi, Abbu, chup ho jaiye na, please.* [Mom, Dad, please keep quiet.]

MURAD: Please, doctor, go on.

CLARINDA: Well, Shazia, I should tell you what your options are.

SHAFIQA: Yes, please …

CLARINDA: We can order mediation, send him to counselling, and/or you can take him back …

SHAFIQA: What?

MURAD: What do you mean?

SHAFIQA: These are options?

SHAZIA: I am not sure.

CLARINDA: You are not sure of what?

MURAD: That we are a burden?

SHAZIA: I am not sure if I want him back anymore.

MURAD: Oh!

CLARINDA: Are you sure?

SHAZIA: I am not sure if I am sure.

CLARINDA: There is something else you can do.

SHAZIA: What?

SHAFIQA: Yes, doctor, please ...

CLARINDA: You can withdraw his sponsorship.

MURAD: You mean immigration sponsorship? Halfway through?

CLARINDA: It's a sure way of getting him out of your life.

SHAZIA: Pardon me?

CLARINDA: Deporting him!

MURAD: Good riddance. I never liked that fellow.

SHAZIA: Send him out of the country? That isn't right.

CLARINDA: What's right? Get beat up and live like a lame duck? Look, many men ... bring a bride from "back home," beat her up, and if she complains, blackmail her by threatening to send her back ... "back home." I see no reason why you can't do the same. I'm not suggesting that's what you should do. I'm telling you that it is one thing you could do.

MURAD: Yes, that's what she will do, doctor.

SHAFIQA: That's right, thank you, doctor.

MURAD: Yes, that's a good option, doctor.

CLARINDA: Thank you, but I'm not a doctor.

SHAZIA: When must I decide?

CLARINDA: Shazia, my motto is zero tolerance. My concern is for you, not him.

SHAZIA: But if I don't do this, do I have to live with him?

CLARINDA: Do you think he will leave you alone? (silence) ... I don't think so.

SCENE 4

The police station. PROUGAULT is busy completing a file. MOOLCHAND enters and waits for PROUGAULT to acknowledge him.

PROUGAULT: Can I help you?

MOOLCHAND: If you don't mind helping a coloured man?

PROUGAULT: Try me.

MOOLCHAND: I want to see a man by the name of Shapoor Farhadi.

PROUGAULT: The guy from Iran?

MOOLCHAND: That's right, the guy from Iran.

PROUGAULT: Your client assaulted his wife.

MOOLCHAND: Come on, you're talking like a judge, as though my man is already proven guilty.

PROUGAULT: What's your name?

MOOLCHAND: Moolchand. Mr. Moolchand Misra. Shapoor called me. What would you say is your name?

PROUGAULT: Gilles Prougault.

MOOLCHAND: The president of the Police Brotherhood?

PROUGAULT: Yeah.

MOOLCHAND: Lovely symbolism. Union, solidarity, brother ... HOOD. Hoods, I like that ...

PROUGAULT: What do you want?

MOOLCHAND: What were we talking about? Shapoor, Mr. President, so what are you going to do with Shapoor?

PROUGAULT: I don't know, arrest him, walk the guy around the block. Mediate. But you might have a problem: the arresting officer feels your client should be locked up.

MOOLCHAND: A white officer?

PROUGAULT: Would you like to see him now?

MOOLCHAND: You didn't take that personally, did you, Mr. Prougault? But you have to agree with me that a large number of citizens are uncomfortable with the way white officers treat other people.

PROUGAULT: Other people?

MOOLCHAND: People of colour! People from other countries, cultures, traditions, and histories ...

PROUGAULT: Mister ...

MOOLCHAND takes a step away from PROUGAULT and the scene transforms into the courtroom: MOOLCHAND addresses the unseen judge.

MOOLCHAND: I thought that white people always brought up their past. They are always telling you how their ancestors fought a war in a coloured country. (as though he is reminded by the judge) Yes, Your Honour, Mr. Prougault seemed quite nervous when I introduced myself. Nervous? Yes, like always hiding something from you. I cannot believe that I have to put my trust in men like him ...

Flashback to the police station. MOOLCHAND and PROUGAULT are present.

PROUGAULT: You mean, you're not his lawyer?

MOOLCHAND: Would it help if I said that I ... I am a member of the race tribunal.

PROUGAULT: All right. (*calling*) Shapoor Farhadi.

SHAPOOR enters.

MOOLCHAND: Shapoor!

SHAPOOR: Mr. Moolchand, please help me.

MOOLCHAND: I will. (*to PROUGAULT*) Excuse us. (*taking SHAPOOR aside*) Sit down. What happened?

SHAPOOR: I don't know ... I uh ... uh ...

MOOLCHAND: Where is she?

SHAPOOR: I don't know.

MOOLCHAND: Is there anything you do know?

SHAPOOR: I don't know. The police came and I am here. The last time ...

MOOLCHAND: Shapoor, you have been here before?

SHAPOOR: Yes. That time we just talked to some woman and Shazia and I just went home. Oh, Mr. Moolchand ...

MOOLCHAND: Why are you in jail now? Why should an East Indian wife behave in such a strange way?

SHAPOOR: I slapped her.

MOOLCHAND: You should not have.

SHAPOOR: Oh God, I know, oh God.

MOOLCHAND: What did she do?

SHAPOOR: She said insulting things about my father.

MOOLCHAND: Why?

SHAPOOR: I don't know! ... I don't know.

MOOLCHAND: I thought mothers and fathers sent their children to Canada to know everything. What happened to you? ... Shapoor, I'm sorry, I can't help you.

MOOLCHAND starts to exit. SHAPOOR stands up.

SHAPOOR: Come on, you know my father has put me in a fix.

MOOLCHAND: (*looking at PROUGAULT*) It's all right, Mr. Prougault. (*to SHAPOOR*) The carpets?

SHAPOOR: They're already on the dock. A hundred thousand dollars' worth of Persian carpets ...

MOOLCHAND: I told you to advise your father that we have rules in Canada.

SHAPOOR: I tried, and my wife advised him, too. But then I got back on the phone and he said, "Son, what kind of man have you become? Is your wife going to advise me or are you going to tell her to listen?" I tried, Mr. Moolchand, I tried to tell her ... and here I am. And if I ...

MOOLCHAND: And if you anger your father, he'll have a heart attack. Then your mother will tell you, "Son, do you want to disgrace your father by disobeying him so that he has his heart attack now instead of later?"

SHAPOOR: It's not a joke! He really does have a heart problem.

MOOLCHAND: This is more interesting than Aladdin and his carpets. Shapoor, all right ... didn't you take care of what we talked about? Do you have a place to store them? A licence to sell them? Did you manage the loan?

SHAPOOR: No, my wife won't ...

MOOLCHAND: What? Brilliance like that could only have come from a Concordia graduate.

SHAPOOR: I'm sorry.

MOOLCHAND: Now I understand why your wife must have thrown a fit. You know what will happen? Your carpets are going to rot on the docks and then they'll be auctioned off.

SHAPOOR: I wish I could just send them back. I need to talk to Shazia.

MOOLCHAND: On the other hand, not many people have an eccentric father who is willing to stuff a business with a 500 per cent profit potential down his son's throat.

SHAPOOR: Can you get me out of here?

MOOLCHAND: I could have if you hadn't hit your wife.

SHAPOOR: (*almost in tears*) Oh God, if my father finds out about this ...

MOOLCHAND: Did the cop rough you up?

SHAPOOR: What?

MOOLCHAND: (*whispering*) Did he make the crime you committed the fault of your race or your culture? You know, you being Iranian or a Muslim!

SHAPOOR: I hit her.

MOOLCHAND: You have already said that. You hit your wife. It should not happen, but it did. Now, did the cop treat you the same way he would have treated ... say ... a white person?

SHAPOOR: I don't know, he said some ...

Transition back to the present. From some location onstage, GALLIARD addresses the unseen judge.

GALLIARD: It was like it didn't matter what he did – but what I said. I am not a racist – I treat all wife beaters equally.

Immediately from another location, CLARINDA addresses the unseen judge.

CLARINDA: No! She didn't kill him. I'm sorry, Your Honour. When I first heard the accusations of Shazia killing her husband, I almost believed it. He never really seemed honest and if she did kill ...

Flashback to the police station. MOOLCHAND has come to free SHAPOOR. CLARINDA enters.

MOOLCHAND: I expected to see somebody black and blue.

CLARINDA: Sorry, just black.

MOOLCHAND: No, no. What I meant was, I was expecting to see Shazia with you.

SHAPOOR: Is she here?

CLARINDA: She decided she can't face her tormentor under the circumstances.

CLARINDA starts to exit. MOOLCHAND rushes to stop her and takes her aside.

MOOLCHAND: Ms. Ms. ... from what I hear, Shazia is not even bruised.

CLARINDA: She doesn't have to be.

MOOLCHAND: You're quite right. But ... but don't you think that's a good reason why these children should forgive and forget the whole thing.

CLARINDA: Is that what you wanted to tell her?

SHAPOOR: No ...

MOOLCHAND: No, Madam, I wanted to say he'll apologize to her in front of you and me.

SHAPOOR: I am really sorry. I am. I admit it.

CLARINDA: Is that it?

SHAPOOR: But, but ...

MOOLCHAND: A good man sometimes makes a mistake and a good woman must forgive.

SHAPOOR: Yes, tell her to forgive me.

CLARINDA: Tell her?

MOOLCHAND: Does this look like the face of a wife beater to you?

CLARINDA: Is this his real face?

MOOLCHAND: Madam ...

CLARINDA: Clarinda Keith.

MOOLCHAND: Ms. Keith, I understand you. In fact, I agree with you.

CLARINDA: Don't patronize me.

MOOLCHAND: I am not. I too have a problem with men like him ... they give us a bad name. I can't even believe he did it. You know, we joke about him because in his everyday life, he is so docile, so domesticated ... He is pretty liberated for an Iranian, you know.

CLARINDA: So liberated that he hit her because she wouldn't take out a loan for his carpet business!

MOOLCHAND: They are a family.

CLARINDA: She doesn't want to be his family anymore.

MOOLCHAND: What do you mean?

CLARINDA: She's decided to end the marriage.

SHAPOOR: She said this?

CLARINDA: She's withdrawing his sponsorship.

SHAPOOR: No. She said this? Please, no.

MOOLCHAND: It's all right, Shapoor ...
Ms. Clarinda –

CLARINDA: She is absolutely firm about it.

MOOLCHAND: Shapoor ...

SHAPOOR: Oh my God! My parents ... My parents ... what will happen to them?

CLARINDA: They won't be Shazia's burden now.

MOOLCHAND: Is there something I don't know?

MOOLCHAND looks at SHAPOOR inquisitively. SHAPOOR has an embarrassed look on his face.

CLARINDA: He hides things from you, too? He put in an application to bring his father and mother to Canada without telling his wife.

MOOLCHAND: In the family class? Why did you do that?

SHAPOOR: I can't say no to my father.

MOOLCHAND: I thought I told you –

CLARINDA: If you'll excuse me ... (*heads for the exit*)

SHAPOOR: Yes. But ...

MOOLCHAND runs to stop her.

MOOLCHAND: Ms! ... Ms!!! ... Please, so what if he wants his parents with him. What's the problem?

CLARINDA: There's no problem. He'll have his parents with him – when he's back in Iran.

SHAPOOR: No, why would ...

MOOLCHAND: Okay, okay. He went about it in the wrong way. Let's punish him, but not destroy his life ...

CLARINDA: It's not my decision. Shazia has made up her mind.

SHAPOOR: She said this?

MOOLCHAND: She has? Or did someone? ...

CLARINDA: (*to SHAPOOR*) That's why you shouldn't have hit her. Especially because you, your father, and mother depended on her in order to come here. But you got her mad.

SHAPOOR: She got me madder.

CLARINDA: Then you both are mad people. (*exits*)

PROUGAULT: Farhadi!

MOOLCHAND: Shapoor.

SHAPOOR: Shazia wouldn't say that.

MOOLCHAND: You are a certifiable idiot. Why in the family class? With that kind of money they are investors before they are your family.

SHAPOOR: What?

MOOLCHAND: They should be put in the "investor class." You fool. If you had listened to me by now your father would have been buying up real estate in Laval. Now you can't transfer them to a different class.

SHAPOOR: Oh God, I am such an idiot. Please, can't you do something?

PROUGAULT steps forward.

PROUGAULT: Farhadi, let's go.

SHAPOOR: Mr. Moolchand.

MOOLCHAND: Wait, Mr. President, I'll take responsibility for him. What forms must be signed? Who do I see? This boy needs to go home and clear his mind.

PROUGAULT: He will, as soon they can book a flight.

MOOLCHAND: What? What are you saying?

PROUGAULT: I've said enough, you're not his lawyer. Let's go.

MOOLCHAND: Where are you taking him?

PROUGAULT: He will be in detention until deported home.

SHAPOOR: No!

MOOLCHAND: Hold on ... deported?

SHAPOOR: No – you can't do that!

PROUGAULT: Those are the immigration rules.

SHAPOOR: Please let me talk to Shazia.

MOOLCHAND: One more coloured man out of Canada, eh, Mr. President? What is going on here?

SHAPOOR: Where's Shazia?

MOOLCHAND: (*turning to SHAPOOR*) Shapoor, let me handle this.

SHAPOOR: Shazia! Shazia! I am sorry, Shazia ...

SHAPOOR runs out the door.

PROUGAULT: Sergeant!

SHAPOOR: Please forgive me, Shazia.

There is loud shouting and screaming offstage. GALLIARD brings SHAPOOR back. He pushes SHAPOOR forcefully and SHAPOOR falls down on the floor.

GALLIARD: Hey! Get back in the room.

MOOLCHAND: Shapoor, Shapoor ...

SHAPOOR: (*to MOOLCHAND*) I only wanted to tell her ...

MOOLCHAND: There, there, enough said ...

SHAPOOR: Please, sir, I beg you. I am sorry. I promise I will never ...

MOOLCHAND: Shapoor ...

GALLIARD: Too late, you should have –

PROUGAULT: Galliard, shut up!

SHAPOOR: Please, sir, oh please. (*crying*) I am sorry.

MOOLCHAND: Very well, officers. Look at him. You have succeeded in scaring him. He will not strike his wife again. I assure you. Please tell me, what can we do?

PROUGAULT and MOOLCHAND stand facing each other. SHAPOOR stays sitting helplessly between them. The two men exchange tense looks as we move to the next scene.

SCENE 5

CLARINDA's office. She is talking to the family (SHAZIA, SHAFIQA, and MURAD).

SHAZIA: Am I being cruel to him?

SHAFIQA: No, Shazia!

MURAD: Don't be ridiculous.

CLARINDA: You are being kind to yourself. I am very proud of you.

MURAD: Proud of a husbandless woman?

SHAFIQA: Murad!

CLARINDA: She has done something that no battered woman has.

SHAZIA: Clarinda ... I'm not doing this.

CLARINDA: This will send the message loud and clear. 'Cause back home he will have to explain why he was deported. He'll have to face the embarrassment. Everybody will learn the price for hitting a woman. Here or anywhere.

MURAD: Well, good.

CLARINDA: Okay! We still have a few legal things to do.

SHAZIA: I already signed the separation papers, didn't I?

CLARINDA: No, we need to discuss your share of the carpets.

SHAZIA: I don't want a cent from them.

MURAD: You need the money.

SHAZIA: I don't want the carpets!

SHAFIQA: Shazia.

SHAZIA: No, Ma!

SHAFIQA: This girl is stupid. All she wants is to end her unhappy marriage, as if marriage was a happy thing.

MURAD: As if she will become happy after ending her marriage.

SHAZIA: Abbu, please!

Suddenly from some location onstage, PROUGAULT addresses the unseen judge.

PROUGAULT: Yes. I didn't know why he did it. He was always doing things like that. I had warned Sergeant Galliard about his behaviour many times. I am sorry, Guy. I tried to warn you ...

Flashback to the police station. GALLIARD stamps a report and gives it to MOOLCHAND.

GALLIARD: No, no, your man isn't here. You can pick him up downstairs.

MOOLCHAND: That way? Thank you, you have been so kind. (*seeing PROUGAULT*) Oh! Hello – Mr. President!

PROUGAULT: Has Farhadi been released?

GALLIARD: Did you hear that race tribunal guy?

PROUGAULT: Has Farhadi been released? Why did you just send Moolchand downstairs?

GALLIARD: Where does a guy like that get ten thousand dollars' bond money?

PROUGAULT: Sergeant ...

GALLIARD: Colour power.

SHAPOOR enters.

SHAPOOR: Where is Mr. Moolchand?

GALLIARD starts to walk toward SHAPOOR.

PROUGAULT: Guy, what are you doing?

GALLIARD: (*to SHAPOOR*) Listen, asshole, I can't keep you locked up, but if you go anywhere near her I will ship you back to where you came from.

SHAPOOR: Ah ... ah ...

PROUGAULT: That's enough, Galliard. Okay Farhadi, go ...

SHAPOOR starts to exit. GALLIARD grabs his arm and pulls him back.

PROUGAULT: (*under his breath*) Fuck.

GALLIARD: Listen, boy, if you want to live in our country, you live by our rules. You understand that? You don't beat your women in this country! Bond or no bond, you touch her and I will send you to hell.

PROUGAULT: (*to SHAPOOR*) Your friend is waiting downstairs. Ask for Lieutenant Green.

SHAPOOR exits.

PROUGAULT: (*to GALLIARD*) Sergeant, you are too rough. What's the matter with you? Have you never heard of the term "slander suit"?

We return from the flashback to the present time as we move to the next scene.

SCENE 6

CLARINDA's office. SHAZIA, SHAFIQA, and MURAD.

MURAD: No, I'd rather Shazia not be seen outside.

CLARINDA: Don't worry, he can't touch her anymore.

SHAFIQA: No, no, it's because his friends will say, "There goes Rizvi's daughter who has brought shame to his family."

MURAD: Oh, you be quiet.

SHAZIA: Abbu, Ummi, I'll be okay. You can go to Vancouver. Naushad needs you more than I do. I'll be fine.

CLARINDA: Oh, your parents are leaving?

SHAZIA: Yes, they were supposed to fly out tomorrow to see my brother.

SHAFIQA: Yeah, he needs us to babysit his brat so he can look after his video store. But we'll stay until …

From some location onstage, MOOLCHAND addresses the unseen judge.

MOOLCHAND: When I found out Shapoor died, I was not sure. He seemed to love his wife a great deal. But she seemed bent on destroying him. It was not good enough to divorce him. She wanted him deported … gone, maybe dead. I'm not saying she killed him. When he talked to me after I got him released on bond …

Flashback to the front of the police station. MOOLCHAND comes out of the police station finishing his conversation with an officer offstage.

MOOLCHAND: Yes, tell him I'll be waiting outside.

SHAPOOR exits the police station.

SHAPOOR: Thank you very much for getting me out. Did you talk to Shazia?

MOOLCHAND: It's not over yet.

SHAPOOR: Did you tell her how sorry …

MOOLCHAND: You want your parents here, we have got to open a retail store and sell carpets.

SHAPOOR: Mr. Moolchand, how is she doing? I need to go home.

MOOLCHAND: Shapoor, Shapoor …

MOOLCHAND gives SHAPOOR a document.

SHAPOOR: What's this?

MOOLCHAND: Restraining order!

SHAPOOR: What? Fuck!

SHAPOOR starts to rush off. MOOLCHAND grabs him and pulls him back.

SHAPOOR: I have to go.

MOOLCHAND: You can't go. Listen – if you get closer than a hundred yards to her, my friend, they will deport you.

SHAPOOR: Oh God, I look at my hands and I see my father's hands. I feel awful. I shouldn't have hit her.

MOOLCHAND: Yes. Now, do you want me to take care of the carpets?

SHAPOOR: I just want to tell her I didn't mean it. I understand now why she didn't want my parents … my father here. If she had just given me time, I could have understood. I am not my father. Why? Why? I just kept hitting her hoping that she would see. I'm not my father.

MOOLCHAND: Is he that bad?

SHAPOOR: Sergeant Galliard is right. Oh God, I need a policeman to protect my wife from me.

MOOLCHAND: Did he threaten you? Shapoor. Did he? What else did he tell you?

SHAPOOR: He is right. He's right …

MOOLCHAND: He's right about what?

SHAPOOR: Maybe I should be locked up.

MOOLCHAND: Do you know what that fucking cop did to you? Do you think the officer really cares for your wife? Look, my neighbour, a white guy, got drunk and made pulp out of his wife before passing out. The cop tells her, "Call us when he wakes up." Why didn't the cop arrest him?

SHAPOOR: I don't know.

MOOLCHAND: That cop had nothing to gain by arresting one of his own tribesmen. It is only when they find someone "different" that they get all dutiful. And then they get your wife to collaborate with them.

SHAPOOR: If I could talk to her …

MOOLCHAND: Go home, break the restraining order, see what they do!

SHAPOOR: But Mr. Moolchand, maybe she won't …

MOOLCHAND: She is kicking you out of the country.

SHAPOOR: She can't, you have a bond on me.

MOOLCHAND: The bond is to keep you out of the jail – it can't protect you from being deported.

SHAPOOR: What?

MOOLCHAND: Where do you think the bond money came from anyway? (*pause*) Your carpets.

SHAPOOR: All the carpets?

MOOLCHAND: Yes.

SHAPOOR: My father …

MOOLCHAND: Just until this is all settled. That's why we need to open a store and sell those carpets, but to do that I have to keep you in the country. We have to find a way to stop them from making an example of you.

SHAPOOR: What the fuck are you talking about?

MOOLCHAND: Have you ever heard of anyone getting kicked out of the city, let alone the country, for hitting their wife? They're using you to scare us.

SHAPOOR: Why are they doing this to me?

MOOLCHAND speaks the following lines with a Canadian accent instead of his usual East Indian.

MOOLCHAND: I don't know. Because you are Muslim. And they think you are all terrorists, out to get Salman Rushdie, blow up Bay Street ... your people breed like crazy ... might take over Canada. Don't you get it? Your community is a growing concern to them ... taking over entire suburbs, shopping malls, I don't know. Your community is doing pretty good for a minority, but hey, then you utter the word "minority," everybody thinks about blacks only.

SHAPOOR: Mr. Moolchand, what happened to your accent?

The return of the East Indian accent brings us back to the present as MOOLCHAND addresses the unseen judge.

MOOLCHAND: Against the police, the immigration, and the justice system! Shapoor's only fault is that he struck his wife. But that didn't even leave a mark on her body. But then he was also begging her for her mercy ... and yes, Shapoor was about to set up a business, may have created a couple of jobs. What does he get in punishment? Deportation! I say that the system didn't work. This boy did not die in vain and I plan to do something about it. They will see what this minority can do!

SCENE 7

From some location onstage, CLARINDA addresses the unseen judge.

CLARINDA: No! No! No! He did not care about anyone, Your Honour – Shapoor or Shazia. He doesn't know what it's like to be hit 'cause he does all the hitting. If I were you, I'd check where those carpets are now. Who is selling them?

Flashback to CLARINDA's office. MOOLCHAND enters.

MOOLCHAND: No, no, please. First give me an opportunity to greet you.

CLARINDA: All right.

MOOLCHAND: How are you?

CLARINDA: How about you?

MOOLCHAND: Clarinda, I need your help, I really do.

CLARINDA: How?

MOOLCHAND: It's about Shapoor ...

CLARINDA: I'm sorry, Mr. Moolchand, I –

MOOLCHAND: I know how you feel. Please listen – he's a good man with so much potential. I know right now that he can't control his rage, but he needs our help. He can't get help if he is thrown out. What I am saying is – us, the East Indians, the Africans, the Chinese ... you know – people like you and me – if we are to survive, we must be united. Help each other.

CLARINDA: Because we are coloureds?

MOOLCHAND: Without Shazia, Shapoor has nobody here, no family, no support, nothing. Right now he happens to be one of many unfortunate men in this country because he happens to be a man of the wrong colour and culture.

CLARINDA: Nobody's culture equals torture. He hit her because he is a man and she is a woman. It's nothing to do with culture.

MOOLCHAND: Please, listen to me – listen to me ... help us. He is not a typical Canuck, opens a beer, watches hockey, and scores, punches at the wife for fun.

CLARINDA: No, he doesn't play hockey.

MOOLCHAND: He's one of us, see?

CLARINDA: Isn't she also one of us?

MOOLCHAND: That's why she shouldn't deport him.

CLARINDA: And give him an opportunity to attack her again? And turn the crime against her into her own fault? No!

MOOLCHAND: (*pulling out a declaration*) Okay, this thing bears the signatures of some very important ethno-cultural leaders, including a couple of MPs of colour.

CLARINDA: Signatures for what?

MOOLCHAND: Stopping his deportation.

CLARINDA: Where did you get all these?

MOOLCHAND: I'm trying to help Shapoor.

CLARINDA: I'm trying to protect Shazia.

MOOLCHAND: Somebody should try to forgive him.

CLARINDA: Somebody is trying to forget him.

MOOLCHAND: Is that why she has gone public?

CLARINDA: (*sarcastically*) God forbid the victims go public and the world might hear them.

MOOLCHAND: But what do we hear? Victims? No. Miss Clarinda Keith's "zero tolerance" in the *Gazette*. Shapoor's father is a lunatic on the CBC. How about hearing him? No wonder she provokes the hell out of him.

CLARINDA: Provoking ain't a crime, battering is. Got that?

MOOLCHAND: Got it.

CLARINDA: Excuse me, I'm busy.

MOOLCHAND: You know, you're a very determined woman. You'll need to be. (*bringing out another letter*) Some of us want an inquiry.

CLARINDA: I know.

MOOLCHAND: (*giving her the letter*) Look again. Inquiry into a larger problem. Inquiry into what Sergeant Galliard did.

CLARINDA: What?

MOOLCHAND: Galliard is a racist.

CLARINDA: A woman was assaulted here.

MOOLCHAND: He racially assaulted Shapoor.

CLARINDA: You can't be serious. That's not the issue here.

MOOLCHAND: Right here in Montreal, eight men of colour have been shot dead by the police, and you want to tell me the officers aren't racist?

CLARINDA: Galliard isn't one of them.

MOOLCHAND: Just the other day the officers looked very happy because there was a black taxi driver in custody. When officers have that smile on their faces and there is a black man in custody, do you know what's coming?

CLARINDA: Don't teach me what racism is!

MOOLCHAND: Just because you are a shade darker?

CLARINDA: Get the hell out of my office.

MOOLCHAND: Guy Galliard is a chronic racist.

CLARINDA: He saved that woman's life.

MOOLCHAND: I want him removed from his job.

CLARINDA: What kind of man are you? Do you know what you're trying to do here? There is no other officer who runs the domestic unit as well as Galliard does. You take him to the inquiry and I'll be his expert witness. Now get out.

MOOLCHAND: Bravo! Bravo. A black woman, turned activist, turned expert, turned witness for a racist cop! I hate to say it, but there is something wrong with a person who doesn't stand by her own community.

CLARINDA: Shazia's my community.

MOOLCHAND: Every time you open your mouth, whoop ... a cliché spills out of it.

CLARINDA: Out!

MOOLCHAND: Let's both take a deep breath.

CLARINDA: Out!

MOOLCHAND: Don't you think the whites hate us enough already? Do you want to give them one more excuse to hate us?

CLARINDA: Whites don't have time to hate us. They are too busy paying the bills and raising their families.

MOOLCHAND: And you're too busy chasing a poor man of colour out of the country.

CLARINDA: Cut the crap. Canada deports drug dealers, not wife beaters.

MOOLCHAND: Then it's sad you are doing this country's dirty work. (*flashing the paper*) Well, it's my turn to talk to the press. People in the community must know where you stand.

CLARINDA: Get out or I'll call the police.

MOOLCHAND: The police? That confirms where you stand. I am going, but I want you to think about something. There is an immigrant business in the making. There is a troubled young man, there is his sick father. I just want you to remember this. (*exits*)

SCENE 8

From some location onstage, SHAFIQA addresses the unseen judge.

SHAFIQA: No, no, Your Honour, my husband – he was so possessed – shame – he said – our lives were filled with shame. I don't know why he says these things. He is a gentle man, Your Honour. He could not have done that. He could not have killed that poor boy but, Your Honour, he was just so upset with our community.

Flashback to the Rizvi family home. MURAD enters in a bad and irritated mood.

MURAD: Shafiqa ... Shafiqa?

SHAFIQA: (*offstage*) In the kitchen.

MURAD: Come out.

SHAFIQA enters talking.

SHAFIQA: You worried about what goes on in your wife's kitchen?

MURAD: Accidents – and I eat them. Do you know what they are saying in the meeting? Mr. Moolchand ...

SHAFIQA: Don't make it harder for her.

MURAD: Why can't she behave the way daughters behave back home? (*calling*) Shazia! Shazia!

SHAFIQA: She is with Clarinda.

MURAD: The black woman?

SHAFIQA: Yes, to register something.

MURAD: Is Clarinda married?

SHAFIQA: No, she is happy.

MURAD: How can a woman who makes her living breaking families be happy? I'll not allow her in this house.

SHAFIQA: That's enough! Take off your shoes – come and eat.

MURAD: You know, nobody talked to me at the mosque. They all think that the failure of the daughter is due to the failure of the father. Shazia has no shame in being husbandless, but I do.

SHAFIQA: I didn't know you wanted a husband.

MURAD: It's not a joke. I have to take Shazia to the imam.

SHAFIQA: No mullah is going to decide my daughter's fate.

MURAD: You don't live in the real world, do you? What will happen to her? What man will marry her?

SHAFIQA: One who won't hit her! Now come and eat.

MURAD: (*showing her a newspaper*) No, wait – look what they say about her. Look! Do you have any idea who marries a divorced woman? A convict, a handicap, or an old widower with ten children! Is that what you want for her? Shafiqa *begum*,

nobody wants a divorced woman, she is all used up ... nothing left, not even her dignity.

SHAFIQA: Used up? It's our daughter you're talking about. Shame on you! I am ashamed of you.

MURAD: Remember when it happened between my sister and her husband? Didn't my father go to the mullah?

SHAFIQA: (*mocking him*) And that stupid mullah said, "Lock her up, starve her, give her a chance to behave before you smack her."

MURAD: You say what you please, but the next day he bought her an expensive saree and she was fine.

SHAFIQA: No wonder she had so many expensive sarees.

MURAD: That's not the point!

SHAFIQA: My daughter will not go to any mullah.

MURAD: All right then, let's move out of the city, where there is no mullah and no Clarinda.

SHAFIQA: And no Moolchand!

MURAD: Do you know what Moolchand said at the meeting? "We don't need the RCMP to kick out a man of colour. We need a Canadian wife to do that."

SHAFIQA: When you go to the next meeting, tell that mullah and Moolchand if they say a word about my daughter I will chase *them* out of the country. Now come and eat!

We return to the present time.

SCENE 9

From some location onstage, GALLIARD addresses the unseen judge.

GALLIARD: I remember when my dad got mad, my mom got beat up. He kicked the door, ripped the phone out of the wall, threw food, and pulled big handfuls of her hair. My dad was six feet tall, three hundred pounds. When he got started, my brother ran to pull the curtains and I hid behind the door with my hands over my ears and my eyes closed. My mother died and everybody believed it was in her sleep. (*pause*) So when I see someone beat his wife, part of me says, "Send him to hell." Is that racist, Judge?

Flashback to the police station.

PROUGAULT: He's charged you with racial misconduct.

GALLIARD: Bullshit.

PROUGAULT gives GALLIARD a letter.

PROUGAULT: I have tried to warn you, Guy.

GALLIARD: (*reading*) "Cultural Insensitivity or Racism: Police Still White." (*breathing out with relief*) So?

PROUGAULT: Every word that scares the hell out of a white cop is here ... "Used excessive force and racial slurs ..."

GALLIARD: Come on, do you know one cop who doesn't use foul language?

PROUGAULT: Not foul language, Sergeant, racial language.

GALLIARD: The other day, I called a Scotsman a skirt-wearing dyke, and he called me a French toad.

PROUGAULT: You called him an Iranian.

GALLIARD: So?

PROUGAULT: You denied him his "Canadian identity."

GALLIARD: And if I called him Canadian, wouldn't I be denying him his "ethnic roots"? I don't chase words, I chase criminals.

PROUGAULT: You're famous, Sarge! Haven't you seen the paper today? You're on the front page. You're on the front page of every newspaper. And on the chief's desk. When you go home tonight tell your wife and son, "I'm racist." An Iranian made you famous, Guy.

GALLIARD: I'd like to break that currychand's neck.

PROUGAULT: Shut up, Sergeant. I don't need your garbage mouth doing any more damage! Every ethno-cultural leader and bleeding-heart white is calling! Fuck, I don't need another inquiry, not with the union election coming up.

GALLIARD: What inquiry?

PROUGAULT: The chief has ordered an inquiry.

GALLIARD: He thinks I am a racist?

PROUGAULT: He got a call from Bouchard's office. Damage control after Parizeau's ethnic remark!

GALLIARD: Bouchard?

PROUGAULT: You're the first victim, Guy. "We lost the referendum because of the ethnics." The man lost the battle of his life because he didn't have ethnics on his side. Surely Mr. Bouchard has to woo ethnics. How do you expect the chief not to call an inquiry?

GALLIARD: Bullshit!

PROUGAULT: He ain't got the race card up his sleeve. "Will that be cash or credit?" "Put it on my race card, baby." You can charge "justice" to the race card. Used to be blacks. Now, it's every fucking shade of people. Racism has turned into a contagious disease.

GALLIARD: An inquiry, because of this Iranian bastard. Jesus ...

PROUGAULT: (*flashing a document*) Moolchand doesn't know when to stop. Now he's saying, "We should have coloured officers serving coloured criminals."

GALLIARD: Really! When a coloured man smacks his wife, we must find a cop of matching colour and race. Maybe it'd been better if I just killed the guy instead of calling him an Iranian.

PROUGAULT: Sergeant, shut up.

GALLIARD: I ain't a racist. Clarinda knows that and she's black. She and I have worked together plenty of times.

PROUGAULT: Guy, Clarinda is fixated on gender – she wants more ladies on the force because ladies serve ladies better.

GALLIARD: That's great. I will teach my boy – you want something – just blame someone. Women blame men, blacks blame whites, homos blame heteros (*laughs*), but that's fine because I'll do my job.

PROUGAULT: Sarge, you are being removed from the domestic unit until the inquiry clears you.

GALLIARD: What the fuck ...

PROUGAULT: I warned you.

GALLIARD: That ain't fair.

PROUGAULT: I'm sorry.

GALLIARD: Ten years of service, hundreds of citations ...

PROUGAULT: I have no choice. Moolchand got his wish.

SCENE 10

*From some location onstage, **GALLIARD** addresses the unseen judge.*

GALLIARD: I was trained to run the domestic unit. That's my job! And I had to sit around some desk while he ran around. And what if he hit her again? No one would care.

*From another location, **MURAD** addresses the unseen judge.*

MURAD: Your Honour, if you had seen Shazia before she married this ... this man ... We had such hopes for her. Our little chatterbox. We called her that. 'Cause she talked and talked until her jaws began to hurt from talking before she would fall asleep. We were always ...

Flashback to Rizvi family home. SHAZIA is sleeping in her bed, SHAFIQA sitting beside her. MURAD enters.

SHAFIQA: Shh. Don't scream. (*looking at SHAZIA*) Poor girl, came back from the doctor and hasn't said a word.

MURAD kisses SHAZIA's forehead.

MURAD: Shafiqa begum, I never imagined that I would ever smell beer in my daughter's breath. *Baap ray baap* [Father, my father].

Lights fade. In the next scene, lights cross-fade from one location or actor to the other in uninterrupted succession to indicate that events are happening simultaneously.

Lights come up on MOOLCHAND, who is delivering a speech.

MOOLCHAND: Yes, I want people of colour on the force, but not by preferential treatment. I say that if you have ten dollars, you must get the same value for your ten dollars whether you are white or black. Do the non-whites have the same opportunity as their white brothers to earn those ten dollars? That is not me talking. No. That is the Auditor General of Canada ... and no, he is not a whining Mr. Moolchand, he is a white man who has the courage to say the truth.

Lights come up on SHAZIA, who has just woken up. Her parents continue their conversation, unaware she is awake. MURAD pulls out a letter.

SHAFIQA: What's that?

MURAD: (*whispering*) Major Sahib is still shopping for a bride abroad for his son.

SHAFIQA: What will you do when Major Sahib finds out that your daughter is all "used up"?

MURAD: He is our best bet.

SHAZIA gets up.

SHAZIA: Are you betting on me?

MURAD: No, no, *beti* [daughter], I'm not betting on you, but you need a husband.

SHAZIA: I don't need a husband. I have a husband.

MURAD: If I talked to my father like that, *aray baap rey baap* [oh Father, my father].

SHAZIA: *Aray baap rey* what? Why must you find a husband for me? Because I am a misfit, I drink sometimes. I want a divorce and a Muslim woman is not allowed to. Is that your *baap rey* what? Abbu, why must I defend myself? (*breaks into tears and exits*)

MURAD: Shazia ...

SHAFIQA: Beti ...

Lights fade and come up again on MOOLCHAND, who continues with his speech.

MOOLCHAND: I think violence towards women is appalling. In the culture I come from, women are treated with respect.

Lights fade and come up on the family home.

SHAFIQA: Are you happy now?

MURAD: Would you be happy if your daughter scolded you?

SHAFIQA: Murad, we have to help her.

MURAD: I just wanted to find her a new husband so she won't have to ... to live in the fear of the old one.

SHAFIQA: Really?

MURAD: Yes, really! What do you think?

SHAZIA re-enters.

SHAZIA: Abbu, Ummi, you don't have to stay for me. Just go to Vancouver now. (*storms out*)

Lights fade and come up on GALLIARD.

GALLIARD: I'm not guilty! I swore to tell the truth and ...

Lights fade and come up again on the family.

MURAD: Does she really want us to leave?

SHAFIQA: Of course not. She is just upset with you. Come, let's go for a walk. Let her clear her mind. Then I'll talk to her. (*calling*) Beti, lock the door, we will be back soon.

SHAZIA: (*offstage*) Okay.

MURAD and SHAFIQA exit. Meanwhile, SHAPOOR appears and stands near the Rizvi family house.

Lights fade and come up on MOOLCHAND, who is continuing his speech.

MOOLCHAND: That's why I want people of colour in the force, to work side by side with the white cops. So that the white cop will see that the coloured cop next to him is just as human as anybody else. The best way to win over your enemy is to love your enemy.

Lights fade and come up on the family home. Now SHAZIA *is alone. She hears a knock.*

SHAZIA: Who is it? Didn't you take the key, Ma?

She opens the door and finds SHAPOOR *there.* SHAZIA *steps back.*

SHAPOOR: Don't. Please. Don't call the police. Please.

SHAZIA: You shouldn't be here.

SHAPOOR: I just want to talk.

SHAZIA: What?

SHAPOOR: (*pause*) Hi ...

SHAZIA: Hi ...

SHAPOOR: I thought ... maybe you moved.

SHAZIA: Well, I didn't.

Lights fade and come up on CLARINDA's *office. She is in conversation with* GALLIARD.

GALLIARD: Well, at first I just told him not to move.

CLARINDA: Did he?

GALLIARD: Well, no, but it was all very fast. I mean, I didn't know how badly she was hurt.

CLARINDA: Did Shapoor try to run?

Lights fade and come up again on the family home.

SHAPOOR: I called, but you had taken an unlisted number.

SHAZIA: You better go now. My parents will be ...

SHAPOOR: Please, Shazia, don't hate me. I have nobody to turn to. My family ... they're in danger. (*pause*) I would not risk coming here if it weren't serious. (*pause*) Please ... I'm begging. Just listen to me and I'll go.

SHAZIA moves back.

SHAPOOR: I won't move.

SHAZIA stops.

SHAPOOR: Please don't be afraid of me.

SHAPOOR takes a step toward her.

SHAZIA: Don't move. Please.

SHAPOOR: Shazia, how are you?

SHAZIA: What do you want?

SHAPOOR: Shazia.

SHAZIA: Shapoor.

SHAPOOR: My mother and father ... Please let me finish. They're in danger. They had to flee from Iran.

SHAZIA: Where to? Pierre Elliott Trudeau Airport without a visa?

SHAPOOR: They escaped to India. They are in a jail, in Bombay.

SHAZIA: What kind of business is your father doing?

SHAPOOR: The Iranian government put him on the list to be tried.

Lights fade and come up on PROUGAULT.

PROUGAULT: I understand where this Moolchand is coming from. Once I went to Toronto ... on a private visit. I took the bus; the driver was an Indian. Not Indian Indian. East Indian. In Toronto a lot of them are driving buses. He told me that I was a dime short but I was sure that I had put in the right fare. So I dropped another dime. And throughout the ride, that's all that I thought about ... a coloured guy telling me I was a dime short.

Lights fade out and come up again on the family home. SHAZIA *and* SHAPOOR *are talking.*

SHAZIA: Because, you fool of a son, you put them in the family class.

SHAPOOR: He is locked in a jail full of criminals. Shazia, you know my father is very ill. This shock may kill him.

SHAZIA: What do you want? Money?

SHAPOOR: No, the only way I can bring them to safety is if ... if you ... if I'm not deported.

Lights fade and come up again on MOOLCHAND, *who is still making his speech.*

MOOLCHAND: Let's not forget, Shapoor did something wrong, a horrible act that unfortunately so many men do. I don't condone him. But I wish we lived in a society where we learn to understand why the problem exists and heal it. Hate the wrong, not the wrongdoer. That is why I will not allow ...

Lights fade and come up again on SHAZIA *and* SHAPOOR.

SHAZIA: I can't ...

SHAPOOR: I am begging you to just delay the divorce ... so that ...

SHAZIA: Delay? You do want a divorce?

SHAPOOR: Only until you ...

SHAZIA: What am I? A bargaining chip to negotiate your father's escape?

SHAPOOR: No – I love you.

Lights fade and come up on CLARINDA's office, where she and GALLIARD are still talking.

GALLIARD: *A-I-I-R-A-N* ... Yeah, I said that because I knew that he would listen. You know, get his attention.

CLARINDA: Why, what was he doing?

GALLIARD: He was very ... you know ... moving around ... quick, jerky ... agitated. Kind of ... you know.

Lights fade and come up again on SHAZIA and SHAPOOR.

SHAZIA: Why is that policeman under inquiry? Who made them investigate Clarinda's ethics? I can't even see her again until this inquiry is over.

SHAPOOR: I know, I know, I don't know what to do about Moolchand. He's out of control.

SHAZIA: I'm a bar-hopping slut who has no respect for family values.

SHAPOOR: No, I'll tell him to stop. I promise.

SHAZIA: When? When I am dragged into the court?

SHAPOOR: I promise I will break all ties with Moolchand, all right?

SHAZIA: Provided I delay the divorce until your father arrives safely in Canada.

SHAPOOR: Yes, no. Please.

SHAZIA: Get out.

Lights fade and come up again on CLARINDA's office.

CLARINDA: That's all you said? Guy, this inquiry's not a joke. It's important that you remember everything a little more clearly.

GALLIARD: I didn't stop to memorize everything I did. Every situation is different. When you walk in there ... it's not easy, you know. You never know if he is waiting behind some door, has a gun ... you know ...

Lights go out on CLARINDA's office and come back up on SHAZIA and SHAPOOR.

SHAZIA: No. Leave or I'll call ... the police.

SHAPOOR: Don't. I was wrong. I didn't know any better.

SHAZIA: And you never will! Leave.

SHAPOOR stands still, visibly tense and angry.

Lights fade and come up on PROUGAULT. GALLIARD is standing a short distance from him.

PROUGAULT: I mean, this guy remembers his fucking history. Two centuries under the English. Now he thinks it is his turn to get back at them. A kind of show of power!

GALLIARD: Getting back at the English, eh?

PROUGAULT: Do I look English to you?

GALLIARD: You act very French.

PROUGAULT: (*pause*) Yeah ...

Lights fade and come up again on SHAZIA and SHAPOOR. With a sudden outburst of anger, SHAPOOR grabs SHAZIA.

SHAZIA: Let me go! You'll be sorry if you don't ...

SHAPOOR: I am sorry, I said I am sorry ... But you won't listen. I am sorry ... Listen to me ... I am sorry ... my whole goddamn life is sorry ...

SHAZIA: You're hurting me!

SHAPOOR throws her on the bed. Lights fade and come up on MOOLCHAND, who is in the middle of his speech.

MOOLCHAND: Some of my best friends are white. Just the other day a white woman told me she would have married me instead of her fourth husband.

Lights fade and come up again on SHAZIA and SHAPOOR.

SHAPOOR: No. You be sorry, too. Call the newspaper. What's the number? (*picking up the phone book*) Call them, tell them ... (*starts to rip out pages, looking for a number and repeating himself*) I am sorry ... say sorry ...

SHAZIA: Go away!

SHAPOOR: Not before telling everyone.

He tears pages from the telephone book and starts to throw them at SHAZIA. He attacks her violently. She falls to the floor. SHAPOOR stands over her and in an uncontrollable rage stuffs torn pages into her mouth.

SHAPOOR: You are going to call the newspaper and tell them. I want the world to know that my father is dying and you don't give a fuck. (*dialing the phone; to SHAZIA*) Say you are sorry ... you'll – (*to the person on the other end of the line*) Hello, yes ... who writes the front page? What ... What ... NO! Wait. (*holding the phone; to SHAZIA*) Say sorry ... sorry ... sorry ...

SHAPOOR stops. Steps back. SHAZIA tries to get up but falls back. SHAPOOR drops the phone and starts to cry in shame.

Lights fade and come up again on MOOLCHAND, who is still speaking.

MOOLCHAND: My friends, let the truth be spoken: a police force which sees only a criminal in a person of colour is incapable of treating us as human beings.

Lights fade and come up again on the Rizvi family home. SHAFIQA and MURAD return from their walk and find SHAZIA lying on the floor.

SHAFIQA: Oh my God ...

MURAD: Hi Allah ...

Lights fade and come up again on PROUGAULT, who is still talking with GALLIARD.

PROUGAULT: And then, when I was getting off the bus, I saw my dime on the floor. I held it up to him. "Here it is." But he didn't even look. I waved, "Take care, man." He says, "You too."

GALLIARD: He said, "You too," eh?

PROUGAULT: So I understand what Moolchand wants to be and what he is. He is not black, he is not white. He's a mongrel.

Lights fade and come up on the family home. SHAFIQA takes SHAZIA away. MURAD picks up torn pages, and SHAPOOR is whisked away and handcuffed by an unseen cop.

SCENE 11

Lights come up on PROUGAULT, who is talking to CLARINDA.

PROUGAULT: Every cop was tried.

CLARINDA: When was the last cop punished?

PROUGAULT: Have you heard the term "benefit of the doubt"?

CLARINDA: What doubt? Killing's a crime, even if it is done by a cop. That's why Moolchand has become your headache. He is not Galliard's problem, the Brotherhood is. Do yourself a favour. If you get re-elected, clean up the Brotherhood.

PROUGAULT: You know what's funny? Coloureds don't act mistreated unless they are caught breaking the law.

GALLIARD: (*offstage*) Fuck!

CLARINDA: What?

PROUGAULT: What happened?

GALLIARD enters.

GALLIARD: Restraining order, eh? That Iranian attacked his wife again.

CLARINDA: Oh my God. Shazia ...

GALLIARD: (*to CLARINDA*) Queen Elizabeth Hospital.

CLARINDA: Thank you ... Oh God. (*rushes off*)

PROUGAULT: (*in her direction*) Should I send one of my men to arrest him or look for an Iranian cop?

GALLIARD: They just picked him up. He's down the hall ...

GALLIARD starts to go in that direction.

PROUGAULT: Galliard! Get back to your desk. The two of you have done enough damage around here already.

GALLIARD stops. He is visibly angry. PROUGAULT motions to him to go in the other direction.

SCENE 12

From some location onstage, MURAD addresses the unseen judge.

MURAD: Has your daughter ever been beaten to the last thread of her life? (*pause*) I'm sorry. Yes, I am sorry, Your Honour ... It's just, when you hold your little daughter in your arms and you realize she needs your help. I ...

SCENE 13

Detention cell. SHAPOOR is locked up, devastated, distraught, and incoherent. PROUGAULT delivers MOOLCHAND to the cell. MOOLCHAND walks up to SHAPOOR while PROUGAULT stands outside the cell.

SHAPOOR: Mr. Moolchand ...

MOOLCHAND: Shithead ... Iranian shithead ... Complete shithead. Why don't you take on someone your own size? Idiot. What will I tell everybody now? That I'm protecting a proven wife beater?

SHAPOOR: Forgive me, please.

MOOLCHAND: Shut up. We were getting somewhere. We were finally going to have some coloured cops on the force. You were going to give the most important testimony. You blew it. I had Galliard cornered. I could have proven him a racist.

SHAPOOR: You won't have to prove anything anymore. I'm withdrawing the charges against Galliard.

MOOLCHAND: *What?*

> *MOOLCHAND hits SHAPOOR with a rolled newspaper, then hits him again and again. SHAPOOR goes down on the floor.*

MOOLCHAND: *Gaddha!* [donkey!] That is a slap in my face – a big bloody slap.

SHAPOOR: Please. I won't ask anything more. Just get me out of here. I won't go near her, I won't ...

MOOLCHAND: I can't. Not this time.

SHAPOOR: I don't want any more courts, any more Galliards.

MOOLCHAND: The moment you withdraw the charges, they will throw you out of the country.

SHAPOOR: I want to be thrown out of the country. Do it for me.

> *MOOLCHAND slaps SHAPOOR, stunning him.*

MOOLCHAND: I am sorry. How do you think you can get your mother and father out of Tihar Jail in India? You want them alive, you have to stay in Canada.

SHAPOOR: *(tearfully)* I can't fight with my wife anymore. I just can't.

MOOLCHAND: All right, all right.

SHAPOOR: I want to leave this country, please.

MOOLCHAND: Quiet! Let me think.

SHAPOOR: I can't live like this anymore.

MOOLCHAND: Calm down ... please ...

SHAPOOR: *(whispering)* Please help me ... Please get me out of here. I promise I will not come back. Sell all those carpets if you ...

PROUGAULT: *(from outside the detention cell)* Time is up.

MOOLCHAND: Shh ... Shut up – shut up. Don't speak with anyone until I come back.

> *SHAPOOR, like a helpless child, grabs MOOLCHAND with both arms.*

SHAPOOR: Don't go ... No ... Please.

MOOLCHAND: I will be back soon.

> *MOOLCHAND pulls him to his feet, hugs him, and whispers a secret in his ear. PROUGAULT, who was standing outside, steps forward.*

PROUGAULT: Time's up, mister.

MOOLCHAND: *(to SHAPOOR)* Come on, stand up. *(to PROUGAULT)* Yes. Thank you ... Thank you, sir. *(exits)*

> *SHAPOOR is left alone in the cell with PROUGAULT. An awkward silence sets in as PROUGAULT gives SHAPOOR an intimidating stare. Then PROUGAULT starts to whistle, drawing SHAPOOR's attention.*

PROUGAULT: If a hundred thousand French Canadians landed in India, what do you think would happen? They'd screw up the country!

SHAPOOR: I don't know.

PROUGAULT: Here we have a hundred thousand Moolchands in Quebec. And what do you think they are doing?

SHAPOOR: I'm sorry, sir, I don't know!

PROUGAULT: I think you do. Get up.

> *SHAPOOR extends his arms to be handcuffed.*

PROUGAULT: No, I'm not putting any handcuffs on you. *(pointing)* No, that door.

> *PROUGAULT takes SHAPOOR away.*

SCENE 14

From two different locations onstage, CLARINDA and MOOLCHAND in turn address the unseen judge.

CLARINDA: It hurts. It wasn't fair.

MOOLCHAND: When the inquiry was postponed, I was afraid another racist cop would not be punished.

CLARINDA: It didn't seem to hurt Mr. Prougault's union campaign or Moolchand's quest for more people of colour on the force.

MOOLCHAND: With Shapoor's disappearance I had to dig up many more witnesses against Galliard.

CLARINDA: The police knew it, the judges knew it, but they let him slip away. Why bother? She's just a woman.

CLARINDA and MOOLCHAND leave their respective locations onstage as though they have finished their testimonies to the judge. They cross paths as they step out of the courtroom.

MOOLCHAND: Miss Clarinda, we will see each other in two weeks.

CLARINDA: I don't have time for this bullshit. Why didn't Shapoor turn up today for the inquiry?

MOOLCHAND: I don't know.

CLARINDA: What? You're stalling for time?

MOOLCHAND: Okay, if you really want to know, I just found out he fled the country.

CLARINDA: *What?*

MOOLCHAND: I went to post bail for him (*pulling out the paperwork*) but Prougault told me that Shapoor was freed on a stricter restraining order.

CLARINDA: Prougault? How come you didn't mention it in there?

MOOLCHAND: I just got the call from London Heathrow. The boy called to say that he was en route to India.

CLARINDA: Does he know if he flees the country with a criminal charge, he'll never be allowed back in.

MOOLCHAND: That is why I did not believe him on the phone.

CLARINDA: Where are you hiding him?

MOOLCHAND: Why should I hide him?

CLARINDA: Because you're afraid to lose and you didn't want him to face the judge today.

MOOLCHAND: Miss Keith, please learn to trust someone.

CLARINDA: Trust? Did he trust you with his carpets?

MOOLCHAND: Look, I want this inquiry over just as much as you – so we can finally settle this issue ...

CLARINDA: There's a young woman lying in hospital.

MOOLCHAND: Then you should be happy her attacker isn't around. I'm almost happy he left. How do you think it makes me look, defending a wife beater? You wanted him deported, he's gone!

CLARINDA: You're a wretched piece of scum.

MOOLCHAND: There is no need for name-calling. Goodbye. Oh, Ms. Clarinda, there's one thing. Now that he's out of the country and can't harm the girl, could you convince her to drop the charge against the boy so I can get my bond money?

CLARINDA: As if nothing ever happened?

MOOLCHAND: The inquiry was just postponed. That will happen.

CLARINDA: (*bitterly sarcastic*) Without the man who was "racially assaulted by the white cop"? Without your star witness?

CLARINDA starts to exit. MOOLCHAND rushes after her.

MOOLCHAND: (*shouting*) He is gone away, not the racism!

No answer from CLARINDA. MOOLCHAND shrugs his shoulders and exits.

SCENE 15

Rizvi family home. SHAZIA is seated between her parents.

MURAD: Oh my God, oh my God, please help me.

SHAFIQA: Why didn't you tell me?

SHAZIA: I didn't know.

SHAFIQA: You're four months pregnant and you didn't know?

MURAD: Four months?

SHAFIQA: What planet do you live on?

SHAZIA: At first the doctor thought it was stress. I didn't know.

MURAD: Stress?

SHAFIQA: You'll know the meaning of stress when you are a mother.

SHAZIA: I'm going to keep the baby.

MURAD gets up angrily.

MURAD: Now she wants to be a good Muslim.

SHAFIQA: Are you insane, girl?

SHAZIA: I want the baby.

MURAD: What will people say?

SHAZIA: I don't care.

MURAD: Who will marry you now?

SHAZIA: Abbu, please!

MURAD: Don't "please" me ... please. No decent man will marry you.

SHAZIA: I'm still married.

MURAD: And I'll take care of that.

MURAD walks away.

SHAZIA: How? How? How with him so far away. God knows where ... I can't believe he would do this. Just leave. So spineless ... No care for me. Just ... just ... nothing. This is all I have.

MURAD walks back to SHAZIA and holds her in a fatherly manner.

MURAD: No, what have I said? Ah, little chatter-box. My little ...

SHAZIA cries in her father's arms.

SHAFIQA: Murad, you go in the other room.

MURAD exits.

SHAZIA: Ma, I want the baby.

SHAFIQA: What if the baby grows up to be like his father?

SHAZIA: I can't know that.

SHAFIQA: I am afraid, Shazia! With this baby you are inviting the man back into your life.

SHAZIA: I don't want him. I want the baby!

SCENE 16

From some location onstage, PROUGAULT addresses the unseen judge.

PROUGAULT: I mean, it all seemed very suspicious how Farhadi disappeared right before the inquiry. We checked everywhere. We thought Mr. Mool-chand was hiding him. We checked the airlines and found he left the country. But it didn't matter. We had an inquiry, didn't we? (*listens*) What? Yes, I was responsible. No, no, we couldn't keep him in the station any longer. What purpose would that have served?

Flashback to the inquiry. GALLIARD has just come out of the inquiry room. He meets PROUGAULT outside.

GALLIARD: That was a fucking circus, not an inquiry.

PROUGAULT: Sarge, listen to me.

GALLIARD: Goddamn ... makes me sick. I want to get the hell out of here.

PROUGAULT: Wait. Wait a minute, Sarge.

GALLIARD: Don't call me that. I'm not a goddamn sergeant anymore. They wouldn't even let me talk.

PROUGAULT: Inquiries are arbitration, not judgment.

GALLIARD: What am I going to do now? It's not fair.

PROUGAULT: I think you have something to celebrate. The inquiry cost you your job, but granted you 90 per cent of your salary. You can sit home ... or buy a condo in Mexico.

GALLIARD: I don't deserve this.

PROUGAULT: Sarge, nobody would believe that you are guilty. The man who knew most wasn't around ... vanished.

CLARINDA comes out of the inquiry room and watches them from a distance.

PROUGAULT: Sarge, let the dust settle and I promise the Brotherhood will give you your job. I have got to go take care of some business. I will call you. (*exits*)

CLARINDA walks up to GALLIARD.

CLARINDA: Galliard, I am really sorry.

GALLIARD: Yeah, thanks.

CLARINDA: But look, it's not over yet.

GALLIARD: It is.

CLARINDA: Galliard, there are hundreds of women who will testify that you are a very good cop.

GALLIARD: Good enough to let go. You know what I have done for them already – nobody works as ... ah shit ... forget it.

CLARINDA: Wait ... no, wait ... Guy ...

GALLIARD: Thanks, Clarinda, for trying, but I am just a white man.

CLARINDA and GALLIARD exit as SHAFIQA, MURAD, and SHAZIA come out of the inquiry room.

MURAD: Huh, justice?

SHAZIA: It's over.

MURAD: What justice? Making profit out of racism? I wonder whose carpets is he selling?

SHAZIA: Just forget it ... let's go.

MURAD: *Haramzada* [bastard] ...

SHAZIA: Just stop!

MURAD: Do you think a slimeball like him will fight for racial justice without personal benefit?

SHAZIA: I don't want the bloody carpets.

SHAFIQA: I say we sue him. Those carpets belong to her, not Moolchand.

SHAZIA exits.

MURAD & SHAFIQA: Shazia, wait, Shazia ... Shazia ...

MOOLCHAND comes out of the inquiry, answering questions to reporters offstage.

MOOLCHAND: Please, one at a time ...

CLARINDA steps forward and confronts him.

CLARINDA: You were under oath!

MOOLCHAND: I don't have time now, call me ...

CLARINDA: Some of us aren't lucky enough to give testimony on behalf of vanished people.

MOOLCHAND: What's your point?

CLARINDA: You lied.

MOOLCHAND: You've got no right to doubt what I said. What did you say in there?

CLARINDA: Do you care about anybody?

MOOLCHAND: Wake up, woman. Look what has been accomplished. I think you should be celebrating.

CLARINDA: What do you want me to celebrate? Couple of fucking people of colour on the force? A good cop lost his job. How can I celebrate when no one will take battering seriously!

MOOLCHAND: You had your chance.

CLARINDA: I never had a chance, you made sure of that.

MOOLCHAND: You can always appeal.

CLARINDA: When will Shapoor come out of "hiding"?

MOOLCHAND: Miss Keith, why don't you hire a detective? And – oh yes – make sure he is smarter than James Bond.

CLARINDA and MOOLCHAND exit in opposite directions.

SCENE 17

From some location onstage, SHAZIA addresses the unseen judge.

SHAZIA: What? Shapoor called me. Two weeks before, Your Honour. No, no! It was the first time I ever went there. Yes. Yes. Sergeant Galliard was in the room when I arrived. No. What? No! I didn't kill him, I loved ...

Flashback to the Rizvi family home.

SHAFIQA & MURAD: (*calling angrily*) Shazia, Shazia!

She enters. MURAD shows her a letter.

MURAD: Why didn't you tell us?

SHAZIA: What ... You opened my letter?

MURAD: Why Shazia?

SHAZIA: Why what?

MURAD: Don't annoy me.

SHAFIQA: You are writing love letters?

MURAD: While everybody thought Moolchand had your lover locked in his basement.

SHAZIA: He's the father of my child.

SHAFIQA: Father? Huh. He is a *gunda*. A criminal.

MURAD: Where did you find him?

SHAZIA: (*pause*) He asked me to let him come to see his child when it's born and I said yes.

SHAFIQA: You're right. She acts like a spoiled maiden in fairy tales.

SHAZIA: Ma, I have made up my mind.

SHAFIQA: You have lost your mind.

MURAD: And you are pigheaded.

SHAZIA: I can't do this! Yes, I wrote the letter, because ... I can't bring this baby up alone. How will I support him?

MURAD: You will get those carpets.

SHAZIA: Not now. We can't. Moolchand has them and Shapoor is afraid Moolchand might do something. If we want ...

SHAFIQA: We?

SHAZIA: Maybe we could ...

SHAFIQA: We?

SHAZIA: Don't get mad at me, Ma.

SHAFIQA: I am not mad, you are.

SHAZIA: You don't understand ...

MURAD: No, you don't.

SHAZIA: I ... I miss him.

MURAD: Your beast?

SHAZIA: Don't say that.

MURAD: Yes, your beast. Two hands, two fists, two legs, remember the beast? Last time he left you alive, next time he will bury you. Those charges still stand, don't they? I'll call the police. Where is he?

SHAZIA: I dropped the charges.

MURAD: What?

SHAFIQA: Oh God!

SHAZIA: Look, I know how it sounds, but don't you see? I need him.

MURAD: I would rather be in hell.

SHAFIQA: I have had enough of you, girl. If you let that beast come here, I'll kill you. You hear me? I will kill you.

Lights fade. We are back in the present.

SCENE 18

From some location onstage, CLARINDA addresses the unseen judge.

CLARINDA: It really hurt. When I first found out that he had come back into the city and Shazia had dropped the charges, I just cried. I had to give up. How can you help someone who does not want to be helped? But I did tell her they should get those carpets from Moolchand. Maybe that's what he was trying to do before he got killed.

Flashback to the Rizvi family home. SHAPOOR is waiting at the door to be allowed in. MURAD stands in his way. SHAFIQA and SHAZIA stand a short distance away. There is a long pause before anyone speaks.

SHAFIQA: Murad, let the beast in.

MURAD gives SHAPOOR room to step in.

SHAPOOR: Hello.

SHAFIQA: (*to SHAPOOR*) You touch her and I will kill you. (*to SHAZIA*) Shazia, your fool is back.

SHAPOOR: You look good. Sorry, I thought I knew what I was going to say. (*looking at her belly*) I thought you'd be bigger ... That was a stupid thing to say. What's new? You must be so used to my saying stupid things.

SHAZIA: You are not staying here.

SHAPOOR: No, of course not. You had written that to me.

SHAZIA: Then why are you here now? I said after the baby is born. You're lucky my parents haven't killed you.

SHAPOOR: Shazia, I came for one thing ...

SHAZIA: I have heard it before.

SHAPOOR: I understand it now. I do. I can't take anything I did away but ...

SHAZIA: If your father saw you like this, he'd have a heart attack.

SHAPOOR: Shazia ... my father ...

SHAZIA: Is he proud of his son's wife? A machine that pops out babies while the son sells carpets?

SHAPOOR: That is not true.

SHAZIA: Carpet and a wife ... they both get walked on.

SHAPOOR: Shazia, please listen to me.

SHAZIA: No, you listen to me. I'll let you see your son, but I still have a restraining order and it won't matter what colour the officer is. But don't fool yourself – you will not control this baby like your father controls you.

SHAPOOR: He died. (*long silence*) I lost him ... I lost you.

MURAD: And we lost the carpets, you fool. Moolchand is selling them now. Fool.

SHAPOOR: I know. I'm taking care of the carpets. Shazia, look. (*pulling out a document*) I've started therapy. My counsellor says I'm not a wife beater.

MURAD: Then how come she's a battered wife?

SHAPOOR: I am learning to control my temper. I am doing everything I can to correct myself. You know I even meditate. Can you forgive me? I need to know if you can ... if there is a hope, any hope ... that you could forgive ...

SHAZIA: I haven't forgotten anything.

SHAPOOR: Please ... give me a chance one last time. Not now, at this minute. But maybe in time ...

SHAZIA: Shapoor, I'm very scared.

SHAPOOR: Maybe you'll need me. I'll be the baby-sitter. I'll do things other Iranian men don't do. I'll cook, I'll clean ...

MURAD: And call cops racist.

SHAPOOR: That was Moolchand. I'm sorry about that. I called that officer, Sergeant Galliard. I'm seeing him tomorrow to see if there is anything I can do.

SHAZIA: I am afraid.

SHAPOOR: I know. Me too. Here is my number at the Y. I won't call you again until you want me to. When you are ready. I will wait.

*He pulls out his business card to give to **SHAZIA**, but **MURAD** takes it instead. **SHAPOOR** starts to exit.*

SHAZIA: Shapoor ... Come tomorrow.

SHAPOOR: No, you think about it. Goodbye, Shazia. (*exits*)

SHAZIA: Ummi ...

*SHAFIQA does not answer. SHAZIA exits. SHAFIQA takes the business card from **MURAD**, picks up the phone, and dials.*

SHAFIQA: (*on the phone*) Hello, Lieutenant Prougault please ... Hello, sir. Begum Shafiqa Rizvi here. Shazia's mother ... Good. The carpet seller is back in town ... I thought he was her ex, but he is trying hard to become her present ... Help me, sir. I know she said she made a mistake. But there must be something you can do. Yes, yes, he was just here ... he left a number ...

Lights fade on the family as we return to the present.

SCENE 19

MURAD addresses the unseen judge from somewhere onstage.

MURAD: That's all she did. Just gave the police his number. No, that was the last time we saw him. Yes, the last time I saw him. Yes. Yes ...

*From another location, **MOOLCHAND** addresses the unseen judge.*

MOOLCHAND: Well, someone must have them then. I swear I don't. No, he had those papers, I threw them on the bed. Yes. In that YMCA room. And he was very much alive.

*Flashback to **SHAPOOR**'s room at the YMCA (the same room as in Scene 1 where the audience saw **SHAPOOR** dead).*

MOOLCHAND: This is it. All I ever will have to do with you again. (*holding out the papers*) They are in your wife's name.

SHAPOOR: You lied.

MOOLCHAND: What?

SHAPOOR: You lied in the inquiry. I never said those things. I wanted to drop ...

MOOLCHAND: I don't care what you think. Here! You wanted your carpets, here are the papers. Sorry they do not come back 100 per cent. I had expenses in trying to save your sorry head. Now goodbye and please never call me again.

MOOLCHAND throws the papers on the bed and starts to go to the door.

SHAPOOR: Why did you lie?

MOOLCHAND: You want to undo everything I did?

SHAPOOR: I wanted to drop those charges against Galliard. Why did ...

MOOLCHAND: You fucking wife beater, you broke the restraining order, you beat the hell out of her. You ask me why?

SHAPOOR: I told you to drop those ...

MOOLCHAND: We finally have some coloured cops on the force to help people like you. Do you want to know what I said in the inquiry? What they did not want to hear! Should I have waited for you to come back? I didn't need you anymore. I had better witnesses against that cop. You don't get it, do you? What would have happened if I lost the inquiry? Revenge from the cops! More racism! People would have laughed at us. No person of colour would have dared talk about racial justice in this city. Drop the charges? ... Fuck you!

*MOOLCHAND starts to exit. **SHAPOOR** runs to the door.*

SHAPOOR: Bastard. You used me. What I did to my wife was wrong. I was wrong. But you manipulated me. You turned my crime against my wife into a crime against the colour of our bloody skin. You abused us. You wanted to win. It didn't matter about anybody else, did it? Well, you won, you bastard. You're a big shot today. What about me? How do I get back my wife?

MOOLCHAND storms out. We return to the present.

SCENE 20

*From some location onstage, **MOOLCHAND** addresses the unseen judge.*

MOOLCHAND: Then I left. I swear he was holding them. What would I gain? The carpets were in his wife's name. I mean, why would I care what happened to him? He had lost his life the moment he hit that woman.

*From another location, **SHAZIA** addresses the unseen judge.*

SHAZIA: I keep thinking if only I had got there even ten minutes earlier. I know he ... he did things to me. But he didn't deserve to die. If only I had got there before Sergeant Galliard ...

*Flashback to the YMCA room. **SHAPOOR** is on the phone. As he puts down the phone, **PROUGAULT** enters. **SHAPOOR** is surprised to see him.*

SHAPOOR: Oh, ah ... Hi, sir, is there something wrong?

PROUGAULT: You seem surprised.

SHAPOOR: Yes, I was expecting Galliard. I just called him. I just wanted to tell him ...

PROUGAULT: Why do you need to talk with him? Haven't you destroyed his life enough already?

SHAPOOR: No, no, Moolchand said those things. See, that's why I need to talk –

PROUGAULT: Quiet. I thought we had an understanding.

SHAPOOR: I know we did, I know. I just wanted to apologize to him. I thought it wouldn't matter if I came back now.

PROUGAULT: Don't you think that might be a little dangerous?

SHAPOOR: What? Why?

PROUGAULT: What are you going to do? Clear his name?

SHAPOOR: Well, no. But if I could ...

PROUGAULT: You want to reopen the inquiry?

SHAPOOR: No, I just want to say sorry to him.

PROUGAULT: I smell a plot.

SHAPOOR: What? You have no reason.

PROUGAULT: What's the last thing you said to me? You forgot that? You want me to remind you?

Lights fade as we return to the present.

SCENE 21

*From some location onstage, **GALLIARD** addresses the unseen judge.*

GALLIARD: (*visibly nervous*) When? The second time he was arrested? What? It was ... I don't know. Ah ... when Shapoor ... It was just before he took the plane back to India. What? I ... uh, I don't ... All right ... All right! (*pause*) Prougault had him in this room, I just happened to be there. I overheard them ... It wasn't my idea. I was actually ...

*Flashback to the detention cell. The audience should see **SHAPOOR** and **MOOLCHAND** as they were in Scene 13 (when **SHAPOOR** was in a detention cell after breaking the restraining order and attacking*

SHAZIA). It is a replay of that scene and should be played exactly as before.

SHAPOOR: (*whispering*) Please help me ... Please get me out of here. I promise I will not come back. Sell all those carpets if you ...

PROUGAULT: (*from outside the detention cell*) Time is up.

MOOLCHAND: Shh ... Shut up – shut up. Don't speak with anyone until I come back.

SHAPOOR, like a helpless child, grabs MOOLCHAND with both arms.

SHAPOOR: Don't go ... No ... Please.

MOOLCHAND: I will be back soon.

MOOLCHAND pulls him to his feet, hugs him, and whispers a secret into his ear. PROUGAULT, who was standing outside, steps forward.

PROUGAULT: Time's up, mister.

MOOLCHAND: (*to SHAPOOR*) Come on, stand up. (*to PROUGAULT*) Yes. Thank you ... Thank you, sir. (*exits*)

SHAPOOR is left alone in the cell with PROUGAULT. An awkward silence sets in as PROUGAULT gives SHAPOOR an intimidating stare. Then PROUGAULT starts to whistle, drawing SHAPOOR's attention.

PROUGAULT: If a hundred thousand French Canadians landed in India, what do you think would happen? They'd screw up the country!

SHAPOOR: I don't know.

PROUGAULT: Here we have a hundred thousand Moolchands in Quebec. And what do you think they are doing?

SHAPOOR: I'm sorry, sir, I don't know!

PROUGAULT: I think you do. Get up.

SHAPOOR extends his arms to be handcuffed.

PROUGAULT: No, I'm not putting any handcuffs on you. (*pointing*) No, that door.

Repeat of the scene ends. We now see PROUGAULT bringing SHAPOOR into another interrogation room. He sits him down on a stool.

PROUGAULT: So, I heard you planning a little escape. Yeah, the walls are paper thin. I can't believe you were talking about leaving without an apology.

SHAPOOR: I wasn't planning ...

PROUGAULT: No, no. Don't say anything ... Remember what your friend said? You know ... I'm hurt.

SHAPOOR: Sir, listen ...

PROUGAULT: No. Please don't say anything now. It's too late for apologies. I just can't believe an Iranian ... I said that right, didn't I? An Iranian and an Indian are holding us ransom.

SHAPOOR: Please, sir, I'm not ...

While the scene is unfolding, GALLIARD walks up to the door. He stands there without being noticed by PROUGAULT and SHAPOOR. He listens in on what PROUGAULT is telling SHAPOOR.

PROUGAULT: Shh ... He said don't talk. You beat your wife, didn't you?

SHAPOOR nods.

PROUGAULT: Is that fair? You assaulted a woman and I have to treat you better than the prime minister? Bad example, eh? And now ... this inquiry ... what do you think will happen if I don't get re-elected? This inquiry is causing me concern. Or maybe it doesn't matter. Maybe we should elect an Iranian as the president of the Brotherhood. You guys can't even run your own fucking country, right? Damn, I am mad. I got all these problems. Why? Why? I know, I know. (*staring directly at SHAPOOR*) You drop all your racial charges against us.

SHAPOOR: I tried. I would, but Mr. Moolchand, he ... Oh please, my father is in jail in India. He's dying ... Please sir, let me go there. I will never come back here, promise.

PROUGAULT: Moolchand wouldn't have much of an inquiry without you, would he?

SHAPOOR: No sir ... I beg you. Just let me out. I just need some money. I can take the next plane ...

PROUGAULT: Whoa ... hold the camel, we have rules here. What'd you think – I just open the door and out you go?

PROUGAULT turns around and notices that GALLIARD is listening to their conversation.

Oh hello, Guy – doing a little eavesdropping? Hey, maybe you can escort our friend here to the airport.

GALLIARD: What?

PROUGAULT: We've got to get him out of the country before the inquiry.

GALLIARD: Sir, he can't go. There's no bond.

PROUGAULT: You want your fucking job back?

GALLIARD: But ... it's not legal.

PROUGAULT: We'll let him out on a stricter restraining order.

SHAPOOR: You let me go, I will keep my mouth shut. I promise. Nobody will know anything. Even Mr. Moolchand won't know what ...

GALLIARD: This isn't right.

PROUGAULT: We'll make it right.

GALLIARD: I don't know about this.

SHAPOOR: I promise.

PROUGAULT: This might save both our asses!

GALLIARD: Sir ... you can't.

SHAPOOR: Sir, thank you, sir, thank you ...

PROUGAULT: Shut up. You can both count yourselves lucky. Now, Galliard, take him to the airport. I'll book the flight.

PROUGAULT exits, gesturing to GALLIARD to follow his orders. We return to the present.

SCENE 22

From some location onstage, GALLIARD addresses the unseen judge.

GALLIARD: That's what he said – "I'll book the flight." No. I didn't know. I did it because I wanted my job back. He was the one who was afraid Shapoor would talk.

PROUGAULT: (*offstage*) That's a lie. You're a goddamn liar. Whose name was on the purchase of the tickets?

GALLIARD: (*to the unseen judge*) Yeah, I put it on my Visa. He was supposed to pay me back. He said ...

PROUGAULT: (*offstage*) I am not on trial here. You are. You're the one.

Meanwhile MOOLCHAND, dressed in a tuxedo and bow tie, delivers a speech to an imaginary crowd.

MOOLCHAND: Thank you for honouring me as Indo-Canadian of the year. Thank you. Honourable guests, friends, and dear community leaders, Canada is the best country in the world and it couldn't be the best without us making it best ...

Lights cross-fade from MOOLCHAND to the YMCA room. PROUGAULT is talking to SHAPOOR.

PROUGAULT: I think I'm going to have to put you back on the plane again.

SHAPOOR: You can't.

PROUGAULT: I can't?

SHAPOOR: Please, Lieutenant, I will keep my mouth shut about what happened. I promise. I won't tell anyone anything.

PROUGAULT: Why should I believe you? Didn't you already break your promise by coming back?

SHAPOOR: Look, I don't want any trouble with the police.

PROUGAULT steps in the direction of SHAPOOR, who takes a step back fearfully.

SHAPOOR: Here, take my carpets. Please, I will not say anything to anyone. Please!

The audience sees PROUGAULT lunging at SHAPOOR with vengeance. SHAPOOR tries to protect himself as the lights cross-fade from the YMCA room to MOOLCHAND. He continues his speech.

MOOLCHAND: Some years ago, I was already a Canadian citizen, had a degree from McGill and one from New Delhi, and an immigrant's discipline. But I was bumped out of a job. Why? "Mr. Moolchand belongs in a behind-the-desk job at the census bureau, for example, where many of his countrymen are doing wonderful work ..."

As MOOLCHAND continues his speech, dim lights fade in on the YMCA room. SHAPOOR is lying on the bed as in the opening scene. PROUGAULT leaves the room, making sure nobody has seen him. GALLIARD enters as in the opening scene. As MOOLCHAND continues with his speech, the opening scene is replayed in dim light and at low volume.

Lights cross-fade from the YMCA room to MOOLCHAND, who continues his speech.

MOOLCHAND: "He is not a suitable candidate for the classroom." I guess it was my Bombay-wallah accent and my lack of humour. Do you think I lack humour? The reason was they will let you get only so far ahead and then they will cut you down. And we still need more people of colour on the force. Let's not forget; the man shouldn't have hit his wife, and I didn't know the answer to his problem! But that didn't give a police officer the right to bully him because of his race. It is as simple as that. I still don't feel safe in their company. If my car stops at a red light and I see a cop car, I want him to notice that I have broken no law because I know the cops are in the habit of prejudging us as law violators. Anthony Griffin was prejudged as a shoplifter; Albert Johnson was prejudged as a murderer. Marcellus François as a drug dealer. Barnabé as a lunatic. And the list goes on. The result is always the same – we lose our citizenship or we lose our lives ... always in "self-defence" ... 'n always a case of "mistaken identity." But I promise you that, with your support, no Shapoor will have to leave the country, and no Farhadi will lose his life! That is why we want a strong voice for racial justice.

Gradually, the lights go out on the YMCA. Then the spot on MOOLCHAND slowly shrinks until the entire stage is in complete darkness.

END

In a 1998 interview with Carole Corbeil, George F. Walker explained the impulse behind many of his plays. The only "idea that made any sense to me," he said, "was that we're all really, really pathetic, but we should try anyway! And I thought, well, that's enough." Except for the B-movie megalomaniacs in the plays of his first decade, most of Walker's protagonists have been of the pathetic variety: the down-and-out, the eccentric, the mad, the drunk, the fearful. On the receiving end of the social-Darwinist aggression that passes for civilized behaviour in Walker's urban jungles, they survive, if at all, by improvising wildly and hoping for the best. And if that holds true for the inhabitants of the darkly comic east-end neighbourhood of so many of his plays – characters with roots in the community who have something more to fight for than just their own survival – it holds doubly true for the temporary tenants of *Suburban Motel*.

In the six one-acts that make up this play cycle, the losing and the lost circulate through one dingy motel room waiting for news which, when it comes, will only be bad. Daniel De Raey, the first director of *Problem Child*, describes the place as "a drab, camouflaged circle of hell with an ice machine." *Toronto Star* critic Vit Wagner sees it as "an uninviting way station on the road from nowhere good to somewhere worse." The characters typically speak of themselves as being in hell or in a horrible nightmare, "very deeply in the shit" or simply "fucked." Uprooted and virtually resourceless, they recognize how pathetic they really are. Under those circumstances they face an important variation on Walker's fundamental theme. *Should* they try anyway? *Is* that enough? Or is the whole exercise pointless? Walker confronts those questions head-on in *Problem Child*, one of the bleakest, funniest, and most powerful plays in his substantial canon.

Walker grew up in Toronto's working-class east end. He was driving taxi in 1970 (so the story goes) when he saw a flyer soliciting scripts for Ken Gass's new Factory Theatre Lab, billed as "The Home of the Canadian Playwright." The play he submitted, *Prince of Naples*, was his first attempt at writing drama, and when he attended its opening in 1971, it was only the second play he had ever seen. Despite Walker's inexperience, Gass made him resident playwright from 1971–76, an invaluable apprenticeship and the start of an enduring association that has seen most of Walker's plays premiere at the Factory.

Prince of Naples and *Ambush at Tether's End* (1971) were absurdist exercises, derivative of Ionesco and Beckett. With *Sacktown Rag* (1972) and *Bagdad Saloon* (1973), Walker began to find his own voice, planting increasingly exotic landscapes of the mind with oddly chosen pop icons like Gary Cooper and Gertrude Stein. This phase of his work climaxed with *Beyond Mozambique* (1974) and *Ramona and the White Slaves* (1976). The former features a B-movie jungle locale populated by a drug-addicted priest, a disgraced Mountie, a porn-film starlet, and a demonic Nazi doctor whose wife thinks she is Olga from Chekhov's *Three Sisters*. *Ramona*, a murder mystery–cum–opium dream that marked Walker's directing debut, takes place in a Hong Kong brothel in 1919.

Walker took his next three plays to Toronto Free Theatre. *Gossip* (1977), *Zastrozzi* (1977), and *Filthy Rich* (1979) were less obscure and more accessible than his previous work. *Zastrozzi*, a stylish, anachronistic gothic romance and revenge melodrama about "the master criminal of all Europe," has been produced across the United States and Canada, in London, Australia, and New Zealand. It was staged by Joseph Papp for the New York Shakespeare Festival in 1982 at the end of Walker's year as playwright-in-residence there, and had a major 2009 remount at the Stratford Festival. It remains one of Walker's most popular plays. *Gossip* and *Filthy Rich*, heavily indebted to Humphrey Bogart and Raymond Chandler, were the first of his plays in film-noir style. Along with *The Art of War* (1983), they were published under the title *The Power Plays* (1986), featuring a character named Tyrone Power as a cynical, shabby investigative reporter or private eye, reluctantly involved in sorting out political intrigue and murder. Related in theme and mood is the Floyd S. Chalmers Canadian Play Award–winning *Theatre of the Film Noir* (1981), a bizarre murder mystery set in wartime Paris.

Exotic locales feature prominently in *Rumours of Our Death* (1980), an antiwar rock musical parable, and *Science and Madness* (1982), a turn-of-the-century gothic melodrama. But Walker increasingly focused his attention on the modern city he had explored in the first two Power plays. *Criminals in Love*, winner of the 1984 Governor General's Literary Award; *Better Living* (1986); and *Beautiful City* (1987) were published as *The East End Plays* (1988), set in what is transparently the east end of Toronto itself. The nihilism of Walker's earlier work gives way in these political comedies to tenuous hope for a life of simple happiness in a city salvaged from the powerful and greedy.

Love and Anger (1989) and *Escape from Happiness* (1991), a sequel to *Better Living*, continue Walker's championing of women, the oppressed, and the marginal against the patriarchal centre. These two Chalmers Award–winning comedies have had critical and popular success across Canada and the United States. But the play that first cemented Walker's reputation outside Canada was *Nothing Sacred* (1988), his adaptation of Ivan Turgenev's 1862 novel, *Fathers and Sons*. Set in pre-revolutionary Russia, *Nothing Sacred* won a batch of major Canadian theatre awards and became so popular among American regional theatres that the *Los Angeles Times* named it play of the year. In 1993, Walker wrote *Tough!* for Vancouver's Green Thumb Theatre, a comedy about sex and gender relations among three young people. *The East End Plays* have since been repackaged and republished in two parts: *Criminals in Love*, *Better Living*, and *Escape from Happiness* in Part One; *Beautiful City*, *Love and Anger*, and *Tough!* in Part Two.

After taking time off from theatre to write TV scripts for *The Newsroom* and *Due South*, Walker returned in triumph to his first theatrical home. Having nearly folded, Toronto's Factory Theatre was once more under the artistic directorship of Ken Gass, who revived the theatre in 1997 by presenting Walker's six new one-acts under the title *Suburban Motel*. All set in the same shabby motel room, *Problem Child*, *Adult Entertainment*, *Criminal Genius*, *Featuring Loretta*, *The End of Civilization*, and *Risk Everything* (which brings back *Problem Child*'s R.J. and Denise, and introduces Denise's mother) run the gamut from bitter drama to wacky comedy. They played in repertory format, two plays a night, directed by Walker himself. The plays were a major success, winning multiple Chalmers and Dora Awards and acclaim for subsequent productions in Montreal, Vancouver, and elsewhere. Walker also wrote the screenplay for a 2006 film adaptation, *Niagara Motel*. Other film versions of his plays are *Better Living* (1998) and a French production of *Beyond Mozambique* set in contemporary Montreal, titled *Rats and Rabbits* (2000).

Walker rang in the millennium with *Heaven* (2000), a bitter revenge comedy whose characters come back from the dead, premiered by Toronto's Canadian Stage. For the next decade he worked primarily in television, co-writing and producing with Dani Romain TV dramedies very much in sync with the themes of his later plays: *This Is Wonderland* (2004–05) chronicles the law and disorder of the Canadian legal system, its victims, and minions; *The Line* (2008) is a gritty cop show; and *Living in Your Car* (2010) looks at corporate corruption and the urban underclass.

But Walker has never forsaken the stage. Of the writers who helped establish modern Canadian theatre in the decade after 1967, only he and Michel Tremblay continue to generate new plays for production on a regular basis. His flurry of new theatrical work began with an unemployed middle-class couple, their schizophrenic daughter, and the ghost of Kurt Vonnegut in *And So It Goes* (Factory, 2010). *King of Thieves*, adapted from John Gay's eighteenth-century classic, *The Beggar's Opera*, premiered at Stratford in 2010, commissioned by Festival artistic director Des McAnuff, Walker's old friend from the 1970s Toronto theatre scene. Walker stuck with another old friend when Ken Gass was fired by the Factory Theatre board in 2012. Walker pulled his new play, *Dead Metaphor*, from the 2013–14 Factory season in protest, opening it in San Francisco. *Dead Metaphor* would have its Canadian premiere at Gass's Canadian Rep Theatre in 2013, along with new plays by Judith Thompson and Wajdi Mouawad. Theatre Passe Muraille and Green Thumb co-produced *Moss Park* (2013), in which Walker revisits two of the young characters from *Tough!* who now have a baby. Like *Problem Child*'s Denise and R.J., they struggle to build a life for themselves against substantial odds.

Problem Child has become one of Walker's most popular plays, with productions from 2008–2012 in Victoria, Vancouver (in English and French), Calgary, London (Ontario), and St. John's, Philadelphia and San

Francisco, Limerick, Munich, Frankfurt, and London (England). Walker's personal successes include his appointment as the National Theatre School of Canada's first resident playwright in 1991, the Order of Canada in 2006, and the Governor General's Performing Arts Award for Lifetime Achievement in 2009.

Although an extremely funny play, *Problem Child* dramatizes a serious battle driven by a mother's very high stakes. In his excellent book on Walker, Chris Johnson cites Kate Taylor's 1997 *Globe and Mail* review of the play in which she asks, "How far would you go to win back your child?" Johnson's own answer is "pretty damn far," and the play certainly establishes audience empathy with Denise's plight. But despite flirting with stereotypes of the stage social worker in his portrayal of the uptight, overbearing, judgmental Helen, Walker also gives her position substantial credence. We are only too familiar with horrible incidents of severe abuse or even murder of children in which social services somehow failed to intervene aggressively enough to save them from their own parents. Helen's invocation of "Christian" values – her accusation that Denise doesn't cook or go to church – can likely be dismissed (at least in Canada) as Helen's personal dogma, tangential to the issue at hand. That Denise has abused drugs and turned tricks might be stronger grounds for questioning her responsibility as a parent, although Walker allows Denise reasonable arguments in her own defence. Still, enough questions remain about Denise's motives and the adequacy of her mothering skills to warrant some of Helen's caution. When a child's welfare is at stake, surely it is better to be safe than sorry.

Whatever the merits of her arguments or her strategies for attempting to get her child back, Denise genuinely feels that without the child her life has no meaning or value. She can only go through the motions. Her deep despair at the end of the play is predicated on the conviction that things won't work out, because "for people like us" they never do. This pessimism is grounded in more than just psychological depression. *Problem Child* and all the other plays in the *Suburban Motel* cycle appear to support her assumption. The liminal site of the motel (neither urban nor rural) and the transitional situation of Denise and R.J. ("we've got a new life"; "Everything is a possibility") may suggest productive potential. But at some profound level Denise understands that she and R.J. are doomed: by class, education, economics, and even appearance. Helen's comic refrain in *Problem Child*, "buried alive," really describes *their* condition and the condition of people like them. Their attempts to dig themselves out of the hole and fix their lives lead to comic chaos and the kind of failure that is not funny at all, but never to a successful outcome. As Denise says, "We've been found guilty. And no one ... is going to all of a sudden find us not guilty ..." So why bother?

R.J. has a variety of answers: because he loves Denise, because if you don't bother "then it all falls apart," because he believes in justice. Phillie practically gets hysterical at the mention of "justice." He finds the concept much too threatening. It means having to get involved in the world, and he has tried to make himself immune, drinking himself unconscious and insisting that he doesn't "give a shit." A hilarious character, Phillie is also, sadly, what Denise might easily become. For a moment in the play, stirred to action, he tentatively commits to her project. But what a feeble ally he makes. Tellingly, Phillie provides the only help Denise can afford, her implicit response to R.J.'s remark that "we're trying to be the kind of people who get lawyers in circumstances like this." Meanwhile, R.J. becomes ever more deeply involved with the TV talk shows where his interventions seem to have some actual effect. "Life is disgusting," he says, and "I can't do anything about life." So he pours his energies into life's absurd surrogate, content with the illusion of making a difference, while Denise sinks quietly, deeper and deeper, into hell.

Problem Child

George F. Walker

Problem Child was first produced by Rattlestick Productions at Theatre Off Park in New York City on May 13, 1997, with the following cast:

R.J.	Christopher Burns
DENISE	Tasha Lawrence
PHILLIE	Mark Hammer / Alan Benson
HELEN	Kathleen Goldpaugh

Directed by Daniel De Raey
Set Design by Van Santvoord
Lighting Design by Chad McArver
Costume Design by Rachel Gruer
Sound Design by Laura Grace Brown

This revised version of *Problem Child* was first produced by the Factory Theatre in Toronto on October 25, 1997, with the following cast:

R.J.	Shawn Doyle
DENISE	Kristen Thomson
PHILLIE	James Kidnie
HELEN	Nola Augustson

Directed by George F. Walker
Set and Costume Design by Shawn Kerwin
Lighting Design by Rebecca Picherack
Sound Design by Jonathan Rooke and Evan Turner

CHARACTERS

R.J.
DENISE
PHILLIE, the motel caretaker
HELEN, a social worker

SETTING

A slightly rundown motel room.

SCENE 1

R.J. REYNOLDS is watching TV. DENISE is in the washroom taking a shower. There are two old suitcases on the floor and a small baby crib up against the wall beside the bed.

R.J.: Ah man, will you look at that. That guy is too ugly for that woman. When they bring that woman out she's gonna pass out. You can't do stuff like that. Bring in some good-looking woman and tell her she's got a secret admirer then bring her out in front of millions of people to see some ugly guy with pimples on his ears just smiling at her. She's gonna freak out when she sees him. She's gonna be embarrassed. The studio audience is gonna be embarrassed. It's a weak concept for a show so it's gotta be handled just right. Oprah never does this shit.

DENISE comes out of the bathroom drying her hair, wearing a large man's shirt.

DENISE: Can't you do anything besides watch those things.

R.J.: This is life, Denise. Don't be a snob. Just because it's on TV doesn't mean it's not real.

DENISE: Gimme a break ... Mothers who confront their cross-dressing sons. That's your idea of real, eh.

R.J.: What? You think that doesn't happen. When was that anyway.

DENISE: Yesterday.

R.J.: Which one. Jerry Springer? Montel?

DENISE is putting on a pair of jeans.

DENISE: How the hell should I know ... There was that guy in a black garter belt and fishnet stockings and his mother wailing, "I don't mind that he dresses like a woman, but does he have to dress like a slut!"

R.J.: Garter belt, yeah. Sitting next to his mother in a garter belt. Sad. Kind of touching. But too extreme for daytime. What a cool thing for her to say though.

DENISE: (*shaking her head*) Yeah, cool, sure. Man, you are losing your perspective. Turn that thing off. Take a shower. Let's get out of here. Get a meal.

R.J.: Can't leave. She might call.

DENISE: It's been a week, R.J. I'm beginning to lose –

R.J.: A week isn't long. She could still call.

DENISE: We could get the guy in the office to take a message. Whatsisname.

R.J.: Philips. Phillie Philips. Yeah right. I really want to put our future in the hands of a brain-damaged drunk.

DENISE: But I'm going a bit nuts. Maybe I'll go out for a –

R.J.: You gotta stay. She told us to stay put. She was specific. We're on ... you know ... probation or something. We gotta obey. We'll order in. Something different ... We'll order Siamese.

DENISE: Siamese? What's that.

R.J.: Not Siamese. The other one.

DENISE: What? Szechuan?

R.J.: No ... Indian.

DENISE: Indian? How do you get Indian confused with Siamese?

R.J. points at the TV.

R.J.: Shush. They're bringing her out. This is gonna be awful. The audience knows. Look at their faces ... It's gonna be really embarrassing ... I hate it when it's this embarrassing ... No, I can't watch ...

R.J. pulls his sweater over his head.

DENISE stands in front of a wall mirror, brushing her hair.

DENISE: What is Siamese food anyway ... I mean, is there such a thing ... I guess there must be ... They gotta eat, don't they ... the Siamese, I mean.

R.J. pulls down his sweater.

R.J.: Oh man. She's laughing. She's pointing. She's laughing. She's putting her fingers in her mouth. She's making the puking sound. Oh ... oh that's just cruel. Look at the guy. He's devastated. He's

ruined for life. Fuck you. Fuck you, Ricki Lake. Enough is enough.

R.J. turns the TV off.

R.J.: I'm disgusted. Did you see that.

DENISE: No.

R.J.: I think I'll write a letter. Yeah. Right now. We got any paper?

DENISE: We don't have anything, R.J. ... A change of clothes. That's it.

R.J.: Yeah but ... I have to write that letter!

DENISE: Why are you getting so worked up.

R.J.: Because I'm disgusted ... Life is disgusting.

DENISE: That wasn't life, R.J. It was a TV talk show.

R.J.: Hey, that's no more disgusting than life, that show. Life is disgusting like that. Life is the place where dopes like that guy get to be humiliated ... Life is the place that fucks people like you and me up. Life is just like that show.

DENISE: No it's not.

R.J.: Yes it is ... Okay no it's not. It's worse. But I can't do anything about life. I can write that show a letter ... Paper!

DENISE: Look. Calm down.

R.J.: Forget the letter. I'll call.

DENISE: Who you gonna call? You gonna call Ricki Lake?

R.J.: The network ... Hey, I've done this before.

R.J. walks over to the phone.

DENISE: You have?

R.J.: Once. I called Geraldo. When they had that KKK guy on with his grandchild. The old prick had the little kid – eight months old – in a Klan costume. That really disgusted me.

DENISE: I remember that one. That was bad. You called, eh. Why didn't you tell me.

R.J.: Well I didn't get through ... So there was nothing to tell ... But maybe this time I'll – shit!

He holds the phone to his ear.

DENISE: What's wrong?

R.J.: It's not working. It's dead.

DENISE: No way. Jesus.

She scrambles over the bed. Grabs the phone. Listens.

DENISE: Ah no. No ... When was the last time you used the phone?

R.J.: I can't ... remember. (*pacing*) What is this. Is this fate. Is this a kick in the face from fate. What is it. What.

DENISE: Calm down. We'll get it fixed. We can't do anything except get it fixed. Maybe Phillie will fix it.

R.J.: If he can. If he's even around.

DENISE heads for the windows.

DENISE: I can see if he's in the office from here.

She throws back the drapes. And screams because PHILLIE PHILIPS's unshaven face is pressed against the window. DENISE backs up in horror.

DENISE: Jesus. Holy shit. Look at him. Look at him. What's he doin'.

PHILLIE: (*yelling*) Your phone is broken! Your phone is broken!

R.J. runs to the door. Opens it.

R.J.: Why are you on the window, man! What are you doin'!

R.J. goes to PHILLIE. We can see through the window as R.J. pushes HIM.

R.J.: I asked you what the hell you're –

PHILLIE falls over.

R.J.: Shit!

R.J. bends over. DENISE strains to see but tries not to get too close. When R.J. straightens, he has PHILLIE under his arms and is dragging him toward the door.

DENISE: R.J.? R.J. What are you doing.

R.J.: He's unconscious.

DENISE: Why are you bringing him in here.

R.J.: So he can fix the phone.

DENISE: Like that?

R.J.: Well first we have to revive him.

R.J. manages to get PHILLIE in a chair.

DENISE: God. Look at him. He's so ... he's so ... Whatya think is wrong with him.

PHILLIE: (*eyes closed*) Drunk! He's drunk.

DENISE and R.J. look at each other.

PHILLIE: (*opens his eyes*) Yeah he's drunk. He's so drunk he just passed out against our window.

Smells too. (*stands unsteadily*) Smells bad. Well why shouldn't he? Do you think he bathes. Not often. Look at him he's so ... he's so. Well what I think is fuck it, wastin' all our time tryin' to figure out what brought him to this sorry state. Let's just shoot him. Bring him out back under the billboard, near the trash in the place where rats live. Fuck it ... (*focuses on DENISE*) Oh yeah, a lady called ... Your phone's busted. Couldn't put her through. Bitch got all ... unpleasant ... What did she want. Oh yeah. Something about ... something ...

DENISE: A baby?

PHILLIE: A what?

DENISE: A baby?!

PHILLIE: What about a baby?! Oh yeah, baby ... She was callin' about a baby!! (*grabs his head*) Shit. All this excitement has made me nauseous.

He rushes into the washroom. Retching sounds.

R.J. goes to DENISE. Puts his arms around her.

DENISE: This is not good. You told me everything would be all right ... This is not all right.

DENISE moves away from R.J. Another loud retching sound. R.J. goes toward DENISE.

DENISE: No. Just stay away from me. Suppose she doesn't call back ... I said stay the fuck away from me.

R.J.: I was gonna ... comfort you. You know?

DENISE: You wanna comfort me? Get the phone fixed.

A retching sound. R.J. gestures toward the bathroom.

R.J.: It'll probably be a minute or two more ... I dunno.

DENISE continues to pace. PHILLIE continues to wretch. R.J. continues to look helpless.

Blackout.

SCENE 2

HELEN MACKIE stands just inside the open door. Wearing a business suit. Carrying a briefcase. DENISE and R.J. stand and stare at her.

HELEN: Can I ... sit down.

DENISE: Where's the baby ...

HELEN: I'm sorry?

DENISE: You didn't bring the baby.

HELEN: We're a long way from that yet ... Can I sit down.

R.J.: Sure. There.

He points to a chair.

HELEN: Actually over at the table would be better. I've got some paper work.

She sits at the small table in the corner. DENISE has started to pace.

DENISE: What's she mean we're a long way from that ... Ask her what she means.

HELEN: Did you think this would be easy, Denise.

DENISE: Look, I ... I just want to know what she meant.

HELEN: (*to R.J.*) What's wrong with her.

R.J.: Nothing. She's just –

HELEN: She looks pretty ... edgy. (*to DENISE*) Are you on any ... medication, Denise.

R.J.: No, she's – Well, we thought you'd be bring-ing – Look, we've been cooped up in here for a week.

HELEN opens her briefcase. Puts papers on the table. A notepad.

HELEN: Why.

DENISE: Why? Waiting for you.

R.J.: Yeah. And we didn't go anywhere. We never left.

HELEN: Never left? I don't get it.

R.J.: You told us to stay put. We stayed put.

HELEN: I never meant you couldn't go out. I just said I'd need a week to get things moving. So you should just –

DENISE: Where's the baby!

HELEN: Denise ... Denise, come over here. Sit down.

DENISE: No.

R.J.: Denise.

DENISE: No. I'm not sitting. I'm not doing anything until she tells me where the baby is.

HELEN stands. Goes to DENISE.

HELEN: She's in the same place she's been in for the last six months. She's in a loving foster home. And we can't just take her from a place where she's secure and loved and give her back to you

unless we're sure she's going to be okay ... And making sure she's going to be okay takes time. Do you understand. Time and consideration. And ... some questions.

R.J.: We'll answer questions. I've already told you that. Any questions.

HELEN: Good ... Now Denise, are you on any medi-cation ... Lift your head. Look at me.

DENISE obeys.

HELEN: Denise, what's that expression on your face supposed to mean. All that ... attitude. You think that's helpful? I'm just doing my job.

DENISE: I just ... I just thought you were bringing the baby ... I guess I got that wrong.

R.J.: (*to HELEN*) That's my fault. I heard you wrong. Or I misunderstood ... We both got pretty worked up ... The phone was broken ... We were cooped up ... Things ... things ...

DENISE: I'm not on anything. I haven't been on anything for a long time. We've got doctors' papers. (*to R.J.*) Show her.

R.J.: Where are they.

DENISE: In my suitcase.

R.J. gets the suitcase.

R.J.: Yeah we've got doctors' papers. We've got a social worker's letter. We've got a letter from our landlord.

DENISE: He's got a job.

R.J.: Yeah. I've got a job ... It's ... good ... It's –

DENISE: Okay. It's an okay job. He works for a builder. He does drywall.

R.J.: It's almost a trade ... I've got a letter from my boss.

He hands HELEN a large envelope.

R.J.: They're all in there. All the letters.

HELEN: What about you, Denise.

DENISE: I've been looking. I had a part-time wait-ress thing. A small restaurant ...

R.J.: Well you know, it's a small town. There's not a lot of places where – She put in some applica-tions ... but ...

HELEN: You like life in a small town?

R.J.: Yeah. It's cool.

HELEN: Denise?

DENISE: It's okay. It takes getting used to. I'll be okay. Look, what are you asking. Do you wanna know if I turn tricks. Do I put stuff in my veins.

R.J.: That's not happening, Miss ... Miss ...

HELEN: Helen. Just Helen is okay ...

R.J.: Okay, Helen ... Look. Look at the letter. The letter will tell you we've got a new life in that town. It was hard at first. You know? But we did it. We went away from everyone we knew. Everything we ... did. And we started ... I mean it was hard. Denise was great. What she did was so hard. It was –

DENISE: We need our baby back. It's not gonna work if we don't get Christine back. I won't make it.

HELEN: What do you mean by that, Denise. Do you think you'll start back on drugs, Denise. Do you feel that's a possibility.

DENISE: Of course it's a possibility. Everything is a possibility. I'm not a new person. They didn't throw out the old Denise and make a new one. It's a repair job. I'm just ... repaired ... (to R.J.) She doesn't get it.

R.J.: (to HELEN) She needs the baby. Everything she's done these past few months she's done for the baby.

HELEN's cellphone rings. She answers it.

HELEN: (into phone) Yeah? ... Yeah. Okay ... Okay sure. About a half-hour. (putting the cellphone back in her briefcase) Look, I'm needed somewhere. Why don't I just take these letters away. Look them over. Call you. Set something up.

R.J.: Set something up like what?

HELEN: A meeting. We'll talk some more.

R.J.: We thought it was set. The court said it was okay ... I mean here we are in this dump. We've come back and –

HELEN: Look, the court needs our approval. If we say it's –

DENISE: We?

HELEN: Me ... If things look okay to me then the court is just a rubber stamp. Listen, I'm sorry if I gave you the wrong impression but we can't rush this. We're going to have to ... get to know each other a bit better. We'll have to reveal a few things. Rehash a few things probably. Do you understand what I'm saying, Denise.

DENISE shrugs. Turns away.

HELEN picks up her briefcase.

R.J.: We'll ... just wait then.

HELEN: I'll call you.

HELEN looks for a moment at both of them. Leaves.

R.J. looks at DENISE. Goes to the open door. Yells after HELEN.

R.J.: Goodbye ... (to DENISE) She waved ... She turned and waved.

DENISE: This is not going to happen.

R.J.: Ah don't –

DENISE: Nah, we've got a judgment against us. We've been found guilty. And no one, especially her, is going to all of a sudden find us not guilty, throw that judgment away and say here, here's your kid, start over, make a family ... Ah, aren't you cute – We thought you were the scum of the earth but really you're cute. We're sorry ...

R.J.: (moving toward her) Listen, are you tired. You're probably hungry and tired so –

DENISE: Ah please stay away from me. I can't do this. I can't let you get my spirits up. I'm not up to getting positive. It's hard. Sometimes it's just like – I don't know ... bullshit. Can't you just let me feel like it's all bullshit and leave it at that.

R.J.: No ... I can't ... Because then it all falls apart, Denise.

DENISE: I'm going out. (grabs a jacket) If I don't get out of here for a while I'll go –

R.J.: It's okay. You go out. I'll stay. I'll be here if she calls. There was something in the way she waved goodbye. I think she'll call soon. Maybe she felt sorry or something but ... she'll call. Don't worry ... I'll be here.

He sits on the couch.

DENISE: Yeah ... I know you will ... You're a rock or something. How'd that happen. I mean you used to be as messed up as me and now ... now you're some kind of solid thing.

She leaves. R.J. just stares straight ahead.

R.J.: Bullshit ...

He lowers his head.

Blackout.

SCENE 3

PHILLIE is vacuuming the room. R.J. is watching the TV.

PHILLIE: (*shouting*) This bothering you?

R.J. gestures that it's okay.

PHILLIE: 'Cause I could turn it off. Come back later.

R.J. gestures again. PHILLIE turns off the vacuum.

PHILLIE: Are you sure.

R.J.: Definitely. Just do your job, man. It's okay.

PHILLIE: I appreciate that.

R.J.: Yeah ... By the way, it's good to see you sober.

PHILLIE: It's Wednesday. I clean the rooms on Wednesdays. It's almost impossible to do that under the influence.

R.J.: I bet ...

PHILLIE: I mean it can be done ... But I gotta tell you, cleaning toilet bowls when you're smashed ... is kind of ... unnatural.

R.J.: Yeah.

PHILLIE turns on the machine. Vacuums a while. Something on the TV grabs his attention. Turns off the machine.

PHILLIE: Why are those three chubby women crying.

R.J.: They're sisters ... See the skinny guy with the skimpy beard next to them? He's been having sex with all of them. And today they've finally confronted him.

PHILLIE: Yeah? Confronted? So how come they're crying. And he looks ...

R.J.: Kinda pleased with himself? ... Because there's no justice in the world, man. None. He thinks he's the cock of the walk. He's on national TV and he's a winner and the women are ... fools. Crying fools. There is definitely hardly any justice in the world.

PHILLIE: You think I don't know that? I know that ... The thing about me is I don't give a shit.

R.J.: I give a shit. I think justice is the only thing. Fair behaviour for fair behaviour. You know? Even breaks for everyone.

PHILLIE: No no ... Don't take me there, man. I can't get into that. Next thing I'll just get upset. I'm capable of some pretty self-destructive behaviour. I gotta concentrate on doing my job. I'm lucky to have this job. If it wasn't for my cousin Edward ... No ... No, I can't get into that justice shit. The lucky and the unlucky. The haves and the have-nots. The fuckers, the fuckees – oh man. Let me just suck up some dirt. Let me just do what I can do, and suck up what little dirt I can here.

PHILLIE turns on the machine. Vacuums a while. PHILLIE turns off the machine.

PHILLIE: Who's the guy in the suit.

R.J.: The expert. They always have an expert.

PHILLIE: What? A social worker.

R.J.: Sometimes. Or a doctor. Or someone who's written a book.

PHILLIE: So. Yeah? Is he supposed to solve this. Is he supposed to bring justice to this situation ... I really don't think so!

PHILLIE unplugs the vacuum. Gathers his cleaning supplies.

PHILLIE: Look. Here's the truth. I can't do anymore. It's that ... justice thing. Once it's in your head you can't ignore it. You just can't ... It colours everything ... It makes all work futile.

He starts off.

R.J.: Sorry ... It looks pretty clean though.

PHILLIE: There's a stain on the carpet. It's permanent. Other than that, yeah, it's pretty clean ... The bathroom is spotless ... not that I give a shit!

He gets choked up and leaves, not closing the door.

R.J. turns back to the TV.

R.J.: ... Oh yeah right. Take it out on her. Like it's her fault. Look at him. Look at that grin. Get serious, man ... No no it's not about sibling rivalry you twit, it's about the guy and his dick. It's about the dick ... Go ahead ask him. Ask him about the dick! The truth is in the dick!

DENISE appears in the doorway. Doesn't come in. Just leans against the frame watching R.J. She looks a little messed up.

R.J.: Ah man ... Enough. Look she's crying. She's really crying. Okay – Host intervention! Host intervention! Come on! Come on! Fair is fair. Come on, for Chrissake. Intervene!

DENISE: Hey!

R.J. turns to DENISE.

DENISE: Calm down! It's just a fucking TV show!

R.J. looks at DENISE. At the TV. At DENISE.

R.J.: Yeah.

He turns off the TV. Stands.

R.J.: Hi.

DENISE: I mean don't we have enough problems of our own. Real ones? You have to go looking for something to get upset about on a ... a fucking TV show?!

R.J.: Where you been?

DENISE: Downtown.

R.J.: How far downtown?

DENISE: All the way.

R.J.: You see your mother?

DENISE: She wasn't there ... I went over to your place. Your mother wasn't there either. Hey, there's a show idea you can send in: "Mothers Who Aren't There When You Need Them."

R.J.: You on something?

DENISE: Ah you're gonna wanna talk about that, aren't you. I wanna talk about where our mothers are when our life is going down the toilet but you'll have to get into that "let me see your eyes" bullshit.

R.J.: I'm not gonna look in your eyes. I don't have to look in your eyes. You can't even stand up.

DENISE: Says who.

She stands. Falls back against the door frame.

R.J. sits on the bed. Hangs his head between his legs.

DENISE: Ah don't go falling apart on me. Hanging your head like that. It's just booze. Six beers. Nothing. I needed to feel better than I felt.

She staggers a bit as she moves toward him.

DENISE: I was feeling so bad ... I was afraid I wouldn't be able to ... you know ... make good choices ... because the way I was feeling was – fuck it ... So I thought – hey, feel better. Make better choices so ...

She sits next to him. Rubs his head.

DENISE: So really it's okay ... I'm not falling. I'm really not falling ... I'm still ... hopeful. Look there's still hope in me ... Look at me. Look at me. Come on.

She lifts his head.

DENISE: Now is this the face of an ... optimistic person ... a basically optimistic person ... or ... isn't it. I say it is.

R.J.: Well, you must know ... Why'd you go see your mother.

DENISE: Ah ... 'Cause it's hard not to go see your mother when you think ... "God I sure could use a little mother talk!" Even when you remember your mother's kind of written you off. Even when you remember it was your mother who called in "the government" and had them take away your kid ... so ... so I went to talk ... But ... well ...

R.J.: She wasn't there. Big surprise. When was she ever.

DENISE: Hey don't get uppity. Neither was yours.

R.J.: Yeah but mine has an excuse. She's dead.

DENISE: Holy shit. You're right.

R.J.: Just six beers?

DENISE: Or more ... Holy shit. That's right. She died just after I got pregnant ... I forgot. How could I forget that ... I walked over to your building. Took the elevator to the twelfth floor. Went down the hall to 1209. Knocked. Waited. Left ... I just forgot.

R.J.: It's been a rough year.

DENISE: Ah look who's trying to cheer me up. Doesn't it ever just wear you down ... Trying to make sure I'm ... okay? (*kisses his face*) Really. How could I forget your mother is dead. Do you think I've got permanent brain damage. Memory loss?

R.J.: Maybe you were just ... drunk.

DENISE: That's my man. Always got the right answer. Always looking to let me off the hook. Always looking for ... a reason ... Why?

R.J.: I don't know. I love you. I ... love you.

He kisses her. He puts his hand under her sweater. She kisses him back.

DENISE: Are we gonna have sex now?

R.J.: It's better than ...

DENISE: What.

R.J.: Thinking ... about the baby ... About mothers. I mean *your* mother. Of all the hypocritical bullshit in the world ... Your mother gets us busted ... your mother, the biggest screw-up in the universe gets to play Miss Citizen and –

DENISE: I did that. (*kissing him*) Shush. I did that.

R.J.: What.

DENISE: That "my mother's gotta go to hell" thing. After the six beers ...

R.J.: Or more.

DENISE: Yeah. Anyway it's been done. She's in hell. I sent her in my mind to hell. You know maybe I didn't go to see her to talk ... Maybe I went to kill her. Yeah. I think I actually went to kill her.

R.J.: Yeah. Sure.

DENISE: No really. I mean why else would I buy a gun.

R.J.: What? Get real.

DENISE: No ... No. I bought it off ... Billy Richards. Remember him? I ran into him and he says, "Hey ... So? What's new" ... All that shit. And I find myself asking if he's got any weapons I can purchase ...

R.J.: Denise ... What is this –

DENISE: It's in my bag. Over there somewhere.

R.J. walks over to the door. Bends. DENISE's canvas bag is on the floor. He empties the contents onto the table. A few things. No gun.

R.J.: So?

DENISE: No gun? I guess I musta made it up.

R.J.: And why would you do something like that, Denise.

DENISE: Your worst fear, dear. What is it. Something like that? Denise gets a gun. Goes on a rampage. Takes revenge on her mother. Then ... what? Turns the gun on herself. Well whatever ... Your worst fear ... I was just putting it out where we could both see it ... I don't know ... I don't know ...

R.J.: Maybe I should go get us some coffee.

DENISE: I guess ...

R.J.: How about food ...

DENISE: Food ... No ... Look ... I'm just going to crash ... You go out. Eat.

R.J.: No, I'll –

DENISE: No, I went out. You go out. It's probably good ... I mean you are talking to the TV. So ...

R.J.: Yeah ... Yeah maybe I'll just go get a –

DENISE: Take your time. I'm just going to sleep.

R.J.: She didn't call by the way. Helen. The social worker? She didn't call.

DENISE: No?

R.J.: But ... you didn't ask me if she called. Why not.

DENISE: I don't know.

R.J.: Sure you do ... You're preparing for the worst.

DENISE: Maybe.

R.J.: You are ... What's the good of that ... Denise?

She shrugs. Turns away. He leaves. She takes off her jacket. Reaches inside her pocket. Takes out a small gun. Puts it under the mattress. Lies down on the bed. Takes the bedspread. Pulls it over herself. Rolls in it until she is wrapped tight.

Blackout.

SCENE 4

HELEN stands over the bed. Watching DENISE sleep ... She begins to look casually around the room. Pokes at a pile of newspapers. Looks in one of the dresser drawers. Eventually, she goes into the bathroom. We hear glass objects being shifted. DENISE stirs. A glass crashes in the bathroom. DENISE sits up quickly.

DENISE: R.J.?

HELEN: (*coming out of the bathroom*) No ... it's just me ... I broke a glass ... Hi ... I was just ... just ...

HELEN wraps her hand in a towel. DENISE is up.

DENISE: Searching?

HELEN: Searching? ... No, I was thirsty. So I –

DENISE: Is that a bad cut.

HELEN: I don't know.

DENISE: You're bleeding.

HELEN: A little ... Yes. There's glass all over the floor. Do you want me to ...

DENISE: I'll get it later.

HELEN: I can do it.

DENISE: I said I'll get it later! I'll do it! (*smiles*) It'll get done. Honest.

HELEN: Sure. Fine. Thanks ... So ... Can I sit down.

DENISE: Yeah, sit down ... I'll sit down too. We'll both sit down.

DENISE sits at the table.

HELEN: What's wrong.

DENISE: Nothing. Sit down.

HELEN: (*sitting*) You look tired –

DENISE: Do I? ... You look fine ... You look just fine. Well, you've got a bad cut on your hand. And you're bleeding all over the table but other than that –

HELEN: Oh dear, I better –

HELEN starts to stand. DENISE grabs her wrist.

DENISE: Where you going?

HELEN: I don't ... well, to the bathroom. I'm bleeding.

DENISE: Stay put. Just for a minute.

HELEN: But I'm bleeding on the table.

DENISE: Hey it's okay. Stay put. Can you just stay put. I need to talk to you.

HELEN: Well, I need to talk to you too. But –

DENISE: So good. Let's talk. It's just that I've been worried you know. Worried that you were out there doing your investigation without having all the –

HELEN: It's not really an investigation.

DENISE: Yes it is. We're suspects. And you're investigating us.

HELEN: I'm doing my job. I'm just trying to determine if you're capable of caring for your child. You're not a suspect. It's not a criminal –

DENISE: Hey, we're suspected of being inadequate. Let's not argue over the fucking word here. Look I'm sorry. But I was just worried you were out there "doing your job" without knowing something essential about me. And that is ... I need my baby. I *need* her.

HELEN: I know that.

DENISE: No you don't.

HELEN: Yes –

DENISE: No you don't! I didn't tell you. I should have told you how much I need her. And how much I love her. And that I never would do anything to hurt her ... And how what happened before wasn't really what they said happened. My mother ... you know, we were fighting and to get back at me she made it look like I was neglecting the baby and called you people.

HELEN: Look, all that's on record.

DENISE: Some of it. Not all of it.

HELEN: The point is, it doesn't matter how we got involved. We're involved.

DENISE: Yeah but listen –

HELEN: No, *you* listen. We were called. We got involved. We saw things we didn't like. We took action.

DENISE: Pretty drastic though ... I mean the action you took was ... pretty fucking drastic.

HELEN: Were you or were you not a drug addict.

DENISE: Hey Helen, that sounded pretty ... you know "legal." Like a lawyer, that "were you or were you not" stuff.

HELEN: Were you or were you not a prostitute.

DENISE: I turned a few tricks. It happened. Hey I thought I should pay the rent.

HELEN: Please.

DENISE: Please? What's that mean. Did that sound feeble to you. I mean as an excuse.

HELEN: I didn't want to go backwards here, Denise. We have enough to deal with in the present.

DENISE: I just want to make sure you ... got it clear. I mean maybe you don't. Maybe you don't know R.J. was in jail. I was alone. Did you know that.

HELEN: Yes.

DENISE: So I was alone. I'd had this baby. My husband was in prison. I was broke.

HELEN: You were receiving welfare.

DENISE: It wasn't enough.

HELEN: Look, I've told you I don't want to rehash –

DENISE: It wasn't enough. I wasn't making it.

HELEN: Others do.

DENISE: I wasn't. It wasn't enough. The rent was too high. I couldn't get them to lower it. I had expenses.

HELEN: Drugs ... Crack, speed, what else.

DENISE: No! ... No, you see, this is what makes me think you don't really know everything you should. I'd been clean since I got pregnant.

HELEN: Not according to your mother.

DENISE: My mother yeah. See? I told you. We've got to investigate my mother's part in this. I think if you were to examine her in more detail you'd see –

HELEN: Your mother isn't an issue.

DENISE: Sure she is.

HELEN: No. No, *you're* the issue. You're a drug addict and a prostitute who wants her daughter back and that makes you the *only* issue ...

DENISE is up. Moving around.

DENISE: I was never a prostitute. I turned a few tricks and even if I was a prostitute, who says a prostitute can't raise a child.

HELEN: I do.

DENISE: You do?

HELEN: Yes, I do.

DENISE: Is that an official position there, Helen.

HELEN: No.

DENISE: But it's your position.

HELEN: Yes.

DENISE: Is this getting personal here, Helen. It sounds like you take this personally.

HELEN: I want to talk about your new life, Denise. I've read the letters you've given me. I've made a few calls.

DENISE: I was a drug addict though. You were right about that. I mean I kind of messed around with drugs all through my teens. I stopped when I got pregnant. But when you took my baby away I became a drug addict. That's when I became a drug addict! For the fucking record! Okay?!

HELEN: So. What strikes me about your new life in this small town is that it's really not your life. It's R.J.'s. I mean, all the reference letters are about him. He seems to have become a real member of that community. But there's no reference to you at all. What do you do up there, Denise.

DENISE: I stay at home and take drugs. Sometimes I go out and fuck people for money. The guy who runs the hardware store. The mayor. The scout-master. I fuck them all!

HELEN: Do you think that smart-ass mouth is going to help you out here, Denise. Do you think you're going to impress me into giving you back your baby with that smart-ass talk? Come here and sit down.

DENISE: I feel better here.

HELEN: Come here!

> *DENISE sits ... but not on the chair Helen has pointed to.*

DENISE: Okay?

HELEN: So? ... What do you do. Look for work? Watch TV?

DENISE: I look for work.

HELEN: What kind. Waitressing?

DENISE: Yeah.

HELEN: What about at home. Do you cook?

DENISE: Cook?

HELEN: Meals. Do you cook meals for R.J. Do you cook his dinner when he comes home from work.

DENISE: Ah ... no.

HELEN: No? Why not.

DENISE: He doesn't like my cooking. It's not very good. He cooks better.

HELEN: So he comes home, cooks his own dinner.

DENISE: And mine. He cooks for me too, Helen. I mean he doesn't just cook for himself. That would be cruel.

HELEN: Do you clean.

DENISE: Clean. You mean vacuum? I vacuum.

HELEN: How often.

DENISE: What? What is this crap.

HELEN: I notice R.J. joined a church last month. I guess he did that to impress us.

DENISE: Probably ... But with R.J. you never know. It's possible he found God. Prison changed him. He discovered the TV talk shows in prison. Maybe he discovered God there, too.

HELEN: I'm assuming he did it to impress us. That's okay. It's still a good thing no matter how you come to it.

DENISE: You think so? You think church is a big deal.

HELEN: It can be. You don't think so, though. I mean, you wouldn't even make the effort to impress us, I mean let alone actually sincerely looking for some true religious experience –

DENISE: I'm getting a really uneasy feeling about you, Helen.

HELEN: Oh really. Why? Do you think I might be questioning your values, Denise. Do you have values, Denise. Do you know what values are, Denise.

DENISE: This is personal isn't it, Helen.

HELEN: You want me to give you back the baby so you can hang out with her, Denise? Maybe take her to the mall? Train her to give you a hug when you're feeling low ... Is that why you want the baby, Denise. You need a "friend"?

DENISE: I want her because she's ... mine!

HELEN: Well frankly, I think she's better off where she is. She's in a real family.

DENISE: I want her!

HELEN: (*standing*) Well, I don't think you're going to get her. I really don't.

> *DENISE leans over the table. Grabs HELEN's injured hand. HELEN yells.*

DENISE: I want her! I want her!

HELEN: Let ... go of my hand. You're hurting me.

DENISE: You shouldn't have made it personal.

HELEN: Let go!

> *DENISE lets go.*

HELEN: Ah. It's really bleeding now.

> *HELEN goes into the bathroom.*

DENISE: What gave you the right to make it personal.

> *DENISE goes to the bed. Takes the gun from under the mattress.*

HELEN: (*from bathroom*) Ah, damn. It's bleeding pretty badly.

DENISE: I mean what kind of position does that put me in? You think I should go to church and become a better cook or I'll never see my kid again. What kind of shit is that.

HELEN: (*from bathroom*) Look. You better help me. I'm feeling a ... little ... light-headed ...

> *DENISE stares at the gun.*

> *PHILLIE comes in. Carrying a pile of towels.*

PHILLIE: Oh. Sorry. Should have knocked. (*hits himself on the head*) Moron. Learn. Why can't you learn! You wanna lose this job? Do you? (*hits himself again, looks at DENISE, smiles*) I brought some fresh towels.

> *HELEN groans loudly in the bathroom. Passes out with much noise and spilling of things. PHILLIE looks toward the bathroom. DENISE stands. Puts the gun in her waistband. Walks over to PHILLIE. Takes the towels.*

DENISE: Thanks.

> *DENISE and PHILLIE both look into the bathroom. DENISE looks at PHILLIE intently.*

DENISE: What's your name again?

> *Blackout.*

SCENE 5

> *R.J. is on the phone and he is very upset.*

R.J.: No, I won't calm down. No ... No. I've had it. It's gross, man. It's fucking pathetic and gross. Are you watching this shit. Are you watching that big prick scream at his mother. You let some big piece of garbage come on national television and humiliate a helpless pensioner. Are you nuts. Are you people insane. No! Bullshit ... No! Fuck you. It's gotta be ... stopped ... Oh really ... Oh right ... No! No! Mothers Who Never Visited Their Sons in Prison is a fucking stupid idea for a show. Ah look at that. What's he gonna do? Hit her? Do you just let him hit her? Well it looks like he's gonna hit her ... I want the producer. Get me the producer! Get me the producer! I need to tell him something ... Get him. Get him! Get him! Get him!!

> *PHILLIE and DENISE come in. They are both a bit messed up. R.J. sees them.*

R.J.: I'll call you back.

> *He hangs up.*

DENISE: Who was that.

R.J.: No one.

DENISE: You're losing it, right? You're flipping out.

R.J.: Come here. (*points to TV*) Look at that. Piece of shit! Piece of shit won't stop!! It's not her fucking fault he was doing eight to ten. (*to TV*) I mean a fucking reality check might be in order here, son. I didn't blame *my* mother when I was inside. I mean I didn't even know anyone who blamed their mother. (*to DENISE*) I mean where did they dig this guy up ... Look at her face. Look at that poor woman's hurt and confused face. It's a crime. I can't believe they syndicate this shit.

DENISE: Do you mind if I turn it off.

R.J.: No. Please. Turn it off. I want you to turn it off. Do you think I like watching this stuff. It's fucking infuriating.

> *DENISE turns off the TV.*

PHILLIE: It's the injustice that gets to him.

R.J.: Yeah ... yeah ...

> *DENISE has taken HELEN's briefcase from under the bed.*

PHILLIE: Yeah ...

R.J.: You're both covered in mud ... or something.

DENISE: I'll explain later ... I've got to give Phillie something ...

R.J.: Whose briefcase is that. Is that whatshername's.

DENISE: In a minute, okay?

DENISE has taken an address book from the briefcase. Looks through it. Tears out a page. Hands it to PHILLIE.

DENISE: It's the one on top ... Do you know where that is.

PHILLIE: Yeah. It's on top ...

DENISE: But do you know ... where it is.

PHILLIE: It's on top ...

DENISE: But do you know how to find it.

PHILLIE: Yeah.

DENISE: Do you think you can do this.

PHILLIE: Do you.

DENISE: Yeah, I think you can. But you have to be sure you want to ...

PHILLIE: I want to ...

DENISE: Okay then ... Go.

PHILLIE: Yeah. Okay ... I'm going.

He starts off. Stops.

PHILLIE: I feel good.

DENISE: I'm glad.

PHILLIE nods. Leaves.

R.J.: What's going on. Where you been. Where's he going ... What's going on.

DENISE: Things got a bit weird when you were out before. I'm trying to think of how to explain this to you. Trying to think if maybe there's some TV show I can compare it to for you.

R.J.: Gimme a break.

DENISE: I don't know, man. Life is just crawling all over us here and you're putting all your energy into that crap you watch on that stupid box. So I'm wondering maybe you're not really capable of understanding what I have to tell you unless ... I don't know maybe I should go on TV and sit on one of those stupid chairs. Cry. And then you'll see me and hear my story and your heart will go out to me and you'll understand. But if I just tell you how it happened and I'm just me and you're just you ... I don't know, I don't know ...

R.J.: How bad is this.

DENISE: She's dead.

R.J.: Who's dead.

DENISE: Helen.

R.J.: Helen? Helen the social worker?

DENISE: Yeah ... She's dead ... She fell down and hit her head against the toilet.

R.J.: The toilet ... Our toilet?

DENISE: Yeah ... the bowl ... you know.

R.J. walks into the bathroom. Walks out.

R.J.: She's not in there.

DENISE: No. She's ... gone.

R.J.: I was afraid to look. I had my eyes closed. But when I opened them she wasn't there.

DENISE: Yeah.

R.J.: A lot of blood though.

DENISE: Yeah. Some of that's from her head. Some of it from when she cut her hand.

R.J.: She cut her hand?

DENISE: On a glass. I had nothing to do with that.

R.J.: Oh. Did you have anything to do with her hitting her head.

DENISE: Not directly. I think I sped up the flow of blood from her hand when I squeezed it and that might have made her woozy. I think that's what happened ...

R.J.: Why were you squeezing her hand.

DENISE: Look we gotta skip all that and get to the important thing. I didn't shoot her. I wanted to shoot her. I didn't. She told me we weren't getting our child back. She told me to basically forget it and I thought okay, I'll forget it. I'll put a bullet in you and then one in myself and it'll be forgotten. But I didn't. Of course maybe she made the decision for me by falling and hitting her head on the toilet bowl. But I don't think so. I think I'd already decided not to use the gun. To remain hopeful. I mean I can't be sure because the timing was ... tight. But I think I'd already decided. And then Phillie was standing there with the towels and my mind started to race. You know how it races sometimes when I'm upset. Like that. But different. Because this time it was clear. My mind. It had purpose. So I knew the first thing I had to do. And I did it.

R.J.: You got rid of the body.

DENISE: No. I got Phillie on my side ... I mean I had to ... He was right there so I had to get him on my side. It wasn't hard really. Because really he's one of us …

R.J.: What's that mean, "one of us"?

DENISE: Scum of the earth. So he knows. He knows about getting screwed … Because it's just so easy to screw us, people can do it without even trying really.

R.J.: No. Justice.

DENISE: What.

R.J.: He's just got a thing about justice. He thinks it's something that's … forbidden or something.

DENISE: No. He knew her. He knew her type, that's all. I told him what she said to me. That I won't be getting the baby 'cause I don't go to church and I don't cook.

R.J.: She said that?

DENISE: Yeah she said that.

R.J.: She said, "I'm sorry, Denise, but you can't have your child back because we've found out you're a lousy cook"?

DENISE: Yes! She said that! Exactly!

R.J.: And so you killed her?!

DENISE: I didn't kill her.

R.J.: No you didn't kill her. You thought about killing her with the gun you told me you didn't have but you didn't really kill her. Oh you squeezed her hand a little. But that was it. Come on, Denise. There's a lot of blood in that bathroom. A lot!

DENISE: I didn't kill her. I didn't kill her, I'm telling you!

R.J.: Good thing I didn't go in there unprepared. If I'd gone in there not knowing … All that blood. Good thing I went right for the TV. I mean you're down on me watching television but it's a damn good thing I wanted to watch television instead of taking a piss, or I might be really fucked up now! Because I would've thought that was your blood. Your blood. And I would've thought you'd hurt yourself. Really bad … And I would have freaked … Okay. But that didn't happen. Something else happened. Let's try and stay with what really happened.

DENISE: Good idea …

R.J.: She died?

DENISE: Yeah.

R.J.: Accidentally.

DENISE: Ah … Yeah …

R.J.: You got Phillie on your side and he helped you get rid of the body.

DENISE: Yeah.

R.J.: Because you had to … because you couldn't call the goddamn police or a goddamn ambulance like most people … even though it was a fucking accident you had to get rid of the body. Sure. That makes sense! Oh my God. Oh my God, what have you done. We could have appealed. She wasn't the only social worker in this city. We could have appealed. (*grabs DENISE*) You didn't have to kill her. Killing her was not the right thing to do.

DENISE: Listen to me!

R.J.: It was a bad idea! Bad bad bad –

DENISE: Listen to me. Listen!

R.J.: Bad!

DENISE: Listen! Listen it was over before she fell. We were finished as parents. Our life. Our future. Everything we wanted to do was over. She was going to make sure it wasn't going to happen. I didn't kill her. But … it would've maybe looked like I had … so we buried her …

R.J.: Where.

DENISE: Out back.

R.J.: We could've gotten a lawyer. We're trying to be the kind of people who get lawyers in circumstances like this, Denise.

DENISE: Please. No. No lawyers. No law. No official investigation. We're not going that route. It's not our route. Listen to me. We're doing it our way. The only way we've got … really.

R.J.: Where'd you send Phillie.

DENISE: She had their names in her address book. The foster parents …

R.J.: Ah no –

DENISE: He can do it.

R.J.: Ah. No, he can't.

DENISE: I gave him the gun.

R.J.: You sent him to get our baby. And you gave him a gun?

DENISE: No bullets. Just the gun. Something to … produce if he meets resistance. I think it'll be okay. They don't know him. He'll just ring the doorbell. They'd recognize me probably. She's probably described me to them. Thought I might pull something … So I couldn't do it myself … Because she prepared them.

R.J.: Are you nuts.

DENISE: What.

He grabs her.

R.J.: Are you fucking nuts?!

DENISE: Yes! Yes I am. I'm out of my fucking mind. I want my baby. I can't sleep, I can't eat without her. I can't live without her. And I want her now! I want her. That's all I want. Just let me have her and it will be okay. I promise. Let this happen and it will be okay. Just … please let this happen!

She buries her head in his chest.

DENISE: Please …

R.J. stares off into space. Rubs DENISE's back.

Blackout.

SCENE 6

R.J. and DENISE are waiting for the phone to ring. He paces. She sits on the bed staring at the phone.

R.J.: He said he'd call? You're sure?

DENISE: Yeah.

R.J.: And you think he … understood.

DENISE: Yeah … Understood what?

R.J.: To call.

DENISE: I said, "Call when you've got her."

R.J.: There could've been a problem.

DENISE: Yes … Lots of them.

R.J.: The chances are slim he got her out of there.

DENISE: I thought he could do it. I mean they're just a nice suburban couple. They're not the mob or anything. They're not protected. He shows up. Shows the gun if he has to … Says, "Give me the kid" … They should cooperate … It's human nature to cooperate.

R.J.: Yeah? Would you give her over to someone.

DENISE: I did. Remember? People came into our apartment and I gave her to them. And they didn't have a fucking gun. They just had a piece of paper.

R.J.: Well we'll see … we'll see how reckless you've been. Why doesn't he call … Why … It's been enough time.

DENISE: Shit … Oh shit.

She stands and heads for the door.

DENISE: There's no one in the office to put the call through.

R.J.: Is that how it works.

DENISE: Yes. That's how it fucking works.

She leaves. Slams the door behind her.

R.J. paces a while. Looks at TV. Paces. Goes to TV. Turns it on. Flips the channels. Flips. Flips. A knock on the door. R.J. goes to the door. Opens it. PHILLIE is standing there.

PHILLIE: I saw Denise leave. I've been waiting. Can I come in.

R.J.: Yeah come in. (*pulling PHILLIE in*) Have you got her?

PHILLIE: The baby?

R.J.: Yeah, the baby!

PHILLIE: No … no. I didn't do it. I mean I thought about doing it. But I couldn't. It was a wild idea. It was like an idea from my youth. In my youth I could've done it. I had guts then. But not now. I tried though. Got in the car. Headed in the right direction. Five or six blocks. But then I stopped. Reality stopped me. I mean what am I. I'm a drunk. I'm not a kidnapper. There's a difference.

R.J.: Yeah.

PHILLIE: You understand?

R.J.: Yeah.

PHILLIE: I mean I couldn't say this to Denise … She was wild. Intense and wild. You got anything to drink?

R.J.: No.

PHILLIE: Because I need a little something.

R.J.: I'm sorry.

PHILLIE: That's okay. Don't feel bad. I was telling you about Denise … She was wild. She was intense. (*hits himself*) Well, which was it. Wild or intense? She couldn't be both … She was intense. Yeah. Focused. "Why are we burying this body?" I asked her. I mean she fell. I heard her. It was an accident. (*shrugs*) You use hair tonic? I could go in the bathroom and you wouldn't have to watch me drink or anything. I'd just go in there if that's where it is. Anyway I was telling you about Denise. What Denise said about the body was: "I can't take any chances" … So what about that hair tonic … Aftershave …

R.J.: There's nothing like that in there.

PHILLIE: But I need something …

R.J.: You want me to go get you a bottle?

PHILLIE: You might have to ... I mean I have to face Denise. I've let her down.

R.J.: It's okay.

PHILLIE: I don't think so. I don't think it's okay.

R.J.: Denise isn't ... She's not thinking clearly.

PHILLIE: Yes. She is. She's trying to survive. Look, nothing I've said should be taken as criticism of Denise. She's just trying to ... what's the word I'm looking for. Survive?

R.J.: Yeah but she's ... Look, we've got to go dig up that body ... Call the police. Get it straight.

PHILLIE: Dig up the body?

R.J.: Yeah.

PHILLIE: Tell the police?

R.J.: Yeah.

PHILLIE: Tell the police what? We buried a body. But now we think that was unwise.

R.J.: Well, it *was* unwise. It was really, really ... unwise. Why didn't you call the police.

PHILLIE: Denise couldn't take a chance. That's what she said. They come in. They see the situation. They find out the social worker was going to make a bad report about her. They make Denise a suspect. She couldn't let that happen. She couldn't. Don't you know that, man. God, are you her husband or not. Can't you see she's right! Denise was doing it right, man. She's gotta get that baby. And the two of you gotta take that baby and disappear. And make a great life. That's the only way for justice to be served. Okay I'm goin'. I'm going this time for sure.

R.J.: Where.

PHILLIE: To get the baby.

R.J.: No, no. No!

He grabs PHILLIE.

PHILLIE: No listen. It's okay. I can do it. I'm worked up. I can do it.

R.J.: No, I don't want you to do it.

PHILLIE: But if I do it, I'll feel better about myself. I think it's something I could take pride in.

R.J.: Someone could get hurt.

PHILLIE: It'll be all right. I'll get her. Don't you want her. She's your baby too. Don't you want her.

R.J.: Yes. Yes I want her. But not like this. I want her in a way that'll be okay ...

PHILLIE: That can't happen. Nothing is ever going to be truly okay again. Everything is wrong. Everything in the world is wrong. There is no justice. Not really. There's only grab and run! ... Everyone for themselves. I gotta do this.

R.J.: I can't let you.

PHILLIE: Look. I gotta.

He pulls the gun from his pocket.

PHILLIE: I'm sorry. But I'm doing this so stay back.

R.J.: That isn't loaded.

PHILLIE fires a shot into the floor.

PHILLIE: What gave you that idea.

PHILLIE runs out of the room.

R.J. is about to follow when the phone rings. He runs over. Answers it.

R.J.: (*into phone*) Yeah ... yeah speaking ... Yeah. Really. How'd you get my number ... I did? Oh yeah, right – Yeah ... yeah well it was about that Mothers Who Didn't Visit Their Sons in Prison show. I mean don't you think you went a bit too far with that one. There was real pain on that woman's face. She didn't need ... Well sure she has free will but do you think she expected to be treated like that by her own son. I mean –

DENISE bursts through the door.

DENISE: Jesus Christ! What is wrong with you?!

She rushes over. Grabs the phone. Hangs up.

DENISE: I mean you left your number with the network? I put the call through because at first I thought ... then I thought what the hell was that. Is that all you've got on your mind considering the circumstances of our life right now.

R.J.: I made the call earlier. Things were okay when I made the call.

DENISE: You made the call six months ago? 'Cause that's the last time I remember things being okay.

R.J.: No, I made the call before you killed the social worker.

DENISE: Look, for the last time. I didn't kill the social worker. I just buried the social worker.

R.J.: You know what though ... It's gonna turn out to be the same thing. I think it's gonna have basically the same impact on our lives as if you'd killed her. So let's just say you did. Okay?!

DENISE: Why? Because it'll sound better on TV? You thinking ahead 'til when we're invited on one of those shows. Look, I can't talk to you anymore. I'm waiting for Phillie's call.

R.J.: He's not calling.

DENISE: He'll call. Have faith.

R.J.: He was here.

DENISE: When.

R.J.: Just now.

DENISE: Did he have Christine.

R.J.: No, he couldn't do it.

DENISE: Shit ... Shit ... Okay okay, we'll have to do it ... We'll go get her ourselves. Come on.

R.J.: No, he's doing it.

DENISE: You just said he wasn't doing it.

R.J.: He changed his mind. He went to do it. He's ... doing it.

DENISE: He changed his mind?

R.J.: He convinced himself. It's something he has to do. He says it'll make him feel better.

DENISE: It will ... It'll be an accomplishment.

R.J.: He's got a gun.

DENISE: I know.

R.J.: It's loaded.

DENISE: So?

R.J.: You told me it wasn't.

DENISE: I did?

R.J.: Suppose he hurts someone.

DENISE: It's a risk worth taking. Hey R.J., it's our life we're talking about here.

R.J. goes to the phone.

DENISE: What are you doing.

R.J.: I have to call that TV guy back.

DENISE: You're kidding.

R.J.: You hung up on him. He took the time to call me and you hung up on him ... He might never take the time to call anyone again. That would be a shame. Because improvements can be made in how things are done and he's in a position to make them ... Probably all he needs is encouragement ... and, you know ... input.

DENISE: You're too much.

R.J.: So are you, Denise. So are you.

He dials the phone.

Blackout.

SCENE 7

R.J. and DENISE are near the bathroom door. Looking tense. The door is closed and someone is having a shower. DENISE becomes exasperated, throws her arms in the air, and begins to pace. R.J. puts his head against the bathroom door. Listens. The water stops running. R.J. gestures to DENISE. She stops pacing. They wait. Suddenly the bathroom door opens. Steam pours into the room. They wait.

HELEN comes out of the bathroom. Wet hair. Wearing one of R.J.'s shirts.

HELEN: That feels better ... A lot better. (*to R.J.*) Thanks for the shirt.

R.J. nods. HELEN looks at herself in the wall mirror. Touches her forehead.

HELEN: Nasty little bump. (*to DENISE*) Do you have a brush I could borrow.

DENISE gets a brush from the bedside table. Takes it to HELEN.

HELEN: Thanks ... I said thanks.

DENISE: You're ... welcome.

HELEN sits at the table. Begins to brush her hair.

HELEN: (*brushing*) It's important to be polite ... Politeness is a cornerstone of civilized behaviour. I guess no one ever taught you that ... That's just one of the things you weren't taught ... Politeness. Moderation ... Reasonable behaviour. I don't think people know these things intuitively. They have to be taught. So as I was lying in that mud under that pile of leaves and debris under that billboard out back afraid to move – not knowing if I were paralyzed, how seriously injured I was – I thought about your lack of education. Why didn't Denise call for help. Why has she taken the criminal route in this. Why hasn't she taken the reasonable moderate – yes, even polite approach – and called an ambulance. And then of course I remembered all my training and everything I've been taught about people like you and I decided you just don't know any better.

R.J.: Are you going to call the police.

HELEN: (*brushing*) I don't know yet. Probably. I mean, it is the reasonable thing to do. I was just buried alive.

R.J.: You see, what happened was, she panicked.

HELEN: I was buried alive! I had to claw my way up through garbage and leafy smelly muddy things because I was buried alive in a deep hole.

DENISE: (*to herself*) Not deep enough.

HELEN: I heard that.

R.J.: She didn't mean it.

HELEN: Oh she meant it.

R.J.: (*to DENISE*) Tell her you didn't mean it.

DENISE: (*to HELEN*) I didn't mean it.

HELEN: Yes you did! You meant it. What's wrong with you. Don't you have any civilized instincts left in you. Have they all been dulled or killed by your senseless self-indulgent lifestyle.

DENISE: Look I'm sorry. Don't start ... with that judgment crap. I can't take it.

HELEN: Well, look who's going on the offensive. I mean, talk about inappropriate responses. I mean, who buried who alive.

DENISE: It wasn't personal. Why are you always making it personal. I didn't do it to punish you. I thought you were dead. I was just –

R.J.: She panicked.

DENISE: I didn't panic. I thought it through. I was taking precautions. I did what I thought I had to do ... so we could get on with our life.

HELEN: (*standing*) You're a bad girl, Denise. That's all you are. Someone should have just told you this a long time ago. You're a very bad girl.

DENISE: Ah shut up.

HELEN: I won't shut up! (*rubs her head*) I have a job here. I'm a representative of our government. And what government represents to me is the people's will to have a civilized society. And what that means is dealing with people like you and getting you back in line. You're out of line, Denise. Way out of line!

HELEN rubs her head. Wobbles.

HELEN: Ooh. I have to sit down.

She sits.

R.J.: Are you all right.

HELEN: No. I have a serious concussion. And I was buried alive. I'm not all right ... Did you call a doctor as I asked, Denise.

DENISE: Yes.

HELEN: Did you.

DENISE: Yes!

HELEN: Did you really?!

DENISE: No! No I didn't!

HELEN: No you didn't! Couldn't you see I was maybe giving you a second chance to do the right thing. Why didn't you call a doctor, Denise. It would have been the right thing for you to do ... So why didn't you do it?

DENISE: Because! ... I needed to know if you were going to tell the police.

HELEN: Protecting yourself.

DENISE: Yes.

HELEN: At any cost.

DENISE: Yes.

HELEN: Bad bad girl! Bad girl! Wicked girl!

DENISE: Oh please shut up. (*to R.J.*) Make her shut up.

R.J.: How.

DENISE: Any way you can.

HELEN: Don't get him to do your dirty work. Maybe it's time you stopped dragging him down, Denise. He's trying to do better things with his life. Why don't you let him do them ... these better things.

DENISE: (*to R.J.*) She's impressed with you because you joined the church.

HELEN: Or maybe I'm impressed because he doesn't bury people alive!

R.J.: (*to HELEN*) The church thing. I just did it to make points with you people ... It's not real.

HELEN: It could be, R.J. Just open up your heart. I know you want to. I know you've got the ... right things in you.

DENISE: (*to R.J.*) I told her you could cook. She thought that was great. Well she thought it was sad you had to cook your own supper after working hard all day. She thought I was some demon bitch for making you do that. But the fact that you could cook, she thought that was cool.

R.J.: (*to HELEN*) I like to cook.

HELEN: I'm sure you do. The desire to cook. To serve. To nurture. These are good things. The things civilized people feel.

R.J.: Denise has been sick. Really sick. Sick about losing the baby.

HELEN: That's not an excuse.

R.J.: Yes it is.

HELEN: Not enough of an excuse.

R.J.: Yes it is. Losing the baby made her life ... made her feel her life was ... didn't have any value. And she hated herself ... She'd cry all night. Night after night for weeks and months.

DENISE: No no I don't want you telling her this stuff.

R.J.: She should know. She thinks you're just some punk kid who –

DENISE: (*to R.J.*) No no listen. I don't want to ... it's not what I'm worried about, what she thinks of me. (*to HELEN*) I just want to know if you're going to tell the police.

HELEN: I ... don't know.

DENISE: When *will* you know.

HELEN: I don't know when I'll know! I mean I'm trained, you know. Trained to think things through ... Act in the best interests of people. The people in this instance are your child, R.J. here and even you, Denise. I have to weigh intent with possibility. And possibility with harsh reality.

DENISE: I don't know what you're talking about.

HELEN: Is it better if I just let this pass. Or is it better for everyone if you're put away! I have to think about these things ... And then of course there's the issue of ... compassion ... I am a Christian. I believe in Christian things.

R.J.: That's ... good ... I don't know much about it ... I mean I just started to learn and I wasn't paying a lot of attention. But I got the general feeling it was a good thing to be ... a Christian.

DENISE: Oh please ... I just want to know what she's going to do ... Maybe you can ask her. Christian to Christian. I'm tired.

DENISE sits on the bed.

HELEN: (*to R.J.*) Can you get my briefcase. All my muddy clothes are on the bathroom floor. Can you stuff them all in my briefcase. Can you take a twenty-dollar bill out of my wallet. And put it in my hand. Can you take me and my possessions to the street and hail a cab for me. Can you get started on those things now.

R.J.: Yeah ... yeah.

He goes about his tasks

HELEN: Good ... because I think I need to have an X-ray. I feel that would be the best thing for me to do right now. Go to the hospital and get an X-ray.

R.J.: (*from bathroom*) I'm coming. I'm coming.

HELEN: Good ... Denise?

DENISE: What.

HELEN: Stay put ... I'll let you know what I decide.

DENISE: Sure.

HELEN: I mean, the chances of you getting your child back now are slim. Very slim.

DENISE: Right.

HELEN: I mean, you have really messed up ... But we'll see ... I've reclaimed worse people than you ... I have ... I'm trained ... And it's ... possible ... We'll have to meet ... and meet again.

DENISE: Here?

HELEN: Here or in prison ... Wherever. We'll see ...

R.J. comes out of the bathroom.

R.J.: Okay ... Ready?

PHILLIE walks by the window. Sees HELEN.

HELEN: I need some help.

R.J.: Okay.

He helps her up. They start off. HELEN holds R.J. for support. They are leaving.

HELEN: Denise?

DENISE: What.

HELEN: Remember. Hang in.

DENISE: Sure ...

HELEN: But stay put.

They are gone.

DENISE goes into the bathroom. Runs water. Comes out drying her face vigorously.

PHILLIE comes in.

PHILLIE: Wow. That was weird. Good thing I looked through the window before coming in. So ... she's alive. Well I guess that's better in the long run.

DENISE: I don't know. How did you get on.

PHILLIE: Did you talk to R.J. ... You know I didn't go the first time?

DENISE: Yeah ... But you went back ... So?

PHILLIE: I got up to the front porch ... I looked in the window. I saw her.

DENISE: You saw her? Really?

PHILLIE: Yeah. She looks like you. She's cute. She was playing with blocks. Blue and red and orange blocks. She looked ... happy ... I couldn't go in. I would've scared her.

DENISE: Yeah.

PHILLIE: We've got to think of a way that won't scare her.

DENISE: Yeah ...

PHILLIE: I'll be in touch ... ah ... Wednesday ... Wednesdays are my best days ... So ... we'll talk ... I mean I'm committed to this project. I think it's good ... I feel good about it.

DENISE: I'm glad.

PHILLIE: See ya.

DENISE: Yeah.

> *She closes the window. PHILLIE disappears. R.J. comes back in. DENISE just leans against a wall.*

R.J.: I think she's bleeding internally.

DENISE: Really.

R.J.: I mean her eyes are bloodshot ... If that's a sign ... I don't know for sure.

DENISE: Me neither.

R.J.: So ... what do you think's gonna happen.

DENISE: I don't know.

R.J.: I mean should we stay here. Should we go back home. Should we go on the run.

> *DENISE shrugs.*

R.J.: I mean if Phillie grabs Christine we can just take off like you said ... I'm up for that if we have to ...

DENISE: I wouldn't count on that happening.

R.J.: No?

DENISE: No.

R.J.: You know something I don't?

DENISE: Yeah.

R.J.: You wanna tell me what it is?

DENISE: No. Not really ... No point ... Later maybe ...

R.J.: So ... (*shrugs*) so ...

> *The phone rings. R.J. looks at DENISE but she seems far away so he goes to the phone. Picks it up.*

R.J.: Hello ... Yeah hi, Phillie ... Oh ... wait a sec. (*covers the receiver*) It's that guy from the television network. Can I talk to him. Will it piss you off.

> *DENISE looks at R.J. for a long time.*

DENISE: (*shaking her head*) Go ahead.

R.J.: Thanks ... (*into phone*) Put him through, Phillie.

> *R.J. smiles at DENISE. DENISE smiles sadly at R.J.*

> *There is a lighting change. DENISE is alone in a light. Everything else is in darkness or shadow. And DENISE is talking to us.*

DENISE: We stayed in that motel room for six months. We hardly left. R.J. watched his shows and took a lot of calls from network executives. They seemed to think he had some special understanding of what their shows were trying to do and they called him to ask for his advice. He'd suggest ideas and plead with them for a more human handling of their guests. He spent a lot of time explaining to these shows how it wasn't necessary to treat people like shit just to boost their ratings. And he told me he had a feeling that gradually they were coming around to his way of thinking. Phillie made a few more feeble attempts to grab Christine ... Once he made it as far as her bedroom. But she was asleep. And he didn't want to wake her up ... Anyway he was crying so hard he could barely see. Because the book she had open on her sleeping body was the same book his aunt Jennie used to read to him when he was about Christine's age. And his aunt Jennie was the only person other than his cousin Edward who ever treated him with justice and a fair heart ... Helen spent seven weeks in the hospital recovering from a ... subdural hematoma ... She called me from the hospital daily ... And continues to do so. Asking me questions and counselling me about moderate civilized behaviour. And I have learned to listen patiently and sigh pleasantly like I agree and like I am truly trying to change ... But I'm not agreeing with her or even thinking about what she's saying any more than I'm listening to R.J. on the phone with his TV people or even when I'm watching those shows with R.J. and listening to those sad, desperate people and all those experts telling them how to live better and everything else and blah, blah, blah ... I'm not really listening ... Because I'm not really there. I'm in hell. I'm more desperate than anybody I ever hear on those shows and I'm trapped in a sadness and an anger so deep I know I'll never get out. Because I'm just slipping deeper into the sadness. And deeper into the anger ... I have horrible thoughts about doing horrible things to people. If I were on one of those shows and I told people how I really felt and what

I really wanted to do ... they wouldn't be able to give me any advice ... they wouldn't even be able to talk ... Maybe they'd just cancel the fucking show ... If I leaned over in bed and told R.J. what I felt about everything ... about life ... about our life and everyone else's life and how really useless and stupid it all is ... he'd die probably. He'd give up and die ... So I don't tell him. I tell him I'm waiting. I'm being a good girl. Seeing if things work out. I tell him maybe there's still a chance we'll get Christine ... But I know ... things don't work out ... Not for people like us. They just get worse ... Until ... well, you can't take it anymore ... Then you really do get bad ... Helen thinks she knows how bad I am. She probably thinks she knows how sad I am and how angry I am too. She's wrong ... She hasn't got a clue ... She might find out though ... Maybe I'll just ... come up with a way of letting her know ...

> *DENISE* shrugs. Lights up on *R.J.* watching TV. Smiling. *DENISE* shakes her head sadly.

DENISE: You okay, R.J.?

R.J.: Yeah. How about you. Still with me? Still hangin' in?

DENISE: Yeah.

R.J.: Thata girl.

> *DENISE* smiles.

> *Blackout.*

END

DJANET SEARS

(b. 1959)

One of the genuinely exciting developments in English-Canadian theatre was the emergence of a vibrant African Canadian theatre culture in the 1990s. The historical record of black involvement in Canadian theatre reaches back at least to 1849 when the Toronto Coloured Young Men's Amateur Theatrical Society performed a Restoration drama and scenes from Shakespeare. On the other side of the curtain, attempts by black audiences to integrate theatres in Victoria in the early 1860s met with white resistance and led to a series of near race riots. Canada's first black professional company, the Negro Theatre Guild, established itself in Montreal in 1941, and during the headiest period of Canadian alternate theatre, from the late 1960s to the early 1980s, new companies regularly came on stream: Toronto's Black Theatre Canada and Theatre Fountainhead, Vancouver's Sepia Players, Winnipeg's Caribbean Theatre Workshop, and Kwacha Playhouse in Halifax, among others. Canada's longest-running black theatre company, Montreal's Black Theatre Workshop, celebrated its fortieth anniversary in 2012. But until recently, African Canadian plays were still a rarity in Canadian theatres.

The 1990s witnessed a flourishing of African Canadian playwrights and play production reflecting the many facets of that multi-faceted culture: native-born Ottawans, Torontonians, Montrealers, and Africadians from Nova Scotia; first-generation Canadians from Africa, England, and the Caribbean writing about life in Africa, the Caribbean, Canada, and the United States – George Seremba, Archie Crail, Walter Borden, George Boyd, George Elliott Clarke, Diana Braithewaite, ahdri zhina mandiela, maxine bailey, sharon m. lewis, Lorena Gale, and Andrew Moodie. The next decade introduced Joseph Jomo Pierre, Lisa Codrington, Trey Anthony, Michael A. Miller, d'bi.young anitafrika, and more.

In the midst of this ferment, Djanet Sears has been a significant creative force as actor, director, producer, teacher, anthologist, and playwright. Her own plays grapple with what George Elliott Clarke calls the "poly-consciousness" of African Canadian identity, its tangled roots, and multiple cultural influences, with the addition, in Sears's case, of a black feminist, or womanist, perspective. *Harlem Duet*, her self-described "rhapsodic blues tragedy," tackles love and race, slavery and minstrelsy, vengeance and friendship through the lens of Shakespeare's *Othello*, refracted through the experience of Othello's black wife in contemporary Harlem and two other historical settings.

Born in England of Guyanese and Jamaican parents, Janet Sears came to Canada at the age of fifteen, spent her teens in Saskatoon and Oakville, then moved to Toronto where she earned a B.F.A. in theatre at York University and began work as an actor. Her first play, *Shakes*, a love story about work and relationships, was staged at York in 1982. Following a trip to Africa, Sears wrote and performed *Afrika Solo*, produced by Factory Theatre and Theatre Fountainhead in 1987. A fictionalized musical autobiography, or "autobio-mythography," as she calls it, the play recounts her confusions about personal and cultural identity, her search for and discovery of her African roots, and her decision to rename herself Djanet. It climaxes around a jungle bonfire in Zaire where she serenades her BaMbuti pygmy hosts with a soul-gospel version of "O Canada," a revelation of her polyvalent, post-colonial self as "the African heartbeat in a Canadian song," authentically African Canadian. *Afrika Solo* had a very successful series of runs on stage in Toronto and Ottawa, and won two international prizes for its CBC radio adaptation.

Double Trouble, dealing with life in public housing, was produced by Toronto Workshop Productions and toured schools in 1988. Sears collaborated with Crossroads Theatre on *The Mother Project* (1990), which examined African American female storytelling. Ground Zero Productions' *Who Killed Katie Ross?* (1994) toured Ontario, exploring the ramifications of an Aboriginal woman's violent death. *Harlem Duet* was developed during Sears's 1996 tenure as playwright-in-residence at Joseph Papp's Public Theater in New York. It premiered at Tarragon Theatre in 1997, produced by Nightwood Theatre and directed by Sears, winning four Dora Mavor Moore Awards (including outstanding production, direction, and new play), the Floyd S. Chalmers Canadian Play Award, and the Governor General's Literary Award for Drama. The play has subsequently been produced in Halifax and Montreal, New York, St. Louis, and Miami, with a major revival directed by Sears at the Stratford Festival in 2006. *The Adventures of a Black Girl in Search of God* (2002), directed by Sears and co-produced by Nightwood, was the first show for Toronto's Obsidian Theatre, a new company Sears co-founded in 2000 to profile and produce the work of black theatre artists. She took her title from George Bernard Shaw to tell the powerful, funny, moving story of a black woman in Ontario whose daughter has just died. Her father is also dying and her marriage is falling apart. As she tries to make sense of her life, her father and his friends go around "liberating" racially offensive lawn ornaments. A large chorus provides musical accompaniment.

The versatile Sears has been playwright-in-residence at Nightwood and Factory Theatre in addition to New York's Public Theatre; associate director of Canadian Stage; writer-in-residence at the Canadian Film Centre and University of Guelph; and adjunct professor at University of Toronto. As an actor, she has received both Dora and Gemini (TV) award nominations. Feature film performances include *Milk and Honey*, *April One*, and Clement Virgo's *One Heart Broken into Song*. Among her notable directing credits are ahdri zhina mandiela's *dark diaspora ... in dub* and Monique Mojica's *Princess Pocohontas and the Blue Spots*. In addition to her role as founding member of Obsidian Theatre, Sears has been artistic director of *Negrophilia: An African American Retrospective, 1959–71*, and the AfriCanadian Playwrights Festival. She has edited the two-volume *Testi-fyin'*, an anthology of African Canadian drama (2000, 2003), and *Tellin' It Like It Is* (2000), the first collection of African Canadian monologues for actors. In 2003, she received Black Theatre Workshop's Dr. Martin Luther King Jr. Achievement Award, and the Stratford Festival honoured her with its Timothy Findley Award in 2004.

Nearly a decade before *Harlem Duet*, a little-known Ann-Marie Mac-Donald had revisited *Othello* in her incisive feminist comedy *Goodnight Desdemona (Good Morning Juliet)* (included in *Modern Canadian Plays*, vol. 1). Also produced by Nightwood, Canada's foremost feminist theatre company, MacDonald's play re-visions Shakespeare's portrait of the tragic female protagonist, imagining a Desdemona utterly unlike the passive victim of Shakespeare's play. MacDonald's Desdemona is a fearless warrior who categorically rejects the gender roles and imagery assigned to her. Her battle cry is "bullshit!"

Similarly, Sears uses the template of *Othello* to explore the female position in a relationship in which power is skewed in favour of the male. But she focuses on gender only secondarily. Primarily, Sears foregrounds race. What is the impact on Othello's black wife, Billie, of his leaving her for a white woman? What larger cultural and ideological ramifications does Othello's decision have? The personal is very much the political in this play. Signifying on Shakespeare's *Othello*, Sears not only makes the jealous female the central figure and aggressor, but reduces Desdemona to Mona, the play's only white character, an offstage voice invisible to the audience but for the brief appearance of her hand through a door. More-over, Sears fractures the chronology of the play. Not content just to reset the story in contemporary Harlem, she utilizes fantasy or dream sequences or snatches from the African American collective unconscious – the status of these scenes is never entirely clear – to reframe Billie and Othello as slaves in the immediate pre-Civil War South and as actors in the dressing room of a Harlem theatre in 1928. The result is a wide-ranging examina-tion of some of the many ways in which race still inevitably matters, as much as we might like to think otherwise.

Othello is the play's primary intertext but certainly not its only one. The 1928 scenes evoke the American theatrical tradition of minstrelsy, the cultural travesty marked by the use of grotesque blackface makeup, which some black actors themselves eventually embraced in order to secure a place in the theatrical market. The soundscapes that preface each scene introduce the voices of Martin Luther King and Malcolm X, whose names mark the Harlem streets at the crossroads of which sits Billie's apartment. Their ideological differences and divergent strategies for advancing the cause of African Americans are reflected in Othello and Billie's contrasting views on assimilation, as are the voices of Jesse Jackson and Louis Far-rakhan. But the political soundtrack is not synchronized to the time frame of the scenes. For example, we hear Reverend King's "I Have a Dream" speech in 1928 and Marcus Garvey's 1920s Afrocentric nationalism in the present day. In more recent productions, other voices, including that of Barack Obama, have joined the soundscape. Like the relevance of the *Othello* story, the struggle for racial dignity in its many forms is ongoing.

The musical prefaces also deepen and expand the tensions conveyed in the play's central plot. Billie (whose real name is Sybil but whose nickname suggests Billie Holiday) certainly has the blues. The prefatory riffs range from the deep country blues of the Mississippi delta to sophisticated urban jazz, spanning the African American experience in time and place. But the instruments (played live onstage) are cello and bass, more evocative of the European string tradition than the vernacular blues voice of African American culture, a tension again suggestive of Billie and Othello's clash and of the latter's upwardly mobile, assimilationist aspirations. Toward the end, the sound loop becomes increasingly distorted, a cacophony of strings and voices reflecting Billie's heightened emotional state as her desperate revenge plot approaches fruition. The last sonic preface includes the Langston Hughes poem "Harlem," a commentary on what happens to "a dream deferred" too long. It speaks of Billie's final condition, refers back, through Hughes, to the Harlem Renaissance of the 1920s, and contains in one of its lines the title of Lorraine Hansberry's *A Raisin in the Sun*, the play that Djanet Sears says inspired her to become a playwright.

Although the emotional arguments of *Harlem Duet* are heavily weighted against Othello, Sears gives him a good deal of counterweight (his impassioned monologue in Act One, Scene Nine, for example). She also reserves ample sympathy for Billie's father, the symbolically named Canada, who admits that he was a bad drunk and a worse parent. The father-daughter reconciliation cuts across generations, gender lines, and national borders. "Canada freedom come," the slaves' cry of hope as they looked northward, expresses Billie's dream of forgiveness, healing, and self-repossession. The play ends with a reconfigured duet, a celebration of the rose that grows in Spanish Harlem – in this case an African-American-Canadian hybrid.

Harlem Duet

Djanet Sears

Harlem Duet premiered on April 24, 1997, as a
Nightwood Theatre production at the Tarragon
Theatre, Extra Space, Toronto, with the
following cast:

BILLIE (SYBIL)	Alison Sealy-Smith
OTHELLO	Nigel Shawn Williams
MAGI (MARJORIE)	Barbara Barnes Hopkins
AMAH / MONA	Dawn Roach
CANADA	Jeff Jones
Double Bass	Lionel Williams
Cello	Doug Innis

Directed by Djanet Sears
Set and Costume Design by Teresa Przybylski
Lighting Design by Lesley Wilkinson
Music and Sound Design by Allen Booth
Music Composition and Arrangement by Lionel
Williams

> That handkerchief
> Did an Egyptian to my mother give.
> She was a charmer …
>
> …
>
> … there's magic in the web of it.
> A sibyl …
> In her prophetic fury sew'd the work.
>
> Othello, III. iv. 55–72

CHARACTERS

OTHELLO, *a man of forty, present day*
HE, *OTHELLO, 1928*
HIM, *OTHELLO, 1860*
BILLIE, *a woman of thirty-seven, present day*
SHE, *BILLIE, 1928*
HER, *BILLIE, 1860*

CANADA, *BILLIE's father, sixty-seven*
AMAH, *BILLIE's sister-in-law, thirty-three*
MAGI, *the landlady, forty-one*
MONA, *a white woman, thirties (an offstage voice)*

SETTING

Late summer

Harlem, 1928: a tiny dressing room

*Harlem, the present: an apartment in a renovated
brownstone, at the corner of Dr. Martin Luther
King Jr. and Malcolm X Boulevards (125th Street
and Lenox Avenue)*

Harlem, 1860: on the steps to a blacksmith's shop

PLAYWRIGHT'S NOTE

Ellipsis marks vary; this is intentional.

ACT ONE

PROLOGUE

*Harlem, 1928: late summer – night. As the lights
fade to black, the cello and the bass call and respond
to a heaving melancholic blues. Martin Luther King's
voice accompanies them. He seems to sing his
dream in a slow polyrhythmic improvisation, as he
reaches the climax of that now-famous speech given
at the March on Washington in 1963. Lights up on a
couple in a tiny dressing room.* **SHE** *is holding a large
white silk handkerchief, spotted with ripe strawberries.* **SHE** *looks at* **HE** *as if searching for something.*
HE *has lathered his face and is slowly erasing the
day's stubble with a straight razor.* **SHE** *looks down
at the handkerchief.*

SHE: We keep doing this don't we?

HE: I love you … But –

SHE: Remember ... Remember when you gave this to me? Your mother's handkerchief. There's magic in the web of it. Little strawberries. It's so beautiful – delicate. You kissed my fingers ... and with each kiss a new promise you made ... swore yourself to me ... for all eternity ... remember?

HE: Yes. Yes ... I remember.

Pause.

SHE: Harlem's the place to be now. Everyone who's anyone is coming here now. It's our time. In our place. It's what we've always dreamed of ... isn't it?

HE: Yes.

SHE: You love her?

HE: I ... I wish –

SHE: Have you sung to her at twilight?

HE: Yes.

SHE: Does your blood call out her name?

HE: Yes.

SHE: Do you finger-feed her berries dipped in dark and luscious sweets?

HE: Yes.

SHE: Have you built her a crystal palace to refract her image like a thousand mirrors in your veins?

HE: Yes.

SHE: Do you let her sip nectar kisses from a cup of jade-studded bronze from your immortal parts?

HE: Yes.

SHE: Does she make your thoughts and dreams and sighs, wishes, and tears ache sweet as you can bear?

HE: Yes.

SHE: Do you prepare her bed, deep in fragrant posies, rosemary, forget-me-nots, and roses, anoint her feet with civet oil, lotus musk, and perfumes, place them in gossamer slippers with coral clasps, amber beads, and buckles of the purest gold, kiss her ankles and knees, caress her fragrant flower, gently unfolding each petal in search of the pearl in her velvet crown?

HE: Yes.

SHE: You love her.

HE: Yes. Yes. Yes.

He wipes his face with a towel. She stares at the handkerchief lying in her bare hand.

SHE: Is she white? (*silence*) Othello? (*silence*) She's white. (*silence*) Othello ...

She holds the handkerchief out to him. He does not take it. She lets it fall at his feet. After a few moments, he picks it up.

SCENE 1

Harlem, the present: late summer – morning. The strings thump out an urban melody blues/jazz riff, accompanied by the voice of Malcolm X, speaking about the nightmare of race in America and the need to build strong black communities.

MAGI is on the fire escape, leaning on the railing, reading a magazine with a large picture of a blonde woman on the cover. As the sound fades, she closes the magazine, surveying the action on the street below.

MAGI: Sun up in Harlem. (*spots the postman*) Morning, Mr. P.! Don't bring me no bill now – I warned ya before, I'm having a baby. Don't need to get myself all worked up, given my condition ... I'm gonna have me a Virgo baby, makes me due 'bout this time next year ... I can count. I just haven't chosen the actual father/husband candidate as yet. Gotta find me a man to play his part. I wanna conceive in the middle of December, so I've booked the Convent Avenue Baptist Church for this Saturday. The wedding's at three. You sure look to be the marrying kind. What you up to this weekend, yourself sweetness? Oh well then, wish your wife well for me. Package from where? California? Oohh. Yeh, yeh, yeh. I'll be right – Hey, hey, Amah girl ... Up here ... Let yourself in ... (*throws a set of keys down to AMAH*) Mr. P., give that young lady the package ... Yeh, she'll bring it up for me. (*beat*) Thank you, sugar. (*beat*) You have yourself a nice day now. All right, sweetness. Mmn, mmn, mmn!

AMAH unlocks the door, enters, and makes her way to the fire escape.

AMAH: Magi, look at you, out on the terrace, watching the summer blossoms on the corner of Malcolm X and Martin Luther King Boulevards.

MAGI: Nothing but weeds growing in the Soweto of America, honey. (*shouting out*) Billie!

AMAH: Where is she?

MAGI: I didn't want to wake her up 'til you got here. She didn't get to sleep 'til early morning. I could hear her wailing all the way downstairs.

AMAH: I can see a week. A couple of weeks at the most. But what is this?

MAGI: Two months – it's not like she's certifiable, though. (*shouting gently to BILLIE in the bedroom*) Billie! Billie, Amah's here!

AMAH: Well, least she sleeps now.

MAGI: She's stillness itself. Buried under that ocean of self-help books, like it's a tomb. Like a pyramid over her. Over the bed. (*calling out once more*) Billie!

> *BILLIE's body moves slightly and an arm listlessly carves its way to the surface, shifting the tomb of books as several drop to the floor. MAGI and AMAH make their way inside. On a large table is a vase filled with blossoming cotton branches. There is also a myriad of bottles and bags, and a Soxhlet extraction apparatus: laboratory flask, extractor and thimble, condenser, and siphoning hoses, all held up by two metal stands. A Bunsen burner is placed under the flask.*

MAGI: I'm just making her some coffee, can I get you a cup?

AMAH: (*inspects the table and searches for a space to put the small package*) Thanks, Magi. Where d'you want this? It looks like a science lab in here.

MAGI: Some healing concoction I've been helping her make – but she's way ahead of me these days. She's got a real talent for herbs, you know. She's been sending away for ingredients – I can't even figure out what most of them are. Put the package down anywhere.

AMAH: If I can find a space.

MAGI: Right there. On top of that alchemy book – right in the middle. Yeh. Thanks for doing this, Amah. For coming. It'll make her feel like a million dollars again.

AMAH: Please. Billie and me go so far back, way before Andrew. Besides, sister-in-laws are family too, you know. Jenny's been simply begging to come and see her, you know, for their once-a-week thing. They eat sausages, mashed potatoes, and corn. Some Canadian delicacy I guess –

MAGI: Aren't you guys vegetarians?

AMAH: Vegan.

MAGI: Vegan?

AMAH: We don't eat anything that has eyes. The sausages are tofu. You know they eat exactly the same thing every time. I was glad for the break. I guess I was kinda ... well ... it bugged me. Jenny's always full of auntie Billie this, auntie Billie that. Now I miss our one night a week without her. I mean – our time alone. And I see how it's a kind of security for her.

MAGI: Security for who?

AMAH: Oh, I can't rent your ground floor. They won't give me any insurance 'cause I don't have a licence. And I can't get a licence until I get a cosmetician's certificate. And I can't get a cosmetician's certificate until I finish this two-year course on how to do white people's hair and makeup. I told them ain't no white people in Harlem. I'd learn how to do work with chemical relaxers and Jheri curls. Now, I do dreadlocks. And do they teach that? Oh no. They're just cracking down on people who do hair in private homes – something about lost tax revenues. I don't know ... I want my own salon so bad I can taste it. "The Lock Smiths."

MAGI: "The Lock Smiths."

AMAH: Billie's supposed to be helping me with the business plan. Besides, we've started trying for kid number two. I need the space.

MAGI: You're trying?

AMAH: I'm ten days late.

MAGI: No!

AMAH: It's still early. Don't tell Billie ... you know. *I'll* tell her.

MAGI: Good for you, girl! Did I tell you I was having a baby?

AMAH: Oh yeh. How was he, that new candidate you were telling me about ... Warren, no Waldo –

MAGI: Wendel? Wedded Wendel, as I've discovered.

AMAH: He didn't tell –

MAGI: Oh no. He believes that the nuclear family is the basis for a healthy society. That's why he's married. He keeps his own personal nuclear family at home in the event that he might someday want to spend time with it.

AMAH: Why'd you stop seeing George. I liked George.

MAGI: Well, I liked him too.

AMAH: You two looked pretty serious there for a while.

MAGI: We'd been seeing each other the better part of …… what … two years. I'm just not getting any younger. I mean, I kept dropping hints I was ready for him to pop the question. Seems like he don't know what question I'm referring to. So I decided to give him some encouragement. See, I've been collecting things for my trousseau, and I have this negligée … all white, long, beautiful lacy thing. Looks like a see-through wedding gown. So, I'm out on my balcony – you know, 'cause it's too hot inside, and I still ain't got around to putting in air conditioning. Anyway, I see him coming up the street. So I rush in and put on the wedding dress negligée, thinking, he'll see me in it, all beautiful like – want to pop the question, you know. So I open the door, me in the negligée, and he … He stands there. Mouth wide open. And he says, he guess he should go get a bottle of wine, seeing how this was gonna be some kind of special occasion an' all. Now I don't know whether he got lost … or drunk … But I ain't seen or heard from him since.

AMAH: Aahh nooo.

MAGI: I should have margarined his butt when I had the chance.

AMAH: Margarined his backside?

MAGI: If you want to bind a man –

AMAH: You don't mean, what I think you mean?

MAGI: If you want to keep a man then, you rub his backside with margarine.

AMAH: And it works?

MAGI: I don't know. When I'd remember, I could never figure out how to get from the bed to the refrigerator.

AMAH: Margarine, huh?

MAGI: But you've got to be careful. He might be a fool. You don't want to be dragging no damn fool behind you the rest of your days.

AMAH: You're a regular charmer, girl.

MAGI: Don't get me wrong. I don't cut the heads off chickens, or anything now.

AMAH: You know, a Jamaican lady told me about one where you rinse your underwear and use the dirty water to cook the meal.

MAGI: Nooo! Really?

AMAH: Really.

MAGI: Ooh, I like that. Boil down some greens in panty stock. Hmm!

AMAH: Once I buried his socks under the black-berry bush by the front door. Sure enough, he always finds his way back home.

MAGI: How is True Drew?

AMAH: Oh, Andrew's real good. You know him. He was up here 'til late, night before last even, playing broad-shouldered brother.

MAGI: Yep, he's a good man. They're rare. And he went all the way down to D.C. for the Million Man March. Yeh, he's one in a million. If you ever think of trading him in …

AMAH: Don't even think about it!

MAGI: Can't blame a girl for trying. (calling out again) Billie! Billie, you up yet? (gets no response; goes into the bedroom) Billie? Billie, sorry to wake you, but Amah's here. She waiting.

BILLIE emerges. We recognize her as the woman in the prologue. She slowly makes her way to the edge of the bed.

BILLIE: If I could only stop dreaming, I might be able to get some rest.

MAGI: You should jot them down. They're messages from other realms, you know.

BILLIE: Jenny's in a large white room – the walls start pressing in all around her …

MAGI: You okay?

BILLIE: Mm mm. Yeh. I'm fine. I'm good.

MAGI: (gently) Come on sweetheart, Amah's waiting.

BILLIE: Let me just wash my face, and my mouth.

MAGI leaves BILLIE to join AMAH, who is now on the fire escape.

MAGI: She's coming … (AMAH hands MAGI a cup of coffee.) Ooh … Thanks.

AMAH: How is she?

MAGI: Better. Dreaming hard, though. Like she's on some archeological dig of the unconscious mind.

AMAH: His words hit her hard, huh.

MAGI: Like a baseball bat hits a mango. Like he was trying for a home run or something. The bat breaks through the skin, smashing the amber flesh, propelling her core out of the park, into the clouds. And she lays there, floating.

AMAH: Feeling sorry for herself.

MAGI: A discarded fruit sitting in a dish, surrounded by its own ripening mould.

AMAH: She feels so much.

MAGI: Yeh. Each of her emotions sprout new roots, long, tangled things, intersecting each other like strangle weed.

AMAH: She should go out though, get some fresh air once in a while.

MAGI: She does. Her trips out into the real world are brief, though. The grocer's for tubs of things you add water to, she calls food; the pharmacy for the pills; and the bookstore. All her money goes up in smokes and writings that tell her she really ain't out of her mind. They'd make her feel better, more beautiful, more well, until she'd see some nice chocolate brown-skinned man, dangling his prize in front of her. 'Cause all the rot inside her would begin to boil, threaten to shoot out. So she comes home, takes some pills, and sleeps again that fitful sleep 'til she wakes.

AMAH: So she knows?

MAGI: Ooh she knows. She knows she's still up there in the clouds.

AMAH: She never used to be like that, you know, about colour.

MAGI: Guess it ain't never been personal before.

AMAH: But it seems bigger than that ...

MAGI: Girl, you've been married what ... six years?

AMAH: Seven this February coming ...

MAGI: How'd you feel if Drew just upped and left you?

AMAH: I can't even imagine ...

MAGI: They've been together nine.

AMAH: She still moving?

MAGI: So she say ... asked me to pick up some boxes.

AMAH: (*quietly*) Rumour has it he's getting married.

MAGI: So soon. He hasn't told her anything. He still hasn't even moved his stuff yet.

AMAH: And she sacrificed so much. Gave up her share of the trust from her mother's life insurance to send him through school.

MAGI: No!

AMAH: So when it's her turn to go ... All those years.

MAGI: And those babies.

AMAH: Yeh, thank God they didn't have any babies.

MAGI: No, no ... Twice ...

AMAH: No!

MAGI: First time, he told her he believed in a woman's right to choose, but he didn't think that the relationship was ready for –

AMAH: We didn't –

MAGI: Nobody did. Second time she miscarried.

AMAH: When? I don't –

MAGI: 'Bout the same time he left – no, it was before that. She was by herself ... Set down in a pool of blood. She put it in a zip-lock bag ... in the freezer ... all purple and blue ...

AMAH: Ooh God ... No ... Really?

MAGI: Yeh.

AMAH: Nooo ... For real. I'm serious ...

MAGI: Yeh!

AMAH: Show me.

MAGI turns toward the living area and heads for the kitchen; AMAH follows closely behind. They approach the fridge and MAGI is about to open the freezer door when BILLIE enters from the bedroom. AMAH and MAGI stop abruptly, as if caught in the act.

AMAH: Billie!

MAGI: (*overlapping*) Hey girl! (*BILLIE waves to them as she exits into the bathroom. MAGI turns to AMAH.*) Or maybe I lied. Gotcha!

AMAH: You ... You ... little heifer –

MAGI laughs. AMAH gets infected and joins her.

SCENE 2

Harlem, 1860: late summer – twilight. The instruments sing a blues from deep in the Mississippi Delta, while a mature northern American voice reads from the Declaration of Independence. HIM steeps hot metal in cool water. He places the shackles on an anvil and hammers the metal into shape. HER is using a needle to make repairs to a shawl.

HER: I pray Cleotis is in heaven.

HIM: Yeh ... I ... um ... I ...

HER: You think Cleotis went to heaven?

HIM: Well, I ... I don't ...

HER: You think he's in hell?

HIM: No. No.

HER: Probably somewhere in between, though. Not Hades. Not God's kingdom. He's probably right there in the hardware store. Probably right there watching every time that Mr. Howard proudly hoists the Mason jar. Every time they pay their penny to see through the formaldehyde. Cleotis is probably right there watching them gawk at his shrivelled, pickled penis ... You seen it?

HIM: No.

HER: You know who did the cutting, though?

HIM: No ... Oh no ...

HER: In France they got the vagina of a sister entombed for scientific research.

HIM: No!

HER: Venus, the Hottentot Venus. I read it in one of Miss Dessy's books. Saartjie – that's her real name, Saartjie Baartman. When Saartjie was alive they paraded her naked on a pay-per-view basis. Her derrière was amply endowed. People paid to see how big her butt was, and when she died, how big her pussy was.

HIM: Woo!

HER: Human beings went and oohed and aahed and paid money to see an endowment the creator bestowed on all of us.

HIM: That's ... that's ... so ... so ...

HER: They probably go to a special place, though – Cleotis and Venus, Emmett. Purgatory. Venus and Cleotis fall in love, marry, but have no tools to consummate it. Must be a lot of us there walking around in purgatory without genitals.

Beat.

HIM: I've been meaning to ... I want ... (*laughing to himself*) I would like to ...

HER: Yes ...?

HIM: Talk. We should talk.

HER: Talk-talk?

HIM: Talk-talk.

HER: About what ...? What's wrong?

HIM: Why must something be wrong –

HER: I ... I just figured ... figure ...

HIM takes HER's hand and kisses it, then places a white handkerchief into her palm.

HIM: My heart ...

HIM closes HER's fingers around the handkerchief. He kisses her fingers. Opening her hand, she examines the cloth.

HER: Little strawberries on a sheet of white. Berries in a field of snow ... (*sighing*) Ah silk. It's beautiful.

HIM: It was my mother's. Given her by my father ... from his mother before that. When she died she gave it me, insisting that when I found ... chose ... chose a wife ... that I give it to her ... to you, heart.

HER: Oh ... It is so beautiful.

HIM: There's magic in the web of it.

HER: So delicate ... so old.

HIM: A token ... an antique token of our ancient love.

HER: My ancient love ...

HIM: My wife. My wife before I even met you. Let's do it. There's a war already brewing in the south. Canada freedom come.

HER: Yes?

HIM: Yes.

HER: We're really gonna go?

HIM: People will come to me and pay me for my work.

HER: Yes sir, Mr. Blacksmith, sir.

HIM: Can we have us a heap of children?

HER: Four boys and four girls.

HIM: And a big white house.

HER: A big house on an emerald hill.

HIM: Yeh ... a white house, on an emerald hill, in Canada. (*pause*) I want to be with you 'til I'm too old to know. You know that.

HER: Even when my breasts fall to my toes?

HIM: I'll pick them up and carry them around for you.

HER: And when I can't remember my own name?

HIM: I'll call it out a thousand times a day.

HER: Then I'll think you're me.

HIM: I am you.

HER: And when I get old, and wrinkled, and enormously fat, you'll –

HIM: Fat? Naw. If you get fat, I'll have to leave your ass. (*kisses inside the crook of HER's arm*)

HER: Oh-oh. You're prospecting again.

HIM: I'm exploring the heightening Alleghenies of Pennsylvania. (*kisses HER*) The curvaceous slopes of California. (*kisses HER*) The red hills of Georgia, the mighty mountains of New York. (*kisses HER again*) I'm staking my claim.

HER: I don't come cheap, you know.

HIM: I know ... I'm offering more than money can buy.

HER: How much more?

HIM: This much. (*kisses HER*)

HER: I could buy that.

HIM: Could you buy this? (*kisses HER deeply*)

HER: Beloved ... (*kisses HIM*)

SCENE 3

Harlem, the present: late summer – morning. Strains of a melodious urban blues jazz keeps time with an oral address by Marcus Garvey on the need for African Americans to return to Africa.

MAGI: No, I hate it.

AMAH: Come on. No one hates it.

MAGI: I do.

AMAH: Bah humbug?

MAGI: What?

AMAH: Scrooge?

MAGI: Oh no, no, no. You know what I hate about Christmas? Seven days to New Year's Eve. And I hate New Year's Eve. And you know what I really hate about New Year's Eve? It's not the being alone at midnight. It's not the being a wallflower at some bash, because you fired your escort, who asked for time and a half after 10:00 p.m. It's not even because you babysat your friend's kids the previous two. I really hate New Year's Eve because it's six weeks to Valentine's Day. And what I really really hate about Valentine's Day – well, maybe that's too strong. No. I really hate it. What I really hate about Valentine's Day is ... it's my birthday. Don't get me wrong, now. I'm glad I was born. But I look at my life – I'm more than halfway through it and, I wonder, what do I have to show for it? Anyway ...

AMAH: Well, you come and spend Kwanzaa with us this year.

MAGI: I don't know about the seven days, girl? Look, I gotta go. I'm seeing a certain minister about a certain wedding.

AMAH: Whose wedding?

MAGI: Mine. And don't say a thing – you know, about him getting married, or anything. (*indicates the refrigerator*)

AMAH: Sealed.

MAGI: I'll drop by later.

AMAH: All right.

MAGI: (*shouting*) Billie? I'm gonna drop by later with some boxes, okay?

BILLIE: (*offstage*) Thanks, Magi.

MAGI exits. AMAH goes to the table and examines the small chemical factory.

AMAH: Saracen's Compound ... woad ... hart's tongue ... Prunella vulgaris ... (*picks up a book lying among the small packages and vials*) Egyptian Alchemy: A Chemical Encyclopedia ... (*puts the book back in its place and picks up another vial*) Nux vomica. Warning: Extremely poisonous. Can be ingested on contact with skin ...

AMAH quickly replaces the vial, wiping her hand on her clothes. She turns her attention to the kitchen. She cautiously approaches the refrigerator and is about to open the freezer section when BILLIE comes out of the bathroom.

BILLIE: Hey Amah.

AMAH: Oh – hi girl, how you feeling?

BILLIE: Thanks for making the house call, Amah.

AMAH: Child, you look so thin.

BILLIE: Well, I'm trying to lose a little baby fat before I die.

AMAH: Coffee?

BILLIE: Oh ... Thanks. (*pours coffee*) You didn't have to come. I'm fine you know.

AMAH: You're very welcome. Come sit down. (*hands her the cup*)

BILLIE: I didn't mean ... Thank you.

AMAH: You washed your hair?

BILLIE: Yesterday.

AMAH: Good. A package came for you this morning.

BILLIE: Where?

AMAH: I put it beside the chemistry set. What is all that?

BILLIE: Don't touch anything!

AMAH: All right – all right. I –

BILLIE: No. No. I – I mean, some of this stuff can be deadly unless mixed ... or ... or diluted. Some ancient Egyptian rejuvenation tonic. If it don't kill me, it'll make me brand new – or so it says. How's my baby?

AMAH: Jenny's fine. Andrew's taking her to her first African dance class today. You should see her in the little leotard …

BILLIE: I should be there.

AMAH: She's dying to come over for sausages and mashed potatoes.

BILLIE: Yeh, yes, soon. Real soon.

AMAH prepares to twist BILLIE's hair. She opens a jar of hair oil and takes a generous portion, rubs it onto her hands, and gently works it into BILLIE's hair.

AMAH: She was so cute, today – you know what she did? She overheard me talking to Andrew about you, and I was saying I thought your breakdown was –

BILLIE: You told her I had a nervous breakdown?

AMAH: Oh – no. No. She overheard me –

BILLIE: I am not having a nervous breakdown.

AMAH: She didn't really understand. She thinks you've broken your legs and can't walk, you can't dance. She thinks you've broken your throat, and that's why she can't talk to you on the phone, that's why you don't sing to her on the phone anymore.

BILLIE: Please don't tell her I'm crazy.

AMAH: I never said you were crazy.

BILLIE: I've just been … tired. Exhausted. I … I didn't want her to see this in me. She'd feel it in me. I never want her to feel this …

AMAH: I know.

BILLIE: But I'm fine now. Really, I'll be fine. I registered for school, I'm only taking one course this term, but that's cool. And first thing next week, I'm redoing the business plan for the salon.

AMAH: You need to give me some of that tonic too, girl. That's the best kind of revenge, you know – living the good life.

BILLIE: I thought I was living that life.

AMAH: Maybe you were just dreaming.

AMAH takes a new lock of BILLIE's hair. Taking a large dab of oil, she applies it to the lock, rubbing the strand between her palms.

BILLIE: Remember when we moved in? The day Nelson and Winnie came to Harlem, remember? Winnie and Nelson – our welcoming committee.

They'd blocked off the whole of 125th – it took us forty-five minutes to convince the cops to let us through. And me and you and Othe and Drew went down to hear them speak. And Drew went off in search of some grits from a street vendor. And you asked me to hold baby Jenny while you went to the restroom, when this man came up to us and took our picture. Asked to take our picture. Jenny in my arms. Othello beside me. "The perfect black family." That's what he called us. "The perfect black family."

The phone rings.

AMAH: I'll get it.

BILLIE: No. Let it ring. I know who it is. I can still feel him – feel when he's thinking of me. We've spoken … must be three times, in the last two months. Something about five hundred dollars on my portion of his American Express card, which they'd cancel if I didn't pay the bill. Seems I did me some consumer therapy. Last time he called – mad – to announce that the card had been cancelled by Amex, and that he hoped that I was pleased. (*beat*) And I was. Is that crazy?

AMAH: Don't sound crazy. Hold the hair oil for me.

BILLIE: I used to pray that he was calling to say he's sorry. To say how he'd discovered a deep confusion in himself. But now … (*phone stops ringing*) I have nothing to say to him. What could I say? Othello, how is the fairer sexed one you love to dangle from your arm the one you love for herself and preferred to the deeper sexed one is she softer does she smell of tea roses and baby powder does she sweat white musk from between her toes do her thighs touch I am not curious just want to know do her breasts fill the cup of your hand the lips of your tongue not too dark you like a little milk with your nipple don't you no I'm not curious just want to know.

AMAH: You tell Jenny colour's only skin deep.

BILLIE: The skin holds everything in. It's the largest organ in the human body. Slash the skin by my belly and my intestines fall out.

AMAH: Hold the hair oil up. (*takes a dab of oil from the jar*)

BILLIE: I thought I saw them once, you know – on the subway. I had to renew my prescription. And I spot them – him and her. My chest is pounding. My legs can't move. From the back, I see the sharp barber's line, separating his tightly coiled hair from the nape of the skin at the back of his neck. His skin is soft there ... and I have to kick away the memory nudging its way into my brain. My lips on his neck, gently ... holding him ... Here, before me – his woman – all blonde hair and blonde legs. Her weight against his chest. His arm around her shoulders, his thumb resting on the gold of her hair. He's proud. You can see he's proud. He isn't just any Negro. He's special. That's why she's with him. And she ... she ... she flaunts. Yes, she flaunts. They are before. I am behind, stuck there on the platform. My tongue is pushing hard against the roof of my mouth ... trying to hold up my brain, or something. 'Cause my brain threatens to fall. Fall down through the roof of my mouth, and be swallowed up. Slowly, slowly, I press forward, toward them. I'm not aiming for them though. I'm aiming with them in mind. I'm aiming for beyond the yellow line, into the tracks. The tunnel all three of us will fall into can be no worse than the one I'm trapped in now. I walk – no, well hover really. I'm walking on air. I feel sure of myself for the first time in weeks. Only to be cut off by a tall grey man in a grey uniform, who isn't looking where he's going, or maybe I'm not – Maybe he knew my aim. He looks at me. I think he looks at me. He brushes past. Then a sound emanating from ... from ... from my uterus, slips out of my mouth, shatters the spell. They turn their heads – the couple. They see me. It isn't even him.

The phone rings again.

AMAH: It could be your father, you know. He's been trying to get in touch with you. Says he doesn't know if you're dead or alive. He was calling Drew even up to this morning.

BILLIE: My father ... I wouldn't have anything to say. It's been so long. What would I say?

The phone stops ringing.

AMAH: He's been in the hospital, you know. Something about his liver.

BILLIE: He hauled us all the way back to Nova Scotia from the Bronx, to be near Granma when Mama died.

AMAH: I love that Nova Scotia was a haven for slaves way before the underground railroad. I love that ...

BILLIE: He's a sot. That's academia-speak for alcoholic. My dad, the drunk of Dartmouth.

AMAH: You're still his children.

BILLIE: A detail. I'm glad he's recalled.

AMAH: Better late than never.

BILLIE: Too little, too late.

AMAH: Forgiveness is a virtue.

BILLIE: What?

AMAH: Forgiveness is a virtue.

BILLIE: Girl, patience is a virtue.

AMAH: Well ...... forgiveness is up there ...

BILLIE: Did Drew tell you about the time my father sang to me at my high-school graduation dinner?

AMAH: Nooo. That's lovely. My father never sang to me at my graduation.

BILLIE: We were eating. He was standing on top of the banquet table.

AMAH: Nooo!

BILLIE: It's the truth!

Pause.

AMAH: Can I get a glass of water?

BILLIE: Yeh. Yeh, help yourself. (*AMAH goes into the kitchen.*) I've got O.J. in the fridge, if you want.

AMAH: Water will do, thanks. Do you have any ... ice in your freezer?

BILLIE: I'll get it.

AMAH: I can get it.

BILLIE: (*gets up quickly and heads toward the kitchen*) It's okay. It's okay. I'll get it for you. (*opens the freezer and gets her the ice, closing the freezer door immediately behind her*)

AMAH: Thanks. (*beat*) What's in there?

BILLIE: Frozen shit.

The phone begins to ring again. Both women look toward it.

SCENE 4

Harlem, the present: same day – noontime. Accompanying the sound of rushing water and the polyrhythmic chorus of strings, Martin Luther King continues to assert his dream, its relationship to the American Constitution and Declaration of Independence.

OTHELLO: (*offstage*) Billie! (*Silence. He knocks again.*) Billie?! (*to MONA*) I don't think she's there.

OTHELLO unlocks the door. He enters. We recognize him as the man in both 1860 and 1928.

OTHELLO: Billie? Mona and I are here to pick up the rest of my things. Billie? (*He hears the shower, goes over to the bathroom door, knocks.*) Billie? ... (*BILLIE screams. We hear something crash.*) It's just me ... I tried to call. You should get that machine fixed.

BILLIE: (*offstage*) I'll be out in a minute.

> OTHELLO *returns to* MONA *at the entrance. We see nothing of her but brief glimpses of a bare arm and a waft of light brown hair.*

OTHELLO: It's okay Mona, she's in there. Why don't you wait in the car.

MONA: (*offstage*) She'll have to get used to me sometime.

OTHELLO: I'll be down in a flash. It won't take me that long. (*She doesn't answer.*) Hey, hey, hey!

MONA: (*offstage*) Hey yourself. I do have other things to take care of, you know. (*He kisses her.*) Okay ... I still haven't found anything blue. I'll scour the stores. I'll be back in a couple of hours.

OTHELLO: All right.

MONA: (*offstage*) All right.

> *He brings in several large, empty boxes. He closes the door and looks around. He sees a burning cigarette, picks it up, looks at it, then puts it out. He takes off his jacket. Then he takes several albums from a shelf and places them on the floor. He begins to form two piles. He picks up one of the albums and begins to laugh.* BILLIE *enters, dressed in a robe.*

BILLIE: What are you doing here?

OTHELLO: I came over to pack my things. The movers are coming in the morning. I tried to call ...

BILLIE: You took my pot.

OTHELLO: What ...

BILLIE: My pot. The cast-iron Dutch pot.

OTHELLO: Oh ... Well, you never use it.

BILLIE: I want it back.

OTHELLO: You never use it.

BILLIE: The one with the yellow handle.

OTHELLO: We need it to make gumbo.

BILLIE: She uses it?

OTHELLO: I need it to make gumbo.

BILLIE: She needs my pot? The one with the carrying rings.

OTHELLO: It was a gift to both of us.

BILLIE: From my father.

OTHELLO: I'll bring it back tomorrow.

BILLIE: If you don't have it here for me inside of thirty minutes, I will break every jazz recording on that shelf.

OTHELLO: You want me to go all the way back for something you don't even use.

BILLIE: Let me see ...

OTHELLO: You never used it.

BILLIE: Abbey Lincoln ...

> *She takes the album from the table. Takes the record from the jacket and breaks it in two. She reaches for another album.* OTHELLO *picks up the broken record.*

BILLIE: Aah. Max Roach. (*takes the cover off the Max Roach album*)

OTHELLO: The Abbey Lincoln was yours. (*She breaks the Max Roach record, too.*) Okay. Okay, I'll go and get it. (*He picks up his jacket and proceeds to the door.*)

BILLIE: Fine. It's fine.

OTHELLO: Excuse me?

BILLIE: It's fine. Tomorrow's fine.

> *Pause. He turns toward her.*

OTHELLO: Okay. (*Pause. He puts his jacket down again. Pause.*) How are you? You look well.

BILLIE: I'm fine. And you?

OTHELLO: Great ... Good.

> *Pause.*

BILLIE: Well, you know where your stuff is.

OTHELLO: Yep ... Yes.

> *Pause.*

BILLIE: Drink?

OTHELLO: What?

BILLIE: Would you like something to drink?

OTHELLO: Sure ... Yes ... What do you –

BILLIE: Peppermint, fennel, chamomile ... No ... Just peppermint and fennel. Coffee, wine, cognac, water.

OTHELLO: What are you having?

BILLIE: Cognac.

OTHELLO: Oh. Well ... That'll do. (*BILLIE goes to the kitchen.*) Where's my suitcase?

BILLIE: Where you left it.

Pause.

OTHELLO: So you're staying on then?

BILLIE: No.

OTHELLO: Where are you ... You know ... I mean, things are tight, money-wise, but I'll still put money in your account ... When I can ... I mean, I hope we can keep in touch. (*She hands him a glass of cognac.*) Thank you.

BILLIE: You're welcome.

Pause.

OTHELLO: You've lost weight. You look great. (*He takes a large gulp.*) Aaahh! Yes!

> *OTHELLO looks at BILLIE for a moment. He then takes one of the boxes and places it at his feet. He approaches the bookshelf. He takes down a large book.*

OTHELLO: *African Mythology* ... Is this mine or yours?

BILLIE: Mine ... I think ... I don't know.

OTHELLO: This is going to be interesting.

BILLIE: Take what you like. I don't care.

OTHELLO: (*takes another book*) *The Great Chain of Being?*

BILLIE: From man to mollusc. The scientific foundation for why we're not human. An African can't really be a woman, you know. My department agreed to let me take only one course this year – I'm taking a reading course.

OTHELLO: Yours ... Yours ... Mine ... *Black Psychology*, you keeping this?

BILLIE: Yeh. (*takes the books from him*) You'd think there was more information on black people and mental health. You know ... Christ, we've been here, what, four hundred years. No money in it I guess ...

OTHELLO: What's money got to do with it?

BILLIE: You know, grants ... scholarships ...

OTHELLO: Race is not an obscure idea. (*He places several books into a box.*)

BILLIE: In genetics, or the study of what's wrong with people of African descent – the Heritage Foundation will give you tons of dough to prove the innate inferiority of ... The Shakespeare's mine, but you can have it.

OTHELLO: Sure, if you don't –

BILLIE: No. The Heritage Foundation – that's where that guy Murray et al. got most of their money for *Bell Curve* – I think ... There's just no one out there willing to give you a scholarship to prove that we're all mad.

OTHELLO: We're all mad. This is the founding principle of your thesis?

BILLIE: Well, not mad ... I mean ... Well ... Psychologically dysfunctional, then. All cultural groups are to some degree ethnocentric: We – they. But not all inter-cultural relations are of an inferior/superior type.

OTHELLO: Thus we're not all mad. (*He returns to the bookshelf.*)

BILLIE: No, no. In America, this race shit is classic behavioural disorder. Obsessions. Phobias. Delusions. Notions of persecution. Delusions of grandeur. Any one or combination of these can produce behaviours which categorize oneself as superior and another as inferior. You see, this kind of dysfunction is systemically supported by the larger society. Psychology only sees clients who can no longer function in society. We're all mad. We just appear to be functional.

OTHELLO: And your solution?

BILLIE: You'll have to buy my book. (*Pause. They continue packing.*) How's the teaching?

OTHELLO: Fine ... Great ...

BILLIE: Good.

Pause.

OTHELLO: I'll be heading the department's courses in Cyprus next summer.

BILLIE: I thought you told me Christopher ... What's his name?

OTHELLO: Chris Yago?

BILLIE: Yeh, Yago.

OTHELLO: Well, everyone thought he would get it. I thought he'd get it. So a whole bunch of them are challenging affirmative action.

BILLIE: Rednecks in academia.

OTHELLO: No, no ... Well ...... I think it's a good thing.

BILLIE: Pu-leese.

OTHELLO: Using discrimination to cure discrimination is not –

BILLIE: We're talking set-asides of 5 per cent, 5 per cent of everything available to whites. They've still got 95.

OTHELLO: Billie ... Injustice against blacks can't be cured by injustice against whites ... you know that.

BILLIE: And younger people won't have the same opportunities you had.

OTHELLO: Now look who's sounding white.

BILLIE: Who said you sounded white?

OTHELLO: It's implied ... No one at school tells me I don't know how to do my job ... it's implied. I'll be at a faculty meeting, I'll make a suggestion and it'll be ignored. Not five minutes later, someone else will make the exact same suggestion and everyone will agree to it. Mona noticed it, too. They think I'm only there because I'm black. I've tested it.

BILLIE: So let me get this straight, you're against affirmative action in order for white people to respect you.

OTHELLO: For my peers ...... my peers to respect me. You know what it's like. Every day I have to prove to them that I can do my job. I feel that any error I make only goes to prove them right.

BILLIE: Well, you must be perfect. Mona respects you.

OTHELLO: Well, she really sees me. She was the only other faculty to support me on the MLK Day assembly. When we played the video –

BILLIE: The "I Have a Dream" speech?

OTHELLO: They understood. For a moment I got them to understand. (*He picks up several books and places them in a box.*)

BILLIE: "America has defaulted on this promissory note insofar as her ..."

OTHELLO & BILLIE: "... citizens of color are concerned."

OTHELLO: "Instead of honoring this sacred obligation, America has given its colored people a ..."

OTHELLO & BILLIE: "bad check ..."

BILLIE: ... "a check that has come back marked ..."

OTHELLO & BILLIE: ... " 'insufficient funds.' "

BILLIE: The man was a ... a ...

OTHELLO: Poet ... Visionary.

BILLIE: A prophet.

OTHELLO: After all he'd been through in his life, he could still see that at a deeper level we're all the same.

Pause.

BILLIE: I'm not the same.

OTHELLO: In the eyes of God, Billie, we're all the same.

BILLIE: One day, little black boys and little white girls –

OTHELLO: You're delusional.

BILLIE: *You're* the one looking for white respect.

OTHELLO: Wrong again! White respect, black respect, it's all the same to me.

BILLIE: Right on, brother man!

OTHELLO: When I was growing up ...... in a time of black pride – it was something to say you were black. Before that, I'd say ... my family would say we're Cuban ... It takes a long time to work through some of those things. I am a member of the human race.

BILLIE: Oh, that's a switch. What happened to all that J.A. Rogers stuff you were pushing. Blacks created the world, blacks are the progenitors of European civilization, Gloriana ... Constantly trying to prove you're as good, no, better than white people. White people are always the line for you, aren't they? The rule ... the margin ... the variable of control. We are black. Whatever we do is black.

OTHELLO: I'm so tired of this race shit, Billie. There are alternatives –

BILLIE: Like what? Oh yes, white.

OTHELLO: Oh, don't be so –

BILLIE: Isn't that really what not acting black, or feeling black, means.

OTHELLO: Liberation has no colour.

BILLIE: But progress is going to white schools ... proving we're as good as whites ... like some holy grail ... all that we're taught in those white schools. All that is in us. Our success is whiteness. We religiously seek to have what they have. Access to the white man's world. The white man's job.

OTHELLO: That's economics.

BILLIE: White economics.

OTHELLO: God! Black women always –

BILLIE: No. Don't even go there ...

OTHELLO: I ... You ... Forget it!

BILLIE: (*quietly at first*) Yes, you can forget it, can't you. I don't have that ... that luxury. When I go into a store, I always know when I'm being watched. I can feel it. They want to see if I'm gonna slip some of their stuff into my pockets. When someone doesn't serve me, I think it's because I'm black. When a clerk won't put the change into my held-out hand, I think it's because I'm black. When I hear about a crime, any crime, I pray to God the person who they think did it isn't black. I'm even suspicious of the word "*black.*" Who called us black anyway? It's not a country, it's not a racial category, it's not even the colour of my skin. And don't give me this content-of-one's-character B.S. I'm sorry ... I am sorry ... I had a dream. A dream that one day a black man and a black woman might find ... Where jumping a broom was a solemn eternal vow that ... I ... Let's ... Can we just get this over with?

> She goes to the window. Silence. He moves toward her.

OTHELLO: I know ... I know. I'm sorry ...

BILLIE: Yeh ...

OTHELLO: I care ... you know that.

BILLIE: I know.

> *Silence.*

OTHELLO: I never thought I'd miss Harlem.

> *Pause.*

BILLIE: You still think it's a reservation?

OTHELLO: Homeland/reservation.

BILLIE: A sea of black faces.

OTHELLO: Africatown, USA.

> *Pause.*

BILLIE: When we lived in the Village, sometimes, I'd be on the subway and I'd miss my stop. And I'd just sit there, past Midtown, past the Upper West Side, and somehow I'd end up here. And I'd just walk. I love seeing all these brown faces.

OTHELLO: Yeh ...

BILLIE: Since they knocked down the old projects, I can see the Schomburg Museum from here. You still can't make out Harlem Hospital. I love that I can see the Apollo from our – from my balcony.

OTHELLO: Fire escape.

BILLIE: Patio.

OTHELLO: You never did find a pair of lawn chairs and a table to fit in that space.

BILLIE: Terrace.

OTHELLO: I never saw the beauty in it.

BILLIE: Deck. My deck.

OTHELLO: I wish ... (*He looks at her.*)

BILLIE: That old building across the street? I didn't know this, but that used to be the Hotel Theresa. That's where Castro stayed when he came to New York ... Must have been the fifties. Ron Brown's father used to run that hotel.

OTHELLO: I ...... I ...... I miss you so much sometimes. Nine years ... it's a long time.

BILLIE: I know.

OTHELLO: I'm really not trying to hurt you, Billie.

BILLIE: I know.

OTHELLO: I never meant to hurt you. (*He strokes her face.*)

BILLIE: I know.

OTHELLO: God, you're so beautiful. (*He kisses her. She does not resist.*)

BILLIE: I ... don't ... I feel ... (*He kisses her again.*) What are you doing?

OTHELLO: I ... I'm ... I'm exploring the heightening Alleghenies of Pennsylvania. (*kisses her again*) The curvaceous slopes of California. (*kisses her again*) The red hills of Georgia, the mighty mountains of New York. Such sad eyes. (*kisses her again*) I'm an equal-opportunity employer. (*pause*) I am an equal-opportunity employer. (*pause*) I say, "I'm an equal-opportunity employer," then you say, "I don't come ..."

BILLIE: I don't come cheap, you know.

OTHELLO: I'm offering more than money can buy.

BILLIE: How much more?

OTHELLO: This much. (*He kisses her.*)

BILLIE: I could buy that.

OTHELLO: Could you buy this? (*He kisses her deeply.*)

BILLIE: Be ... Be ... Beloved. (*She kisses him.*)

SCENE 5

> *Harlem, the present: same day – early afternoon. The stringed duet croons gently as Malcolm X speaks about the need for blacks to turn their gaze away from whiteness so that they can see each other with*

new eyes. OTHELLO *is lying in the bed.* BILLIE *is in the living room, smoking a cigarette.*

OTHELLO: I've missed you.

BILLIE: That's nice.

OTHELLO: By the looks of things, I miss you even now.

BILLIE: I'm coming.

OTHELLO: I noticed.

BILLIE: Sometimes ... Sometimes when we make love. Sometimes every moment lines up into one moment. And I'm holding you. And I can't tell where I end, or you begin. I see everything. All my ancestors lined up below me ...... like a Makonde statue, or something. It's like ... I know. I know I'm supposed to be here. Everything is here.

OTHELLO: Sounds crowded to me.

BILLIE: It's actually quite empty.

OTHELLO: Not as empty as this bed is feeling right about now.

BILLIE: I'm coming. I'm coming.

She hurriedly stubs the cigarette out and heads toward the bedroom. The apartment buzzer rings. BILLIE *goes to the intercom.*

BILLIE: Hi Magi. I ... er ... I'm kinda busy right now.

MONA: (*through intercom*) It's Mona. Could I have a word with Othello.

OTHELLO: (*overlapping*) Shit!

BILLIE: One second please.

He rushes to the intercom while attempting to put his clothes back on. BILLIE *tries to hold back her laughter. Her laughter begins to infect* OTHELLO. *He puts a finger over his mouth indicating to* BILLIE *to be quiet.*

OTHELLO: Hey, Mone ... Mone, I'm not done yet. There's more here than I imagined. Why don't I call you when I'm done. (*MONA does not respond.* OTHELLO's *demeanour changes.*) Mone? Mona? I'm coming, okay? I'll be right ... Just wait there one second, okay? Okay?

BILLIE *is unable to hide her astonishment.*

MONA: (*through intercom*) Okay.

OTHELLO: Okay. (*He steps away from the intercom to finish putting on his clothes.* BILLIE *stares at him.*) I'll be back in ... uh ... I just have to go straighten ... uh ... She wants to help ... help pack. You'll have to get used to her sometime. I mean ... I ... (BILLIE *continues to stare steadily at* OTHELLO *as he struggles with the buttons on his shirt.*) I'm sorry ... Well ...... I'll be right ... I'll be back.

He exits. BILLIE *does not move.*

SCENE 6

Harlem, 1860: late summer – night. A whining Delta blues slides and blurs while the deeply resonant voice of Paul Robeson talks of his forebears, whose blood is in the American soil. HIM *is hammering a newly forged horseshoe.* HER *rushes in holding a large carry bag.*

HER: Oh ... let me catch – catch my breath ... I thought I was seen ... Oh my ... I ... I've packed a change of clothes for both of us, some loaves ... I liberated the leftover bacon from yesterday's meal, from out the pantry, seeing how it was staring me right in the face when I was cleaning. It won't be missed. I wish I could pack old Betsy in my bag. She'd be sure an' give us some good fresh milk each mornin'. Oh – and I packed a fleece blanket. I hear the nights get good and cold further north you go. And ... did I forget ... no ... Nothing forgotten. Oh yes, I borrowed the big carving knife – for the bacon, a' course. You still working on those shoes for Miss Dessy's stallion ... Let her send it to town, or get some other slave to do that ... She's going to be mad as hell you took off in any event ... May as well not finish the shoes, it won't placate her none ...

HIM *picks up the horseshoe with a pair of tongs.* HIM *inspects it carefully.* HIM *puts the shoe to one side and retrieves the shackles.* HIM *takes a chamois and begins to polish the metal.*

HER: (*pause*) O? O? Othello? The moon'll be rising. We've got to make any headway under cover of dark ... Othello, why you trying to please her. I'm so tired of pleasing her. I'm so tired of pleasing white folks. Up in Canada, we won't have to please no white folks nohow. I hear they got sailing ships leaving for Africa every day. Canada freedom come ... O? Othello? Are you coming?

HIM: I can't.

HER: If we make it to the border there's people there'll help us wade that water – help us cross over.

HIM: I'm not going.

HER: A big white house on an emerald hill ...

HIM: I know.

HER: You need more time, O? I can wait for you. Finish her shoes, I'll ... I can wait –

HIM: No. No.

Pause.

HER: You love her.

HIM: Her father going to war.

HER: You love her?

HIM: I love you. It's just ... She needs me. She respects me. Looks up to me, even. I love you. It's just ... When I'm with her I feel like ... a man. I want ... I need to do for her ...

HER: Do you love her?

HIM: Yes.

HER: Fight with me ...... I would fight with you. Suffer with me, O ... I would suffer with you ...

Silence.

SCENE 7

Harlem, the present: late summer – late afternoon. Dulcet blue tones barely swing as Louis Farrakhan waxes eloquent on African Americans being caught in the gravity of American society.

MAGI: And you know what he says, after turning on the baseball game, in the middle of my romantic dinner? Eyes glued to the screen, he says, "I bet you've never made love to a man with twenty-six-inch biceps!"

BILLIE: (*smiles*) Oh ... no ...

MAGI: I'm telling you, girl. Macho Mack, spot him at any locale selling six-packs. Easily recognizable, everything about him is permanently flexed. His favourite pastime? Weekend NFL football, Monday night football, USFL football – even Canadian foot ... You look like you're feeling better. Amah did a great job with your hair.

BILLIE: What's her motto? We lock heads and minds.

MAGI: Hey, can I borrow that beautiful African boubou – I got me a date with an African prince. The brother has it going on! Oh ... you already have boxes.

BILLIE: (*begins placing some of the wrapped objects in a box*) They're his box –

MAGI: When ... He came over?

BILLIE: I even spoke to her.

MAGI: You saw her?

BILLIE: No. Want this mask?

MAGI: You met her?

BILLIE: No. Want this mask?

MAGI: I'll keep it for you –

BILLIE: I ... er ...... I don't know how long these things will have to stay in storage.

MAGI: You don't have to move, you know. It's not rented yet. I mean, I can always lower the –

BILLIE: No, no ... I'm moving on.

MAGI: Good. Good. To where? Where are you going? You haven't given me a date or anything. I've got bills to pay too, you know. When d'you plan to leave? Where are you going?

BILLIE: I might go ...... stay with Jenny. I could go home.

MAGI: I'll keep it for you –

BILLIE: I don't want anything that's – that was ours. If you don't want it, that's okay, I'll just trash it.

BILLIE throws the mask onto the floor. It breaks into several pieces.

MAGI: Something happened. What happened?

BILLIE: Nothing.

MAGI: Did he tell you about ... What did he say to you?

BILLIE: I'm just tired. Tired of sleeping. Tired of night. It lays over me like a ton of white feathers. Swallows me up. The movers are coming in the morning to pick up his things. It's okay. I'm fine. You know ... I've lived all my life believing in lies.

MAGI: Well, getting your master's isn't a lie.

BILLIE: It's about proving, isn't it? Proving I'm as good as ... I'm as intelligent as ...

MAGI: Nothing wrong with that.

BILLIE: I don't want anything ... believe in anything. Really. I've gotta get out of here. I don't even believe in Harlem anymore.

MAGI: Come on ...

BILLIE: It's all an illusion. All some imagined idealistic ... I dunno.

MAGI: When I go out my door, I see all the beauty of my blackness reflected in the world around me.

BILLIE: Yeh, and all my wretchedness by the time I get to the end of the block.

MAGI: Billie, he's the one who wants to whitewash his life.

BILLIE: Corporeal malediction.

MAGI: Corp-o-re-all mal-e ... Ooh, that's good.

BILLIE: A black man afflicted with Negrophobia.

MAGI: Girl, you on a roll now!

BILLIE: No, no. A crumbled racial epidermal schema ...

MAGI: Who said school ain't doing you no good.

BILLIE: ... causing predilections to coitus denegrification.

MAGI: Booker T. Uppermiddleclass III. He can be found in predominantly white neighbourhoods. He refers to other blacks as "them." His greatest accomplishment was being invited to the White House by George Bush to discuss the "Negro problem."

BILLIE: Now, that is frightening.

MAGI: No, what's frightening is the fact that I dated him.

BILLIE: What does it say ... about us?

MAGI: Who?

BILLIE: You and me.

MAGI: Girl, I don't know. I can't even want to go there.

BILLIE: Ohh ... Oh well ... Least he's happy though. What does he say? Now he won't have to worry that a white woman will emotionally mistake him for the father that abandoned her.

MAGI: Isn't he worried the white woman might mistake him for the butler?

BILLIE: He'd be oh so happy to oblige.

MAGI: I see them do things for white women they wouldn't dream of doing for me.

BILLIE: It is a disease. We get infected as children and ... and the bacteria ... the virus slowly spreads, disabling the entire system.

MAGI: Are we infected, too? (*There is knocking at the apartment door.*) Speaking of white minds parading around inside of black bodies – you want me to stay?

BILLIE: Don't you have a date?

MAGI: Hakim. But I can cancel ...

There is knocking at the door again.

BILLIE: I'm okay. I'm okay. I'm fine ... Truly.

BILLIE opens the door. OTHELLO enters.

OTHELLO: The pot! (*He hands the pot to BILLIE.*) Magi!

MAGI: How's Harlumbia?

OTHELLO: Columbia?

MAGI: Harlumbia – those ten square blocks of whitedom, owned by Columbia University, set smack dab in the middle of Harlem.

OTHELLO: Harlumbia, as you call it, is dull without you.

MAGI: You could steal honey from a bee, couldn't you. Better watch you don't get stung. Well, I'm off to doll myself up. Billie ...

BILLIE: Yeh, I'll get that boubou ...

BILLIE goes into the bedroom. After a few moments of silence ...

MAGI: Why haven't you told her yet?

OTHELLO: About? – Oh yes ... Yeh ... I wanted to ...

BILLIE returns with a beautiful multicoloured boubou.

BILLIE: He won't be able to resist you ...

MAGI: Thank you, thank you. Later you two.

OTHELLO: I'll be in touch ...

BILLIE: I'm keeping my fingers crossed for you.

MAGI: Good, I'm running out of time.

MAGI exits. OTHELLO enters. BILLIE closes the door. There is a long awkward silence. BILLIE continues placing wrapped objects into her boxes. OTHELLO steps on a piece of the broken mask. He picks it up, looks at it, then places it on the mantel. He goes over to the bookshelf and begins to pack more of his possessions into his boxes.

OTHELLO: They're coming at nine.

BILLIE: Oh ... Er ... I'll be out of your way.

OTHELLO: You can be here ...

BILLIE: No. No. No. I have an appointment ...... an early appointment.

OTHELLO: Either way ... (*They continue packing.*) Ah ... I've been meaning to tell you ... things are real ...... money's real tight right now, what with buying the apartment, and moving and everything ... I won't be able to cover your tuition this semester. I'll try and put money in your account when I can. Maybe –

BILLIE: I told you, I'm only taking one course. If you cover that, I won't be taking a full load 'til next –

OTHELLO: I know, that's what I'm saying ... I can't ... I just can't do it right now.

BILLIE: It's one course ...

OTHELLO: It's five thousand dollars.

BILLIE: You promised …

OTHELLO: I'm mortgaged up the wazoo. I don't have it. I just don't have five thousand dollars, right now.

BILLIE: Ooh …… okay.

OTHELLO: I would if I could, you know that. (*He continues to pack.*) I think I brought the bookshelf with me when we first –

BILLIE: Take it all.

OTHELLO: I don't want all of it.

BILLIE: I'm keeping the bed.

OTHELLO: What about the rest …

BILLIE: If you don't want it … I'm giving it away …

OTHELLO: Okay, if you're throwing it out …

BILLIE: I'm keeping the bed.

They continue packing in silence.

OTHELLO: We're getting married. (*pause*) Me and Mona. We're engaged … Officially.

Very long pause.

BILLIE: Congratulations.

OTHELLO: I wanted to tell you … Hear it from the horse's mouth … Hear it from me first. You know …

Pause.

BILLIE: Yeh … Yes. Yes. Congratulations.

OTHELLO: Mona wanted me to tell you.

BILLIE: Yes. Yes. Being a feminist and everything – a woman's right to know – since we're all in the struggle … I thought you hated feminists.

OTHELLO: Well … I didn't mean that. I mean … the white women's movement is different.

BILLIE: Just black feminists.

OTHELLO: No, no … White men have maintained a firm grasp of the pants. I mean, white men have economic and political pants that white women have been demanding to share.

BILLIE: White wisdom from the mouth of the mythical Negro.

OTHELLO: Don't you see! That's exactly my point! You … The black feminist position as I experience it in this relationship leaves me feeling unrecognized as a man. The message is, black men are poor fathers, poor partners, or both. Black women wear the pants that black men were prevented from wearing … I believe in tradition. You don't support

me. Black women are more concerned with their careers than their husbands. There was a time when women felt satisfied, no, honoured being a balance to their spouse, at home, supporting the family, playing her role –

BILLIE: Which women? I mean, which women are you referring to? Your mother worked all her life. My mother worked, her mother worked … Most black women have been working like mules since we arrived on this continent. Like mules. When white women were burning their bras, we were hired to hold their tits up. We looked after their homes, their children … I don't support you? My mother's death paid your tuition, not mine …

OTHELLO: Can't we even pretend to be civil? Can't we? I know this isn't easy. It's not easy for me either. Do you ever consider that?

BILLIE: You like it easy, don't you.

OTHELLO: The truth is, this is too fucking difficult.

BILLIE: You wouldn't know the truth if it stood up and knocked you sideways.

OTHELLO: You don't want the truth. You want me to tell you what you want to hear. No, no, you want to know the truth? I'll tell you the truth. Yes, I prefer white women. They are easier – before and after sex. They wanted me and I wanted them. They weren't filled with hostility about the unequal treatment they were getting at their jobs. We'd make love and I'd fall asleep not having to beware being mistaken for someone's inattentive father. I'd explain that I wasn't interested in a committed relationship right now, and not be confused with every lousy lover, or husband, that had ever left them lying in a gutter of unresolved emotions. It's the truth. To a black woman, I represent every black man she has ever been with and with whom there was still so much to work out. The white women I loved saw me – could see me. Look, I'm not a junkie. I don't need more than one lover to prove my manhood. I have no children. I did not leave you, your mother, or your aunt with six babies and a whole lotta love. I am a very single, very intelligent, very employed black man. And with white women it's good. It's nice. Anyhow, we're all equal in the eyes of God, aren't we? Aren't we?

BILLIE stares at OTHELLO. He continues to pack.

SCENE 8

Harlem, 1928: late summer – night. The cello and bass moan, almost dirge-like, in harmonic tension to the sound of Jesse Jackson's oratory. SHE holds a straight-edged razor in her bloodied palms. HE lies on the floor in front of her, motionless, the handkerchief in his hand.

SHE: Deadly, deadly straw little strawberries it's so beautiful you kissed my fingers you pressed this cloth into my palm buried it there an antique token our ancient all these tiny red dots on a sheet of white my fingernails are white three hairs on my head are white the whites of my eyes are white too the palms of my hands and my feet are white you're all I'd ever and you my my I hate Sssshh. Shhhhh. Okay. Okay. Okay. I'm okay all right don't don't don't my eyes on the shadow sparrow my sense in my feet my hands my head shine the light there please scream no sing sing (*tries to sing*)

> *… and if I get a notion, to jump into the ocean,*
>
> *Ain't nobody's business if I do do do do*
>
> *If I go to church on Sunday then shimmy down on Monday*
>
> *T'ain't nobody's business if I …*

SCENE 9

Harlem, the present: late summer – early evening. The instruments sound out a deep cerulean blues while Malcolm X almost scats the question, "What difference does colour make?" OTHELLO continues to pack. BILLIE sits on the floor by the bed watching him from the bedroom.

OTHELLO: I didn't mean – what I said. You know that. I just … Sometimes you make me so mad I … People change, Billie. That's just human nature. Our experiences, our knowledge transforms us. That's why education is so powerful, so erotic. The transmission of words from mouth to ear. Her mouth to my ear. Knowledge. A desire for that distant thing I know nothing of, but yearn to hold for my very own. My mama used to say, "You have to be three times as good as a white child to get by, to do well." A piece of that pie is mine. I don't want to change the recipe. I am not minor. I am not a minority. I used to be a minority when I was a kid. I mean my culture is not my mother's culture – the culture of my ancestors. My culture is Wordsworth, Shaw, *Leave It to Beaver*,

Dirty Harry. I drink the same water, read the same books. You're the problem if you don't see beyond my skin. If you don't hear my educated English, if you don't understand that I am a middle-class educated man. I mean, what does Africa have to do with me. We struttin' around professing some imaginary connection for a land we don't know. Never seen. Never gonna see. We lie to ourselves saying, ah yeh, Mother Africa, middle passage, suffering, the whites did it to me, it's the whites' fault. Strut around in African cloth pretending we human now. We human now. Some of us are beyond that now. Spiritually beyond this race shit bullshit now. I am an American. The slaves were freed over 130 years ago. In 1967 it was illegal for a black to marry a white in sixteen states. That was less than thirty years ago … in my lifetime. Things change, Billie. I am not my skin. My skin is not me.

SCENE 10

Harlem, the present: late summer, the same day – night. A rhapsody of sound keeps time with Christopher Darden as he asks O.J. Simpson to approach the jury and try on the bloody glove. The apartment is virtually full of boxes. BILLIE is by the chemical factory at the table. The book of Egyptian alchemy sits open upon it. Something is boiling in the flask and steam is coming out of the condenser. With rubber-gloved hands she adds several drops of a violet liquid to the flask. She picks up a large white handkerchief with pretty red strawberries embroidered on it.

BILLIE: I have a plan, my love. My mate … throughout eternity. Feel what I feel. Break like I break. No more—no less. You'll judge me harsher. I know. While Susan Smith … She blamed some imaginary black man for the murder of her two boys and that's why authorities didn't suspect her for nearly two weeks. Stopping every black man with a burgundy sedan from Union, South Carolina, to the Oranges of New Jersey. And you're still wondering what made her do it. What was she going through to make her feel that this was her only way out. Yet I'll be discarded as some kind of unconscionable bitter shadow, or something. Ain't I a woman? This is my face you take for night – the biggest shadow in the world. I … I have nothing more to lose. Nothing. Othello? I am preparing something special for you … Othe … Othello. A gift for you, and your new bride. Once you gave me a handkerchief. An heirloom. This handkerchief, your mother's …… given by your father. From his mother before that. So far back ... And now ... then ... to me. It is fixed in the emotions of all your ancestors. The one who laid the foundation for the road in Herndon, Virginia, and was lashed for laziness as he stopped to wipe the sweat from his brow with this kerchief. Or your great-great-grandmother, who covered her face with it, and then covered it with her hands as she rocked and silently wailed, when told that her girl child, barely thirteen, would be sent 'cross the state for breeding purposes. Or the one who leapt for joy on hearing of the Emancipation Proclamation, fifteen years late mind you, only to watch it fall in slow motion from his hand and onto the ground when told that the only job he could now get was the same one he'd done for free all those years, and now he's forced to take it, for not enough money to buy the food to fill even one man's belly. And more ... so much more. What I add to this already fully endowed cloth will cause you such ...... such ... wretchedness. Othe ... Othello.

The contents of the flask have been transformed from violet to clear. BILLIE places the handkerchief onto a large tray. Then with tongs, she takes the hot flask and pours the contents over the handkerchief. She retrieves a vial from the table, opens it.

BILLIE: My sable warrior ... Fight with me. I would fight with you ... Suffer with me ... I would suffer –

She starts to pour, but the vial is empty. The buzzer rings. BILLIE is surprised. The buzzer rings again. BILLIE turns off the Bunsen burner. She takes the flask into the kitchen and pours it into the sink. The buzzer rings once more. Going back to the table, she carefully takes the tray and heads toward the bathroom. There is a knock at her door.

BILLIE: (*from the bathroom*) You have a key, let yourself in ... Make yourself right at home, why don't you –

MAGI: (*offstage*) Billie? Billie, it's me. Magi.

BILLIE: Magi?

MAGI: (*offstage*) Are you okay?

BILLIE: Yes. Yes. I'm fine. Let me call you later, okay Magi?

We hear the sound of liquid being poured. The toilet flushes. MAGI offstage mumbles something about BILLIE having a visitor.

BILLIE: What?

MAGI mumbles something about a visitor again.

BILLIE: What? Door's open!

MAGI enters and stands in the doorway. She is speaking quietly, as if not wanting someone to hear.

MAGI: Sweetie, you have a visitor. Shall I –

BILLIE: (*entering the living area*) Look, I'm tired. He's been here practically all day already –

MAGI: No, no, no. He said his name is Canada. (*BILLIE turns to MAGI.*) He says he's your father. That's what he said. He said he was your father.

A man in his late sixties brushes past MAGI. He wears a hat and has a small suitcase in his hand.

CANADA: Sybil? Sybil! There's my girl. Come and give your daddy a big hug.

ACT TWO

SCENE 1

Harlem, the present: late summer – night. The cello and bass pluck and bow a funky rendition of Aretha Franklin's "Spanish Harlem" against the audio sound of Michael Jackson and Lisa Marie Presley's interview on ABC's Primetime. *CANADA is sitting on one of the chairs, amid stacks of boxes.*

CANADA: The first time I came to Harlem, I was scared. Must have been '68 or '69. Yeh ... We were living in the Bronx, and your mother was still alive. Everything I'd ever learned told me that I wasn't safe in this part of town. The newspapers. Television. My friends. My own family. But I'm curious, see. I says, Canada you can't be in New York City and not see Harlem. So I make my way to 125th. "A" train. I'm gonna walk past the Apollo, I'm gonna see this place. I'm gonna walk the ten city blocks to Lexington and catch the "6" train back, if it's the last thing I do. So out of the subway, I put on my "baddest mother in the city" glare. I walk – head straight. All the time trying to make my stride say, "I'm mean ... I'm mean. Killed somebody mean." So I'm doing this for 'bout five, ten minutes, taking short furtive glances at this place I really want to see, when I begin to realize ... No one is taking any notice of me ... Not a soul. Then it dawns on me: I'm the same as them. I look just like them. I look like I live in Harlem. Sounds silly now. But I just had to catch myself and laugh out loud. Canada, where did you get these ideas about Harlem from?

The kettle whistles.

BILLIE: How do you like it? (*She heads to the kitchen to make tea.*)

CANADA: Brown sugar. No milk.

BILLIE: I don't even know why I asked, I don't have any milk anyway.

CANADA: You can't take milk. Never could. When your mother stopped feeding you from her milk, that cow's milk just gave you colic. And those diapers ... Now that's an image I'll never forget.

BILLIE: So what brings you to these parts?

CANADA: Just passing through. Since I was in the neighbourhood, thought I'd stop on in.

BILLIE: Nova Scotia's nearly a thousand miles away.

CANADA: Well, I thought I should see my grandchild. Jenny's almost six and I've only talked to her on the phone. And Andrew and his wife, and you. Nothing wrong with seeing family is there?

BILLIE: Strong or weak?

CANADA: Like a bear's bottom.

BILLIE: Polar or grizzly?

CANADA: Grizzly.

BILLIE returns with a tray.

CANADA: Andrew told me what happened.

BILLIE: He did, did he?

CANADA: Said you were taking it kinda hard.

BILLIE: Oh, I'll be fine. I'm a survivor. But then again, you already know that.

CANADA: Tea should be ready. Shall I be mother?

BILLIE: Go ahead.

CANADA pours the tea.

BILLIE: I hear you were in the hospital.

CANADA: My liver ain't too good. Gave out on me. I guess you reap what you sow.

BILLIE: Still drinking?

CANADA: Been sober going on five years now.

BILLIE: Good. Good for you.

CANADA: Don't mean I don't feel like it sometimes though ...

BILLIE: Well ... How long do you plan to be in town?

CANADA: Just a few days. See Andrew and his family. See the sights. I'm staying there – at Andrew's. Went by there earlier ... No one home. Must have given them the wrong time. Left a note though. Told them to find me at Sybil's.

BILLIE: Billie. I've always despised that name. Sybil.

CANADA: I gave you that name. It's a good name. It was your grandmother's name. It means prophetess. Sorceress. Seer of the future. I like it. I don't see anything wrong with that name.

BILLIE: Sounds like some old woman living in a cave.

CANADA: (*reaches for his suitcase*) I brought something for you. (*takes out a small red box*) Go on ... open it. The box is a bit too big, but ...

BILLIE opens the box.

CANADA: It's your mother's ring. I figured she'd want you to have it.

BILLIE: I hardly remember her anymore. I get glimpses of this ghostly figure creeping in and out of my dreams.

CANADA: When Beryl first passed on, I couldn't get her off my mind, like she'd gone and left us somehow. Left me ... with two kids, one a young girl ripening to sprout into womanhood. I was sad, but I was good and mad too. One minute I'd be trying to etch her face into my mind, 'cause I didn't want to forget. Next thing, I'd be downing another shot of rye ... I couldn't carry the weight. I just couldn't do it by myself. That's when we moved to Dartmouth. What's that them old slaves used to say? "I can't take it no more, I moving to Nova Scotia."

BILLIE: I'm thinking of heading back there myself ...

Pause.

CANADA: 'Cause he left you, or 'cause she's white?

Pause.

BILLIE: I remember that white woman ... That hairdresser you used to go with ... The one with the miniskirts ... What was her name?

CANADA: That's going way back ... You remember her?

BILLIE: She was boasting about knowing how to do our kind of hair. And she took that hot comb to my head ... Sounded like she was frying chicken ... Burnt my ears and half the hair on my head. I hated her stubby little beige legs and those false eyelashes. She taught me how to put on false eyelashes.

CANADA: Deborah.

BILLIE: Debbie ... Yes ... Debbie.

Pause.

CANADA: I wish ... I wish things between ...

The buzzer rings.

BILLIE: That must be Drew. (*goes to the console by the door*) Drew?

AMAH: (*through intercom*) It's me. Amah. Is your –

BILLIE: He's here. Come on up.

CANADA: You know, an old African once told me the story of a man who was struck by an arrow. His attacker was unknown. Instead of tending to his wound, he refused to remove the arrow until the archer was found and punished. In the meantime, the wound festered, until finally the poison infected his entire body, eventually killing him ... Now, who is responsible for this man's death, the archer for letting go the arrow or the man for his foolish holding on?

A knock at the door. BILLIE gets up and heads toward it.

BILLIE: The drunk?

CANADA: A drunken man can get sober but a damn fool can't ever get wise.

BILLIE opens the door. AMAH enters carrying some rolls of paper in her arms.

AMAH: (*kissing BILLIE's cheek*) Hi, sweetie. And you must be Canada.

CANADA: Drew's wife ...

AMAH: So very pleased to meet you at last.

CANADA: Delighted ...

AMAH: We weren't expecting you until tomorrow. We ate out tonight. We would have come pick you up. Jenny's so excited.

CANADA: No, no ... No need to fuss. I arrived safe and sound. And Sybil – Billie's been taking good care of me.

AMAH: Drew would have come himself. Jenny insisted he give her a bath tonight. You know, it's a father-daughter thing. (*silence*) Anyway, we should get going. (*to CANADA*) You're probably starving. I can rustle something up for you in no time.

CANADA reaches for his coat.

AMAH: (*to BILLIE*) Look, I'm gonna have to bring that child of mine over here. She's driving me crazy asking for you –

BILLIE: No. No ... not yet.

AMAH: Well, if I go mad, you and Drew will have to take care of her. I want you to know that. Oh, Jenny asked me to give these to you. (*shows drawings*) She made them 'specially for you. She wanted to give you some inspiration. You might not be able to tell, but one's of her dancing, and the other's of her singing.

BILLIE: Tell her I miss her.

AMAH: I will.

BILLIE: Tell her I'll see her real soon.

AMAH: I will.

BILLIE: (*to AMAH*) I still have a bone to pick with you, though. (*indicating CANADA*)

AMAH: No, no. You have a bone to pick with Drew.

CANADA: I'll drop in again tomorrow, if that's okay with you.

BILLIE: Tomorrow might not be so good. He's moving his stuff in the morning. We'd probably be in the way. I won't even be here until sometime in the afternoon.

CANADA: Well then ... We'll see how things go. (*kisses BILLIE on the forehead*)

AMAH: Come join us over something to eat –

BILLIE: No. Thanks. I'm fine.

CANADA: Good to see you, Sybil – Billie.

BILLIE: Well, it certainly was a surprise. Bye y'all.

AMAH and CANADA exit. BILLIE closes the door, then leans against it as she studies the pictures Jenny drew.

SCENE 2

Harlem, the present: the next day – late morning. Lyrical strains give way to an undulating rhythm while Malcolm X recounts the tale of how George Washington sold a slave for a gallon of molasses. The apartment looks empty of furniture, save for the bed, several piles of books, and boxes strewn around the living area. OTHELLO walks into the bedroom with a large green garbage bag. After a few moments, the door is unlocked and BILLIE peers through the doorway. She hears someone in the bedroom. She quietly closes the door behind her and places a small brown paper bag in her pocket. She makes her way into the kitchen area. She waits. OTHELLO exits the bedroom, green garbage bag in tow. He walks to the centre of the living room, where he stands for a few moments taking it all in.

BILLIE: Got everything?

OTHELLO: (*startled*) Ahh! (*dropping the garbage bag, he turns around*) Christ …

BILLIE: Got everything?

OTHELLO: God, I didn't hear you come in.

BILLIE: My meeting ended earlier than I expected. I was able to get what I needed … I didn't see a van. I figured you'd be done by now.

OTHELLO: They just left. I was doing a final check. See if I'd forgotten anything.

BILLIE: So the move went well.

OTHELLO: Yes … yeh. It's amazing how much stuff there is.

BILLIE: Yeh. It's hard to throw things away.

OTHELLO: I know what you mean. We've got a huge place though.

BILLIE: Good. Good for you.

Pause.

OTHELLO: This place looks pretty huge right now, though. Remember when we first came to look at this place?

BILLIE: Yes.

Pause.

OTHELLO: Well … I guess that's it.

BILLIE: I guess …

Pause.

OTHELLO: Anyway … So when do you plan on leaving?

BILLIE: Oh, I don't … I don't know.

OTHELLO: Ah.

BILLIE: I haven't decided.

OTHELLO: I see … Well …

BILLIE: So when's the big day?

OTHELLO: Oh …… Well … er … Three weeks.

BILLIE: So soon?

OTHELLO: Just a small affair.

BILLIE: Good. Good for you. Good for you both.

OTHELLO: Yeh …

BILLIE: I … I've been meaning … Well … I've been thinking.

OTHELLO: Hmn hmn …

BILLIE: I … er … I … um … I want to return something you gave me … centuries ago.

OTHELLO: Oh?

BILLIE: The handkerchief?

OTHELLO: Oh! Really? Wow … No. No. It's not necessary. Really –

BILLIE: No, no, let me finish. I've …… been foolish. I understand that now. You can understand why. And …… I'm sorry. That's what I wanted to tell you. And the handkerchief … it's yours. Held by me for safekeeping really. To be passed on to our children – if we had any. Since we don't, it should be returned to you, to your line …

OTHELLO: Why are you doing this?

BILLIE: I just thought you might … I thought you would … After all … it's the only thing your mother left you …

OTHELLO: I don't know what to say.

BILLIE: I thought you'd be glad.

OTHELLO: Oh, I'm more than glad.

BILLIE: But I have to find it first.

OTHELLO: Are you sure about –

BILLIE: I'm sure. Give me a couple of days, to find it …… clean it up a bit.

OTHELLO: I could come by.

BILLIE: Yes. You should have it before … you know … before your … big day.

OTHELLO: Thank you.

BILLIE: Just trying to play my part well.

OTHELLO: Thanks.

BILLIE: Forgive me …

OTHELLO: I know it's been hard.

BILLIE: Yeh …

OTHELLO: Okay. Well …

He reaches to touch her face. She retreats.

BILLIE: I'll see you in a couple of days then.

OTHELLO: All right.

BILLIE: All right.

OTHELLO: All right. And say hello to Jenny for me. (*silence*) All right.

OTHELLO exits. BILLIE takes the small package out of her pocket. She unwraps it, revealing a small vial of fluid. She goes into the kitchen, vial in hand, turns toward the fridge, opens the freezer door, and stares into it.

BILLIE: Look this way and see … your death … Othe … Othe …

She places the vial in the freezer.

SCENE 3

Harlem, 1862: late summer – night. Indigo blues groan as if through a delta, while echoes of a presidential voice read from the Emancipation Proclamation. The sound fades. HER holds HIM in her arms like Mary holds Jesus in Michelangelo's Pietà. There is a rope around his neck. He does not move.

HER: (*caressing him*) Once upon a time, there was a man who wanted to find a magic spell in order to become white. After much research and investigation, he came across an ancient ritual from the caverns of knowledge of a psychic. "The only way to become white," the psychic said, "was to enter the whiteness." And when he found his ice queen, his alabaster goddess, he fucked her. Her on his dick. He one with her, for a single shivering moment became … her. Her and her whiteness.

SCENE 4

Harlem, the present: late summer – night. A cacophony of strings grooves and collides as sound bites from the Anita Hill–Clarence Thomas hearings, the L.A. riots, the O.J. Simpson trial, Malcolm X, and Martin Luther King loop and repeat the same distorted bits of sound over and over again. BILLIE is alone in the apartment. She opens the freezer and removes the vial. Wearing rubber gloves, she places several drops of a liquid substance onto the handkerchief. She replaces the cap of the vial. BILLIE carefully folds the handkerchief, hesitates for a moment, looks around and spots the red box on the mantle. She puts the handkerchief back down on the tray and, with her hands in the air, like a surgeon scrubbing for surgery, she gets up and goes to the red box. With one hand she takes off one of the gloves. With the ungloved hand she opens the red box and slips her mother's ring on her finger. She then takes the red box with her to the table. She very carefully replaces the one glove, picks up the handkerchief, and neatly places it in the small red box. She works slowly, and is mindful not to touch the sides of the box with the handkerchief itself.

She once more removes a single rubber glove, picks up the cover to the box, and places it on top of the other half. She is still for a few moments, staring at the box.

BILLIE gets up and crosses the room, as if looking for something, only to stop in her tracks and return to the box. She paces. Her pacing appears more methodical than hysterical. Suddenly she stops. She turns to look at the small red box.

She shakes her head and takes a seat on a large, full cardboard box at her feet. Her breathing becomes more apparent as she begins to rock, almost imperceptibly at first. Finally, she places her head in her hands.

After several moments, BILLIE's face slowly emerges from her hands.

She glares at the gloved hand incredulously, as she realizes that she has inadvertently transferred some of the potion onto her own skin. She quickly removes the second glove and proceeds to wipe her face with her own clothes.

BILLIE: (*to herself*) Oh God! Oh my God! Shit! Shit! Shit! Shit!

BILLIE gets up and rushes to the kitchen sink, turns on the tap, and frantically washes her hands and face in the water.

SCENE 5

Harlem, the present: the following day – early evening. In counterpoint to the cello and bass, the distorted sound loop becomes a grating repetition. MAGI and CANADA are on either side of a large box, sitting on two smaller ones. The larger box is covered by a scarf to resemble a tablecloth, on top of which is a small feast. They are eating. MAGI gets up and goes to the door of the bedroom. She peeks in. After a few moments she closes the door and returns to her seat.

MAGI: She's in distant realms. I checked in on her when I got back from church. I thought she was speaking in tongues. I couldn't understand a thing she was saying. I don't think she slept a wink all night. Those pills work like a charm, though. (*beat*) How is it?

CANADA: Mmn! Those greens … She looks like an angel and cooks like one, too.

MAGI: Can I get you some more?

CANADA: No, no, I don't want to appear too greedy now.

MAGI: Here … (*serving him another helping*) There you go. And I won't tell a soul. Promise.

CANADA: I haven't tasted cooking like this in a long time.

MAGI: My mama would say, "Some food is good for the mind, some is good for the body, and some food is good for the soul."

CANADA: Your mama taught you how to cook like this?

MAGI: Once she even taught me how to cook a soufflé. She used to have a restaurant downstairs from as far back as I can recall. And I guess the boys returning home from the war in Europe kept asking for the Parisian food, and it ended up on her menu. She'd say, "Now, this Parisian food ain't good for nothing. Soufflé ain't nothing more than baked eggs. And eggs is for breakfast. Eggs don't do no one no good past noon."

CANADA: So you've lived here all your life?

MAGI: And my mother before me, and her mother before her. My great-grandmother worked for the family that lived here, most of her life. She never married, but she had two children by the man she worked for – seems his wife never knew they were his. One brown baby looks just like another to most white folks. And when the wife died, my great-grandmother just stayed on. Everybody thinking she's just the maid, but she was living like the queen of the manor – him being her babies' father and everything. And his other children were all grown by then. So when he died, he left everything to his white children, 'cept this house. He left it in my great-grandmother's name, and it's been in my family ever since.

CANADA: So the white man's children ever find out? About their brown-skinned relatives.

MAGI: I don't know. The Van Dykes – they were Dutch. We used to watch *The Dick Van Dyke Show*, and my grandmother used to always say, "That there's your relative!" But we didn't pay her too much mind. More greens?

CANADA: If I eat another thing, I will truly burst. This was wonderful. Thank you. Thank you very much.

MAGI: You're more than welcome.

CANADA: When I was a boy, I used to love to sop the pot liquor.

MAGI: It's nearly the best part.

CANADA: You sure know the way to a man's heart.

MAGI: Haven't had any luck so far.

CANADA: Yet.

There is an awkward silence between them, after which they both start speaking at once.

MAGI: (*overlapping*) Well, I better get started with these dishes …

CANADA: (*overlapping*) I should go in and check on Sybil … Let me give you a hand.

MAGI: No, no, it's quite all right. I can handle this.

BILLIE enters.

CANADA: Billie! Marjorie was kind enough to share her dinner with me.

MAGI: Billie, come and have something to eat.

BILLIE: I'm not hungry. I heard voices. I need to go back and lay down … get some reading done.

MAGI: You can't have eaten anything for the day, girl.

BILLIE: I'm fine.

CANADA: What you need is a good meal inside you.

BILLIE: I said I was fine.

MAGI: I'll just take these things downstairs.

(*exits*)

CANADA: I'll make you some tea, okay.

BILLIE: I don't – don't need any tea. I don't want anything to eat. I'm fine. I'm sorry. I don't – don't – don't mean … to be like this … But I haven't seen you in God knows how long … And you just show up, and expect things to be all hunky dory.

Pause.

CANADA: Well, I'll be off then. (*goes for his coat*)

BILLIE: I'm sorry.

CANADA: Me too. (*heads for the door*)

BILLIE: And I am glad you came … Maybe this can be … you know … like a beginning of something … I don't know.

CANADA: I nearly came before … Two or three times … You know, when I heard. I wished your mother was here. I really wished for her … Her wisdom. I mean Beryl would know what to do. A girl needs her mother. And I know you didn't have her all those times … I mean, I couldn't tell you. What could I tell you? I kept seeing your face. It's your mother's face. You've got my nose. My mouth. But those eyes … The shape of your face … The way your head tilts to one side when you're thinking or just listening. It's all her. You've got her moods. I used to call them "her moods." Once 'bout every three months, on a Friday, when she'd have the weekend off, she'd come home from that hospital, take off her clothes, and lay down in her bed and stay there 'til Sunday afternoon. She'd say she'd done turned the other cheek so many times in the past little while, she didn't have no more smiles for anybody. She'd say, better she just face God and the pillow than shower me and the children with the evil she had bottled up inside her. See, if you spend too much time among white people, you start believing what they think of you. So I'd take you and Drew and we'd go visiting. We'd take the whole weekend and visit all the folks we knew, in a fifteen-mile radius ... When we'd get home, she'd have cleaned the house, washed the clothes and even made a Sunday dinner. And after I'd pluck the guitar ... And she'd start to sing ... And you'd dance ... You remember? You'd dance. You'd stomp on that floor like you were beating out some secret code to God or something ... I know you – we don't see eye to eye. I know you haven't wanted to see very much anything of me lately. But I've known you all your life. I carried you in my arms and on my back, kissed and spanked you when you needed, and I watched you start to talk, and learn to walk, and read and I just wanted to come ... I just wanted to come. And I know I can't make everything all right. I know. But I was there when you arrived in this world. And I didn't think there was space for a child, I loved your mother so much. But there you were and I wondered where you'd been all my life, like something I'd been missing and didn't know I'd been missing. And I don't know if you've loved anybody that long. But behind your mother's face you're wearing, I still see the girl who shrieked with laughter, and danced to the heavens sometimes ...

CANADA slowly approaches BILLIE. She does not move. He takes her in his arms. He holds her in his arms for a long time.

SCENE 6

Harlem, 1928: late summer – night. The strident movement of the strings is joined by the rising tempo of the distorted sound loop. HE and SHE are both in a tiny dressing room, as in the prologue. On a counter are a shaving brush, a straight-edged razor, greasepaint, and a top hat. HE wipes his face with a towel. SHE holds the handkerchief out to him. He does not take it. She lets it fall at his feet. After a few moments, he picks it up.

HE: (*referring to the handkerchief at first*) White, red, black, green, indigo ... What difference does it make? That makes no sense ... makes no difference. "If virtue no delighted beauty lack, / Your son-in-law is far more fair than black." Far more fair than black. I want ... I need to do this ... For my soul. I am an actor. I –

SHE: (*kindly*) A minstrel. A black minstrel ...

HE: (*places the towel on the counter beside the toiletries*) It's paid my way.

SHE: (*caresses the towel*) Stay, my sable warrior ... (*Her hand stumbles upon the razor.*)

HE: I'll not die in blackface to pay the rent. I am of Ira Aldridge stock. I am a classical man. I long to play the Scottish king. The Prince of Denmark. "The slings and arrows of outrageous ..." Or ... Or ... "There's a divinity that shapes our ends, / Rough-hew them how we will" ... Those words ... I love those words. They give me life. Mona sees my gift. She's cast me as the Prince of Tyre. She's breathed new life into a barren dream. She ... She ... She has a serene calmness about her. That smile ... I bet they named her Mona because even at birth she had that constant half-smile, like the *Mona Lisa*. Skin as smooth as monumental alabaster ... As warm as snow velvet.

SHE: (*exposes the blade*) My onyx prince ...

HE: Ooohh ...

SHE: (*approaches him from behind*) My tourmaline king ... (*leans her head on his back*)

HE: S'all right ...

SHE: My raven knight ...

She wraps her arms around him. He turns his head toward her.

HE: Oh sweet ...

SHE: My umber squire ...

HE: I wish ... I wish –

Her hand rises, the razor is poised, nearly touching the skin of his neck, just below his ear, within his peripheral vision.

SHE: My Cimmerian lord ...

He turns around, as if to see what she's holding, and in that turn his neck appears to devour the blade. The razor's shaft, at once hidden by his flesh, swiftly withdraws, leaving a rushing river of red like a scarf billowing around his neck and her hands. He yields to gravity.

SCENE 7

Harlem, the present: late summer – night. The plucked strings and the distorted audio loop have become even more dissonant. BILLIE is clutching the small red box.

MAGI: ... You know, Hakim has seven children, and he's never been married. Brother Hakim. Spot him at any street rally where the subject is prefaced by the words "Third World." He's the one with the Lumumba Lives button prominently displayed on his authentic kente cloth dashi – Billie? Billie, what's up? You don't look so good. *(pause)* Billie?

BILLIE: Sybil. I'm Sybil.

MAGI: That's what your daddy calls you.

BILLIE: Yes.

MAGI: Your daddy sure is one good-looking gentleman.

BILLIE: Trapped in history. A history trapped in me.

MAGI: I'm serious. I mean ... I wanna know if you mind? Really. You were still a little girl when your mama died.

BILLIE: I don't remember Beryl's funeral. I see my father dressed in black, sewing a white button onto his white shirt with an enormous needle. He attaches the button and knots the thread so many times it's like he's trying to hold on to more than just the button. Like he can't bear for anything else in his life to leave him.

MAGI: He's a nice man. Would you mind?

BILLIE: Am I nice?

MAGI: Billie, I bet you haven't eaten today.

BILLIE: Can you keep a secret?

MAGI: No, but that's never stopped you before.

BILLIE: Then sorry ...

MAGI: Okay, okay. I promise.

BILLIE: I am about to plunge into very dangerous waters. Give me your word.

MAGI: You're not going to do something stupid, now.

BILLIE: Your word?

MAGI: Yeh, okay.

BILLIE: I've drawn a line.

MAGI: A line? A line about what?

BILLIE: I'm returning the handkerchief – the one his mother give him. The one he gave to me when we first agreed to be together ...

MAGI: I don't understand.

BILLIE: I've concocted something ... A potion ... A plague of sorts ... I've soaked the handkerchief ... Soaked it in certain tinctures ... Anyone who touches it – the handkerchief, will come to harm.

MAGI: Now that is not a line, Billie, that is a trench!

BILLIE: I'm supposed to ...

MAGI: Billie, if this kind of stuff truly worked, Africans wouldn't be in the situation we're in now. Imagine all them slaves working magic on their masters – didn't make no difference. If it truly worked, I'd be married to a nice man, with three little ones by now. But if it makes you feel better –

BILLIE: He's going to marry her ... Officially ...

MAGI: I know ... I know. Remember, what goes around comes around. Karma is a strong and unforgiving force.

BILLIE: I haven't seen it affect white people too much.

MAGI: Is everything about white people with you? Is every living moment of your life eaten up with thinking about them. Do you know where you are? Do you know who you are anymore? What about right and wrong. Racism is a disease my friend, and your test just came back positive. You're so busy reacting, you don't even know yourself.

BILLIE: No, no, no ... It's about black. I love black. I really do. And it's revolutionary ... Black is beautiful ... So beautiful. This Harlem sanctuary ...... here. This respite ... like an ocean in the middle of a desert. And in my mirror, my womb, he has a fast-growing infestation of roaches. White roaches.

MAGI: Billie?

BILLIE: Did you ever consider what hundreds of years of slavery did to the African American psyche?

MAGI: What? What are you ...?

BILLIE: Every time someone mentions traditional values or the good old days – who exactly were those days good for?

The phone rings. BILLIE goes over to it. She sits on the bare floor but does not answer.

BILLIE: Jenny ... Is that you, Jenny. My beauty. My little girl. It's Sybil ... Auntie Sybil ... The woman who lives in the cave. (*laughs*)

MAGI: I'll get it for you.

BILLIE: (*picks up the receiver*) Yes, yes, I'm here. Oh, Othe ... Othello. I didn't recognize your voice. You sound ...... different. No. No, no, you can't pick it up. I mean – I've got it, yes. It's right here. No. No, I won't be in ... No, no. I haven't changed my mind. But – I mean ... I have to go ... Roaches. Yeh, blue roaches. Green roaches. So I have to go now. I – I just have to go. (*replaces the receiver*)

MAGI: He's coming over?

BILLIE: I don't want a Mona Lisa smile ...

MAGI: Oh Billie ... Billie, you're all in bits and pieces.

BILLIE: I know. I know. A tumour. Suddenly apparent, but it's been there, tiny, growing slowly for a long time. What kind of therapy to take? Chop it out? Radiate it? Let it eat me alive? I see roaches all around me. In me. Blue roaches. Green roaches. Aah! Get off! Get it off. I eat roaches. I pee roaches. Help! I'm losing ... I don't don't ... I'm falling ...

MAGI: Billie? Billie?

BILLIE: "I have a dream today."

MAGI: You had a dream?

BILLIE: "I have a dream that one day every valley shall be engulfed, every hill shall be exalted and every mountain shall be made low ..." oh ... oh ... "the rough places will be made plains and the crooked places will be made ..."

MAGI: (*overlapping*) It's gonna be all right, Billie. (*goes to the phone and dials*)

BILLIE: (*overlapping*) "... straight and the glory of the Lord shall be revealed and all flesh shall see it together."

MAGI: (*overlapping*) It's Magi. You all better get over here, now. No, no, no. NOW. All right. All right.

> MAGI *puts down the receiver and returns to* BILLIE. *She gently takes the red box from out of* BILLIE's *hands and places it on the mantel.*

BILLIE: (*overlapping*) "... This is our hope ..."

MAGI: (*overlapping*) It's gonna be all right. I know ... I know ...

BILLIE: (*overlapping*) "... With this faith we will be able to hew out of the mountain of despair a stone of hope ..."

MAGI: (*overlapping*) It's okay. It's okay. Let's start with a little step. Come on. Come with me. (*helps* BILLIE *up*) Come on ... Good. Let's get some soup into you. Warm up that frozen blood of yours. (*leads her to the door*) Warm up your insides. Come ... Come on ... Chase all the roaches out ...

> BILLIE *breaks loose of* MAGI *and rushes to the window.*
>
> MAGI *is no longer in the room.* OTHELLO *appears wearing a brightly coloured dashiki. He is inspecting a broom lying against the fridge. It is now fall, seven years earlier. Save for the broom and the fridge, the apartment is empty.*

BILLIE: Look ... Come, look ... You can see the Apollo from the window. I love it.

OTHELLO: Where?

BILLIE: Over there. See.

OTHELLO: Oh yeh – if I crane my neck.

BILLIE: I could find some lawn chairs and table and we'd have a city terrace.

OTHELLO: On the fire escape?

BILLIE: We'd have our own little balcony.

OTHELLO: Patio.

BILLIE: Terrace ...

OTHELLO: We could buy a house up here.

BILLIE: We can't afford to buy a house until I finish school. If I'm going to go to school full time this fall, like we agreed – you'd go to school, then I'd go to school – how can we afford a down payment on a house?

OTHELLO: I know. I know.

> *Pause.*

BILLIE: I love it. Don't you love it?

OTHELLO: I love you.

BILLIE: I love you and I love it.

OTHELLO: Think Chris Yago and Mona and the other faculty will feel uncomfortable coming up here ... for meetings and the like ...?

BILLIE: It's on the subway line.

OTHELLO: And boy do they need to take the journey. I'll take them on a cultural field trip – blow their minds.

BILLIE: I've longed for this sanctuary.

OTHELLO: I know what you mean.

BILLIE: Black boutiques.

OTHELLO: Black bookstores.

BILLIE: Black groceries.

OTHELLO: Filled with black doctors and dentists. Black banks.

BILLIE: Black streets teeming with loud black people listening to loud jazz and reggae and Aretha ... (*singing*) "There is a rose in Spanish Harlem."

He joins her.

BILLIE & OTHELLO: (*singing*) "A rose in black and Spanish Harlem. Da da da, da da da ..."

BILLIE: Maybe later we could buy a place on "strivers' row," that's where all the rich black folks live.

OTHELLO: Strivers' row.

BILLIE: Owned by blacks hued from the faintest gold to the bluest bronze. That's my dream.

OTHELLO: By then you'd have your Ph.D.

BILLIE: And a small lecturer's position at a prestigious Manhattan university. We might even have enough money to get a small house in the country, too.

OTHELLO: A big house in the country, too?

BILLIE: A big house with a white picket fence.

OTHELLO: On a rolling emerald hill.

BILLIE: I want two-point-five kids.

OTHELLO: (*kisses her lightly*) You're mad, you know that.

BILLIE: That makes you some kinda fool for loving me, baby.

OTHELLO: Let's do it. There's an old broom right over there. Wanna jump it with me? (*retrieves the broom*)

BILLIE: Are you asking me to m –

OTHELLO: Yes ... Yes, I am asking.

BILLIE: Yes ... (*silence*) Then yes.

> *OTHELLO kisses her. He places the broom in the middle of the floor. He takes BILLIE's hand. They stand in front of it.*

BILLIE: What will we use for rings?

OTHELLO: Think them old slaves had rings? Slave marriages were illegal, remember. This broom is more than rings. More than any gold. (*whispers*) My ancient love.

BILLIE: (*whispers*) My soul.

> *OTHELLO kisses her hand. The couple gaze at each other, preparing to jump over the broom. They jump. They hold each other. The landlady enters.*

MAGI: Oh – I'm sorry.

BILLIE: No, no. We were just ... just –

> *OTHELLO picks up the broom and places it to one side.*

OTHELLO: I think we'll take it.

MAGI: I didn't mean to rush you. I can give you another few minutes if you need to make good and sure?

BILLIE: I think we're sure. (*to OTHELLO*) You sure? (*to MAGI*) We're sure.

> *MAGI looks gravely at BILLIE. They are the only ones in the room. We are back in the present. MAGI carefully approaches BILLIE. BILLIE stares at where OTHELLO stood only moments ago.*

MAGI: Come on. Come with me. Come on ... Good. Let's get some soup into you. Warm up that frozen blood of yours. (*leads her to the door*) Warm up your insides. Come ... come on ... Chase all the roaches out ... One by one ... One by one ...

> *They exit.*

SCENE 8

> *Harlem, the present: late summer – afternoon. A lyrical rhapsody swings to the sound of a commentator describing the scene at the Million Man March. The apartment is virtually empty. CANADA is cleaning the kitchen, taking tubs and bags from out of the freezer. He gives them a brief once-over and then throws them into the trash. OTHELLO enters.*

OTHELLO: Billie? Billie?

CANADA: Othello! Othello, good to see you son. (*They shake hands.*) Good to see you.

OTHELLO: I didn't know ... When did you get here?

CANADA: A few days.

OTHELLO: Billie didn't say a word.

CANADA: Well, Billie's in ... she's ... Billie's not here right now.

OTHELLO: (*scanning the apartment*) Did she leave anything for me. An envelope ... A package – (*sees the red box on the mantel*) Oh. Maybe ... (*goes over to it*)

CANADA: Oh, she said no one was to touch that ... I'm supposed to throw it out.

OTHELLO: Great! (*opens the red box and takes out the handkerchief*) It's okay, this is it. It's mine. This is what I was looking for.

CANADA: I was just about to throw it in with the trash from the fridge.

OTHELLO: Just in time, huh?

CANADA: Yeh, some of this stuff's about ready to crawl out by itself.

OTHELLO: I can imagine.

CANADA: I swear, one thing had actually grown little feet.

OTHELLO: Well, Billie wasn't one for cleaning ... I guess neither of us was. (*an awkward silence between them*) Well ... I should be off. (*takes some keys out of his pocket and places them where the red box lay*)

CANADA: She tells me you're getting married.

OTHELLO: I do confess the vices of my blood.

CANADA: I'm real sorry it didn't work out ... Between you and Billie ... I mean ... I was hoping ...

OTHELLO: Yes. I know.

CANADA: She's my child, so –

OTHELLO: I know, I know.

CANADA: You young 'uns don't know the sweetness of molasses ... Rather have granulated sugar 'stead of a deep clover honey or cane-sugar juice from way into the Demerara. Better watch out for that refined shit. It'll kill ya. A slow kinda killin'. 'Cause it kills your mind first. So you think you living the life, when you been dead a long time.

Silence.

OTHELLO: Well, sir ... I should be somewhere.

CANADA: (*nodding*) Well, I hope we can catch up sometime ...

OTHELLO: (*goes to the door*) That would be great. Tell Billie I came by.

CANADA: I'll tell her that. She'll be glad to know.

OTHELLO: Good seeing you.

CANADA: You too ... son ... You too.

OTHELLO takes one last look at the apartment, takes out a tiny cellphone, and exits. CANADA is still for a few moments. From the hallway we hear OTHELLO.

OTHELLO: (*offstage*) Chris Yago, please.

CANADA returns to the fridge and continues to clean.

SCENE 9

Harlem, 1928: late summer – night. The music softly underscores the voice of Paul Robeson speaking about not being able to get decent acting roles in the United States, and how fortunate he feels to be offered a contract to play Othello in England. HE is alone. HE proceeds to cover his face in black grease paint. HE begins to speak, at first as if rehearsing.

HE: "It is most true; true, I have married her.

It is most ...

It is most true; true, I have married her.

For know, but that I love the gentle Desdemona,

(She) questioned me the story of my life

From year to year – the battles, sieges, fortunes,

That I have passed. These things to hear

Would Desdemona seriously incline;

But still the house affairs would draw her thence,

Which ever as she could with haste dispatch

She'd come again, and with a greedy ear

Devour up my discourse. Which I, observing,

Took once a pliant hour ...

And often did beguile her of her tears,

When I did speak of some distressful stroke

That my youth suffered ..."

In the background we can hear a children's song. HE begins to add white greasepaint to his lips, completing the mask of the minstrel.

"... My story being done,

She gave me for my pains a world of sighs.

She wished she had not heard it, yet she wished

That heaven had made her such a man. She thanked me,

She thanked me ...

She thanked me ...

She thanked me ..."

SCENE 10

Harlem, the present: late summer – night. A beryline blues improvisation of "Mama's Little Baby" cascades alongside a reading of the Langston Hughes poem "Harlem." AMAH sits beside BILLIE in the visitors' lounge of the psychiatric ward. AMAH is clearly saddened by BILLIE's state.

BILLIE: (*singing*)

> *... Step back Sal-ly, all night long.*
> *Strut-in' down the al-ley, al-ley, al-ley,*
> *Strut-in' down the al-ley, all night long.*

AMAH & BILLIE:

> *I looked over there, and what did I see?*
> *A big fat lady from Ten-nes-see.*

BILLIE gets up and begins to dance.

> *I bet you five dollars I can beat that man,*
> *To the front, to the back, to the side, side, side.*
> *To the front, to the back, to the side, side, side.*

The two women laugh.

BILLIE: I haven't done that in ... in years.

AMAH: I never knew that one – I just saw Jenny do it the other day.

BILLIE: I even remember the dance. (*singing under her breath*) "... Bet you five dollars I can beat that man ..."

AMAH: It's not so bad here.

BILLIE: You'd think the doctors at Harlem Hospital would be black. Especially in psychiatrics. Most of the nurses are black.

AMAH: But they're nice to you – the doctors?

BILLIE: They help. I don't – don't want any more pills. And that's okay. They don't really understand, though. I had this dream. Lucinda – she's my main doctor. Lucinda was sitting at the edge of a couch and I asked her a question. But she couldn't answer because her eyes kept flashing. Like neon lights. Flash, flash, flash. That was it. That was the dream. I knew it was important, but I didn't get it. And I told her. And she didn't get it either. But it gnawed away at me ... for days ... The flashing eyes. And that was it! The eyes were flashing blue. Her eyes were flashing blue. She could only see my questions through her blue eyes.

AMAH: Something in you really wants to heal.

BILLIE: Exorcism.

AMAH: Pardon?

BILLIE: Repossess.

AMAH: Self-possession?

BILLIE: I hate. I know I hate. And he loves. How he loves.

AMAH: Billie?

BILLIE: Why is that, you think?

AMAH: Some of us spend our entire lives making our own shackles.

BILLIE: Canada freedom come.

AMAH: And the experienced shackle-wearer knows the best polish for the gilt.

BILLIE: I wanna be free.

AMAH: It must be hard, though. I feel for him.

BILLIE: I'm not that evolved.

AMAH: Forgiveness.

BILLIE: Forgiveness ...

AMAH: If I don't forgive my enemy, if I don't forgive him, he might just set up house, inside me.

BILLIE: I just ... I – I despise – I know ... I know ... Moment by moment. I forgive him now. I hate – I love him so – I forgive him now. And now. (*She moves as if to speak, but stops herself.*) And I forgive him now.

AMAH: My time's up, sweetie.

BILLIE: I have a dream ...

AMAH: Sorry?

BILLIE: I had a dream ...

AMAH: Yes ... I know.

BILLIE: Tell Jenny ... Tell her for me ... Tell her that you saw me dancing.

AMAH: I will tell her.

BILLIE: And tell her ... Tell her that you heard me singing.

AMAH: I will.

BILLIE: And tell her ... I'll see her real soon.

AMAH: I will tell her, Billie. I will tell her.

AMAH kisses BILLIE on the cheek and begins to exit. CANADA enters.

BILLIE: (*in the background, singing softly*)

> *Betcha five dollars I can beat that man.*
> *To the front, to the back, to the side, side, side.*
> *To the front, to the back, to the side, side, side.*

CANADA: How's she doing?

AMAH: Mmm, so-so.

CANADA: Okay. Thanks.

AMAH: We'll really miss you when you go – back to Nova Scotia.

CANADA: Oh, I don't think I'm going anywhere just yet – least if I can help it. Way too much leaving gone on for more than one lifetime already.

BILLIE stops singing for a moment, then segues into a version of Aretha Franklin's "Spanish Harlem," more hummed than sung.

CANADA pats AMAH on the back. AMAH turns and exits. CANADA approaches BILLIE and sits down beside her.

Shortly, he joins her in the song. He rests his hand on hers.

After several moments the lights fade to black.

END

RONNIE BURKETT

(b. 1957)

Puppets and performance have gone together for millennia, and performing puppets appear in virtually every culture across the globe. From Balinese shadow puppets, Japanese *bunraku*, and the ceremonials of Northwest Coast First Nations to Italian *commedia dell'arte*, British *Punch and Judy* shows, and popular stage plays like *The Lion King* and *Avenue Q*, puppets have played an important role in the expressive history of live performance. During the past quarter-century, Ronnie Burkett has put his unique personal stamp on theatrical puppetry. He designs, builds, articulates, and interacts with his remarkable marionettes, tells their stories in the sophisticated scripts he writes, and animates them with his extraordinary skills as puppeteer and solo human performer. Breathtaking, exquisite, astonishing, brilliant – these are the adjectives regularly used to describe his work. Its quality and success have inspired the formation of other Canadian puppet theatres, notably Calgary's Old Trout Puppet Workshop. But Burkett's puppetry is in a league of its own. "Ronnie Burkett is one of the world's geniuses," writes Michael Feingold in New York's *Village Voice*. "Seeing his troupe every few years has just become a necessity of civilized theatregoing."

    Street of Blood is Burkett's most audacious play. Reviewing its premiere in the *Calgary Herald*, Martin Morrow lists some of its topics: "loss of religious faith, the Red Cross and the blood crisis, homophobia, the Holocaust, old Hollywood movies, terrorism, growing up gay, pedophilia, AIDS, vampire lore. Not to mention different recipes for jellied salads." He neglects to mention perhaps its most outrageous element: the appearance of Jesus, not embodied in a puppet character but played by Burkett himself, the puppeteer as God. *Street of Blood* is howlingly funny, deeply serious, and powerfully moving. "It feels like a masterpiece," says Canadian critic Robert Cushman, a man not given to excessive praise. "You don't expect a puppet play to be like this. You don't, unless you're very optimistic, expect much theatre of any kind to be like this."

    Ronnie Burkett was born in Lethbridge, Alberta, and grew up in Medicine Hat. He claims to have fallen in love with puppetry at age seven when he opened the *World Book Encyclopedia* to the letter *P* and read about legendary puppet masters Bil and Cora Baird. Becoming obsessed with the art, he began performing his own puppet shows around the province. He took a correspondence course from senior American puppeteer Martin Stevens, joined the Puppeteers of America, and at age fourteen attended the organization's festival in Michigan, meeting many of the masters from whom he would learn and on whose work he would initially model his own. Burkett found in puppetry a profound creative outlet as well as escape from the difficulties of being a gay teenager in a small, conservative prairie community.

After briefly studying musical theatre at Utah's Brigham Young University, he left for New York to work with Bil Baird's company. With the success of Jim Henson's *The Muppet Show*, puppetry in this era was all about TV. Burkett's work on a PBS children's special, *Cinderabbit*, earned him a regional Emmy Award in 1977. But after a few years, feeling the need to find his own theatrical style, Burkett moved back to Alberta, to Calgary, performing improvisational puppet shows in a punk club where he met other young artists like Denise Clark and Brad Fraser, who would soon reshape Calgary's theatre scene. His work, like theirs, was edgy, obscene, outrageous.

In a *Canadian Theatre Review* article, Liz Nicholls describes Burkett, in the mid-1980s, "sculpting, stringing and dressing the most exquisite marionettes the country had ever seen. He was giving them individual voices, setting them in motion, reinventing the marionette vocabulary to find a body language that was revealing, detailed and subtle ..." In 1986, he created his own company, the Ronnie Burkett Theatre of Marionettes, and for the next five years he performed on the newly established Canadian fringe festival circuit, and soon at major theatres across the country. Developing his substantial craft with these campy, jokey shows, Burkett also cemented his persona as "the bad boy of puppetry."

One element of his performance style was especially radical. All his mentors, Burkett recalls, "told me I must never, ever stand on stage, without masking, working the puppets. The marionette operator is always hidden, thereby creating a better illusion. So they said. I introduced the notion that if perhaps the puppeteer wasn't hidden, the audience would get beyond trying to figure out the technique of the show and ease more readily and quickly into the story" ("The Mentored Path"). Standing onstage with his puppets, himself and his technique completely visible to the audience, Burkett not only channels attention to the story but paradoxically makes the puppets seem more expressively alive, more breathtakingly real. "I deny the existence of a puppeteer," Michael Feingold insists. "This is a great ensemble of actors."

One Yellow Rabbit company's Blake Brooker wrote *Fool's Edge* (1986), a *commedia*-style puppet musical performed by Burkett and his marionettes. But soon Burkett took the *auteur* route; like Robert Lepage, he began to write, design, and perform his own shows. Additionally, he was—and remains—master builder. His *Virtue Falls* (1988), a pseudo-Victorian, operatic melodrama, featured a Mountie named Dick Swell. A short, unhappy stint doing a George Bernard Shaw puppet show, *Shakes Vs. Shav*, at the Shaw Festival in 1989 inspired *The Punch Club* (1990), in which a traditional misogynistic *Punch and Judy* show is raided by a radical feminist with an Uzi. *Awful Manors* (1991), described by Nicholls as "a 43-puppet gothic Victorian murder mystery romance musical with pipe organ accompaniment," includes a Canada Council officer named Phyllis Stein.

Tinka's New Dress (1994) marked a radical change of direction. Inspired by a passage in Baird's *The Art of the Puppet* about Czech puppeteers carrying out underground performances during the Nazi occupation, Burkett created a powerful, heartfelt political drama about those artists – a play that also included a long improvisational segment that allowed him to indulge his penchant for bawdy, campy comedy. *Tinka* was Burkett's breakout show. Opening at the Manitoba Theatre Centre and touring for the next eight years, it received six Dora Award nominations in Toronto, winning two, as well as five Elizabeth Sterling Haynes Awards in Edmonton, including Outstanding Performance by a Lead Actor for Burkett himself, a remarkable affirmation of that aspect of his artistry. *Tinka* also won an off-Broadway Obie Award and a UNIMA–USA Citation for Excellence in the Art of Puppetry at the Henson International Festival of Puppet Theatre in New York. It received the *Evening Herald* Award for Best International Show at the Dublin Theatre Festival and the Critics' Award at the Melbourne Festival, where *Tinka* was "retired." All Burkett's subsequent plays have had a limited lifespan, after which he no longer performs them.

Old Friends (1996), a wordless children's play co-produced by Manitoba Theatre for Young People, won the Chalmers Canadian Play Award for Young Audiences. *Street of Blood* (1998) and *Happy* (2000) followed, those plays forming, with *Tinka's New Dress*, what Burkett calls the Memory Dress Trilogy. *Happy*, a play about grief, opened at Toronto's du Maurier World Stage Festival, won best production and best actor awards in both Calgary and Edmonton, and played in Germany and the U.K., where it was retired in 2003.

Now living in Toronto, Burkett wrote *Provenance* (2003), in which a Canadian student's quest for beauty and the historical origins of a painting leads her to a Vienna brothel. *Provenance* opened at Edmonton's Theatre Network (winning the Sterling Award for Outstanding New Play), then toured across Canada and on to the U.K., Austria, Australia, Sweden, and Germany before its 2005 retirement. *10 Days on Earth* premiered at Toronto's Canadian Stage in 2006, toured Western Canada, and played Australia, New Zealand, Austria, the U.K., and Russia. A heartbreaking play about a mentally challenged middle-aged man and the death of the mother with whom he lives, *10 Days on Earth* won Burkett another UNIMA-USA Citation of Excellence and was retired in 2007.

Billy Twinkle: Requiem for a Golden Boy (2008) opened at Edmonton's Citadel Theatre and played across Canada, the U.K., and Australia through 2010, winning Burkett his fourth UNIMA-USA Citation of Excellence; his third was for *Street of Blood*. Like *Street of Blood*, *Billy Twinkle* is autobiographically based, the tale of a cruise ship puppeteer in mid-life crisis and the ghost of his dead mentor. In performance, Burkett manipulated the marionette of puppeteer Billy as Billy operated tiny marionettes of his own. *Penny Plain* (2011) also premiered at the Citadel and toured Canada. Burkett calls it "an apocalyptic gothic comedy." His take on the collapse of civilization includes talking dogs, American survivalists, and the puppeteer Geppetto from *Pinocchio*.

The Daisy Theatre premiered at Toronto's Luminato Festival in 2013, followed by a Canadian tour. With music and lyrics by John Alcorn and vignettes written by ten other Canadian playwrights including Daniel MacIvor and Joan MacLeod, *The Daisy Theatre* is an improvisational comedy cabaret modelled on the underground Czech puppet shows that were the subject of *Tinka's New Dress*. *The Daisy Theatre* stars puppets from Burkett's previous plays, including Edna Rural and Esmé Massengill from *Street of Blood*.

In addition to his many individual play awards, Burkett has received the Calgary Freedom of Expression Award, the President's Award for Outstanding Contribution to the Art of Puppetry from the Puppeteers of America, the Herbert Whittaker / Canadian Theatre Critics Award for Outstanding Contribution to Canadian Theatre, and the Canadian Institute for Theatre Technology Award for Technical Merit. In 2009, he won the Siminovitch Prize – at the time, Canada's richest and most prestigious theatre award. The only person ever nominated in all three categories (Playwriting, Direction, and Design), Burkett won the Siminovitch for Design.

Street of Blood had its premiere at Manitoba Theatre Centre, played Calgary, Edmonton, and Toronto, the Henson International Festival of Puppet Theatre in New York, Stockholm, Brighton, Manchester, and Glasgow, where it was retired in 2002. It won five Betty Mitchell Awards in Calgary for best production, performance, original music, set and costume design. Burkett also won the Elizabeth Sterling Haynes Award in Edmonton for his costumes. The play received a Floyd S. Chalmers Canadian Play Award in Toronto and the GLAAD Media Award for Outstanding Theater Production (Broadway and Off-Broadway) in New York. The reviews were typically glowing: "stage artistry of the highest order" (Morrow), "breathtaking artistry" (Friedlander), "simply exquisite, as near to perfection as one could ask" (Brown). The *New York Times*' Ben Brantley was awed by Burkett's design and technique: "It's not just the finely detailed appearance of the marionettes that astonishes; it is also Mr. Burkett's ability to endow them with such physical eloquence."

Street of Blood features thirty-nine individual marionettes, seventeen alone for Edna Rural and Esmé Massengill, who appear in many different costumes at different ages. The set contains three separate acting areas, each with three levels. In a departure from his previous technique, Burkett "long strung" his marionettes and operated them from *above*, rather than standing with them on the same level. This locates his Jesus (indicated by a lighting special on his face and a "Techno Jesus" musical cue) above the earthly fray, and gives added power to those moments when, as Jesus or Stanley Rural or a rapist, Burkett joins the marionette characters down on their level or violently hauls them up to him.

In his typically baroque script Burkett mixes radically different styles and tones. He plays for broad laughs with campy double entendres while pursuing serious storylines, and alternates between harsh realism and poignant sentiment. At one level this is an AIDS play, written at the height of the epidemic in politically conservative Alberta, citing the Canadian Red Cross scandals in which people contracted HIV through transfusions of tainted blood, and evoking the memorial AIDS quilts that were both inspirational and melancholy features of the 1990s. Note Edna's ironic refrain: "If there's one thing I am, it's positive."

At another level the play is Eden Urbane's quest for self-reconciliation. The lonely gay boy, brutally rejected by his father, turns to Hollywood fantasy for escape, then channels his rage into terrorism, and finally comes home to find forgiveness in an extraordinary scene involving his mother, a vampire, and Jesus. The autobiographical parallels between Ronnie Burkett's life and Eden Urbane's are too many to ignore (though maybe not the terrorism or the vampires). "Eden is me without the therapy," Burkett told Liz Nicholls.

Although Jesus may be the most controversial character (he gets a hard time from many of the others; called a liar, a hypocrite, a pain in the ass, and worse), and Eden and the vampire actors may be flashier, the heart of the play is gentle, modest, old-fashioned Edna Rural. Cushman calls her "one of the great characters of modern drama ... a latter-day Mrs. Alving from Ibsen's *Ghosts*." Nicholls writes: "The moment when Edna relives her wedding day, with its hints of sexual disappointment, will make you hold your breath. The flashback to the moment when Stanley feeds her bacon and eggs as they confront the sadness of her infertility will bring tears to your eyes." Lord love a duck, as Edna would say. She is only the most quietly brilliant of the many extraordinary characters Ronnie Burkett brings vividly to life in *Street of Blood*.

Street of Blood

Ronnie Burkett

Street of Blood premiered at Manitoba Theatre Centre, Winnipeg, on April 8, 1998, produced by Rink-A-Dink Inc. / Ronnie Burkett Theatre of Marionettes, with the following company:

Written and Performed by Ronnie Burkett
Marionettes Designed and Built by
    Ronnie Burkett
Costumes and Set Design by Ronnie Burkett
Music and Sound Design by Cathy Nosaty
Lighting Design by Bill Williams
Stage Managed by Terri Gillis

CHARACTERS

EDNA RURAL, *a prairie widow*
DOLLY, *Edna's dog*
EDEN URBANE, *a karaoke-singing gay terrorist*
ESMÉ MASSENGILL, *a faded Hollywood vampire*
JESUS, *Son of God*
SPANKY BISHOP, *a vampire actor*
UTA HÄAGEN-DAZ, *a silent-screen star vampire*
FLUFFER, *the stage manager*
DON DIVINE, *a retired veterinarian*
OGDEN RAMSAY, *Eden's childhood friend*
CORA JEAN PICKLES, *xylophonist for The Turnip*
    Corners Ladies Orchestrale
TIBBY HARBRECHT, *town busybody and drummer*
WINNIE WISMER, *pianist*
GRETA DEBOER, *guitarist*
ARMINA PHILPOTT, *clarinetist*

SETTING

The fictitious town of Turnip Corners, Alberta. The present [late 1990s].

NOTES ON STAGING

"Bridge" refers to three modified marionette stage catwalks above the three main acting areas stage left, centre stage, and stage right. They are three feet above deck level, each four feet wide, with a two-foot gap between them that Ronnie can straddle to move from one to the other. Most of the marionettes are "long strung," meaning the strings allow the marionette control to be held from this bridge height rather than the standard (Theatre of Marionettes) practice of both Ronnie and puppet being on the same deck level. The play features only a few short-strung marionettes, specifically the young Esmé figures for the film flashbacks.

"Gallows" indicates a system used to hang a marionette onstage. These are steel rods bent into right angles and inserted in pre-drilled holes across the leaning rail, which is slightly lower than Ronnie's waist when he is standing on the bridge. This enables him to hang four or five marionettes in one area at a time, either for group scenes or to leave characters in position while working at another area. "Control" refers to the marionette control to which the strings of the puppet are attached.

The set is primarily exposed steel with a painted wooden floor and three decorative panels onstage composed of inlaid wood, copper, brass, and sheet metal. The panels front the three bridge towers and are three feet high (deck to top of Ronnie's catwalk "floor") by four feet wide. These are the three acting areas, and each represents one of the three main characters (although they are also used for various flashbacks and other scenes). Stage right is Eden Urbane's area, the panel front featuring a prominent sheet metal triangle painted "Pride Pink," distressed and overwashed to cut the colour intensity. Centre stage is Edna Rural's area; the panel features an inlay of sheet metal cross-painted "Red Cross

Red." Stage left is Esmé Massengill's area, the inlay showing a metal star painted yellow gold (distressed and overwashed).

Behind each panel are frames that hide special prop puppets such as the oversize "television face" of young Spanky Bishop or Eden on the cross. The stage-right and stage-left panels both live in tracks on the edge of their bridge towers and can be raised and locked into position, revealing the settings or figures within. The centre-stage panel lowers like a drawbridge, and the reverse side of the panel becomes the floor of Edna Rural's house. Edna's wingback chair is attached to the inside panel or "floor" and lowers with the panel each time the drawbridge comes down. When the drawbridge is lowered, we are instantly in Edna's living room.

All scenic shifts and changes, such as panels in front of the acting areas moving up and down or the band moving in and out, are performed manually by Ronnie or the stage manager.

The deck is a foot above the stage floor. The main area of the deck is wood, painted to resemble (marionette scale) floor planks in stains of oak, sage, and browned purple. The tracks for the bandstands echo the look of train tracks running across the width of the acting area. The sides of the deck and the three entrance points are sheet metal. Behind the acting area and bridge towers is an upstage pass-through area with no decking. At the eight-foot height is a hanging rail for marionettes, most of which are hung offstage. The top of this rail is painted black with highway lanes for the final image in the show. The back of each bridge tower also has hanging rails for the main characters and their duplicates (that is, most of the Esmé puppets are hung on the back of the stage-left bridge tower). On the top three and a half feet of the back wall is a mural of a grain elevator and prairie horizon in the same materials of wood, copper, sheet metal, brass, and steel-mesh screening, all rusted and overwashed to cut intensity.

Props and furniture either live under each bridge tower or on the two side bridges (which are additional to the three main acting bridges). The side bridges serve as structural bracing for the deck and back wall as well as points for the stage manager to climb up and down from the upstage passage. Since all puppets and props are contained within the framework of the set, there is no need for any offstage activity or storage during the performance.

The play is performed solely by Ronnie Burkett. Stage manager Terri Gillis is onstage throughout, calling sound and lighting cues from a wireless headset as well as doing pre-sets of scenes and passing marionettes to and from Ronnie.

When a number appears after a character's name in the stage directions, such as "Edna #3," it indicates a character represented by duplicate marionettes. The same character in a different costume or at a different age requires a separate figure. Esmé Massengill, for example, is represented at three different ages and numerous costume changes by eleven different marionettes.

Cathy Nosaty's score and sound design and Bill Williams's lighting design are integral to the overall design and performance, although sound and lighting notes within this text are referred to only when necessary for the reader.

The play is performed without intermission.

At the five-minute call, Ronnie and the stage manager walk onstage and climb onto the bridge. House lights remain up in their pre-set level. As the audience continues to enter the theatre, Ronnie walks each member of the band – "The Turnip Corners Ladies Orchestrale" – onstage. Each of the Orchestrale members enters separately and "tunes up," the disjointed musical sounds pre-recorded as separate tracks.

The bandstand is actually two separate areas, stage right and stage left. These are two small wagons, which can move across the stage to be joined, or which can slide independently. Stage left houses the piano and xylophone; stage right holds the other three instruments and players.

The Orchestrale is composed of five elderly women, all dressed in faded finery. First to enter is WINNIE WISMER. She walks onstage from the alley between stage-right bridge and side tower and shuffles to centre, where she addresses the audience.

WINNIE: Ladies and gentlemen, the performance will begin in five minutes. There's no intermission, dears, so if you have to piddle, please go now. Thank you.

She turns and shuffles toward the stage-left band area. She sits on the piano bench, assisted by the stage manager, and plunks out a few notes. WINNIE's control is hung from a gallows rod attached to the bandstand (not the bridge) and she is left seated at the piano.

Next in is GRETA DEBOER, who enters from stage left carrying her guitar. She makes her way to the stage-right bandstand, tunes up, and is hung from a gallows.

Miss ARMINA PHILPOTT enters with her clarinet from the alley between the centre-stage and stage-right bridges. She is also walked to the stage-right bandstand, where she warms up and is suspended.

Mrs. TIBBY HARBRECHT enters from the alley between the stage-right bridge and side tower and makes her way to the drums, stage right. She sits behind them and has a go.

The last member of the band to enter (from the alley between the stage-right bridge and side tower) is CORA JEAN PICKLES. She walks to the stage-left bandstand.

Once CORA JEAN has reached the xylophone, it is curtain. House lights and pre-set fade slowly as a lighting special on WINNIE at the piano, stage left, cross-fades up. She begins to play a short piano overture version of "Behold, the Blessed Prairie."

EDNA #1 walks onstage and addresses the audience, standing in front of her panel centre stage.

EDNA: Hello, and welcome to Turnip Corners, Alberta. I'm Edna. Edna Rural. Mrs. Stanley Rural. Now, I'm not an actress. Lord love a duck, no! I'm no one special. I'm just a silly old biddy in a Sears housedress, just like you. Well then, let's begin.

The stage-left bandstand tracks in to centre stage left.

WINNIE: Edna!

EDNA: Oh, hello Winnie dear! That's Winnie Wismer, our pianist.

WINNIE: Edna! What are you doing?

EDNA: Nothing. I'm starting.

WINNIE: Aren't you forgetting something?

EDNA: No. Probably. Yes. What?

WINNIE: Them. (*She looks to the audience.*)

EDNA: No, I've been talking to them, dear.

WINNIE: I mean them and us.

EDNA: Oh yes, of course. That. My apologies. When you're ready, Winnie.

WINNIE: Thank you, Edna. We're ready.

The bandstands track into position centre stage during EDNA's monologue.

EDNA: Ladies and gentlemen, please rise for our national anthem, as played by The Turnip Corners Ladies Orchestrale. Now I'm not kidding, dears. Stand up. Come on. Pretend you're at a hockey game. We're not going any further until we get this over with. This wouldn't be a problem if we were in the United States of America. They might be a war-hungry bunch of bullies, but at least they're patriotic. Now please, stand up! All right, ladies, you may begin.

The ladies begin a spirited, if somewhat awful, version of "O Canada." The audience is encouraged – or bullied, if need be – to sing along. At the conclusion the bandstand splits and returns to far stage right and stage left.

EDNA: Thank you, dears. You may be seated. Well, let's not stand out here. Come on inside.

EDNA's centre-stage panel is lowered, revealing her living room. She sits in her chair. The stage manager places the dog, DOLLY, on the floor by EDNA.

There, that's better. And you have my every assurance that "O Canada" will stand as the sole bit of audience participation for the evening. There will be no singing of "God Save the Queen" at show's end. Lord love a duck, no! I'm off the Royal Family. A bunch of inbred yahoos who can't keep their knickers on straight, if you ask my opinion. Now, I don't blame the Queen. It's hard for a woman to have a full-time job and raise a family, especially when you're married to a layabout la-di-da like Philip, so it's not her fault that she's raised a horsey girl, a fat boy, a fruitcake, and a fairy. No, the Queen's had her hands full, not to mention having to haul her mum and her drunk sister around with her everywhere and all the time. Lord love a duck, that's enough to make anyone a sourpuss with a purse. They had a chance in Diana, and look how they messed that up. Poor Princess Di. I loved that little gal. She took all my risks for me. Too bad the Queen had her murdered in Paris. But none of us, not even the Queen herself, ever know the saints when they're amongst us, do we?

Listen to me! Lord love a duck, I barely know you and I'm talking your ears off. Who am I to talk about Her Majesty the Queen of England?! Who gives a tiddly-boo what I think? I'm just a silly old biddy in a Sears housedress, that's who.

She looks at the dog on the floor beside her.

Isn't that right, Dolly? Poor Dolly, my little Crazydoll. You're not doing too well, are you dear? Pretty soon it'll be time for Saint Diana to gather you into her angel arms and take you to your reward, too.

The stage manager enters and places a section of quilting into EDNA's hands.

Thank you, dear.

Stage manager exits.

Local girl, comes in to help out every now and then. We grow 'em big around here! Although I don't think her marriage prospects are very good. She's been running with a queer crowd lately. Anyways, where was I? Oh yes, speaking of the great beyond, you know what my idea of heaven is? Heaven is a place where you don't worry about money. Ever. Funny how important we make it down here though. I can't honestly remember a day in my adult life when I haven't worried about money. Did I have enough? If I bought this or that, would it throw us off the precarious balance known as getting by and into the pit of eternal debt? Every time I bought myself something, like this dress for instance, it became a question as to whether or not I was worth spending money on. That's been my whole life.

Oh, I know what you're thinking. How on earth does this silly old biddy in a Sears housedress know she's going to heaven? Well my dears, there's no guarantee whatsoever that I will see the Pearly Gates. But I've fed my family three meals a day all these years on a strict budget. I've done more exotic things with macaroni than most women would ever even dream of. And I've worried about money for fifty-one years of my married life. Lord love a duck, that's got to count for something, I'm sure of it. And if there's one thing I am, it's positive.

Light level on her area fades out. Music transitions in. Lights come up stage right as Ronnie places EDEN #1

in front of his panel. The lighting is very dream-like. Suspended around him are clear spheres, each containing a fetus or baby.

EDEN: I've been dreaming of this. I've been dreaming of babies. Really. All these babies, floating. And I'm with them. Not one of them, but there. Seeing things from their point of view. We're floating ... inside. Something. Somewhere. And it's always the same. Whenever we start coming out, it ends. A flash of light too bright, walls of skin – thighs, I think – and then ... And then I can't remember anything. Just that same dream. Over and over.

The baby spheres swing out of the playing area. Light changes to reality.

I got a letter. No return address. No name. Just a note really. Addressed to me, Eden Urbane, care of the Princess of Wales Hospital. I wonder how she even knew to reach me here. Maybe she's been watching me. Maybe she had a private investigator tail me. Cool. How sick and exhilarating to think that she's seen me. That she knows who I am. Well, of course she knows me. Well, not really.

Anyway, now it's my turn. My turn to finally see her. My mother. Not my mother that you've just met, not Edna, that's my mum. My birth mother. The one I've never met. She wants to meet me. All the letter said was, "Turnip Corners. Meet me there. I'm waiting. Your real mother." She wants to meet me. Maybe I'll finally find out what happened after that flash of light. Shit.

Lights out on EDEN and slow fade up on EDNA's area centre stage. Crossing to the centre bridge, Ronnie knocks on the metal siding of the tower. This surprises EDNA.

EDNA: Oh dear, I've pricked myself!

TIBBY: (*offstage*) Edna, have you heard the news?

EDNA: Just a minute, Tibby dear. Oh darn, I'm bleeding.

TIBBY: (*enters*) Can't stay long, Edna, just thought I'd pop in with the news.

EDNA: Cup of coffee, Tibby?

TIBBY: No time, Edna. Gotta spread the word!

EDNA: What word is that?

TIBBY: Two words, Edna. Esmé Massengill. Esmé Massengill is coming to Turnip Corners! Today! She'll be here today!

EDNA: Esmé Massengill the movie star?

TIBBY: The one and only!

Eden and fetus. Photo courtesy Ronnie Burkett Theatre of Marionettes

EDNA: Lord love a duck. I thought she was dead.

TIBBY: That's what the tabloids will have you think, but no. She's alive, she's making a comeback, and she's making it here!

EDNA: Why on earth would anyone come to Turnip Corners?

TIBBY: She's doing a new musical, and they always work the bugs out in Canada before hitting Broadway.

EDNA: You don't say. (*She looks down at her lap.*) Oh, Lord love a duck! I've bled all over my quilting!

TIBBY comes over to EDNA, who is still seated.

TIBBY: It's an interesting design though.

EDNA: It's a special quilt.

TIBBY: No, I mean the blood. It's created quite a picture.

EDNA: Picture?

TIBBY: Yeah, look. It's like ...

EDNA: ... a face. Tibby, do you see what I see?

TIBBY: Edna, you're right.

EDNA: It is a face. There's no mistaking it. It's him, Tibby. It's the face of ...

TIBBY: Mr. Wayne Newton! Bud and I saw him in Las Vegas two years ago.

EDNA: Not Wayne Newton. Tibby, it's him. It's the Son of God!

TIBBY: Edna, that doesn't look a thing like Elvis.

EDNA: Not Elvis, Tibby! It's Jesus.

TIBBY: (*looks again*) Jesus Christ, Edna!

EDNA: Exactly!

TIBBY: Edna, your eyes are strained. That's not Jesus.

EDNA: It *is*, Tibby. It's him. (*She holds up the quilt square.*) It's the Shroud of Turnip Corners.

A soft hint of the "Techno Jesus" music sting (to come later) as a special (the "Jesus special") comes up on Ronnie's face. For the audience, this will be the "shroud" image. For EDNA, the face is still on her quilt square. Ronnie talks to EDNA.

JESUS: Hello, Edna.

EDNA: Oh, don't talk to me, Jesus. Not now. It's too late.

JESUS: Please, Edna. You're bleeding.

EDNA: Go away!

TIBBY: Edna Rural!

EDNA: Not you, Tibby dear, him.

She indicates the quilt square. The Jesus special on Ronnie's face fades out.

TIBBY: Edna, everyone knows that Jesus only appears to Catholics, kooks, and cripples. You're just a creative bleeder, that's all.

EDNA: Yes, Tibby, of course.

TIBBY: You know, Edna, you really should think about coming on a cruise with me and Bud this winter. They're loads of fun.

EDNA: I'm a prairie girl, Tibby. The only sea I need are those fields out there.

TIBBY: Edna, you sit in this house night and day. We all thought that when ...

EDNA: Please Tibby, don't!

TIBBY: Well, Edna, we thought that when you moved into town you'd use your time to do more things.

EDNA: I do plenty, Tibby. I have my quilt to keep me busy.

TIBBY: You've been working on that quilt for years.

EDNA: It's a big quilt, Tibby!

TIBBY starts off, then turns to EDNA.

TIBBY: Suit yourself, Edna, but I don't think that's the face of Jesus. He's got more important things to do than have quilting bees with you.

TIBBY leaves and is hung backstage. Above EDNA, on the bridge, the Jesus special comes up again on Ronnie's face.

JESUS: Edna.

EDNA: You're wasting your time, Jesus. You'd be better off appearing to someone else. Someone who ...

JESUS: Yes, Edna?

EDNA: Has time for this. For you.

JESUS: Edna ...

EDNA: I said not now, thank you very much!

The Jesus special on Ronnie's face fades out.

I'd better phone Eden. This is very important. He'll make a pilgrimage home when he hears the news. He's always been Esmé Massengill's biggest fan.

She stands and exits. Lights down on EDNA's area as music transition begins. The drawbridge of the centre-stage panel is raised and lights come up on

EDEN's area stage right. It is still somewhat dream-like, although the baby spheres have been removed.

EDEN: Do you remember that old Esmé Massengill movie from the 1950s called *Pompeii Afternoon*? She played Mamie Idaho, a spinster librarian who found love in the ruins with a penniless count, played by Italian heartthrob Carlo Biscotti. He was one of those barrel-chested, foreign daddy types, but I never spent much time looking at him. No way. I was too busy looking at Esmé's clothes! Even playing a spinster from Bumfuck, USA, she looked fabulous! Listen to me. I can't believe I just used the word "fabulous." It's so fag hag.

Anyway, there was that scene, y'know the one I mean? Her big acting scene where she was standing up on some mound of rocks or ruins or something, and she extends her hand to the count ...

*Music underscoring begins with seagulls manipu-lated on a pole by the stage manager in front of the centre-stage tower. Ronnie crosses to the centre-stage bridge and walks **YOUNG ESMÉ #1** as **MAMIE IDAHO** onto the upper playing area / catwalk. She wears a 1950s day ensemble and "acts" alone to the unseen COUNT.*

ESMÉ / MAMIE: Oh, Count Calabrese, it's glorious up here. Why, you can see everything and it's all so old! Come see, Count.

COUNT / MALE VOICE: Mamie, please, let us not be so formal after all we have shared, all we have tasted, all we have explored. Call me ... darling.

ESMÉ / MAMIE: Yes. Darling! Oh my darling Count, join me here and feast on these splendid ruins.

COUNT / MALE VOICE: Oh, Mamie, I'm coming!

ESMÉ / MAMIE: I never knew that life could be so delicious. All I've ever known are the love stories in books back in my lonely library. But I've been so hungry. Hungry for real love, with a real man. Be with me now, darling.

COUNT / MALE VOICE: Yes, Mamie, but it's so hard!

ESMÉ / MAMIE: Don't struggle so. Let me help. My hand has a firm grip.

EDEN: And then, just as she bent over for the count, Mamie Idaho lost her footing, and fell ...

The ESMÉ marionette falls to the floor, centre stage.

ESMÉ / MAMIE: Aaaaagghhhhhhhhhhhhhhhhhh-hhhhhhh ...

She hits the floor and lies dying.

COUNT / MALE VOICE: Mamie! Darling! Speak to me!

ESMÉ / MAMIE: There is nothing for me to say, darling. Our love is forever written in these ruins.

COUNT / MALE VOICE: Mamie!

ESMÉ / MAMIE: *Arrivederci*, baby.

She expires and is temporarily hung onstage. Ronnie crosses back to the stage-right bridge to manipulate EDEN.

EDEN: And then she died. A Hollywood death. Looking – well there's no other word for it – fabulous!

Light out centre stage. The stage manager clears the young ESMÉ marionette.

And that's how I feel every time I go onstage. Well, saying I go onstage is a bit of a stretch, I know, but it's how I feel when I perform in these places. Hospitals, hospices, nursing homes. Like I'm somehow extending a hand, yet falling. Into their despair. Their sadness. Okay, I know, they don't ask me to sing, and they don't ask me to feel sad for them, but these dying people need me. I think. I know I need them. Because I'm like Mamie Idaho back in her library. Just living my life through the fictions of other people's lives. And the sadder those lives are, the better.

He exits stage right. Hospital sounds. Dream light cross-fades to his show light. The stage manager places a mirror ball and a stool onstage. EDEN #2 enters from the stage-left side of the stage-right tower. He is dressed in a powder-blue tuxedo jacket and has a microphone in his hand.

EDEN: Good afternoon, ladies and gentlemen. How's everyone doing today? Obviously not so well, or you wouldn't be in a place like this!

"Bad joke" drum sting.

My name is Eden Urbane and I'm the songbird of the sick bay, the crooning chanteur of the ICU, the karaoke king of the cancer ward! I'm here to sing you a few tunes and hopefully bring a little smile to your face. My, what a well-dressed crowd we have today! That's a lovely colostomy bag, Mrs. Spudnicki, but trust me hon, you'll never find shoes to match!

Another drum sting.

Thank you! Allow me to introduce the band.

The stage manager places a boom box on the stool. EDEN looks at the mic.

Mind if I call you Mike? With a head like that, you can call me anything!

Drum sting.

Reminds me of a date I had once. But seriously folks, it's my great honour to be in this fine public health care facility today with all ... (*counts quickly*) eleven of you. Ladies and gentlemen, I would now like to perform for you the love theme from the 1962 horror classic *House of Pain*, in which the incomparable Miss Esmé Massengill played Lotta Payne, a reclusive widow living in a strange hilltop house. Maestro, if you please.

Music intro starts. EDEN sings.

> "HOUSE OF PAIN"
>
> *Your love is scaring me to death*
> *I'm speechless*
> *Scaring me to death*
> *And darling*
> *It's cutting off my breath*
>
> *Your love is making me turn blue*
> *I'm gasping*
> *Making me turn blue*
> *And darling*
> *Strictly entre nous*
> *I love this*
> *I'm blue*
> *And scared by love*
>
> *Yes, my heart has become a house of pain*
> *Each room a prison, a torture cell*
> *This sweet paradise is also my hell*
> *I return to again and again*
> *Yes, my heart has become a house of pain*
> *I should flee, but why bother trying*
> *Why can't you see, my darling, I'm dying*
> *To live in your house of pain*

Lights out. Ronnie hangs EDEN #2 backstage and crosses to stage-left bridge. During this, he continues to speak as EDEN on the musical playout.

Thank you! What a wonderful crowd. My name is Eden Urbane with Karaoke Memory Lane and I'll be performing for you all afternoon.

Lights up on ESMÉ's area stage left. The panel is not raised. In front of it, posed in tableau, are (left to right) UTA HÄAGEN-DAZ, SPANKY BISHOP #1, and FLUFFER, all hung from the bridge or gallows by the stage manager during EDEN's patter and song. There are several old-style trunks and suitcases in front of them.

SPANKY: Oy. This is some place, this Turnip Corners. I haven't seen a town so small since ... well, come to think about it, I've never seen a town this small.

UTA: *Alter Wichser!* [Old jerk-off!] *Du bist ein Peniskopf!* [You're a dickhead!]

FLUFFER: What did she say, Mr. Bishop?

SPANKY: I believe she just called me an old dickhead.

FLUFFER: Oh no, oh no, oh no, that's terrible, Mr. Bishop!

SPANKY: It's all right, Fluffer. Under the circumstances I would tend to agree with her.

UTA: *Verfickte Hurenscheisse!* [Overfucked whore's shit!]

FLUFFER: Mr. Bishop?

SPANKY: Not worth repeating, my dear, not worth repeating. Now Fluffer my darling, why don't you go see what's holding Miss Massengill up ... other than her legs. I love that joke! Get it?

FLUFFER laughs, then pauses.

FLUFFER: Um, no, not really, Mr. Bishop.

FLUFFER exits in the alley between stage-left and centre-stage bridge towers.

SPANKY: Oy.

TIBBY enters from the alley between stage-left and centre-stage bridge towers, handed to Ronnie by the stage manager. She excitedly makes her way toward SPANKY and UTA.

TIBBY: Oh! Thespians! Hello hello hello. Welcome to Turnip Corners! We are so thrilled to have you in our "corner" of the world.

SPANKY: And we are delighted to be in your company, Miss ...

TIBBY: Harbrecht. Tibby Harbrecht.

SPANKY: Charmed, Miss Harbrecht.

Fluffer, Spanky, and Uta. Photo courtesy Ronnie Burkett Theatre of Marionettes

TIBBY: Actually, it's Mrs. Mrs. Bud Harbrecht.

SPANKY: Oy, I've been nipped by the Bud!

TIBBY: Oh, such talk! You'll turn my head!

SPANKY: Later, perhaps. Allow me to introduce myself. Spanky Bishop, at your service.

TIBBY: No! Really? Not *the* Spanky Bishop?! The Wacky Bellhop himself! I saw every one of your movies … *The Wacky Bellhop in Paris, The Wacky Bellhop in Love, The Wacky Bellhop Goes AWOL in Waikiki* … oh, I could go on and on!

SPANKY: No doubt.

UTA: *Schnetzer Laberkopf!* [Loose-lipped gossip!] *Arschkriecher!* [Brown nose!]

TIBBY: Oh, and who do we have here? She's such a tiny little thing, I barely noticed her!

SPANKY: This, my dear Mrs. Harbrecht, is the greatest actress ever to grace the silent screen. Miss Uta Häagen-Daz.

UTA: *Pissende Dummfotze!* [Stupid pissing cunt!]
TIBBY: Oh, how European! And "bidet" to you too, honey!

> *Music sting in.* ESMÉ #1 *enters and is posed dramatically in the alley between stage-left and centre-stage bridge towers. She is fabulous in a Golden Age of Hollywood kind of way. She is wearing her idea of a travelling or day ensemble. Lots of beads and feathers. In one arm is a vicious white poodle.*

ESMÉ: So this is Alberta. Yee-haw.

SPANKY: The one, the only, Esmé Massengill!

ESMÉ: Spanky, remind me to kill my agent.

SPANKY: You already did.

TIBBY: I could just lay down and die right here and now!

ESMÉ: What a soothing thought. But darling, the night is young. Let's save the fun for later.

TIBBY: I'm all tongue-tied. My heart's a-racing!

ESMÉ: Oh, yummy.

TIBBY: We are so honoured to have you in our fair town, Miss Massengill.

ESMÉ: Thank you. We're glad to be … anywhere.

SPANKY: You know the tour's bad when you look forward to Regina.

> *ESMÉ's poodle barks and snarls at* TIBBY.

TIBBY: What an adorable dog. Hello sweetie.

ESMÉ: Please don't touch her. She's an absolute bitch.

TIBBY: What's her name?

ESMÉ: Dorothy Barker. She plays a lamb in my new show.

TIBBY: And what is your new musical about, if I may be so bold?

ESMÉ: It's called *Oh Mary!* The life of the Virgin Mary, told in word and song and dance. I, of course, portray the titular role of Mary, the Virgin. Mr. Bishop here is Joseph.

TIBBY: And Miss Häagen-Daz?

ESMÉ: The angel who appears to Joseph, telling him to take flight to Egypt. It's a dance role.

TIBBY: And the wise men?

ESMÉ: There are no wise men. Especially not in the theatre. No, we're going rather minimalist on this one. Bare bones, pared down, and bold in its simplicity.

SPANKY: Our backer died.

ESMÉ: So sue me, I like a nosh. *Et voilà!* We find ourselves here. Extraordinary talent, a few simple costumes, but no scenery and, alas, no band. A musical without musicians!

SPANKY: Some nosh, it was more like a buffet.

TIBBY: Oh, but that's not a problem! I'm with The Turnip Corners Ladies Orchestrale. We'd be honoured to play for your show!

ESMÉ: Fortune smiles upon us! Lovely. I'll have my stage manager, Fluffer, arrange the rehearsal details with you.

TIBBY: Well, you must be exhausted after your trip.

ESMÉ: Not really, we sleep all day.

TIBBY: How bohemian!

ESMÉ: Technically it's Romanian, but why quibble.

UTA: *Spermaschlucker!* [Sperm swallower!]

ESMÉ: That's enough, Uta! Spanky, be a darling and escort Miss Häagen-Daz to her dressing room.

SPANKY: Certainly.

> SPANKY *and* UTA *exit.*

ESMÉ: And Spanky, keep an eye on her. You know how our Uta gets when she's hungry. (*She turns to* TIBBY.) Speaking of which, any thoughts on where I could get a bite?

Esmé and Dorothy Barker. Photo courtesy Ronnie Burkett Theatre of Marionettes

TIBBY: Well, there's the Red Lantern Café, home of Chinese and Canadian cuisine. Bit of everything on the menu, but I'm sure you'll find something to satisfy you.

ESMÉ: I think I already have. My tastes are so simple.

TIBBY: Lovely! Well then, follow me.

TIBBY leaves and is handed to the stage manager.

ESMÉ: I'm right behind you. Come Dorothy darling, dinner is served! Mummy will save you a bone!

ESMÉ exits. The stage manager clears the luggage. Stage-left lights out. As soon as they begin to dim, we hear the sound of EDNA (pre-recorded) on EDEN's answering service. This message plays over the transition as the stage manager lowers the drawbridge panel into EDNA's living room and places DOLLY #2 on the chair.

EDEN: (*recorded*) Hi, you've reached the voicemail for Eden Urbane and his Karaoke Memory Lane. Please leave your message after the tone and I'll call you back as soon as I can. And remember, follow the bouncing balls! Ciao!

EDNA: (*recorded*) Eden? Edie dear, are you there? Can you hear me? Pick up. Eden, it's me. Pick up. It's Mum. Edie, pick up if you can hear me. Are you listening? (*pause*) Well, I guess you're not there. Are you there? I guess not. Anyways, just thought I'd call to see how you're doing. I'm fine, not much going on. Crazydoll's gonna die soon, Esmé Massengill is in town, and Jesus Christ has appeared to me on a quilt square. No need to call back. Just thought I'd say hi. Okay then, bye-bye.

Sound of the end of the phone call. Lights up centre stage. EDNA #2 is dressed in her nightie and robe, standing stage left of her chair, looking down at DOLLY. Standing stage right of the chair is DON DIVINE, a rather dashing older man.

EDNA: So that's it then, eh?

DON: I'm sorry, Edna. These dogs get to a certain age and there's not much we can do for them.

EDNA: I just hate to see her suffer.

DON: Oh, she's having a bit of a time breathing, but I don't think she's in pain. You're just slowing down, aren't you, Dolly?

EDNA: Do you think we should ... you know ... help her off to sleep?

DON: I think she'll just drift off when it's her time. But if she takes a turn for the worse, Edna, you call Doctor Talbot and he'll make the end easier for you both. Or give me a call and I'll drive the old girl over to him for you.

EDNA: Oh, you've already done more than enough, Doctor Divine.

DON: Please, Edna, it's Don. I'm not a practising veterinarian anymore. And I was hoping you'd start thinking of me as something else.

EDNA: Oh?

DON: A friend. A neighbour. We're both townies now, so we gotta stick together, eh?

EDNA becomes a bit uncomfortable, embarrassed.

EDNA: Lord love a duck! Look at me standing here in my nightie. Practically nude! You must think I'm a terrible old hussy.

DON: Not at all. Perfectly natural to be in your pajamas at this hour.

EDNA: And me calling you over here in the middle of the night! I'm just a silly old biddy, I am. It's just that I was so worried about Dolly and I didn't know what else to do.

DON: You did the right thing, Edna.

There's an awkward pause as they lean into one another over the chair.

DON: Well, I'll let you get some sleep.

EDNA: Let me pay you for your trouble.

DON: Wouldn't hear of it, dear lady.

EDNA: Well, that's awfully kind of you ... Don.

DON: But there is something I would like, Edna.

She retreats a bit.

EDNA: Oh?

DON: There's a dinner and dance for the Prairie Revival Party next week. Oh, these political things can be a bit long-winded, but it's for a good cause. And I would be honoured if you'd attend as my guest.

EDNA: Your guest?

DON: My date.

EDNA: Your date.

DON: Yes.

EDNA: Don Divine! What in Sam Hill do you think I am? Some free-love floozy you can romance like a cheap dame in the movies?

DON: No, of course not. Edna, please, you misunderstand.

EDNA: No Don, you misunderstand. I'm a married woman.

DON: I'm sorry, Edna. I've been so lonely since my Dora died. I guess I thought you'd be interested in some company, too.

EDNA: Company is all fine and well, Don. But dinner and dancing and dates, well, that's just taking it a bit too far. Stanley Rural is the only man I've ever been with, and I intend to keep the vows of my marriage intact.

DON: But Edna, we have to move on.

EDNA: I am a married woman ... Doctor Divine. I will always be a married woman. Now, if you'll excuse me, I have my quilt to finish. Good night.

DON: Good night, Edna.

He leaves. EDNA stares after him momentarily, then turns with a sigh.

EDNA: I guess I'll make myself a NeoCitran. It's the only thing that gets me to sleep these days. Warm milk just gives me gas, and hot toddies make me tipsy. No, a nice, hot Neo is the only thing that knocks me out. Sometimes I have a double, but only if I've watched the CBC news and upset myself.

She exits centre-stage right as light fades out. The stage manager strikes DOLLY and raises the drawbridge of EDNA's panel. Small spot on EDEN #1, stage right.

EDEN: I once knew a male nurse whose cock was so big, every time he got an erection he would faint. Imagine that. A boner so big it drains the blood right out of your brain. Now that's passion!

For six years I lived with the nicest man. Anthony. Eden and Anthony. We were the perfect couple. Everyone told us so. I was in love. Once. A long time ago. But it was brutal. It wasn't Anthony, although I grew to be afraid of him, too.

See, Anthony looked like a gay icon. Like those perfect, ridiculous, empty men in underwear ads. V-shaped, hairless, airbrushed. And that's really fucking hard to be around, man, because it caused me to look at myself a considerable amount more than I prefer. Who can look that much sadness and anger in the face? Not me. Not when it's mine. But we had everything. Except passion. And besides, I couldn't leave him. We had too much stuff.

One Saturday afternoon I was lying on the couch while Anthony was in the basement working out. And there on TV was my sign – my epiphany – in the form of an old Esmé Massengill movie, *No Room for Love*, in which she played Constance Hart, a wealthy society dame married to an abusive banker who forfeits comfort and home and social standing to run off with a long-haul trucker named Butch, played brilliantly by Armand Collier. Butch. Oh, hump-daddy Butch. That guy was as dangerous as day-old sushi.

Light dims somewhat on EDEN as it comes up on YOUNG ESMÉ #2, atop the stage-right catwalk, posed in a spectacular gown. ESMÉ acts alone to an unseen male voice. The flashback is underscored with lush, overly romantic movie music.

ESMÉ / CONSTANCE: I love you, Hy, and I've tried to make you love me. But you've left me, and left me with no choice.

HY / MALE VOICE: I've never left you, Constance. I'm here! Right here, just as I've always been.

ESMÉ / CONSTANCE: No, you're distant, Hy. You've gone far, far away, to a land where love cannot live.

HY / MALE VOICE: I've given you everything a woman could ever want, Connie. Money, clothes, jewels. That's love, isn't it?

ESMÉ / CONSTANCE: No, Hy! We've crowded our lives with things, and left no room for the most important thing of all. We've left no room for love!

The movie music swells dramatically as ESMÉ hits her final pose and exits. Lights fade on the flashback area and restore on EDEN.

EDEN: Once again Esmé came through for me! She was my inspiration. Fuck the house. Screw the stuff. Okay, so I didn't have a long-haul trucker waiting for me, but I had a car. A 1986 powder-blue Monte Carlo. I got up off that couch and packed. Favourite clothes, photo albums, some books, my pipe-bomb stuff, the duvet and two pillows, all the CDs that were mine, a boom box, and almost anything that was battery operated. And the cellphone. I was on the run, true, but I still needed access to my voicemail. Into the car it went. I had found my new home. And my escape. It was decided and done, start to finish, in thirty-five minutes.

Thirty-five minutes. It took six years to build something, to accumulate all the trappings, and thirty-five minutes to end it. But then, destruction is always quicker than creation. And way more noticeable.

I went downstairs to tell Anthony I was leaving. "Keep the house, keep everything, I have to go. I can't stay here anymore. I can't stay with you." And he started to cry. Well, I like to think they were tears, not just sweat running down his face. Eventually he spoke. "It's because I bore you, isn't it?"

Of course I lied. I said no.

And left. But lemme tell ya, life isn't like the movies. In *No Room for Love*, just as Constance and Butch finally hit the road, they both die when the truck skids off a bridge in the rain. My fate was worse. I lived.

In my car. Really. I am one of the intentionally homeless. It's okay, and once you figure out which bathrooms to use, it becomes easier. "No fixed address," that's me. Kind of implies I'm going somewhere, doesn't it? I guess you could say I'm presently between lifestyles. But hey, what fag isn't?

Anyway, I'm going home. Not to Anthony. To Turnip Corners. To visit my mum. And to meet my mother. My real mother. Esmé! Oh shit, I'm afraid again. Maybe I should blow something up before I hit the road. That always makes me feel better. Nah, I'd miss all the press coverage.

Lights out on EDEN, who exits via the alley right off the stage-right bridge. Music in for the "Techno Jesus" sound-and-light show. This segment is loud, chaotic, intense, modern. Ronnie crosses to the stage-left bridge tower, places ESMÉ #2 on her chaise, and as the transition ends there is a blast of smoke from under the catwalk. Ronnie ends on the stage-left leaning rail, arms outstretched. Light up on ESMÉ and the Jesus special on Ronnie's face above.

ESMÉ: Now that's an entrance!

JESUS: Miss Massengill. We need to talk.

ESMÉ: Well, if it isn't the Only Begotten. *Iesus Nazarenus Rex Iudaeorum.*

JESUS: Very good, Esmé! I never would have guessed you to know Latin.

ESMÉ: Pish darling, it's the perfect language for me. Dead.

JESUS: Well, you are starting to look your age, Esmé.

ESMÉ: And you've put on weight, bitch, but did I bring that up?

JESUS: Look, I'm not here to fight.

ESMÉ: Then what brings you here? Surely the good folk of Turnip Corners aren't so important that they warrant an appearance by you.

JESUS: There's two I thought I should keep an eye on.

ESMÉ: To protect them from me?

JESUS: To protect them from themselves.

ESMÉ: Darling, you've been off the circuit for so long people wouldn't recognize you if they saw you. But have you seen what your competition's been up to lately?

JESUS: I keep tabs on him.

ESMÉ: Cable, multinationals, the Moral Majority, all of Hollywood, and of course, Satan's craftiest minion on earth, the Internet. It's gorgeous, and so simple.

JESUS: Don't be fooled by the appearance of simplicity, Esmé.

ESMÉ: But it is simple, darling, and he's the one who figured it out, not you. Give them sex, everywhere! Let them diddle themselves in front of a computer screen, with a video, or on their cellular phones. Swell their loins and drain the blood out of their brains. Let the new millennium sneak up and catch them all with their pants down!

JESUS: All right, Esmé, enough. Why are you here?

ESMÉ: Oh, I'm doing out-of-town tryouts with my new show.

JESUS: Esmé, it's me.

ESMÉ: Well darling, being here is part of the plan. Actually, it *is* the plan.

JESUS: What plan?

ESMÉ: It's blood, darling. Pure, uncontaminated blood. Oh, not for me. I'll drink any plasma you put in front of me. But for stockpiling, for hoarding, for selling, well, for that, I need the quality stuff.

JESUS: Selling?

ESMÉ: Yes. Because he – or rather, she – who controls the blood supply controls the world. You can blood bank on it. And besides, feeding on victim after victim got a bit tedious after a while. So now we still have the thrill of seduction and attack, make the puncture, have a little sip, and drain the rest for storage. And the product tends to be purer in the sticks.

JESUS: Esmé, promise me you'll leave my two people alone.

ESMÉ: We'll see, darling, we'll see.

JESUS: You may have a fight on your hands this time, Esmé.

ESMÉ: Delicious! So you think you're finally up to me?

JESUS: What makes you think I was talking about *me*?

*Light out on Ronnie and **ESMÉ**, stage left. Short "Techno Jesus" sting, dissolving into theme for **EDNA**. Slow cross-fade up on centre stage. The stage manager strikes the chaise and lowers the drawbridge panel. Ronnie hangs **ESMÉ** backstage, crosses to centre-stage bridge tower, and walks **EDNA #2** into the scene.*

EDNA: I've been awake all night. Two NeoCitrans and I still couldn't sleep. Maybe it was the late show that did it. They were showing that old Esmé Massengill movie *Passport to Love*. It was one of my favourites. Esmé played Dixie Carlyle, a waitress in a roadside diner who changes a flat tire for a travelling foreign prince and falls in love. Oh, so romantic. But that was our Esmé. Living, breathing passion!

*Light dims somewhat centre stage. Ronnie leaves **EDNA** sitting in her chair and crosses to stage-left bridge tower, walking **YOUNG ESMÉ #3** onto the catwalk. This is a contained pool of light, revealing **ESMÉ** in a spectacular white satin wedding dress with a pale-pink beaded veil. Again, **ESMÉ** stands alone and the people to whom she is speaking are unseen. This is heavily underscored with movie music.*

ESMÉ / DIXIE: Oh Betty, oh Audrey, oh Delores, why, you're the best friends a gal could ever have. Thanks for coming all the way to this foreign country just to be my bridesmaids. I'll miss you all and the happy times we had at the diner. Oh sure, here they'll call me Princess, but I'll always be Diner Dixie to you. Please know that I will never forget you gals, nor will I ever forget that it was slinging hash that brought me to the palace gates. But now, I say goodbye, my beloved Ladies in Waitressing, for my heart has a new destination and my passport is love! Prince darling, wait for me!

*She turns upstage as the music swells. Sound of honking car horn and screeching tires as stage-left light goes to black. **YOUNG ESMÉ** is hung backstage, Ronnie crosses to centre-stage bridge, and **EDNA's** light restores.*

EDNA: Too bad poor Dixie Carlyle tripped on the train of her dress and got hit by a speeding taxi as she crossed the street to the church. But she died beautifully, and oh, I loved that dress! More than anything I had ever seen. So when my Stanley asked me to help run the farm – which was his idea of a marriage proposal – I just knew that my wedding dress had to be like the one in *Passport to Love*.

I saw that movie three times down at the old Bijoux, trying to doodle the dress in the dark. I clipped every picture I could find of it from the movie magazines. I worked extra hours at Turner's Drugstore during the week, just so I could save enough money to buy five yards of satin and two of lace from the catalogue, shipped all the way from Toronto.

I made my pattern from old newspapers, then I cut it out of sugar sacks, like I use for my quilting, as a kind of test run. Then I scrubbed down the kitchen table, laid out my precious cloth, and cut. Lord love a duck, I had never been so nervous in my whole life. It took me weeks to sew that dress, because I knew that fancy clothes in France were all hand sewn. And since necessity is the mother of invention, I stained the lace veil pink by dipping it in a bucket of diluted Saskatoons I'd put through the sieve.

*Leaving **EDNA** seated in her chair centre stage, Ronnie crosses to stage-left bridge.*

EDNA: I knew I was no Esmé Massengill, and even though I stopped eating the week before the wedding, I was still just lumpy Edna. But when I put on that dress, well, didn't I just feel like a princess.

***YOUNG EDNA #1** enters through the alley between stage-left and centre-stage bridges. She is in her wedding dress, a copy of the one from **ESMÉ's** movie. She walks centre stage left to a phrase of "Here Comes the Bride" and is hung in position there.*

It was a small wedding and I had only one gal stand up with me, not a tribe of bridesmaids like Esmé. There was no money for that, and besides, I didn't have that many friends.

*Light up on **CORA JEAN** at the stage-left bandstand.*

But Cora Jean Pickles, who worked with me at the drugstore, agreed to be my bridesmaid and matron of honour combined. Cora Jean was saving up her money to go to Winnipeg to study the ballet. It was Cora Jean who gave me the beads for my veil. Took them right off one of her dance-recital dresses. I was indebted to her for life because of that.

Light fades out on CORA JEAN. Ronnie crosses back to the centre-stage bridge and EDNA.

I don't remember much about my wedding day. Oh, I know it's supposed to be the most important day in a woman's life, but I had worked and worried so much on an empty stomach that I was in kind of a fog. Mind you, the fog lifted that night when Stanley ... took his husbandly way with me. Suddenly, I didn't feel like a princess anymore. So the next morning I wrapped that dress in tissue paper and put it away in the cedar chest.

Light stage left dims on YOUNG EDNA, but not to black.

And we got on with our married life, which was surprisingly not much different from life before. I even grew to tolerate Stanley climbing on top of me at night, sometimes imagining that he was Armand Collier or Trevor St. Clair or some other movie-star lover. Looking back, I realize now that it never really took that long anyway, although it seemed like an eternity at the time. But it was my duty, and it would hopefully lead to something.

But it never did. After a while, I went to old Doctor Beaton to see if I was doing something wrong. But no, he assured me that we were doing everything right. It was my body that was wrong. It could not, it would not, make a baby. They used to call it barren. Like the prairie when the fields are empty. That was me. Empty, through and through.

When I got home, Stanley was still out doing the chores. To this day I don't know why, but I went to the cedar chest, took out my wedding dress, and put it on. And went upstairs and sat on the bed. It was the only night in my married life when I didn't make supper.

Light up, just barely, on YOUNG EDNA, stage left. The stage manager hands Ronnie a black cap, which he puts on as STANLEY.

Stanley found me sitting there. He didn't say a word. Not a peep. Stood in the doorway staring at me. I couldn't look at him, but I told him. "I can't have a baby," was all I said. Stanley was so quiet. He left the room. I stayed on the bed, memorizing the rag rug on the floor, listening to him downstairs. A terrible racket. I thought he was breaking things, or packing to leave. I didn't know.

Light intensity shifts somewhat in a subtle cross-fade from EDNA in chair centre stage to YOUNG

EDNA, stage left. Centre stage does not fade to black. Continuing EDNA's storytelling, Ronnie leaves the centre-stage marionette, walks stage left and climbs off the bridge to deck level. He is STANLEY RURAL. During the following monologue, Ronnie enacts what EDNA is describing. The bacon and eggs are mimed but the apron is real, and he ties it on to the marionette during the description.

And then he was there again. He set something down on the bureau, walked over to me, and tied an apron around me while I sat. Then he took what he had set on the bureau and put it on my lap. I looked down and there was a plate. Bacon and eggs. He knelt down, took a piece of bacon in his fingers, and held it up to my mouth. That's when we looked at each other. We stayed there for a long, long time. Me in my wedding dress and an apron, Stanley on his knees before me. Me and my man. Mr. and Mrs. Stanley Rural. Crying over a plate of bacon and eggs.

STANLEY ends on his knees, embracing YOUNG EDNA. The tableau of Ronnie and YOUNG EDNA in her wedding dress is held as the stage-left light fades very slowly to black. Ronnie strikes YOUNG EDNA #1 and resumes his place on the bridge, stage left. Lights up on EDEN's area stage right as Ronnie crosses from stage-left bridge to stage right.

EDEN: Do you ever think about those people you called fag in school? No, of course you don't. But we think about you. All the time. Imagine that in every town all over the world there were a few of those kids. Nice kids, whose only hope of survival was to get out. And man, I got out. To the city.

In the city you have access to ... more. More activity, more noise, more movies, more shopping, more people, more stuff, more sex. Oh yeah, I had a lot of sex when I first got there. A lot. I suppose I'm kind of your worst nightmare. A fag who has had as much sex as you think fags have.

Lights cross-fade. Down a bit on EDEN (who is hung from the gallows and remains in position stage right) and up on EDNA in her chair centre stage.

EDNA: It was Thanksgiving 1982. Eden had already been living in the city for several years, ever since he graduated from high school. Like a bullet from a pistol, that's how he got out of this town. So once every now and then, I'd pack my plaid overnight case and take the bus into the city to see him. The train had stopped coming through Turnip Corners years ago, even though we clung to these tracks and the grain elevator as some sort of memento of when the town had had a soul. Same reason I'd go see my Edie. To remind myself that we were a family still.

Now, Mr. Stanley Rural did not join me on these Greyhound adventures. Never cared much for the bus. Certainly did not care for the city. And although it was never discussed, I felt that something had stopped him from caring about Eden, too.

Anyways, a week before Thanksgiving 1982, Eden phoned to say that he was coming home. And bringing a couple of friends. Well, Lord love a duck, didn't that just throw me into a tizzy! Why, there were mattresses to turn, beds to make up, pies and jellied salads to get prepared, the good china to get out and wash up. And I needed Stanley to drive me to the IGA so I could get the biggest turkey they had. Oh, but I didn't mind all the fuss and bother. This was one Thanksgiving I had something to be thankful for. My Eden was coming home.

*Lights cross-fade again. Up on **EDEN**, stage right.*

EDEN: I learned how to make bombs on the Internet. Nothing fancy, just pipe bombs and fire explosives. Simple stuff. I could have gotten more elaborate, I suppose, but I hated surfing through all those militia pages. Hundreds and hundreds of websites devoted to my extinction. Man, I had no idea I was such a threat to them. Cool.

My first bomb was actually intended for a Prairie Revival Party campaign rally. See, they were making all this Christian bullshit noise about the "homosexual agenda." Man, someone should have told them you can't organize fags to agree on anything. But just when we thought it was safe to poke our heads out of the trenches and wave our little rainbow flags, the enemy pounced. And man, those fuckers are organized. And all the gay activists could do was to mount a lame campaign to prove how normal we are. Fuck that. What needed to happen was to prove how dangerous those people are to me. I mean, to us. Look, I'm no activist, okay? I don't ask for my right to be. I'm a radical. I take it.

So I changed my plan and set my first pipe bomb off in the back entrance of Tongue in Cheek, one of the more popular gay bars. It was a Monday night, so there were only a handful of patrons, and I knew they were all in the front bar. The blast didn't cause any injuries and not a lot of damage. But the effect was fucking enormous. A gay bar had been bombed. The cops took it seriously, the press covered it, best

of all, the gay community got scared. Really scared. Junior high scared. And indirectly, fingers started pointing at the Prairie Revival Party. Jackpot!

So that weekend I set off another one at a lesbian coffee shop called Sappho's Grind. I felt kinda bad 'cause it was a nice place. But I had to involve the dykes, too. I mean, think about it. They're gay and female, so there's double the oppression. Which means double the rage. And rage is what I'm interested in.

Tick tick tick tick … kaboom, baby.

*Lights cross-fade. Up on **EDNA**, centre stage.*

EDNA: Eden's friends were, now let me see … there was a pale, skinny boy named Kiki, and a largish girl named Jane spelled d-j-a-n-e with the *D* being silent. They didn't say much to me, and most of what they said to Edie was whispered. Djane sat in the kitchen a few times, not to lift a finger and help out but to lecture me on how degrading my role as a homemaker was to my "woman spirit." She did manage to eat most of the baking I'd put out, although I don't think she realized that this was a direct result of my chosen profession. And she felt that my saying "Lord love a duck" gave too much power to an unseen male force with a controlling agenda. Better, she thought, to say "Goddess love all the ducks, big and small, of all colours and gender persuasions." What a cornflake!

Stanley had found all sorts of work to do out in the Quonset hut. Barely showed his face around the house the whole time we had Edie and his friends. But this was a holiday dinner – a prairie woman's showcase – and I marched myself out to that shed and told Mr. Stanley Rural to wash up, suit up, and show up at my table on time or there would be hell to pay. I put up with a lot, but don't mess with me when there's a turkey involved!

*Lights cross-fade. Up on **EDEN**, stage right.*

EDEN: I knew what my third target would have to be. There's a small alternative high school, and they had a program for gay kids. Kids who had really suffered in the mainstream system. And it was something the community had fought and worked for for a long time, because, well, let's face it man, we all remembered high school.

Ronnie pauses, looks straight out to the audience, and remembers.

RONNIE: Fucking high school.

EDEN: Anyway, it was the only bomb that I ever had second thoughts about, but I knew its impact would be the last straw. It had to be done. So late one night I broke in, set up, and blew the shit out of that school. And I can't tell you how fucking good that felt. And this time I left a calling card. Out on the sidewalk I spray-painted two pink words. "Purse Boy." That's all it said.

Lights up on EDNA, centre stage.

EDNA: Thanksgiving dinner. There we sat, the five of us. Or rather, me and the silent quartet. Now, you may have noticed I tend to go on a bit. And when I'm nervous, well, my chin-wagging just won't stop. So I talked. I passed the turkey and I talked. I passed the dressing and I talked. I passed the gravy boat and I talked. I passed the potatoes, the turnips, the peas, and the corn, and I talked and talked and talked and talked. I was just about to pass around the jellied salad – oh, the clear green one with fruit cocktail in it, not the creamy ambrosia one with the Philadelphia cream cheese and pineapple tidbits – when Eden stood up, cleared his throat, and said:

EDEN: Mum. Dad. I'm gay.

EDNA: I didn't know what to do. I'd planned this for a week and now it had all gone wrong. Maybe there wasn't enough food. I held the jellied salad in front of Djane and said, "This one has fruit in it."

EDEN: Mum! Didn't you hear me? I said I'm gay. Don't you have anything to say about that?

EDNA: Well, for once I was silent. It was dead quiet at that table. That eerie kind of stillness, like right before a big storm. And I could feel him. From the other end of that table, my Stanley, starting to vibrate like a generator getting going. All in his neck, eh? His neck doubling in size and ready to burst. And his face. Eyes crazy like an animal, ready to attack. And getting all red, like every drop of blood in his body had rushed to his head. This had gone terribly wrong. This was all my fault. I should have cooked a ham, too!

Suddenly, Stanley slammed his cutlery down on his plate with a crash. Put both hands on the table and lifted himself up to his full height. He looked bigger than I'd ever seen him before. Like a giant. Like a crazy, unfriendly giant. And his face was so red it looked like a missile would shoot straight out the top of his head at any moment. I had to do something. Say something. Fix this. Come on Edna, you're a smart woman, you read *Chatelaine*. Think Edna, think.

EDNA stands, half from the excitement of her storytelling, half as re-enactment.

Dessert. I had dessert! My saviour! I put the jellied salad down, placed my hands on the table, and stood opposite Mr. Stanley Rural, staring him down. Oh, not as tall but just as strong-willed. His eyes locked with mine, like two gunfighters, fingers twitching for their pistols. I shot first. I spoke. I spoke as calmly and as bravely and as sensibly as any Canadian woman in my situation would. And I said to him, "Stanley Rural, keep your fork! There's pie."

EDNA sits.

He sat down. We finished our meal in silence. I cleared the table. Everyone retained their cutlery. I served dessert. Eden and his friends went back to the city. Stanley went to bed. And I did the dishes, alone. It was an awful Thanksgiving. I didn't even have my slice of the pie.

Centre-stage light fades out.

EDEN: My bombs aren't meant to hurt gay people. They're meant to blow the lid off our bottled rage. So watch out, because now there is a homosexual agenda. Fairies are fighting back. And God help anyone who gets in the way of that fury.

EDEN's light fades out as he exits stage right. Music transition, suggesting time change. Ronnie strikes EDNA #2 and seats EDNA #3 in the chair. This is her good dress, not flashy but from the more expensive part of the Sears ladies wear section. The stage manager places a box wrapped in Christmas paper downstage left of the chair. Sound of a car horn. Lights up centre stage.

EDNA: Eden, is that you?

EDEN #1 enters from the alley between centre-stage and stage-right bridges.

EDEN: No, it's Gloria Cartier, the orphaned young socialite with amnesia from *Midnight in Monte Carlo*!

EDNA: Oh you! Get in here and give your old mum a hug.

He enters EDNA's area, stage right of the chair.

EDEN: Hi Mum.

EDNA: Let me get you something to eat.

EDEN: I'm not hungry, Mum. Sit.

EDNA: You look like a skeleton. How about a grilled cheese?

EDEN: No thanks.

EDNA: I've got some matrimonial cake. Just made it yesterday.

EDEN: Mum, no.

EDNA: Oh, but you always liked my matrimonial cake.

EDEN: Not now, okay?

EDNA: Okay then, I think I've got some rocky road squares with the coloured mini marshmallows in the freezer. Only take a minute to thaw them out ...

EDEN: Mum, stop overfunctioning.

EDNA: Suit yourself, Mr. Scrawny. How's Tony?

EDEN: Mum, it's Anthony. You never abbreviate a fag's name.

EDNA: Oh. How's Anthony?

EDEN: He's ... perfect. (*notices the box on the floor*) Bit early for Christmas.

EDNA: Oh no, dear, that's Dolly.

EDEN: What? You wrapped up the dog?

EDNA: She was gathered, Edie. Middle of the night, she was taken off to her reward.

EDEN: Mum, this is too weird. Why would you gift-wrap a dead dog?

EDNA: Well, you gave her to me as a Christmas present and that's how I'm going to send her off. I've been waiting for you to get here so we could bury her in the backyard. That's why I'm in my fancy dress and wearing my Avon.

EDEN: Poor Crazydoll.

EDNA: I thought you might like to sing that at the service.

EDEN: What?

EDNA: That song. "Crazydoll." From that old Esmé Massengill and Spanky Bishop movie. You used to sing that song at the drop of a hat when you were a kid. Remember?

EDEN: Not really.

EDNA: Sure you do. You'd get up and perform for me, right in front of the television. It was almost like you were on it. Come on, Edie, sing a little bit for me.

EDEN: I don't remember it.

EDNA: Well, I do. I remember everything. We had just bought the colour TV.

Light centre stage dims to very low level as we cross-fade upstage right. The stage manager has pre-set a chair like EDNA's right of the stage-right panel. YOUNG EDNA #2 is pre-set in the chair, dressed in a housedress. Beside her is YOUNG EDEN #1. He is a chubby, pleasant-looking child with the same shock of red hair and glasses. The intro for the song "Crazydoll" plays under the initial dialogue.

YOUNG EDEN: This is *way* better than black and white!

YOUNG EDNA: The Heckler Brothers' pictures were always the most spectacular, Eden. Look at those costumes! I had forgotten how snazzy they were.

YOUNG EDEN: And Esmé looks even more beautiful in colour.

YOUNG EDNA: Shhh, Edie, here comes Spanky's big number. Go turn the set up so we can hear it better.

Lights dim on them, and the area in front of the screen brightens as Ronnie raises the panel in front of the stage-right bridge. It reveals a large face of YOUNG SPANKY BISHOP as the Wacky Bellhop, filling the frame. He is in the movie being watched by YOUNG EDNA and YOUNG EDEN. SPANKY's mouth is manipulated from behind the screen by the stage manager. SPANKY sings.

SPANKY: (*singing*)

> *"CRAZYDOLL"*
>
> *Gather round now, one and all*
> *Come and meet my Crazydoll*
> *She's a dame who's earned her fame*
> *And my heart's back in the game*
> *Come on kids and say her name*
> *Come and meet my Crazydoll*
>
> *Crazydoll!*
> *She's a wacky lady*
> *Crazydoll!*
> *Oh yessirree*
> *Crazydoll!*
> *Crazy 'bout ya baby*
> *Can't you say you're crazy for me*

The music continues with a brief dance orchestra-
tion as YOUNG EDEN *stands up and moves directly*
in front of SPANKY.

YOUNG EDEN: Hey, Mum, look at me! I'm a movie
star too, and I'm in colour!

YOUNG EDNA: Oh Edie!

During the following, Ronnie sings live as YOUNG
EDEN *with the pre-recorded* SPANKY.

YOUNG EDEN: (*singing*)

> *Here I am on bended knee*
> *With the word matrimony*
> *Please say yes that you'll be mine*
> *Hubby's year-round Valentine*
> *Crazy him loves crazy she*
> *Crazydoll please marry meCrazydoll!*
>
> *You're my little Venus*
> *Crazydoll!*
> *My Juliette*
> *Crazydoll!*
> *Nothin' comes between us*
> *Can't you see how crazy I get*
>
> *Crazydoll!*
> *Be my little missus*
> *Crazydoll!*
> *Lemme see you smile*
> *Crazydoll!*
> *Come and get my kisses*
> *Crazydoll!*
> *Oh Crazydoll!*
> *My Crazydoll!*
> *Take a crazy walk with me down the aisle*

YOUNG EDEN *collapses into* EDNA's *arms. They are*
both laughing.

YOUNG EDNA: Oh Eden, that was wonderful!
You're a regular Spanky Bishop you are!

YOUNG EDEN: I'd rather be Esmé Massengill.

YOUNG EDNA: Oh Edie, such a kidder. My little
movie star!

YOUNG EDEN: And you're my Crazydoll, Mum.
Forever.

They cuddle and giggle as the stage-right lights
fade. Ronnie lowers the panel. Centre-stage lights

restore. Stage manager strikes stage-right chair and
marionettes.

EDNA: And that's why you named her Crazydoll.

EDEN: Yeah. I remember.

EDNA: Of course you do, Edie. Your father didn't
see the sense in buying that colour TV, but I held
my ground. I said, "Stanley Rural, it's *my* family
allowance, I'll spend it as I see fit!"

EDEN: Well, he never saw much sense in anything
we liked.

EDNA: Edie, that's not true.

EDEN: Fine, I'm sorry I brought it up. I should
know better than to criticize him in front of you.

EDNA: Oh, you're just mad at him. Just because
he didn't throw his arms around you and say, "Oh,
you're a homo! Isn't that just tickety-boo! Let's go
have a smoke on the porch!"

EDEN: I didn't expect that. I knew he would have
a hard time with it.

EDNA: Then why did you tell him, Edie? To hurt
him?

EDEN: No. Maybe. I don't know.

EDNA: Well, it's hard to mend a fence when you're
sitting on it, Mister Man. And besides, your father
isn't angry.

EDEN: Wasn't.

EDNA: What?

EDEN: Wasn't angry, not isn't.

EDNA: Don't start with me, Eden.

EDEN: Mum ...

EDNA: Fine. Enough. We'll have it your way. It
wasn't anger. It was disappointment that he'd have
no one to pass the farm on to.

EDEN: He never even asked me if I wanted it!

EDNA: Well, of course not, Edie. What would you,
one of you people, want with a farm?

EDEN: There are plenty of gay farmers.

EDNA pauses, shocked, then bursts into laughter.

EDNA: Oh, Lord love a duck! You're pulling my leg
now. Oh you! And I almost fell for it. Gay farmers!

EDEN: And ranchers.

EDNA: Eden!

EDEN: I've been to gay rodeos. Yee-haw! Ride 'em
cowboy!

EDNA: Now that's enough of your smart mouth! Eden, it's not nice to tease your old mum like this. Not now, what with Dolly's passing and Jesus Christ appearing in my quilt square.

EDEN: Hey, Mum, did you ever think that maybe Jesus was gay?

EDNA: Now that's just talk for talk's sake, Eden.

EDEN: Well, you never know. His last dinner party was men only.

EDNA: Lots of men get together for a meal. Look at the Kinsmen! Doesn't mean they're a bunch of poofs. Mind you, I've always had my suspicions about the Shriners. Something not quite right about grown men in harem pants. (*stands*) Now let's get Dolly buried before she starts to smell up the whole house. I'll go get my purse. (*exits*)

EDEN: But we're just going to the backyard.

EDNA: (*offstage*) You never know who's going to see you, Eden.

EDEN: No, you never do. "Turnip Corners. Meet me there. I'm waiting. Your real mother."

EDNA: (*offstage*) Eden, are you coming?

EDEN: I'm already here, Mother. I'm here, Esmé.

> *All light centre stage fades as **ESMÉ** music-and-sound theme comes in. **EDEN** and the box are removed and the drawbridge panel raised up. Cross-fade into a single light on stage left. It's the effect of a work light on a rehearsal stage; the stage manager has placed a prop version of it left of the stage-left panel. **ESMÉ #3** walks slowly into the light. Music out.*

ESMÉ: I'd forgotten how quiet you were, old friend. Not like a sound stage at all. No. That's chaos, that's dazzle, all brighter than life. Not like you, the theatre. Dark. Quiet. Secret. (*looks around her*) I grew up on you. Places like you. Long before I made my choice. Long before my life became an eternity of dark and quiet and secrets. A little girl. Just a normal little girl. A little girl who found such a dark world. "Baby Esmé. Songs and Dances from the Bible."

> *ESMÉ is hung in place in her spot. We hear music, vaguely Arabian, somewhat striptease, like the accompaniment to a silent film. **BABY ESMÉ** appears from the centre-stage right alley entrance. She is a beautiful child, maybe five years old, dressed in a harem-type costume. The overall image is unsettling. She dances on, gyrating seductively. Adult **ESMÉ** talks while the child version of her dances.*

I played a lot of halls like this. And churches. Mother was very clever that way. They particularly liked my Salome. Dancing for the head of John the Baptist. A little girl, practically naked, dancing like a whore. Oh, they paid to watch and they loved me. The ministers' wives would cuddle me afterward and call me their living doll. Their husbands would cuddle me later, when no one else was around. Presbyterians were the worst. They always smelled damp. "Baby Esmé. Songs and Dances from the Bible."

> *The child dances off. Music ends.*

I was pushed into the dark. Forced, by a woman who had stopped breathing in the very act of my conception. A woman who drew life from me. From what she lived through me. Yes, I wanted you, old friend. I wanted to be on the stage. And lucky for me, because I would have been pushed out here anyway.

After a while, it was the only safe place. I knew what was lurking in the wings. In the alley. In the pulpit! And until I could figure out how to suck the life out of those who had pushed and prodded and fingered me, I stayed here. In your false, warm, protective light. My oldest friend. My saviour.

> *Slow musical sting of **ESMÉ**'s eerie theme as the work light fades out; then a wild blast of the "Techno Jesus" sound-and-light show erupts. During this, Ronnie clears **ESMÉ** and hangs her behind the stage-left bridge tower, the stage manager strikes the work light and lowers the centre-stage drawbridge, and Ronnie seats **EDEN** in **EDNA**'s chair. There is a blast of smoke from under the centre-stage catwalk. Light up centre stage and on Ronnie as **JESUS** above.*

JESUS: Eden.

> *EDEN jumps up from the chair and sees him.*

EDEN: Holy shit!

JESUS: Eden, we need to talk.

EDEN: This isn't real. This is *not* real.

JESUS: I am very real, Eden.

EDEN: You don't scare me.

JESUS: Good. I'd like to see you without your fear.

EDEN: You're wasting your time. Go away.

JESUS: I can't. Your pain is what brought me here.

EDEN: Oh fuck off. If you throw that Leviticus shit in my face, I'll ...

JESUS: You'll what?

EDEN: I'll come right up there and nail you, man, I swear.

JESUS: Come on, Eden!

Ronnie strikes a sudden and harsh crucifixion pose with his free hand. He catches himself and softens.

JESUS: Sorry. Sorry.

EDEN: I know why you're here, man, and believe me, those bombs did more good than harm.

JESUS: Eden, you're hurting people.

EDEN: I just woke them up. No one got hurt.

JESUS: Everyone got hurt.

EDEN: Oh right. We're all supposed to play by your rules.

JESUS: My rules? No one lives by my rules.

EDEN: Yeah, well, they don't work for me.

JESUS: You never even tried them.

EDEN: I did so!

JESUS: You did not!

EDEN: Did!

JESUS: Didn't!

EDEN: Yes I did!

JESUS: When?

EDEN: I went to Sunday school!

Ronnie laughs. The mood lightens somewhat.

EDEN: What's so fucking funny?

JESUS: You are. You need to lighten up, Eden.

EDEN: So you came here to laugh at me? Some saviour. Man, you don't even look like you. I thought you'd look, you know …

JESUS: Like a picture in Sunday school?

EDEN: Fuck off. I'm just used to the beard and long hair, okay? That looked good. Real good. I used to have such a crush on you. You were so hot. Well, him. That Sunday school Jesus. But this aging club-boy thing doesn't really work on someone your age.

JESUS: I forgive you for that, Eden. I thought I'd try a new image.

EDEN: Keep working on it, honey.

JESUS: Maybe you could help me.

EDEN: Let's not pretend we're pals. We have nothing in common. You're the Son of Man, I'm … I'm the son of Stan.

JESUS: So we have a lot in common. Silent fathers and saintly mothers.

EDEN: Oh please! Leave them out of it. My rage is enormous. Too big to pin on my parents. They're simple people. My rage is very complicated. And it's all mine.

JESUS: Rage is not self-contained.

EDEN: You fucking hypocrite. You peddled fear and rage yourself, didn't you? But oh, I forgot, you smokescreened it all with magic and hocus-pocus.

JESUS: Okay, yes, I thought that if people were impressed with the spectacle, maybe they'd listen. But that obviously hasn't worked out like I had hoped, so I think I need a more personal approach.

EDEN: So what are you gonna do, man? Talk to people one at a time?

JESUS: Yes.

EDEN: Fuck off.

JESUS: It's true.

EDEN: Yeah right. You're gonna talk to everyone on earth, one at a time.

JESUS: I'm talking to you, aren't I?

EDEN: Well, I'm not listening.

JESUS: Well, I am.

EDEN: I've got nothing to say to you.

JESUS: But there's something you need to hear.

EDEN: What?

JESUS: You tell me.

EDEN: What?

JESUS: The truth.

EDEN: Man, you're a pain in the ass.

JESUS: Sorry. It's my job. Eden?

EDEN: What?

JESUS: Remember.

EDEN: What?

JESUS: When you weren't afraid.

There is a pause.

EDEN: We were in this room, playing.

JESUS: Who?

EDEN: Me and Ogden. Ogden Ramsay, the only kid in school who ever bothered with me. Well, the only boy, anyway. But that was okay. He was the only boy I noticed. He was thin and quiet and … beautiful. Not like me at all. Yet, here he was, in my house playing with me.

JESUS: Did you love him?

EDEN moves to one side of the area, as if watching.

EDEN: What? No. I don't know. I was just a little kid. What did I know about love, except for what I saw in movies? We were just playing. To me, he was ... someone else. It was pretend. It was all just pretend ...

Jesus special on Ronnie out. Short musical sting / memory transition. We stay in the same area but it is now another time, years earlier. A subtle yet distinct lighting change enhances this memory. A marionette of YOUNG EDEN #2 runs in, wearing an exact replica of EDNA's wedding dress. It is too big on him and there is no veil. It is crucial that during this scene the character does not show his back to the audience. He has a purse over one arm.

YOUNG EDEN: Okay, Ogden, I'm ready. Are you ready?

OGDEN: *(offstage)* Yeah. I guess.

YOUNG EDEN: Well, are you ready or not?

OGDEN: *(offstage)* I'm ready. I just feel stupid, Eden. What if your mum walks in?

YOUNG EDEN: I already told you, she's at a church meeting in town.

OGDEN enters. He is, as described, a beautiful boy. He is dressed in his underclothes.

OGDEN: I guess this is what a dad would wear. It's what my dad wears to bed.

YOUNG EDEN: In the movies they wear silk pajamas!

OGDEN: Huh. I don't got those.

YOUNG EDEN: It's okay. You look nice, Ogden.

OGDEN: Thanks. What's that you're wearing?

YOUNG EDEN: It's my mum's wedding dress.

OGDEN: Do you want to be a girl?

YOUNG EDEN: No.

OGDEN: Then why are you dressed like one?

YOUNG EDEN: I'm not dressed like a girl. I'm dressed like a star!

OGDEN: You want to be a star?

YOUNG EDEN: Yes.

OGDEN: But you're dressed like a girl star.

YOUNG EDEN: The only stars are girl stars.

OGDEN: Then you want to be a girl.

YOUNG EDEN: I dunno. No.

OGDEN: Doesn't matter. You look nice, Eden. What's in the purse?

YOUNG EDEN: Nothing.

OGDEN: Then why do you have it?

YOUNG EDEN: 'Cause I like it. It goes.

OGDEN: So, what should I call you?

YOUNG EDEN: I dunno. You could call me ... your wife.

OGDEN: Nah, that's weird.

YOUNG EDEN: Yeah. That's weird.

OGDEN: I know. I'll call you ... Purse Boy!

YOUNG EDEN: Okay.

Suddenly a strong, harsh backlight shines on Ronnie on the centre-stage bridge. He is STANLEY RURAL. The light outlines his size, massive compared to the two small boys beneath.

OGDEN: It's your dad!

STANLEY: Go home, Ogden.

OGDEN: We were just playing.

STANLEY: Put your clothes on and go home, Ogden.

OGDEN: Yes, Mr. Rural. *(He starts to exit, then turns to EDEN.)* See ya, Eden.

STANLEY: Now!

OGDEN exits.

STANLEY: What are you doing, boy?

YOUNG EDEN: Nothing. Honest. Playing.

STANLEY: Playing? What?

YOUNG EDEN: Nothing. Wedding.

STANLEY: Wedding?

YOUNG EDEN: I was being ...

STANLEY: Who?

YOUNG EDEN: Mum. I was Mum, Dad.

STANLEY: Come here.

YOUNG EDEN: Except she was like a movie star.

STANLEY: Come here.

YOUNG EDEN: And Ogden was sort of ... you, Daddy.

STANLEY: Take that dress off and come here. Now!

YOUNG EDEN: No, we were just playing.

STANLEY: How dare you touch that dress, you little bastard.

YOUNG EDEN: I'll put it away, Daddy. Just like I found it.

STANLEY: Come here.

YOUNG EDEN: No ... (*He starts to move.*)

STANLEY: I said come here!

Ronnie grabs the strings of the marionette and violently pulls the puppet of YOUNG EDEN up to his level.

Look at you. Look at ... this. Eden, the spoiled fruit!

YOUNG EDEN: Daddy, no! Please, Daddy!

Music sting. Short, brutal, loud. YOUNG EDEN is "thrown" down to the stage level, bent over the chair and facing upstage, revealing the bloodstained back of the wedding dress.

EDEN: My mother's wedding dress was covered in blood. And I had lost the only man I ever loved. I hated him for that.

YOUNG EDEN exits slowly.

And that's when I learned the power of rage.

EDEN sits in the chair.

JESUS: Eden ...

EDEN: Leave me alone. I have nothing to say to you.

Ronnie sits on the centre-stage catwalk, feet dangling into EDEN's playing area. Cross-fade from top light to catwalk light. He sings.

JESUS: (*singing*)

> "MIDNIGHT IN MONTE CARLO"
>
> *All I remember*
>
> *Is midnight and moonlight*
>
> *You're but a ghost in the mist*
>
> *All I remember is*
>
> *Midnight and moonlight*
>
> *Starlight and candles*
>
> *Champagne and whispers*
>
> *And then*
>
> *Am I right?*
>
> *I'm kissed at midnight*
>
> *With the heavens aglow*
>
> *I was kissed at midnight in Monte Carlo*

EDEN: You know that?

JESUS: *Midnight in Monte Carlo.* Gloria Cartier was one of Esmé's best performances.

EDEN: Fuck off, you know Esmé?

JESUS: I've been watching her for years. Just like you.

EDEN: That's so wild.

JESUS: Not really. See Eden, we aren't that different.

EDEN: She's my blood.

JESUS: I am your blood.

EDEN: No man, she's my mother.

JESUS: What?

EDEN: That's why she's here. I got a note. She wants to meet me.

JESUS: Oh Eden, no.

EDEN: I'm finally going to meet my birth mother and she's Esmé Massengill!

JESUS: Eden, I wouldn't do that if I were you.

EDEN: Well, you're not me, are you? See, we don't have a bloody thing in common.

"Techno Jesus" music transition begins. Light out centre stage. Ronnie hangs EDEN backstage and the stage manager raises the centre-stage drawbridge panel. Stage-left acting area light comes up. The panel stays down and the stage is bare, with no furniture props. Ronnie walks FLUFFER onstage. Music ends.

FLUFFER: Okay everyone, places please for rehearsal. We'll start at the top of Act Two. I need Mr. Bishop onstage in costume as Joseph. Places, please.

SPANKY enters dressed as Joseph with long robes and sandals. He's running lines.

SPANKY: Okay Mary, lemme get this straight. When we got married, you were a virgin. Right? Now all of a sudden you tell me you're with child. *Bist meshugeh?* [Are you crazy?] I haven't even touched you! Believe me, a man remembers details like that.

FLUFFER: Bravo, Mr. Bishop! I think you finally have that speech nailed.

SPANKY: Thank you, Fluffer. And where is my delightful co-star?

FLUFFER: Oh, Miss Massengill is just getting into her Virgin Mary costume.

ESMÉ #4 enters from stage left wearing her Mary costume. This looks nothing at all like the Virgin

Mary, but instead is a scanty Ziegfeld-like concoction of beads and feathers. With fishnets.

ESMÉ: Sorry to keep you waiting, darlings, but the duct tape on my ass keeps slipping. Fluffer, make a note to bone my derrière after rehearsal.

FLUFFER: Um, sure thing, Miss M.

ESMÉ: Is something wrong, Fluffer? What are you staring at?

FLUFFER: That certainly is a lot of cleavage for the Virgin Mary, Miss Massengill.

ESMÉ: She was pregnant, darling. Her tits would have been enormous.

FLUFFER: Oh. Do you need a pillow for pregnancy padding?

ESMÉ: Padding? When will you learn, Fluffer? I'm not an actress, I'm a star!

FLUFFER: But you just said she was pregnant.

ESMÉ: Well, it's not a literal interpretation. Allow me some licence. Christ, it's a musical!

FLUFFER: Sorry, Miss Massengill, I just thought that ...

ESMÉ: No one cares what you think, you stupid dyke.

FLUFFER: I am not a dyke. I am a professional stage manager from Toronto.

ESMÉ: Oh, excuse me. I wasn't aware that there was a difference! Now please, let's get on with it.

FLUFFER: Okay, let's take it from the top of the flight scene. Places please.

*FLUFFER moves aside to stage left and **ESMÉ** and **SPANKY** take centre stage.*

When you're ready, Mr. Bishop.

SPANKY / JOSEPH: Oy Mary, it's true I tell you. What, I should lie to you about such a thing? May God strike me dead should I lie to my wife. I should *plotz* right before you, a lie crosses my lips. There was this angel. Gorgeous! A blonde *shiksa* angel. She comes to me, a vision I tell you, and she says, "Joseph, get your wife and your ass outta town. Herod, that schmuck, he's killing all the babies." *Oy vey iz mir!* Just when you get yourself shtuped by the big guy, such a decree!

ESMÉ / MARY: But Joe, my crazy madcap Joe, where oh where will we go?

SPANKY / JOSEPH: To Egypt, my darling! We'll leave this *farkakt* place and find peace. Mind you,

given your condition, Mary, it appears you already found a piece!

ESMÉ: Spanky! That's not in the script!

SPANKY: I know, but it works.

ESMÉ: Fine. Whatever. Enough! Let's just skip to the duet.

FLUFFER: Oh no, oh no, oh no, we can't!

ESMÉ: No? Why not, Fluffer?

FLUFFER: Because three of the band members are missing.

ESMÉ: Three? Spanky!

SPANKY: Don't look at me.

ESMÉ: Spanky ...

SPANKY: Honest. Here, check my breath.

He breathes, wheezing, onto her.

ESMÉ: Fine. Where's Uta?

SPANKY: I thought she was with you.

ESMÉ: No. Well, don't just stand there, go find her! And get her into costume. We have to rework the angel sequence without the German Tourette Syndrome.

SPANKY: I warned you about taking her on the road.

ESMÉ: What was I to do? Lock her in her casket? I owe her everything!

SPANKY: Oy, for such a life we're thankful? (*exits*)

ESMÉ: Let's get on with it, Fluffer. We'll rehearse my solo. The show-stopping road to Bethlehem number, "My Ass is Killing Me." Where's the donkey?

The stage manager places a chair onstage which has a prop donkey head made from a sock attached to it.

ESMÉ: Fluffer, what's that?

FLUFFER: Your ass. I made it myself!

ESMÉ: Obviously. I thought I was getting real livestock!

FLUFFER: Oh no, oh no, oh no! People are very protective of their animals ever since fourteen cows were found mutilated and drained of all their blood!

ESMÉ: Damn that Uta! I need a drink! (*exits right*)

FLUFFER: But Miss Massengill, it's not time for an Equity break yet. Oh no. Well, the show must go on.

FLUFFER looks around, strokes the prop donkey head, and begins "acting."

Oh Joe, oh Joe, my crazy madcap Joe! Looking for a room to let, but everyone says oh no, oh no, oh no!

ESMÉ: (*offstage*) Fluffer!

FLUFFER: Coming!

FLUFFER runs off. Lights out stage left. During the following voice-over, Ronnie hangs ESMÉ and FLUFFER backstage while the stage manager strikes the donkey chair prop and lowers the centre-stage drawbridge panel. Ronnie places EDEN #1 in EDNA's chair and EDNA #1 standing stage left of him.

ANNOUNCER / MALE VOICE: (*recorded*) In other news, city police report that there are no new developments in the Purse Boy bombings. While many community leaders are pointing fingers at the Prairie Revival Party for the rash of bombings targeting gay and lesbian businesses, an uncon-firmed source hints that this may be the work of a homosexual person. This comment has inflamed gay rights activists who denounce it as continued fear-mongering from the Prairie Revival Party.

Light up on centre stage.

EDNA: Lord love a duck, who would do such a thing?

EDEN: Me.

EDNA: Oh Edie!

EDEN: It's true. I did it.

EDNA: There you go again with your teasing, Mis-ter Man.

EDEN: Don't you remember, Mum? What kids used to yell at me. What they called me?

There is a pause as EDNA remembers. She speaks softly.

EDNA: Purse Boy.

EDEN: Yeah, Purse Boy. See, it's me. I did it, Mum.

EDNA: Lord love a duck. What would your father say about this?

EDEN: Why don't you ask him, Mum?

EDNA: Don't be cheeky.

EDEN: I'm not. You talk to him every day, don't you?

EDNA: He's my husband.

EDEN: Was.

EDNA: Is.

EDEN: Mum ...

EDNA: Eden, don't start! Not this. Not now.

EDEN: Mum, please.

EDNA: What do you want from me, Eden? Why have you come home? To upset me? To make fun of me?

EDEN: No. I came to find myself.

EDNA: You think too much. Find yourself. Lord love a duck! You know who you are.

EDEN: No, I don't.

EDNA: Well, I know who you are, Edie. You're my son.

EDEN: No, I'm not.

EDNA: What?

EDEN: I'm someone else's son.

EDNA: No! You're my son. I may not have given you life but I gave you my life. And I've nothing left to give, Eden.

EDEN: How about the truth? Come on, Mum, say it. Please. Please, Mum. Damn you, say it!

Silence. EDNA turns away.

Yeah, well. I guess that says it all.

EDEN leaves, walking to the stage-right area where he is hung from the gallows. He is in dim light dur-ing EDNA's monologue. Her light centre stage has become that of an inner dialogue or dream state. Not dim, just not "real."

EDNA: We sold the farm in 1988. Not because Eden didn't want it. Four years before, my Stanley took ill. A heart attack. It seems that all those years of my sensible prairie cooking had not sustained my man as intended, but instead clogged his arteries to the point where his well-hidden heart simply could not get the blood it needed.

There were four or five important moments in our married life. Our wedding day. The time we were told I could not have children. The occasion of Eden coming into our home and our lives. And this. They weren't all happy, they were just impor-tant. And Stanley's illness was very important.

The Jesus special comes up on Ronnie's face atop the centre-stage bridge.

JESUS: The important moments live on because they live within love.

EDNA: Jesus dear, I'm trying to tell a story. Now if you insist on interrupting, I'll never get through it.

JESUS: Sorry, Edna. What was I thinking. Mind if I listen?

EDNA: Suit yourself.

Jesus special out. EDNA sits in her chair.

Stanley needed an operation. I have never been so afraid in all my life. Stanley saw it all as just a nuisance, like a piece of machinery that was screwy but you didn't have time to fix. I made him make time. And he made me promise not to worry. Nothing to worry about, he'd say. Government health care and the Red Cross. Stanley said you couldn't be in better hands.

So, on October 13, 1984, Stanley had a triple bypass. It was risky, but the doctor tried to make me think it was all going to go just tickety-boo. What none of us expected, including the doctor, was that Stanley would have another heart attack once they had him on the table, which is exactly what happened.

There was a lot of bleeding that complicated matters. To this day I still don't understand all the fancy medical words, but what we learned later was that he had been injected with a clotting agent made from blood the morning after surgery to stop the bleeding. And as bad as it had all been, within a week Stanley seemed to be on the road to recovery. And courtesy of medical science, government health care, and the Red Cross, I brought my man home.

But Stanley never had the new lease on life you hear others talk about. There was no new awakening of his spirit, no realization of the good fortune of having a second chance. I think he realized that while his life wasn't over, the life he had always known had changed. And my Stanley did not like change. He's an Albertan. Change disappointed him.

But that man is the other half of my Velcro. And whether he admitted it or not, he needed me. And I realized how much I needed him.

Light cross-fades from centre stage to stage right.

EDEN: July 1986, my father was back in the hospital. His heart was fine. It was pneumonia. Pneumonia in July. PCP. It was a symptom I had heard of many times.

My father had not spoken to me much since the infamous Thanksgiving-jellied-salad-coming-out

party. Not that he had spoken to me much before that. I grew up in a household where silence really was golden. No one spoke. Ever, except to say, "Pass the potatoes." I guess that's why the movies became so important to me. Up there, on the screen, was a world of people doing the strangest thing. They were talking. To one another. And sometimes, it felt like they were talking to me.

A pool of light comes up on the stage-right catwalk. YOUNG ESMÉ #4 enters, dressed in another dazzling gown. She acts alone, playing the scene with an unseen man. EDEN remains facing front. He doesn't need to watch; it's in his head.

ESMÉ / AMANDA: Rex, before I leave you – and I am leaving you, Rex – there's something you must know.

REX / MALE VOICE: You can't leave me, Amanda. I love you, woman!

ESMÉ / AMANDA: But I don't love you. I've never loved you, Rex!

REX / MALE VOICE: Amanda!

ESMÉ / AMANDA: No Rex, don't! Our liaison was madness, beating like a heart, but without blood. Passionless. Let me go, Rex, let me go!

REX / MALE VOICE: Then go. Go to him! That's it, isn't it? There's someone else, isn't there, Amanda? Who is he? I'll kill the varmint!

ESMÉ / AMANDA: No! For without him I will die!

REX / MALE VOICE: Who is he, Amanda? Answer me!

ESMÉ / AMANDA: He's my one true love! My Eden! (*turns to EDEN and beckons to him*) Eden, come to me. I have so much to tell you.

EDEN: I went to see my father in the hospital. I got as far as the doorway to his ward. He saw me standing there. And turned his head and looked out the window. I left, without saying a word.

ESMÉ: Eden, come home.

YOUNG ESMÉ exits and is hung up. Lights down on EDEN, and cross-fade up again on EDNA as Ronnie crosses to the centre-stage bridge.

EDNA: I thought it was awfully queer, a man like Stanley getting pneumonia in the summer. But the doctor said he was just run down. And sure enough, in three weeks my man was home again. I don't think Eden even considered coming home, but he phoned. He phoned almost every day. He phoned every day and kept pestering me to get some blood tests done on his father. He wouldn't let up on that, day after day. I finally just had to tell him, Lord love a duck, Edie, we've got a medical doctor, government health care, and the blessed Red Cross on our side. I think if we needed a bunch of fancy tests they would have let us know by now.

It was the one time he hung up on me.

But Christmas of that year, our family was together again. I worked like a madwoman! I loved Christmas. And Eden gave me the most wonderful present. A puppy! Called her Crazydoll, after one of those old Esmé Massengill movies. Can you imagine that? A dog named after a movie! I called her Dolly. She was a frisky bundle that Christmas Day, but she brought some life back into this house.

And that night, Stanley even started feeling a little perky. You know, down there. Whispered to me in bed, "Edna, I got another present for you." I said to him, Lord love a duck, Mr. Stanley Rural, what in Sam Hill are you thinking? I've got turkey gas something terrible! But he was gentle. I don't remember him ever being so gentle on top of me. Maybe it was his condition. Maybe it was out of respect for my gas. Whatever it was, I felt like his wife again. No. I felt like his partner. We'd get through this.

Christmas 1986. I thought I was so happy.

Light up again on **EDEN**, *stage right and downstage centre.*

EDEN: Boxing Day my father got sick. We already knew the symptoms, so it was just a matter of getting him to the hospital so they could tell us it was the pneumonia again. It was the one and only time in my life I saw my mother angry. I walked into the kitchen late that night and, in the dark, with only the opened refrigerator for light, I saw her standing at the table with a knife in her hand. She was stabbing the leftover turkey carcass, over and over. Not crying, not screaming, just stabbing. And with each plunge of the knife she whispered, "Happy birthday, happy birthday, happy birthday." At some point I must have moved or she realized I was there, watching. Without turning, without stopping her stabbing, she just said:

Centre-stage light up.

EDNA: Go to bed, Edie. This is between me and him.

EDEN: I went to the hospital the following day. To forgive my father. To ask him to forgive me. But in true Rural fashion not a word was spoken. I didn't make it on time.

EDNA: I've never said goodbye to my Stanley. I couldn't bear to live in this house alone.

EDEN: We greeted 1987 with a funeral. And the results of an autopsy, which I had insisted on. It was exactly what I had known all along. I guess the only saving grace was that Mum and Dad were so old that, well, you know, at least she wasn't at risk.

EDNA: After all those years of married life I can't let him go. He's inside of me. He is my blood.

EDEN: But we don't talk about it. It's not the kind of thing anyone would believe anyway. Not in Turnip Corners. Fuck this town. Fuck this family. I'm going to meet Esmé. I am her blood.

EDEN exits. His light goes out.

EDNA: All right. If it's so important, I'll say it for you, Eden. Your father … My husband, Stanley Rural, is dead. He died of complications brought about by AIDS.

EDNA: I said it out loud. I said it out loud, Eden. (*She stands.*) Eden?

Light slowly fades on **EDNA**, *centre stage. She is hung backstage. Music transition. Ronnie makes his way to stage-left bridge. He slowly raises the stage-left panel, revealing* **EDEN #3**, *nude and hung on a cross à la the crucifixion. This is a special figure, fastened to the cross and with a modified control for moving only* **EDEN's** *head, which is operated from behind by the stage manager. Smoke and light inside the bridge tower.* **ESMÉ #5** *enters from the stage-right side of the stage-left area and stands before him.*

EDEN: Why are you doing this to me?

ESMÉ: I could have impaled you on a stake like my predecessor Vlad, but we vampires have such an aversion to stakes. (*She laughs.*)

EDEN: But this. The cross. You can't look at it, not if you're a vampire.

ESMÉ: Dear boy, you are so damaged by Hollywood. Once, yes, the sign of the cross was repellent to us. Back when people believed in him. Believed in the possibility of his redemption. But no one really believes in him anymore, so the imagery is benign.

EDEN: But he's here.

Edna and her dog, Dolly. Photo courtesy Ronnie Burkett Theatre of Marionettes

ESMÉ: Of course. But do you believe in him, even now? (*EDEN is silent.*) Precisely. Oh, he and I have so much in common.

EDEN: What? You're a monster and he's ...

ESMÉ: Yes?

EDEN: He's him.

ESMÉ: And we're both cursed by a public far more interested in the myth of us rather than the reality. You know, seeing you on the cross, like he was so long ago, makes me think I should put the crucifixion scene back in the show. Poor Mary, sobbing her ass off at the base of the cross.

EDEN: Please. Don't do this. Not to me. I've loved you my whole life.

ESMÉ: Well, your whole life has been shit! You don't have a life. What, you think you're special? A lonely little faggot who lived his life through movies? Darling, that's neither a life nor special. That's common. That's boring. That's general fucking public. You could have done something. Been somebody. But no, you let me do all the work while you watched. Well, sweetie, now I'm watching you. Die.

EDEN: But you're my ...

ESMÉ: What? Your mother?

EDEN: You said so.

ESMÉ: No, you believed so. I just didn't deny it.

EDEN: Why not?

ESMÉ: Because I'm hungry! I'm always hungry. And there's always one of you around. So willing to please me. To feed me.

EDEN: I wanted you to be my mother.

ESMÉ: Well, I'm not, so get over it. You already have a perfectly good mother. A woman so good not even I would fuck with her. But that didn't stop you, did it, darling?

EDEN: No. She is perfectly good, isn't she.

ESMÉ: How lovely. You've had your redeeming moment of insight before dying.

EDEN: No. Please, I want to live!

ESMÉ: You are so dreary. I said that line first! When I played Sissy Mink, an innocent society dame framed for murder in *Cell-Block Celebrity*. Listen to you. You're pathetic. You even steal from me when you're begging for your life. There's nothing original about you.

SPANKY #1 enters.

SPANKY: Esmé, we got trouble. (*He sees EDEN on the cross.*) What's this? I thought we cut the crucifixion scene.

ESMÉ: Spanky darling, join me for a drink?

SPANKY: Who is this?

ESMÉ: A fan. He was dying to meet me.

SPANKY: Why this, Esmé? Why now? We got Jesus Christ in town, he's watching us, and you do this? You think this is funny? You push too far, Esmé. We already got enough trouble on our hands.

ESMÉ: A few dead cattle. Relax, Spanky. They'll just blame it on aliens, like always.

SPANKY: Uta's running all over town feeding on the locals!

ESMÉ: What? Well, did you catch her?

SPANKY: I'm an old man, I haven't fed in days. Now you think I should run a marathon after a crazy, blood-drunk Hun?

ESMÉ: Fine! I'll go.

She starts to exit, then turns back. She looks first at EDEN, then to SPANKY.

Oh, and Spanky, if this one dies while I'm out, don't worry. The little faggot was empty to begin with. (*exits*)

EDEN: Please ...

SPANKY: Shh, don't talk. It's easier that way.

EDEN: Please ...

SPANKY: Kid, don't get me involved. Please.

EDEN is faint and delirious. He starts to sing, softly.

EDEN: "Gather round now one and all ..."

SPANKY: What did you say?

EDEN: "Come and meet my Crazydoll ..."

SPANKY: Well, I'll be.

EDEN: "She's a dame who's earned her fame ..."

SPANKY: "And my heart's back in the game / Come on kids and say her name / Come and meet my crazy Crazydoll."

EDEN: Hi, Mr. Bishop.

SPANKY: Who are *you*, kid?

EDEN: I'm Eden. Eden ... Rural.

SPANKY: Rural? Say, this Edna Rural, the one with the Shroud protecting her ... you related?

EDEN: Yes. She's my ... Crazydoll.

SPANKY: Oy. This is some situation you got your-self into, my friend. It may be too late, but come on, let's get you home.

He moves toward the cross, close to EDEN.

EDEN: Are you going to feed on me, too?

SPANKY: Nah, you're a good kid, I can tell.

EDEN: How?

SPANKY: Trust me, I got a nose for these things.

Lights dim as SPANKY's hands reach up to EDEN. Music transitions in. Ronnie lowers the stage-left panel and crosses to centre-stage bridge. Centre-stage drawbridge down. Light slowly comes up on EDNA in her nightie and robe. SPANKY stands stage left of her.

EDNA: Mr. Bishop, there's a lot I don't understand in this world, and I don't understand any of this. But I thank you. Because I know, somehow, you didn't have to bring my boy home to me.

SPANKY: I heard you were a good woman, Edna Rural. Terrible things happen in the world, I know. But family, that's important. And I thought maybe this terrible thing shouldn't happen to yours, Edna Rural.

EDNA: It's too late for that, I'm afraid.

SPANKY: I'm sorry.

EDNA: Don't be. Everything happens for a reason, I'm sure. And if there's one thing I am, Mr. Bishop, it's positive.

SPANKY: I could tell.

EDNA: Oh? How?

SPANKY: I got a nose for these things. Edna Rural, I'm a vampire!

EDNA: Oh yeah, eh?

SPANKY: You're not afraid?

EDNA: Children fear things of the night, Mr. Bishop. When you're an adult, you learn to fear the monsters that live in daylight.

SPANKY: I've seen these monsters.

EDNA: Why would you give up Hollywood star-dom for such a life, Mr. Bishop?

SPANKY: Please, it's Spanky.

EDNA: Spanky.

SPANKY: Because I had a rage, Edna Rural, not unlike your Eden. And when Uta and Esmé offered me this life, I embraced it as my passport to vengeance.

EDNA: But you were Spanky Bishop! Everyone loved you.

SPANKY: My dear lady, even when I was larger than life on the screen, there were many people who hated me. Who hated what I was.

EDNA: Who could hate the Wacky Bellhop?

SPANKY sits in EDNA's chair as the stage manager climbs onto the stage-left bridge.

SPANKY: We started hearing rumours around the lot. At first, vague threads, nothing concrete. Jews were being shipped away overseas. We were used to being hated, no news in that. A writer on con-tract with the studio, his family still in Europe, he cracks one day in his bungalow. Shoots himself in the head. Of course, the studio covered it up. Said he was a drunk. Edna Rural, I'm telling you, I barely knew the man, but he was no drunk. He had sent someone money to get his wife and kids out, but they're not there. The apartment is in shambles. Gone. Shipped, like cattle. I ask you, Edna Rural, what person wouldn't go crazy with such news?

EDNA: Lord love a duck.

Ronnie hangs SPANKY and EDNA onstage and crosses to the stage-left tower. The stage manager hands him a pair of sunglasses, which he puts on, and the marionette of YOUNG SPANKY dressed as the Wacky Bellhop. Cross-fade, lights down on centre stage and upstage left on YOUNG SPANKY. Front light on Ronnie in sunglasses above. During the following speech he is a studio boss.

SPANKY: So I go to the studio bosses, straight from the set. I say we gotta do something. All of a sudden the door closes, things get serious. They say to me, "Spanky," they say, "it's true. They're killing all the Jews." So I say we gotta tell someone. And they say to me, "Tell who, Spanky?" The government, our government! "Spanky," they tell me, "the govern-ment knows. They don't care." Then the people. We gotta tell the people! "How would we do that, Spanky? How would we convince people of such fantastic horror?" You're in the movie business, I scream. You sell horror and fantasy and craziness to people every day. Make a newsreel. Tell the people!

Ronnie flips sunglasses up as he speaks for EDNA and (old) SPANKY.

EDNA: Good for you, Spanky, good for you!

SPANKY: Good for me? Who was I? I was nobody.

EDNA: You were Spanky Bishop.

Sunglasses down again.

SPANKY: No. I was Schmool Bischovsky, the low serf of low slapschtick from the Lower East Side. Hollywood made me Spanky Bishop, to the world. But to them I was still just Schmool Bischovsky. And they said to me, "Spanky, don't make trouble. Don't make waves. People don't want to hear about this. And they don't want to hear bad news from a goofy-looking Jew like you. Be funny, Spanky. The world loves you when you're funny. We love you … when you're funny." And with that the meeting was over.

Light on Ronnie out as he hands sunglasses to the stage manager.

EDNA: That's terrible.

SPANKY: What's terrible, Edna Rural, is that these were Jews saying this to me. The Heckler brothers themselves, telling me to keep my mouth shut. I just couldn't be funny anymore. It was over for me.

Stage-left light out. Ronnie hands YOUNG SPANKY to the stage manager and crosses back to centre bridge as light centre stage restores.

EDNA: I'm confused.

SPANKY: Don't worry, it's part of your charm.

EDNA: No, I mean why did you become a vampire?

SPANKY: To kill the monsters of daylight. To kill Nazis. But there were too many, even for a thirst like mine. Eight million members of the Nazi party. Eight million guilty Germans with blood on their hands.

EDNA: But isn't Miss Häagen-Daz a German?

SPANKY: Uta is an actress. And once, a great star. We came alive at night, drinking the applause of our audience. You get drunk on that, addicted, but it's a fix you need daily. Long before this life I was already a vampire of sorts. Not many people understand that. But Uta did. So you see, Edna Rural, to me she's family.

EDNA: It's too bad you didn't know that earlier, Spanky.

SPANKY: What?

EDNA: That family isn't always about blood.

SPANKY: Edna Rural, do an old man a favour. End it. Drive a stake through my heart!

EDNA: Oh Spanky, not in the living room!

SPANKY: Please, Edna Rural. I can't go on. I'm finished!

EDNA: No, you're not! Listen to you. Finished! Shame on you, Spanky, shame on you. Why,

there are lots of monsters still walking free. Getting away with murder in broad daylight. And too much unfinished business that no government commission or inquiry will ever set it right. Lord love a duck, we need solutions with some teeth in them. So you get up, Spanky. Get up and go on. Go on for my Eden. Go on for me.

SPANKY: You're one hell of a woman, Edna Rural. I'd kiss you, but I got my teeth in.

EDNA: Just tell me one last thing, Spanky.

SPANKY: Anything for you, Edna Rural.

EDNA: What does "oy" mean?

SPANKY: Oy. Well, it's Yiddish for what you say, Edna Rural. "Lord love a duck."

EDNA: Well, Lord love a duck! Good luck, Spanky Bishop.

SPANKY: Good luck, Edna Rural.

They embrace. SPANKY exits left and is hung up backstage.

EDNA: Happy hunting! And Spanky … go east.

EDEN #4 enters right, dressed in pajamas and a robe. His neck is bandaged.

EDEN: Mum?

EDNA: Eden, oy! What are you doing up? Go back to bed!

EDEN: I need to tell you something.

EDNA: Later, you're too weak.

EDEN: No, now.

EDNA: All right then, but you come sit down.

EDEN: (*sits*) I thought Esmé Massengill was my mother. You know, my birth mother.

EDNA: Oh Eden. You've watched too many movies, dear.

EDEN: I should have just asked you, but you never wanted to talk about it. You were so ashamed that I was adopted.

EDNA: Is that what you think?

EDEN: Yes.

EDNA: Oh Eden, no. No. I was always so proud of you. That you were my little boy.

EDEN: Really?

EDNA: Eden, most people who can have children are stuck with what life hands them. Your father and me got a special baby. It's like … well, you know when you go to the IGA and want to buy a roast? The butcher doesn't just hand you any old piece of meat. No, he puts them all on display and lets you choose the best one. Well, that's what your father and me did. We chose the prime cut. We chose you, Edie.

EDEN: Mum, you're so weird. I always thought you were ashamed of me because I wasn't part of you.

EDNA: You *are* a part of me. But Eden, it was different when I was younger. We didn't have the talk shows telling us how to think, or what was right. We had something worse. Ladies' church groups. A bunch of mean-spirited women who said one thing to your face and another behind your back. And if you couldn't have a baby, those holier-than-thou mothers looked at you as if you were broken. They whispered things about you. They made you … they made me … feel less than a whole woman.

It's true, Edie, I couldn't talk about this because I was ashamed. But not of you. Of me. I'm ashamed of broken, barren Edna.

EDEN: You're not broken. You're a beautiful woman.

EDNA: Listen to you, bending my ear like some Carlo Biscotti in a movie! No, Edie, I'm just a silly old biddy in a Sears housecoat. But your mother, the woman who brought you into this world, she was beautiful.

EDEN: Mum, you don't have to do this.

EDNA: Yes, I do. I'm tired, Edie. Tired of secrets. You should know. It's true.

EDEN: What, Mum?

EDNA: That your mother was the most beautiful gal in all of Turnip Corners.

EDEN: You knew her?

EDNA: She was my maid of honour.

EDEN: Miss Pickles?

EDNA: Cora Jean. As lovely as those ballerinas in a windup jewellery case.

Light centre stage dims and comes up stage left. EDNA and EDEN are hung onstage as Ronnie goes to CORA JEAN at the bandstand. As he crosses, he takes a black toque from the stage manager. Xylophone music plays during the scene, although CORA JEAN does not play it herself. She leaves the instrument and steps off the bandstand as EDNA continues talking.

EDNA: After your father and I got married, Cora Jean took the train to Winnipeg. It was big news in Turnip Corners, one of our own going off to the city. Winnipeg and the ballet! It all seemed so exotic then. We knew she would make something of herself.

CORA JEAN dances for a moment, then stops as the music becomes darker.

EDNA: But the real world outside isn't as sugar-coated as the ballets that lived inside her mind. But Cora Jean didn't know that. She was always off in her beautiful world. Always seeing painted scenery in front of her eyes, not reality. And so of course she didn't see him. Even when he was practically beside her, I don't think she ever knew he was there.

EDEN: Who?

EDNA: The man. Some man. Walking home from her class one night, Cora Jean was … raped.

Ronnie yanks the toque onto his head and jumps down off the bridge, standing in the alley between the stage-left side tower and the stage-left bridge. He is the man. As the music reaches its strange, violent crescendo, he grabs the puppet. There is a scream – CORA JEAN's – and he covers her mouth. Saturated red light and music peak as Ronnie thrusts forward. He releases CORA JEAN, quickly climbs back on the bridge, and removes the toque.

EDNA: Beaten and raped by a man she never knew and never saw again. And I don't think she ever saw that beautiful scenery in her mind again.

CORA JEAN walks slowly off in the alley between the stage-left side tower and bridge. Ronnie crosses to the centre-stage bridge as light restores there.

EDNA: She came home. It was kept quiet. Everyone knew, but not a word was spoken, not even in private. But when her time came I sat with her. I owed her that. I don't know if she recognized me, but she squeezed my hand and stared at me the whole time. She was quiet so long, it's like a dream ended when that baby came out hollerin'. You woke me up from that dream, Eden. I was the first person to hold you. And I named you. Eden. Because what was barren had become bountiful.

EDEN: That was you in the light.

EDNA: Poor Cora Jean. I don't even think she remembers.

EDEN: Yes, she does. She sent me a note.

EDNA: No, Eden. I sent you that note.

EDEN: You? Why?

EDNA: Because I was so lonely, with your father gone and Dolly dying. I needed you, Edie. I may not be your flesh and blood, but you're my heart and soul. I knew you wouldn't come home just to see me, but I thought you might come to her. Your mother. Your beautiful mother.

A moment of silence, then EDEN places a hand on EDNA's arm.

EDEN: You are my mother. My only mother. And I am your son. Tell anyone who thinks differently to fuck off.

EDNA: Eden!

EDEN: Mum, tell them.

EDNA: Eden, don't.

EDEN: Mum, I'm really sick. So I need you to promise me you'll tell them to fuck off. Promise?

EDNA: I promise.

EDEN: Then say it.

EDNA: Eden ...

EDEN: Please, Mum. Say it out loud. If you're proud, it's not a secret and they can't use it against you anymore.

EDNA is silent, then slowly.

EDNA: This is my son. And I ... I am not a broken woman. So fuck off, you church bitches!

EDEN: That's my girl!

EDNA: Now you do something for me.

EDEN: Anything for you, Crazydoll.

EDNA: Stop being so angry.

EDEN: I can't. I'm filled with rage.

EDNA: Eden, that's not rage. It's disappointment. The curse of the Rural men.

EDEN: Forgive me, Mum.

EDNA: It's not my forgiveness you need, dear. You know what you have to do.

EDEN: Oh Mum, come on. You don't believe in that.

EDNA: Eden, he's in town. It won't hurt to ask!

EDEN: (*looks up*) Hey. Are you up there? I'm sorry.

Light on Ronnie's face.

JESUS: I don't need your apology, Eden.

EDNA: He wants your forgiveness. Give it to him.

JESUS: He already has it, Edna. What do you expect me to do?

EDNA: What do I expect? I expect you to heal him. That's what you do, isn't it?

JESUS: Sometimes, yes.

EDNA: Yes, sometimes. When you feel like it. When you need some attention. I guess you didn't care for any publicity when Spanky's people were being herded off like cattle. A bit too messy for you, dear? Where were you during the Holocaust? Funny, I thought you were a Jew. Didn't you need attention when Cora Jean was raped? Didn't you hear her screams? Obviously you didn't need attention when my Stanley was dying. Oh no, he was ... what was he to you? You and your cross. Your bloody red cross! What was my man then? A sacrifice? An example? I am talking to you! I've talked to you my whole life and you never answered me. Well, you're in my house now, mister, and you will answer to me!

JESUS: I'm sorry I disappoint you, Edna.

EDNA: I am not disappointed, don't you accuse me of that! I'm *angry* at you. My boy is ill. And you can fix it, in the twinkling of an eye. Well, then do it. Heal him. Why do you want him so soon? Why now? You took my man, you took my dog, well, take *me* next, but not my son. I'm not like your family. Your father. I can't watch my boy suffer and die just to teach a lesson that no one will ever learn.

JESUS: Let him learn peace, Edna. With me.

EDNA: Peace? You've got some cheek, waltzing into this house and using that word, mister! All the slaughtering and hatred and sacrifice made in your name. You call that peace? Once I thought all paths led to you, but I see you for what you really are. You're nothing. Nothing more than a road of sadness. Of despair. Damn you! Damn you and your street of blood!

JESUS: Stop blaming me! I'm tired of being blamed for everything. I'm not to blame. Eden started this, Edna, not me. All I can offer him is the road home.

EDNA: Well, that's not good enough for me! Shame on you. I wonder what your mother would think of you now.

She turns away. EDEN looks up.

EDEN: I'm sorry.

JESUS: Shut up, Eden.

YOUNG EDEN #2, wearing the wedding dress, appears in the alley between the stage-right and centre-stage bridges.

JESUS: Tell him.

EDEN: Who is that?

JESUS: It's Purse Boy. Washed in blood. Tell him.

EDEN: I'm sorry.

YOUNG EDEN: I forgive you.

YOUNG EDEN exits. Intro to "Behold, the Blessed Prairie" starts as underscore.

EDEN: I forgave myself. Mum? Mum!

EDNA: Shh, Eden, it's all right.

EDEN: Mum, where am I?

EDNA: Oh Edie. You're home. (*She sings to him softly.*)

> "BEHOLD, THE BLESSED PRAIRIE"
> *At dusk the dormant sky turns flame*
> *A gentle breeze stirs wild again*
> *And all around the eyes can see*
> *How this our land is strong and free*
> *Let us rejoice, with grateful voice*
> *Behold*
> *Behold*

EDEN sings the last line.

EDEN: Behold, the blessed prairie.

EDNA: Sure is nice to hear you sing again, Edie.

EDEN: Mum?

EDNA: Yes dear?

EDEN: I'm not afraid.

EDNA: That's good, Edie, that's real good.

EDEN gasps quietly, thrusting forward a bit, then slumps back into the chair. He is dead. EDNA holds him close.

EDNA: My little boy.

The tableau is held for a moment, then lights snap out centre stage and up on Ronnie's Jesus special above.

JESUS: Esmé!

Jesus special snaps out as the "Techno Jesus" sound-and-light show begins again. Ronnie clears the two marionettes and removes the gallows hanging rods as he crosses to the stage-right side tower. The stage manager places a duplicate cross downstage left and hangs (a short-strung) ESMÉ #6 in front of the stage-left panel. Ronnie jumps off the side tower, enters the acting area stage right, crosses to centre, and slams the drawbridge shut.

JESUS: Why have you done this? He was mine!

He crosses to ESMÉ, taking the control in his hand and playing the scene on her level.

He was lost. And now he's found.

ESMÉ: No darling, now he's dead. In his mama's arms. Oh, that must bring back a lot of memories for you!

Ronnie kneels, grabs ESMÉ by the throat, and lifts her straight up to his eye level.

JESUS: Don't you dare!

They are eye to eye for a moment. He slowly puts the marionette down again.

I gave my blood for you.

ESMÉ: I wonder how much I could get for a pint of that.

JESUS: It's not for sale.

ESMÉ: Oh please! The world has been paying the price for your blood far too long.

JESUS: I gave it freely.

ESMÉ: Look, sweetie, that myth may wash with the desperate and discouraged, but I don't buy it. You should stay down here with these people for a while. You won't be crowned in glory. You'll be covered in dirt and shit and blood.

JESUS: It's not time.

ESMÉ: Well, don't wait too long. Comebacks get harder the longer you wait, believe me. And look, there's your cross.

He picks up the cross.

JESUS: What is this, Esmé?

ESMÉ: Home sweet home.

JESUS: Stop it.

ESMÉ: What's the matter? Don't you recognize it?

He throws the cross down.

JESUS: I said stop.

ESMÉ: That's it, isn't it? Oh, I know that most of your history was rewritten to serve the scare tactics of Rome, but you never really died on the cross, did you?

JESUS: What are you saying?

ESMÉ: You are a liar. An illegitimate bastard who invented a fantasy life for himself to protect his whore mother!

JESUS: I'm warning you!

ESMÉ: What's the matter, darling? Finding it hard to turn the other cheek?

JESUS: I died on the cross.

ESMÉ: Liar.

JESUS: I rose again.

ESMÉ: Liar.

JESUS: I am sanctuary. I am forgiveness. I am love.

ESMÉ: You are a liar!

JESUS: What do you want?!

ESMÉ: Proof.

JESUS: Of what?

ESMÉ: Your splendid pain.

JESUS: I can't. Not again.

ESMÉ: Show me.

JESUS: Once. He said just once.

ESMÉ: Show me.

He lifts the cross and holds it, remembering.

JESUS: I was all alone up there. That's why I appear, one at a time. I know the longing. I know the loneliness.

ESMÉ: I want to know your pain. Let me drink from your holy cup.

She crawls onto him. As the following seduction becomes more intimate, her mouth gets closer to his neck.

JESUS: You want my pain?

ESMÉ: Yes.

JESUS: You want my suffering?

ESMÉ: Yes.

JESUS: You want my blood?

ESMÉ: Yes darling. Give it to me.

JESUS: Then know it. And to hell with you!

He raises the cross and violently thrusts it into her. Shrill sound-and-music sting. Red light fills the area.

ESMÉ: Why?!

JESUS: Now you know my pain. And you are free.

ESMÉ dies, her control thrown to the floor. Ronnie leans and kisses her on the lips. He then holds the cross in front of him, clasps each side with his hands, and stares into the audience.

JESUS: Fine. I'm back.

Music begins as Ronnie thrusts upward. The stage manager is above on the stage-left bridge and takes the rising cross from his hands as the "Techno Jesus" sound-and-light show begins again. Ronnie clears

ESMÉ and hangs her backstage right. He climbs back up on the bridge level and he and the stage manager position three rolled-up quilt panels on each bridge leaning rail. Music changes. Lighting rebuilds to a daytime wash. EDNA #4 enters from the alley entrance stage left of the centre bridge tower. She is dressed in a hat and coat, carrying her purse.

EDNA: I haven't slept in days. Needed to finish my quilt. Needed it to be done and out of my hands. But I feel good. I feel calm. Okay dear, let 'er rip.

The stage manager unties two cords on the stage-left leaning rail and a quilt panel unrolls, covering the entire area from the leaning rail to the deck floor. The centre of the panel reads, "Stanley Rural, 1924–1986." There is a cloth appliqué of a plate of bacon and eggs.

EDNA: This is for my Stanley. My bacon-and-eggs man. A remembrance panel in honour of his life. Hung here for all of Turnip Corners to see.

She begins to cross to stage right.

The whole quilt was supposed to be for Stanley. I guess I figured if I made it so big that it would never be finished then I would never have to acknowledge why it was being made in the first place. But life had another plan and I had to cut it into a manageable size. I had to hang my quilt up for everyone to see. And if they don't like it, or can't deal with it, or if it makes them angry, well then, as Eden would have said, fuck them.

The stage manager unties another panel on the stage-right bridge leaning rail. It reads, "Eden Urbane, 1957–2001." There is a cloth appliqué of musical notes.

This is for my Eden. I wasn't sure how best to tell the world about him. He was a complex boy. Man. But those notes are music that he loved. The beginning of the chorus to "Midnight in Monte Carlo."

(*singing softly*): "All I remember / Is midnight and moonlight / You're but a ghost in the mist ..."

My Edie. He always loved this purse.

She walks toward centre stage.

So here I am, flanked by my men. And forever a part of them. It was a long time in the making, but we were ... no, we are the Rural family.

Ronnie unties a third quilt panel, which unrolls directly behind EDNA, centre stage. It reads, "Edna Rural, 1927–?" There is a cloth appliqué of a fork sewn onto the centre of the quilt, shadowed by the familiar red AIDS ribbon.

Yes, I made my own panel. Can't assume that anyone else will acknowledge how I die, much less care. Turnip Corners is a funny place that way. It's a hard town to be positive in, if you catch my drift. And Lord love a duck, who would care about an HIV-positive old biddy in a Sears housedress anyway!

Jesus special up on Ronnie's face.

JESUS: I do.

EDNA turns and looks up.

EDNA: I know that. Now. Thanks for appearing in my quilt, Jesus.

JESUS: Thank you for recognizing me, Edna. I hope the road is clearer now.

EDNA: Oh, I don't know if it's any clearer, dear, but at least I know which direction I'm headed in. When you see your mum, tell her I think she should be very proud of you.

The light fades out on Ronnie.

I always thought that when my quilt was done, it would be finished. But I don't think that's true, necessarily. Eventually, hopefully, someone will take that big question mark off of my panel and replace it with a date. I could have left it blank, I suppose, but somehow that question mark is reassuring to me. A great big sign saying, "Well, Edna, what's it going to be? What sweet adventure will you take today?"

So I'm going to dance while the music is still playing. And I won't worry if there's no one to dance with. I'm going to turn the TV off and look at things in three dimensions. I'm going to switch off the radio and listen to my own thoughts. I'm going to take a nap in the middle of the day and not feel guilty about it. I'm going to call up Don Divine and ask him for a date. I'm going down to the Red Lantern Café and have myself a plate of french fries for supper. And I'm saving room for dessert, because this time I'm going to have a slice of the pie!

FLUFFER appears in the entrance alley just left of the centre-stage bridge.

FLUFFER: Mrs. Rural!

EDNA: Oh Fluffer dear, don't you look pretty today!

FLUFFER: Oh thanks, Mrs. Rural. Hey, we got a postcard from Mr. Bishop!

EDNA: Oh Spanky! How's he doing?

FLUFFER: Well, he lost Miss Häagen-Daz in Montreal, but he made it to Ottawa and he says he's never eaten better in his life.

EDNA: Good for him. I hope he gets to dine at 24 Sussex.

FLUFFER: I've got Eden's Monte Carlo loaded with all the gear, Mrs. Rural. We'd better shake a leg if we're gonna make the show on time.

EDNA: Thank you, Fluffer dear. I'll just say my goodbyes.

FLUFFER: I'll wait in the car, Mrs. Rural.

EDNA: Fluffer, when we're in public, I think you should call me by my stage name, dear.

FLUFFER: Sure thing … Miss Edna Urbane! (*exits*)

EDNA: Well, I'd best be off. I've taken over Eden's Karaoke Memory Lane business, and Fluffer and I got ourselves a gig at a hospice in the city. Oh, I know, I'm just a silly old biddy. But I think it'll work out just fine. And if there's one thing I am, it's positive.

Sound of a car horn.

Did you hear that? It's life calling me again. Wish me luck, dear, and remember, no matter what happens to you, keep your fork because I guarantee … there's pie.

All right, Winnie dear, you can play us out now.

Music in, a piano version of "Behold, the Blessed Prairie." EDNA exits as acting area light fades, leaving a special on the fork motif of the centre quilt panel. Ronnie crosses to the stage-left side tower, picks up a miniature blue Monte Carlo, and attaches it to a string running along the "highway" atop the upstage puppet hanging rail. The stage manager, on the stage-right side tower, begins to pull the string, causing the car to drive in front of the upstage prairie horizon. Music swells and the horizon glows as Ronnie waves goodbye.

Blackout.

END

JOAN MACLEOD

(b. 1954)

Teenage bullying has become a central issue of our time, not just in Canada, but maybe especially in Canada, and particularly in British Columbia. The highly publicized 1997 killing of Victoria schoolgirl Reena Virk by a group of her classmates, mostly female, and the YouTube confessional of bullied Vancouver-area teen Amanda Todd, who took her own life in 2012, made headlines around the world. Though certainly not a new problem, schoolyard bullying seems to have become more prevalent or more acute in recent years, and the ability of social media to make it vividly present has magnified the issue. In the wake of the Reena Virk tragedy, and having written plays about teenage girls with autism (*Toronto, Mississippi*) and eating disorders (*Little Sister*), Joan MacLeod took on the subject of girl-on-girl violence. Commissioned and toured internationally by Vancouver's Green Thumb Theatre, one of North America's foremost TYA (Theatre for Young Audiences) companies, *The Shape of a Girl* has become a modern Canadian classic – widely produced in this country and abroad, for audiences of all ages – and a touchstone for discussions of bullying and responsibility.

Joan MacLeod was born and grew up in Vancouver, earning degrees in creative writing from the University of Victoria (B.A., 1978) and the University of British Columbia (M.F.A., 1981). While attending a poetry workshop at the Banff Centre in 1984, she met playwright Alan Williams who encouraged her to try her hand at drama. The result was the monologue *Jewel*, which she sent to Tarragon Theatre in Toronto. Tarragon invited her to join its Playwrights Unit in 1985 and subsequently premiered her first four plays. MacLeod remained playwright-in-residence there for six years. Her first produced work, however, was the libretto for a chamber opera, *The Secret Garden*, presented by Toronto's COMUS Music Theatre in 1985. Based on the classic children's novel, it won MacLeod a Dora Mavor Moore Award for best new musical.

Jewel premiered at Tarragon in 1987. Set in 1985, it takes the form of a widow's moving valentine to her husband who drowned in the sinking of the oil rig *Ocean Ranger* three years earlier. *Jewel* received Chalmers Award and Dora Mavor Moore Award nominations for best new play. It also marked MacLeod's first (and last) experience as a stage actor when, the day before opening and with no previous experience, she replaced the actress who had been rehearsing the part. She later reprised the role for radio. Retitled *Hand of God*, the radio adaptation of *Jewel* garnered honourable mention in the prestigious Prix Italia competition, and has been produced in five languages. The female monologue would become one of MacLeod's favourite theatrical formats.

Tarragon also premiered *Toronto, Mississippi* (1987) and *Amigo's Blue Guitar* (1990). MacLeod's first full-length stage play and a national success, *Toronto, Mississippi* (collected in *Modern Canadian Plays,* vol. 1) is a rich family comedy focused on an autistic teen and her father, a professional Elvis imitator. In *Amigo's Blue Guitar* a political refugee from El Salvador comes to live with a family in British Columbia's Gulf Islands, his experience of torture and horror challenging their inadequate Canadian liberalism. The play was subsequently produced across Canada as well as in Chicago, London, Mexico, and Alaska. The published text of *Amigo's Blue Guitar* won the Governor General's Award for Drama in 1991.

Next came *The Hope Slide* (1992), a widely staged one-woman play about an actress who assumes the characters of three dead Doukhobors in an attempt to comprehend the deaths of her friends from AIDS, and to rally her own crumbling hope. The Tarragon production won a Chalmers Award, and the play was produced across Canada. *Little Sister* (1994), a TYA play about body image and eating disorders, co-produced by Vancouver's Green Thumb and Toronto's Theatre Direct, also won the Chalmers. Ottawa's Great Canadian Theatre Company first produced MacLeod's millennial comic drama *2000* (1996). Set on the border between city and wilderness in North Vancouver, *2000* combines West Coast mysticism with the concerns of an upper-middle-class couple wrestling with mid-life crisis.

The Shape of a Girl was co-produced in 2001 by Green Thumb Theatre and Alberta Theatre Projects (ATP) at Calgary's PanCanadian playRites Festival (now the Enbridge playRites Festival of New Canadian Plays). With *Homechild* (2006), premiered by Toronto's CanStage, MacLeod radically shifted generations, telling the story of elderly characters who relive their traumatic past as orphaned and abandoned young children who were transported from Britain to Canada in the early twentieth century. In *Another Home Invasion* (2009), first co-produced by Tarragon and ATP at the Enbridge playRites Festival, eighty-year-old Jean faces a literal home invasion and a more profound metaphorical one as she struggles with her husband's dementia. One of MacLeod's great female monologues, *Another Home Invasion* was nominated for best new play awards in Toronto and Calgary as well as the Governor General's Award for Drama, and has played across Canada. Another premiere at the Enbridge playRites Festival, *The Valley* (2013) is MacLeod's exploration of a teenage boy's depression and the challenges faced by police in having to deal with the mentally ill.

In addition to writing for the stage, MacLeod has published poetry and fiction in more than a dozen literary journals, written radio plays and multiple episodes of the TV series *Edgemont,* and adapted *Jewel* and *Amigo's Blue Guitar* for television. She is currently a professor in the department of writing at the University of Victoria, where she has taught since 2006. In 2011, MacLeod received the Siminovitch Prize for playwriting, Canadian theatre's richest award.

The Shape of a Girl won best new play awards in Calgary and Vancouver. Olivier Choinière's French translation, *Cette fille-là* (Théâtre La Licorne, 2004), won Montreal's Masque Award for Best Franco-Canadian Production. The play has been widely produced and toured across Canada in both English and French; in New York, Chicago, San Francisco, and Seattle; as well as in Australia, Ireland, Germany (in German translation), Iceland (in Icelandic), France, Martinique, and Guadeloupe (in French). Canadian actresses Jenny Young, Jennifer Paterson, and Sophie Cadieux have earned extravagant praise for their portrayal of Braidie in various productions.

Although intelligent, witty fifteen-year-old Braidie reads and writes poetry, she's also a normal adolescent trying to figure out how to fit into the world. Unable to connect with her distant father ("Planet Dad") and the mother who drives her crazy ("the voice of Mum"), Braidie addresses her funny, anguished confession to her absent older brother, Trevor, who has recently left home to live on his own. On the cusp of adulthood, she is about to leave home as well, figuratively, and faces a critical challenge to her adolescent values. Friendship, loyalty, and popularity are high school essentials. In addition to being Braidie's best friend since childhood, Adrienne is one of those high-status kids whose friendship wins you points. And squealing on anyone to an adult authority is a major taboo.

But Sofie's torment and torture have become much too troubling for Braidie to ignore, especially in light of the story she has been following on TV about another bullied teenage girl, this one killed by her peers in Victoria. (Reena Virk is never mentioned by name but the circumstances of the story are identical.) "Those girls," those slutty low-lifes who beat up the victim and burned her with cigarettes and drowned her – Braidie is so not them. Yet, to her horror, she gets it. She realizes that the girls who did it are in some ways "regular" girls. "A monster in the shape of a girl" (the line slightly altered from Adrienne Rich's poem "Planetarium") could be the tormentor or the one who watches and does nothing. Braidie understands the behaviour because, in her own way, she's part of the culture: "I know the way in." The question is whether she can conjure a way out.

The Shape of a Girl is a powerful piece of theatre, a wonderful role for a young actress, and an important teaching tool for educators wanting to engage students in discussion about the self-imposed silence, willful blindness, conformity, peer pressure, and other issues associated with teen bullying that can lead to tragedies like Reena Virk's. In an excellent essay, sociologist Michele Byers argues that *The Shape of a Girl* and two other fictionalized accounts of the Virk murder distort its reality by eliding the racialized nature of the violence against dark-skinned Reena, daughter of South Asian parents. Race hardly enters into MacLeod's equation, I would argue, because it hardly enters into Braidie's. Braidie and her friends are all the same colour, so race is extraneous for her. She sees the Virk story as a mirror in which girls of any colour, herself included, can reveal their reflection in the shape of a monster.

The Shape of a Girl

Joan MacLeod

The Shape of a Girl was commissioned by Green Thumb Theatre and first produced in February 2001 at Alberta Theatre Projects in Calgary, a co-production with Green Thumb, as part of the PanCanadian playRites Festival, with the following cast:

BRAIDIE   Jenny Young

Directed by Patrick McDonald
Costumes Design by David Boechler
Lighting Design by Brian Pincott
Set and Properties Design by Scott Reid
Music Composed by Ian Tamblyn
Stage Managed by Rhonda Kambeitz

PRODUCTION NOTE

The Shape of a Girl is a one-act, one-character play. Braidie is a fifteen-year-old female. The running time is approximately eighty minutes; there is no intermission.

SETTING

An island off the coast of British Columbia, near Vancouver. The late 1990s.

SET

The original set was a gravel beach with a large and beautiful driftwood tree upstage.

Darkness, a bell sounds from the distance. Spot up on BRAIDIE. She speaks to her absent brother, Trevor.

BRAIDIE:

I woke up this morning to this sound. This sound that feels far away one second, then from right inside my gut the next. Very pure with the potential to be extremely creepy. But before I've even opened my eyes this other thing worms its way in and wreaks its usual havoc: the voice of Mum.

I tell you, Trevor, she's gotten even worse since you left. She is yelling that THIS *is* IT. What IT is I still haven't figured out. At this point in my life being kicked out would be incredible. All I know is her voice chiselled, no, burrowed into my brain before I was fully conscious. By the time I'm actually awake the voice of Mum has reached this pitch that is making the panelling beside my bed vibrate. *Braidie, I have had* IT!

And then I remembered that day, that truly outstanding day, Trevor, when you told Mum that in another life her voice is going to come back as an earwig. I was thinking of that exact thing when that sound comes again, and this time I know what it is. The blind are back, back at their summer camp across the bay – which is highly weird because it's hardly April. That sound is the gong that tells the blind folks to get up or come for porridge. It just seems like it's really close, sound carrying across water and all that.

And for some reason today, on this particular morning, at this particular point in time, after living on this stupid island my whole life, I am acutely aware for the first time that sound carries across water BOTH ways. Did that ever dawn on you? Did you ever have this really ugly image of Mum's voice snaking around the blind camp? There they are: lying on their bunk beds, innocent as pie. *You're your own worst enemy!* That'll get them sitting up or worse yet shuffling off to the cookshack, Mum's voice attacking them from above like some crow gone nuts. *Keep your shoulders back! You are walking like an ape!*

I am thinking of all these things, Trevor, and how I wish I could talk to you about it. I wish you were here, asleep in your room. You, big brother, with the unparalleled ability to sleep until three in the afternoon three months in a row; you who can drive all the way to your place in Whistler using only your peripheral vision. I am thinking of all this stuff then all of a sudden this seaplane lands, right outside the deck. I pretend, just like we always did, that the plane is here to kill us. BAM! BAM! BAM! – it'll dive-bomb the whole island. Bullets will explode the mattress around me, outline my arms, my legs.

That is how my day begins, that is how I greet the morning. And from across the water the gong from the camp sounds again. I think, briefly, very briefly, about actually going to school. I also contemplate apologizing to Mum for the basic snarkiness of my disposition – all inherited, of course – but she's already left for work. Then I'm pretending we're all Muslims or Buddhist monks or anything except who we are. And that the gong is calling us to prayer or at least ending this round.

That the sound means – STOP, don't move a muscle, help is on the way.

———◆———

I watch the school bus come and go. I haven't been to school in a week now. Adrienne always waits until the last minute to climb aboard. She looks tall and grumpy. Mum says I need to make more friends. She reminds me that in grade five I almost had a heart attack because Adrienne and I had different teachers for the first time, the first time since preschool. In preschool Annie made a point of trying to let other kids sit beside Adrienne at circle and I'd just freak. And Annie and me, we'd have to go off together for a quiet time in her rocking chair. She smelled like playdough. I'd bury my head in her shirt and I'd blubber all over Annie. The world was ending. I love Adrienne so much I used to worry I was a lesbian and when Dad would say stuff like: *You two sure are joined at the hip!* I thought he was worried that I was a lesbian, too.

– *If Adrienne jumped off the Lions Gate Bridge, would you?* All over the world, parents have been posing this question to their children forever. I used to think I'd want to be dead if Mum or Dad

died. Now I actually imagine them dead so that I'll be able to stay out late and do what I want. If Adrienne jumped off the Lions Gate I wouldn't follow BUT – I would spend the rest of my life writing poems about her short one. And explaining the devastating effect that her death had on, well, her obviously. And me. I'm not the suicidal type. Even if I was a complete mess and my brain had turned to Jell-O I wouldn't want anyone pulling the plug.

Mum would pull the plug on me in a second. Remember that, Trevor. Make sure Mum doesn't pull the plug.

So the bus is gone and Mum is gone and even though it is my intention to at least try and write a poem I end up flipping on the TV. I watch one of those really bad shows about really bad things that happen to really depressingly normal people. We're still not allowed cable so the reception is just rancid – everybody's foreheads have gone alien and bodies all shivery – like when you'd try to zap down something racy from Pay. The show's called MOST DANGEROUS AND AWFUL MOMENTS EVER.

They're showing this speedboat, this speedboat in Florida somewhere and it's heading full speed, dead ahead, for this big bleacher full of spectators. God knows what the problem with the boat is, but the guy driving it is yelling and waving his hands, warning the people in the stands to get the hell out of the way. The boat smashes right into the crowd – chaos I tell you – blood and guts and totally nuts.

And I was thinking of this poet, this poet I have recently discovered called Stevie Smith. Not a guy Stevie, a girl Stevie. I was thinking of this thing she said that I loved, that reminded me of my friends and me. This thing about not waving but drowning. I was thinking of that when the rabbit ears sort of shake, almost like they're one of those divining things, and all of a sudden the whole scene changes on the TV.

And there we are. A group of girls – just like me and Adrienne and Jackie and Amber. A group of girls with hair and jeans and jackets. *They are not waving, they are drowning.* And this group of girls on the TV starts waving, right on cue. Weird, I'm thinking. This is highly weird.

And what feels even stranger is that the picture is actually clear for once, from the neck down at least. But their faces are blurry, smudged, almost as though someone has taken an eraser and tried to rub them out.

And then I realize who these girls are. They are supposed to look distorted because they are young offenders and we aren't allowed to see who they are. They are accused of assault, accused of murder, accused of killing another girl – a fourteen-year-old girl. One is wearing these big high-heel runners like Amber's. They are all standing out front of the courthouse while the judge is taking a break. They are laughing like maniacs. Me and Adrienne often laugh like maniacs. Honestly, totally unprovoked.

Then the news guy starts talking about how one saw her dad murdered when she was six. And another girl's dad was also murdered. And I feel stupid to have ever thought we have anything in common. In fact it pisses me off that they are trying to pass themselves off as normal. And even though it's illegal to do so, I can imagine their faces: slutty eyes, chapped lips. Then one girl waves again and yells *hi* and you just know she's making goofy faces just like Adrienne and me did when we saw the Canucks, when we thought we were making our debut on national television.

I don't know why I have to find out more about those girls, I just do. They are all over the news. Always in a group, always from the back or with their jackets pulled over their heads. I don't want to look at the victim, it's too depressing. But she is everywhere, too – as a baby with her dad, as a regular weird kid on holiday, then one of those blown-up yearbook pictures that always mean someone is either a movie star or dead.

And then that gong across the bay starts ringing again. Except this time it sounds like a summons, like someone is calling me.

Lights up on the set. **BRAIDIE** *is on a beach, perhaps leaning against a log, looking out at the water. She is wearing jeans and a warm jacket. A tangle of blackberry vines and bush rises up steeply on the bank behind.*

Hello! I'm here ... Attention: Braidie has landed.

BRAIDIE *looks upstage.*

But up at the camp the shutters are all still up, the flagpole is bare, not a blind guy in sight. And you know that gong? It's just the same old bell. I was expecting something out of *Tarzan*. So it's me, solo. Braidie on the beach. Remember how much we used to love coming here to spy?

BRAIDIE *holds her arms straight out in front.*

Trevor, let's be blind. (*shutting her eyes*) Shut your eyes and you can hear the summer. The little kids arriving, so wired up. And the older ones with their dogs, those outstanding dogs. I love Buster but I've always felt he was an inferior species of animal. I mean, I've never seen a seeing eye dog eating goose shit or sniffing up another retriever.

A bell rings softly in the distance. **BRAIDIE** *opens her eyes and looks up the bank, watching a memory from years ago.*

Trevor? Did you hear that? Do you see? It's Sofie, twelve years old. The camp is deserted like now. It's winter. I am below her, also twelve. Adrienne is up the hill beside Sofie, always nearly one year older. Sofie wants to ring the bell because she thinks Adrienne might kill her and I think Adrienne might kill Sofie, too. I watch Adrienne watching Sofie. Adrienne is so mad her mouth is shaking. Sofie is watching me. She has no idea my body has turned to concrete. I can't move and I can't shout. All I can do is see.

———◆———

BRAIDIE goes back in time. She is eight years old. She gallops around and around until she falls over, exhausted and happy.

We are in love, we are all forever in love. We spend hours drawing them. We call ourselves by our new names in secret: Rainbow Rider, Lucky Lady, Thunder. We cram our pockets and lunch kits with them – piles and piles of ponies. Little brushes for their tiny pink manes, their purple tails.

Sofie is the new girl in grade two. Her horse name is Trotter and Toto and Lala and Gypsy. Because Sofie doesn't just fall in love with horses and have a horse name like the rest of us. Sofie becomes a horse or sometimes an entire herd of horses. She gallops out to the playground for recess; she trots down the halls. She talks by doing whinnies and stomping her feet. She even eats her lunch like it's a feed-bag, without using her hands.

We are amazed by Sofie, how she can spend hours, entire afternoons, down there on all fours. How she never cares about who sees. *Good little horsey.* That's what Adrienne says and then Adrienne is flying, having been bucked by Sofie the horse onto the couch. And then Rachel has a turn on Sofie's back and Sofie sends her flying, too. We love Sofie the horse. We make tiny braids all over her head; we paint rainbows on her cheeks.

And then one day, one normal un-special day, Adrienne comes to school and announces that it's penalty day. We don't know what penalty day is. Adrienne explains that on penalty day one girl is chosen and everyone is mean to that one girl for the whole day. *Why?* Adrienne doesn't know. It's just a part of school. Adrienne offers to go first. We get to be mean to her first. I want to go first, too.

At first penalty day is hard to figure out. There are a lot of rules. The person we have to be mean to has fleas, of course. Everyone has to write FP for "flea proof" on their hand.

BRAIDIE as a teenager again.

You know something, Trevor? By the end of grade four penalty day had become as complex as World War Two. But who the enemy was had become entirely simple. Now all the girls had FP written on their hands, all the girls but one. I don't know why it was Sofie. It just was.

———◆———

The next day. BRAIDIE is settling in on the beach.

THE VOICE OF MUM came in weak today, this annoying little signal that was barely registering. I believe I told her I was sick – perhaps I surfaced long enough to tell her school was out of the question. I sense she senses that school and myself are on our last legs. Maybe I'll be like you, try home-schooling. Maybe I'll move up to Whistler, too.

Mum and me did have a big blowout last night, a major blowout. She says to me, all weird and cheery: *The teen centre is having a dance this weekend. Why don't you go?* I point out I went last time and that it was BEYOND repulsive.

She points out that I never actually went inside, that I hung out with Adrienne in the parking lot. How does she know?

Because she drove by – MORE than once. She cruised the teen centre like an undercover cop or a pervert. Life with her is unbearable, a lesson in indignity.

In today's papers there are no pictures of those young offenders. I tell you – it's almost a relief. You remember when the girl was killed, Trevor, you were still living here. How she was beat up by a group of girls and this guy and then finished off a

few minutes later by that boy and this one girl who went back for more. The ones that watched the girl get beat up, they aren't accused of anything. To be accused you have to have gotten in there, down and dirty. I suppose that to be a teenager, even to be a little kid, is to often see very hideous behaviour from your peers.

If you reported everyone you would certainly have to watch your back at all times and look no one in the face, ever. You would have to go through your entire life using only your peripheral vision.

The girls who beat her up, the girls who are on trial for assault, they used to hang out at Walmart. They also hang out UNDER COVER. This sounds way cooler than it is. Because under cover really is just that – a covered area at the school just like we had for playing hopscotch when it rained. But these really are tough girls. They make like they are a gang and that they're all hooked up with the gangs in New York and L.A.

On Granville Mall once Adrienne and me were followed by some tough girls, these wipe out girls. They wanted us to give them some money and Adrienne said no way. They said they were going to get us. One gobbed on the back of Adrienne's jeans. But we weren't afraid of them. We just thought they were idiots.

These girls in Victoria, they're a mess. Some are in foster care; some have been doing the McFamily thing for a long, long time. Some have already been up on charges, one for lighting fire to another girl's hair. The fight with the dead girl starts when someone butts out a cigarette on her forehead. This is terrible enough in itself but it also opens a door. *Look what I did? Now just watch, just wait and see …* It's surreal. And that's not fair to say because it's exactly the opposite – it's totally real. I mean it happened. And what scares me, what freaks me right out, Trevor, is that I know the way in. I don't know how else to put it. I know the way in.

The human body is what? Eighty per cent water? That kills me. We're like these melons with arms and legs. Well, eighty per cent of the female brain is pure crap. We're constantly checking each other out, deciding who goes where, who's at the bottom.

When I look at her picture, when I look at the picture of the dead girl in the paper, part of me gets it. And I hate it that I do; I hate to be even partly composed of that sort of information. But right now, if you put me in a room filled with girls, girls my age that I've never seen before in my life – I could divide them all up. I could decide who goes where and just where I fit in without anyone even opening their mouth. They could be from this island, they could be from Taiwan. It doesn't matter. Nobody would have to say a word. You know something, Trevor? I could have divided up a room like that when I was in grade two. Grade fucking two.

———◆———

When the lights come up, BRAIDIE is ten years old, being Adrienne, perhaps standing up the bank, up high.

– No one is to have contact of any kind with IT from first period until lunch. If you have to address IT do so during homeroom. On the school bus IT has to sit on the fourth seat on the left. If IT talks to any boys it will be dealt with by me. IT's lunch today will be divided between Amber, Braidie, and Jackie. Case closed. IT will make no comments and will not be allowed to look at me anymore as of now.

BRAIDIE leaps down.

Adrienne then turns her back on Sofie to show us she means business. Adrienne always means business. So the five of us sit there, waiting for the school bus.

Yesterday means nothing now; it means nothing that we spent all day Sunday together and had a good time. There is a brand new code every day. I spend most of my time trying to figure out what the code is.

– What if she …

– IT.

– What if IT has to go to the bathroom.

This is Amber interjecting when she shouldn't. Adrienne ignores her. Adrienne often ignores what isn't important. And it works.

Yesterday we let ourselves into one of the houses Adrienne's mum is trying to sell. *Let's take off our tops.* Adrienne is lifting up her T-shirt. She is wearing a white bra covered in tiny pink flowers. Mine is identical. Sofie yanks up her blouse. She is wearing a rolled-up undershirt.

– IT'S A SPORTS BRA, says Sofie.

– IT thinks that's a bra.

– DON'T CALL ME THAT.

– Don't call me that.

The house is freezing. The beds are all bare. The mattresses and the ocean silver. Something shitty's going to happen. Something shitty could happen here. *Tell IT to get us something from the fridge.* And Sofie does. She comes back with a box of baking soda and a jar of relish. The lousy food is Sofie's fault. Maybe she should've broken in early and stocked the fridge. I would've. I would've done that if I was in her position. But Sofie doesn't have a clue. She has no sense of how to avoid anything.

– A sports bra, says Adrienne, *is a defence against guys. The really high-end sports bras repel guys, totally impenetrable. A good sports bra will catapult guys across the room.* THAT *is* NOT *a sports bra. It's a Little Miss Undie undie shirt.*

– Ha ha. Another one of Sofie's bad habits, ha-ha-ing all the time. She sticks her fingers into the jar of relish. *Ooohhhh, gross.* Adrienne practically has a heart attack. It is gross. Sofie slopping up a jar of hamburger relish. Except now Adrienne also finds it funny. And all of a sudden everyone is laughing and Sofie is allowed to be our friend again.

So we sit there all afternoon in our bras or our phony bras, fingers in the relish. Last year we took off all our clothes and sat together in a dry bathtub. I don't know why. We just did.

– You have to swim across this lake to get there. Then you'll come to a little door in the side of a tree.

This is Adrienne, doing what we always do. Designing a place, a home for the four of us. A dream house where we will all live together forever.

My dream house always looks the same – one big room that is divided by gauzy white curtains, sort of like a swishy hospital ward. There are no mothers and our dads will show up with supplies only when we want them to. Boys are banished. We do not want boys like the ones we see now, getting on the school bus. Adrienne, Sofie, Amber, and me are first picked up and last home every day on the school bus.

BRAIDIE as a teenager again.

You were there too, Trevor. At the back with the boys: throwing pencil cases and shoes and sweaters out the window. You had a handmade slingshot that was the envy of everyone. And a pocketful of smooth black stones. You were always pummelling each other, always mouthing off to Gustaf the driver. So you probably didn't notice how we sat around Sofie. And how still she was, with her eyes straight ahead. Behind her Jackie was kicking her calves, something was smeared in her hair. The girls across from her were chanting but you'd have to listen hard to hear it. While you boys in the back were slugging it out we were in the front, almost still, always the good little girls.

———◆———

A few days later.

The voice of Mum and I went out for dinner last night. As usual Dad – also known as Planet Dad – is away on business, so it's going to be, and I quote – *just us girls.*

One would think that dinner would mean ordering food, eating food, paying for food. Not so. Mum insists, first, that we sit at the same table. Two, that I don't read. Three, four, and five that I get my hair out of my face, sit up properly, and stop looking as though I'm planning my escape. And six, she wants us to *reconnect*, have ourselves a little chat. I explain, patiently, that I'd rather be shot from a cannon than hang around and see what she really has up her stupid sleeve.

And so it comes out: the school has phoned her at work. They are seeking an explanation for my unexplained absences. I explain, patiently, that I am now home-schooling.

All apparently news to Mum. And news to the school.

I am partway through stating just what I think home-schooling should be when the voice of Mum jumps to her feet and starts doing the famous whisper-shriek. *This is the last straw, the end of the road, the end of the rope, the absolute limit.* Then she goes. Leaves me sitting there alone with Terry the cook. Terry leers from the kitchen. He cleans his teeth with a business card and winks at me.

The Braidie Institute of Higher Learning. Lesson One – Current Events:

BRAIDIE holds up a newspaper.

Girls Turning on Each Other

Bullied to Death

Girls Killing Girls

These are the headlines; these are what put us on the map. Like the Stanley Cup riots, only worse, way worse.

The articles go on and on about how girls are getting meaner. The attacks more vicious. I look at those girls. I look at the pictures of those young offenders until the newspaper goes all squirrelly. If you look at them in bits, they are regular girls: these lips, that hair, those kinds of jeans.

If someone could invent a laser to zap the rotten parts they would be entirely normal. Young offenders. *Sorry – I didn't mean to offend you!* Adrienne and me would run into people on purpose on the ferry so that we could say that. *Oooops! No offence ...* We thought that was hysterical.

A girl in the shape of a monster

A monster in the shape of a girl

That, Trevor, is poetry. It is also a riddle that gets played out in Victoria. Because that's how they treat her – like a monster. Only they're the monsters, get it? Because they phoned her up. *Guess what we're doing? Wanna come?* It's like wolves pretending to be some animal that's hurt, maybe a little calf or a goat. This wasn't a case of someone in the wrong place at the wrong time. This was planned, organized.

And the girl, she knows they're one scary bunch but she goes. Maybe she is pleased that someone phoned, someone wanted her to do something. *Let's meet here ...* She even brings her pajamas. Her pajamas and diary and Charlie perfume are buckled into her black pack.

BRAIDIE goes back in time. She is twelve years old.

Sofie walks like a cripple, little quarters of blood on her heel, soaking into her white socks. Sofie wears her runners too small because her feet are too big. She is accused of watching the girls get undressed in gym. But I watch, too. I want to see who else has hair under their arms or who has thighs as big as mine. I talked to her after volleyball. I told her, I did the best I could.

– *Sofie, don't go on the field trip.* See – I said it: in plain English.

– *Why?*

– *Just don't.*

– *But we have to write an essay.*

This is pure Sofie, putting homework ahead of life or death. I tell you – she's an extremely exasperating person. We are all going to see *Hamlet* for the field trip, at a theatre in town. It's not the real *Hamlet*; it's a phony version for kids.

FOR EMERGENCY ONLY – SORTIE DU SECOURS. I have studied that sign ever since I can remember. It is written over top of some windows in the bus. I sit three rows down from Sofie. Jackie and Adrienne are behind me.

Sofie is sitting with Lorna. Lorna's dad owns the store on our island; sometimes she works there. We don't know Lorna. We don't even think of Lorna as an actual person.

The ocean shrinks and glitters as we head over the Lions Gate. You can see where we live, lying out there in the strait, all wrapped up in mist. It looks uninhabited, prehistoric. Adrienne and Lorna have switched places. Adrienne is whispering something to Sofie. Sofie is looking dead ahead. Adrienne leans into Sofie so that Sofie is squished up against the side. Sofie's face turns grey.

FOR EMERGENCY ONLY. Sofie pushes the window on the bus. It fans out unnaturally from the bottom. Sofie hoists herself up, her head is out. Sofie is going to jump out the window. The ocean is hundreds of feet below.

I shut my eyes. And Sofie is falling, cannonballing over the side of the bridge, her clothes parachute around her, a gigantic flower. I open my eyes. Sofie hasn't gone over the side of anything. Her bum is stuck in the window of the bus.

Amber and Adrienne and me and Jackie – we laugh so hard we nearly puke. Sofie is all weird and breathing heavy. Then she pushes out a sound that is hardly human. *Ha-ha.*

The bus driver is grabbing Sofie by the sweater. He pulls her in. *What the hell do you think you're doing?* Adrienne watches Sofie. *Nothing,* Sofie says. *Fooling around.*

Sofie isn't allowed to see the play. We watch Ophelia load herself up with flowers and sail off to meet her maker. We make burp noises except when Hamlet's around. Hamlet's cute.

When Hamlet gets going on one of his long speeches we go *oh oh oh oh* like we are Hamlet's own girlfriend. Then this lady usher comes and tells us we have to be quiet. She's a total bitch.

---◆---

A few days later.

The first week is now history at the Braidie Institute. Two weeks now without Adrienne.

This is me without my friends. I am nothing, zero, zip. A black mark on the horizon.

If I had to, I could live on this beach for a long time – live on berries and fish and kelp. Trevor, remember how we'd plant ourselves up there on the bank? The perfect camouflage – we would spy on the blind just doing their everyday stuff: the little kids going ballistic, the old guys sucking back the lemonade. Remember them swimming? Bobbing around in their lifejackets, unaware that the sun is descending in some spectacular fashion. They had that way of turning their faces up to the sky – all weird and happy.

It floored me, Trevor. I mean, I'm sure their lives are usually even more dull and shitty and hideous than the rest of us but I used to imagine myself blind – how careful I would be. For my eighteenth birthday I would be given a dog. I would call him Henry. *There goes Henry and Braidie.* I never think about all the stuff I wouldn't be able to do, what I wouldn't be able to see. For once I am focusing on only the positive. The voice of Mum would be proud of me.

BRAIDIE goes back in time. She is twelve years old.

We are blind: Adrienne, Amber, Jackie, and me. We have made a huge pile of sand and leaves. We cover our eyes with a pair of old pantyhose and leap off the bank. We turn each other around and around to see if we can point in the right direction – at the beach, the mountains, each other. We feel each other's faces, stomachs, breasts. *Definitely Braidie.* If it wasn't winter I would swim away, swim blind into the middle of the sea.

– *This is boring.* Adrienne takes off her blindfold. We take off ours. We climb up the bank and hide in the laurel leaves. We think about going to the store to steal something: gum, matches, bath-oil bubbles that squish in our pockets and leak all over our shirts. Sometimes Adrienne steals change and cans of beer from the people she baby-sits for. I confine my crimes to the general store and believe I am a slightly less bad person.

Adrienne goes to light a smoke then stops. *Look ...* And we look out on the beach and there is Sofie. *What is IT doing?* We haven't seen Sofie in ages. *God, look at IT!* Adrienne makes it sound as if Sofie is out there killing something. I squint in on her but Sofie is just hunched over a little book. Maybe Sofie still draws pictures of horses. Maybe she also likes trying to write poems and stories. The possibility that Sofie and I might have even one thing in common makes a little shift in me.

– *I'm going to get IT*. Adrienne is climbing down the vines. Sofie looks up and in the wrong direction: pure Sofie. And Adrienne is right there, grabbing Sofie by the ponytail.

– *What do you think you're doing?*

– *Nothing.* Sofie slams her book shut, she examines her feet.

– *What's in the book?*

– *Nothing.*

And Sofie tries to run, to bolt down the beach. Adrienne still has a hold of her hair, she pushes Sofie down. Sofie's head makes a little smack sound on the rock. It sounds phony – like a slap in the movies. And then her head is bleeding and the blood looks phony too. And then we are all around Sofie. This is it. Adrienne is going to do something. And we are going to see. Then Adrienne is holding a covered elastic and a tangle of Sofie's hair.

Sofie is gone, running. And then everybody is running after her, someone is yelling *No No No* ... It isn't me.

Sofie mashes open her jeans falling on the barnacles. She starts climbing back up the blackberries and Adrienne is right there, grabbing on to her ankle.

I understand too now what Sofie wants to do. Sofie is going to ring the bell at the blind camp. You can hear that bell all over the island. But then Adrienne screams and we all stop breathing.

We watch Adrienne slide down the bank while Sofie scrambles away. We peer down at Adrienne on the sand, all curled up and quiet. *She's dead*, Amber announces.

BRAIDIE as a teenager again.

But I knew Adrienne had just been stalled, shot, hit by a smooth black stone. And that you were there, you were with us, Trevor, up in the maple tree. How much did you know all along? How much did you see? Adrienne came back from the dead a moment later. *Your brother is such an asshole.* Adrienne knew it was you but somehow it becomes Sofie's fault, too. *Sofie and Trevor probably do it together, do it twenty times a day.*

We all lay there on the sand, joined at the head, spokes in a wheel. In my pocket a pink plastic diary and a key. Of course it belonged to Sofie. I

didn't show it to anyone. But I felt entitled, I found it, it was mine to keep and mine to see.

What was Sofie doing as we lay there on the beach? Were the others thinking about her, too? How she might be stumbling in the back door of her house, trying to keep the blood and the dirt from getting over everything. *I fell, I slipped, I whacked my head on an alder tree.* We all understand that Sofie telling the truth isn't even a remote possibility.

BRAIDIE goes back in time. She is twelve years old.

Jackie shifts down, rests her head on my stomach. I place my head on Adrienne's. We make a chain. First Amber laughs, then Jackie, all around the circle. I can feel the laughter and the skin of Adrienne's body, warm against my ear. And then I'm laughing too and when we stop there's just our breath, rising and falling. I match my breath to Adrienne's perfectly.

———◆———

The next day.

Mum comes thundering down the stairs last night to announce she has given up. I point out, as calmly as possible *If you're going to give up on someone you just give up. You don't tell them about it.* Mum goes berserk. All this screaming and crying and gnashing of teeth. Then she notices the pictures, some of the newspaper clippings tacked up around my room. *I'm studying.*

And then she's screaming: *Cut the lip! Cut all the nonsense about home-schooling.* And she is inside my room, mine, for the first time in a year and a half. A complete violation of my rights. What is this stuff? She is looking at this cover from the Vancouver *Province*:

– *At least* SHE *has a nice haircut.*

– *She's a killer*, I tell her.

And Mum takes me by the shoulders: *Look.* She stares right into me, then her eyes fill up and she touches my cheek. *Braidie?* It's worse than anything, the voice of Mum trying to be my buddy, trying to be halfway sweet.

– *Get out.* Her hands drop to her side. *This is my room.* But she isn't moving. She gets me so pissed off I just start flailing.

– *Braidie, use your words.*

– *All right. Fuck you, Mother.*

And she gets it, she finally gets it. She slams the door behind her. She's giving up on me.

I look at the girl, the picture of the girl who did it. The one in Victoria who held her head underwater until all was quiet. The one who held a smoke in one hand and held the girl under with the other, her foot on her back. She bragged about it. Maybe she made the telling of it into a joke because she doesn't know how else to try it out. *Did you hear the one about …* Maybe she just snapped. I do that. I look at the picture again: she's a regular girl.

And she's hanging out on a Friday night in November 1997 – the moon is full, the air is clear. Usually the stars get lost in winter here. But on this night the stars are out, everyone is out, *under cover*, passing a joint, drinking vodka and Sprite mixed in a can. Some are watching the sky and waiting because a Russian satellite is going to break through the earth's atmosphere tonight, right over Victoria. It will explode, light up all that black.

But this girl, this regular girl and one other girl are waiting for something else; they are waiting to teach someone a lesson. They've already phoned her up, they've called her out.

Because she is big, because she likes *that* boy. Because she is brown and she lost their book; because she doesn't fit and she lies. Because they can.

The girl they're going to get is miserable, that much is clear. Four different schools and two different foster homes in the past year. She keeps returning to family – her parents, her grandma and grandpa. And she keeps running away. And she doesn't know, doesn't get the plot, doesn't understand her part. So it starts.

The ones who watched, maybe they thought it wasn't real. Maybe as they yelled out or laughed they were actually frozen. Maybe they were so glad to not be that girl – whose hair is being held up to a lighter now – that they don't even know how to imagine shouting *stop*. Maybe they think that silence is the ticket, the only way to never end up like the girl.

Even the ones who didn't watch, who just heard about what happened, they carry the silence, too – a dark present, passed hand to hand. When they get home maybe they will dream about being blind. Because they can't stand the replays anymore – how the girl looked up and begged for help.

Or maybe it's that boy in Burnaby last winter, how he wrote his goodbye note and climbed the rails on the Pattullo Bridge.

Or maybe it's Sofie. Because just when you think it was all ancient history it starts again.

Trevor – remember how I went through the first five years of life hiding behind Mum's bum whenever we were out in public? That's the trouble with staying silent. I can't move, even when I want to. And I start thinking Adrienne acts for me.

———◆———

BRAIDIE goes back in time. She is fourteen years old.

It is dark now by 4:30. We miss the school bus on purpose so that we can hang out longer in town. *Mum, I'll be on the 6:30 ferry, pick me up …* I'm doing what I do every day after school, what I did practically every day in grade eight and in grade nine, too. I am in the parking lot behind the school and I am waiting for Adrienne. High school is just like how movie stars describe making movies – there's a lot of waiting around.

It's raining hard; my hair is soaking wet – unbelievably ugly. There are about thirty of us hanging out. Some of the older guys have cars. These little pools of light – vibrating with music and bodies and smoke. And with Adrienne.

Right now she is in Justin Hannah's Dodge Caravan. She loves Justin and Justin, of course, treats her terribly. I think Justin is sort of an idiot. In fact I find a lot of Adrienne's guys are fairly gross.

Across from the parking lot everyone else lines up for the bus – shoving and smoking and fooling around. Except for one still shape, holding on to the bus sign like it's some sort of anchor. Sofie always has her hood up, rain or shine. From the back she looks like this giant version of E.T. Sofie is something Adrienne seems to have forgotten. At lunch Sofie doesn't go to the cafeteria or behind the gym or the parking lot like the rest of us. She slinks along the edges of the halls; she walks away from the school. She walks around and around. She often eats lunch in a bus shelter, six blocks from our school. She doesn't hang out with other kids. She is certainly doing her very best to be invisible.

I have no idea why I feel I have to keep tabs on Sofie. I just do. Sometimes I follow her around. She has no idea; she has always been a fairly clued-out individual. I go to the bus shelter after she's left to check it out. There are little rocks lined up along the sides and she's carved her initials – S.G. – into the seat. No doubt it all is charged with meaning in the weird world of Sofie. Maybe I'll give back her diary. I keep it at the back of my locker, just on the verge of handing it over. I never even finished reading the whole thing. It was too boring – just a regular girl. She doesn't let anyone in on anything.

I watch Sofie board the bus, always first on so that she can sit directly behind the driver. I watch the bus pull away just as Adrienne gets out of Justin's van.

Adrienne lights a cigarette and glares at me. Justin was supposed to give us a ride to the ferry but apparently now this is completely and totally out of the question. We walk – two and a half miles. I get home four hours late, the voice of Mum waiting on the dock to tear a strip off of me.

—◆—

A girl in the shape of a monster

A monster in the shape of a girl

It all starts again just three weeks ago, in the girls' bathroom. Right after homeroom. I walk in. I'm not doing anything, I'm minding my own business, I just have to pee. Sofie is there. Applying this goofy blue eyeliner in a goofy blue line. Then guess-who comes kicking her way out of the end cubicle. Adrienne's been crying; her eyes are rabbity pink. No doubt there has been some new atrocity between her and Justin. *Let's go.* That's me, trying to head her off, but Adrienne has already seen Sofie.

– *What are you looking at?* Sofie goes blank. She turns and fixes her sights on the Tampax machine. *I asked you a question.* But Sofie is still in statue mode, uninhabited. No doubt Sofie's entire school life is an out-of-body experience.

Adrienne drops her atlas on Sofie's foot. Sofie doesn't blink.

– *Pick it up.*

– *Let's go.*

– *I said pick it up.*

Do something, say something, anything, fight. Do something, say something, anything, fight …

But Sofie just bends over. And I hate her. As soon as she does it I know she's lost. Adrienne kicks Sofie down on all fours. All the work she'd put into

being invisible, down the drain. Sofie is entirely visible – her legs are pink, her underwear covered in little blue circles.

– *Lovely. Sofie the horse.* Sofie tries to get up and Adrienne's boot comes down in the centre of Sofie's back. *Did I say you could get up?* Sofie tries to turn her head around but Adrienne grabs her by the shirt. *Maybe the horse needs a drink of water.* Adrienne pulls Sofie over to the toilet.

And yes, finally. Sofie's head is turning, twisting away from Adrienne, and … turning toward me. *Braidie please.*

You do what you have to do.

You look down.

Like this.

And then you navigate your way to the door using only your peripheral vision.

When I walk down the hall I feel all weird and pukey. I feel like everyone is staring at me. I don't go to English; I just walk around. And then I don't go to Math or P.E. At lunch I go looking for Sofie. I go to the bus shelter. S.G. still carved into the bench. Why wouldn't it be?

After school, when I get on the bus, Adrienne is waiting, waiting for me.

– *Adrienne. What happened?* But she doesn't know what I'm talking about, can't remember, just a regular day. *What happened to Sofie?*

– *Nothing happened.* I see the empty seat behind the driver on the bus, Sofie's seat. A tremor starts, way down low on the floor of the ocean. *With someone like Sofie you never have to actually DO anything.* My hands are shaking, the bus pulls out. *Shut up*, says Adrienne. *Stop breathing like a pervert.*

But Adrienne seems miles away now, deflated, her face behind her hair all white and skinny.

And she's gone. The friend I loved is gone. All that's left is the shape of a girl.

FOR EMERGENCY ONLY. I push out the window and it fans out from the bottom unnaturally. I puke all down the side of the bus. The driver lets me off. I walk back to school. I go right into the girls' bathroom. I wash my face. When I turn off the tap I hear a sound, from the last cubicle.

Sofie is sitting on the lid of the toilet. Her lips all puffed up and purple. When she sees who it is, she covers her head. *Don't worry* … She's acting like I'm going to hit her, which is so crazy. *I never did anything.* I bet she wishes you were there, Trevor, hiding out behind the Tampax machine, waiting to get off a good shot at me.

Sofie rocks back and forth then all of a sudden she smashes her head into the side of the stall.

We did a good job. Even Sofie hates Sofie.

A bell sounds as in the beginning.

Sound carries across water. On that full-moon night, in Victoria, the word goes out that a girl was killed, that girl. Maybe there are groups of kids in schoolyards, malls ... *Really?* And by the time her body is found – hundreds of kids know and hundreds of kids don't tell. Who is the one who told the unthinkable to their mum or their teacher? Who marched into the police station and said, *See here, enough is enough?* I'll bet you a million dollars everyone thinks it wasn't a girl.

I always thought it was the voice of Mum that made you escape, Trevor. But I'm wondering now if you moved to Whistler to get away from me. In fact you might be ecstatic to know I am well on my way to becoming the official island outcast. I just wanted you to know one thing. One tiny thing that'll probably be the end of me.

Mum is forcing me to abandon home-schooling. I agreed, on the condition that the voice of Mum no longer speak to me. So yesterday the now-defunct Braidie Institute went on our first and last field trip – to the Island Community Preschool. Remember preschool? Remember what a big deal it was?

They have this snazzy new building now. I'm hanging out at the fence like some kind of psycho. Watching all these kids smash into each other on their trikes and kicking around in the mud puddles. All these nutty four-year-olds doing their usual things. And Annie comes out. Her hair is all grey now. But she is still the same because this boy is hanging off her arm by his teeth and she doesn't even notice. You can tell she still thinks all kids are just dandy.

Then Annie spots me. *Braidie!* You'd think I was God or something. You'd think I was the greatest thing she's ever seen. And Annie comes running over. She smells like playdough. She opens the gate for me.

A spot shines brightly in front of **BRAIDIE**. *She steps into the light.*

And I understand for the first time what I have to say and how long I've been practising.

– *I wish to report the behaviour of ...*

– *I fear for ...*

– *I'm scared. Scared for the safety of another girl. That she might do something crazy. Her name is Sofie. She has been treated in a despicable way by many people ... including me.*

Annie doesn't say anything. For the longest time she just nods. And then when she finally does speak it's in this weird whisper because she probably hates me. She will go with me to my school, to the principal. I tell her – o*kay.*

She holds me tightly. Maybe she thinks I'm going to escape. Her arms still fit around me.

A bell sounds again, then **BRAIDIE** *looks up.*

Sound carries across water. The girl in Victoria is discovered after eight days, her body seen floating from the air above. The stories were endless, the stories about how it all happened. Most of them weren't true. The only real story is the one told by her body, silently. This bruising beneath her eyes, the black nose and cheeks. The broken arm and the star burned into her forehead.

A bell sounds fourteen times.

Sometimes I dream she got away, swam straight out into the ocean, maybe floated off on a log boom. Where? Not south to the States, not here. I don't know how to imagine it; I don't know where her safe place might be. I only know how to go backwards.

BRAIDIE goes back in time. She is eight years old.

We are eight years old. We are all planting our toes in the edge of the water. We're at the blind beach, it's summer, the water is foamy and brown around our feet. We are all wearing life jackets. Adrienne, Amber, Sofie, and me. The jackets make us feel like we can go anywhere, do anything – deep water, waves, you name it, all these possibilities.

We are brave, we are perfect – girls.

END

ROBERT
CHAFE

(b. 1971)

Newfoundland occupies a unique place in Canadian culture. At the risk of offending regional sensibilities, I would describe it as second only to Quebec in its distinctiveness. Now officially called Newfoundland and Labrador, the final province to enter Confederation (in 1949) has retained much of its special flavour despite the new prosperity built upon its off-shore oil resources. One factor is geography: its isolation out in the North Atlantic, the rugged, unforgiving landscape, the stormy outports so long dependent on fishing and sealing. Another is its people with their idio-syncratic language and wry humour, legendary warmth, generosity, and toughness. David French has provided the best known theatrical portraits of this culture in his five Mercer family plays, including *Leaving Home* (in *Modern Canadian Plays*, vol. 1). The outport dramas of Michael Cook and the satirical work of the CODCO company in the 1970s also helped shape theatre in Newfoundland. Actor/comedian Mary Walsh, a CODCO alumna, has put Newfoundland's stamp on Canadian television with a vengeance.

Playwright/actor Robert Chafe and director Jillian Keiley are the contemporary stars of Newfoundland theatre. Separately and together, often under the umbrella of the St. John's company Artistic Fraud, they have created a body of work that honours Newfoundland's people, geog-raphy, history, and cultural traditions while significantly expanding its theatrical vocabulary. Their collaboration on *Tempting Providence* both humanizes and mythicizes Nurse Myra Bennett and the people she meets and treats on Newfoundland's remote Northern Peninsula. Elegant in its simplicity, the straightforward, understated script presents a character who accomplishes remarkable things with the few resources at her dis-posal. The *mise en scène* utilizes directorial magic and the talents of a small cast of actors to evoke a similar sense of accomplishment, marrying the ordinary with the extraordinary. The resulting production has toured for more than a decade, leaving superlatives in its wake. "Keiley's innovative staging ... and Chafe's urgent command of language," Paula Citron wrote in the *Globe and Mail*, "combine to produce a powerful theatricality that is as good as it gets on the stage."

Robert Chafe discovered theatre while studying philosophy at New-foundland's Memorial University. He wrote his first play, *Urbanite* (1993), about growing up just outside his birthplace of St. John's, performing it solo at that city's Resource Centre for the Arts. *Lemons* (1996), directed by Danielle Irvine, who would become Chafe's second most frequent col-laborator, was produced by Artistic Fraud, founded two years earlier.

Chafe first partnered with Keiley on Artistic Fraud's remarkable *Under Wraps: A Spoke Opera* (1997), a gay love story in which he also starred as one of only two characters visible to the audience. The other sixteen cast members act as a chorus, performing under a sheet transformed by lighting and the actors themselves into various shapes and objects, accompanied by Petrina Bromley's music. To describe her formal technique of harmonizing colour, movement, and sound, Keiley would coin the term "kaleidography." Toured to Halifax and western Canada, and revived in St. John's in 2013, *Under Wraps* took Chafe, Artistic Fraud, and Keiley's signature directorial style outside Newfoundland for the first time.

In 1998–99, Chafe's one-act comedies *Round Robin* and *Fatboy* premiered at Calgary's Lunchbox Theatre, but nearly all his work before and since has originated in Newfoundland. *Empty Girl* (1998), a play about carnival sideshow acts, was directed by Keiley with performers in front of a curtain interacting with the shadows of others behind it. Chafe and Irvine joined forces again for *Place of First Light* (1997), a historical pageant about the miners of tiny Bell Island, produced on the island and staged partly inside a mine; *Charismatic Death Scenes* (1998), a one-man show exploring a writer's life, performed by Chafe; and *Butler's Marsh* (2001), a two-hander also set on Bell Island about a woman seeking to unearth her mother's story. Chafe was named 1998 Emerging Artist of the Year by the Newfoundland and Labrador Arts Council.

Tempting Providence was commissioned by Corner Brook's Theatre Newfoundland Labrador (TNL) and premiered in 2002 at its Gros Morne Theatre Festival in Cow Head, Newfoundland, then was co-presented with Artistic Fraud in St. John's. Frequently remounted, the TNL / Artistic Fraud production has toured Newfoundland and the rest of Canada multiple times, as well as the United Kingdom and Australia, with a highly successful run at the Edinburgh Fringe in 2004. That year *Tempting Providence* and *Butler's Marsh*, published together as *Robert Chafe: Two Plays*, received a Governor General's Award nomination, and Jillian Keiley won the prestigious Siminovitch Prize for Direction.

This was an especially fertile period for Chafe and his theatrical partners. Artistic Fraud appointed him playwright in residence in 2003 and produced his *Burial Practices of the Early European Settlers through to Today* (2004), a play about cultural responses to death, directed by Keiley in a St. John's church, and *Belly Up* (2005), a solo show about a blind man and his goldfish, performed by Chafe in sync with music and digital video under Keiley's kaleidographic direction. Chafe wrote and Keiley directed a theatrical biography of Newfoundland fiddler Émile Benoit, produced by the Stephenville Theatre Festival as *Vive la rose* (2004), and later remounted under the title *Émile's Dream*; and *Nightingale*, a play about local opera singer Georgina Stirling, which premiered in 2006 at the Magnetic North Theatre Festival in St. John's. Chafe reunited with Irvine for *Isle of Demons* (2004), commissioned by Theatre Newfoundland Labrador, about a sixteenth-century Frenchwoman abandoned on an island off the Newfoundland coast.

Through the body of work built up by Chafe and his Newfoundland directors, plus the repeated tours of *Tempting Providence*, they and Artistic Fraud have emerged as more than just a regional force. *Fear of Flight*, developed by Chafe and Keiley for Artistic Fraud with students at Corner Brook's Grenfell College, includes monologues written by Judith Thompson, Daniel MacIvor, Marie Clements, and Guillermo Verdecchia among other major playwrights. It premiered in St. John's in 2008, then travelled to Toronto's Factory Theatre and Vancouver's 2010 Cultural Olympiad. Keiley used handheld lighting and an electrified stage to illuminate Artistic Fraud's production of *Afterimage*, adapted by Chafe from a Michael Crummey short story about fire, photography, electrocution, and human connection. It opened at Toronto's Harbourfront, part of World Stage 2009, and the published play won Chafe the 2010 Governor General's Literary Award for Drama. The next year he was shortlisted for the Siminovitch Prize for Playwriting. In 2012, Keiley was appointed artistic director of the National Arts Centre's English Theatre in Ottawa, shortly after getting rave reviews for directing Chafe's powerful *Oil and Water* (2011), based on the true story of a black U.S. Navy sailor shipwrecked off the Newfoundland coast during World War Two, his impact on the locals who save him, and their effect on him.

Tempting Providence's Nurse Myra Bennett was also a real person with an inspirational tale. She had come from England to Newfoundland's Great Northern Peninsula in 1921 to provide basic medical services to isolated communities without doctors, nurses, or roads along hundreds of miles of rugged coastline. Bennett's home in Daniel's Harbour was adjacent to Gros Morne National Park, where Theatre Newfoundland Labrador holds its annual festival. When TNL's artistic director, Jeff Pitcher, decided to commission a play about her, he asked Chafe, whom he had met at a TV writer's workshop in Toronto a few years earlier, to write it. "We wanted to design a play that was very simple," Pitcher says, "that could easily play in our intimate Warehouse Theatre and tour – the dream was a play that we could put on the road through rural Newfoundland and Labrador that would play in schools, church halls and community halls."

From a variety of perspectives, primarily those of Nurse Bennett and her husband Angus, the play tells a story of quiet heroism and culture shock. Nurse, as she insists on being called, has to overcome the folk prejudices of her patients as well as their reluctance to put themselves in the hands of a woman "from away." At the same time, she struggles with her own homesickness and melancholy, what she calls her "sad little, sore little heart." The sweet, simple lyricism of that phrase is typical of Chafe's gently humorous style, and congruent with Nurse's own self-effacing modesty and pragmatism. No matter how remarkable her achievements, she insists she is simply "being useful." The play offers a single instance of high drama near the end, which serves to cement Nurse's heroic competency and illustrate how her evolving love for this place and its people became reciprocal. Denise Lynde's introduction to the published play describes *Tempting Providence* as "a quintessentially Newfoundland saga of isolation and deprivation transformed by the goodness of heart, dedication, and courage found in both individuals and the community."

Chafe wrote a script for four actors (one of whom, Deidre Gillard-Rowlings, has played Myra in every performance of the play to date) and a single set. He proposed that there be no costume changes, and that shifts in time and setting be indicated by lighting and sound. Keiley stripped things down further, removing all sound cues and establishing a design of stark simplicity. A wooden table, four chairs, and a tablecloth, along with the actors, became the sole elements of her minimalist production aesthetic. In a sequence of tightly choreographed movements, the actors transform set pieces into the components of Nurse's life. In the performance I saw at Vancouver's 2006 PuSh Festival, the tablecloth in one sequence became first bread dough, then a medical bag, then a sheet covering a woman in childbirth, then the infant she bears. Combining the cloth with chair or table produced a backpack, a cradle, a rowboat, or a sleigh. The play's thematic principle of practical transformation is directly reflected in its acting and staging – the ability to change, grow, and use what resources you have to make things work, and make them better. In an article titled "Igniting Imaginations with Actor-Manipulated Designs," Keiley asks: "Can we offer up a design that our actors use to create new worlds on stage? Can we ask the audience to look at a cloth or a box or a set of stairs in a new way? And then can we ask them to look at the same set of stairs in sixteen new ways?" *Tempting Providence* answers all those questions in the affirmative, the characteristic mode of Nurse Myra Bennett: "I am completely here, and ready, and able."

Tempting Providence

Robert Chafe

Tempting Providence was commissioned by Theatre Newfoundland Labrador and premiered at their Gros Morne Theatre Festival in Cow Head, Newfoundland, on June 1, 2002. It was subsequently remounted and co-presented with Artistic Fraud in St. John's, Newfoundland, in December 2002, with the following cast:

MYRA	Deidre Gillard-Rowlings
ANGUS	Daniel Payne
MAN	Peter Rompkey
WOMAN	Melanie Caines

Directed and Design Concept by Jillian Keiley
Lighting Design by Walter J. Snow
Costume Design by Barry Buckle
Stage Managed by Karla Biggin

CHARACTERS

MYRA, *age thirty-one at the beginning of the play, which progresses through approximately ten years of her life. Stern, though caring; serious, though quick-witted*

ANGUS, *late twenties at the beginning of the play. Thoughtful, playful, charming, down to earth. The perfect man. A working man. A warm heart and dirty hands*

MAN, *various distinct male characters, age fourteen to eighty*

WOMAN, *various distinct female characters, age nineteen to eighty*

SETTING

Daniel's Harbour, Newfoundland, 1921 to 1961

The stage should be relatively bare, with limited use of props and costumes. The play is actor-driven. Myra and Angus are constant characters. MAN and WOMAN denote a variety of characters who become self-evident in the dialogue and minor stage directions. It is strongly recommended that these characters themselves be actor-driven, not reliant on costuming.

All actors should remain on stage unless otherwise noted. While not in a given scene they should be visible, giving focus to the action. It may be desired to have Myra and Angus in constant character, even when not in scene. MAN and WOMAN may be omnipotent, and at times become watchers of the event.

Set and time change should be executed primarily with lighting, if at all. The play is written to move swiftly through scenes. The text does the work. Pause should only be taken where noted. Fun, fast, playful and, above all, theatrical.

ACT ONE

ANGUS alone.

ANGUS: Who knows the answer to that? A person's inner thoughts like that. It's a forbidden domain. She was a thoughtful woman, and a private one. So, as for what she was thinking, what was on her mind, who can say. I don't pretend to know everything. Why she decided to stay, was content to stay. Put down roots here, of all places. Here.

MYRA stares out to sea.

MYRA: Daniel's Harbour.

ANGUS: Smack in the middle of three hundred miles of sparsely occupied coast. Daniel's Harbour.

MYRA: Though there is really no harbour at all. The sharp land as straight and fierce as the long horizon that it dutifully stares down. A collection of houses sit at the top, where the grass begins. A collection of people in front of them. Waiting. I am late. What a horrible way to make a first impression. Three weeks late but only as a result of the ungovernable will of God. Pack ice so thick and a late spring thaw has meant that my passage north was to be late beyond being fashionable. The stranger arrives to the strange land. On the *SS Home*.

A weak smile.

The *Home* carries the first provisions the area has seen since autumn. People scramble for the food first, and then later to me for introductions. A long thin hand falls into mine and its loose skin, its thinness makes me recall that of my grandmother's. A comforting thought on my first day here if not for the fact that this dainty hand is attached to the arm of a forty-year-old man. Many are sick. They will not tell you such, but it is clear enough. Many near starvation. It takes little of my formal experience and training to identify why I have been placed here. It takes no time at all to see a most urgent need for a nurse.

MAN and WOMAN enter.

WOMAN: Well, she insisted, you see.

MAN: Yes, insisted.

WOMAN: From the very first day. First time she stepped her foot off the boat.

MAN: And there were some ...

WOMAN: Oh there were.

MAN: That were none too delighted to be told that, to be commanded, right?

WOMAN: And that's what she did, too. Commanded, yes sir.

MAN: No sir, there were some that needed to be told twice, but few a third time, and even fewer a fourth.

WOMAN: You just didn't cross her. Not when she made her wishes known.

MAN: No, not when she made her wishes known.

WOMAN: She was a strong woman.

MAN: Strong, powerful woman.

WOMAN: A strong woman, so you listened.

MAN: You listened, all right.

WOMAN: You listened to what she told you.

MYRA: You will refer to me as Nurse. Nurse. Nurse Grimsley, if you prefer, but never Miss. And certainly not Mrs. I would demand your respect just as I'm sure that you would expect to have mine.

I will be seeing patients as soon as humanly possible. I trust you all know where to find me.

ANGUS: I don't think she even knew where she was staying at that point. The minister had her all set up over at George Moss's place. School teacher at the time. Now George's place wasn't big, sir, by no stretch, but they did manage to find her room in the parlour for a nice little clinic, and the patients, they were to wait in the kitchen. Well, that's the way it was. She landed and she was hardly unpacked before people were over with every ailment under the sun. A good few of them simply there to meet her, check her out. People were just glad she was finally here, glad to finally have a nurse. And I guess I counted among them.

WOMAN enters and stares at MYRA.

MYRA: Hello.

No response.

ANGUS: But us, we never met that day.

He steps aside as MYRA approaches the WOMAN.

MYRA: I'm Nurse Grimsley.

No response.

MYRA: And you are?

No response.

MYRA: My first patient.

WOMAN: Knows it all, do ya?

MYRA: Pardon me?

WOMAN: Thinks ya knows it all.

MYRA: Well, I've certainly never said that.

WOMAN: Oh yes, you knows it all, all right.

MYRA: Perhaps enough to help. What is the trouble?

WOMAN: Where you from?

MYRA: Madam –

WOMAN: Not Newfoundland.

MYRA: No.

WOMAN: Where?

MYRA: I ask the questions. What is the trouble?

WOMAN: Where are you from?

MYRA: None of your business.

WOMAN: You're all up in my face about my troubles.

MYRA: And the day I come to your place of work, where you have set aside some of your time to speak to me about where I am from, where I originate, then that day, madam, you shall know every last detail of my history and upbringing, but as long as you walk through my door, as long as you stand in my place of work, I will ask the questions, and I will refuse to be apologetic about it or my personal privacy.

A short pause. The WOMAN starts a slow chuckle that turns into a laugh.

WOMAN: You're all right.

MYRA: Thank you.

WOMAN: Pain in my hip.

MYRA: Well, good. Not your pain, but your co-operation.

WOMAN: Some tongue on you.

MYRA: Yes, well, I apologize.

WOMAN: No, girl. Good to hear. Good to hear. Good to have another one like myself around.

MYRA: Yes. Okay.

WOMAN: That what it takes?

MYRA: Pardon me?

WOMAN: I have to invite you over to my place of work, set aside some time to find out where you're from?

MYRA: What if I said yes?

WOMAN: I'd have to invite you over for tea, then, wouldn't I?

MYRA: Why, yes, I suppose you would.

WOMAN: Well, that's it then.

MYRA: Yes, I suppose it is. Mrs.?

WOMAN: House.

MYRA goes to her and begins to examine her hip.

WOMAN: Ow. Yeah, that's it right there.

MYRA alone.

MYRA: There is a cautious curiosity here. I must remember that. I must remember that these people, not only have they never had any formal medical aid, but they also rarely meet someone new. I am standing in front of Mrs. House's, and I am watched by my new neighbours. They look at me from the paths. They whisper as they walk. They exist in this sublime world of friends and relatives. So, of course, there will be a trust issue,

with a stranger in town. A stranger barking commands. And this is fine. I'm not here to make friends. That is not my intent. I must remember that, too. As I knock on this door. As I start to talk pleasantries.

MYRA at MRS. HOUSE's for tea.

WOMAN: What difference does it make?

MYRA: Honestly, I don't know. But my mother would have it no other way.

WOMAN: Foolishness really. It is.

MYRA: There is a difference in the taste. It's noticeable.

WOMAN: Just because you put the milk in first? Tea is tea is tea, my dear.

MYRA: Call it a habit then.

WOMAN: We all got them. Habits. You might be having to break some of yours.

MYRA: I'll just start some new ones. (*beat*) You're smiling.

WOMAN: Lovely accent, girl. It is. Not polite to say that, I suppose.

MYRA releases a small, tight smile.

WOMAN: You bake?

MYRA: Bake?

WOMAN: Bread.

MYRA: I've never had much occasion to.

WOMAN: Now see. That's gonna change.

MYRA: Is it?

WOMAN: Got to. You got to bake. No self-respecting woman on this coast that don't bake. Sew. Knit.

MYRA: Really.

WOMAN: Yes. The crowd around here won't be paying you no mind with your do this and don't do that if they finds out you can't even do that stuff. I can hear Wallace Carter now. Yes now, go and see her, have her mend my body when she can't even mend a pair of socks.

MYRA: So, I've got some learning to do?

WOMAN: Yes, girl, women round here got skills, do anything. Knit a house they could. Predict the weather.

MYRA: Soothsayers too, eh?

WOMAN: Not all, no. But some, girl. Some of them are right spooky. There's a few of them on this coast can tell, just by looking at you, if you're with child.

MYRA smiles.

WOMAN: It's true as I'm sitting here. Tell a young one she's pregnant before she even knows herself.

MYRA: Do you believe that?

WOMAN: Some of them. I tell ya. Lean over the table and say, do you know you're pregnant? Just like that.

MYRA: And they are always correct?

WOMAN: (*smiles*) Well, who can say, eh? No one really keeps track of who said what and when and who was right or no. But you'll come to see all that yourself by and by. You'll come to see that all soon enough. Break a few habits. Make a few new ones. Fit right in, eh?

MYRA: Learn to bake. Knit a house.

WOMAN: Don't go worrying about that. I can help you out with that stuff easy enough. You'll be a good hand at it all when I'm done with ya.

MYRA gives a small smile.

MYRA: I believe it.

ANGUS alone.

ANGUS: There was nothing much to speak of. At first. And it's hardly my story. But if you want to know the facts of it. Where I was, where she was. The circumstances of us being in the same place at the same time. The series of events that caused her to be shaking my hand. For her to be in my house. For Alex to have gone and fetched her.

MYRA alone. MAN enters.

MAN: Nurse?

MYRA: Yes.

MAN: You busy?

MYRA: I make a point to always be busy, sir. I haven't met you.

MAN: Alex, ma'am. Alex Bennett.

MYRA: Yes, Alex Bennett, how may I help you?

MAN: I don't mean to disturb.

MYRA: Not at all. Just beginning some baking. I've been feeling the need to diversify my talents while here. Do you bake?

MAN: No, ma'am.

MYRA: I'm led to believe that it may not be good enough to just be a nurse on this coast. I'm led to believe that any woman worth her weight can bake a batch of bread and darn a pair of socks. Do you believe that, Alex Bennett?

MAN: I don't know, ma'am.

MYRA: Could you refer to me as Nurse, please, Mr. Bennett. I applaud your formality, but when it comes out of your mouth as "ma'am" it makes me feel much older than my years demand.

MAN: Yes, ma'am. Nurse.

MYRA: Are you sick, Mr. Bennett?

MAN: Me? Oh no.

MYRA: I see. Well?

MAN: Yes?

MYRA: To what do I owe the pleasure?

MAN: Oh, my mother. She's having a baby?

MYRA: Yes?

MAN: Uh, now.

MYRA: Now? She's in labour?

MAN: I'm no doctor but –

MYRA: But she's in pain, she is sweating and crying? Swearing?

MAN: Yeah.

MYRA: And how long were we going to discuss the weather, Mr. Bennett?

She frantically collects her supplies and washes her bread-making hands.

Lessons learned, remember this. They are a charming people. They will give you the clothes off their back. They will sleep on the floor as to give you their beds. Their last piece of bread will be yours sooner than theirs. They are as kind and gentle and welcoming as any group you will ever encounter. They are good. And they will panic over a toothache as though it is the mark of death itself, and they will suffer through wracking coughs and chest pains rather than seek medical advice. And they will saunter, oh yes, take their bloody sweet time, to collect the nurse for a mother and child as close to parting ways as the bubbling red sea.

She runs into the Bennett house.

ANGUS: She came running through the door with Alex.

MYRA: Where?

MAN: Just in here.

ANGUS: Ran right past me. Don't even think she saw me.

MYRA: Mrs. Bennett? How are you today, ma'am?

WOMAN: Oh, girl, I've been better.

ANGUS: There was a formality to her step, the very speed at which she walked that demanded respect. That made you not only feel obliged to give it, but happy to do so.

MYRA: Alex?

MAN: Yes, Nurse?

MYRA: Get out.

MAN: Ma'am? Nurse?

MYRA: It is your home, and normally I would never dare, but I must insist that you both leave. Your mother and I would prefer to be alone. I hope I don't speak out of turn, Mrs. Bennett.

WOMAN: Alex, get out. Take Angus with you.

MAN: Yes, ma'am.

ANGUS: And that was that. Hardly a word spoken and she had myself and Alex out. Feet scraping on the porch. Ears perked to hear over the wind. The scatter noise from behind that fat door and our mother in labour. Our mother in labour and our hands in our pockets. Wearing a path with unlaced boots and not so much as a sweater. But we didn't get back in that house, sir, until Nurse saw fit. And when we finally walked through the door, here was this sight, you know. Mom with little Margaret. And this woman. She was walking slower. Her hands and mouth not moving as fast. She was off duty, see. All done. And it was then that she took the time, and only then, to shake my hand.

MAN: Nurse, Nurse, this is my brother Angus.

MYRA: Mr. Bennett.

ANGUS: Nurse.

They shake hands. They continue to shake hands through the following.

MYRA: I've only signed on for two years, after two years who knows where I will be. I've come here to help people. I've come here to be of assistance. I have found myself a place of respect, with these people, with this town. I have done good work. I truly believe that. I have taught people, I have saved lives. I have just delivered my first baby in this town. My second since arriving on this coast. That, that is why I am here. Not this hand. Not this arm, and shoulder. Not this.

They stop shaking hands.

MYRA: Some fresh bedding and a pot of tea, please, Mr. Bennett.

She returns to Mrs. Bennett. ANGUS remains staring at her.

ANGUS: That's all. There was just nothing much to speak of. In that other way. She was all about the work. There was nothing much happening within her but that. Work. Not then. Not when we first met. That was going to be up to me to change.

MYRA at MRS. HOUSE's for tea.

WOMAN: You like it here?

MYRA: I've only been but six months. Too early to say.

WOMAN: I ask 'cause, this crowd, the crowd around here can give a bad first impression. Don't mind them though. Give you the shirt off their backs.

MYRA: I have no doubt.

WOMAN: How long do you plan to stay?

MYRA: I've signed on for two years. That's all the budget will allow for right now.

WOMAN: Not gonna change the world in two years. Not that easy.

MYRA: I'm aware.

WOMAN: Lot of coast here. People are spread out.

MYRA: I'm aware of that, too. And it doesn't daunt me in the slightest. It hasn't killed me yet, so.

WOMAN: Well, yes, you'll get back and forth easy enough in summer. Footpaths all up and down the coast. And of course by boat. Fast, easy. But winter, my dear. Now that's another story.

MYRA: Ice?

WOMAN: No going by boat then.

MYRA: Footpath then?

WOMAN: You're braver than I, my dear. To even be out there in the likes of that come January.

MYRA: I've heard stories of your winter.

WOMAN: They're all true. Every last one of them. The winter here. Long as the coast itself. Cold. Even on the good days, wind coming from the west, and not the North, well sir, she's still whipping across that sea there like there's no tomorrow. Picking up water and salt. Flinging it at ya from October to May. Scaring ya?

MYRA: No roads at all.

WOMAN: No, my dear. Be cold day in hell too before the crowd in St. John's sees fit to dump that kind of money on this coast.

MYRA: Well.

WOMAN: Two years, eh? Think you'll last that long.

MYRA: I don't know. Think you'll have a road in two years? Can't leave you without a nurse. Without a sensible road. It wouldn't be right.

WOMAN: I'm gonna ask you that question again. In February.

She smiles. MYRA, it would seem, cannot.

ANGUS alone.

ANGUS: It was just a joke. I was up in the woods. When the steamer brought her up back in May. The first sensible day of cutting since the snow had gone. Nice day all around. Saw the boat from the top of the hill on the way back and I slapped Alex right hard on the back. That's the nurse, I said. We got ourselves a nurse now. Think I'll marry her.

MYRA on a footpath. Two heavy bags.

MAN: You're the nurse.

MYRA: Correct you are.

MAN: Where you going?

MYRA: Parson's Pond.

She drops one of the bags. He watches her pick it up.

MAN: You walking?

MYRA: That was the plan.

MAN: Nice ways.

MYRA: Yes, it has been in the past.

MAN: Nice day for it though.

MYRA: How old are you?

MAN: Fourteen.

MYRA: Isn't there something you should be doing?

MAN: Could be. Always could be, I suppose.

MYRA: Well?

MAN: Well.

She gives a disgruntled sigh.

MYRA: Goodbye then.

MAN: Okay.

He begins to walk away.

MYRA: Were you even going to offer?

MAN: Pardon.

MYRA: Assistance. Were you even going to offer, in politeness.

MAN: Truth be told, Nurse, that's why mother sent me down the path. Saw you wobbling under the bags. Thought you could use a hand down the shore.

A short pause.

MYRA: She did?

MAN: Her express orders. Not to offer. Make yourself be known and if she needs you she'll ask. She said she wouldn't have a fine independent woman like yourself bothered by the likes of me. The nurse made that trip countless times already, she said. Don't you dare insult her to even offer to carry a bag. Don't you touch a thing. Unless you needed the help, that is. Asked for it expressly.

MYRA: I see. Well. I'm sorry.

MAN: No, no need for that.

They stand and smile at each other for a moment.

MYRA: Well, you will have to remind me to thank your mother.

She holds one of her bags out for him to take.

MAN: Will do. Good day.

He turns and exits. MYRA stares after him in disbelief and lets the heavy bag fall to the ground. ANGUS steps in behind her.

ANGUS: Heart's in the right place.

MYRA: Mr. Bennett.

ANGUS: Not the sharpest knife in the drawer but none of his crowd ever were.

MYRA: I suppose. I mean he did mean well.

ANGUS: You going far?

MYRA: Parson's Pond.

ANGUS: Emergency?

MYRA: No. No, nothing terribly urgent.

ANGUS: I shouldn't break our necks in haste then.

MYRA: Excuse me?

ANGUS: Them bags look as heavy as you. Not fit to be carrying by yourself.

MYRA: You don't have to really.

ANGUS: No trouble.

MYRA: Really, I would prefer it if you –

ANGUS: You prefer it if I ran back and got that little fella for ya.

A silent standoff.

ANGUS: Well. Good.

MYRA: It's just very kind, excessively kind of you. I mean, it is a long walk.

ANGUS: I knows how long a walk it is. Too long to walk it alone. Should never have to travel alone.

MYRA: I'm quite used to it.

ANGUS: Still doesn't make it right. It's too quiet out here. Gives you a false sense of safety.

MYRA: Am I in danger?

ANGUS: Never said that either, but you can't be too careful.

MYRA: I've never equated silence with danger, Mr. Bennett.

ANGUS: No?

MYRA: Peril wears many masks, but none so pretty as this.

ANGUS: (*smiles*) Peril?

MYRA: Excuse me?

ANGUS: You've come face to face then. With danger, peril.

MYRA: Do you think women are immune to ugliness, Mr. Bennett?

ANGUS: What, angry patients? Babies screaming in your ears?

MYRA: My first years doing this sort of thing, in England, back in Woking during the Great War. Do you know nothing of war?

ANGUS: I know my share. I was a merchant marine.

MYRA: Well then, you know enough to know that women still have children, and people get sick and people get hurt. With surprising frequency.

ANGUS: And?

MYRA: And, you go. Regardless. Sirens and blackouts, bombs.

A short pause.

ANGUS: And you're out in all that. By yourself, walking around.

MYRA: Biking around.

ANGUS: That's something.

MYRA: Had to be done. Someone is sick, someone is in labour –

ANGUS: You go. Brave woman.

MYRA simply stares at him.

ANGUS: What? I say so.

MYRA: It's not like that. Bravery, it doesn't come into it. You just did it. Can't adequately explain it. I just remember that. No room for fear.

ANGUS: I don't believe that. You're just being humble.

MYRA: Excuse me?

ANGUS: You are.

MYRA: Mr. Bennett, I hardly find it funny.

ANGUS: I didn't –

MYRA: It was an exceptionally odd time, and sensation.

ANGUS: I'm sure –

MYRA: It was near impossible to feel anything at all. Things were so bleak, stripped bare. It was a place and time of action and reaction and little else. You couldn't allow yourself to feel anything, because if you started to cry, or scream, or, or laugh, then you would find yourself never having occasion to stop. (*short pause*) Emotion was scant. Like there was nothing left to lose. You must think me heartless.

ANGUS: No. No, not at all.

MYRA: It. It just was. It just was what it was. And it made me appreciate, made me see the value of all this. Of quiet walks in the country.

ANGUS: Yes. I suppose it would.

He smiles. A long uncomfortable pause, as they look ahead.

MYRA: Lovely day. Your country really is quite beautiful.

ANGUS: I still think you shouldn't have to.

A pause as she looks at him again. He remains staring ahead.

ANGUS: Travel alone.

She turns back out and smiles in spite of herself.

ANGUS alone.

ANGUS: I told Alex I was going to marry her. And like I said, it was a joke. And Alex wasn't going to hold me to it, so I certainly wasn't thinking much about it. But that day, our first walk, to hear her talking like that. War and such. It was something.

It left me curious. How many times this woman in front of me had truly felt afraid. And what forces it would take to inspire it in her. I was thinking of what good stuff would have to be waiting in the wings for her to finally have the courage to really feel something. To be scared. To bawl. To eventually stop. I was thinking of that, and somehow that joke about courting and marriage, it wasn't all that much a joke anymore.

MYRA with a young male patient and his mother.

WOMAN: Go on, tell her.

MYRA: Hello to you, too.

WOMAN: Go on, tell her, she's a busy woman.

MYRA: Is there a problem?

WOMAN: Fell off the fence. Go on, tell her. Tell her you fell off the fence.

MYRA: You fell off a fence?

WOMAN: Fell off the fence, after walking up and down the length of it. Walking up and down the length of it after me going blue in the face for lack of breath for having wasted it on telling you not to go walking up and down the length of it. Go on, tell her.

MYRA: Madam –

WOMAN: Go on, tell her where you fell. Tell her.

MAN: Mom.

MYRA: Madam –

WOMAN: Tell her. Blue in the face. Telling him he's gonna ruin himself. Telling him he's gonna ruin himself and what does he go and do. Tell her.

MYRA: Madam –

WOMAN: Walked up and down the fence, walked up and down the fence and fell. Fell and ruined himself no doubt. Ruined himself. Go on, tell him. Tell him he ruined himself.

MYRA: Madam! Please, if you would. A second alone with the patient.

WOMAN: Oh, that's all right girl, nothing I haven't seen before. Take off your pants, Henry.

MYRA: Madam –

WOMAN: Four boys. Four fine boys, nothing I haven't seen before. Go on, Henry, take off your pants and show the nurse where you fell on yourself.

MYRA alone.

MYRA: I'm sure it is bred out of concern. I am sure that it stems from a maternal instinct so strong, made so strong by the elements, the harshness of their surroundings. The need to protect, nurture beyond an age that is more than reasonable. And not just children. Brothers. Husbands, parents, grandparents. I'm sure there is a reason why here they all are, travelling in packs, travelling in packs to the nurse to have their bodies exposed, examined, picked apart for fault. Their none too delightful and often embarrassing conditions diagnosed and treated with extended family in tow. Leaning over my shoulder to get the best possible look. I'm sure there is a reason for it. But I'm sorry. Privacy. If I'm not to have roads, sensible supplies, at least give me privacy. I demand it for their sake as much as my own. And yet, they are looking at me with long faces of hurt and disappointment like I'm spoiling the family picnic. It strikes me, it strikes me as almost – I'm going to say it – selfish.

MAN and WOMAN alone.

WOMAN: Painfully clear it was.

MAN: Indeed it was.

WOMAN: Painfully clear to anyone who was looking.

MAN: Looking close enough.

WOMAN: And for us.

MAN: Yes us, we were looking.

WOMAN: And for us it was clear as the nose on your face.

MAN: The nose on your face, sir.

WOMAN: He, suddenly all interested in the health care.

MAN: And she ten times as short with him as anyone.

WOMAN: Oh, she'd deny it to this day.

MAN: Of that I'm sure.

WOMAN: Deny it black and blue, to and fro.

MAN: Inside out.

WOMAN: But it was clear.

MAN: Crystal clear.

WOMAN: Clear as what I'm saying to you here. There was something on the go from the start.

MAN: From the very start.

WOMAN: There was something on the go between them two.

MYRA and ANGUS step out on the porch.

MYRA: My Lord, it is hot in there.

ANGUS: Is that why we are out here?

MYRA: You people, it's amazing. This perfectly nice house, with a perfectly nice parlour, couches, chairs, and you all insist upon squeezing into a kitchen the size of a closet.

ANGUS: It's a proper dance, my dear. Can't stray from the kitchen.

MYRA: Really.

ANGUS: You complaining?

MYRA: What?

ANGUS: You weren't having fun?

MYRA: I simply said it was hot.

ANGUS: Think I didn't notice the circle you were spinning around that room with Alex? Cut a path right into the floorboards, no doubt. I told Mother not to invite you, you would only do damage.

MYRA: I didn't say I wasn't enjoying myself, Mr. Bennett.

ANGUS: You're just hot.

MYRA: Warm. Yes. Too warm.

ANGUS: Now see, that sounds like the words of a woman who is not planning on walking back into that kitchen for one more dance.

MYRA: I honestly don't think I'm up for it.

ANGUS: You are going home after having the last dance with Alex. That's not a slap in the face, is it.

MYRA: Your brother was very insistent.

ANGUS: Runs in the family. Just like our dancing. Give me half the chance, I'll prove it.

MYRA: Your insistence?

ANGUS: You're not going home yet.

MYRA: Excuse me?

ANGUS: Unless you want half the town thinking you're only after younger men.

MYRA: Inappropriate, Mr. Bennett.

ANGUS: I agree. Doesn't become you.

MYRA: Stop it. What do I have to say? What would you have me do?

ANGUS: Take five minutes. Long enough to catch your breath.

Another silent standoff. She holds his gaze, and then looks up at the sky.

MYRA: Lovely night. You have a lot of them here.

ANGUS: Yes. I keep forgetting that our beloved nurse has only been with us since the spring. She has not had the pure pleasure of a Newfoundland winter.

MYRA: You all have this big talk about winter. Like it's a terror. You're not frightening me. I don't scare off that easily.

ANGUS: No?

MYRA: I, my dear man, have battled and braved worse foes than your much vilified Newfoundland winter.

ANGUS: So you think.

MYRA: You are so smug, Mr. Bennett. How can you be sure that I do not have a fondness for a little snow and wind?

He laughs.

MYRA: How can you be sure, Mr. Bennett, that your lengthy winter is not one of the reasons I chose to come to Newfoundland in the first place?

ANGUS: Was it?

MYRA: As a matter of fact, yes.

ANGUS: Our winters and our kitchen parties. *(short pause)* What were your reasons?

MYRA: What?

ANGUS: Why did you come here?

A short pause.

MYRA: No great secret, I wanted to help. I wanted to help people.

ANGUS: Newfoundlanders.

MYRA: Newfoundlanders. Anybody.

ANGUS: Could of helped anybody in England. Didn't need to come all the way over here to do that.

MYRA: It was a question of need. There was a great and saddening need here. I read a story about a family in Saskatchewan. I originally applied to go there. And was told I was needed more here.

ANGUS: One story about one family and you packed up your life?

MYRA: A young mother, her first child. Her and her husband lived quite a distance out. Quite a few days' travel to anybody else. He left to get help. Left as soon as they thought the baby might be on its way. Weather set in. Help was too far away. Hours turn into days. Story has a sad ending.

ANGUS: And that was that? Duty calls?

MYRA: Stories about mothers and babies deserve only the happiest of endings.

A short pause. He smiles at her.

ANGUS: They are all afraid of you, you know. Terrified. Gotta do what the nurse says or else.

She looks at the sky silently.

ANGUS: It's just the way you talk to them.

MYRA: It's necessary sometimes, to make myself clear, and listened to.

ANGUS: Oh, you don't have to tell me. It's just … I think they see this one side of you. They see this nurse. A very good nurse, well respected, don't get me wrong. But they just see that side. And that's a shame. Because … I get the feeling that Nurse Grimsley has a depth that would make the very Atlantic blush with shame.

She remains staring at the sky.

MYRA: Mr. Bennett –

ANGUS: Your five minutes are up.

She looks at him.

ANGUS: Do you have your breath?

A warm pause.

MYRA: I believe so.

ANGUS: Yes?

MYRA: Take me back to your hot and crowded kitchen. If you must.

ANGUS: *(laughs)* If I must?

MYRA: If you must, take me to your kitchen, sir. Dance me until my legs themselves plead for clemency.

Fast dancing and music. ANGUS breaks away.

ANGUS: She stayed for two more hours that night. Only danced with me twice. Danced with every other guy there. With Alex four or five times. Didn't matter though. She could have danced with anyone she pleased. She could have refused me a dance outright. For she smiled at few of them. She talked to even less. And with me, with me she took her five-minute breaks, which stretched to twenty. Empty porch step. Cold colouring our breath. Long talks circling nothing. Stars the only witnesses.

ANGUS joins up with her again. Dancing and music dissolve into MYRA sitting by herself. Tired and slow.

MYRA: My hands and shoulders are very tired. I don't often realize the strain I put on them. It is different with teeth. Pulling teeth. There is less at stake, so you can … more of your mind can wander to your joints and muscles and bones. Take stock of yourself. But with birthing it is much more involved. So you don't often realize your own fatigue, pain until everyone else is comfortable. Until the only pain in the room is your own. But today, I walk out of that house, clean myself. Get myself home. Make supper. Sit on my bed, and close my eyes and force it out. And then, then I feel this ache in my arms. Only after all of that. She was crying when I left. The same for Roy. Their first child. And there is no consoling them that there will be more. There's no talk of breech birth, by way of explanation, of umbilical cords, of suffocation. There is no explanation. There is no consoling. You just leave, and clean yourself, and make supper. And then, only then, do your arms hurt.

MYRA walking alone.

WOMAN: Good day, Nurse.

MYRA: Good day …

WOMAN: Mary.

MYRA: Mary, yes. Forgive me. How are things today?

WOMAN: Good, Nurse. Killing my back, but good.

MYRA: Potatoes?

WOMAN: Turnip. Bit of cabbage over there. Next spring gonna plant more potatoes though. Never puts down enough. Says it every year. Never learn.

MYRA: Hard work.

WOMAN: All hard work on this coast. Nobody gets it easy. I would say especially yourself.

MYRA: Normally I'd feign humility, but these past days.

WOMAN: Dorothy Walsh. Tough going.

MYRA: This is a very small town, isn't it.

WOMAN: How is she?

MYRA: Surviving.

WOMAN: Poor soul. Her first too, eh?

MYRA: It was a hard day. Dorothy had it hard.

WOMAN: Like I told ya. All hard work on this coast.

MYRA: It's true, isn't it. You can't do anything easily.

WOMAN: Would if I could. But most times you don't even get the option. Feet out first? Dorothy? Breech is it you calls it?

MYRA: She had it hard.

WOMAN: My mother, the very same.

MYRA: Yes?

WOMAN: And my sister-in-law. A bugger of time, both of them had.

MYRA: It's as common as the grass, it would seem. I've never seen the like. And I'm completely at a loss.

WOMAN: Good Lord got a weird sense of humour when it comes to this place, Nurse. Summer, land of milk and honey and beautiful sun and sea. Winter, a slap in the face for six months. Same with everything else. The most beautiful babies in the world. And the labour that hard to almost make it not worthwhile.

MYRA: All hard work on this coast.

WOMAN: You better believe it.

MYRA: Better let you get back to yours.

WOMAN: Good day to you.

MYRA: Yes, Mary, take care.

She begins to leave.

WOMAN: Nurse.

MYRA: Yes.

WOMAN: Regardless of how hard it was, the birthing I mean. It was worse before. You know that, right? It was all much worse before you got here.

A short pause and a weak smile.

MYRA: I'll take some of those turnip if you're willing to sell.

WOMAN: Always willing.

MYRA alone.

MYRA: It is a crisp night in late September. The summer is almost gone now. The fall itself will not last long, I am told. The air feels thick in my lungs. Thick with water and cold. Thick with autumn. It is a little past midnight and I am sitting on a rock overlooking the non-existent harbour of Daniel's Harbour. The moon is yawning and stretching on the water, like it too will sleep. Like this town, like this entire world, it seems. While I sit here, and marvel, at this beautiful, beautiful land and how fundamentally, how utterly, unfamiliar it is to me. When I arrived it was novelty, and excitement, and it bore its way into my head and heart and hands. It was present in my work, in my work day, that excitement, and it left me to sleep soundly. Now. Now. I enjoy it here, I truly do. But here there is nothing that catches my eye, my peripheral vision, and makes me forget where I am, forget my age. Nothing that makes me sink in comfort, in the secure and peaceful comfort of home. There is an absence here. A telling absence. I can feel it. As sure as I can feel the air leave my lungs, I can feel it. But try as I might, I cannot, I cannot name it. I have a sad heart. I have a sad little, sore little heart. It would seem that there is a wound here that the nurse cannot mend.

ANGUS alone.

ANGUS: It was becoming regular. Our trips together. Me going with her up and down the coast. It was becoming regular and expected. Which was fine with me. Summer was giving it up, calling it quits. The woods were growing colourful and serious. As were our talks. Fall was taking over. Days growing smaller. Seas growing bigger.

MYRA and ANGUS in a boat.

MYRA: The day I left, the day the ship left port to cross the spring Atlantic, it was Friday the thirteenth of April. So, yes, I know of superstition, know its power. Grown men that day practically weeping. Begging to set sail the day following. Tempting providence, they claimed, to set out on the thirteenth.

ANGUS: And you? What were you thinking? What were you feeling?

MYRA: Me? Many, many things. But not fear.

ANGUS: Really.

MYRA: Really. Excitement more than anything else. Nothing could happen to me to spoil the huge adventure upon which I was embarking.

ANGUS smiles and begins to chuckle.

MYRA: What? Why is that funny?

ANGUS: Just never heard anyone refer to Daniel's Harbour as an adventure before.

MYRA: You just have to be on the outside looking in. You ever been there?

ANGUS: On the outside? Yeah. Yeah, I have.

MYRA: It's a confusing place.

ANGUS: Can be.

MYRA: This was, and continues to be, a huge adventure. Believe you me. As different from my world as night and day. My old world.

ANGUS: You getting anxious to get back?

MYRA: Doesn't matter. I'm contracted for another year and a half yet. And then, maybe longer. No roads in place.

ANGUS: What does that have to do with it?

MYRA: Give you two years of sensible help. Give you that and then leave here. Not even a road to get help down the coast, or up. You can't behave that way, think that way, and call yourself a Christian.

ANGUS: No. I suppose not.

MYRA: No.

ANGUS: So you're here until they lay a road.

MYRA: See the adventure? You see it now? Gobbles you up. Two years turn to four turn to eight.

ANGUS: Or longer.

MYRA: Or longer. You just hope that, that that adventure is your fate. That grand story you're falling into is what is meant to be. How tragic otherwise. Fated to be elsewhere, providence tugging at your sleeve. And you not listening.

ANGUS: You believe in fate then. Providence.

She smiles at him.

ANGUS: I guess I do, too. It gets jumbled up sometimes. Confusing. Needs to be sorted out. Needs you to take action. Decisions to be made.

MYRA: Is that so?

ANGUS: Yes. Very much so. I mean, my decision to move back here. To leave the merchant marines. To come back here. It's all fine and good to say that it was fate, but I could have just as easily walked away from it, been scared off by it. Stayed away. There are decisions involved, and, and I guess a person is never sure whether what they are doing is what is right, what is written. Who can say, whether I was supposed to come back here, and open a store. Get married. Have kids.

MYRA: Is that what you want? Do you know?

ANGUS: I think so. I don't know. Yes. Yes, that is what I want.

MYRA: Then. That is fate.

A short pause.

ANGUS: And what do you want?

MYRA: To help people.

ANGUS: For yourself. Do you know what you want for yourself?

She smiles and turns away from him.

MYRA: That, Mr. Bennett, is the problem entirely. Wouldn't you agree?

ANGUS alone.

ANGUS: I remember hearing those words. Her saying she was duty bound. Here. For as long as it took to get a road. No two-year contract. No deadline. And sir, wasn't that a scary thing. Hearing that. Didn't that put things into another light. I there listening to that, and all I could sound was some talk of decisions, taking action. A collection of words falling out of my mouth like they were put there by someone else. I got to speak them. Then I got to pick them up, and bring them home to think about what they meant. Decision. Action.

MYRA and HELEN.

WOMAN: She was only three, you know. When Marie was born. That's young. And while she said she always wanted a sister, well, they say that. They always do, until it's there, until there is another face to look at, another attention-getter. So we expected some trouble. Had been warned about it in fact. Had been told that she would act up. Heard every story under the sun. But when she saw Marie. Oh my. Break your heart. The softest little voice. She spoke with the softest little voice in telling us to shut it up, we'd wake the baby. And she was like that. Always on about the baby. Don't make a racket, you'll wake the baby. Wanting to feed the baby. Wanting to hold the baby. You wouldn't know but she was a woman of forty the way she got on. You wouldn't know it at all. (*pause*) Yeah, she was a charmer.

MYRA: How is Marie?

WOMAN: Fine, girl. Five months old last Tuesday. Soon off the milk, please God. Big head a hair on her now, too. Takes after her father for sure.

MYRA: Is she well?

WOMAN: Oh yes, girl. Finest kind.

MYRA: Dennis?

WOMAN: He's good. Working himself to death dragging in wood. Convinced it's gonna be a bad one this year. No talking him out of it.

MYRA: And you? How are you?

WOMAN: Good. I'm fine. (*pause*) Not much of a liar. I'm tired, girl. Hard year.

MYRA: Hard week.

HELEN stands and walks away from her.

WOMAN: More tea?

MYRA: No, no, thank you, Helen.

WOMAN: You sure?

MYRA: Helen. Physically. How are you?

WOMAN: There's a lovely bit of bread there, Nurse, some jam.

MYRA: Helen, please. Any pain? Discomfort? Coughing?

WOMAN: Nurse.

MYRA: It's important.

WOMAN: No. I'll not have you at that. It's too soon.

MYRA: Helen, there is a very real danger –

WOMAN: No. Sit here and let you frighten the wits out of me. No, Nurse. It's too hard. Cassie only gone four days now. Four days and you talking the like of that.

MYRA: She died of a disease called TB, Helen, a very dangerous, very easy-to-catch disease –

WOMAN: Don't presume me ignorant, Nurse. I know full well what she died of. I know full well too that we are fine. I know full well many a family that suffered through what we just did, suffered through it and lost but the one. The only thing this week, I swear to God the only thing this week that kept my body out of that hole with Cassie was the little one I had in my arms and the man standing next to me. So don't you dare presume me ignorant, and don't you dare frighten me with the thought of that happening all over again.

MYRA: Helen –

WOMAN: Goodbye, Nurse.

A small tense pause.

MYRA: I'm not trying to upset you. Helen, I'm not. I'll go, just ... Please, just humour me. Let me take a look at you. Listen to your lungs. Helen.

WOMAN: We're fine, Nurse. We are. All of us. Now you're welcome to more tea, but I've got to get on the go. Dennis will be home the once. Marie needs to be fed.

HELEN takes up baby Marie and rocks her. She sings softly.

MYRA: I thought myself fully prepared for any emergency, any medical emergency or situation that would, that could present itself here. And yet this place, these people, in all of their glory manage to surprise me. Not in the condition with which they present themselves, not with the illnesses. But with the stubbornness. The sheer stubbornness when it comes to taking care of themselves, with heeding my words. I had not foreseen having to lecture on the contagious nature of the tubercular patient.

HELEN begins to breastfeed Marie.

MYRA: It is like they think, or want to believe, that I am trying to scare them, assert some sort of authority which they assume I have given myself because of my title. Knowledge is, and has been, my only authority. More than anything I want to share it. It is often exceedingly difficult to do so.

At the clinic.

ANGUS: Nurse?

MAN: Nurse?

WOMAN: Nurse?

MYRA: One at a time. One at a time. Yes?

WOMAN: Nurse, warts. Warts, Nurse.

MYRA: What about them?

WOMAN: My grandmother said to rub a bit of meat on 'em and throw it to the dog. That work?

MYRA: Yes, of course. If by meat you mean wood file, and by rub you mean saw off. Otherwise you can rub whatever you want for however long you want, but the only thing you'll be doing is feeding the dog. Next.

ANGUS: Nurse?

WOMAN: Nurse?

MAN: Nurse?

MYRA: Yes?

MAN: The wife gets the wicked nosebleeds. She swears to warding it off by tying a green ribbon about the neck.

MYRA: Absolutely.

MAN: Yeah?

MYRA: Just make sure you tie it tight enough.

ANGUS: Nurse?

MAN: Nurse?

WOMAN: Nurse?

MYRA: Yes, yes?

WOMAN: My youngest got the asthma. Now, they says that you should pluck a hair from the head, take her height on the wall, put the hair in a hole at just that spot, just at her head height, and plug it up, and once she grows past that hole, the hole with the hair in the wall what was her height, that she'll never have the asthma again. Now. What do you think of that?

MYRA: Madam, who told you this?

WOMAN: Young Charlie Payne, God rest his soul.

MYRA: Perhaps you should bring the child with you in the future. Next.

ANGUS: Nurse.

WOMAN: Nurse?

MAN: Nurse?

MYRA: Yes?

MAN: Father gave me a fishbone to carry in my pocket on account of my toothache.

MYRA: And does your father have any teeth left?

MAN: No.

MYRA: Lie down.

> *He lies on her table as she quickly produces her dental instruments.*

MAN: Nurse!

ANGUS: Nurse?

WOMAN: Nurse?

MYRA: Yes. Yes. One at a time, please.

MAN: Nurse!

WOMAN: Nurse?

ANGUS: Nurse?

MYRA: Yes. I'm busy.

WOMAN: Nurse?

ANGUS: Nurse!

> *She turns angrily from the young man's mouth.*

MYRA: Yes?

ANGUS: Would you consider marrying me?

MYRA: Yes.

> *She turns back to the young man's mouth and gives a hard yank. The young man cries with pain. Lights out.*

ACT TWO

> *ANGUS alone.*

ANGUS: They will tell you now, they will tell you when you ask that she was hopelessly in love. Love at first sight is what they will tell you. They will tell you that that first time we met at Mom's house was the beginning of everything. An inevitable chain of events in which she was a helpless pawn to something bigger than herself. They will tell you that, and they are wrong.

> *MYRA and MRS. HOUSE.*

MYRA: Our marriage, our courtship is one of practicality. Plain and simple. Angus is without wife. I am without husband. I am in need of assistance in travel, the practicalities of getting to the patient.

ANGUS: I, apparently, was in need of a cook, a baker, a darner of socks, all of which she was becoming acquainted with by the way.

MYRA: It is a practical decision. Despite how it looks. And how he looks.

ANGUS: So, do not listen to them when they tell you that. When they speak of true love and fate and such nonsense.

MYRA: Angus Bennett is a very nice man whom it makes perfect sense to make my husband. Yes, that's what I'm talking about. It just makes sense.

ANGUS: And she'd say it to my face. Partly because she believed it. But partly because deep down she knew that I knew there was more there than that. Caution, excitement, determination. Pride. Like a shy child building a house of cards.

WOMAN: Well, it's wonderful. It is.

MYRA: It is that.

WOMAN: Yes. Certainly. Everyone thinks so.

MYRA: Yes.

WOMAN: Of course, all my crowd are climbing the walls over it. Ready to burst. Saying I told you so this, and I knew they'd get together that.

MYRA: It is a sound idea.

WOMAN: It's a wonderful thing.

MYRA: And a practical thing. Angus has been most helpful to me in the past months, getting back and forth. Assisting with patients.

WOMAN: Yes.

MYRA: And it would only make sense to make it official, our partnership as it were. And he needs a wife, a good wife.

WOMAN: He most certainly does.

MYRA: He needs that.

WOMAN: Nurse, are you all right?

A short pause.

MYRA: One could think it distasteful, this behaviour. To be anything but overjoyed, to be sitting here stewing in questions.

WOMAN: Jitters, my child.

MYRA: Really. I mean, teeth, babies, this I can do. A household, cooking, baking.

WOMAN: Now your bread is fine. It is. It will be better, someday. With practice.

MYRA: With time. Which I may not have. Which I may never have. Running back and forth dealing with half of the coast. Is that fair? Honestly. Do you think that is fair?

WOMAN: Honestly?

MYRA: Honestly.

WOMAN: Honestly, I would have to say that Angus is many things, but slow he is not. Agreed.

MYRA: Certainly.

WOMAN: So then don't you think, don't you agree that in the last four months of helping you and your bags up and down this sorry coast it would have crossed his mind that this behaviour, this annoying behaviour of yours of wanting to help everyone and their sheep would be a behaviour that was not going to change quickly. Or at all. Don't you think he has the slightest idea of what he's getting himself into?

MYRA: I suppose so.

WOMAN: So what then, my dear, is the problem?

MYRA: I don't know. Perhaps, perhaps I don't know what I'm getting myself into.

WOMAN: Jitters.

MYRA: You think so?

WOMAN: Look, Nurse, despite your claims that this marriage makes sense, that it is all about sense, I can assure you that it is bloody well not. Two people promising to stand by each other through anything, partners for life. Promises like that don't get made unless you're that drunk on each other that nothing else matters. Sense got nothing to do with it. If it was about sense, if you were all about sense, you probably wouldn't of even set foot in this place. Right? Right?

A short pause.

WOMAN: Nurse. Be happy. And be done with it.

MAN and WOMAN alone.

MAN: Oh, she was all nerves, I hear.

WOMAN: Oh yes, I heard that.

MAN: What with her being from Britain and –

WOMAN: And Angus being from home.

MAN: Too different, see.

WOMAN: Afraid they'd be too different, culturally, eh.

MAN: But sure she was one of us by that point.

WOMAN: Yes, practically one of us.

MAN: What with her keeping the chickens.

WOMAN: And the garden.

MAN: Making the boots and the floor mats.

WOMAN: And the jam, and the partridge, and the fish.

MAN: Shearing the sheep and weaving the wool.

WOMAN: She was never idle.

MAN: No, sir. Not one second.

WOMAN: She wasn't cooking, she was cleaning.

MAN: She wasn't cleaning, she was birthing.

WOMAN: Or at the church, organizing the choir.

MAN: Playing the organ.

WOMAN: And then the medical stuff, what with the diarrhea.

MAN: And the flu.

WOMAN: And the pneumonia.

MAN: And the whooping cough.

MAN & WOMAN: Tuberculosis.

WOMAN: Bloody stuff.

MAN: Pulling out fish hooks.

WOMAN: Draining abscesses.

MAN: Stitching cuts.

WOMAN: Applying salves.

MAN: Sure, it's a wonder the poor woman had the time to breathe let alone start a family.

WOMAN: That's for bloody well sure. It's a wonder they found time to have Grace at all.

MYRA enters on ANGUS at home. He sits wearily. A short pause as she looks at him.

MYRA: She down?

ANGUS: Finally. Didn't think she was going to sleep at all tonight.

MYRA: Misses her mother.

ANGUS: You look tired.

MYRA: No.

ANGUS: You've been on your feet all day.

MYRA: Nothing out of the ordinary.

ANGUS: You walk? Back from Portland Creek?

MYRA: Yes.

ANGUS: Sit.

MYRA: Angus.

ANGUS: No, sit. Let me get you some tea.

He leaves for tea. She is very much alone. A short pause.

MYRA: She must love you.

ANGUS: (*off*) What?

MYRA: She must love you. Spending all day with her. Spending most days with her.

ANGUS: (*off*) She's barely three months old. I don't think she even knows who I am yet.

She speaks quietly to herself. ANGUS re-enters and hears her.

MYRA: I think she does. I think she knows who you are.

A short pause.

ANGUS: Well, she will. Someday. She will know who I am. And you. And she'll boast about the two best parents on the coast. And her mother, the nurse.

MYRA smiles and turns away.

ANGUS: Work is work, my dear. You do what you can. And the rest. The rest you ask for help.

MYRA: I can't take her with me.

ANGUS: And you can't not go. So. So we deal with it.

MYRA: It's that simple.

ANGUS: It's not simple. It just is. The fact of the matter is ... Nurse, the fact of the matter is that child is never going to feel unloved, or unkept, or in need. Of anything. Is she.

MYRA: I love my husband very much.

ANGUS: Yeah?

MYRA: I love my husband very, very much. Beyond words. Beyond report.

ANGUS: Better.

MYRA: I love my husband. And my baby. My beautiful little girl. And my beautiful little house.

ANGUS: Oh, now, don't start.

MYRA: It is, Angus. It is a lovely little house you've built. I do love it.

ANGUS: Why?

MYRA: What?

ANGUS: Why do you love it? What about it do you love?

MYRA: That. That it's ...

ANGUS: Yeah?

MYRA: Mine.

He smiles.

ANGUS: Ours.

MYRA: Ours. Ours.

A small soft kiss. A noise. He speaks softly to her.

ANGUS: Kettle's boiled.

He slowly rises to fetch it.

ANGUS alone.

ANGUS: It's foolishness to think that a wedding, a child will completely cure a person of homesickness. Of that loneliness. It's foolish to think that great happiness equals complete happiness. I never saw her as happy as she was the year Grace was born. I also never saw her as distant. She worked harder, to push it down, to keep it at bay. But you could see it in her eyes. As frustrating as it was, you could see it in her eyes. Watching her out on the hill by herself. Wrapped in a blanket, watching the moon and the sea. And it was foolish to think it was just going to go away like that. As foolish as thinking that all it was was a little case of homesickness.

MYRA alone on the hill.

MYRA: I have biked through bomb raids. I have watched people starve. I have watched children die. I have done all this with a pervasive sense of duty pushing me onward. I have done all of this without succumbing to sentiment. I have never been soft, as a person that word has never defined me. I have also never stood over a patient and truly felt consequence, truly felt that my actions would have repercussions. They do certainly, always for the patient, their family. But I have never felt at risk, personally. As a person. That my soul lies in the balance, that it could very well split. I have never felt that. Not once. Not once. So what does that make me? Heartless? Cold? I feel love. Now more than ever. I do feel love and that helps dispel these concerns. Angus helps. Angus helps everything. Marrying him was the best thing I have ever done. I don't doubt that. But. But I feel very alone here. Yes, that is it. Sometimes I feel very alone, maybe, maybe just because of the sheer distance, separation from what I used to be, where I came from. Angus helps. Angus, and the work itself. The sheer frequency of it. And the variety.

MYRA enters on MAN.

MAN: This way, Nurse. She's in here.

MYRA: How long has she been this way?

MAN: A day or so. Longer than a day. Too long.

MYRA: She's in pain?

MAN: Appears to be.

MYRA: I need you to relax. Everything is going to be okay.

MAN: Yes. Of course.

MYRA: Just tell me everything.

MAN: Well, I came in to check on her yesterday. 'Cause, 'cause she's been quiet lately. And I haven't been thinking anything of it. I mean she is quite old. It's natural she would have spurts like that. You know, quiet spurts like that.

MYRA: Of course.

MAN: I didn't think anything of it.

MYRA: It's all right, Fred.

MAN: And when I checked on her yesterday she was breathing strangely. Thick deep breaths. And stopping in between. Like she couldn't, couldn't catch her breath, or something. And her eyes were closing. Dropping. Like she was weak. Too weak to stand.

MYRA: She was lying down?

MAN: No, standing. But barely.

MYRA: She's been eating well?

MAN: Less than usual. Yes, that's for sure, less than usual.

MYRA: Is she jumpy?

MAN: Regularly, yes. Won't let no one near her but me. Now, who knows.

MYRA: I need to know. I need to know for my safety.

MAN: She, I guess she will be fine. I don't know.

MYRA: Anything else I should know?

MAN: Her stool is loose. Very loose, and, plentiful.

MYRA: Plentiful?

MAN: A bucket each time. Give or take. And.

MYRA: And?

MAN: Her mane is thinning. Thinning quite a bit.

MYRA: All right. I'll do what I can.

She moves to go to the patient.

MAN: Nurse. Cleo is old. I know that. She's been good to us, and, and if this is all for her, I guess that's it and I should be grateful. But. But it's going to be awfully hard for us. This winter. Without her. It's gonna be hard getting the wood in. There's only me. Maud is no good for that stuff. It's gonna be awfully hard without her. Damn near impossible. I just ...

MYRA: I'll do what I can, Fred.

MAN: Yeah. I know. I know.

ANGUS alone.

ANGUS: What was she supposed to do? That's what she'd ask. Sit around and laze away the time. Turn people away at the door. Watch people around her lose their babies, their very lives. Because her contract ran out. She knew when she came here that she only had two years. But she said it herself. Leave people with no road, and no nurse. So, there you go. We got married, she settled down for the long haul knowing that, officially, her time here would run out. And when it did, her life was here. For better or worse, her life was here, and she was working. That's how it went. She went along as usual. Treating who needed to be treated. Helping who needed to be helped. Take payment when she could. More often not. Sometimes just taking what could be offered.

MYRA by a field.

WOMAN: Nurse.

MYRA: Mary, how are you?

WOMAN: Can't complain, girl. Howard see you this morning?

MYRA: I've not been home, Mary, I have to confess. Is his jaw bothering him?

WOMAN: No, finally stopped his whining. Thanks to you. He was going to drop over payment.

MYRA: Now, Mary, I told Howard –

WOMAN: I'm full aware what you told Howard, and it's appreciated. But fair is fair.

MYRA: If you insist. A sack of potatoes it is.

WOMAN: Potatoes?

MYRA: Yes, when Howard was over to finally have that tooth pulled he offered me a sack of potatoes.

WOMAN: He did?

MYRA: Yes. Was he wrong to do so?

WOMAN: No. No, girl, it's not that it's …

MYRA: What?

WOMAN: Sure you got your own potatoes. Lovely field of 'em, I can see it from here.

MYRA: Yes.

WOMAN: More potatoes over there than your crowd would eat all winter.

MYRA: You obviously don't know my crowd.

WOMAN: Nurse.

MYRA: Yes?

WOMAN: Howard didn't offer you potatoes. He knows you don't need potatoes. I told him, I told him to pay you proper.

MYRA: And proper payment is a sack of potatoes.

WOMAN: Nurse.

MYRA: Mary, I'm not going to barter with you, I'm sorry, the tooth was pulled and you said so yourself, fair is fair.

WOMAN: Nurse. We can afford it. We can. We had a good year. Better than last. And your generosity is noted, it's very kind. But, but we'd like to be square with you.

MYRA: Mary.

WOMAN: I'm serious, Nurse. We want to be square.

MYRA: And I want you to be. I've more use for your fine potatoes than I do for that bit of money. What am I going to spend it on? Something at my own husband's shop?

WOMAN: Nurse –

MYRA: Ah Mary, just give me the potatoes. You don't want to see me angry.

WOMAN: You are as stubborn as they say.

MYRA: Not stubborn, Mary. Just a lover of a fine potato. How are you otherwise?

WOMAN: Good, girl. Not long for this stuff now.

MYRA: No, I wouldn't say. What are you, eight months?

WOMAN: Eight and a half.

MYRA: Shouldn't be at it at all, really.

WOMAN: Got to get done, girl. It all got to get done.

MYRA: I suppose so.

WOMAN: How is little Grace?

MYRA: Growing like a weed. They do that, you know.

WOMAN: Can't wait.

MYRA: Take care of yourself, Mary.

MYRA goes to leave.

WOMAN: Yes, girl. Going to have to call it quits the once. Can barely bend over anymore.

A pause as MYRA turns back to watch her work.

WOMAN: No easy work on this coast.

MYRA: She is a fine person. Her husband as well. Generous with what they have. Their first child is due, and it is no secret to anyone who knows them that their glory days are ahead. Wanted children since they were children. It's a nice excitement that way. When people are excited to the point that others are excited for them. It's nice. Because they have worked hard for it. For everything. She continues to work hard. Tending a garden in her ninth month. Bending and tending with a belly full with child. A belly full with child with only so much room to move.

MYRA walks back to her.

Mary. Stoop. Like this. Don't bend.

WOMAN: What?

MYRA: Humour me. Don't bend at your hips like that. Stoop, with your legs, lift with your legs like this.

WOMAN: Why?

MYRA: It might help. Be easier. For everyone.

WOMAN: What?

MYRA: Humour me.

WOMAN: Like this?

MYRA: Yes.

WOMAN: Stooping.

MYRA: Instead of bending.

ANGUS enters.

ANGUS: Breech births at a frequency seemingly unheard of. Especially in the late summer, early fall. So many other problems here with nutrition and sickness, I suppose for the longest while she just assumed it was part and parcel of the bigger picture. And then one day she gets it. Fall, and the harvest, and the bending and the babies.

MYRA: Mothers themselves unwarily forcing their little ones to turn in the womb. Forcing them out feet first.

ANGUS: It was such common sense you think some of our crowd would have come up with it. But no, sir. Sharp as a tack she was. For picking up on that. Everyone thought so. Sure, they published her ideas on that stuff in some fancy medical journal. Which is good. Very good. Only thing better is the number of normal births that wouldn't have been otherwise. Number of mothers with a bearable amount of pain in labour. Number of babies to live to thank her one day.

MYRA alone on a path. A pause.

MYRA: It is not my surroundings. Cause is virtually non-existent. But the feeling is there. I am standing in the middle of the path and it feels like, it feels like something is going horribly wrong. Or has already. That loneliness. It happens when I'm travelling alone like this. When my mind has reign to drift. I am standing in the middle of the path and there is not a breath of wind or sound of any kind. And there is nobody near. And I feel this well of doubt. A sense of absence. That none of this was meant to be. And in the midst of that, in the middle of that horrible sensation, my mind is as calm as the wind. My emotions as still as the grass. (*short pause*) It. It is troubling, that.

ANGUS enters.

ANGUS: You could see it on her face. Plain as day. And you were helpless to change it. Because it was never about you. It wasn't about anything you could touch or talk about. But it was real, and it was there. And you could see it on her face. Until that night.

MYRA and ANGUS in bed. A long silent pause. MYRA awakens.

MYRA: I have learned to sleep with my ears active. Alive to the night.

A pause as her eyes dart around the room.

They learned to filter. They learned to separate the common from the extraordinary. The wind rocking the windows from the knock on the door. The sea on the beach from the clatter of approaching hooves. The rattle of Angus's sleeping breath from sleigh bells beating a path through the woods. Angus, wake up.

ANGUS: What?

MYRA: Listen.

MAN comes bursting in.

MAN: Nurse! Nurse Bennett!

MYRA: What's happened?

MAN: Accident, ma'am.

MYRA: Where?

MAN: Horrible accident, ma'am.

MYRA: Where?

MAN: Logging camp. Logging camp, ma'am. Angus.

ANGUS: No.

MAN: It's Alex.

ANGUS: No.

MYRA: And that's that. We run. We get ourselves, as though by instinct, not even thinking, we get ourselves into the sleigh and we ride. We are hours out. And yet the urgency, the sheer need of us getting there as quickly as possible has us in a sweat. Angus is like I've never seen him. That worry. In his eyes. In his body, everywhere. I can even see it in myself. We are all grabbing onto something. The sleigh, the reins, my medical bag, clutching tightly as though we ourselves, our exertion, could affect the speed of the horse that leads us. And as we ride we listen. To the story. To what awaits us.

MAN: He was safe, Nurse. He was always safe. But it was icy. Ice everywhere. And he slipped. His foot, he went under the saw. But he was fine. He was safe. He landed, his foot landed safely in the dust pit below the blade. But his reflexes, he couldn't help but jump, pull back. And the blade caught him. Across the ankle. I believe it's gone. I believe his foot is gone clear off.

ANGUS: And all I could think about was Alex the silly fool dancing with the nurse at that party. Throwing her around the kitchen like there was no tomorrow. I don't think I was worried. I don't think I ever really worried when she was near.

MYRA: And we are there. In the middle of the woods. The middle of the night. And there are men everywhere. And everyone is strangely quiet. Just looking at me as if to say, get on with it. And the lanterns are hitting the snow and lighting up the place, bouncing off the trees. And all I can see is this huge black spot in the middle of it all. Everyone is looking at this huge black spot in this sea of white. And I realize it is Alex. And then I realize it is Alex's blood. Hello, Alex.

MAN: Nurse.

MYRA: And the light is closer now and you can see the colour of it. All red, and white of snow. Strangely like Christmas, and the thought of it makes me so sad and sick. And lying in the middle of it all is sweet, sweet Alex. So in shock by that point he didn't even know what was what.

MAN: I told them they shouldn't bother you.

MYRA: No?

MAN: No. This time of night. Don't even hurt anymore.

MYRA: Alex, your foot.

MAN: Yes, girl. Something, ain't it. Weird looking.

MYRA: We have to get you up. And on the sleigh.

MAN: I can't walk, I don't think.

MYRA: That's all right.

MAN: Don't even hurt anymore though. Shouldn't have bothered you. Could have all waited until morning.

MYRA: It is no different. Fundamentally. It is no different. A patient is a patient. You function as you were taught. Your mind races for a practical solution even though one is probably not to be found. You file through procedures, interventions in your mind. Pages of textbooks, voices of mentors and teachers, doctors, in your ears. Stop the bleeding. Save the foot if you can, but stop the bleeding. This is all I think about on the way back to the house. My husband is beside me. His brother's blood on his shirt and I am too busy. My mind is too busy to offer consolation.

ANGUS: We arrived back at the house and she was barking commands.

MYRA: Angus. Go wake Mrs. House and Mrs. Buckle. I need them immediately.

ANGUS: Yes, Nurse.

MYRA: Mrs. House. Take this lint. I need you to sew bags, bags about this size. Quickly, you need not be tidy.

WOMAN: Yes, Nurse.

MYRA: Angus. Get your shovel. Fill the bags as they are ready. Fill them with snow.

ANGUS: Yes, Nurse.

MYRA: Mrs. House. Pack the bags around Alex's leg. Here and here. As many as you can. They start to melt and you replace them. You understand?

WOMAN: Yes, Nurse.

MYRA: Angus. Boil the kettle. Sterilize some water and these instruments. Quickly.

ANGUS: Yes, Nurse.

MYRA: Alex. I'm going to clean your leg. You may feel discomfort.

MAN: Yes, Nurse.

MYRA: I'm going to sew your foot back on, Alex. I'm going to sew your foot back on. These bags, these bags of ice will help with the pain. They will help but not entirely. You must trust me, Alex. You must remain calm and trust me. Trust me. Trust me.

ANGUS & WOMAN & MAN: Yes, Nurse.

ANGUS: And that's what she did. She sewed, she stitched his foot back on. Cleaned it as best she could. Fragments of bone and old blood. Deadened his leg with lint bags filled with snow. And did her best. Did all she could do.

MYRA: He needs a doctor. A proper doctor to look at it. He's not going to bleed to death. I've seen to that. But I am no surgeon. And what I did tonight … Angus, I have no aspirations of saving his foot. My instincts tell me that he will lose it. But he must see a doctor. An injury like that, infection is all too possible. He. He is not safe yet. He needs to see a doctor.

MYRA, ANGUS, and WOMAN at telegraph office.

ANGUS: It was that next day she sent the telegram to the doctor in Bonne Bay.

MYRA: Young man with severed right foot. In need of your attention immediately. Request you come as soon as possible. Instructions for interim care vital.

ANGUS: It was the day after that when she got her reply.

WOMAN reads to her

WOMAN: Can do more for him here. Sounds like an amputation case.

MYRA: Well?

ANGUS: Well.

MYRA: Sixty miles, Angus.

ANGUS: At least.

MYRA: Do you think we can make it?

ANGUS: I don't know.

MYRA: I checked him this morning. Took off his bandages to see if … He's looking better. His foot is taking some blood. At least. He might be able to make it through. Make that sixty miles.

ANGUS: Yeah.

MYRA: And he might not be able to make it otherwise.

ANGUS: Good then. We go.

MYRA: You think.

ANGUS: I'll get us there.

MYRA: I know you'll try.

ANGUS: I'll get us there. Okay?

MYRA: Yes.

He walks away from her.

Angus?

ANGUS: Yeah.

A short pause.

MYRA: Nothing.

MYRA and ANGUS travelling.

MYRA: We have done this before. That is what I keep telling myself. We have made this trip before. Maybe not this early in the year. Maybe not with this kind of cold. This much snow. Maybe not this distance, in such a very real hurry. Maybe not with my brother-in-law silent on a sleigh. Maybe not with all of that. But we have made this trip before. That is what I keep telling myself. Angus. Angus, the snow is too deep. Too soft. She going in with every step. Angus, she is going in with every step.

ANGUS: Maybe by the coast.

MYRA: The drift ice.

ANGUS: Maybe clearer.

MYRA: Maybe? Angus.

ANGUS: I know.

MYRA: Slippery, Angus. At all angles.

ANGUS: I know.

MYRA: It will be hard.

ANGUS: It'll be all right.

MYRA: And that's what we do. I am walking. There is no time to stop. There is no time to pause and properly survey my surroundings. I am walking and my head is turning and eyes are scanning and I see nothing. Oh God, I see nothing. Countless times I have made this trip, or others like it. We have done this before. But never, never when I have travelled with Angus have I seen the emptiness. The vastness of what we are trying to conquer. Never has a distance seemed so great or impassable. Never have I felt secretly, so secretly that I will not make it. That this vastness will be the end of me. Of us. Of Alex. I am watching Angus and his bravery, and Alex and his pain, and I am feeling so thoroughly … afraid. I will admit it. Terrified of where I am. Where I have gotten myself. I love Angus, I do not doubt that, but I am having fear attack me on all sides. My God, there is nothing out here, and this man, this man, my brother, Alex, his foot, his life rest with me. And I have known that responsibility, I have held that power in my hands, fought it, conquered it, lost to it. But now, here, I don't want to live if I lose. I cannot live to see Alex die, to see Angus see Alex die. I am afraid like never before, because I've never had so much to lose. I've never had so much to lose. I will not lose this, Angus! I will not lose this! Angus!

ANGUS: Nurse. Look.

A long, long motionless pause.

MYRA: And. There they are.

ANGUS: Help.

MYRA: Eight beautiful souls trekking toward us over the ice.

ANGUS: Parson's Pond. Must have intercepted our wire.

MYRA: Intercepted our wire and immediately mobilized to help.

ANGUS: I was getting afraid for a minute we wouldn't make it. The mare.

MYRA: I have had doubts, since I've been here, creeping in and begging an audience. I have seen myself in England, in a quaint country hospital. I have seen safety and convention and sanity and God help me I have wanted it. My feet have been cold, tired, my legs dying. I have lost patients to the stupidest of reasons. And amidst it all I have seen a life that could well have been and it looked so good. And put me out here, strip it all away until there is nothing left here but something to lose, and the means to lose it. And let me see it, see this. Eight men coming toward us. Shaking our hands. Unhitching our mare. Lifting Alex. Eight men with their strength and generosity as much a part of this place as the snow and the wind. Let me see that, and every doubt is all gone. And I am completely here, and ready, and able. And I can stare down the devil himself.

MYRA near a stove.

WOMAN: How are ya, maid?

MYRA: Cold.

WOMAN: No doubt. Here.

MYRA: Thank you.

WOMAN: Heard the wire, no way we couldn't help. In some way.

MYRA: Alex.

WOMAN: He's resting fine. Get yourself warmed up before you worries about him.

MYRA: How much farther?

WOMAN: Eh?

MYRA: To Bonne Bay.

WOMAN: Forty. Forty-five mile.

A short pause.

MYRA: All right.

ANGUS alone.

ANGUS: And that was the way it was. We went like that. From Parson's Pond. To Sally's Cove. From Sally's Cove to Bonne Bay. Sixty miles in all.

MYRA: Long way to have come.

ANGUS: People offered assistance at every step. Food, shelter. Word made its way down the coast ahead of us. Always ahead of us. And it was like, as fast as we were moving, something was moving faster. Jumping the rocks and the tuckamore, the ice and snow. Burning a trail of hope and good humour. Something as light and real as the air filling your lungs. Don't know what you'd call it.

MYRA and WOMAN alone.

WOMAN: Here. Drink this.

MYRA: You are an angel.

WOMAN: Well, that's high praise. Coming from you. Miracle worker.

MYRA: I don't know about that.

WOMAN: That's really something. What you did. Sixty miles. Sixty miles in that. Walking. And his foot. You, you sewed it on, eh? Just sewed it on.

MYRA: Yes.

WOMAN: With a needle and thread like that. That's all.

MYRA: That's all.

WOMAN: You got some stomach on ya, girl. I wouldn't want to be at that.

MYRA: One does what one has to do.

WOMAN: You warm enough?

MYRA: I'm fine, thank you.

WOMAN: Doctor will have me killed if I don't afford you every comfort.

MYRA: I couldn't be better.

A short pause.

WOMAN: Can I ask you a question?

MYRA: By all means.

WOMAN: It's a personal one, is all. Don't mean to pry.

MYRA: It's all right. Ask.

WOMAN: Do you know you're pregnant?

A short pause.

MYRA: Yes.

WOMAN: Well. Ain't that something.

MYRA: Three months.

WOMAN: Ain't that something. Sixty miles.

A short pause. All smiles.

WOMAN: Well. Congratulations.

MYRA: Thank you.

ANGUS and MYRA.

ANGUS: To hear people talk of it now. The big deal they will make. The big story they will make of it. Talk about the cold and the ice like they were there themselves, the blood on the snow. Tell you how the doctor didn't need to amputate after all. That she had done a good enough job of it stitching it on that circulation resumed. Talk about how she saved Alex's foot. Against all odds.

MYRA: They'll tell you all that.

ANGUS: She would say.

MYRA: But they won't tell you that he still walks with a limp.

ANGUS: (*smiles*) It was what it was. And she never had time for praise. A patient in need of a doctor. So you bring him. That's it.

MYRA: People get foolish about that kind of thing. Tell stories. Draw attention to it.

ANGUS: No big story to hear her tell it. That night. That long cold trip down the coast. That fact that she was pregnant with Trevor. None of it. Just happened. Like anything else. Like everything up to that point. Young Nurse moves to the edge of the world for two years. Marries humble, and devilishly handsome, local. Has family. Pulls teeth. Delivers babies. Saves lives.

He looks at her.

ANGUS: And stays.

MYRA: Being useful. Sure, that's why any one of us is put here. To make use of the time we're given. A person couldn't expect praise for it.

MAN and WOMAN alone.

MAN: Nurse Myra Bennett.

WOMAN: Honorary Member, Association of Registered Nurses of Newfoundland.

MAN: Doctor of Science, *Honoris Causa*, Memorial University of Newfoundland.

WOMAN: Medal of the British Empire.

MAN: King George V Jubilee Award.

WOMAN: The Order of Canada.

MAN: King George VI Coronation Medal.

WOMAN: Queen Elizabeth II Coronation Medal.

MAN: Extractor of more than five thousand teeth.

WOMAN: Midwife to more than seven hundred births.

MAN: Mother of three.

WOMAN: Foster mother of four.

MAN: Died April 26, 1990.

WOMAN: (*smiles*) Age one hundred years.

MAN: Her secret for a long life?

WOMAN: Hard work, a sense of humour particularly, more or less contented mind, ordinary food, no booze, no cigarettes. That's all.

MYRA looking out. ANGUS walks up behind her.

ANGUS: You hungry?

MYRA: No, but you must be.

ANGUS: I can wait.

MYRA: A few more minutes.

ANGUS: They will be here for a few days yet.

MYRA: Yes. Slow work.

ANGUS: It can be.

MYRA: A great deal of bog to contend with.

ANGUS: And rock.

MYRA: And rock.

ANGUS: They'll rip out a path, fill it, then lay down gravel for the road.

She smiles.

ANGUS: Good bit of work to be done. And plenty of time to see it. Come in. They will still be here tomorrow.

MYRA: I know.

ANGUS: And so will you.

MYRA: Yes.

They slowly begin to walk offstage.

MYRA: I darned your lovely socks Mrs. House made for you. They have toes again.

ANGUS: You're a good hand, girl, you're a good hand.

They leave the stage.

END

WAJDI MOUAWAD

(b. 1968)

Third in a triumvirate of world-renowned francophone playwrights from Quebec, Wajdi Mouawad has taken the theatrical legacies of Michel Tremblay and Robert Lepage in new directions. Looking with a nationalist's eye at a Québécois society in rapid transition, Tremblay put Quebec on the international theatre map in the 1970s and '80s. Lepage came along in the late 1980s with a bilingual family background and international vision, his multimedia stage work connecting Quebec to virtually every corner of the globe in the plays he writes, directs, designs, performs, and tours. Mouawad appeared in the 1990s, his work marked by different but no less potent forms of internationalism, interculturalism, and theatrical élan. The biographical note in his published plays in English translation describes him as "Lebanese in his childhood, French in his way of thinking and Québécois in his theatre. That's what happens when you spend your childhood in Beirut, your adolescence in Paris and then try to become an adult in Montreal."

Playwright, actor, director, artistic director, and theatrical provocateur, Mouawad became the first Quebecker to win France's prestigious Molière Award for playwriting, and then turned it down to protest the difficulty of getting contemporary work performed on the French stage. Mouawad has been described as a rock star in France, his second theatrical home. In Canada, he has made his mark in French-language theatre as artistic director of two major companies, acclaimed director and adapter, and author of some of the most striking plays of our time. *Incendies* in French, *Scorched* in English, and *Incendies* again in its Academy Award–nominated film version remains his most acclaimed work, a powerful mystery about love, family, and war crimes.

Wajdi Mouawad was born in 1968 in the Lebanese village of Deir el Qamar and grew up in Beirut, speaking Arabic. Caught up in Lebanon's brutal civil war, which left more than a hundred thousand fatalities in its sixteen-year-long wake, his family left for Paris in 1978 and came to Montreal five years later. Graduating from the French acting division of Canada's National Theatre School in 1991, Mouawad co-founded Théâtre Ô Parleur and began working as an actor, performing solo in *Alphonse* (1993), his own wildly imaginative first play about childhood, storytelling, and the imagination.

A surreal marriage of tragedy and farce, *Journée de noces chez les Cro-Magnons* (1994) (translated as *Wedding Day at the Cro-Magnons'*) was Mouawad's first attempt to stage the horrors of civil war. After serving in

1996–97 as writer-in-residence at three theatres in Quebec and Paris, he returned to his Lebanese subject (although Lebanon is never mentioned by name in any of his plays) with *Littoral* (1997), which he directed for Théâtre Ô Parleur in Montreal, then in France at Limoges and the Festival d'Avignon. *Littoral* won the Governor General's Literary Award for French-language Drama (2000) and France's Molière Award for Best Playwright (the one Mouawad refused) in 2005, the year its English-language version, *Tideline*, premiered at Toronto's Factory Theatre. Mouawad also directed the film version, *Littoral* (2004). The dream-like saga of a son trying to bury his estranged father in the father's war-torn homeland includes a recurring film crew, an Arthurian knight, and a talking corpse. *Littoral / Tideline* would be the first play in Mouawad's *Le sang des promesses* tetralogy. *Incendies / Scorched* would be the second.

Mouawad wrote, directed, and performed in *Willy Protagoras enfermé dans les toilettes* (1998) for Théâtre Ô Parleur, an absurdist comedy about a young man who locks himself in the family toilet, given Best Production and Best Actor awards by the Quebec Theatre Critics Circle and remounted for a French tour in 2007. He directed a *joual* version of *Trainspotting* (1998) and a Bedouin version of Sophocles's *Oedipus Rex* (*Oedipe roi* [1998]), a play evoked in *Tideline* and again in *Scorched*. *Don Quichotte*, his 1998 adaptation of *Don Quixote* for Théâtre du Nouveau Monde, won the Quebec Theatre Critics Circle Award and Masque Award for best Montreal play. Mouawad caused a firestorm at its 1999 remount when he threatened in the program notes to piss and shit on the billboards advertising the theatre's corporate sponsors.

In *Les mains d'Edwidge au moment de la naissance* (1999), a young woman in rural Quebec refuses to believe her sister is dead, and in *Pacamambo* (2001), a play for young audiences that Mouawad later rewrote as an opera, a girl confronts her grandmother's death. *Rêves* (1999), translated as *Dreams*, which he directed for Montreal's Festival de théâtre des Amériques and France's Festival international des francophonies, is about a blocked writer, his alter ego, and his unwritten characters. It recalls Pirandello's *Six Characters in Search of an Author*, which Mouawad adapted and directed for Montreal's Théâtre de Quat'Sous in an acclaimed 2001 production, set amid a terrifying civil war. He served as artistic director of Quat'Sous from 2000 to 2004, published a novel, *Visage retrouvé* (2002), and was honoured with France's Chevalier de l'Ordre des Arts et des Lettres in 2002 and Prix de la francophonie in 2004.

Un obus dans le coeur (2003), a monologue for young audiences first produced in France and translated as *A Bomb in the Heart*, introduces some of the central characters and key incidents of *Incendies*, which premiered in 2003 under Mouawad's direction, produced by Théâtre de Quat'Sous in conjunction with a number of other companies in France and Quebec. *Incendies* was a major success on both continents, getting rave reviews in Paris, the Critics' Choice Award for Best Production in Montreal, and a Governor General's Award nomination. *Scorched*, Linda Gaboriau's astutely lyrical English translation, opened to similar acclaim in 2006 at the National Arts Centre in a co-production with Toronto's Tarragon

Theatre and has since been produced across Canada and the United States, including New York, Chicago, St. Louis, and San Francisco, and at London's Old Vic (in tunnels beneath Waterloo Station). The script presented here is Mouawad's most recent revision, a slightly trimmed-down version of the Gaboriau translation originally published in 2005. The film adaptation, *Incendies*, written and directed by Denis Villeneuve, won Canada's Genie Award for Best Picture and was nominated for the 2011 Academy Award for Best Foreign Language Film.

In 2005, having left Quat'Sous, Mouawad established two new companies to develop his own work, Abé carré cé carré in Quebec and Au carré de l'hypoténuse in France. Their first result was *Forêts*. The third play of *Le sang des promesses* premiered in Limoges and toured France in 2006, where it was lauded before opening in Montreal in 2007. An epic drama about seven women set in the Ardennes Forest of Belgium, the play evokes the horrors of twentieth-century wars and atrocities in the spirit of Greek tragedy. Tarragon premiered the English version, *Forests* (2011), which won Linda Gaboriau the Governor General's Literary Award for Translation.

Assoiffées (2006), translated as *Starved*, a play for teen audiences, was followed by *Seuls* (2007), an extraordinary autobiographical piece written, directed, and performed by Mouawad in France, Montreal, and at Ottawa's National Arts Centre (NAC) in 2008, where he had been appointed artistic director of its French-language theatre, a post he retained until 2012. In *Seuls*, Mouawad engages with the Lebanese civil war, his father, Robert Lepage, and Rembrandt.

The theme of his 2008–09 NAC season was "We are at war," meaning, Mouawad explained, "you're active, you're fighting, you're awake." He took his own words seriously, publically blasting Prime Minister Stephen Harper and his Conservative government for its cuts to arts funding. *Le soleil ni la mort ne peuvent se regarder en face* (2008), his adaptation of tragedies from Aeschylus, Sophocles, and Euripides, opened in Bordeaux, played the NAC in 2009, and was nominated for the Governor General's Award.

Prestigious Festival d'Avignon made Mouawad associate artist and honoured him by remounting *Littoral*, *Incendies*, and *Forêts* in 2009 (presented together in a twelve-hour marathon), along with *Ciels*, the concluding play in his *Sang des promesses* tetralogy, a drama about an anti-terrorist squad. All four were remounted at Montreal's 2010 Festival TransAmériques. *Temps* (2011), a family drama set in northern Quebec, premiered in Berlin. *Des femmes* (2011), a tragic trilogy adapted from Sophocles, provoked outrage when Mouawad announced that he was casting French rock musician Bertrand Cantat, recently released from prison for killing his girlfriend. The show played Festival d'Avignon and the NAC *sans* Cantat. Mouawad has also written a series of miscellanies that include drawings, essays, poetry, commentary, dialogues, and puzzles: *Les tigres de Wajdi Mouawad* (2009), *Le sang des promesses* (2009), and *Le poisson soi* (2011). He published his second novel, *Anima*, in 2012.

In the press release announcing the NAC's 2011–12 season, his last as artistic director, Mouawad wrote: "The purpose of theatre is to provide a poetic clearing in the heart of the urban forest. A space where the simple song of a bird reminds us of this truth: 'A busy life does not a full life make.' The freer an artistic gesture, the freer those who witness it. And that is why it is dangerous." *Scorched* speaks to many of the ideas embedded in this typically oblique Mouawadism. It explores the miracle of song, the nature of the full life, and the dangerous liberating power of artistic truth to provide witness and a clearing in the heart.

The twins, Janine and Simon, go on a quest that reveals the hidden mysteries of their mother's awful, eventful life as well as their own origins. Their journey, along with the flashbacks that piece together Nawal's scorching life in her native country – thinly disguised, civil war–ravaged Lebanon – leads them and us into the heart of darkness, a place where "childhood is a knife stuck in the throat," where people do unspeakable, unthinkable things to each other in a tragic cycle of violence and revenge that must be broken. Nawal's progress from ignorance and poverty to guerilla warfare, song, silence, and finally to a strategy to "break the thread" provides the spine of the play. Her legacy, though, has to live on through her children. Canada, in *Scorched*, is where the violent old world comes to be redeemed and reborn.

Theatrically, *Scorched* alternates shocking action, painful narrative, and eloquent testimony. The horrific bus massacre, recreated as a symphony of horror, even drowns out Alphonse Lebel, the play's avatar of comic relief. Elsewhere, action swirls around the still centre of Janine, listening to tapes of her dead mother's long silence, or the heartbreaking symbolism of a little clown nose. But Nawal's spirit and enduring presence dominate *Scorched*, in part through Mouawad's decision to have her played at ten different ages by three different actresses. In the letter her children read at the end, she suggests that they try to understand her story and theirs, with "its roots in violence and rape," as a love story. The play's ability to sustain such hope in the midst of such horror is among the qualities that led the *Globe and Mail's* J. Kelly Nestruck to call *Scorched* "an artful, humanist anti-polemic" that "may be the best piece of theatre this country has produced this millennium."

Wajdi Mouawad
Translated by Linda Gaboriau

Scorched

Incendies was first presented in France on March 14, 2003, at l'Hexagone Scène Nationale de Meylan, and subsequently in Montreal on May 23, 2003, at Théâtre de Quat'Sous as part of the Festival de théâtre des Amériques, with the following cast:

NAWAL (*age fourteen to nineteen*)	Isabelle Roy
NAWAL (*age forty and forty-five*)	Annick Bergeron
NAWAL (*age sixty and sixty-five*)	Andrée Lachapelle
HERMILE LEBEL	Richard Thériault
JANINE	Isabelle Leblanc
SIMON	Reda Guerinik
NIHAD	Éric Bernier
SAWDA	Marie-Claude Langlois
ANTOINE DUCHARME	Gérald Gagnon

Directed by Wajdi Mouawad

Scorched (*Incendies*, translated by Linda Gaboriau) was first produced in English at the National Arts Centre, Ottawa, in a co-production with Tarragon Theatre, Toronto, April 4, 2007, with the following cast:

NAWAL (*age fourteen to nineteen*)	Janick Hébert
NAWAL (*age forty and forty-five*) **/**	
JIHANE	Kelli Fox
NAWAL (*age sixty and sixty-five*) **/**	
NAZIRA	Nicola Lipman
ALPHONSE LEBEL	Alon Nashman
JANINE	Sophie Goulet
SIMON / WAHAB	Sergio Di Zio
NIHAD / RALPH	Paul Fauteux
SAWDA / ELHAME	Valerie Buhagiar
ANTOINE / DOCTOR / ABDESSAMAD / MILITIAMAN / TOURIST GUIDE / JANITOR / PHOTOGRAPHER / CHAMSEDDINE / MALAK	David Fox

Directed by Richard Rose
Set and Lighting Design by Graeme S. Thomson
Costume Design by Teresa Przybylski
Sound Design by Todd Charlton
Stage Managed by Kathryn Westoll

CHARACTERS

NAWAL MARWAN, *ages fourteen to sixty-five*

JANINE, *Nawal's daughter and Simon's twin*

SIMON, *Nawal's son and Janine's twin*

ALPHONSE LEBEL, *a notary*

SAWDA

NIHAD

ANTOINE DUCHARME

WAHAB

JIHANE

NAZIRA

ELHAME

ABDESSAMAD

MALAK

RALPH

CHAMSEDDINE

DOCTOR, MILITIAMEN, MUSEUM GUIDE, JANITOR, PHOTOGRAPHER

SETTING

Quebec and a war-torn Middle Eastern country, last half of the twentieth century.

NAWAL'S FIRE

1. NOTARY

Day. Summer. Notary's office.

ALPHONSE LEBEL: For sure, for sure, for sure, I'd rather watch birds in the sky. But you have to call a spade a spade: from here, instead of birds, you see cars and the shopping centre. When I was on the other side of the building, my office looked out over the highway. It wasn't the Taj Nepal, but I finally hung a sign in my window: *Alphonse Lebel, Notary.* At rush hour it was great publicity. Now I'm here on this side and I've got a view of the shopping centre. A shopping centre's not a gaggle of geese. Your mother's the one who taught me that geese live in gaggles. I'm sorry. I hate to mention your mother because of the tragedy that has struck, but we have to face the music. Life goes on, as they say. C'est la vie. Come in, come in, come in, you can't stay in the hall-way. This is my new office. I'm just moving in. The other notaries have left. I'm all alone in this building. It's much nicer here because there's less noise, with the highway on the other side. I've lost my rush-hour advertising, but at least I can keep my window open and that's lucky, because I don't have air conditioning yet.

Right. Well ...

For sure, it's not easy.

Come in, come in, come in! Don't stand there in the hallway, it's the hallway!

Even though I understand, I understand you might not want to come in.

I wouldn't come in.

Right. Well ...

For sure, for sure, for sure, I would've preferred to meet you under other circumstances, but hell isn't paved with good circumstances, so these things are hard to foresee. Death can't be foreseen. You can't negotiate with death. Death breaks all promises. You think it will come later, but death comes when it pleases. I loved your mother. I'm telling you that, straight and narrow: I loved your mother. She often talked to me about the two of you. Actually, not often, but she did talk to me about you. A bit. Occasionally. Just like that. She'd say: the twins. The twin sister, the twin brother. You know how she was, she never said anything to anyone. I mean long before she stopped saying

anything at all, she already said nothing and she didn't say anything about the two of you. That's how she was. When she died, it was raining. I don't know. I was really sad that it was raining. In her country it never rains, so a will, you can imagine all the bad weather in a will. It's not like birds, someone's will, for sure, it's different. It's strange and weird, but it's necessary. I mean it remains a necessary evil. I'm sorry.

He bursts into tears.

2. LAST WILL AND TESTAMENT

A few minutes later. Notary ALPHONSE LEBEL with twin brother and sister, SIMON and JANINE.

ALPHONSE LEBEL: The Last Will and Testament of Madame Nawal Marwan. The witnesses who attended the reading of the will when it was registered are Monsieur Trinh Xiao Feng, owner of the Vietcong Burgers restaurant and Madame Suzanne Lamontagne, waitress at Vietcong Burgers.

That's the restaurant that used to be on the ground floor of the building. In those days, whenever I needed two witnesses, I'd go down to get Trinh Xiao Feng. And he'd come up with Suzanne. Trinh Xiao Feng's wife, Hui Huo Xiao Feng, would take care of the restaurant. The restaurant's closed now. It's closed. Trinh died. Hui Huo Xiao Feng remarried, she married Réal Bouchard who was a clerk in this office, with my colleague Notary Yvon Vachon. That's how life is. Anyway.

The opening of the will takes place in the presence of her two children: Janine Marwan and Simon Marwan, both twenty-two years of age and both born on the twentieth of August 1980 at the Saint-François Hospital in Ville-Émard ... That's not far from here ...

According to Madame Nawal Marwan's wishes and in keeping with her rights and the regulations, Notary Alphonse Lebel is named executor of her last will and testament ...

I want you to know that that was your mother's decision. I was against it myself, I advised her against it, but she insisted. I could have refused, but I couldn't.

The notary opens the envelope and reads the will.

"All my assets are to be divided equally between the twins Janine and Simon Marwan, my off-spring, flesh of my flesh. I leave my money to them in equal shares, and I want my furniture to be disposed of according to their wishes and mutual consent. If there is any dispute or disagreement, the executor of my estate will sell the furniture and divide the proceeds equally between the twin brother and sister. My clothing will be donated to the charity chosen by my executor.

Special bequests:

I leave my black fountain pen to my friend, Notary Alphonse Lebel.

I leave the khaki jacket with the number 72 on the back to Janine Marwan.

I leave the red notebook to Simon Marwan."

The notary takes out the three objects.

"Burial:

To Notary Alphonse Lebel.

My notary and friend,

Take the twins with you

Bury me naked

Bury me without a coffin

No clothing, no covering

No prayers

Face to the ground.

Place me at the bottom of a hole,

Face first, against the world.

As a farewell gesture,

You will each throw

A pail of cold water

On my body.

Then you will fill the hole with earth and seal my grave.

Tombstone and epitaph:

To Notary Alphonse Lebel.

My notary and friend,

Let no stone be placed on my grave

Nor my name engraved anywhere.

No epitaph for those who don't keep their promises

And one promise was not kept.

No epitaph for those who keep the silence.

And silence was kept.

No stone

No name on the stone

No epitaph for an absent name on an absent stone.

No name.

To Janine and Simon, Simon and Janine.

Childhood is a knife stuck in the throat.

It can't be easily removed.

Janine,

Notary Lebel will give you an envelope.

This envelope is not for you.

It is for your father,

Your father and Simon's.

Find him and give him this envelope.

Simon,

Notary Lebel will give you an envelope.

This envelope is not for you.

It is for your brother,

Your brother and Janine's.

Find him and give him this envelope.

Once these envelopes have been delivered to their recipients

You will be given a letter

The silence will be broken

And then a stone can be placed on my grave

And my name engraved on the stone in the sun."

Long silence.

SIMON: She had to piss us off right to the very end! That bitch! That stupid bitch! Goddamn fucking cunt! Fucking bitch! She really had to piss us off right to the very end! For ages now we've been thinking, the bitch is going to croak any day now, she'll finally stop fucking up our lives, the old pain in the ass! And then, bingo! She finally croaks! But *surprise*! It's not over yet! Shit! We never expected this. Christ! She really set us up, calculated everything, the fucking whore! I'd like to kick her corpse! You bet we're going to bury her face down! You bet! We'll spit on her grave.

Silence.

At least I'm going to spit!

Silence.

She died, and just before she died she asked herself how she could fuck up our lives even more. She sat down and thought hard and she figured it out! She could write her will, her fucking will!

ALPHONSE LEBEL: She wrote it five years ago.

SIMON: I don't give a shit.

ALPHONSE LEBEL: Listen! She's dead. Your mother is dead. I mean she is someone who is dead. Someone none of us knew very well, but someone who was someone nevertheless. Someone who was young, who was an adult, who was old and who died! So there has to be an explanation in all that somewhere! You can't ignore that! I mean, the woman lived a whole life, for heaven's sake, and that has to count for something somehow.

SIMON: I'm not going to cry! I swear I'm not going to cry! She's dead! Who gives a shit, for Chrissakes! Who gives a shit if she's dead. I don't owe that woman a thing. Not a single tear, nothing! People can say what they want. That I didn't cry over my mother's death! I'll say she wasn't my mother! That she was nothing! What makes you think we give a shit, eh? I'm not going to start pretending! Start crying! When did she ever cry over me? Or Janine? Never! Never! She didn't have a heart, her heart was a brick. You don't cry over a brick, you don't cry! No heart! A brick, goddammit, a brick! I don't want to think about her or hear about her again, ever!

ALPHONSE LEBEL: Yet she did express a wish concerning the two of you. Your names are in her last will and testament –

SIMON: Big deal! We're her children and you know more about her than we do! So what if our names are there. So what!

ALPHONSE LEBEL: The envelopes, the notebook, the money –

SIMON: I don't want her money, I don't want her notebook ... If she thinks she can touch me with her goddamn notebook! C'mon! What a joke! Her last wishes: "Go find your father and your brother!" Why didn't she find them herself if it was so fucking important?! Why didn't she worry more about us, the bitch, if she was so concerned about a son somewhere else? When she talks about us in her goddamn will, why doesn't she use the word "my children"? The word "son," the word "daughter"! I mean, I'm not stupid! I'm not stupid! Why does she always say the twins? The twin sister, the twin brother, "the offspring of my flesh," like we

were a pile of vomit, a pile of shit she had to get rid of! Why?!

ALPHONSE LEBEL: Listen. I understand!

SIMON: What can you understand, you dickhead?

ALPHONSE LEBEL: I can understand that hearing what you just heard can leave you stranded high and low, thinking what's going on, who are we, and why not us! I understand, I mean I understand! It's not often we find out that the father we thought was dead is still alive and that we have a brother somewhere in this world!

SIMON: There's no father, no brother. It's all bullshit!

ALPHONSE LEBEL: Not in someone's will! Not things like that!

SIMON: You don't know her!

ALPHONSE LEBEL: I know her in a different way.

SIMON: Anyway, I don't feel like discussing this with you!

ALPHONSE LEBEL: You have to trust her.

SIMON: I don't feel like it –

ALPHONSE LEBEL: She had her reasons.

SIMON: I don't feel like discussing this with you. I don't feel like it. I've got a boxing match in ten days, that's all I care about. We'll bury her and that's it. We'll go to a funeral home, we'll buy a coffin, we'll put her in the coffin, put the coffin in a hole, some earth in the hole, a stone on the earth and her name on the stone, and we'll get the hell out of there.

ALPHONSE LEBEL: That's impossible. Those are not your mother's last wishes and I will not allow you to go against her wishes.

SIMON: And who are you to go against us?

ALPHONSE LEBEL: I am, unfortunately, the executor of her will and I don't share your opinion of this woman.

SIMON: How can you take her seriously? C'mon! For years, she spent day after day at the courthouse, attending the trials of all sorts of perverts, sickos, and murderers, then, from one day to the next, she shuts up, never says another word! Never! For years! Five years without a word, that's a helluva long time! Not another word, not a sound, nothing ever comes out of her mouth again. A loose wire, a short circuit, she blows a fuse, whatever, and she invents a husband still alive who's been dead for ages, and another son who never existed, the perfect fantasy of the child she wished she'd had, the child she could've loved, and now the goddamn bitch wants me to go find him! How can you talk about her last wishes –

ALPHONSE LEBEL: Calm down!

SIMON: How can you try to convince me that we're dealing with the last wishes of someone who hasn't lost her mind –

ALPHONSE LEBEL: Calm down!

SIMON: Jesus Christ! Goddamn sonofabitching fucking shit, shit, shit ...

Silence.

ALPHONSE LEBEL: For sure, for sure, for sure, but still, you have to admit it suits you to see things that way ... I don't know, it's none of my business ... you're right ... nobody understood why she stopped talking for such a long time and yes ... yes ... at first glance, it seems like an act of madness ... but maybe not ... I mean, maybe it was something else ... I don't want to upset you but if it were an act of madness she wouldn't have spoken again. But the other day, the other night, you know that, you can't deny it, they called you, she spoke. And you can't tell me that was a coincidence, a mere fluke! Personally, I don't believe that! I mean, it was a present she was offering you! The most beautiful present she could give you! I mean, that's important. The day and the hour of your birth she spoke again! And what does she say? She says, "Now that we're together, everything feels better. Now that we're together, everything feels better." I mean, that's no ordinary sentence! She didn't say, "You know, I'd love to have a hot dog, all-dressed." Or "Pass me the salt!" No! "Now that we're together, everything feels better." C'mon! The nurse heard her. He heard her. Why would he make that up? He couldn't have. Couldn't have made up something that true. You know it, I know it, we all know it, a sentence like that resembles her, like two peas in a pot. But okay, I agree with you. It's true. She shut up for years. I agree and I also agree if things had stayed like that, I would've had my doubts, too. I admit it. But still, we can't forget, I believe we have to take it into consideration. She acted rationally. "Now that we're together, everything feels better." You can't deny it. Deny your birthday! That's not the kind of thing you can deny. Now you're free to do what you want, that's for sure, for sure, for sure, you're free not to respect your mother's last wishes. Nothing obliges you to. But you can't ask the same of other people. Of me.

Of your sister. The facts are there: your mother is asking each of us to do something for her, those are her wishes, and everyone can do what he wants. Even someone sentenced to death has a right to his last wishes. Why not your mother ...

SIMON exits.

The envelopes are here. I'll keep them. Today you don't want to hear about them, but maybe later. Rome wasn't built in the middle of the day. Some things take time. You can call me when you're ready ...

JANINE exits.

3. GRAPH THEORY, PERIPHERAL VISION

Classroom where JANINE teaches. Overhead projector. JANINE turns it on. Course begins.

JANINE: There's no way of knowing today how many of you will pass the tests ahead of you. Mathematics as you have known them so far were all about finding strict and definitive answers to strict and definitively stated problems. The mathematics you will encounter in this introductory course on graph theory are totally different since we will be dealing with insoluble problems that will always lead to other problems, every bit as insoluble. People around you will insist that what you are wrestling with is useless. Your manner of speaking will change and, even more profoundly, so will your manner of remaining silent and of thinking. That is exactly what people will find the hardest to forgive. People will often criticize you for squandering your intelligence on absurd theoretical exercises, rather than devoting it to research for a cure for AIDS or a new cancer treatment. You won't be able to argue in your defence, since your arguments themselves will be of an absolutely exhausting theoretical complexity. Welcome to pure mathematics, in other words, to the world of solitude ... Introduction to graph theory.

Gym. SIMON with RALPH.

RALPH: You know why you lost your last fight, Simon? And you know why you lost the one before that?

SIMON: I wasn't in shape, that's why.

RALPH: You're never going to qualify if this keeps up. Put on your gloves.

JANINE: Let's take a simple polygon with five sides labelled a, b, c, d, and e. Let's call this polygon

Polygon k. Now let's imagine that this polygon represents the floor plan of a house where a family lives. And one member of the family is posted in each corner of the house. For the time being, let's replace a, b, c, d, and e by the grandmother, the father, the mother, the son, and the daughter who live together in Polygon k. Now let's ask ourselves who, from his or her position, sees whom. The grandmother sees the father, the mother, and the daughter. The father sees the mother and the grandmother. The mother sees the grandmother, the father, the son, and the daughter. The son sees the mother and the sister. And the sister sees the brother, the mother, and the grandmother.

RALPH: You're not looking! You're blind! You don't see the footwork of the guy in front of you. You don't see his defence ... That's what we call a peripheral vision problem.

SIMON: Okay, okay!

JANINE: We call this application the theoretical application of the family living in Polygon k.

RALPH: Warm up!

JANINE: Now, let's remove the walls of the house and draw arcs between the members of the family who can see each other. The drawing this creates is called the visibility graph of Polygon k.

RALPH: There are three things you have to remember.

JANINE: So there are three parameters we'll be dealing with over the next three years: the theoretical application of polygons ...

RALPH: You're the strongest!

JANINE: The visibility graphs of polygons ...

RALPH: No pity for the guy you're facing!

JANINE: And finally, polygons and the nature of polygons.

RALPH: And if you win, you become a pro!

JANINE: The problem is as follows: for every simple polygon, I can easily draw its visibility graph and its theoretical application, as I have just demonstrated. Now, how, working from a theoretical application like this one, for instance, can I draw the visibility graph and the corresponding polygon? What is the shape of the house where the members of the family represented in this application live? Try to draw the polygon.

Gong. SIMON attacks immediately and punches into his trainer's hands.

RALPH: You're not there, you're not concentrating,

SIMON: My mother died!

RALPH: I know, but the best way to get over your mother's death is to win your next fight. So go in there and fight! You'll never succeed otherwise.

JANINE: You'll never succeed. All graph theory is essentially based on this problem, which remains for the time being impossible to solve. And it's this impossibility that is beautiful.

Gong. End of training session.

4. THE HYPOTHESIS TO BE PROVEN

Evening. Notary's office. ALPHONSE LEBEL and the twin sister JANINE.

ALPHONSE LEBEL: For sure, for sure, for sure, there are times in life like this, where you're stuck between the devil and the Blue Danube. You have to act. Dive in. I'm glad you've come back. Glad for your mother's sake.

JANINE: Do you have the envelope?

ALPHONSE LEBEL: Here it is. This envelope isn't for you, it's for your father. Your mother wants you to find him and give it to him.

JANINE prepares to leave the office.

She also left you this khaki jacket with the number 72 on the back.

JANINE takes the jacket.

Do you believe your father is alive?

JANINE exits. Pause. JANINE returns.

JANINE: In mathematics, one plus one doesn't equal 1.9 or 2.2. It equals two. Whether you believe it or not, it equals two. Whether you're in a good mood or feeling miserable, one plus one equals two. We all belong to a polygon. I thought I knew my place in the polygon I belong to. I thought I was the point that only sees her brother Simon and her mother Nawal. Today, I found out that, from the position I hold, it is also possible for me to see my father; and I learned that there is another member of this polygon, another brother. The visibility graph I've always drawn is wrong. Where do I stand in the polygon? To find out, I have to prove a hypothesis. My father is dead. That is the hypothesis. Everything leads us to believe this is true. But nothing proves it. I never saw his body or his grave. It is therefore possible, between one and infinity, that my father is still alive. Good-bye, Monsieur Lebel.

JANINE exits.

NAWAL (age fourteen) is in the office.

ALPHONSE LEBEL walks out of his office and calls from the hallway.

ALPHONSE LEBEL: Janine!

NAWAL: *(calling)* Wahab!

ALPHONSE LEBEL: Janine! Janine!

ALPHONSE LEBEL comes back into the office, takes out his cellphone, and dials a number.

NAWAL: *(calling)* Wahab!

WAHAB: *(in the distance)* Nawal!

NAWAL: *(calling)* Wahab!

WAHAB: *(in the distance)* Nawal!

ALPHONSE LEBEL: Hello, Janine? It's Notary Lebel. I just thought of something.

NAWAL: *(calling)* Wahab!

WAHAB: *(in the distance)* Nawal!

ALPHONSE LEBEL: Your mother met your father when she was very young.

NAWAL: *(calling)* Wahab!

ALPHONSE LEBEL: I just wanted to tell you, I don't know if you knew that.

WAHAB: *(in the distance)* Nawal!

5. SOMETHING IS THERE

Dawn. A forest. A rock. White trees. NAWAL (age fourteen). WAHAB.

NAWAL: Wahab! Listen to me. Don't say a word. No. Don't speak. If you say a word, a single word, you could kill me. You don't yet know the happiness that will be our downfall. Wahab, I feel like the minute I release the words about to come out of my mouth, you will die, too. I'll stop talking, Wahab, so promise me you won't say anything, please, I'm tired, please, accept silence. Shhhh! Don't say anything. Don't say anything.

She falls silent.

I called for you all night. I ran all night. I knew I'd find you at the rock where the white trees stand. I'm going to tell you. I wanted to shout it so the whole village would hear, so the trees would hear, so the night and the moon and the stars would

hear. But I couldn't. I have to whisper it in your ear, Wahab, and afterwards I won't dare hold you in my arms, even if that's what I want most in the world, even if I'm sure I'll never feel complete if you remain outside me, and even if I was just a girl when I found you, and with you I finally fell into the arms of my real life, I'll never be able to ask anything of you again.

He kisses her.

I have a baby in my belly, Wahab! My belly is full of you. Isn't it amazing? It's magnificent and horrible, isn't it? It's an abyss, and it's like freedom to wild birds, isn't it? And there are no more words. Just the wind! I have a child in my belly. When I heard old Elhame tell me, an ocean exploded in my head. Seared.

WAHAB: Maybe Elhame is wrong.

NAWAL: Elhame is never wrong. I asked her. "Elhame, are you sure?" She laughed. She stroked my cheek. She told me she's the one who has delivered all the babies in the village for the last forty years. She took me out of my mother's belly and she took my mother out of her mother's belly. Elhame is never wrong. She promised she wouldn't tell anyone. "It's none of my business," she said, "but in two weeks at the most, you won't be able to hide it anymore."

WAHAB: We won't hide it.

NAWAL: They'll kill us. You first.

WAHAB: We'll explain to them.

NAWAL: Do you think that they'll listen to us? That they'll hear us?

WAHAB: What are you afraid of, Nawal?

NAWAL: Aren't you afraid? *(beat)* Put your hand here. What is it? I don't know if it's anger, I don't know if it's fear, I don't know if it's happiness. Where will we be, you and me, in fifty years?

WAHAB: Listen to me, Nawal. This night is a gift. It might be crazy for me to say that, but I have a heart and it is strong. It is patient. They will scream, and we will let them scream. They will curse and we will let them curse. It doesn't matter. After all that, after their screams and curses, you and I will remain, you and I and our child, yours and mine. Your face and my face in the same face. I feel like laughing. They will beat me, but I will always have a child in the back of my mind.

NAWAL: Now that we're together, everything feels better.

WAHAB: We will always be together. Go home, Nawal. Wait till they wake up. When they see you, at dawn, sitting there waiting for them, they will listen to you because they will sense that something important has happened. If you feel scared, remember that at that very moment, I'll be at my house, waiting for everyone to wake up. And I'll tell them, too. Dawn isn't very far away. Think of me like I'll think of you, and don't get lost in the fog. Don't forget: now that we're together, everything feels better.

WAHAB leaves.

6. CARNAGE

In NAWAL's house. NAWAL (age fourteen) with her mother, JIHANE.

JIHANE: This child has nothing to do with you, Nawal.

NAWAL: It's in my belly.

JIHANE: Forget your belly! This child has nothing to do with you. Nothing to do with your family. Nothing to do with your mother, nothing to do with your life.

NAWAL: I put my hand here and I can see his face.

JIHANE: It doesn't matter what you see. This child has nothing to do with you. It doesn't exist. It isn't there.

NAWAL: Elhame told me. She said, "You are expecting a baby."

JIHANE: Elhame isn't your mother.

NAWAL: She told me.

JIHANE: It doesn't matter what Elhame told you. This child does not exist.

NAWAL: And when it arrives?

JIHANE: It still won't exist.

NAWAL: I don't understand.

JIHANE: Dry your tears!

NAWAL: You're the one who's crying.

JIHANE: I'm not the one who's crying, your whole life is pouring down your cheeks! You've gone too far, Nawal, you've come back with your spoiled belly, and you stand here before me, in your child's body, and tell me, I am in love and I am carrying my love in my belly. You come back from the woods and you tell me I'm the one who's crying. Believe me, Nawal, this child does not exist. You're going to forget it.

NAWAL: A person can't forget her belly.

JIHANE: A person can forget.

NAWAL: I won't forget.

JIHANE: Then you will have to choose. Keep this child and this instant, this very instant, you will take off those clothes that don't belong to you and leave this house, leave your family, your village, your mountains, your sky, and your stars, and leave me ...

NAWAL: Mother.

JIHANE: Leave me, naked, with your belly and the life it is carrying. Or stay and kneel down, Nawal, kneel down.

NAWAL: Mother.

JIHANE: Take off your clothes or kneel.

NAWAL kneels.

JIHANE: You will stay inside this house, the way this life lies hidden inside you. Elhame will come and take this baby from your belly. She will take it and give it to whoever she wants.

7. A KNIFE STUCK IN THE THROAT

NAWAL (age fifteen) with her grandmother, NAZIRA.

NAWAL: Now that we're together, everything feels better. Now that we're together, everything feels better. Now that we're together, everything feels better. Now that we're together, everything feels better. Now that we're together, everything feels better.

NAZIRA: Be patient, Nawal. You only have one more month to go.

NAWAL: I should have left, Grandmother, and not knelt, I should have given back my clothes, everything, and left the house, the village, everything.

NAZIRA: Poverty is to blame for all of this, Nawal. There's no beauty in our lives. No beauty. Just the anger of a hard and hurtful life. Signs of hatred on every street corner. No one to speak gently of things. You're right, Nawal, you lived the love you were meant to live, and the child you're going to have will be taken away from you. What is left for you? You can fight poverty, perhaps, or drown in it.

NAZIRA is no longer in the room. Someone is knocking on the window.

WAHAB: (*offstage*) Nawal! Nawal, it's me.

NAWAL: Wahab!

WAHAB: (*offstage*) Listen to me, Nawal. I don't have much time. At dawn, they're taking me away, far from here and far from you. I've just come back from the rock where the white trees stand. I said goodbye to the scene of my childhood, and my childhood is full of you, Nawal. Tonight, childhood is a knife they've stuck in my throat. Now I'll always have the taste of your blood in my mouth. I wanted to tell you that. I wanted to tell you that tonight, my heart is full of love, it's going to explode. Everyone keeps telling me I love you too much. But I don't know what that means, to love too much, I don't know what it means to be far from you, what it means not to have you with me. I will have to learn to live without you. Now I understand what you were trying to say when you asked, "Where will we be in fifty years?" I don't know. But wherever I am, you will be there. We dreamed of seeing the ocean together. Listen, Nawal, I'm telling you, listen, the day I see the ocean, the word "ocean" will explode in your head, it will explode and you will burst into tears because you will know that I'm thinking of you. No matter where I am, we will be together. There is nothing more beautiful than being together.

NAWAL: I hear you, Wahab.

WAHAB: (*offstage*) Don't dry your tears, because I won't dry mine from now to dawn, and when you give birth to our child, tell him how much I love him, how much I love you. Tell him.

NAWAL: I'll tell him, I promise you I'll tell him. For you and for me, I'll tell him. I'll whisper in his ear: "No matter what happens, I will always love you." I'll tell him for you and for me. And I'll go back to the rock where the white trees stand and I'll say goodbye to childhood, too. And my childhood will be a knife stuck in my throat.

NAWAL is alone.

8. A PROMISE

Night. NAWAL is giving birth. NAZIRA, JIHANE, and ELHAME.

ELHAME hands the baby to NAWAL (age fifteen).

ELHAME: It's a boy.

NAWAL: No matter what happens, I will always love you! No matter what happens, I will always love you.

NAWAL slips a clown nose into the baby's swaddling clothes. They take the child away from her.

ELHAME: I'm going south. I'll take the child with me.

NAZIRA: I feel like I'm a thousand years old. Days go by and months are gone. The sun rises and sets. The seasons go by. Nawal no longer speaks, she wanders about in silence. Her belly is gone and I feel the ancient call of the earth. Too much pain has been with me for too long. Take me to my bed. As winter ends, I hear death's footsteps in the rushing water of the streams.

NAZIRA is bedridden.

9. READING, WRITING, COUNTING, SPEAKING

NAZIRA is dying.

NAZIRA: Nawal!

NAWAL (age sixteen) comes running.

NAZIRA: Take my hand, Nawal!

There are things we want to say at the moment of our death. Things we'd like to tell the people we have loved, who have loved us ... to help them one last time ... to tell them one last time ... to prepare them for happiness ...! A year ago you gave birth to a child, and ever since you've been walking around in a haze. Don't fall, Nawal, don't say yes. Say no. Refuse. Your love is gone, your child is gone. He turned one. Just a few days ago. Don't accept it, Nawal, never accept it. But if you're going to refuse, you have to know how to talk. So be courageous and work hard, sweet Nawal! Listen to what an old woman on her deathbed has to say to you: learn to read, learn to write, learn to count, learn to speak. Learn. It's your only hope if you don't want to turn out like us. Promise me you will.

NAWAL: I promise you I will.

NAZIRA: In two days they will bury me. They'll put me in the ground, facing the sky, and everyone will throw a pail of water on me, but they won't write anything on the stone because no one knows how to write. When you know how to write, Nawal, come back and engrave my name on the stone: Nazira. Engrave my name because I have kept my promises. I'm leaving, Nawal. My time has come. We ... our family, the women in our family ... are caught in the web of anger. We have been for ages: I was angry at my mother, and your mother is angry at me, just as you are angry at your mother. And your legacy to your daughter will be anger, too. We have to break the thread. So learn. Then leave. Take your youth and any possible happiness and leave the village. You are the bloom of this valley, Nawal. You are its sensuality and its smell. Take them with you and tear yourself away from here, the way we tear ourselves from our mother's womb. Learn to read, write, count, and speak. Learn to think. Nawal. Learn.

NAZIRA dies.

She is lifted from her bed. She is lowered into a hole. Everyone throws a pail of water on her body. It is nighttime. Everyone bows their head in silence.

A cellphone starts to ring.

10. NAWAL'S BURIAL

Day. Cemetery. ALPHONSE LEBEL, JANINE, and SIMON at a graveside.

ALPHONSE LEBEL answers the phone.

ALPHONSE LEBEL: Hello, Alphonse Lebel, Notary.

Yes, I called you. I've been trying to reach you for two hours! What's going on? Nothing. That's the problem. We were supposed to have three pails of water at the graveside, and they're not here. Yes, I'm the one who called for the pails of water.

What do you mean, "What's the problem, there's no problem." There's one big problem. I told you we requested three pails of water and they're not here. We're in the cemetery, where do you think we are, for crying out loud! How thick can you get? We're here for Nawal Marwan's burial.

Three pails of water!

Of course it was understood. Clearly understood. I came myself. I notified everyone: a special burial, we only need three pails of water. It didn't seem that complicated. I even asked the custodian: "Do you want us to bring our own pails of water?" He said, "Of course not. We'll prepare them for you. You've got enough on your mind already." So I said fine. But here we are, in the cemetery, and there are no pails of water, and now we've got a lot more on our minds. I mean. This is a burial! Not a bowling party. Honestly! I mean, we're not difficult: no coffin, no tombstone, nothing. The bare minimum. Simple. We're making it very simple, we're only asking for three miserable pails of water, and the cemetery administration can't meet the challenge. Honestly!

What do you mean you're not used to requests for pails of water? We're not asking you to be used to it, we're asking for the pails of water. We're not asking you to reinvent the deal. That's right. Three. No. Not one, three. No, we can't take one and fill it three times. We want three pails of water filled once.

Yes, I'm sure.

Fine, what can I say? Make your calls.

He hangs up.

They'll make some calls.

SIMON: Why are you doing all this?

ALPHONSE LEBEL: All what?

SIMON: All this. The burial. The last wishes. Why are you the one doing all this?

ALPHONSE LEBEL: Because the woman in that hole, face to the ground, the woman I always called Madame Nawal, is my friend. My friend. I don't know if that means something to you, but I never realized how much it meant to me.

ALPHONSE LEBEL's cellphone rings. He answers.

Hello, Alphonse Lebel, Notary.

Yes, so, what's happening?

They were prepared and placed in front of another grave.

Well, that was a mistake ... Nawal Marwan ... Your efficiency is overwhelming.

He hangs up. A man arrives with three pails of water. He sets them down. Each one picks up a pail. Empties it into the hole. NAWAL is buried and they leave without placing a gravestone.

11. SILENCE

Day. On the stage of a theatre. ANTOINE is there.

JANINE: Antoine Ducharme? Janine Marwan, I'm Nawal Marwan's daughter ... I went by the hospital and they told me that you stopped working as a nurse after my mother's death. That you're working in this theatre now. I've come to see you because I want to know exactly what she said ...

ANTOINE: I can still hear your mother's voice ringing in my ears. "Now that we're together, everything feels better." Those were her exact words. I called you immediately.

JANINE: I know.

ANTOINE: She had been perfectly silent for five years. I'm really sorry.

JANINE: Thank you anyway.

ANTOINE: What are you looking for?

JANINE: She always told us that our father died during the war in the country where she was born. I'm looking for proof of his death.

ANTOINE: I'm glad you've come, Janine. Ever since she died, I've wanted to call you, you and your brother. To tell you, to explain to you. But I hesitated. And here you are in this theatre. In the course of all those years spent at her bedside I got dizzy listening to your mother's silence. One night I woke up with a strange idea. Perhaps she speaks when I'm not there? Perhaps she talks to herself? I brought in a tape recorder. I hesitated. I had no right. If she talks to herself, that's her choice. So I promised myself I'd never listen to the tapes. Just record without ever knowing. Just record.

JANINE: Record what?

ANTOINE: Silence, her silence. At night, before leaving her, I'd start the recording. One side of a cassette lasts one hour. That was the best I could do. The next day I'd turn the cassette over, and before leaving her I'd start recording again. I recorded more than five hundred hours. All the cassettes are here. Take them. That's all I can do for you.

JANINE: (*takes the box*) Antoine, what did you do with her all that time?

ANTOINE: Nothing. I often just sat beside her. And talked to her. Sometimes I played some music. And I danced with her.

ANTOINE puts a cassette in the tape recorder. Music.
JANINE exits.

CHILDHOOD ON FIRE

12. THE NAME ON THE STONE

NAWAL (age nineteen) at her grandmother's grave. She is engraving NAZIRA's name on the stone in Arabic.

NAWAL: Noûn, aleph, zaïn, yé, rra! *Nazira.* Your name lights up your grave. I came into the village by the low road. My mother was standing there, in the middle of the street. She was waiting for me, I think. She must've expected something. Because of the date. We stared at each other like two strangers.

The villagers gathered around. I said, "I've come back to engrave my grandmother's name on her tombstone." They laughed. "You know how to write now?" I said yes. They laughed. One man spit on me. He said, "You know how to write but you don't know how to defend yourself." I took a book out of my pocket. I hit him so hard I bent the cover and he passed out. I went on my way. My mother watched me until I reached the fountain and turned, on my way up here to the cemetery to come to your grave. I've engraved your name, now I'm leaving. I'm going to find my son. I kept my promise to you, I'll keep my promise to him, the promise made the day of his birth: "No matter what happens, I will always love you." Thank you, Grandmother.

NAWAL exits.

13. SAWDA

NAWAL (age nineteen) on a sun-parched road. SAWDA is there.

SAWDA: I saw you. I watched you from afar, I saw you engrave your grandmother's name on her gravestone. Then you stood up suddenly and ran off. Why?

NAWAL: What about you, why did you follow me?

SAWDA: I wanted to see you write. To see if it really existed. The rumour spread so fast this morning. You were back, after three years. In the camp people were saying: "Nawal is back, she knows how to write, she knows how to read." Everyone was laughing. I ran to wait for you at the entrance to the village but you'd already arrived. I saw you hit the man with your book, I watched the book tremble in your hand, and I thought of all the words, all the letters, burning with the heat of the anger on your face. You left, and I followed you.

NAWAL: What do you want?

SAWDA: Teach me how to read and write.

NAWAL: I don't know how.

SAWDA: Yes, you do. Don't lie. I saw you.

NAWAL: I'm leaving. I'm leaving the village. So I can't teach you.

SAWDA: I'll follow you. I know where you're going.

NAWAL: How could you know?

SAWDA: I knew Wahab. We're from the same camp. We came from the same village. He's a refugee from the South, like me. The night they took him away, he was shouting your name.

NAWAL: You want to find Wahab.

SAWDA: Don't be silly. I'm telling you, I know where you're going. It's not Wahab you want to find. It's your child. You see, I'm right. Take me with you and teach me how to read. I'll help you in exchange. I know how to travel and we'll be stronger together. Two women, side by side. Take me with you. If you're sad, I'll sing, if you feel weak, I'll help you, I'll carry you. There's nothing here for us. I get up in the morning and people say, "Sawda, there's the sky," but no one has anything to say about the sky. They say, "There's the wind," but no one has anything to say about the wind. People show me the world but the world is mute. And life goes by and everything is murky. I saw the letters you engraved and I thought: that is a woman's name. As if the stone had become transparent. One word and everything lights up.

NAWAL: What about your parents?

SAWDA: My parents never say anything to me. They never tell me anything. I ask them: "Why did we leave our country?" They say, "Forget that. What's the point. Don't think about it. There is no country. It's not important. We're alive and we eat every day. That's what matters." They say, "The war won't catch up with us." I answer, "Yes, it will. The earth is being devoured by a red wolf." My parents don't say anything. I tell them, "I remember, we fled in the middle of the night, men came and chased us from our house. They destroyed it." They tell me, "Learn to forget." I say, "Why was my father on his knees crying in front of our burning house? Who burned it down?" They answer, "None of that is true. You dreamt it, Sawda, you dreamt it." So I don't want to stay here. Wahab was shouting your name and it was a miracle in the middle of the night. If they took me away, no name would fill my throat. Not a single one. How can we love here? There is no love, no love. They always tell me, "Forget, Sawda, forget," so I will forget. I'll forget the village, the mountains, and the camp and my mother's face and the despair in my father's eyes.

NAWAL: We can never forget, Sawda, believe me. Come with me anyway.

They exit.

JANINE is listening to her mother's silence.

14. BROTHER AND SISTER

SIMON is facing JANINE.

SIMON: The university is looking for you. Your colleagues are looking for you. Your students are looking for you. They keep calling me, everyone's calling me: "Janine has stopped coming to the university. We don't know where Janine is. The students don't know what to do." I've been looking for you, I've been calling you. You don't answer.

JANINE: What do you want, Simon? Why have you come to my house?

SIMON: Because everyone thinks you're dead.

JANINE: I'm fine. You can leave.

SIMON: No, you're not fine and I won't leave.

JANINE: Don't shout.

SIMON: You're starting to act like her.

JANINE: How I act is my own business, Simon.

SIMON: No. I'm sorry, but it's my business, too. I'm all you have left, and you're all I have left. And you're acting like her.

JANINE: I'm not doing anything.

SIMON: You've stopped talking. Like her. One day she comes home and she locks herself in her room. She sits there. One day. Two days. Three days. Doesn't eat. Or drink. She disappears. Once. Twice. Three times. Four times. Comes home. Refuses to talk. Sells her furniture. Your furniture's gone. Her phone rang, she wouldn't answer. Your phone rings, you won't answer. She locked herself in. You lock yourself in. You refuse to talk.

JANINE: Simon, come sit beside me. Listen. Listen for a bit.

JANINE gives SIMON one of her earphones and he presses it to his ear. JANINE presses the other earphone to her ear. They both listen to the silence.

JANINE: You can hear her breathing. You can hear her move.

SIMON: You're listening to silence!

JANINE: It's her silence.

NAWAL (age nineteen) is teaching SAWDA the Arabic alphabet.

NAWAL: Aleph, bé, tä, szä, jïm, ha, khâ ...

SAWDA: Aleph, bé, tâ, szâ, jîm, hâ, khâ ...

NAWAL: Dâl, dââl, rrâ, zâ, sîn, shîn, sâd, dââd ...

SIMON: You're going crazy, Janine.

JANINE: What do you know about me? About her? Nothing. You know nothing. How can we go on living now?

SIMON: How? You throw the tapes away. You go back to the university. You give your courses and you finish your Ph.D.

JANINE: I don't give a damn about my Ph.D.!

SIMON: You don't give a damn about anything!

JANINE: There's no point in trying to explain it, you wouldn't understand. One plus one equals two. You don't even understand that.

SIMON: I forgot, we have to talk to you in numbers! If your math professor told you you were going crazy, you might listen to him. But your brother – forget it! He's too dumb, too slow!

JANINE: I don't give a damn about my Ph.D. There's something in my mother's silence that I want to understand, something I need to understand.

SIMON: And I'm telling you there's nothing to understand!

JANINE: Fuck off!

SIMON: You fuck off!

JANINE: Leave me alone, Simon. We don't owe each other anything. I'm your sister, not your mother. You're my brother, not my father!

SIMON: It's all the same thing.

JANINE: No, it's not the same.

SIMON: Yes, it is!

JANINE: Leave me alone, Simon.

SIMON: The notary is expecting us in three days, we have to sign the papers. Are you going to come ...? You're going to come, Janine ... Janine ... answer me, are you going to come?

JANINE: Yes. Leave now.

SIMON leaves.

NAWAL and SAWDA are walking side by side.

SAWDA: Aleph, bé, tâ, szâ, jîm, hâ, khâ, dâl, dââl, rrâ, zâ, sîn, shîn, sâd ... tââ ... oh, no ...

NAWAL: Start over.

JANINE is listening to her mother's silence.

JANINE: Why didn't you say anything? Speak to me. Say something. You're alone. Antoine isn't with you. You know that he's recording you. You know that he won't listen to anything. You know that he'll give us the cassettes. You know. You've

figured it all out. You know. So speak. Why won't you say something to me? Why won't you say something to me?

JANINE smashes her Walkman on the ground.

15. ALPHABET

NAWAL (age nineteen) and SAWDA on a road in the sun.

SAWDA & NAWAL: Aleph, bé, tâ, szâ, jîm, hâ, khâ, dâl, dââl, rrâ, zâ, sîn, shîn, sâd, dââd, tââ, zââ, ainn, rain, fa, kââf, kaf, lâm, mime, noun, hah, lamaleph, wâw, ya.

NAWAL: That's the alphabet. Twenty-nine sounds. Twenty-nine letters. Those are your weapons. Your bullets. You have to remember them. And how to put them together, to make words.

SAWDA: Look. We've reached the first village in the South. The village of Nabatiyé. The first orphanage is here. Let's go ask.

They pass JANINE. JANINE is listening to silence.

16. WHERE TO BEGIN

JANINE walks onto the stage in the theatre. Loud music.

JANINE: (calling) Antoine ... Antoine ... Antoine!

ANTOINE appears. The music is too loud for them to talk. He gestures for her to wait. The music stops.

ANTOINE: Sorry, we're doing sound checks for the show tonight.

JANINE: Help me, Antoine.

ANTOINE: What do you want me to do?

JANINE: I don't know where to begin.

ANTOINE: You have to begin at the beginning.

JANINE: There's no logic.

ANTOINE: When did you mother stop talking?

JANINE: In the summer of '97. In August. On the twentieth. The day of our birthday. Mine and Simon's. She came home and she refused to talk. Period.

ANTOINE: What happened that day?

JANINE: I don't know. At the time she was following some preliminary hearings at the International Criminal Tribunal.

ANTOINE: Why?

JANINE: They were related to the war in the country where she was born.

ANTOINE: And on that particular day?

JANINE: Nothing. I read and reread the minutes a hundred times, trying to understand.

ANTOINE: You never found anything else?

JANINE: Nothing. A little photograph. She'd already shown it to me. Her, when she was thirty-five, with one of her friends. Look.

She shows him the photo. ANTOINE studies the photo.

NAWAL (age nineteen) and SAWDA in the deserted orphanage.

SAWDA: There's no one here, Nawal. The orphanage is empty.

NAWAL: What happened?

SAWDA: I don't know.

NAWAL: Where are the children?

SAWDA: There are no more children here. Let's go to Kfar Rayat. That's where the biggest orphanage is.

ANTOINE keeps the photo.

ANTOINE: Leave the photo with me. I'll have it blown up. I'll study it for you. I'm used to looking for little details. That's where we have to begin. I miss your mother. I can see her. Sitting there. In silence. No wild look in her eyes. No lost look. Lucid and piercing.

JANINE: What are you looking at, Mama, what are you looking at?

17. ORPHANAGE IN KFAR RAYAT

NAWAL (age nineteen) and SAWDA in the orphanage in Kfar Rayat with a DOCTOR.

NAWAL: There was no one in the orphanage in Nabatiyé. We came here. To Kfar Rayat.

THE DOCTOR: You shouldn't have. There are no children here either.

NAWAL: Why?

THE DOCTOR: Because of the war.

SAWDA: What war?

THE DOCTOR: Who knows ... Brothers are shooting their brothers and fathers are shooting their fathers. A war. But what war? One day 500,000 refugees arrived from the other side of the border and said, "They've chased us off our land, let us live side by side." Some people from here said yes, some people from here said no, some people from here fled. Millions of destinies. And no one knows who is shooting whom or why. It's a war.

NAWAL: And where are the children who were here?

THE DOCTOR: Everything happened so fast. The refugees arrived. They took all the children away. Even the newborn babies. Everyone. They were angry.

SAWDA: Why did the refugees take the children?

THE DOCTOR: Out of revenge. Two days ago the militia hanged three young refugees who strayed outside the camps. Why did the militia hang the three teenagers? Because two refugees from the camp had raped and killed a girl from the village of Kfar Samira. Why did they rape the girl? Because the militia had stoned a family of refugees. Why did the militia stone them? Because the refugees had set fire to a house near the hill where thyme grows. Why did the refugees set fire to the house? To take revenge on the militia who had destroyed a well they had drilled. Why did the militia destroy the well? Because the refugees had burned the crop near the river where the dogs run. Why did they burn the crop? There must be a reason, that's as far as my memory goes, I can't retrace it any further, but the story can go on forever, one thing leading to another, from anger to anger, from sadness to grief, from rape to murder, back to the beginning of time.

NAWAL: Which way did they go?

THE DOCTOR: They were headed south. To the camps. Now everyone is afraid. We're expecting retaliation.

NAWAL: Did you know the children?

THE DOCTOR: I was their doctor.

NAWAL: I'm trying to find a child.

THE DOCTOR: You'll never find him.

NAWAL: I will find him. A boy of four. He arrived here a few days after his birth. Old Elhame delivered him from my belly and took him away.

THE DOCTOR: And why did you give him to her?

NAWAL: They took him away from me! I didn't give him away! They took him from me. Was he here?

THE DOCTOR: Elhame brought many children.

NAWAL: Yes, but she didn't bring many in the spring four years ago. A newborn boy. From the North. Do you have records?

THE DOCTOR: No more records.

NAWAL: A cleaning woman, a kitchen worker, someone who would remember. Remember having found the child beautiful. Having taken him from Elhame.

THE DOCTOR: I'm a doctor, not an administrator. I travel around to all the orphanages. I can't know everything. Go look in the camps, down south.

NAWAL: Where did the children sleep?

THE DOCTOR: In this ward.

NAWAL: Where are you? Where are you?

JANINE: Mama, what are you looking at?

NAWAL: Now that we're together, everything feels better.

JANINE: What did you mean by that?

NAWAL: Now that we're together, everything feels better.

JANINE: Now that we're together, everything feels better.

Night. Hospital. ANTOINE comes running in.

ANTOINE: What? What? Nawal? Nawal!

SAWDA: Nawal!

ANTOINE: What did you say? Nawal!

ANTOINE picks a tape recorder up off the floor beside NAWAL (age sixty-four).

NAWAL: If I could turn back the clock, he would still be in my arms ...

SAWDA: Where are you going? Where are you going?

ANTOINE picks up the phone and dials a number.

ANTOINE: Janine Marwan ...?

NAWAL: South.

ANTOINE: Antoine Ducharme, your mother's nurse.

SAWDA: Wait! Nawal! Wait!

ANTOINE: She just spoke. Nawal just spoke.

NAWAL exits.

18. PHOTOGRAPH AND SOUTHBOUND BUS

ANTOINE and JANINE at the university. The photograph of NAWAL (age thirty-five) and SAWDA is projected on the wall.

ANTOINE: They're back in your mother's country. It's summertime, you can tell from the flowers behind them. Those are the wild herbs that bloom in June and July. The trees are parasol pines. They're found throughout the region. And there's something written on the burnt-out bus in the background, you see. I asked the grocer at the corner of my street, he comes from there, and he read: Refugees of Kfar Rayat.

JANINE: I've done research on the history of the hearings. One of the longest chapters concerns a prison built during the war in Kfar Rayat.

ANTOINE: Now look. You see that, just above her hand ...

JANINE: What is it?

ANTOINE: The butt of a gun. Her friend has one too, you can see the outline under her blouse.

JANINE: What were they doing with guns?

ANTOINE: We can't tell from the photo. Maybe they were working as guards in the prison. What year was the prison built?

JANINE: 1978. According to the tribunal records.

ANTOINE: Good. Now we know that your mother, towards the end of the seventies, was in the vicinity of the village of Kfar Rayat where a prison was built. She had a friend whose name we don't know and both of them carried guns.

Silence.

Are you all right? Janine? Are you all right?

JANINE: No, I'm not all right.

ANTOINE: What are you afraid of?

JANINE: Of finding out.

ANTOINE: What are you going to do now?

JANINE: Buy an airplane ticket.

NAWAL (age nineteen) is waiting for the bus. SAWDA is at her side.

SAWDA: I'm leaving with you.

NAWAL: No.

SAWDA: I can't leave you alone!

NAWAL: Are you sure there's a bus on this road?

SAWDA: Yes, it's the one the refugees take back to the camps. You see that cloud of dust down there, that must be it. Nawal, the doctor said you should wait. He said there'll be trouble in the camps, because of the children who were kidnapped.

NAWAL: So I have to be there!

SAWDA: What difference can one day make?

NAWAL: One day more to hold my child in my arms. I look up at the sun and I think he's looking at the same sun. A bird flies by, perhaps he sees the same bird. A cloud in the distance, and I think it's passing over him, that he's running to escape the rain. I think of him every minute and every minute is like a promise of my love for him. He turned four today. He knows how to walk, he knows how to talk and he must be afraid of the dark.

SAWDA: And if you die, what's the point?

NAWAL: If I die, it will be because he was already dead.

SAWDA: Nawal, don't go today.

NAWAL: Don't tell me what to do.

SAWDA: You promised you'd teach me.

NAWAL: We must go our separate ways now.

The bus arrives. NAWAL climbs aboard. The bus leaves. SAWDA is left standing at the roadside.

19. LAWNS IN THE SUBURBS

ALPHONSE LEBEL's house. In his backyard. ALPHONSE, JANINE, and SIMON. Noise of traffic and jackhammers close by.

ALPHONSE LEBEL: Not every day is Sunday, for sure, but once in a while, it does you good. I get to the office and the landlord is there. Right away I thought, watch out, there's some fishing going on here. He says, "Mr. Lebel, you can't go in, we're taking up the carpet and redoing the floors." I say, "You could have let me know, I have work to do, I'm expecting clients." He says, "You're always busy, what's the difference, today or tomorrow, you would've complained anyway." "I'm not complaining, I just would've liked to know," I say, "especially since I'm in a rush period." So then he looks at me and he says, "That's because you're not well-organized." Wait. Me, not well-organized. "You're the one who's not well-organized. You show up like a fly in the appointment, and you announce: 'I'm going to redo your floors.'" "Whatever!" he says. So I said, "Whatever!" back to him and I left. Good thing I was able to reach you.

Come out, come out, come out, it's nicer outside, it's too hot to stay in the house. Come out in the yard. I'll turn on the sprinklers to water the lawn. That'll cool us off.

ALPHONSE turns on the faucet to water his lawn. JANINE and SIMON join him. Sound of jackhammers.

They're redoing the street. They'll be at it till winter. Come out, come out, come out. I'm happy to see you here in my home. It was my parents' house. There used to be fields as far as the eye could see. Today there's the Canadian Tire store and the hydro plant. It's better than a tar pit, for sure. That's what my father said just before he died: "Death is better than a tar pit." He died in his bedroom upstairs in this house. Here are the papers.

Sound of jackhammers.

They've changed the bus route because of the construction work. Now the bus stop is right there, just the other side of the fence. All the buses on this line stop here and every time a bus stops I think of your mother ... I ordered a pizza. We can share it. It comes with the special: soft drinks, fries, and a chocolate bar. I ordered all-dressed without the pepperoni because it's hard to digest. It's an Indian pizzeria, the pizzas are really good, I don't like to cook so I order out.

SIMON: Okay, fine. Can we get this over with? I've got a fight tonight and I'm already late.

ALPHONSE LEBEL: Good idea. While we're waiting for the pizza, we can settle the paperwork.

JANINE: Why do you think of our mother every time a bus stops?

ALPHONSE LEBEL: Because of her phobia!

JANINE: What phobia?

ALPHONSE LEBEL: Her ... bus phobia. Here are the papers and they're all in order. Didn't you know?

JANINE: No!

ALPHONSE LEBEL: She never took a bus.

JANINE: Did she tell you why?

ALPHONSE LEBEL: Yes. When she was young, she saw a bus full of civilians riddled with machine-gun fire, right in front of her. A horrible sight.

JANINE: How do you know that?

Sound of jackhammers.

ALPHONSE LEBEL: She told me.

JANINE: Why did she tell you that?

ALPHONSE LEBEL: How do I know? Because I asked her!

ALPHONSE hands them the papers. JANINE and SIMON sign where he indicates.

ALPHONSE LEBEL: So these papers settle your mother's estate. Except for her last wishes. At least, in your case, Simon.

SIMON: Why in my case?

ALPHONSE LEBEL: Because you still haven't taken the envelope to be delivered to your brother.

SIMON glances at JANINE.

JANINE: Yes, I've taken mine.

SIMON: I don't get it.

Sound of jackhammers.

JANINE: What don't you get?

SIMON: I don't get what you're up to.

JANINE: Nothing.

SIMON: Why didn't you tell me?

JANINE: Simon, it's hard enough as it is.

SIMON: What are you going to do, Janine? Run around everywhere shouting, "Papa, papa, where are you? I'm your daughter." This is no mathematical problem, for Chrissakes. You won't find the solution. There is no solution. There's nothing left …

JANINE: I don't want to discuss this with you, Simon.

SIMON: … no father, no brother, just you and me.

JANINE: Exactly what did she say about the bus?

SIMON: What are you going to do? Fuck! Where are you going to start looking for him?

JANINE: What did she say?

SAWDA: (*screaming*) Nawal!

SIMON: Forget about the bus and answer me! Where are you going to find him?

Sound of jackhammers.

JANINE: What did she tell you?

SAWDA: (*screaming*) Nawal!

ALPHONSE LEBEL: She told me she had just arrived in a town …

SAWDA: (*to JANINE*) Have you seen a girl named Nawal?

ALPHONSE LEBEL: Travelling on a bus …

SAWDA: (*screaming*) Nawal!

ALPHONSE LEBEL: Packed with people.

SAWDA: (*screaming*) Nawal!

ALPHONSE LEBEL: Some men came running up, they blocked the way of the bus, doused it with gasoline, and then some others arrived with machine guns and …

Long sequence of jackhammer noise that entirely drowns the sound of ALPHONSE LEBEL's voice. The sprinklers spray blood and flood everything. JANINE exits.

NAWAL: (*screaming*) Sawda!

SIMON: Janine! Come back, Janine!

NAWAL: I was in the bus, Sawda, I was with them! When they doused us with gas, I screamed: "I'm not from the camp, I'm not one of the refugees from the camp, I'm one of you, I'm looking for my child, one of the children they kidnapped." So they let me off the bus, and then, then they opened fire, and in a flash the bus went up in flames, it went up in flames with everyone inside, the old people, the children, the women, everyone! One woman tried to escape through a window, but the soldiers shot her, and she died there, straddling the window with her child in her arms in the middle of the blaze, her skin melted, her child's skin melted, everything melted and everyone burned to death. There is no time left, Sawda. Time is like a chicken with its head cut off, racing around madly, every which way. Blood is flowing from its decapitated neck, and we're drowning in blood, Sawda, drowning.

SIMON: (*on the phone*) Janine! You're all I've got left, Janine. I'm all you've got left. We have no choice. We have to forget. Call me back, Janine, call me back!

20. THE VERY HEART OF THE POLYGON

SIMON is dressing for his fight.

JANINE, with a backpack, is holding a cellphone.

JANINE: Simon, it's Janine. I'm at the airport, Simon. I'm calling to tell you that I'm leaving for her country. I'm going to try to find this father of ours, and if I find him, if he's still alive, I'll give him the envelope. I'm not doing it for her, I'm doing it for myself. And for you. For the future. But first we have to find Mama, we have to discover her past, her life during all those years she hid from us. She blinded us. Now I'm afraid of going crazy. I have to hang up, Simon. I'm going to hang up and tumble headfirst into a world far from here, far from the strict geometry that has defined my life. I've learned to write and count, to read and speak. Now all that is of no use. The hole I'm about to tumble into, the hole I'm already slipping into, is that of her silence. Simon, are you crying? Are you crying?

SIMON's fight. SIMON is knocked out.

JANINE: Where are you leading me, Mama? Where are you leading me?

NAWAL: To the very heart of the polygon, Janine, to the very heart of the polygon.

JANINE places her earphones on her ears, slips a new cassette into the recorder, and starts to listen to her mother's silence again.

JANNAANE'S FIRE

21. THE HUNDRED YEARS WAR

NAWAL (age forty) and SAWDA. A building in ruins. Two dead bodies lie on the floor.

SAWDA: Nawal!

NAWAL: They went to Abdelhammas's house too. They killed Zan, Mira, Abiel. At Madelwaad's they searched the whole house and didn't find him so they slit everyone's throat. The whole family. And they burned his eldest daughter to death.

SAWDA: I've just been to Halam's. They were at his house, too. They couldn't find him so they took his daughter and his wife away. No one knows where.

NAWAL: They killed everyone who contributed money to the newspaper. Everyone who worked at the newspaper. They burned the printing press. Burned the paper. Threw out the ink. And now look. They've killed Ekal and Faride. We're the ones they're searching for, Sawda, they're after us and if we stay here another hour, they'll find us and kill us too. So let's go to the camps.

SAWDA: We'll go to my cousin's house, we'll be a bit safer there.

NAWAL: Safer …

SAWDA: They even destroyed the homes of people who read the newspaper.

NAWAL: And it's not over yet. Believe me. I've thought it through. We are at the beginning of the hundred years war. At the beginning of the last war in the world. I'm telling you, Sawda, our generation is an "interesting" generation. Seen from above, it must be very instructive to see us struggling to name what is barbarous and what isn't. Yes. Very "interesting." A generation raised on shame. Really. At the crossroads. We think this war will only end with the end of time. People don't realize, if we don't find a solution to these massacres immediately, we never will.

SAWDA: Which war are you talking about?

NAWAL: You know very well which war. The war pitting brother against brother, sister against sister. The war of angry civilians.

SAWDA: How long will it last?

NAWAL: I don't know.

SAWDA: The books don't say?

NAWAL: Books are always way behind the times, or way ahead. It's all so ridiculous. They've destroyed the newspaper, we'll start another one. It was called the *Morning Light*, we'll call the next one the *Rising Sun*. (*beat*) Words are horrible. We can't let them blind us. We have to do as our ancestors did in ancient times: try to read in the flight of birds the presages of things to come. Divination.

SAWDA: Divine what? Ekal is dead. All that's left is his camera. Shattered images. A broken life. What kind of a world is this where objects have more hope than we do?

Beat. SAWDA sings a song like a prayer.

22. ABDESSAMAD

JANINE is in NAWAL's native village. ABDESSAMAD is standing with her.

JANINE: Are you Abdessamad Darazia? They told me to come see you because you know all the tales of the village.

ABDESSAMAD: The true and the false, too.

JANINE: Do you remember Nawal? (*showing him the photo of NAWAL [thirty-five] and SAWDA*) Her. She was born and grew up in this village.

ABDESSAMAD: There is Nawal who left with Sawda. But that's a legend.

JANINE: Who is Sawda?

ABDESSAMAD: A legend. They called her the girl who sings. A deep, sweet voice. She always sang at the right moment. A legend.

JANINE: And what about Nawal? Nawal Marwan.

ABDESSAMAD: Nawal and Sawda. A legend.

JANINE: And what does the legend say?

ABDESSAMAD: It says that one night they separated Nawal and Wahab.

JANINE: Who is Wahab?

ABDESSAMAD: A legend! They say if you linger too long in the woods, near the rock where the white trees stand, you'll hear their laughter.

JANINE: The rock where the white trees stand?

WAHAB and NAWAL (age fourteen) at the rock where the white trees stand. NAWAL is unwrapping a present.

WAHAB: I brought you a present, Nawal.

NAWAL: A clown nose!

WAHAB: The same one we saw when the travelling circus came to town. Remember how hard you laughed! You kept saying, "His nose, his nose! Look at his nose!" I loved to hear you laugh like that. I went to their campsite, I almost got eaten alive by the lion, trampled on by the elephant, I had to negotiate with the tigers, I swallowed three snakes, and I walked into the clown's tent. He was sleeping, his nose was on the table, I grabbed it and ran!

ABDESSAMAD: In the cemetery, the stone still stands where, according to the legend, Nawal engraved her grandmother's name. Letter by letter. The first epitaph in the cemetery. She'd learned to write. Then she left. Sawda went with her and the war began. It's never a good sign when the young people flee.

JANINE: Where is Kfar Rayat?

ABDESSAMAD: In hell.

JANINE: More specifically.

ABDESSAMAD: South of here. Near Nabatiyé. Follow the road.

ABDESSAMAD exits. JANINE makes a phone call.

JANINE: Hello, Simon, it's Janine. I'm calling from the village where Mama was born. Listen. Listen to the sound of the village.

She walks off holding her phone aloft.

23. LIFE IS AROUND THE KNIFE

SAWDA and NAWAL (age forty) are leaving the village. Morning. A MILITIAMAN appears.

MILITIAMAN: Who are you? Where are you coming from? The roads are closed to travellers.

NAWAL: We've come from Nabatiyé and we're on our way to Kfar Rayat.

MILITIAMAN: How do we know you're not the two women we've been looking for? Our entire company is looking for them, and the soldiers who've come from the South are looking for them, too. They know how to write and they're putting ideas into people's heads.

Silence.

MILITIAMAN: You are those two women. One writes and the other sings. (*beat*) You see these shoes? I took them off the feet of a corpse last night. I killed the man who was wearing them in a one-on-one fight, looking him in the eye. He told me, "We're from the same country, the same blood," and I smashed his skull and stripped off his shoes. In the beginning my hands shook. It's like everything else. The first time you hesitate. You don't know how tough a skull can be. So you don't know how hard you have to hit. And you don't know where to stab your knife. You don't know. The worst isn't stabbing the knife, it's pulling it out, because all the muscles contract and hold on to the knife. The muscles know that's where life is. Around the knife. So you sharpen the blade and then there's no problem. The blade slips out as easily as it slips in. The first time is hard. Then it gets easier, like everything else.

The MILITIAMAN grabs NAWAL and holds a knife to her throat.

MILITIAMAN: I'm going to slit your throat and we'll see if the one who knows how to sing has a pretty voice, and if the one who knows how to think still has any bright ideas.

SAWDA takes out a gun and fires one shot. The MILITIAMAN falls.

SAWDA: Nawal, I'm afraid he's right. You heard what he said: "The first time is hard, then it gets easier."

NAWAL: You didn't kill him, you saved our lives.

SAWDA: Those are just words, nothing but words.

SAWDA fires another shot into the MILITIAMAN's body.

24. KFAR RAYAT

JANINE in the Kfar Rayat prison. A GUIDE is with her. She is taking photos.

GUIDE: This prison was turned into a museum in 2000, to revive the tourist trade. I used to be a guide up north, I did the Roman ruins. My specialty. Now I do the Kfar Rayat prison.

JANINE: (*showing him the picture of NAWAL and SAWDA*) Do you know these two women?

GUIDE: No, who are they?

JANINE: Maybe they worked here.

GUIDE: Then they fled at the end of the war with the torturer, Abou Tarek. This is the most famous cell in Kfar Rayat prison. Cell number 7. People make pilgrimages here. It was the cell of the woman who sings. She was a prisoner here for five years. When the others were being tortured, she'd sing –

JANINE: Was the woman who sings named Sawda?

GUIDE: No one knew her name. They just had serial numbers. The woman who sings was number 72. It's a famous number around here.

JANINE: Did you say number 72?!

GUIDE: Yes, why?

JANINE: Do you know anyone who worked here?

GUIDE: The janitor at the school. He was a guard here back then.

JANINE: How long ago was this prison built?

GUIDE: 1978. The year of the massacres in the refugee camps of Kfar Riad and Kfar Matra. That's not far from here. The soldiers surrounded the camps and they sent in the militia. The militiamen killed everything in sight. They were crazy. Their leader had been assassinated. So they didn't fool around. A huge wound in the flank of the country.

JANINE exits.

25. FRIENDSHIPS

NAWAL (age forty) and SAWDA.

SAWDA: They entered the camps. With knives, grenades, machetes, axes, guns, and acid. Their hands were not shaking. Everyone was fast asleep. They plunged their weapons into their sleep and they murdered the dreams of the men, women, and children who were sleeping in the great cradle of the night!

NAWAL: What are you going to do?

SAWDA: Leave me alone!

NAWAL: Where are you going?

SAWDA: I'm going into every house.

NAWAL: To do what?

SAWDA: I don't know.

NAWAL: Are you going to fire a bullet into every head?

SAWDA: An eye for an eye, a tooth for a tooth, that's what they say!

NAWAL: Not that way.

SAWDA: There's no other way! Now that death can be contemplated in cold blood, there's no other way!

NAWAL: So now you want to go into houses and kill men, women, and children!

SAWDA: They killed my parents, my cousins, my neighbours, my parents' distant friends! It's the same thing.

NAWAL: Yes, it's the same thing, Sawda, you're right, but think about it.

SAWDA: What's the point of thinking about it. Thinking about it can't bring anyone back to life.

NAWAL: Think about it, Sawda. You are a victim and you're going to kill everyone who crosses your path, and then you'll be the murderer. Then, in turn, you'll be the victim again! You know how to sing, Sawda, you know how to sing!

SAWDA: I don't want to sing! I don't want to be consoled, Nawal. I don't want your ideas, your images, your words, your eyes, the time we spent side by side – I don't want all that to console me after everything I've seen and heard! They stormed into the camps like madmen. The first screams woke the others and soon everyone heard the fury of the militiamen! They began by throwing children against the walls, then they killed every man they could find. They slit the boys' throats and burned the girls alive. Everything was on fire, Nawal, everything was on fire, everything went up in flames. Blood was flowing through the streets. Screams filled throats and died, another life gone. One militiaman was preparing the death of three brothers. He lined them up against the wall. I was at their feet, hiding in the gutter. I could see their legs shaking. Three brothers. The militiamen pulled their mother by the hair, stood her in front of her sons, and one of them shouted: "Choose, choose which one you want to save. Choose or I'll shoot all three of them. I'm going to count to three, and at three, I'm going to kill all three of them. Choose!" Listen to me, Nawal, I'm not making this up. I'm telling you the pain that fell at my feet. I could see her, through her sons' trembling legs. Unable to speak, unable to think, shaking her head, looking from one son to the next! With her heavy breasts and her body ravaged by having carried them, her three sons. And her entire body was shouting, "What was the point of bearing them, just to see their blood splattered against a wall?" And the militiaman kept shouting, "Choose! Choose!" Then she looked at him and said, as a last hope, "How dare you, look at me, I could be your mother." And he hit her. "Don't insult my mother! Choose!" Then she said a name, she said, "Nidal. Nidal!" And she collapsed and the militiaman shot the youngest two. He left the eldest son alive, trembling! He just left him there and walked away. The two bodies lay at his feet. The mother stood up, and in the middle of the town in flames, weeping in its fumes, she began to wail that she had killed her sons. Dragging her heavy body, she kept screaming that she was her sons' assassin!

NAWAL: I understand, Sawda, but you can't just strike back blindly. Listen. Listen to what I'm saying: we have blood on our hands and in a situation like this a mother's suffering is less important than the terrible machine that is crushing us. That woman's pain, your pain and mine, the pain of those who died that night is no longer a scandal, it is an accumulation, an accumulation too monstrous to be calculated. So you, Sawda – you who were reciting the alphabet a long time ago on the road to the sun, when we were travelling side by side to find my son born of a love story the likes of which is no longer told – you can't add to this monstrous accumulation of pain. You simply can't.

SAWDA: So what can we do? What can we do? Just fold our arms and wait? And tell ourselves this has nothing to do with us, let the idiots fight it out among themselves! Are we supposed to stick to our books and our alphabet where everything is so nice, so beautiful, so extraordinary, so interesting?! "Nice, beautiful, interesting, extraordinary." That's like spitting in the victims' faces. Words! What good are words if I don't know what I should do today? What can we do, Nawal?

NAWAL: I can't answer that question, Sawda. There are no values to guide us, so we have to rely on makeshift values ... on what we know and what we feel. This is good, that is bad. But I know one thing: we don't like war, and we are forced to be part of it. We don't like unhappiness and we are drowning in it. You want to take revenge, burn down houses, make people feel what you feel so

they'll understand, so they'll change, so the men who have done this will be transformed. You want to punish them so they'll understand. But this idiotic game feeds off the madness and the pain that are blinding you.

SAWDA: So we don't make a move, is that it?

NAWAL: Who are you trying to convince? Can't you see that there are men who can no longer be convinced? Men who can no longer be persuaded of anything? The guy who was shouting "Choose!" at that woman, forcing her to condemn her own children, do you think you can convince him that he made a mistake? What do you expect him to do? Tell you, "Oh, Mademoiselle Sawda, your argument is very interesting, I'm going to change my mind, my feelings, my blood, my world, my universe, my planet, and I'm going to apologize immediately." What do you think? That you're going to teach him something by spilling the blood of his wife and son? Do you think that from one day to the next, with the bodies of his loved ones lying at his feet, he's going to say, "This gives me food for thought, now I can see that the refugees deserve a home. I'll give them mine and we'll live in peace and harmony, all of us together!" Sawda, when they yanked my son from my body, tore him from my arms, from my life, I realized that I had a choice: either I lash out at the world or I do everything I can to find him. I think of him every day. He's twenty-five now, old enough to kill, old enough to die, old enough to love and to suffer. So what do you think I'm thinking when I tell you all that? I'm thinking of his probable death, of my ridiculous search, of the fact that I will be forever incomplete because he left my life and I will never see him standing before me. Don't think I can't feel that woman's pain. It's inside me like a poison. And I swear, Sawda, that I would be the first to grab the grenades, to grab dynamite, bombs, and anything that could do the most damage, I would wrap them around me, I would swallow them, and I would head into the midst of those stupid men and blow myself up with a joy you can't imagine. I swear I'd do it, because I have nothing left to lose and my hatred for those men is deep, so deep! I see my life in the faces of the men who are destroying our lives. I'm etched in every one of their wrinkles and it would be so easy to blow myself up so I could tear them to shreds, right to the marrow of their soul, do you hear me? But I made a promise ... I promised an old woman I would learn to read, to write, and to speak, so I could escape poverty and hatred. And this promise is going to guide me. No matter what. Never let hatred be your guide, never, reach for the stars, always. A promise made to an old woman who wasn't beautiful or rich or anything special, but who helped me, who cared for me, and who saved me.

SAWDA: So what can we do?

NAWAL: Let me tell you what we can do. But you have to hear me out. You have to promise me you won't argue. That you won't try to prevent anything.

SAWDA: What are you thinking of?

NAWAL: Promise!

SAWDA: I'm not sure.

NAWAL: Remember, a long time ago, you came to me and said: "Teach me to read and write." I said yes, and I kept my promise. Now it's your turn to promise me. Promise.

SAWDA: I promise.

NAWAL: Listen. We're going to strike. But we're going to strike a single spot. Just one. And we're going to hurt. We won't touch a single man, woman, or child, except for one man. Just one. We'll get him. Maybe we'll kill him, maybe we won't, that doesn't matter, but we'll get him.

SAWDA: What are you thinking of?

NAWAL: I'm thinking of Chad.

SAWDA: The paramilitary leader. We'll never get to him.

NAWAL: The girl who teaches his children used to be my student. She's going to help me. I'm going to replace her for a week.

SAWDA: Why are you saying "I"?

NAWAL: Because I'm going alone.

SAWDA: And what will you do?

NAWAL: At first, nothing. I'll teach his daughters.

SAWDA: Then?

NAWAL: Then? The last day, just before leaving, I'll fire two shots at him, one for you, one for me. One for the refugees, one for the people from my country. One for his stupidity, one for the army that has invaded us. Two twin bullets. Not one, not three. Two.

SAWDA: And then what? How will you get away?

Silence.

I refuse. It's not up to you to do that.

NAWAL: Who is it up to, then? You maybe?

SAWDA: Why not?

NAWAL: Why are we doing this? For revenge? No. Because we still want to love with passion. And in a situation like this, some people are bound to die and others not. Those who have already been passionately in love should die before those who have never loved. I have lived the love I was meant to live. I had the child I was meant to have. Then I had to learn, and I learned. Now all I have left is my death and I have chosen it and it will be mine. You have to go hide at Chamseddine's house.

SAWDA: Chamseddine is as violent as the rest of them.

NAWAL: You have no choice. Don't betray me, Sawda. You have to live for me, and go on singing for me.

SAWDA: How can I go on living without you?

NAWAL: And how can I go on living without you? Remember the poem we learned a long time ago, when we were still young. When I still thought I would find my son.

They recite the poem "Al Atlal" in Arabic.

Recite it every time you miss me, and when your courage fails, you can recite the alphabet. And when my courage fails, I'll sing. I'll sing, Sawda, the way you taught me to. And my voice will be your voice and your voice will be my voice. That's how we can stay together. There is nothing more beautiful than being together.

26. THE KHAKI JACKET

JANINE and the school JANITOR.

THE JANITOR: I'm a school janitor.

JANINE: I know, but before … When the prison was still a prison.

THE JANITOR: You have outstayed your welcome.

JANINE takes out the khaki jacket. The JANITOR grabs it from her.

JANINE: There's a number printed on the back. Number 72 …

THE JANITOR: The woman who sings.

JANINE: (*handing him the photo*) Is that her?

THE JANITOR: (*studying the photo*) No, that is.

JANINE: No! That's her!

THE JANITOR: I saw that woman for more than five years. She was always in her cell. The woman who sings. I was one of the few people to see her face.

JANINE: Please. Are you sure that this woman, the one with the long hair who's smiling, is the woman who sings?

THE JANITOR: That is the woman I knew in her cell.

JANINE: And who is this?

THE JANITOR: I don't know her.

JANINE: Sawda. She is the woman who sings! Everyone told me that.

THE JANITOR: Well, they lied to you. The woman who sings is this one.

JANINE: Nawal? Nawal Marwan?

THE JANITOR: No one ever spoke her name. She was simply the woman who sings. Number 72. Cell number 7. The one who assassinated the paramilitary leader. Two bullets. The whole country quaked. They sent her to Kfar Rayat. All her friends were captured and killed. One of them reached the café where the militia hung out and she blew herself up. Only the woman who sings survived. Abou Tarek handled her. The nights when Abou Tarek raped her, we couldn't tell their voices apart.

JANINE: Oh, I see, she was raped!

THE JANITOR: It was very common around here. And inevitably, she got pregnant.

JANINE: What?!

THE JANITOR: That was common, too.

JANINE: Of course, she got pregnant ...!

THE JANITOR: The night she gave birth, the whole prison fell silent. She gave birth all alone, crouching in a corner of her cell. We could hear her screams and her screams were like a curse on us all. When it was over, I entered the cell. Everything was dark. She had put the child in a pail and covered it with a towel. I was the one who always took the babies to the river. It was winter. I took the pail, I didn't dare look in it, and I went out. The night was clear and cold. Pitch-black. No moon. The river was frozen. I went to the ditch and I left the pail there and started back. But I could hear the child crying and I could hear the song of the woman who sings. So I stopped and thought, and my conscience was as cold and dark as the night. Their voices were like banks of snow in my soul. So I went back, I took the pail and I walked and walked, until I ran into a peasant who was returning with his flock to the village higher up, near Kisserwan. He saw me, he saw my grief, he gave me some water, and I gave him the pail. I told him, "This is the child of the woman who sings." And I left. Later on, people found out. And they forgave me. They left me alone. And today I work in this school. Everything worked out.

Long pause.

JANINE: So she was raped by Abou Tarek.

THE JANITOR: Yes.

JANINE: She got pregnant and she had the child in prison.

THE JANITOR: Yes.

JANINE: And you took the child and instead of killing it, like all the others, you gave it to a peasant? Is that right?

THE JANITOR: Yes, that's right.

JANINE: Where is Kisserwan?

THE JANITOR: A little farther west. Overlooking the sea. Ask for the man who raised the child of the woman who sings. They'll know him. My name is Fahim. I threw a lot of children into the river, but I didn't throw that one. His crying touched me. If you find him, tell him my name, Fahim.

JANINE puts on the jacket.

JANINE: Why didn't you tell us? We would have loved you for it. Been so proud of you. Defended you. Why didn't you ever tell us, Mama? Why did I never hear you sing?

27. TELEPHONES

JANINE is in a phone booth. SIMON is at the gym. The following two speeches overlap.

JANINE: Listen, Simon, listen! I don't give a damn! I don't give a damn about your boxing match! Shut up! Listen to me! She was in jail. She was tortured! She was raped! Do you hear me! Raped! Do you hear what I'm saying? And our brother is the child she had in jail. No! Fuck, Simon, I'm halfway round the world, in the middle of nowhere, there's a sea and two oceans between us, so shut up and listen to me ...! No, you're not going to call me back, you're going to see the notary, you're going to ask him for the red notebook, and you're going to see what's in it. Period.

SIMON: No! No! I'm not interested in that. My boxing match! That's all I care about! I'm not interested in knowing who she was! No, I'm not interested! I know who I am today, and that's enough for me. Now you listen to me! Come home! Come home, fuck, right away! Come home, Janine ...! Hello? Hello ...? Fuck! Don't you have the number of your goddamn phone booth so I can call you?

She hangs up.

28. THE REAL NAMES

JANINE at the peasant's house.

JANINE: A shepherd directed me to you. He said, "Go up to the pink house and you'll find an old man. His name is Abdelmalak, but you can call him Malak. He will take you in." So here I am.

MALAK: Who sent you to the shepherd?

JANINE: Fahim, the janitor at the school in Kfar Rayat.

MALAK: And who told you about Fahim?

JANINE: The guide in the Kfar Rayat prison.

MALAK: Mansour. That's his name. Why did you go to see Mansour?

JANINE: Abdessamad, a refugee who lives in a village up north, directed me to the Kfar Rayat prison.

MALAK: And who sent you to see Abdessamad?

JANINE: At this rate, we'll go back to the day of my birth.

MALAK: Perhaps. Then we'll find a beautiful love story. You see that tree over there, it's a walnut tree. It was planted the day I was born. It's a hundred years old. Time is a strange beast, isn't it? So?

JANINE: Abdessamad lives in the village where my mother was born.

MALAK: And what was your mother's name?

JANINE: Nawal Marwan.

MALAK: And what's your name?

JANINE: Janine Marwan.

MALAK: So what do you want from me? Who do you want me to direct you to now?

JANINE: To the child that Fahim gave you one day, on behalf of my mother.

MALAK: But I don't know your mother.

JANINE: You don't know Nawal Marwan?

MALAK: The name doesn't mean anything to me.

JANINE: What about the woman who sings?

MALAK: Why are you talking about the woman who sings? Do you know her? Has she come back?

JANINE: The woman who sings is dead. Nawal Marwan is her name. Nawal Marwan is the woman who sings. And she is my mother.

The old man takes JANINE into his arms.

MALAK: Jannaane!

NAWAL (age forty-five) is there, facing MALAK, who stands holding two babies in his arms.

MALAK: The word spread around the country that you had been released.

NAWAL: What do you want from me?

MALAK: I want to give back your children. I cared for them as if they were my own!

NAWAL: So keep them!

MALAK: No, they are yours. Take them. You don't realize what they will be for you. It took many miracles for them to be alive today, and many miracles for you to be alive. Three survivors. Three miracles looking at each other. Not often you see that. I gave them each a name. The boy's name is Sarwane and the girl is Jannaane. Sarwane and Jannaane. Take them and remember me.

MALAK gives the children to NAWAL.

JANINE: No! No, that can't be us. That's not true. My name is Janine and my brother is Simon.

MALAK: Jannaane and Sarwane.

JANINE: No! We were born in the hospital. We have our birth certificates! And we were born in the summer, not in the winter, and the child born in Kfar Rayat was born in the winter because the river was frozen, Fahim told me, that's why he couldn't throw the pail into the deep water.

MALAK: Fahim is mistaken.

JANINE: Fahim isn't mistaken. He saw her every day! He took the child, he took the pail, the child was in the pail, and there was only one child, not two, not two!

MALAK: Fahim didn't look carefully.

JANINE: My father is dead, he gave his life for this country, and he wasn't a torturer, he loved my mother and my mother loved him!

MALAK: Is that what she told you? Why not, children need bedtime stories to help them fall asleep. I warned you, the question-and-answer game can easily lead back to the birth of things, and it's led us back to the secret of your birth. Now you listen to me: Fahim hands me the pail and he goes running off. I lift up the cloth covering the child, and what do I see, two babies, two newborn babies, red with anger, pressed against each other, clinging to each other with all the fervour of the beginning of their lives. I took the two of you and I fed you and named you. Jannaane and Sarwane. And here you are. You've come back to me after your mother's death, and I can see, from the tears running down your cheeks, that I wasn't so wrong. The offspring of the woman who sings were born of rape and horror, but they will restore the lost cries of the children thrown into the river.

29. NAWAL SPEAKS

SIMON opens the red notebook.

NAWAL (age sixty) is testifying before the tribunal.

NAWAL: Madam President, ladies and gentlemen of the tribunal. I wish to make my testimony standing, my eyes wide open, because I was often forced to keep them closed. I will make my testimony facing my torturer. Abou Tarek. I speak your name for the last time in my life. I say it so you know that I recognize you. So you can entertain no doubt about that. There are many dead who, if they arose from their bed of pain, would also recognize you, recognize the horror of your smile. Many of your men feared you, although they were nightmares, too. How can a nightmare fear a nightmare? The kind and just men who come after us might be able to solve this enigma. I recognize you, but you might not recognize me, despite my conviction that you can place me perfectly since your job as a torturer required an excellent memory for family names and given names, for dates, and places and events. Nevertheless, let me remind you of my face, because my face was what you cared least about. You remember much more clearly my skin, my smell, the most intimate details of my body which you treated as a territory to be massacred, bit by bit. There are ghosts speaking to you through me. Remember. Perhaps my name will mean nothing to you, because all the women were nothing but whores to you. You used to say whore number 45, whore number 63. That gave you a certain style and elegance, a know-how, a weight, an authority. And the women, one after another, felt fear and hatred awake inside them. Perhaps my name will mean nothing to you, perhaps my whore number will mean nothing, but there's one thing you haven't forgotten, something that still rings in your ears despite all your efforts to prevent it from drowning your heart, one thing will certainly burst the dike that allows you to forget: the woman who sings. Now do you remember? You know the truth of your anger towards me, when you hanged me by the feet, when the water and the electrical current … the shards under my fingernails … the gun loaded with blanks against my temple … The gunshots and death that are part of torture, and the urine on my body, yours, in my mouth, on my sex, and your sex in my sex, once, twice, three times, so often that time was shattered. My belly growing big with you, your ghastly torture in my belly, and left alone, all alone, you insisted that I be alone to give birth. Two children. Twins. You made it impossible for me to love the children. Because of you, I struggled to raise them in grief and in silence. How could I tell them about you, tell them about their father, tell them the truth which, in this case, was a green fruit that could never ripen? So bitter. Bitter is the spoken truth. Time will pass, but you will not escape the justice that escapes us all: these children we gave birth to, you and I, are alive, they are beautiful, intelligent, sensitive, bearing their own share of victories and defeats, already seeking to give meaning to their lives, their existence … I promise you that sooner or later they will come and stand before you, in your cell, and you will be alone with them, just as I was alone with them, and like me, you will lose all sense of being alive. A rock would feel more alive than you. I speak from experience. I also promise that when they stand before you, they will both know who you are. You and I come from the same land, the same language, the same history, and each land, each language, each history is responsible for its people, and each people is responsible for their traitors and their heroes. Responsible for their executioners and their victims, for their victories and their defeats. In this sense I am responsible for you, and you are responsible for me. We didn't like war or violence, but we went to war and were violent. Now all that is left is our possible dignity. We've failed at everything, but perhaps that's one thing we still can save: dignity. Speaking to you as I am today bears witness to the promise I kept for a woman who once made me understand the importance of rising above poverty: "Learn to read, to speak, to write, to count, learn to think."

SIMON: (*reading from the red notebook*) My testimony is the result of this effort. To remain silent about your acts would make me an accomplice to your crimes.

SIMON closes the notebook.

30. RED WOLVES

SIMON and ALPHONSE LEBEL.

ALPHONSE LEBEL: What do you want to do?

SIMON: I don't know what I want to do. A brother ... What's the point?

ALPHONSE LEBEL: To know –

SIMON: I don't want to know.

ALPHONSE LEBEL: Then for Janine. She can't go on living if she doesn't know.

SIMON: But I'll never be able to find him!

ALPHONSE LEBEL: Of course you'll be able to find him! You're a boxer!

SIMON: An amateur boxer. I've never fought a professional fight.

ALPHONSE LEBEL: I'll help you, we'll go get our passports together, I'll go with you, I won't leave you alone. We'll find your brother! I'm sure of it. Maybe what you learn will help you live, will help you fight, and win, and become a professional. I believe in that kind of thing ... it's all in the cosmos. You have to have faith.

SIMON: Do you have the envelope for my brother?

ALPHONSE LEBEL: Of course! You can count on me, I swear, you can count on me. We're beginning to see the train at the end of the tunnel.

ALPHONSE exits. NAWAL (age sixty-five) is with SIMON.

NAWAL: Why are you crying, Simon?

SIMON: It feels like a wolf ... it's coming closer. He's red. And there's blood on his jaws.

NAWAL: Come now.

SIMON: Where are you taking me, Mama?

NAWAL: I need your fists to break the silence. Sarwane is your real name. Jannaane is your sister's real name. Nawal is your mother's real name. Abou Tarek is your father's name. Now you must discover your brother's name.

SIMON: My brother!

NAWAL: Your blood brother.

SIMON is left alone.

SARWANE'S FIRE

31. THE MAN WHO PLAYS

A young man on the roof of an apartment building. Alone. Walkman (1980s model) on his ears. Using a telescopic rifle in lieu of a guitar, he passionately plays the first bars of "The Logical Song" by Supertramp. NIHAD is wielding the "guitar" and shouting the instrumental opening at the top of his lungs. When the lyrics begin, his rifle becomes a microphone. His English is approximate. He sings the first verse. Suddenly, something in the distance attracts his attention. He raises his rifle and quickly takes aim while continuing to sing. He fires one shot, reloads immediately. Shoots again while changing position. Shoots again, reloads, freezes, and shoots again. NIHAD hastily grabs a camera. He aims it in the same direction, focuses, and takes a picture. He begins singing again. Suddenly he stops. He falls to the ground. He grabs his rifle and takes aim at something close by. He leaps to his feet and fires one shot. He runs towards the place he shot at. He has dropped his Walkman, which goes on playing. NIHAD comes back, dragging a wounded man by the hair. He throws him on the ground. (NIHAD and the man are speaking in French. NIHAD's French is fluent, while his English is broken.)

PHOTOGRAPHER: No! No! I don't want to die!

NIHAD: "I don't want to die!" "I don't want to die!" That's the dumbest sentence I know!

PHOTOGRAPHER: Please, let me go! I'm not from around here. I'm a photographer.

NIHAD: Photographer?

PHOTOGRAPHER: Yes ... a war photographer.

NIHAD: Did you take my picture?

PHOTOGRAPHER: I wanted a shot of a sniper ... I saw you shoot ... I came up here ... But I can give you the film ...

NIHAD: I'm a photographer, too. My name is Nihad. War photographer. Look. I took these.

NIHAD shows him photo after photo.

PHOTOGRAPHER: Very nice ...

NIHAD: No, it's not nice. People usually think it's shots of people sleeping. They're not sleeping, they're dead. And I'm the one who killed them! I swear.

PHOTOGRAPHER: I believe you.

Searching through the *PHOTOGRAPHER's* bag, *NIHAD* takes out an automatic camera equipped with a trigger cord. He looks through the viewfinder and fires off some shots of the *PHOTOGRAPHER*. He takes some heavy adhesive tape and tapes the camera to the end of his rifle.

PHOTOGRAPHER: What are you doing?

The camera is well-secured. NIHAD attaches the trigger cord to the trigger of his gun. He looks through the viewfinder and aims at the man.

Don't kill me! I could be your father, I'm the same age as your mother …

NIHAD shoots. The camera goes off at the same time. We see the photo of the PHOTOGRAPHER at the moment when the bullet hits him. NIHAD performs for the dead man. He imitates an interview on a U.S. talk show in his broken English.

NIHAD: Kirk, I very habby to be here at *Star TV Show* …

Thank you to you, Nihad. So Nihad, wath is your nesxt song?

My nesxt song will be love song.

Love song!

Yes, love song, Kirk.

This something new on you career, Nihad.

You know, I wrote this song when it was war. War on my country. Yes, one day a woman that I love die. Yes. Shooting by a sniper. I feel big crash in my hart. My hart colasp. Yes, I cry. And I write this song.

It will be pleasure to heare you love song, Nihad.

No problem, Kirk.

NIHAD stands up again, takes his pose, using his rifle as a mic. He adjusts his earphones, turns on his Walkman.

One, two, one, two, three, four!

He sings out the thirty-two drumbeats of "Roxanne" by The Police, shouting "Da, na, na, na, na …" Then he sings the song, twisting the words.

32. DESERT

ALPHONSE LEBEL and SIMON in the middle of the desert.

SIMON: There's nothing in that direction.

ALPHONSE LEBEL: But the militiaman told us to go that way.

SIMON: He could've told us to pound sand, too.

ALPHONSE LEBEL: Why would he have done that?

SIMON: Why not?

ALPHONSE LEBEL: He was very helpful. He told us to go find a man named Chamseddine, the spiritual leader of the resistance movement in the South. He told us to head that way, so we'll head that way.

SIMON: And if someone tells you to shoot yourself …

ALPHONSE LEBEL: Why would anyone tell me to do that?

SIMON: Great, so now what do we do?

ALPHONSE LEBEL: What do you want to do?

SIMON: Let's open the envelope I'm supposed to give my brother! And stop playing hide-and-go-seek.

ALPHONSE LEBEL: That's out of the question!

SIMON: What prevents me from doing it?

ALPHONSE LEBEL: Listen to me, young man, because I won't repeat it from now to Bloomsday. That envelope isn't yours. It belongs to your brother.

SIMON: Oh yeah, so what?

ALPHONSE LEBEL: Look me in the bright of the eyes! Doing that would be like raping someone!

SIMON: Well, that makes sense. I have a precedent. My father was a rapist!

ALPHONSE LEBEL: That's not what I meant.

SIMON: Okay. Fine! We won't open the goddamn envelope! But fuck! We'll never find him!

ALPHONSE LEBEL: Mr. Chamseddine?

SIMON: No, my brother.

ALPHONSE LEBEL: Why not?

SIMON: Because he's dead! I mean, for Chrissake! At the orphanage, they said in those days the militiamen kidnapped the kids to blow them up in the camps. So he's dead. We went to look in the camps and they told us about the 1978 massacres. So again, he must be dead. We went anyway to see a militiaman who came from the same orphanage and he told us he can't remember much, except for one guy like him, who had no mother, no father, who took off one day and he figures he must've died. So if I know how to count, he died blowing up like a bomb, he died with his throat slit, and he disappeared and died. That's a lot of deaths. So I think we can forget Sheik Chamseddine.

ALPHONSE LEBEL: For sure, for sure, for sure! But if we want to get to the bottom of it, the militia-man told us to go see Mr. Chamseddine, who was the spiritual leader of the resistance during the war against the army that invaded the South. He must have contacts. Those people are way up in the hierarchy. Those political types know the business. They know everything. I mean, why not? Your brother might still be alive, I mean, we can't know for sure. We found out his name, that's a start. Nihad Harmanni.

SIMON: Nihad Harmanni.

ALPHONSE LEBEL: Harmanni, right, and there are as many Harmannis as there are Tremblays in the phone book, but still, we're pretty close to finding him. Mr. Chamseddine will tell us.

SIMON: And where are we going to find Mr. Chamseddine?

ALPHONSE LEBEL: I don't know … in that direction.

SIMON: There's nothing but desert in that direction.

ALPHONSE LEBEL: That's right! Exactly! The perfect hiding place! Those people have to hide! I mean, Mr. Chamseddine, I bet he's not a member of the local video club, and he doesn't call and have them deliver Hawaiian pizzas! No, he's in hiding! Maybe he's watching us right now, so let's get a move on, and sooner or later he'll show up and ask us what we're doing on his land!

SIMON: What movie are you in?

ALPHONSE LEBEL: Please, Simon! Sarwane! Let's give it a try and maybe we'll find your brother! You never know. Maybe your brother's a notary like me. We can chat about notarized minutes and deeds. Or maybe a greengrocer, a restaurant owner, I don't know, take Trinh Xiao Feng, he was a general in the Vietnamese army, and he ended up selling hamburgers on Curé-Labelle Boulevard, and Hui Huo Xiao Feng got married again with Réal Bouchard! I mean, you never know! Maybe your brother is married to a rich American from San Diego and they have eight kids, and that makes you an uncle eight times over! Who knows. Let's get going!

They continue on their way.

33. A SNIPER'S PRINCIPLES

NIHAD, with the camera attached to the end of his rifle, is shooting. A first photo of a man on the run appears. NIHAD takes another step, shoots again. A photo of the same man, mortally wounded, appears.

NIHAD: You know, Kirk, sniper job is fantastic job.

Excellent, Nihad, can you tell us about this?

Yeah! It is very artistic job. Because good sniper don't shoot just any way, no, no!

I have lot of principles, Kirk! First, when you shot, you have to kill, immediate, for not make suffering the person.

Sure!

Second, you shoot all person. Fair and same with everyone. For me, Kirk, my gun is like my life.

You know, Kirk,

Every bullet I put in gun

Is like a poetry.

And I shoot a poetry to the people, and it is precision of my poetry that kill people and that's why my photos is fantastic.

And tell me, Nihad, you shoot everybody.

No, Kirk, no everybody …

I suppose you don't kill children.

Yes, yes, I kill children. No problem. It like pigeon, you know.

So?

I don't shoot woman like Elizabeth Taylor. Elizabeth Taylor is good actress. I like very much and I don't want kill Elizabeth Taylor. So, when I see woman like her, I no shoot her …

You don't shoot Elizabeth Taylor.

No, Kirk, sure not!

Thank you, Nihad.

Welcome, Kirk.

NIHAD stands up, aims his gun, and fires again.

34. CHAMSEDDINE

SIMON and ALPHONSE LEBEL facing CHAMSEDDINE. NAWAL (age forty-five).

ALPHONSE LEBEL: Talk about searching! We searched! Here, there, and everywhere! Mr. Chamseddine is here, Mr. Chamseddine is there, no answer. You're as famous as Shakespeare's Skylock, but you're not easy to find.

CHAMSEDDINE: Are you Sarwane?

SIMON: I am.

CHAMSEDDINE: I've been waiting for you. When I heard that your sister was in the region a while ago, I thought, "If Jannaane doesn't come to see me, Sarwane will." When I heard that the son of the woman who sings was looking for me, I knew that she had died.

NAWAL: The next time you hear about me, I will have left this world.

SIMON: I'm looking for the son she had before us. They said you could help me.

CHAMSEDDINE: I can't.

SIMON: They told me you know everyone.

CHAMSEDDINE: I don't know him.

SIMON: His name was Nihad Harmanni.

CHAMSEDDINE: Why are you talking about Nihad Harmanni?

SIMON: One of the militiamen knew him as a child. They joined the militia together, then he lost track of him. He told us, "Chamseddine must've caught him and killed him." He told us you flayed every militiaman and every foreign soldier your men caught.

CHAMSEDDINE: Did he tell you that Nihad Harmanni was the son of the woman who sings, the one born of her relationship with Wahab who no one ever laid eyes on?

SIMON: No. He didn't know anything about that. Never heard of the woman who sings. He simply said that Nihad Harmanni passed through these parts.

CHAMSEDDINE: So how can you say that he is the son of the woman who sings?

ALPHONSE LEBEL: If I may say so, I think I can explain. Alphonse Lebel, notary and executor of the estate of the woman who sings. Now, Mr. Chamseddine, I can tell it to you the way it is: all the details add up.

CHAMSEDDINE: Speak!

ALPHONSE LEBEL: A real puzzle! First we went to Madame Marwan's native village. That led us to Kfar Rayat. There, we followed some leads based on the arrival dates of several boys in the orphanage. Toni Moubarak, but it's not him, he was reunited with his parents after the war, an unpleasant character and not at all helpful. Toufic Hallabi, but it's not him either, he makes great shish taouk up north, near the Roman ruins, he doesn't come from these parts, his parents died, it was his sister who placed him in the orphanage in Kfar Rayat. We followed two other bad leads and we finally found a more serious one. This lead led us to the Harmanni family who have since passed away. The grocer told us about their adopted son. Told us his name. I went to see a colleague, Notary Halabi, very nice man who handled the Harmanni family affairs. He recorded that Roger and Souhayla Harmanni, unable to have children of their own, had adopted, on their way through Kfar Rayat, a boy they named Nihad. The child's age and the date of his arrival at the orphanage coincided perfectly with what we know about Madame Nawal. And most important of all, this boy was the only one of our candidates brought to the orphanage by the midwife from Madame Nawal's village. A certain Elhame Abdallâh. With all that, Mr. Chamseddine, we were pretty sure we were right.

CHAMSEDDINE: If the woman who sings chose to trust you, you must be noble and worthy. But step outside. Leave us alone.

ALPHONSE LEBEL exits.

CHAMSEDDINE: Sarwane, stay with me. And listen to me. Listen carefully.

35. THE VOICE OF ANCIENT TIMES

ALPHONSE LEBEL and JANINE.

ALPHONSE LEBEL: He still hasn't said a word. He stayed with Chamseddine and when he came out, Janine, your brother had the same look in his eyes as your mother. He didn't say a thing all day. Or the next day. Or the day after that. He wouldn't leave the hotel. I knew you were in Kfar Rayat. I didn't want to disturb your solitude, but Simon refuses to speak, Janine, and I'm afraid. Maybe we pushed too hard to discover the truth.

JANINE and SIMON sit facing each other.

SIMON: Janine, Janine.

JANINE: Simon!

SIMON: You always told me that one plus one equals two. Is that true?

JANINE: Yes. It's true ...

SIMON: You didn't lie to me?

JANINE: No! One plus one equals two!

SIMON: It can never be one?

JANINE: What did you find, Simon?

SIMON: Answer me! Can one plus one equal one?

JANINE: Yes.

SIMON: How?

JANINE: Simon.

SIMON: Explain it to me!

JANINE: Fuck! This is no time for math, tell me what you found out!

SIMON: Explain how one plus one can equal one! You always said I didn't understand anything. So, now's your chance. Explain!

JANINE: Okay! There's a strange hypothesis in math. A hypothesis that's never been proven. You can give me a figure, any figure. If it's an even number, you divide it by two. If it's uneven, you multiply it by three, and you add one. You do the same thing with the figure you get. This theory posits that no matter what number you start with, you'll always end up with one. Give me a figure.

SIMON: Seven.

JANINE: Okay. Seven is uneven. You multiply it by three and add one, that makes –

SIMON: Twenty-two.

JANINE: Twenty-two is even, you divide by two.

SIMON: Eleven.

JANINE: Eleven is uneven, you multiply by three, you add one –

SIMON: Thirty-four.

JANINE: Thirty-four is even. You divide by two, seventeen. Seventeen is uneven, you multiply by three, you add one, fifty-two. Fifty-two is even, you divide by two, twenty-six. Twenty-six is even, you divide by two, thirteen. Thirteen is uneven. You multiply by three and add one, forty. Forty is even. You divide by two, twenty. You divide by two, ten. Ten is even, you divide by two, five. Five is uneven, you multiply by three and add one, sixteen. Sixteen is even, you divide by two, eight, you divide by two, four, you divide by two, two, you divide by two, one. No matter what number you start with, you always end up with ... No!

SIMON: You've stopped talking. The way I stopped talking when I understood. I was in Chamseddine's tent, and in that tent I saw silence come and drown everything. Alphonse Lebel had stepped outside. Chamseddine came over to me.

CHAMSEDDINE: Sarwane, it's not mere chance that has led you to me. Your mother's spirit is here. And the spirit of Sawda. The friendship of women

like a star in the sky. One day a man approached me. He was young and proud. Try to imagine him. Can you see him? He is your brother, Nihad. He was searching for the meaning of his life. I told him to fight for me. He accepted. He learned how to use guns. A great marksman. Deadly. One day, he left. "Where are you going?" I asked him.

NIHAD: I'm headed north.

CHAMSEDDINE: And what about our cause? Fighting for the people here, the refugees? The meaning of your life?

NIHAD: No cause. No meaning!

CHAMSEDDINE: And he left. I tried to help him. I had him watched. That's when I realized he was looking for his mother. He searched for years, and never found her. He started to laugh at nothing. No more cause. No more meaning. He became a sniper. He collected photographs. Nihad Harmanni. A real reputation as an artist. He could be heard singing. A killing machine. Then the foreign army invaded the country. They came all the way north. One morning, they caught him. He had killed seven of their marksmen. He'd shot them in the eye. The bullet in their scopes. They didn't kill him. They kept him and trained him. They gave him work.

SIMON: What work?

CHAMSEDDINE: In a prison they had just built, in the South, in Kfar Rayat. They were looking for a man to take charge of the interrogations.

SIMON: So he worked with my father, Abou Tarek?

CHAMSEDDINE: No. Your brother didn't work with your father. Your brother is your father. He changed his name. He forgot Nihad and became Abou Tarek. He searched for his mother, he found her, but he didn't recognize her. She searched for her son, she found him and didn't recognize him. He didn't kill her because she sang and he liked her voice. Yes, that's right. The earth stops turning, Sarwane. Abou Tarek tortured your mother, and your mother was tortured by her son, and the son raped his mother. The son is the father of his brother and his sister. Can you hear my voice, Sarwane? It sounds like the voice of centuries past. But, no, Sarwane, it is the voice of today. The stars fell silent inside me the second you pronounced the name of Nihad Harmanni. And I can see that the stars have now fallen silent inside you, Sarwane. The silence of the stars, and your mother's silence. Inside you.

NIHAD: I don't contest anything that has been said at my trial over these past years. The people who claimed I tortured them – I did torture them. And the people I am accused of having killed – I did kill them. In fact, I would like to thank them all, because they made it possible for me to take some very beautiful photographs. The men I hit, and the women I raped, their faces were always more moving after the blow and after the rape. But essentially, what I want to say is that my trial has been tedious, boring beyond words. Not enough music. So I'm going to sing you a song. I say that because dignity has to be preserved. I'm not the one who said that, it was a woman, the one every-one called the woman who sings. Yesterday she came and stood before me and spoke of dignity. Of saving what is left of our dignity. I thought about it and I realized she was right about something. This trial has been such a bore! No beat, no sense of showbiz. That's where I find my dignity. And always have. I was born with it. The people who watched me grow up always said this object was a sign of my origins, of my dignity, since, accord-ing to the story they tell, it was given to me by my mother. A little red nose. A little clown nose. What does it mean? My personal dignity is a funny face left by the woman who gave birth to me. This funny face has never left me. So let me wear it now and sing you one of my songs, to save dignity from the horror of boredom.

He puts on the clown nose. He sings.

NAWAL (age fifteen) gives birth to NIHAD.

NAWAL (age forty-five) gives birth to JANINE and SIMON.

NAWAL (age sixty) recognizes her son.

JANINE, SIMON, and NIHAD are all together.

36. LETTER TO THE FATHER

JANINE gives the envelope to NIHAD. NIHAD opens the envelope. NAWAL (age sixty-five) reads.

NAWAL:

I am trembling as I write to you.

I would like to drill these words into your ruthless heart.

I push down on my pencil and I engrave every letter

Remembering the names of all those who died at your hands.

My letter will not surprise you.

Its only purpose is to tell you: Look:

Your daughter and your son are facing you.

The children we had together are standing before you.

What will you say to them? Will you sing them a song?

They know who you are.

Jannaane and Sarwane.

The daughter and the son of the torturer, children born of horror.

Look at them.

This letter was delivered by your daughter.

Through her, I want to tell you that you are still alive.

Soon you will stop talking.

I know this.

Silence awaits everyone in the face of truth.

The woman who sings.

Whore number 72.

Cell number 7.

In the Kfar Rayat Prison.

NIHAD finishes reading the letter. He looks at JANINE and SIMON. He tears up the letter.

37. LETTER TO THE SON

SIMON hands his envelope to NIHAD, who opens it.

NAWAL:

I looked for you everywhere.

Here, there, and everywhere.

I searched for you in the rain.

I searched for you in the sun.

In the forest

In the valleys

On the mountaintops

In the darkest of cities

In the darkest of streets

I searched for you in the south

In the north

In the east

In the west

I searched for you while digging in the earth to bury my friends

I searched for you while looking at the sky

I searched for you amidst a flock of birds

For you were a bird.

And what is more beautiful than a bird,

The fiery flight of a bird in the sunlight?

What is more alone than a bird,

Than a bird alone amidst the storm clouds,

Winging its strange destiny to the end of day?

For an instant, you were horror.

For an instant, you have become happiness.

Horror and happiness.

The silence in my throat.

Do you doubt?

Let me tell you.

You stood up

And you took out that little clown nose.

And my memory exploded.

Don't be afraid.

Don't catch cold.

These are ancient words that come from my deepest memories.

Words I often whispered to you.

In my cell,

I told you about your father.

I told you about his face,

I told you about the promise I made the day of your birth:

No matter what happens, I will always love you.

No matter what happens, I will always love you.

Without realizing that in that very instant, you and I were sharing our defeat.

Because I hated you with all my being.

But where there is love, there can be no hatred.

And to preserve love, I blindly chose not to speak.

A she-wolf always defends her young.

You are facing Janine and Simon.

Your sister and your brother

And since you are a child of love

They are the brother and sister of love.

Listen

I am writing this letter in the cool evening air.

This letter will tell you that the woman who sings was your mother

Perhaps you too will stop talking.

So be patient.

I am speaking to the son, I am not speaking to the torturer.

Be patient.

Beyond silence,

There is the happiness of being together.

Nothing is more beautiful than being together.

Those were your father's last words.

Your mother.

NIHAD finishes reading the letter. He stands. JANINE and SIMON stand and face him. JANINE tears up every page in her notebook.

38. LETTER TO THE TWINS

ALPHONSE LEBEL is holding a third envelope, addressed to the twins.

ALPHONSE LEBEL: The sky is overcast. It's going to rain, for sure, for sure, for sure. Shouldn't we go home? Mind you, I understand how you feel. If I were you, I wouldn't go home. This is a beautiful park ... In her will your mother left a letter to be given to the two of you, if you fulfilled her wishes. And you have more than fulfilled them. It's going to rain. In her country it never rains. We'll stay here. It will cool us off. Here's the letter.

SIMON opens the letter.

NAWAL:

Simon,

Are you crying?

If you are crying, don't dry your tears

Because I don't dry mine.

Childhood is a knife stuck in the throat

And you managed to remove it.

Now you must learn to swallow your saliva again.

Sometimes that is a very courageous act.

Swallowing your saliva.

Now, history must be reconstructed.

History is in ruins.

Gently

Console every shred

Gently

Cure every moment

Gently

Rock every image.

Janine,

Are you smiling?

If you are smiling, don't stifle your laughter.

Because I don't stifle mine.

It's the laughter of rage

That of women walking side by side

I would have named you Sawda.

But this name remains, in its spelling

In every one of its letters,

An open wound in my heart.

Smile, Janine, smile

We

Our family

The women in our family are trapped in anger.

I was angry with my mother

Just as you are angry with me

And just as my mother was angry with her mother.

We have to break the thread.

Janine, Simon,

Where does your story begin?

At your birth?

Then it begins in horror.

At your father's birth?

Then it is a beautiful love story.

But if we go back farther,

Perhaps we will discover that this love story

Has roots in violence and rape,

And that in turn,

The brute and the rapist

Had his origin in love.

So,

When they ask you to tell your story,

Tell them that your story

Goes back to the day when a young girl went back to her native village to engrave her grandmother's name

Nazira on her gravestone.

That is where the story begins.

Janine, Simon,

Why didn't I tell you?

There are truths that can only be revealed when they have been discovered.

You opened the envelope, you broke the silence

Engrave my name on the stone

And place the stone on my grave.

Your mother.

SIMON: Janine, let me hear her silence.

JANINE and *SIMON* listen to their mother's silence.

Torrential rain.

END

MARCUS
YOUSSEF

(b. 1969)

GUILLERMO
VERDECCHIA

(b. 1962)

CAMYAR
CHAI

(b. 1968)

It could be argued that the twenty-first century really began for North Americans not on January 1, 2000, but on September 11, 2001. The so-called War on Terror, the wars in Iraq and Afghanistan, rendition and torture, the development of elaborate security apparatuses at borders and airports, and increased ethno-religious paranoia have been among the most dramatic consequences. Of course, Canadians experienced that watershed moment and its aftermath differently than Americans. Canada was not directly attacked on 9/11. And Canada remained on the sidelines when Prime Minister Jean Chrétien refused to join President George W. Bush's "Coalition of the Willing" in the U.S.–led 2003 invasion of Iraq and its subsequent disastrous occupation. Yet, like so many other such critical moments in the history of Canadian-American relations, Canada has been deeply implicated in the post-9/11 politics, policies, and experiences of the nation with which we share what used to be called the world's longest undefended border.

The Adventures of Ali & Ali and the aXes of Evil takes place on a figurative border where Canada and the United States intersect with what Mexican performance artist Guillermo Gómez-Peña, in his book The New World Border, terms the Fourth World: "a conceptual place where the indigenous inhabitants of the Americas meet with the deterritorialized peoples, the immigrants, and the exiles." The Canadian authors of Ali & Ali, with their distinctly non-Anglo-Saxon names, examine the experience of exile and deterritorialization from a unique Fourth World vantage point, asking hard questions about the post-9/11 Canadian imaginary: how and what do we imagine ourselves to be, and whom do we imagine when we (as I have done so carelessly throughout this introduction) use the pronoun "we"? Ali & Ali is smart, radically self-conscious Canadian political theatre, a metatheatrical transnational agitprop comedy that Seattle critic Joe Adcock called troubling, poignant, and "the funniest exposition of American foreign policy ever devised."

The play is a product of three individual playwrights, two companies, and their collective synergies. Born in Iran, Camyar Chai (a.k.a. Chaichian) came to Vancouver as an adolescent and founded Neworld Theatre in 1993 while completing a B.F.A. in acting at the University of British Columbia. He wrote and produced a number of Persian-themed plays over the next decade; and with Guillermo Verdecchia as dramaturg, he wrote and performed *I Am Your Spy* (2000), a play about nuclear scientist Mordechai Vanunu, imprisoned for revealing Israel's nuclear arsenal. Montreal-born Marcus Youssef, son of an American mother and Egyptian father, landed in Vancouver in 1992 after graduating from the National Theatre School. Verdecchia, born in Argentina and raised in Ontario, joined them in 1994 after studying theatre at Ryerson and establishing himself as a Chalmers and Governor General's Award–winning playwright and actor in Toronto, most notably with *The Noam Chomsky Lectures* (with Daniel Brooks, 1990) and *Fronteras Americanas* (1993), funny, seriously political, imaginatively metatheatrical plays. *Chomsky* asserts that "the real Canadian traditions are quiet complicity and hypocritical moral posturing," while the autobiographical *Fronteras* explores the complexities of negotiating cultural stereotypes and "learning to live the border" as a hyphenated Canadian.

In 1995, the three collaborated on *True Lies*, a play about video surveillance, and *A Line in the Sand*, which reimagines the torture and murder of a Somali boy by Canadian soldiers. Both were produced in Vancouver and Toronto (*A Line in the Sand* winning a Chalmers Award), co-written by Verdecchia and Youssef, directed by Verdecchia, with Chai in both casts. Returning to Toronto, Verdecchia became artistic director of Cahoots Theatre Projects (1998–2003), and in 2004 the three co-wrote *The Adventures of Ali & Ali and the aXes of Evil*, co-produced by Neworld and Cahoots, directed by Verdecchia, and performed by Youssef and Chai in Vancouver, Toronto, Montreal, Edmonton, and Seattle. In 2009, the same credits appeared on a sequel, *Ali & Ali 7: Hey Brother, Can You Spare Some Hope and Change?* The title changed to *Ali & Ali: The Deportation Hearings* for its 2010 Toronto production.

Verdecchia remains a major figure in Toronto theatre. He directed Rahul Varma's *Bhopal* (2003) for Cahoots and Sunil Kuruvilla's *Rice Boy* at the Stratford Festival (2009), and became an artistic associate of Soulpepper Theatre for which he reprised *Fronteras Americanas* (2011) while working on his Ph.D. in theatre at University of Guelph. His play *bloom* (2006) looks at wars around the world, based on T.S. Eliot's *The Wasteland*. Chai earned his M.F.A. in directing from UBC (2007), wrote the libretto for *Elijah's Kite* (2008), an opera for young audiences, acted in TV and film, and continued to run Neworld for another few years. Youssef, with an M.F.A. in creative writing from UBC (2001), has worked as a freelance writer, actor, and college instructor. While artistic director of Neworld since 2005, he has been involved in some of Vancouver theatre's most compelling projects: co-writing *Peter Panties* (2011), an adaptation of *Peter Pan*, with

Niall McNeil, a performer with Down Syndrome; co-writing, performing, and touring *Winners and Losers* (2012), a semi-autobiographical two-hander with Theatre Replacement's James Long; writing and performing with his son Zak, *How Has My Love Affected You?* (2013), an autobiographical play about his relationship with his mother.

In 2005, Youssef and Chai wrote *Adrift*, directed by Chai, adapted from an Egyptian novel by Naguib Mahfouz. It premiered at the Magnetic North Festival in St. John's and won the Alcan Performing Arts Award in Vancouver. In their program note for the 2007 Vancouver production they wrote, "we believe it is important for those of us with roots in both the West and Middle East to try to find ways for those different histories and cultures to speak to – and through – each other." Neworld and Cahoots echo similar sentiments on their websites. "Neworld productions investigate borders between cultures, styles, and disciplines ... We create plays and performances that are about 'here' (Canada) and 'there' (other parts of the world) and 'us' (people we identify with) and 'them' (people we are told are different from us)." Cahoots "investigate[s] the complexities of Canada's cultural diversity, and examine[s] the intersections of these cultures ... Our work questions, challenges and transforms our notions of contemporary Canadian life, and explores our evolving connection to the world around us."

In the wake of the 9/11 attacks, racial profiling of men with brown skin and Middle Eastern names was rampant. Invited by Vancouver's CBC Radio to provide multicultural commentaries on their post-9/11 experiences, Youssef and Chai wrote a series of short, satirical radio sketches which they performed in the guise of refugees Ali and Ali. Following the invasion of Iraq, they and Verdecchia expanded the skits into the full-length stage play in which Ali Hakim and Ali Ababwa, stateless refugees from the fictional Middle Eastern country of Agraba (a synthesis of Iraq, Egypt, and Iran, with a touch of Uzbekistan thrown into the mix), are seeking asylum in Canada.

The cartoon home of Disney's Aladdin is called Agrabah, and Ali Hakim is the name of a stage-ethnic character in the musical, *Oklahoma!* Very conscious of the ways media and popular culture – theatre included – help construct images of ethnic and racial Otherness, the playwrights themselves utilize pop music, video, TV-style infomercials, and a Hollywood film scenario, not to mention PowerPoint and the hilariously obscene Classical Puppet Theatre of Agraba, to score their own political points. All this is contained within the larger metatheatrical structure of the cabaret that Ali and Ali put on to persuade the Canadian audience – "the good people of Real Life Canada" – to help them become, as Ali Hakim says, "real like you. Prosperous like you. Legal like you." Their arguments with the Scottish-Canadian theatre manager, the ethnic Canadian father-son scenes-within-the-play that they perform, the conflation of American and Canadian media coverage (CBCNN), and even Tim / Tom's film demo reel all contribute to the play's examination and critique of Canadian culture and the ways performance itself may exacerbate problems rather than help create solutions.

The play presents a brutally funny attack on the stupidities and absurdities of George W. Bush and his brain trust, their obsession with coded security levels (Double Double, Boot Cut), weapons of mass destruction, and the Axis (or aXes) of Evil. Osama Bin Laden appears onstage "rant[ing] in fundamentalist gibberish," but also allowing the playwrights to educate their audience about the American military-industrial public relations complex. And to mock it, along with Canadian theatre's propensity for corporate sponsorships. Nothing in this play is sacred, not even religion. Consider the description of Agraba's Sammi sect of Islam. And no one of any ethnicity is spared. The Alis themselves, their security expert Dr. Mohandes, Duncan, and Tom are all ridiculous characters. But the play has its serious moments when anger and desperation break through, when Ali Hakim drops his clown mask to attack the audience or when we learn of his pregnant wife's languishing without papers in a Maltese detention camp. The real pain of statelessness and exile never lies far from the surface.

Because of its topicality, *Ali & Ali* has evolved, often in typically fearless ways, to keep up with current events and address specific audiences. So the script reproduced here – its most up-to-date incarnation – is only one particular version of the play. For its 2007 remount the playwrights substituted Barack Obama, then a contender in the Democratic Presidential primary, for Donald Rumsfeld in the (very brief, silhouetted) masturbation scene, screaming, "Debate this, Hillary!!!" They added references to the latest conflict in Lebanon, evangelist Jerry Falwell's death, and the New Orleans flood. They cut a video segment of Verdecchia parodying arcane French critical theory, and added the video clip of Jesus in diapers in response to the controversy over satirical Danish cartoons of Mohammed. For the Seattle production they substituted "United Statesian" for "Canadian" and replaced references to CBC newsman Ian Hanomansing with CNN's Sanjay Gupta. And they changed the ending a number of times. This version's ending imagines a utopian Agraba, transformed and reborn in a dream – then blown up. Political theatre like this must be able to dream of a transformative future. But these guys know that dreams are not enough.

The Adventures of Ali & Ali and the aXes of Evil
A Divertimento for Warlords

Marcus Youssef,
Guillermo Verdecchia,
and Camyar Chai

The Adventures of Ali & Ali and the aXes of Evil was co-developed and co-produced by Neworld Theatre and Cahoots Theatre Projects. It premiered on February 13, 2004, at the Vancouver East Cultural Centre with the following cast:

ALI HAKIM /
DR. MOHANDES PANIR ALI ZIA   Camyar Chai
ALI ABABWA   Marcus Youssef
TIM / DUNCAN / OSAMA   Tom Butler
JEAN PAUL JACQUES BEAUDERRIÈREDADA
          Guillermo Verdecchia

Directed by Guillermo Verdecchia
Set and Costume Design by Marina Szijarto
Lighting Design by Sharon Huizinga
Music and Sound Design by Alejandro Verdecchia
Props Design by Rob Lewis
Signs, Graphics, and Pillowcases by Richard Lawley
Video by Andrew Laurenson
Stage Managed by David Kerr

CHARACTERS

ALI ABABWA, *stateless refugee from Agraba; a Copt*

ALI HAKIM, *stateless refugee from Agraba; a Sammi*

DR. MOHANDES PANIR ALI ZIA, *security expert (on video screen only)*

TIM, *Ali & Ali's servant*

DUNCAN, *Scottish-Canadian theatre manager*

OSAMA BIN LADEN

SETTING

The stage is more or less bare. The rear wall is a vaguely tent-like structure onto which video is projected throughout. There is a worn carpet centre stage and some laundry (socks, some underwear) drying on the set.

Music expressing the happiness of brown people in liberated zones plays as the audience enters and passes through the Ali and Ali security apparatus.[1]

Totally funky, vaguely Arabic-Persian-Indo-world-fusion-cuisine music kicks in. The sound of a crowd roaring rises and falls. It could be a rock concert.

VOICEOVER: You've heard the rumours: fresh from their sold-out tour of East Monrovia and the jungle encampments of Congolese bauxite smugglers ... on their way to the unacknowledged detention centres of Axerbaijan ... They're here, they're live, and they've got a Korean! Are you ready, Mogadishu? Butt out your cigars and wipe the buckets of sweat from your really black black brows, put your stumps and prostheses together and give a GREAT BIG CLASH OF CIVILIZATIONS WELCOME TO ALI AND ALI!

ALI & ALI enter.

ALI ABABWA: We know you're not Somalia.

ALI HAKIM: We know where we are.

---

1   Pre-show videos used over the course of multiple productions included John Ashcroft, Attorney General of the United States of America, singing his original composition, "Let the Eagle Soar"; George W. Bush and Tony Blair singing Diana Ross and Lionel Richie's "Endless Love" (by Johan Söderberg) and/or "Gay Bar" (by Electric Six). You can Google them.

ALI ABABWA: We had a little trouble at the border.

ALI HAKIM: No time to redo intro.

ALI ABABWA: And we know how much you were looking forward to see us perform with a real-life Korean, as advertised in the intro, but we don't have one.

ALI HAKIM: Friday Kim Chee. We lost him in Mogadishu.

They make the Agrabanian "Piña Majorca" gesture (lightly touching the forehead, then looking up and raising hands as if to ward off something falling from above) to acknowledge his passing.

ALI HAKIM: He had a "fishing" accident.

ALI ABABWA: In Mogadishu.

ALI HAKIM: One must be so careful with the daughter of a heavily armed ... warlord.

ALI ABABWA: So we had to hire a new guy.

ALI HAKIM: Come.

TIM enters.

ALI ABABWA: Off!

TIM exits.

ALI HAKIM: And now the show –

ALI ABABWA: But Holy Hummus did they love us in Mogadishu, huh? What a show. They were falling in the aisles, hooting and screaming, killing themselves. Ali Hakim told this joke –

ALI HAKIM: Ali Ababwa, let us do –

ALI ABABWA: No, seriously. It was great. You're so funny. In Agraba, he was big star. Hey! You should tell them the joke.

ALI HAKIM: Not now. I don't think this is the sort of aud- –

ALI ABABWA: Fine, I'll tell it. I'll mess it all up. Okay, so, this fat guy walks into the Arctic, he's Italian –

ALI HAKIM: No no no! Stop! You're ruining it.

ALI HAKIM reluctantly finishes the joke.

So. There is – this pisshole ... in the desert. And there is a warlord taking a piss. Suddenly, a small white man – yay high – with red hair, comes, stand beside warlord, also taking piss. Warlord, who surprisingly for black man has small penis, looks over and notices that small man – yay

high – has large penis. Yay big. Warlord say, "How is it that small white man like you have so large a penis?" Small man say, "Easy lad. I'm a leprechaun. I wished it upon myself." Warlord say, "Can you wish one of these upon me?" Leprechaun say, "Sure, lad. But I'd have to have me way wid ya first." Warlord does not like this idea but imagines the many beautiful women that he could have with his new, much larger penis and so he agrees. Warlord bend over. Leprechaun climbs on top and begins business.

"So, what's your name, lad?"

"Abdul."

"Tell me, Abdul, what do you do for a living?"

"I am a warlord."

"And how old are you, Abdul?"

"I'm forty-four."

"Well, Abdul the Warlord, isn't that a bit old to be believin' in leprechauns?"

ALI ABABWA bursts into hysterics.

ALI ABABWA: Come on – that's funny! Laugh! Okay. If you didn't like that, you should leave now because it's only going to get worse. I see. No warlords in this audience tonight, no! This is a refined –

Sirens go off. Lights flash. TIM runs around, scared.

Ladies and gentlemen, please do not be alarmed.

The video screen flickers and comes to life. MOHANDES appears on the screen. He is in full security guard garb. A box of Tim Hortons Timbits is displayed prominently in the frame.

MOHANDES: Attention, theatregoers! Attention, theatregoers! I regret to inform you that the risk of a violent attack has increased considerably since these two gentlemen entered the stage.

ALI HAKIM: Ali and Ali Security Expert.

ALI ABABWA: Mr. Zia.

MOHANDES: No, say my full name. I am Dr. Mohandes Panir Ali Zia Gandhinehrukhomeinijinnah.

ALI HAKIM: Doctor, what exactly is the level of threat?

MOHANDES: The level of threat is determined by up-to-date information gathered by me, Dr. Mohandes Panir Ali Zia Gandhinehrukhomeinijinnah.

ALI ABABWA: Yes yes, we know.

MOHANDES: These threat assessments are, of course, code-named for maximum clarity. Based on the latest top-secret information, the security threat is now … Boot Cut.

ALI ABABWA: Boot Cut?

MOHANDES: Yes. This level of the Mohandes Panir Threat Level Assessment System is now proudly brought to you by the Gap.

ALI HAKIM: The Gap?

MOHANDES: The Corporate Relations Adviser seemed most enthusiastic to nurture relationship with someone of my accent.

ALI ABABWA: But doesn't the Gap subcontract to filthy factories in lawless free-trade zones?

MOHANDES: Don't be cheeky, Bangalore Breath! We are facing a Boot Cut Risk of Terrorist Attacks!

MOHANDES reveals his security level chart.

As you can see, The Mohandes Panir Security System includes five levels of security risk: Decaf, Double Double, Very High, Boot Cut, and Extremely High. I am now test-marketing a new sixth threat level.

ALI ABABWA: But what security level could be higher than extremely high?

MOHANDES: I'm thinking: You-and-All-Your-Loved-Ones-Are-Going-to-Fucking-Die-ANY-FUCKING-MOMENT! Level. My extensive research proves that people who are bored are far more likely to commit terrorist atrocities. This, of course, is why so many terrorist attacks occur in the theatre. But mine is not the realm of politics (or aesthetics) my friend. I am here to provide security, not evaluate the righteousness of a cause.

ALI HAKIM: And we are grateful to have you.

MOHANDES: Yes. Fortunately for you, I have just deployed my most recent innovative invention, the Dr. Mohandes Panir Panopticon. Knowledge Is Power, my friends. Be on your guards. Trust no one. Watch your backs. Eat Timbits. Dr. Mohandes Panir Ali Zia Gandhinehrukhomeinijinnah, Head of Ali and Ali Security. Over and out.

Video screen goes black.

ALI HAKIM: Dr. Mohandes is former employee of Agraba's airport, Jafar Ali International.

ALI ABABWA: Head of Security, Domestic Departures, Left-Hand Side Metal Detector.

ALI HAKIM: We have brought him to protect you from terrorist attack.

ALI ABABWA: Not to mention the aXes of Evil –

ALI HAKIM: Oh please. Do not burden sophisticated Western audience with this superstitious and primitive mumbolo-jumbolo.

ALI ABABWA: Mumbolo-jumbolo?

ALI HAKIM: Shut up.

ALI ABABWA: What about the death of our Korean, Friday Kim Chee? Or the premature and inexplicable death of former U.S. President Ronald Reagan?[2] The signs are everywhere.

ALI HAKIM: Pah! Peoples, please feel safe. You are completely cared for. Nothing can happen to you as we have sealed all the exits.

ALI ABABWA: And finally, if anyone is here a doctor, perhaps he or she could look at my bum?

ALI HAKIM: You donkey, the good people of Real Life Canada do not want to know about your bum.

ALI ABABWA: Hath not an Agrabanian eyes, organs, senses, dimensions, afflictions, a bum …?

ALI HAKIM: What is wrong with your bum now? Is it gas?

ALI ABABWA: I don't know. It hurts. Please, Ali Hakim, take a look.

ALI HAKIM: People in Real Life Canada, please small moment.

ALI HAKIM takes ALI ABABWA aside.

You fool of a Copt, I have told you: do like the Sammis. Use hand-and-water technique. But you rub and rub and scrape your delicate pink asshole with harsh papers. It is small wonder.

Back to the audience.

But NOW … the show. Please, ladies and gentlemen, sit back, relax, and enjoy.

MUSIC:

"Gonna Build a Mountain" by Sammy Davis Jr.

The lights shift to something snazzy. ALI & ALI briefly "jazz" dance.

---

2   Or relevant, topical absurdity. For a subsequent tour, we used "the proposed *Exorcist* theme park in Iraq," for example.

ALI ABABWA & ALI HAKIM: Shazzam Hassan al-muta!

Hello, People in Real Life Canada!

ALI HAKIM: Do Not Be Afraid!

ALI ABABWA: And thank you for coming to Vancouver East Church Basement.[3]

ALI HAKIM: I am Ali Hakim.

ALI ABABWA: And I'm not.

ALI ABABWA & ALI HAKIM: Here are our papers.

ALI ABABWA: We are stateless refugees.

ALI HAKIM: From Agraba.

ALI ABABWA: You know, Agraba?

ALI HAKIM: Land of the clamstones, the Sammis, Kreskin's assistant?

ALI ABABWA: Agronium-rich republic poking into Sea of Agraba?

ALI HAKIM: We are come

ALI ABABWA: to explain.

ALI HAKIM: To spread peace and goodwill, win hearts and minds.

ALI ABABWA: Maybe get married. I am single and in search of wife. Hello ... Hi.

ALI HAKIM: To build bridges, mend fences.

ALI ABABWA: Mow lawns?

ALI HAKIM: Rebuild trust between our peoples.

ALI ABABWA: Maybe stay a little while?

ALI HAKIM: You see, we wish nothing more than to be real like you. Prosperous like you. Legal like you. But, as we say in Agraba, the littlest camel does not make the biggest ... how you say ... poo?

ALI ABABWA: Or most effective refugee application.

ALI HAKIM: You can dream big but start small. And so with seed money from the United Furniture Warehouse of Nations we are proud to bring to you

ALI ABABWA: and the people of Mogadishu, Bosnia, the Congo, Liberia, Senegal, Gaza Strip, and South Surrey–White Rock[4]

ALI HAKIM: our show:

---

3   This was a site-specific reference for the Vancouver East Cultural Centre. In Toronto, at Theatre Passe Muraille, we said, "Thank you for coming to Theatre Past Its Prime." In Montreal, Seattle, and Edmonton, something else.

4   Another site-specific reference. In Toronto, we said Rose-dale. In Montreal, Verdun–West Island. In Edmonton, Sherwood Park. People love that shtick.

ALI ABABWA & ALI HAKIM: *World Dreaming Together.* Starring Don –

TIM: Tom.

ALI ABABWA & ALI HAKIM: Tim ... Butler!

They sing.

"THE WORLD DREAMING TOGETHER SONG"

From the towers of Calcutta
To the sewers of U.S.A.
To all the men and women
And yes, even the gay
From the old man who lost his nutter
To the child allergic to peanut butter
From the clamstone diver in the sea
To you and you and me

This is the World Dreaming Together Show
We are hoping for a sunny day with lovely weather throughout the week
A great big chickpea we're baking
To feed the soul of everyone
Do they know it's dreaming together time right now?
Do they know it's dreaming together time right now?

Overcome with emotion, they embrace.

ALI HAKIM: Pretty good so long, huh?

ALI ABABWA: You must forgive our English; is not always 100 per cent. Fortunately, we have technology. VoxTec Phraseolator. Very nice. Is "machine translator" used by Americans to communicate with liberated civilians in occupied zones.

A demonstration. Let us say we wished to discuss the complexities of contemporary geopolitics, perhaps the impact of holding oil reserves in euros instead of dollars. We simply type in the Agrabanian and ... jumping jinnis, here comes the translation:

ALI HAKIM types. The machine responds.

PHRASEOLATOR (*voiceover*): PUT DOWN THE GOAT!

ALI ABABWA: You see? Excellent tool for trans-cultural negotiations.

ALI HAKIM: Tim?!

TIM enters.

Take this away.

He follows TIM off, blaming him for the phraseolator's malfunction.

ALI ABABWA: Yes, friends, here at Ali and Ali we make every effort to communicate with you in ways to which you are culturally accustomed and so provide many opportunities to purchase merchandise and commemorative memorabilia like *this* ...

PROJECTION:

A commemorative plate

... authentic "Royal Doulton" plate.

Interested in franchise, investment, or sponsorship opportunities? Please check our website – www dot

ALI HAKIM ululates.[5]

dot com. As graduates of the Agrabanian Institute of Niche Marketing, Cross-Pollinization, and Higher Colonics, we understand how to synergize our product to extract full value in the post-deal phase.

ALI HAKIM: But don't worry. We will not be harassing you.

ALI ABABWA: Or involving you in the show.

A big light shines on a portion of the audience.

ALI HAKIM: Or shining a big light on you.

ALI ABABWA: Or singling you out.

ALI HAKIM: Or in any way embarrassing you like in stupid clown shows.

ALI ABABWA: NO.

The audience light fades.

ALI HAKIM: Whew. That sure made me hungry. (*to ALI ABABWA*) Did you speak to manager? No? I wish I had a pizza. Oh, pizza. I love pizza. (*to audience*) You like pizza? You do? Great.

He enters the audience and addresses one person in particular.

Give me twenty dollars and we get pizza. Come on. Give me twenty dollars. I thought you said

5   The crazy-ass tongue-wailing that Arab types do in moments of emotional intensity.

you like pizza. (*He improvises, depending on audience response.*) How 'bout you put it on gold card. You get points; I get pizza. What, you ate before the show? Must be nice.

He returns to stage.

They think nobody else needs to eat.

ALI ABABWA: Now before we go any further, any peoples who are with Immigration Department, please please identify yourselves to us after the show; we have special packages for you.

ALI HAKIM: Nothing big.

ALI ABABWA: Humble really. Just a way for us to say we really really appreciate anything you can do to keep us from going back to miserable stink hole detention centre in Axerbaijan. (*sotto voce*) Ali Hakim!

ALI ABABWA gestures to back of the audience.

Is that him?

ALI HAKIM looks to where ALI ABABWA indicated.

ALI HAKIM: Oh my Sammi!

Ladies and gentlemen: We are tickled pink to announce that tonight in the audience we are blessed with presence of major Canadian media personality, host of *Canada Now* on CBCNN, and our hero ...

ALI ABABWA & ALI HAKIM: Ian Handsomemanthing!

They dance lewdly to sexy music.

PROJECTION:

A snazzy promotional photo of Ian Hanomansing.

They ululate and do a brief tribal dance.

ALI ABABWA: I knew you would come, Ian!

ALI HAKIM: Holy Hookahs, you are big cheese in Agraba.

ALI ABABWA: That face. Look at your face. And your skin! Rich brown nuttiness.

ALI HAKIM: We are very great admirers of you, Successful Brown Person, and have a proposition for you! Perhaps you are looking to make lateral move in world of entertainment, from handsome brown anchor to handsome brown actor?

ALI ABABWA: We propose a modest proposal of interest to you and all entertainment industry peoples here tonight. We at Ali and Ali have idea for movie vehicle.

ALI HAKIM: It's an action movie.

ALI ABABWA: An epic.

ALI HAKIM: A love story.

ALI ABABWA: A quiet drama of personal fortitude.

ALI HAKIM: The movie opens. No credits.

ALI ABABWA: Some bad motherfuckers come to town, yes?

ALI HAKIM: Some of the worst motherfuckers.

ALI ABABWA: They're dirty.

ALI HAKIM: They have greasy hair.

ALI ABABWA: Ugly clothes from Walmart.

ALI HAKIM: They're dark.

ALI ABABWA: With a dark purpose.

ALI HAKIM: Swarthy.

ALI ABABWA: Greasy hair.

ALI HAKIM: Their underarms are pungent.

ALI ABABWA: They're religious.

ALI HAKIM: Fanatics.

ALI ABABWA & ALI HAKIM: SO.

ALI ABABWA: They come to town, these very bad men.

ALI HAKIM: Any town.

ALI ABABWA: Hometown.

ALI HAKIM: Your town.

ALI ABABWA: For what purpose we do not yet know.

ALI HAKIM: We know only they are fanatics.

ALI ABABWA: Because they are always praying and muttering and looking sideways out of their squinty suspicious eyes with jealousy and envy at the material wealth and FREEDOM the people of Hometown enjoy which the bad men call decadence but secretly LONG FOR. They go to a STRIP BAR.

ALI HAKIM: Sick disgusting pigs; they do not tip after the lap dance.

ALI ABABWA: And the next day in a devastating act of criminal monumentality they kill themselves somehow and kill many many tender sweet innocent people who have children or pets or are children or pets themselves.

ALI HAKIM: Sick.

ALI ABABWA: People are understandably upset.

ALI HAKIM: They weep.

ALI ABABWA: They search for their loved ones among the rubbles.

ALI HAKIM: Calling out the names. Sally!

ALI ABABWA: Tercel!

ALI HAKIM: Atanarjuat!

ALI ABABWA: They cry out:

ALI HAKIM: Who has done this?

ALI ABABWA: Who is responsible?

ALI HAKIM: Smash cut to

ALI ABABWA: your boys.

ALI HAKIM: Good boys.

ALI ABABWA: And some girls, too.

ALI HAKIM: In they come.

ALI ABABWA: They do not want revenge.

ALI HAKIM: No. They want justice.

ALI ABABWA: They want to liberate people of small dusty country that had absolutely nothing to do with the unspeakable crime we just saw, a few minutes ago in the movie.

ALI HAKIM: They have no quarrel with PEOPLE of small dust country.

ALI ABABWA: No.

ALI HAKIM: Therefore, they kill by the dozens.

ALI ABABWA: The hundreds.

ALI ABABWA: The thousands. Tanks crush houses.

ALI ABABWA: Dusty brainwashed people rush to defend their city.

ALI HAKIM: Some of them are burned alive. Or mangled by machine-gun fire.

ALI ABABWA: In broken-down alleys they fight hand to hand.

ALI HAKIM: A mouthful of dusty teeth meet the butt of a rifle.

ALI ABABWA: Gums bleed.

ALI HAKIM: Eyes pop.

ALI ABABWA & ALI HAKIM: Women scream.

ALI ABABWA: The bodies and pieces pile up.

ALI HAKIM: Here a leg.

ALI ABABWA: There an arm.

ALI HAKIM: Everywhere a dead man.

ALI ABABWA: And then your boys surrounded by the dead and dying villagers, call the remaining people of small dusty country together

ALI HAKIM: and your boys give the peoples bottles of water.

ALI ABABWA: And the skies open up and it rains –

ALI HAKIM: think *Black Hawk Down* meets *Singing in the Rain* –

ALI ABABWA: it rains Pop-Tarts!

ALI HAKIM: We push in close to the face of a small dusty old woman.

Poignant violin music sneaks in.

ALI ABABWA: Her face is worn.

ALI HAKIM: Sorrowful.

ALI ABABWA: She looks at the bottle of water in one hand and the Pop-Tarts in the other,

ALI HAKIM: and then at the soldier –

ALI ABABWA: this is you, Ian –

ALI HAKIM: nicely backlit by the setting sun –

ALI ABABWA: and her eyes fill with tears

ALI HAKIM: of thankfulness,

ALI ABABWA: of wonder.

ALI HAKIM: She understands.

ALI ABABWA: This is no ordinary war. These are not soldiers such as they know from before.

Act Two: In the city there is a boy, Ali.

ALI HAKIM: He cares nothing for politics or this or that.

ALI ABABWA: No.

ALI HAKIM: He cares only for football.

ALI ABABWA: Soccer, as you say.

ALI HAKIM: This boy plays in the dusty alleys with other boys using a ball made of rags from his older brothers' shirts.

ALI ABABWA: But this boy, playing soccer, does not notice

ALI HAKIM: the anti-personnel land mine

ALI ABABWA: that has been left behind by your boys –

ALI HAKIM: good boys! –

ALI ABABWA: and so on.

ALI HAKIM: Ali loses his legs and arms and some of his face and –

ALI ABABWA: Enough! Ali lies in a hospital bed.

ALI HAKIM: He has an indomitable spirit.

ALI ABABWA: And your boys are beside themselves when they find out what has happened to Ali for they used to watch him playing with his friends and marvel at his speed and grace and agility. They go to see Ali in the hospital. One of your boys weeps –

ALI HAKIM: this is you, Ian –

ALI ABABWA: "This damned war."

ALI HAKIM: But Ali is not angry. He is peaceful.

ALI ABABWA: For he has seen how your boys have already transformed his country; how his friends, the urchins of the streets, are happier, even though their schools are destroyed and they have no running water and their parents are being sexually tortured in the prisons of the former dictator.

ALI HAKIM: As Ali lies in his hospital cot he speaks of soccer and his hero, the great English metrosexual soccer player, David Bendham, and how he dreamed of one day playing against Bendham and, of course, losing but that would be okay because after the game he would trade shirts with Bendham, having won his respect, having played so valiantly.

ALI ABABWA: SO,

ALI HAKIM: your boys climb in a Jeep

ALI ABABWA: and set off hundreds of kilometres

ALI HAKIM: across dangerous territory

ALI ABABWA: where surely they will encounter pockets of fierce resistance

ALI HAKIM: to find the British soldiers.

ALI ABABWA: And when the British soldiers hear the story of Ali they give your boys Bendham's shirt.

ALI HAKIM: And when your boys set off again

ALI ABABWA: one of the Brits is heard to say,

ALI HAKIM: into the darkness of the desert night,

ALI ABABWA: "This damned war."

ALI HAKIM: Back in our Jeep there is silence.

ALI ABABWA: The sort of silence you get when it's dark and men drive a Jeep through hostile territory to deliver a soccer shirt to a boy with no arms. Suddenly,

ALI HAKIM: an ambush.

ALI ABABWA: Incoming RPG!

ALI HAKIM: The Jeep explodes in a fireball of fire.

ALI ABABWA: Your boys rush out of the Jeep, weapons at the ready.

ALI HAKIM: And then they realize:

ALI ABABWA: the soccer shirt.

ALI HAKIM: It's still in the flaming Jeep.

ALI ABABWA: And meanwhile the enemy is advancing.

ALI HAKIM: Scary gibberish music plays.

Scary gibberish music plays.

ALI ABABWA: One of your boys plunges into the maelstrom that is the flaming Jeep –

ALI HAKIM: this is you, Ian –

ALI ABABWA: while the others keep the enemy at bay.

ALI HAKIM: They're outnumbered

ALI ABABWA: but they fight on.

ALI HAKIM: For Ali.

ALI ABABWA: For Bendham.

ALI HAKIM: For transcendence.

ALI ABABWA: For reasons of personal integrity we may never understand.

ALI HAKIM: And they hear you call,

ALI ABABWA: "I've got the shirt!" And it's untouched.

ALI HAKIM: It had been under a flameproof something or other.

ALI ABABWA: And in your excitement you wave the shirt

ALI HAKIM: and the enemy sees the movement

ALI ABABWA: and –

A loud gunshot.

ALI HAKIM: A single shot splits the still desert night.

ALI ABABWA: And you fall.

ALI HAKIM: Still clutching the shirt.

ALI ABABWA: Your friends rush to you,

ALI HAKIM: but you say,

ALI ABABWA: "Take the shirt. Get it to Ali, I'll hold them off, get out of here, go!"

ALI HAKIM: But the leader of the group –

ALI ABABWA: this is perhaps Paul Gross –

ALI HAKIM: says, "None of my boys get left behind."

ALI ABABWA: And forming a crude stretcher out of bits of the Jeep,

ALI HAKIM: they put you, Ian, on it

ALI ABABWA: and go berserk.

They ululate.

ALI HAKIM: Except in English.

ALI ABABWA: Charging in slow motion, the shells expelled from their guns in a languid and glorious balletic choreography.

ALI HAKIM: And the enemy is overwhelmed

ALI ABABWA: even though the boys are in slow motion.

ALI HAKIM: Your boys

ALI ABABWA: good boys

ALI HAKIM: the best boys

ALI ABABWA: jog the hundreds of remaining kilometres back to the city

ALI HAKIM: carrying you on the stretcher

ALI ABABWA: back to the hospital where they left Ali.

ALI HAKIM: They made a promise after all.

ALI ABABWA: But when they get there Ali is dead already.

ALI HAKIM: The pretty brown nurse in the starched white uniform with the button missing here and the shapely legs and the pillowy –

ALI ABABWA: Salma Hayek perhaps –

ALI HAKIM: she says Ali died happy knowing they'd bring the shirt only he couldn't wait that long, they needed him in heaven to play soccer, and she cries, falling into your manly arms, Ian.

ALI ABABWA: You are healing quickly.

ALI HAKIM: And the boys their faces are hard.

ALI ABABWA: The things they've seen.

ALI HAKIM: The prices they've paid.

ALI ABABWA: And it's too much for one of them and he tears off his Special Forces shirt and puts on the soccer jersey crying out, "I am Ali!"

ALI HAKIM: This is you, Ian!

ALI ABABWA: You feel a special bond with the young Ali.

ALI HAKIM: And crazed with grief and sorrow you rush into a machine-gun nest and with your bare brown hands you tear it apart. The enemy attacks you but you squish them like so many mosquitoes.

ALI ABABWA: In a moment of great heroism and poignancy you pass from this world to the next. You are transcendent. You fulfill your destiny.

ALI HAKIM: Back at the base

ALI ABABWA: it is Asian Heritage Night and the soft sounds of a Hawaiian luau drift into the tent where the rest of the company sits in a circle.

We hear the soft sounds of Hawaiian luau music.

ALI HAKIM: They are solemn now, slouched against their cots.

ALI ABABWA: Some smoke, some stare numbly at their hands, but it is you, Ian, that they think of, their fallen comrade: the one who dared to die for something a little bit more ...

ALI HAKIM: And as we pull back from the tent up high into the air, the hot desert wind blows, whipping the tattered remains of a child's soccer jersey up from the dusty street, up above the pre-fabricated tents, up past Old Glory herself, but in the distance we hear the thin wail of the muezzin

From off we hear the muezzin call in gibberish.

calling the faithful to prayer.

We hear the muezzin sing, "Kill all the white guys."

The End.

ALI ABABWA: I think I smell an Oscar.

ALI HAKIM: Do you?

Enter DUNCAN.

DUNCAN: Excuse me. Can I have some light here? (*He addresses the audience.*) I apologize for the interruption, ladies and gentlemen.

ALI ABABWA & ALI HAKIM: Theatre's manager!

DUNCAN: My name is Duncan McVingoe and I'm the Artistic and Managing Producer here at the Vancouver East Cultural Centre. And first, I'd like to thank everyone for coming. Thank you. It's an honour to have you. Welcome. I'd also like to make it clear that our mandate to represent, accommodate, dignify, and empower cultural communities through theatrical productions of high artistic quality doesn't mean that – well ...

ALI HAKIM: Ask him.

ALI ABABWA: You.

DUNCAN: Well, it means we have a responsibility to you, our audience, a responsibility we tek seriously, which is why I've taken the extraordinary step of interruptin' and ... Excuse us please. Excuse me.

He turns to ALI & ALI.

ALI ABABWA & ALI HAKIM: Mr. Manager! Salaam alaikum.

DUNCAN: Could we speak ah privately fer a moment?

ALI ABABWA & ALI HAKIM: Sure.

They step upstage. In a furious whisper DUNCAN berates ALI & ALI.

DUNCAN: Right then. (*to audience*) Ladies and gentlemen, again I apologize for the unorthodox interruption. However, as part of our proactive education and outreach mandate, I feel it is necessary to facilitate ongoing dialogue for personal and intercultural exploration.

ALI & ALI nod vigorously and give thumbs-up.[6]

DUNCAN: Ye see, we had agreed that they would present a new ethnic family drama. Hadn't we?

More vigorous agreement from ALI & ALI.

After all, that's what ye came to see – an ethnic family drama that offers you a window onto our nation's cultural diversity yet resonates with universal themes. So tha's what they're goin' to be doin' now ... (*with a significant glance at ALI & ALI*) Right?

ALI ABABWA: Mr. Manager, small moment before we –

DUNCAN: Right?

ALI ABABWA: Right.

DUNCAN: Back to our show, ladies and gentlemen.

ALI ABABWA & ALI HAKIM: Huah!

ALI & ALI prepare the stage.

ALI ABABWA: (*to audience*) Apologies. The esteemed Manager is, of course, correct. We agreed to present to you a manycultural peoples' ancestral drama, which we will do in due course.

---

6   Though in some parts of the Middle East the "thumbs-up" gesture is rude, Ali and Ali are conversant with North American idioms.

It is just, you know, with you and us all in the same room, together, we get excited and make mischief.

VOICEOVER: Ladies and girls, boys and men, Ali and Ali proudly present a new Canadian play: *Grasshopper White Eyes Dreams of Home.*

TIM enters, wearing a coolie hat with authentic pigtail sewn into it and an apron, and carrying a butcher knife. He plays DAD. ALI HAKIM plays CHARLIE.

DAD: Son, I understand you're feeling conflicted.

CHARLIE: You understand? You understand??!! Did you go to school in an all-white neighbourhood when you were growing up in Dao Dong Long province? Did you have to endure bad jokes about the shape of your eyes, the colour of your skin, or your bad driving habits? Did you have kids in your cafeteria puking their guts out just because you had a chicken claw snack pack?

You understand? You understand? Do you understand what it feels like to feel like a fruit – a banana – yellow on the outside but white on the inside?

He moves to a window special.

Do you feel your soul ripping to pieces because there are two people battling inside of you? A battle that cannot be won because one side is screaming with passion: I am Charlie Chew! I like pitch and putt. And the other side is screaming with equal passion: I am Chew Mao Dong Hung! Grasshopper Stands Firm Against Foreign Devil Oppressor!

Do you understand that I am burning in the flames of internalized racism? Fuck your understanding. I'm tired of seeing the world through white eyes! I'm a chink and I'm proud! Fuck you, Daddy! Fuck you! I hate you! I hate you! I hate you, Daddy!!

DAD: Son, I love you no matter wha'.

CHARLIE breaks down into his father's arms, crying.

CHARLIE: I love you, Daddy. I love you. I love you. I'm Canadian, dammit. I'm Canadian.

DAD: There there, we're all Canadian, Charlie. We're all Canadian.

Moving to embrace CHARLIE, DAD accidentally impales his son with the butcher knife.

CHARLIE: Daddy?

DAD: Charlie?

CHARLIE dies. DAD moves to the window special.

DAD: Damn you, Canadian Dream!

Weeping, DAD commits seppuku,[7] carving a maple leaf into his belly. ALI ABABWA applauds. Actors leap up and take a bow.

ALI ABABWA: Wasn't that wonderful? Ladies and sons, please remember that here at Ali and Ali we have a fine selection of wide merchandise available for purchase. Remember at the top of show when Ali Hakim said,

TIM: "Aren't you a little old to be believing in leprechauns?"

ALI ABABWA: Why not remember that moment forever, with a commemorative Ali and Ali Irish Culture Pillowcase? Only $24.99 for a full set.

PROJECTION:

Pillowcase set with a depraved-looking leprechaun on it.

ALI ABABWA: Or a

TIM ululates ("Lebulebulebulebu!").

Mug.

PROJECTION:

A coffee mug with "Lebulebulebulebu" embossed on it.

ALI ABABWA: It's like

TIM does Homer Simpson.

TIM: D'oh!

ALI ABABWA: But better. Or perhaps some of you are Middle East history buffs? Remember when Jafar Ali Salim led the Agrabanian General Strike of 1968? This pivotal moment in Middle East history is commemorated forever in this bauxite miniature lovingly handcrafted by fairly compensated wood elves from the Brown Forest.

PROJECTION:

Miniature of General Strike.

It can be yours for only $99.99 of your pretty Canadian dollars.

Pause.

---

7   Ritual suicide by disembowelment formerly practised by Japanese samurai. Also called hara-kiri. Look it up.

No? That's okay, we can haggle. We're a haggling people. $17.99. And I'll throw in the commemorative strikebreakers. Hoo, you're good. Drive hard bargain. No accident Western world is on top, huh? $12.99. I pick up GST. God, you're killing me here.

ALI HAKIM: *(storming back on)* How about five bucks for a meatball sandwich?

ALI ABABWA: Calm down, Ali Hakim. Is okay. Is free market. *(to audience)* Too bad you don't want to buy because tonight only we are going to donate 1 per cent of every purchase to Agraba City Fire Department. Perhaps you don't know about Agraba City Fire Department. They are very short on equipment. You know, like infrared sensors, breathing apparatus, engines, hoses, ladders, a pole. Water.

ALI HAKIM: Stop. That's enough, all this bullshit. There's no fire department in Agraba. Provisional Authority disbanded fire department. For being part of old regime. Only fire department I will give money to is the one making fire in occupiers' tanks.

ALI ABABWA: *(laughs exaggeratedly)* Oh. Ali Hakim is having the irony. My friends, there is great need for modern fire department in Agraba today, to put out all the explosions. If you buy pillowcase we give you Agraba City Fire Department decal for proud display in Hummer. Come on.

ALI HAKIM: Cheap bastards. You Canadians – you can't buy me a slice of pizza? How much did you make selling weapons to Americans, huh? Who armed the fundamentalists!

ALI ABABWA: You mean the Zionists? 'Cause they're still arming the Zionists.

ALI HAKIM: No, I mean the other fundamentalists! *(He speaks in Agrabanian.)* Our fundamentalists!

ALI ABABWA: Ali Hakim. They do not speak your language.

ALI HAKIM: My language?

Pause. ALI HAKIM turns to the audience.

They have done this to us. Long live the Revolutionary Front for the Liberation of Agraba. And fuck you!

ALI ABABWA: Ali Hakim. No no no. TIM!

ALI HAKIM: Fuck all you in your peaceful West. Oh sure, you think I am violent and disrespectful, huh? Why don't I embrace your fucking democracy? I wonder?! One hundred years ago you called it civilization, and you're still shoving it down our throats!

TIM runs on and tranquilizes ALI HAKIM with a needle in the neck. ALI HAKIM instantly collapses. TIM drags him off to a corner and revives him.

ALI ABABWA: My friends, please. Ali Hakim is very – aroused? He has much on his serving dish, many worries, responsibilities. But let us not let that trouble us now. Hey! Please, good peoples, take your time choosing what is right for you and your lifestyle. You may at any time during the show signal your interest in buying something simply by calling out, "Hey, I'd like to buy that pillowcase," or these shirts that we are wearing, or that life-like civet cat featured in *Grasshopper White Eyes Dreams of Home*. Whatever you desire. We are – due to circumstances beyond our control – practising neo-liberals, and will sell pretty much anything for a price.

ALI HAKIM is successfully revived by TIM.

ALI HAKIM: Oh, I had the most beautiful dream. I was with my Ana in Agra – *(He sees TIM and the audience. To TIM)* What are you doing, fool? Go bring the goods for Ababwa to sell to good people of Real Life Canada. *(He kicks TIM and turns to ALI ABABWA.)* What?

ALI ABABWA: They're not buying.

ALI HAKIM: Nothing?

ALI ABABWA: They don't like us.

ALI HAKIM: Why? What did you do?

ALI ABABWA: Me? *(shakes his head)*

ALI HAKIM: They look frightened. Are you frightened? Did Ali Ababwa make intestinal wind? Ask you to examine his bum? I am sorry.

ALI ABABWA: It is you, Ali Hakim. You are so aggressive.

ALI HAKIM: When? No no! Ali Ababwa, you indigenous monkey – of course! It is because you are blue![8] *(turning to audience)* It is off-putting, no? *(back to ALI ABABWA)* We must explain. They know nothing of the Sammites and the Copts.

ALI ABABWA: I don't know.

ALI HAKIM: For sure. It's important that they understand. Context is everything. *(He addresses the audience.)* Agraba is a predominantly Muslim society.

ALI ABABWA: Not Shia.

8   Ali Ababwa's face – or a good part of it – is blue. See Disney's *Aladdin*.

ALI HAKIM: Not Sunni.

ALI ABABWA: But Sammi.

ALI HAKIM: As you know, the Shia Muslim believe that at some point there will appear in the world a Twelfth Imam to carry on the work of the Prophet Mohammed, peace be upon him.

ALI ABABWA: The Sunnis believe something else.

ALI HAKIM: The Sammis, on the other case, believe that there is a Thirteenth Imam who has already appeared.

ALI ABABWA: In Vegas.

ALI HAKIM: He has come to Earth and assumed the form of a dynamic

ALI ABABWA: one-eyed

ALI HAKIM: black

ALI ABABWA: Jewish

ALI HAKIM: entertainer

ALI ABABWA: named

ALI HAKIM: Sammy.

ALI ABABWA: Davis Junior.

A burst of "Gonna Build a Mountain" by Sammy Davis Jr. plays.

ALI HAKIM: Sammis are the eponymous followers of Sammy Davis.

ALI ABABWA: Eponymous?

ALI HAKIM: Yes, you know, it means …

PHRASEOLATOR (*voiceover*): PUT DOWN THE GOAT!

ALI HAKIM glares offstage and hisses at TIM to turn off the phraseolator.

ALI ABABWA: The holy book of the Sammis is the Bojang, which interprets many of the lyrics of Sammy Davis's best songs. I've never actually read it but …

ALI HAKIM: It is full of good advice.

ALI ABABWA: Be good. Share and co-operate.

ALI HAKIM: Use your words not your fists.

ALI ABABWA: Talk to animals.

ALI HAKIM: It is a religion of moderation, kindness, tolerance … and martinis.

ALI ABABWA: But in Agraba there is a group of fanatical Sammis.

ALI HAKIM: A *small* group. Fundamentalists. Known as Sammites, they poke out their left eyes and, in the throes of religious ecstasy, tap dance

until their feet are mere bloody stumps. Years ago with the aid of the U.S., the Sammites gained control of Agraba and imposed a theocratic state. In addition to reducing the legal status of women to that of camels they began sweeping oppression of Agraba's minority Christians, an ancient sect known as the Copts.

ALI ABABWA: COPTS. Not cops. Cop-t-s. There's a T. (*He indicates the projection.*)

PROJECTION:

> Copt / kɒpt/ / n.
> A Christian of the Coptic Church.
> [French Copte from Modern Latin Coptus from Arabic al-kibt, al-kubt]

PROJECTION:

> Coptic Church n.
> Of the Jacobite sect upholding the Monophysite Doctrine, condemned by the Council of Chalcedon; for eleven centuries have had possession of the patriarchal chair of Alexandria.

ALI ABABWA: Moderate Sammis didn't put up much fight.

ALI HAKIM: Which is why we must now!

ALI ABABWA: In an orgy of violence known to us as Coptellnacht, the Sammite religious police desecrated our temples, scattered our icons, and poisoned our Pope. Agraba's few Copts were hunted down and our faces were dipped in vats of blue dye to signify our outsider status.

ALI HAKIM: Once again, Ali Ababwa, on behalf of all Sammis, I am truly sorry.

ALI ABABWA: I know. Still, my friends, you must not underestimate us. Despite hailing from a country hijacked by an oppressive theocratic regime, Agrabanians are well-educated and forward-thinking people, poised to take advantage of a growing and dynamic global economy. We are here, and available to work in many capacities.

ALI HAKIM looks at ALI ABABWA curiously; ALI ABABWA makes reassuring noises and presses on with his pitch.

We have very impressive and wide range of employment experience. For example, as event caterers, when Rumsfeld met Saddam in Baghdad.

PROJECTION:

*Photo of U.S. Defense Secretary Donald Rumsfeld's visit to Baghdad when Iraqi President Saddam Hussein was still a buddy, with **ALI HAKIM** inserted in the background.*

ALI HAKIM: But we are not available for employment here as we must return to Agraba as soon as –

ALI ABABWA: (*intently studying the photograph*) One moment, Ali Hakim, what is this in picture …?

ALI HAKIM: What?

ALI ABABWA: This shadow. It was not in original image.

ALI HAKIM: TIM! Prepare the enhancer. (*exits*)

ALI ABABWA: Scan northwest 27,000 degrees. Zoom. Give me 50 per cent. Ten more. Enhance.

With each instruction the image changes until some words can be dimly discerned. Finally, the message becomes clear: THE DARK AXES ARE COMING!

Oh my God Oh my God Ali Hakim, ALI HAKIM –

ALI HAKIM: (*re-entering*) What, Ali Ababwa?

ALI ABABWA: The Dark aXes are coming! It said so in the picture. The Dark aXes of el Mutah. The aXes of Mass Destruction.

ALI HAKIM: Holy Hummus, Ali Ababwa! On picture – is nothing – just shadow of moon on lens.

ALI ABABWA: What did you say? Shadow of moon?!

ALI HAKIM: So?

ALI ABABWA: You know the prophesy as well as I.

He recites.

"I'm being followed by a moonshadow

Moonshadow, moonshadow

Leaping and hopping on a moonshadow

Moonshadow, moonshadow."

ALI HAKIM: Oh my Sammi! You are right! I am shitting myself! What should we do?

ALI ABABWA: TIM! BRING THE BIG BUTTON!

TIM runs out with the security alert button.

ALI ABABWA & ALI HAKIM: Shazaaaaam!

*They press the button. **ALI HAKIM** kicks **TIM** off the stage. The screen flickers to life. **MOHANDES** is eating a doughnut and reading Bob Woodward's*

Bush at War. Behind him, an image of a bikini babe is on his computer screen.

MOHANDES: This is Mohandes Panir Ali Zia … One moment please.

He swallows the remains of the doughnut.

… Gandhinehrukhomeinijinnah. Have you caught a terrorist?

ALI ABABWA: We have an important mission for you.

MOHANDES: What are you talking about, Madras Man? I am very busy profiling potential terrorist suspects.

MOHANDES looks back to his computer screen and attempts to shut it off.

ALI ABABWA: You must increase the security threat assessment!

MOHANDES: Don't tell me what the level of threat should be. I am Mohandes Panir Ali Zia Gandhinehrukhomeinijinnah! The absence of evidence does not necessarily indicate the evidence of absence.[9]

ALI ABABWA: Shut up! The Evil aXes have been deployed. You must find them. The fate of the world hangs in the balance.

MOHANDES: Evil aXes? Oh yes. My intelligence sources have indicated that these aXes of Evil would be used. These terrorists are very wily. They will stop at nothing. They are within my grasp. I will find them!

MOHANDES gets up and exits the frame.

(*from off-screen*) Hey Bindi! You want double double from Tim Hortons?

ALI ABABWA: Okay, now, back to show.

ALI HAKIM: Ladies and gentlemen, we are proud to bring to you one of our country's beautiful artistic traditions: The Classical Puppet Theatre of Agraba.

*With **TIM**, they assume their positions at the puppet theatre. The "puppets" are photocopied faces of President George W. Bush, Vice-President Dick Cheney, Secretary of Defense Donald Rumsfeld, and Secretary of State Colin Powell, on sticks, against a background photo of the Oval Office. The puppet show is projected onto the screen by a live camera.*

---

9   An actual quote from U.S. Defense Secretary Donald Rumsfeld.

DUBYA: Okay, so what's on the agenda?

CHENEY: Mr. President, we need to discuss the report.

DUBYA: Oh yeah. (*pause*) Which report?

CHENEY: The Comprehensive Analysis of Challenges in the Occupation of Iraq report.

DUBYA: Oh yeah. What's it about?

CHENEY: It's about the challenges in the occupation of Iraq.

DUBYA: Right. Did you read it, Rummy?

RUMMY: It's bullshit.

DUBYA: Summarize it for me, would you Dick?

CHENEY: Mr. President, it's seventeen volumes of densely –

DUBYA: Try, Dick.

CHENEY: Well, basically, sir, it says that given ideal conditions we could be successful in Iraq.

DUBYA: I like that.

RUMMY: I love it.

DUBYA: Me too, I love it too, actually.

SEMI-COLIN: (*entering*) Hey are you guys having a meeting without me?

RUMMY: Irie, man.

DUBYA: Oh hi, Semi-Colin.

RUMMY: 'Sup dog?

SEMI-COLIN: Mr. President, the media are having a field day with the prison abuse –

RUMMY: Fuck 'em. Keeps their mind off the really nasty shit we're doing. Hehehe.

DUBYA: I saw those Abu Gayrab pictures. Didn't I?

CHENEY: You did, sir.

DUBYA: Can I see them again?

RUMMY: No, sir.

CHENEY: I want to know what kind of fairy-tale world people are living in. So our boys piled a bunch of naked guys together –

RUMMY: Or made some guy wear some woman's underwear –

CHENEY: Or made some guys jerk off in public –

RUMMY: Or jammed a light up some guy's ass –

CHENEY: I mean, what do they expect?

RUMMY: Yeah!

CHENEY: Hell, I look at way better stuff than that on the Internet all the time.

RUMMY: Amen, Fatty!

CHENEY: Like Rush Limbaugh said, "These soldiers were just blowing off a little steam."

RUMMY: Flush is a good guy.

CHENEY: I like him.

RUMMY: Me too. We should have him over.

CHENEY: Let him know we appreciate what he does.

RUMMY: Thank him.

CHENEY: I'd like to shake his hand.

RUMMY: I'd give him a pat on the back.

CHENEY: I'd like to pinch his ass.

RUMMY: Put a clamp on his balls.

CHENEY: Let him suck my dick.

RUMMY: While Semi gives it to his old lady from behind.

CHENEY: And we watch!

DUBYA: Oh, just like those frat parties we used to go to.

CHENEY: That's right, sir.

SEMI-COLIN: Mr. President, this tort – uh, abuse –

DUBYA: Semi? You ever talk to God?

SEMI-COLIN: Uh … uh … uh …

DUBYA: Dick?

CHENEY: Not face to face.

DUBYA: Rummy?

RUMMY: Oh yeah. We go *way* back.

DUBYA: Laura and I give thanks to Him for clearing up my hemorrhoids.

Murmurs of congratulations.

You know what He told me last night?

CHENEY: What, sir?

DUBYA: He told me that freedom is His gift to every man and woman in this world. And He said that as the greatest power on the face of the earth, we have an obligation to help the spread of freedom.

Agreement.

He told me that the coming apocalypse in the Middle East will herald the beginning of the Second Coming. He said there would be peace in the valley and the Jews could be converted to Christianity. And Jesus is gonna sleep over in the Lincoln Bedroom. What do you say to that?

I say let's get to it.

SEMI-COLIN: To what, Mr. President?

DUBYA: To spread freedom, we should …

> *RUMMY whispers the answers to DUBYA one phrase at a time; DUBYA repeats what he has been told.*

Enslave Palestinians in the West Bank … bank-roll some dictators … give more tax breaks to our really rich friends … oh yeah, no bugging the Russians about Chechnya and …

RUMMY: … and put more black guys in jail!

DUBYA: That's it.

RUMMY: No offence, Leroy.

DUBYA: Why would he take offence? Semi's not black.

SEMI-COLIN: Mr. President uh, I'm uh African-American.

DUBYA: You see?

SEMI-COLIN: Mr. President, I don't think those are the sort of measures your father would have approved of.

RUMMY: His father worked for the CIA! He was an establishment pussy. Fucking weenie.

DUBYA: Yeah. So, I been thinking.

> *Murmurs of congratulations.*

Listen to this you guys. In the War on Terror, retreat is not an onion.

RUMMY: Option.

DUBYA: Ah, I was gonna say that! I was gonna say "option" but then at the last minute I … I didn't.

CHENEY: I wish I had seven cheeseburgers.

> *He leaves the office, presumably to get seven cheeseburgers.*

DUBYA: Semi-Colin?

SEMI-COLIN: Sir.

DUBYA: I want a report on that whole apocalypse in the Middle East, Second Coming, Jesus return-ing to the Holy Land thing. I want it on my desk by noon tomorrow and I want it now!

SEMI-COLIN: Sheeeit, what up, dog? Sho, stick it to de Negro. I ain't no mothafuckin' office boy. I'n

de mothafuckin' secretary of the mothafuckin' state. I'n take dat report and shove it up yo skinny white ass, mothafucka. And Rumsfeld, you moth-afuckin' cracker, any more lip from you and I'n fuck you up, mothafucka. *(beat)* I mean, I'll get my people on it, sir. Right away.

DUBYA: Good.

> *As SEMI-COLIN exits, we hear …*

SEMI-COLIN: Yo! Condoleezza, get your ass over here, girl!

DUBYA: Let me make it very clear. The War on Terror is not a figure of speech. It's more like a bumper sticker.

RUMMY: Mr. President, let us pray.

> *MUSIC: "Ride of the Valkyries" bursts on. A dart appears stage left in the puppet theatre and impales itself in RUMMY's head. The music stops.*

Is that all you got, ya infidels? Bring it on, camel jockeys!

> *He begins to sing.*

> Sharif don't like it!
> Rock the casbah!
> Fuck the casbah!

> *Blackout.*

VOICEOVER: Ali & Ali present a response to insult-ing depictions of the Prophet Muhammed Peace Be Upon Him.

> *VIDEO: A widely disseminated mid-2000's Internet video in which a guy in L.A., dressed up as Jesus, lip-synchs Gloria Gaynor's 1978 disco hit, "I Will Survive," and then gets hit by a bus.*

DUNCAN: *(entering)* Hang on, hang on. What was tha'?

ALI ABABWA: Yes, this is very insulting to me as a Christian.

ALI HAKIM: What? I just like the part where he gets hit by bus.

DUNCAN: Look, this is not the place, and I'm sure you *(audience)* agree with me, NAE the place for your local, petty, feudal grievances, yer decon-textualized finger-pointing. The theatre is where we explore the timeless verities of the human condition. Ladies and gentlemen, I apologize once again. I turn my back for a few minutes to get a falafel and –

ALI HAKIM: Falafel? Did you finish it?

DUNCAN: This, of course, is part of the challenge of doing intercultural work and we know that ye support the work we're doing here and we thank ye and want ye to know that we are constantly striving to improve.

Behind DUNCAN, ALI & ALI hold a heated discussion.

DUNCAN: And I'm sure we'll be right back on track momentarily. (*to ALI & ALI*) So, where's that play ye started?

ALI HAKIM: Uh, play?

DUNCAN: The one specified in the contract, remember?!

ALI HAKIM: Ah yes, the contract ...

ALI ABABWA: Entertaining you should mention the contract, because we –

DUNCAN: So let's get back to it, shall we? The father and the boy and the ... Ladies and gentlemen, again I apologize for the interruption but isn't this wha' makes the theatre so special? It's live. Anything can happen. Though usually – and preferably – not with such frequency.

He leaves.

ALI HAKIM: Why didn't you say something?

ALI ABABWA: Why didn't you? Why must it always be me who does the saying?

ALI HAKIM: You? (*in Agrabanian*) I always have to get the money.

ALI ABABWA: No, Ali Hakim. I tell you. Here I am speaking the English.

ALI HAKIM: Pah! I am always attaining the money. Who made warlord certify cheque in Congo?

ALI ABABWA: Who pawned watch to bury Friday Kim Chee?

ALI HAKIM: Who bribed the guards in camp in Axerbaijan? And who bought passports to get out of Jerkistan?

ALI ABABWA: (*remembering audience*) Ali Hakim ... little camels have big ears ...

ALI HAKIM: Them? – pah! They don't know what's going on. They think this is part of show.

ALI ABABWA: Arguing this way will not help us obtain money we are owed from manager.

ALI HAKIM: Call Tim.

ALI ABABWA: Tim?

ALI HAKIM: He wants to be pay, he can speak to manager. Besides, they are same tribe.

ALI ABABWA: We must speak to manager. Tim is our hireling. He must never know our financial insecurity.

DUNCAN: (*from off*) We're still waiting ...

ALI & ALI scramble.

VOICEOVER: Ladies and gentlemen, Ali and Ali extremely dearly proudly present a new Canadian play: *A Day in the Life of Ivan Scarberia, or The Gulag East Etobicoke.*

DAD (TIM) slurps borscht. VLADIMIR, his son (ALI ABABWA), watches in disgust.

VLADIMIR: Dad, I want to talk to you.

DAD: Vladimir, eat first, then talk.

VLADIMIR: No, Dad, I have something to say. I will not be silenced. This is a democracy we live in here, not a communist dictatorship. Right? That's why you left and came here, isn't it? Isn't it?

DAD: Eat your borscht.

VLADIMIR: You're a gangster. You kill people. You trade in small armaments and enslave poor Siberian girls in local strip clubs. I'm not eating that borscht, Dad. I won't be a part of it anymore. Fuck you Daddy! Fuck you! I hate you! I hate you! I hate you Daddy!!

DAD moves to window special.

DAD: What do you know, Vladimir? Did you come to new country with only shirt on your back? Did you build home for your family with only two hands and an old Soviet army pistol? You're a pussy, Vladimir.

He cruelly strikes his son, though the timing of the stage hit is off.

You're soft.

He cruelly strikes him again.

If we were in Mother Russia I'd shoot you in the head.

He puts pistol to VLADIMIR's head, cruelly.

VLADIMIR: But we're not in Mother Russia, Daddy.

VLADIMIR punches his father, who catches and crushes VLADIMIR's fist.

VLADIMIR: Is that the only tool you have for expressing tenderness and affection towards me?

DAD crushes his fist some more.

Go ahead Dad, crush every bone in my body.

And more.

Can't you see that I am drowning in a tidal wave of Old World, neo-Stalinist, patrio-masculinist repression?

Stung by the truth, DAD releases VLADIMIR.

DAD: You are right, Vladimir. Now I see. I love you, Vladimir.

VLADIMIR: I love you too, Daddy. I'm Canadian, dammit. I'm Canadian.

DAD: There, there Vladimir, don't cry. We're all Canadian. We are all Canadian. Come.

They move to the window special.

I take you to club. It's time for you to meet your mother.

VLADIMIR: Mother?

DAD walks VLADIMIR offstage. He trips and accidentally shoots VLADIMIR.

DAD: (*off*) Vladimi-i-i-i-i-ir! Damn you, Canadian Dream!

Another gunshot.

PROJECTION:

Blood splatter in the shape of a maple leaf.

ALI HAKIM: Bravo, Ali Ababwa! (*indicating to ALI ABABWA that the manager is off in the wings*) Now, we must do scene three of … ethnic peoples' manyculture play …

ALI ABABWA: Ah yes, scene three. It is called … *Jimmy Two Feathers Runs with Pizza Box,* or

He makes Native American ululation sound.[10]

West Edmonton Mall.

They set the scene again. DUNCAN enters while they set up and stands upstage, arms crossed, regarding them skeptically. ALI & ALI see him and give an enthusiastic thumbs-up. ALI ABABWA plays DAD; ALI HAKIM plays JOHNNY. DAD pretends to

chop something on the tabletop. His chopping becomes a rhythmic drumming pattern. He begins to "sing" Native-style.

DAD: HihowareyaareyaareyaHihowareyaarey-aareya Hihowareya. Son, where's my smokes?

JOHNNY: You understand?

DUNCAN: Oh come on! What do ye take me for? They're all the same, those scenes!

ALI HAKIM: No no my friend, is different.

DUNCAN: I cannae see any difference.

ALI ABABWA: Because you my friend as a member of the dominant culture, have a totalizing and homogenizing gaze that erases difference.

DUNCAN: I won't have tha kind of language in my theatre! We have a contract.

ALI ABABWA: Yes, about the contract –

DUNCAN: A legally binding agreement. I don't want this to become a legal matter and I'm sure you don't either. I prefer to speak to you as creative partners, but I won't let you take advantage of my – of our – broad-mindedness, our patience.

ALI HAKIM: Please my friend, don't be angry. We'll give you something different.

ALI ABABWA: Mr. Manager, please, this way. Do you like impressions?

DUNCAN: Yes, I do.

ALI ABABWA: Oh you're going to love this.

DUNCAN: Is it Sean Connery?

ALI ABABWA: Almost.

He signals the booth and leads the manager offstage.

VOICEOVER: Ladies and gentlemen, the Secretary of Defense for the United States of America, Donald Rumsfeld.

ALI HAKIM appears in shadow on rear (tent) wall as DONALD RUMSFELD masturbating.

DONALD RUMSFELD: Who's in power now, Hillary?!!!!!

DUNCAN: No NO NOO!!!! Yer foul, out of bounds, disgustin' –

ALI HAKIM: No, is beautiful. Like you and I, they are real human beings.

ALI ABABWA: This is universal human truth.

DUNCAN: We're not morons. We know when we're being had, played around with, manipulated. I

---

10   That "whoo-whoo-whoo" sound made by movie Injuns in moments of emotional intensity.

mean, if you were doin' a play that told us some-thing about where ye came from, about your people, to eliminate the prejudice. But this, this fabricating and the pornography, it's outrageous.

Ye've got to respect your audience. Ye understan' that? RESPEC'. It's part of our culture. There's certain things you just don't do.

ALI ABABWA: Oh come on, Mr. Manager, you never do this? You know, give quick pull in office when no one is looking?

He demonstrates.

I know I do.

He finds a man in the audience and points him out.

I'm sure he does.

DUNCAN: Tha's it. You people. We give ye this opportunity and ye just push our tolerance 'til it snaps. So, out ye get. Oot of my theatre. And you'll be hearing from my lawyer! Ladies and gentlemen, my sincerest apologies. These two will refund yer money. I'm very sorry they've wasted yer valuable time.

ALI ABABWA & ALI HAKIM: No no no –

DUNCAN traps ALI HAKIM and begins to push him out of the theatre.

ALI ABABWA: Mr. Manager. Where are you from?

DUNCAN: Please. The time for talk has past.

ALI ABABWA: From Bulgaria?

DUNCAN: (*still pushing ALI HAKIM*) Please leave.

ALI ABABWA: From the Shire.

DUNCAN: *The Shire?!*

ALI ABABWA: You have hair on knuckles.

DUNCAN: Look, ye, I'm not a bloody hobbit! I'm a Sco'.

ALI ABABWA: Of course ... a Sco'! Oh yes, from the fair realm of ...?

DUNCAN: SCOTLAND, you stewpid twit!

ALI ABABWA: Yes, Scotland. (*aside to ALI HAKIM*) I saw this movie. (*to DUNCAN*) Where the coura-geous and brave-hearted ...

DUNCAN: Sco's.

ALI ABABWA: Yes, looked death in the face against ... uh against ...

DUNCAN: The ruthless English bastards. (*to audi-ence*) No offence.

ALI ABABWA: Yes, bastards. The Sco's ... led by the brave ... hearted ...

DUNCAN: William Wallace of Ellerslie!

ALI HAKIM: Oh, he was great hero this Walrus.

DUNCAN: And a true patriot. The people were with him, you see? And with them he resisted the cruel invader Edward Longshanks.

ALI ABABWA: Longsnacks, yes! This was the Great Battle of ...

DUNCAN: Falkirk!

ALI ABABWA & ALI HAKIM: Falkr.

ALI ABABWA: In the fateful year of ...

DUNCAN: 1298.

ALI ABABWA & ALI HAKIM: 1298.

ALI & ALI sidle back to make room for DUNCAN.

DUNCAN: Wallace had never before faced such an army or fought a large battle without a natural defence. He may have sensed this was the end, for he made no great exhortation, but spoke simply and bluntly to his men. "Now, I haif brocht ye to the ring – hop gif ye can!"

And at that moment the heavily mailed English cavalry fell with a tremendous shock on the charged spears of the schiltron units of the Scots.

ALI HAKIM: Schiltron?

PHRASEOLATOR (*voiceover*): PUT DOWN THE GOAT!

ALI HAKIM: (*sotto voce*) Tim, turn that off.

ALI ABABWA: (*to DUNCAN*) I am sorry, you were saying.

DUNCAN: The schiltron was a fantastic device for goring and eviscerating the English dogs. No offence intended. Foot soldiers carrying twelve-foot spears were arranged in tight phalanx formations. In front of these spears, great pointy stakes were hammered into the ground.

Using the schiltron, the brave-hearted Scots with-stood the attack of the English dogs – no offence intended – and their Irish vassals – no offence – hammering English skulls with great battle-axes, war hammers, and the mace. Until ...

DUNCAN is momentarily overcome with emotion but then masters himself.

Red John Comyn quit the field. We were betrayed. Wallace was captured.

They dragged him around London, hanged him, then cut him down while he was still alive. Then they slit him open, pulled out his entrails, and burned them before his own eyes. Then they stuck his head on a pike and placed it above London Bridge. Then they killed him. Finally, they quartered him and scattered the four pieces at Newcastle, Berwick, Aberdeen, and Perth.

DUNCAN collapses with grief, then sings.

"LAMENT OF WALLACE"

Farewell, ye dear partners of peril! Farewell!

Though buried ye lie in one big bloody grave,

Your deeds shall ennoble the place where ye fell,

And your names be enrolled with the sons of the brave![11]

DUNCAN weeps.

I cannae tell ye how that makes me feel. It's validatin' you know, to have your own people, their history, their sufferin' up here on the stage. That's what we want to see. That's why the people come. To get in touch with some basic human emotions ...

ALI ABABWA: I know, my friend.

DUNCAN: This is the sort of thing that, well ... you know, this is why we do it.

He puts his arms around ALI & ALI.

I'm really proud of what we've done here. We had our moments, I know, our misunderstandings, but we persevered. We really ... I wish my mother could see this.

ALI HAKIM: You are fine actor.

DUNCAN: Och, it's been a long time, but yes ...

ALI ABABWA: Mr. Manager ...

DUNCAN hugs ALI ABABWA tight.

DUNCAN: I love this guy.

Encouraged, ALI ABABWA puts his arm around the manager.

ALI ABABWA: According to contract –

ALI HAKIM: Contract, right.

DUNCAN hugs ALI HAKIM tight.

DUNCAN: Love this guy, too.

ALI ABABWA: We were to have been paid, on signing, a small sum, a mere pittance really, 3 per cent plus sundry minor but necessary expenses. We are in great need of this money for lodgings and food –

DUNCAN: What are ye sayin' to me, lad? You don't think I was going to pay ye? It's different here, you know, in the West. There's nae corruption, like yer used to. Relationships here, they are built on trust. Besides, as a Sco', it hurts me, when ye imply that I'm cheap.

He leaves.

Sirens. Lights. Bells. Whistles. Onscreen, MOHANDES interrupts. He is in great pain, on the verge of death.

MOHANDES: I have been attacked. Sabotaged by terrorists ... poison on pages of *Bush at War* ... but I have located the location of the Evil aXes ...

ALI ABABWA: Where are they, Mohandes? Tell us.

MOHANDES: At great cost – nah.

He collapses. A piece of paper falls from his hand.

ALI HAKIM: Don't die, Mohandes.

MOHANDES gestures to the floor.

ALI ABABWA: He's trying to tell us something.

ALI HAKIM: They're on the floor? In the basement? Australia?

The camera zooms in on the paper. MOHANDES, making a heroic effort, turns it over. It is out of focus.

ALI ABABWA: That paper. Perhaps is code.

ALI HAKIM: Australia?

ALI ABABWA: Arkansas?

ALI HAKIM: Antigua?

ALI ABABWA: Antilles?

ALI HAKIM: Kuantanabongo?[12]

ALI ABABWA: Huh?

ALI HAKIM: Uh, Copenhagen.

We can make out the message. It reads: theatr. ALI & ALI attempt to decipher it. They are unsuccessful. MOHANDES rises for one last gasp.

MOHANDES: In ... the ... audie-ence.

---

11   Adapted from a poem by Robert Tannahill (1774–1810).

12   Agrabanian province near the Uzbeki-Lebanese border.

MOHANDES begins to die.

ALI ABABWA & ALI HAKIM: Theatre audience.

ALI ABABWA: Of course.

MOHANDES continues to die.

ALI HAKIM: Stupid us.

ALI ABABWA: Thought you could pull one over on the blue guy.

MOHANDES is still dying.

ALI HAKIM: I suspected it all along.

MOHANDES finally expires.

ALI ABABWA: TIM. Bring the Jeeps.

TIM produces tiny white cardboard Jeeps. They all suit up.

ALI HAKIM: Cool helmets.

ALI ABABWA: Check.

ALI HAKIM: Ray guns.

ALI ABABWA: Check.

ALI HAKIM: Clip-on ID cards.

ALI ABABWA: Check.

ALI HAKIM: Wait, Ali Ababwa. Is this right to violate liberties of audience by entering them in this way?

ALI ABABWA: For sure. Ends justify means, my friend. One need only look at benefits of War on Terror for Afghanistan. Twenty years ago there was dirty communist government in Kabul propped up by Soviet Union and dirty rapist heroin-smuggling warlords running the rest of the country.

ALI HAKIM: Now there is dirty capitalist government in Kabul propped up by Americans and dirty rapist heroin-smuggling warlords still running rest of country.

ALI ABABWA: Let us not get preoccupied with these insignificant details of the left brain.

ALI HAKIM: You are right. TIM! This is no time for fence-sitting. Remember Mohandes.

ALL: Huah!

They tool around in their Jeeps and enter the audience.

ALI HAKIM: Hello! We are here to investigate your Weapons of Mass Destruction, particularly the Dark aXes of el Mutah. If you do not co-operate fully, we will leave the country and you will have

the shit bombed out of you. If you do co-operate fully, we will leave the country and you will have the shit bombed out of you.

ALI ABABWA: If you actually have the aXes of Mass Destruction, however –

ALI HAKIM: We'll leave you alone. We represent the Coalition of the If You Say So. He's Mauritian. Tim's Polish. And I'm from Alderaan.

ALI ABABWA: We represent the will of a tiny percentage of the international community.

ALI HAKIM goes into the audience. Picks someone out. Hands him a whip.

ALI HAKIM: Ah, the leader of the audience. Greetings, Mr. President.

He interviews the leader.

Will you surrender your Weapons of Mass Destruction? Do you really cut off people's ears? Do Koreans really eat dogs? Typically cagey, their leader refuses to answer my probing questions.

Meanwhile, in another part of the audience …

ALI ABABWA: Madam, open your purse please. I am an inspector with the United Furniture Warehouse of Nations. Please, open your purse. *(to ALI HAKIM and TIM)* She's obfuscating.

ALI HAKIM: Must have something to hide. Put it in your report.

ALI ABABWA: Semi-Colin Powell will hear about this, my dear. You can be sure of that.

He steals the purse.

Ha! Sneaky, no? Let's see what she was hiding.

Pulls out some lipstick.

Well, it is not the aXes of Evil – but this is certainly a weapon of mass destruction to some poor little bunny who had it shoved up his EYEBALL!

ALI ABABWA throws the lipstick to TIM.

Tim, test the lipstick.

TIM begins to put on the lipstick.

No, no. Test the range of the lipstick.

TIM throws the lipstick.

Look – it travels further than twenty-eight feet. That's illegal under United Furniture Warehouse of Nations Resolution 699, no down payment,

YOU DON'T PAY UNTIL 2010! I am confiscating this purse.

ALI HAKIM finds a "centrifuge" next to some innocent person.

ALI HAKIM: Look! A centrifuge! They mix uranium in these things you know! How dare you! Are you not human? Do you not think and feel the same things we do? Tim, take this to Semi-Colin Powell. And fool, take my Jeep and give him some water. Mission accomplished. The area is secure. Start shopping.

ALI ABABWA: I will focus group the audience. So, how are you liking democracy so far? Is intoxicating, no? What, looting? There's no looting going on here.

TIM is looting.

ALI ABABWA: Oh, dear. Ali Hakim, Tim is looting.

ALI HAKIM. shoots TIM.

TIM: Friendly fire, friendly fire!

ALI HAKIM: Alert CBCNN! We will hold press conference.

Globe and Mail. No, we never said the audience *was in possession of* the Evil aXes. However, let me be perfectly clear. We believe people with white skin can govern themselves and we'll just stay here until you learn how to do so. No more questions.

A beat.

Well my friend, how 'bout now you buy me pizza? I work hard for you, yes. I drive Jeeps, make joke ...?

TIM enters with a cellphone. He tries to get ALI HAKIM's attention as ALI HAKIM attempts to get money from audience. ALI ABABWA enters from the other side and sees TIM standing there. He shoos TIM offstage.

ALI HAKIM: I'm so hungry. You don't believe me? No? Look, my friend. (*He lifts his shirt.*) Listen to my stomach growl. Put your ear there.

ALI ABABWA interrupts with the cellphone.

ALI ABABWA: Ali Hakim?

ALI HAKIM: What? I'm busy –

ALI ABABWA: It's Ana.

ALI HAKIM takes the phone and speaks quietly in Agrabanian to Ana.

ALI ABABWA: Ali Hakim's bride. She is phoning from detention centre in Malta. She traded food for phone call. They were separated in the confusion and the pig of a smuggler took her money and instead of taking her and her family across the mountains to meet Ali Hakim, he drove her straight to Maltese detention centre where she is stranded without papers and expecting a baby in a few months. I am to be godfather. But how will she get out? Ali Hakim is wandering Agrabanian: stateless. He cannot send for her. Crazy life.

ALI HAKIM: Ali Ababwa. The baby is kicking.

ALI ABABWA: Tell Ana to take care of herself. She must eat for two. Not waste food on phone calls.

He turns back to audience.

Look at Ali Hakim, he is smiling. Oh my friend is a lucky man.

ALI HAKIM goes offstage to continue his call in private. ALI ABABWA tiptoes to centre stage.

So. I'm single, pretty smart, sometimes amusing, and somewhat exotic. I like long walks, dancing a bit strangely, and going to the theatre if I can leave at intermission. When they have an intermission.

On the liability side, my bum is more or less constantly sore and though I have no children of my own (*sighs*), I do have dependents, many dependents, all of whom depend on me to send money home to buy food, water, and medicine.

He sings an excerpt from "I Want to Be Loved by You."

So – any takers? Ian, what do you say? Is okay, I am very open-minded. No, you are right. Two famous handsome brown men in one household – it would be all ego.

He picks a woman from the audience and approaches her.

How about you, madam? What do you say? Is easy, if immigration interrogates you, all you have to do is convince them of our intimacy. And believe me, once you've had Agrabanian you never go back. Please. I don't want to go back.

He retreats.

Oh sure. Typical. You Canadians. You're so nice and liberal and support same-sex marriages and when you walk down the street and see a woman with a dot on her forehead, you think that's pretty cool and maybe you even have dot envy. But when it comes to blue Agrabanians, well that's a whole different story now, isn't it? Oh yes you believe blue Agrabanians should share the same rights and privileges as you and no you would never discriminate against blue Agrabanians and yes you think hate crimes legislation should be rewritten to include blue Agrabanians but do you think blue is sexxxxxyyyy?

He returns to the woman.

Kiss me and I'll shut up. Is true. Just one. On the cheek. Blue is permanent – won't come off on lips, I promise.

Ad libbing as necessary until she – or he – does.

(*after kiss*) Be still my beating heart.

VOICEOVER: According to Agrabanian Traditional Law, if a woman kisses a man they are deemed to have been married since they were thirteen – and all property reverts to the male.

ALI ABABWA: May I have keys to late model luxury sedan? Credit card? You will find that I can adapt quickly to your carefree lifestyle. Please, I beg you, take me with you.

Enter ALI HAKIM.

ALI HAKIM: What are you doing? Madam, people, please, there is no such thing as traditional law in Agraba.

ALI ABABWA: Ha! Just a joke.

ALI HAKIM: You have no shame, no respect.

ALI ABABWA: What? Is part of show.

ALI HAKIM: You think I can't hear you from back there? You want to stay here then. For real.

ALI ABABWA: Ali Hakim.

ALI HAKIM: You will just forget us? Forget Ana, forget Souad? Me?

Silence.

You forget who you are.

ALI ABABWA turns away angrily from ALI HAKIM.

Roll video, please.

PROJECTION:

A map of Agraba.

PROJECTION:

Agraba: A People's History.

ALI HAKIM: Ladies and gentlemen, Agraba has a long and complicated and beautiful history but I will only tell you of the Agraba we grew up in. Agraba was a country of few haves and many have-nots. The "government" was a corrupt oligarchy supported by imperial powers who controlled Agraba's agronium mines.

1968. In comes Agraba's great reformer: Jafar Ali Salim, head of the Agronium Miners' Union, who calls for a nationwide general strike.

PROJECTION:

The Agrabanian Flag.

I remember getting up in the morning to find my father still at home and I said to him, "Poopa, what is wrong? Why are you at home?" And he explained to me that he was not going to work, he was on strike. For as long as I could remember my mother and father were always worrying about money and whether my father's job would last and there they were jeopardizing everything.

The strike went on for months. Everybody went out in the end. Almost everybody. The general strike was the watershed. The oligarchy –

ALI ABABWA: (*sotto voce*) donkey shitters –

ALI HAKIM: collapsed. And Jafar Ali Salim became Agraba's first democratically elected leader. What days those were. The conversations. The poetry. The music. The street corner debates. The promise.

For first time ever, agronium profits stay in country. Health care is free. Education is free. University. This is where I meet Ali Ababwa. He is leader of student union. We are in charge of our country, our lives, he says in big speech. We must work to make our future happen. Everyone claps, cheers.

ALI ABABWA: This was long time ago, Ali Hakim.

ALI HAKIM: He had hippy clothes. Big hair. (*beat*) That's when you met Souad. Remember?

ALI ABABWA: I remember.

A moment of silence.

ALI HAKIM: Of course it couldn't last.

ALI ABABWA: The Sammites

ALI HAKIM: backed by the CIA

ALI ABABWA: started to make trouble.

ALI HAKIM: Then the coup d'état.

ALI ABABWA: Jafar Ali Salim died defending our revolution.

ALI HAKIM: His soul ascended to the golden shores of Piña Majorca.

ALI ABABWA: You can be sure.

ALI ABABWA & ALI HAKIM: May we all find ourselves in Piña.

They make the Piña Majorca gesture.

ALI HAKIM: With Jafar. And Souad.

ALI ABABWA nods in acknowledgement.

ALI ABABWA: The Sammite extremists established the Theocratic State of Agraba.

ALI HAKIM: These clerics who had renounced the material world were now driven around in the latest model Mercedes and lived in palatial homes, waited on hand and foot.

ALI ABABWA: People got together and tried to resist this new alliance between the clerics and the oligarchy. Who knows how things might have worked out?

ALI HAKIM: But then came the business with the flight schools and the Thin Towers and the need to vaporize every tent in Afghanistan. And while you were all watching Gulf War Two: The Sequel on CBCNN, the U.S.A. launched top-secret mission Operation Agrabust. Under U.S. command, coalition troops from Mauritius and the Solomon Islands invaded Agraba and seized control one more time.

ALI ABABWA: Of the agronium mines and the water.

ALI HAKIM: Of the palaces and remnants of the CIA–trained secret police.

ALI ABABWA: Of the decayed power plants and children begging in the streets.

ALI HAKIM: Opening up an exciting emerging market. Today in Agraba City is two-mile lineup for gasoline. They say is liberation and they close newspapers and blow up hospitals, sell off national industries. Call it reconstruction. Put up shiny new fence of barbed wire around my sister's village. No one is allowed to come or go without permission of Provisional Authority. When my sister complain, they bulldoze her house. I haven't heard from her since.

Today in Agraba City, the same religious police who murdered Ali Ababwa's Souad now make successful applications to Provisional Authority for lots of new guns.

ALI ABABWA: Is a very big mess, my friends.

ALI HAKIM: Very big.

A moment of quiet, then music sneaks in. They sing the national anthem of Agraba.

ALI ABABWA & ALI HAKIM:

> *"NATIONAL ANTHEM OF AGRABA"*
> *Oh I'm proud to be Agrabanian*
> *There's no food but there's lots of tea*
> *And I won't forget all the men*
> *From whom I bummed smokes for free*
>
> *My country's two kilometres*
> *From sea to oily sea*
> *Thank God for our Agraba*
> *And my sister's black-and-white TV*

Please join us …

Onscreen, a karaoke version begins.

> *I'm proud to be Agrabanian*
> *Not a stinking Turkish dog*
> *I love to eat the chickpea*
> *And have forsworn the hog*
>
> *Oh Agraba, oh Agraba*
> *Long live the green and chrome*
> *'Til we get to Piña Majorca*
> *Our one and only home*

ALI ABABWA & ALI HAKIM: May we all find ourselves in Piña.

They do the Piña Majorca gesture.

ALI ABABWA: I need a break.

He leaves.

ALI HAKIM: So do I. TIM!

TIM enters.

ALI HAKIM: (*glaring at audience*) Keep an eye on them. Make sure they don't try to steal anything. If they do, it comes out of your pay, Tim.

ALI HAKIM leaves. A long pause.

TIM: It's *Tom*. My *name* is Tom.

He turns to the audience.

I'm sorry about this. I'm not responsible – these guys they, well, you've seen how they treat me. I'm a professional actor. I did *The X-Files*. Two episodes.

PROJECTION:

A scene from *The X-Files* with Tom Butler in it.[13]

I worked with Meryl Streep.

PROJECTION:

A scene from Meryl Streep movie with Tom Butler in it.

I did two feature films in China.

PROJECTION:

A scene from Chinese movie with Tom Butler.

Freddy vs. Jason.

PROJECTION:

A scene from *Freddy vs. Jason* with Tom Butler in it.

I was in *Josie and the Pussycats*.

PROJECTION:

A scene from *Josie and the Pussycats* with Tom Butler in it.

Did you see that? Maybe your kids saw it? I love kids. Making them laugh.

He pulls out the Ali and Ali promotional postcard.

But you know, there's no work. The Keep It in America campaign is just killing us up here and stupid us for never developing our own industry and always relying on the Americans. Like we thought they wouldn't abandon us when things got tough or the dollar went too high? And now the Terminator is governor.

So I'm reduced to this. Working for these two ... just to put food in my daughter's horse's stable.

PROJECTION:

TIM's daughter's horse.

I love the theatre. I studied at the National Theatre School. You know I was around in the original TWP days. Been doing this a while. But these two

they're ... I don't know what kind of Muslims they're supposed to be; they're always trying to get me to buy them martinis. And that blue one, I don't know, I don't think it's real, the blue. And the play ... There's so much they could be doing with this material: I mean really showing the suffering and exposing the connections of the American elite, you know, George W. and Arbusto Energy; Dick Cheney and Haliburton Oil; Condoleezza Rice and Chevron – she even had an oil tanker named after her. And Poindexter and Abrams getting a pardon for Iran-Contra. And did you hear about the Bush administration insuring American corporations in Iraq with taxpayers' money, because the private companies are too smart to take the risk? That's how we would have done it at TWP [Toronto Workshop Productions] –

ALI & ALI return.

ALI ABABWA: What are you doing, fool? Shut up. Is the name of this show *Tim & Tim and the aXes of Evil*? No. It's *Ali & Ali and the aXes of Evil*. Shut up. Off.

TIM protests. ALI HAKIM produces a black hood, such as was used by U.S. soldiers on inmates at Abu Ghraib prison (and probably elsewhere).

TIM: No, please, not the hood. I'm not gonna wear that again.

ALI HAKIM escorts TIM off.

ALI ABABWA: Don't mind him, he's from Ottawa. Now, ladies and gentlemen, as we approach the end of our show we are very pleased to welcome onto the stage our newest, no, our very first corporate sponsor. You know we asked a lot of people for support and, surprisingly, not many were interested. We asked, for example, CAE, big Canadian weapons manufacturer. We thought it was a good fit. They make all those weapons being used where we come from and the show is all about that but they weren't interested. Not even a postcard.[14]

ALI HAKIM runs on excitedly.

ALI HAKIM: He's here! I brought him out of the taxi myself.

ALI ABABWA: Ladies and gentlemen, please join us in extending a warm clash of civilizations

---

13   If an actor playing Tim has suitable film, TV, or video credits, they can be substituted. If not, some other device might be called for.

14   They also asked Saddam Hussein, who *was* interested, but unfortunately he'd had a bad year and felt this wasn't the right time for him to give.

welcome to the president of al Qaeda, Mr. Osama bin Laden.

OSAMA enters. He is carrying an AK-47 and a suitcase.

OSAMA: Thank you very much. Begging your indulgence, I am Osama bin Laden and I am the leader of al Qaeda.

From the beginning, art has been a part of all our lives. Or so I am told. As a Wahhabi, I take a dim view of art, among other things. But hey, I am willing to try something new. As Omar the Mullah likes to say, "You take what you can get before you get to the virgins."

It is not enough to blow up big buildings once every ten years. We must win the hearts and minds of the infidel. It is for this reason that we have begun our first strategic partnership with the poor and downtrodden members of the state-less migrant artistic community.

And so, Dan, on behalf of al Qaeda, I'm very pleased to present Ali and Ali with this gift to support your production, *The Adventures of Ali & Ali and the Taxis of Evil*.

He hands over the suitcase.

ALI ABABWA: Actually, it's the aXes of Evil.

OSAMA: Yes. Congratulations.

ALI & ALI look at the audience.

ALI ABABWA: What? You don't like our sponsor?

ALI HAKIM: Mr. ...

OSAMA: Call me Osama.

ALI HAKIM: Please, small moment.

OSAMA checks his watch, then sits. They all sit on the rug together.

ALI HAKIM: Though it may come as a surprise to you, most people in these parts perceive al Qaeda as a loose band of unwashed murderous terrorists who also like to oppress women.

OSAMA rants in fundamentalist gibberish.

ALI ABABWA: Okay, it's okay if you don't want to stop jihad because, from what we can tell, here in the postmodern, post-industrial West, it is not your actions that count so much as your image.

ALI HAKIM: Perhaps what you are facing is image problem.

ALI ABABWA: No no, perceptual challenge.

ALI HAKIM: Many groups have them.

ALI ABABWA: Monsanto, for example.

ALI HAKIM: Pfizer.

ALI ABABWA: Shell.

ALI HAKIM: Dow Chemical.

ALI ABABWA: Or GE. Making and selling all those weapons to Israel, Kuwait, and Egypt. How many people do they kill?

ALI HAKIM: Or Lockheed Martin, maker of F-16. How many people do they kill?

ALI ABABWA: Or Raytheon. Maker of wide variety of missile. How many people do they kill?

ALI HAKIM: Or Ronald Reagan. Or Madeleine Albright and Bill Clinton. How many people did they kill? Or Henry Kissinger.[15]

ALI ABABWA: How many people did he kill?

ALI HAKIM: Like you, a very rich man and also wanted in several countries.

ALI ABABWA: Just as these shady individuals and organizations utilize the tools of public relations to minimize the consequences of their crimes, so too can you and your organization, Mr. Osama.

ALI HAKIM: Perhaps they need a new name.

ALI ABABWA: Al Qaeda has a lot of negative connotations.

ALI HAKIM: But I don't think he wants to give up al Qaeda altogether.

ALI ABABWA: Top marks for visibility.

ALI HAKIM: You can't buy that kind of recognition.

ALI ABABWA: But you could, you know – change it.

ALI HAKIM: Make it fresh.

ALI ABABWA: Different.

---

15   The revision of history was in full swing when we performed in Edmonton (June 2004) and so we added some names to respond to events. Ronald Reagan had finally died and was (virtually) everywhere being hailed as a great man who had brought peace and stability to the globe. His responsibility for the U.S.-sponsored terrorist war on Nicaragua in the 1980s (along with his war on the poor) was conveniently dumped in the Memory Hole.

Madeleine Albright, you may recall, was Clinton's Secretary of State who, when asked how she felt about the half-million Iraqi children dying as a result of U.S.-imposed sanctions (after the first War on Iraq), answered, "It's a tough choice but we think it's worth it."

ALI HAKIM: New.

ALI ABABWA: New al Qaeda!

ALI HAKIM: New is good. But also kind of old. How about al Qaeda 2.0? Or AQ2.

ALI ABABWA: Yes! You know it's al Qaeda but you don't.

ALI HAKIM: And easier to spell.

ALI ABABWA: Sure, my client drove some big planes into some tall buildings but who here hasn't made mistakes.

ALI HAKIM: Like U.S.A. – getting into bed with Shah of Iran, with Saddam Hussein, with Taliban. These are mistakes anyone can make.

ALI ABABWA: You say – whoops – is all different now.

ALI HAKIM: You could still win the Nobel Peace Prize.

ALI ABABWA: Like Henry Kissinger.

ALI HAKIM: Or Peres, Rabin, and Arafat.

ALI ABABWA: But to get to this level I think you also need to rebrand *yourself*.

ALI HAKIM: Osama bin Laden?

ALI ABABWA: Unh nuh nuh.

ALI HAKIM: How about ... Osama bin ... Oprah.

ALI ABABWA: Ahhhh! Yin and yang.

ALI HAKIM: New and old.

ALI ABABWA: Black and kind of yellow. It appeals to a broad spectrum. Good, no?

OSAMA: No.

ALI HAKIM: Okay. You're right. Goodbye – thanks for the briefcase. Can we apply two years in a row?

OSAMA: (*off*) Omar, quick, bring the taxi.

ALI HAKIM: Let's see how much Osama left us, shall we?

They pick up the briefcase. It's heavy. Ticking is heard.

ALI HAKIM: Ali Ababwa.

ALI ABABWA: Ali Hakim.

ALI HAKIM: I had the most

ALI ABABWA: beautiful dream.

ALI HAKIM: I was at my sister's house

ALI ABABWA: back in Agraba.

ALI HAKIM: Only the whole world was Agraba.

ALI ABABWA: And everyone was there. You

ALI HAKIM: Ana

ALI ABABWA: Souad was alive.

ALI HAKIM: Spring had come.

ALI ABABWA: The snow melted

ALI HAKIM: and the village overflowed

ALI ABABWA: with children.

ALI HAKIM: Our words had grown taller than our swords.

ALI ABABWA: The battlefields were green with grass.

ALI HAKIM: And everyone had meaningful work.

ALI ABABWA: And food enough.

ALI HAKIM: And clean water.

ALI ABABWA: And it was all

ALI HAKIM: so easy,

ALI ABABWA: so simple.

A beat.

ALI ABABWA: This must have been Piña Majorca.

ALI HAKIM: No, Ali, I think perhaps it was the future.

ALI & ALI turn to the audience, questioning. They turn to each other. There is a lengthy, deafening, and terrifying explosion. Lights blind the audience.

VOICEOVER: Ladies and gentlemen, please remain seated. This was not a real explosion; it is only theatre, an illusion. There is no immediate danger to you. Please stick around and buy a commemorative program, have a drink in the upstairs bar. We repeat: this is not a real explosion.

The actor who plays TIM / OSAMA appears in a pool of light, peeling off his Osama beard and moustache.

TIM: (*overlapping*) We repeat: this is not a real explosion. Had this been a real explosion from, say, a five-thousand-pound laser-guided penetrator smart bomb or a twenty-two-year-old Chechen widow with six kilograms of explosives strapped to her body, you would not be hearing this announcement. Your children would have been left father- or motherless, any friends living in the immediate vicinity would have been wiped out. We repeat: this is not real. Look, there you are. There's your hand, still good for taking your daughter's hand, writing a poem, scratching your bum. There's your lover, your friend, your dad, a stranger beside you. You see. It's only an illusion.

*The lights shift to reveal **ALI HAKIM** smoking a hookah while **ALI ABABWA** prepares for bed.*

ALI HAKIM: (*singing to himself*)

This is the end
My Semitic Friend, the end
Of our elaborate plans, the end

He turns to the audience.

It really is. The end. Thank you for coming.

He sings again.

I'll never look into her eyes again.

ALI ABABWA: Don't be so pessimistic.

He removes his "show" shirt and puts on a T-shirt.

ALI HAKIM: I'm hungry.

ALI ABABWA: Have a smoke, it dulls the hunger.

To audience.

Ah, good night. We're going to ... Ali Hakim, they're just sitting there.

ALI HAKIM shrugs.

ALI ABABWA: My bum hurts.

ALI HAKIM: Have a smoke. It dulls the pain.

ALI ABABWA: Really, this is the only thing, just to sit quietly, like this.

ALI HAKIM: Ali Ababwa ... you are really wishing to stay here with them?

ALI ABABWA: I don't know, Ali Hakim. (*a pause*) I don't know –

*He notices **ALI HAKIM** has fallen asleep. He turns to the audience.*

When you decide to go, please leave quietly as Ali Hakim is sleeping. Good night.

He draws on the narghileh. His eyes close. The light dims. Music (Souad Massi) plays.

END

LINDA
GRIFFITHS

Feminism on the modern Canadian stage has a rich history. Volume One of this anthology features plays by Sharon Pollock, Ann-Marie MacDonald, and Sally Clark whose women characters, historical and fictional, refuse to conform to standard patterns or perform to accepted norms. Linda Griffiths and her plays fall into a similar category. One of the few Canadian playwrights to have emerged in the 1970s and remained active well into the twenty-first century, Griffiths has created a substantial body of theatre that includes memorable portraits of Margaret Trudeau, Wallis Simpson, and poet Gwendolyn MacEwen, all powerful, rebellious, contentious women. With *Age of Arousal*, the most successful of her recent plays, Griffiths reaches back to the suffragist era in late-nineteenth-century England to dramatize a group of "odd" women – and a man – on the cusp of momentous historical change, struggling to reconcile their feelings with their ideologies. The desire for sex, the desire for love and security, the desire for children, and received notions of gender come crashing up against the politics of emancipation. *Age of Arousal* treats all its characters and their complexities with respect, intelligence, and delightful wit, offering an erotic portrait of a turbulent era and raising fascinating questions about the feminist project.

Born in Montreal, Linda Griffiths studied at Dawson College, the National Theatre School (briefly), and McGill University. In 1975 she moved to Saskatoon, working as an actor with 25th Street Theatre. When director Paul Thompson came out from Toronto that year with his Theatre Passe Muraille ensemble to collectively create *The West Show*, Thompson did what he would often so valuably do: "seed" local theatre by encouraging, and minimally funding, local artists to create their own shows about their community and its history. The result was 25th Street's collectively improvised *If You're So Good, Why Are You in Saskatoon?* (1975), directed by Thompson with Griffiths as a performer and creator. It established Griffiths's talent for fruitful collaboration and improvisation, and marked the beginning of her productive relationship with Thompson and Theatre Passe Muraille.

In 1977, she played a key role in the 25th Street Theatre collective that created and performed *Paper Wheat*, an exuberant ensemble piece about the development of Saskatchewan's Co-op movement and Wheat Pool. *Paper Wheat* went on to sold-out tours of the province and the country while Griffiths rejoined Thompson back east to work on Passe Muraille collectives. One of the roles she played in *Les maudits anglais* (1979) in

Montreal was Prime Minister Pierre Elliott Trudeau. With Thompson's collaboration and direction, she developed his character into the full-length *Maggie & Pierre* (1980). Griffiths performed all three characters: Pierre, his wife Margaret – a celebrity in her own right – and a fictional journalist. *Maggie & Pierre* was a breakout success, winning Dora Mavor Moore awards for best new play and lead performance. Griffiths toured the show across Canada, played it off-Broadway and in an acclaimed 1997 Toronto revival. Its primary theme, the conflict of reason and passion, recurs everywhere in her work – in a major way in *Age of Arousal*.

Griffiths also performed in her next play, *O.D. on Paradise* (1982), written with Patrick Brymer. It premiered in Saskatoon and won another Dora Award for best new play in Toronto. Her third Dora for new play (along with a Chalmers Canadian Play Award and best production at the Quinzanne International Festival in Quebec City) came in 1986 with *Jessica*, a revised version of a script Griffiths first developed and wrote in collaboration with Thompson and Métis author Maria Campbell for 25th Street and Passe Muraille in 1982. Following the 1986 production, Griffiths and Campbell wrote an extraordinary book about their difficult collaboration with its issues of guilt and shame, race, gender, and spirituality, appropriation, betrayal, and self-hatred. It was published along with the revised script as *The Book of Jessica: A Theatrical Transformation* (1989).

Griffiths acted with Alan Williams in her two-hander *The Darling Family: A Duet for Three* (1991), which he directed. A powerful, popular play about a couple fighting over whether to have a child or an abortion, it introduced Griffiths's "thoughtspeak" technique, used extensively in *Age of Arousal*, in which characters speak their subtextual thoughts aloud. *The Darling Family* was nominated for the Governor General's, Chalmers, and Dora Awards, and Griffiths wrote and starred in a 1994 feature film version. She also starred in the title roles of *The Duchess: a.k.a. Wallis Simpson* (1996) and *Alien Creature: A Visitation from Gwendolyn MacEwen* (1999), a solo show. *Alien Creature*, co-produced with Passe Muraille by her new company, Duchess Productions, earned her a fifth Dora, second Chalmers, and second Governor General's Award nomination. In 1999, seven of her early plays, from *Maggie & Pierre* to *The Duchess*, were published in a volume titled *Sheer Nerve*.

Toronto's Factory Theatre produced *Chronic* (2003), a play about illness with Eric Peterson as the Virus. *Age of Arousal* premiered in Calgary in 2007, winning the Betty Mitchell Award for Best New Play, followed the same year by Nightwood Theatre's Toronto production and the U.S. premiere in Philadelphia. It has since played across Canada, in Texas, North Carolina, and Virginia, Edinburgh and Glasgow, gathering rousing reviews almost everywhere. Daniel MacIvor directed Griffiths in *The Last Dog of War* (2009), a solo show for Theatre Projects Manitoba (Winnipeg) about her relationship with her RAF pilot father. In 2013, Theatre Passe Muraille plans a production of *Heaven Above, Heaven Below*, a sequel to *The Darling Family* with Griffiths again in the cast. *Games*, a play about parents and their video gamer son, is scheduled for the 2014 Enbridge New playRites Festival of New Canadian Plays in Calgary.

Along with her playwriting and stage acting, Griffiths has worked extensively in TV and film. She played the title role in John Sayles's 1983 feature, *Liana*; was nominated for a series of acting awards for television, winning a Gemini; and hosted CBC-TV's *Opening Night* (2000–01). She also teaches a popular course called Visceral Playwrighting, based on the strategies she uses for improvising her own new work.

Age of Arousal is based on – or as Griffiths prefers, "wildly inspired by" – George Gissing's 1893 novel, *The Odd Women*. Gissing's title refers to the surplus of women to men in 1880s England, which inevitably left many women unmarried, therefore prone to experimenting with alternative ways of being a woman, hence "odd." Griffiths adds to this mix the politics of women's suffrage, seriously heating up in England at that time, along with the sexual heat she assumes Gissing's characters must have felt beneath the repressive demands of their Victorian mores. In the Coach House Press edition, Griffiths explains why she set *Age of Arousal* in 1885: "I wanted the fusty velvets, the tight corsets, the claustrophobia of a world about to ignite. I wanted a blast of modernity to come from underneath the dust bunnies of Victorian England" (136). Her title speaks to the various forms of arousal her characters experience.

Former militant suffragist Mary Barfoot's secretarial school provides a space for women to learn skills that might offer them a sense of competency and potential financial independence. She calls her Remington type machines "our secret weapon in the battle for equal opportunity." But the battlefield turns out to be a lot more complicated. The women, including three sisters (that magical theatrical number), struggle with their feelings for each other – desire, envy, jealousy, resentment, love, loyalty among them – the conventions of marriage and imperatives of biology, and the sexual feelings they are forbidden by their education, upbringing, or feminist militancy to act on. Some succeed in breaking their own taboos by embracing lesbianism, cross-dressing, or sexual promiscuity. Others vacillate between transgression and conformity. A new world is dawning and with it a new set of rules that no one yet understands. Everything is up for grabs. Even Everard, the play's lone male, finds himself besieged by internal conflict, his growing intellectual enlightenment wrestling with his Victorian notions of masculinity and femininity, and his rampant sexuality.

Sexuality is rampant throughout the play, often revealed through italicized "thoughtspeak" in outbursts that comically contrast with the characters' buttoned-down, corseted demeanours. In the midst of a serious conversation Everard and Rhoda are having about her relationship with Mary, he suddenly thinks/says, "*The swell of her breasts –*" and Rhoda: "*The bulge in his trousers –*" But just because they can't help thinking about sex doesn't mean that Griffiths trivializes the significance of what they are talking about at the same time. "I imagine a world where we might rage and cry, give birth, weep for a kitten, then oversee a transaction worth millions," says Mary. Griffiths understands that we are many things simultaneously. Lust and intellectual rigour need not be mutually exclusive.

As Monica says, "Erotical freedoms are historically inseparable from the discourse of liberation."

Griffiths has great fun with some of the conventions of Victorian behaviour – the inspired fainting sequence in the play, for instance. Her women seem awfully modern in that scene, implicitly understanding that gender is performative. In fact, the play consciously conflates Victorian ideas with those of our own age. In three instances, Griffiths admits in a note at the end of the Coach House text, her characters are actually quoting Germaine Greer. Progress can be very gradual; everything old is new again. No wonder one of the play's biggest laugh lines in production is its last, referring to the emancipation and equality of women: "In thirty years it will all be accomplished."

Age of Arousal

Linda Griffiths

Age of Arousal premiered at Alberta Theatre Projects' playRites Festival in Calgary, associate produced by Duchess Productions, on February 9, 2007, with the following cast:

MARY BARFOOT	Dawn Greenhalgh
RHODA NUNN	Irene Poole
VIRGINIA MADDEN	Valerie Planche
ALICE MADDEN	Elinor Holt
MONICA MADDEN	Gemma James-Smith
EVERARD BARFOOT	John Kirkpatrick

Directed by Karen Hines
Set Design by Scott Reid
Costume Design by Jenifer Darbellay
Lighting Design by David Fraser
Original Music and Sound Design by Richard McDowell
Stage Managed by Rhonda Kambeitz

CHARACTERS

MARY BARFOOT, *sixty years old – definitely not an old lady. Charismatic, egocentric, sexy. Enjoys young women's attention and admiration. An ex-militant suffragette who now runs a school for secretaries. In love with Rhoda.*

RHODA NUNN, *thirty-five years old. An orphan who has become a New Woman with a tendency to zeal. Loyal, idealistic, physically passionate – about to burst into flower. Mary's lover and a teacher at her school.*

VIRGINIA MADDEN, *forty years old. Anxious, agitated, and hyperbolic. Impoverished ex-governess and alcoholic. Confused about her sexuality – secretly desires to dress as a man.*

ALICE MADDEN, *forty-six years old. Ex-governess and sister to Virginia. The take-charge older sister – deeply conservative but full of inner passion. Chastity is more than comfortable for her.*

MONICA MADDEN, *twenty-one years old. Delectable younger sister to Alice and Virginia. Provocative and playful. Struggles with an intense natural sexuality which becomes a revolutionary perspective.*

EVERARD BARFOOT, *thirty-five years old. Sensual, confident, enticed by the New. Cousin to Mary Barfoot. Ex-doctor just beginning a life of leisure. Falls in love with Rhoda and the Woman Question.*

SETTING

London, 1885. A time of enormous political, emotional, and sexual change. People are bursting their corsets with unbridled desire. There are half a million more women than men living in England. The women's suffrage movement is fuelled by sheer numbers. Women demand rights. Those who protest are "unsexed." But the tide is too strong. Passions erupt and confusion reigns …

STAGING

The actors sit on either side of the stage area, watching the action. A large white screen illuminates the back wall. When they must change costume, the characters go behind the screen. The female characters wear the undergarments of Victorian dress on the outside – crinoline cages, bustle forms of all kinds – some resemble the spines of reptiles. Their upper bodies are more modern.

ACT ONE

Lights up on a stage containing one large chaise, bed, or couch.

SCENE 1: THE DREAM

MARY BARFOOT's sitting room. MARY is shaking in RHODA's arms.

RHODA: Shhhhh ... shhhhhhh ...

MARY: I can't –

RHODA: What can't you?

MARY: I still can't breathe –

RHODA: Yes you can. See, you can. It was a dream.

MARY: Not a dream, a nightmare of epic proportions.

RHODA: All right, a nightmare.

MARY: That's better.

RHODA: Don't be angry.

MARY: I'm not angry, I've just had a nightmare of epic proportions –

RHODA: Because you are an epic woman.

MARY: Bollocks.

RHODA: That's better.

MARY: Is it?

RHODA: You know it is.

MARY: You are irritating in the extreme.

RHODA: I am.

MARY: It's embarrassing to be so terrorized by a dream.

RHODA: Nightmare.

MARY: Stop.

RHODA: Is it the one about the force-feeding?

MARY: I haven't dreamt of it for ages, then the dream returns and "unmans" me.

RHODA: Tell me.

MARY: You know it all.

RHODA: I don't.

MARY: Three matrons, one of them very young, enter with the instruments, pry my mouth open, wrench the clamp between my teeth (breaking two), I feel the blood running down my face, then the feeding tube – this is silly –

RHODA: It's not. Tell me.

MARY: I won't, you love the gory details too much, which reveals a very female attraction to suffering. It's the suffocation when they shove the tube down, the blind panic, gasping and straining to breathe, you writhe like an animal –

RHODA: It was torture.

MARY: That's not what haunts me. It is the feeling of loss, as if I failed to stand up to the test. The dream reminds me of what a coward I was.

RHODA: Coward! I hate it when you say that. You marched, were beaten, imprisoned, went on hunger strikes and all for –

MARY: The rights of women? Or for my own glory? I was always terrified and finally I fled.

RHODA: I won't hear this.

MARY: You don't know me.

RHODA: I do.

MARY: A weak warrior.

RHODA: An Amazon. (*gets a brush*)

MARY: You're dressed. Hadn't you come to bed yet?

RHODA: I was up when I heard you.

MARY: Up after midnight? How poetic of you. Ohhhhhh lovely. (*raises her head to be brushed*) Why couldn't you sleep?

RHODA: I was restless.

MARY: Restless.

RHODA: Are *you* never restless?

Slight pause.

MARY: (*lowers her head*) Ohhhh ... wonderful.

RHODA: It's still so lovely and thick.

MARY: (*raises her head*) Still?

RHODA: I didn't mean –

MARY: Still? Still thick?

RHODA: I only meant that –

MARY: Do you see a few grubby pieces of hair sticking out like the stubble from a field of wheat? A few measly, greasy strands –

RHODA: (*laughing*) Stop, I am warning you.

MARY: The last time they kicked me out the prison door, I could barely walk. I couldn't help thinking of the rich women who always had a carriage waiting, pillows for their arses, new dresses to complement their slim figures.

RHODA: You felt the gap between rich and poor within the struggle.

MARY: I found I wanted money. I wanted it, I wanted women to have it. You don't know me. Laying down my sword to open a school for secretaries.

RHODA: You chose a path away from militancy to further women's financial emancipation.

MARY: Or I chose the coward's path because I could no longer endure militancy.

RHODA: Never speak of being a coward again. You were privileged to be on the front lines. You engaged in battle. I only wish I had the same opportunity to prove myself.

MARY: Do you? You want to know how you'd react under fire?

RHODA: I'm afraid I would run away as soon as I was truly challenged.

MARY: Not you, brave heart.

RHODA: You don't know me.

MARY: Shall I torture you to find out? Whip you? Tie you up with my old Votes banner?

RHODA: You'd have to arrest me first.

MARY: Come here. I arrest you and demand bail for your release. I demand … a kiss. (*They kiss.*) Shall we leave this place of business and retire to my rare and sinister boudoir?

RHODA: Your boudoir is ever a garden of delights, but you are upset, I am restless, and the accounts have been piling up. Let's do some sinister business.

MARY: That's what you were doing? The accounts?

RHODA: What does it matter? Yes, I started on the accounts. We must run this school as a proper business.

MARY: I am awake, I might as well help you.

RHODA: (*sorting through papers*) A great pile of outstanding loans.

MARY: My cousin Everard is back from abroad.

RHODA: The hedonist?

MARY: Wicked, I shouldn't have called him that.

RHODA: He's not a hedonist?

MARY: I do not know what he is.

RHODA: Will we see him?

MARY: I believe we must. (*back to papers*) Violet is coming along –

RHODA shivers.

RHODA: Not really. *What has happened? Has something happened? A moment, a perfectly ordinary moment and yet as if some certainty is disappearing –*

MARY: *She's going to leave me, perhaps not yes, she will, she doesn't know but I know –*

RHODA: *Just a draught of cold air, a shiver, yet my eyes lose focus, the floor tilts, there is no ground under my feet –*

MARY: *I'm on the brink of old age, all my flirting done / oh Lord what a fate –*

RHODA: *What has happened?*

MARY: *Do not pack a bag in the middle of the night, do not tell me in a mature and confiding womanly way / that would send me to the grave –*

RHODA: *Hero, teacher, lover, she awakened me, too timid to find my own body till she opened its secrets –*

MARY: *I've filled her head, done nefarious acts to her body –*

RHODA: *Saved me from poverty, blindness, mediocrity –*

MARY: *The icy breath of change.*

RHODA: *Nothing has changed. Nothing has changed.*

MARY: *Don't hate me when it's done.* I'm going back to bed. Are you coming?

RHODA: I'll just finish this note to Bella.

MARY: Don't be long. (*exits*)

SCENE 2: THE BUMP

A London street outside Victoria Station. VIRGINIA is drunk. RHODA is not. VIRGINIA and RHODA smack loudly into each other. VIRGINIA lands heavily on the ground.

RHODA: Ughhhh!

VIRGINIA: Ahhh!

RHODA: I beg your pardon!

VIRGINIA: I've been hit by a train, a horse, a great black steed, my limbs / are severed, my arm is falling off –

RHODA: No, not a train, a person, we bumped into each other, are you hurt / let me help you up –

VIRGINIA: Not hurt, not hurt –

RHODA: Virginia? Virginia Madden? It's Rhoda Nunn.

VIRGINIA: Nunn?

RHODA: Rhoda. We knew each other as girls.

VIRGINIA: Rhoda Nunn. Of course. You argued with my father about Parliament –

RHODA: How are your sisters?

VIRGINIA: Two are dead.

RHODA: My condolences –

VIRGINIA: There's only Alice and pretty Monica left –

RHODA: So many tragedies.

VIRGINIA: Ohh, dizzy ...

RHODA: There's a tea shop just around the corner –

VIRGINIA: Tea shop? You think I can afford tea shops on five pence a day? Ohh, faint –

RHODA: Let me help you. Where do you live?

VIRGINIA: When Father died the whole world became a jungle, he was the lion and now there is nothing / but weeping spinsters as far as the eye can see ...

RHODA: Put your arm over my ... not that way ... no, no, turn towards me – Virginia? Do you feel my arm?

VIRGINIA: Arm.

RHODA: Do you feel its strength?

VIRGINIA: Lovely. Yes.

RHODA: Then lean into me and I will take you home.

SCENE 3: BEDSIT

*Three chairs represent a barren bedsit. **ALICE** has a bad cold. **VIRGINIA** and **RHODA** enter.*

ALICE: Achoo!

VIRGINIA: Alice! Look who I met on the street –

ALICE: Virginia! Where were you? I woke up from a nap and you were gone –

VIRGINIA: Alice, look! It's Rhoda Nunn, she was passing by –

ALICE: You cannot go wandering about by yourself, what would father have said? Rhoda who?

VIRGINIA: Rhoda Nunn!

ALICE: How could you have brought a guest / a guest! Rhoda who?

RHODA: Alice, we knew / each other as girls –

VIRGINIA: I was taken ill and she put out / her strong arm and –

RHODA: I have no intention of bothering you / but your sister –

ALICE: Ill? Are you ill? Do we need a doctor?

VIRGINIA: I am better now. It's Rhoda –

ALICE: Of course, Rhoda Nunn, from a happier time, forgive me, forgive my illness, forgive this room. We must sit down. We must be pleasant and civil. A visit. How gay.

RHODA: Perhaps we should visit at some other time –

ALICE: Pray be seated. Virginia, you are ill, lie down. I am in my nightdress.

VIRGINIA: Shall we have tea?

ALICE: Tea? Are you insane?

VIRGINIA: There must be some leaves left –

ALICE: No tea.

RHODA: I wrote when your father passed away but then moved house and –

ALICE: You were our poor little orphaned friend.

RHODA: Orphaned and poor? Yes, I suppose I was.

ALICE: Father, who was the whole world to us, where is his protection, oh God, his protection.

VIRGINIA: She looks pink cheeked and prospective. Parsimonious?

ALICE: Prosperous.

RHODA: I have been fortunate. And ... you?

ALICE: Father died. Then sister Martha died.

VIRGINIA: Sister Isabel expired horribly in the madhouse.

ALICE: Our guardian, Mr. Humelford, died of the putrid fever.

VIRGINIA: The house was sold, all our belongings sold.

ALICE: There is nothing left. We have recently lost our positions and presently are at leisure –

VIRGINIA: We did work. Have you ever been a governess? Five children looked after for room and board, not a penny of salary, and then they all went to Paris without me. They want certificates now. Formal education. The children were so much larger than I was, even the baby. Very very large.

RHODA: (*dizzily*) I must go.

ALICE: You will not.

VIRGINIA: Now Rhoda is looking faint.

RHODA: I am not given to fainting – *run from the cloying air, the genteel starvation, the stink of* *lavender, sweat, and something else, something with yeast –*

ALICE: *She was a priggish girl even then, as if she were above us, as if she was going to get away, I'd like to smack her in the puss.*

RHODA: *But for a few bits of luck I could be them – I feel the sisters pulling at me, trying to drag me down, don't you dare, I've come too far, too hard –*

VIRGINIA: *I can smell the meat on her, mighty hunks of beef, grizzling platters of lamb –*

ALICE: We are not destitute, however it may appear. When our father died he left us eight hundred pounds.

RHODA: Eight hundred pounds? Not riches, but a fair sum.

ALICE: To be divided among five sisters. Three left. None married.

RHODA: Three? Of course, there was a little girl.

VIRGINIA: Our dear little Monica.

ALICE: Six pence a day for food. Fourteen shillings and tuppence a week. Two pounds, sixteen shillings, and eight pence a month for three months and then ... and then ...

RHODA: Eight hundred pounds could be invested in any number of enterprises.

ALICE: We were advised by the guardian our father appointed never to touch the / principal.

VIRGINIA: Never touch the principal.

ALICE: It is our only security, the only bit of ground we stand on –

VIRGINIA: When we grow old and useless –

ALICE: When no one will give us even board and lodging for our services –

VIRGINIA: Then the principal will be all that keeps us from –

ALICE: The workhouse.

VIRGINIA: The workhouse.

RHODA: Women must stop leaving money matters to male guardians and protectors.

VIRGINIA: Father always said that no woman, old or young, should ever have to think about money.

ALICE: Monica is employed in a shop. They work her half to death, but she is pretty and she will marry.

VIRGINIA: Monica is pretty, Monica will marry.

RHODA: *(standing)* But how? How will she marry? Is it possible you aren't aware of it? For the first

time in recorded memory there is an imbalance in the population of such enormity that it must be a sign from God, if you believe in God. Half a million more women than men in this land. Some say a curse, we say a miracle. The greatest opportunity has been given to us, as though someone were saying, "I take away your props, your supports, your income, aye your slavery and degradation. You cannot marry, you cannot have children, you must rise up – you must be odd!"

Pause.

VIRGINIA: Is that chair uncomfortable? Try this one. I will move here, and you can move there.

ALICE: Too hard a chair. She needs a pillow, would you like a pillow?

VIRGINIA: She should have a pillow.

ALICE: Not that pillow.

VIRGINIA: It's the only pillow unless we use the bed pillow.

ALICE: We cannot use the bed pillow.

RHODA: No pillow! Forgive me. I've been told that I'm something of a zealot – get red in the face when I get going.

ALICE: Nothing of the kind – *very red.*

VIRGINIA: *So pleasantly red.*

ALICE: "Odd," as in ...?

RHODA: Women who will never be paired.

ALICE: Oh. You're not married?

RHODA: I am not.

VIRGINIA: You sound proud of it.

RHODA: I am.

VIRGINIA: You support yourself?

RHODA: I work for a woman of independent means. My employer and I run a school for odd women, meaning –

ALICE: Your employer is a woman?

RHODA: Women must come to grips with two things in this age. Loneliness and money. I must go. I invite you to visit my employer, Miss Mary Barfoot. She's a remarkable woman who may be able to assist you.

ALICE: Well, we / might ...

RHODA: Good, it's settled. And please bring Monica. Sunday next?

VIRGINIA: Ah ...

RHODA: Good –

ALICE: Then you are odd, Miss Nunn?

RHODA: Ferociously odd. Good day.

RHODA exits.

ALICE: *Something is changing, a tonic that makes the eyes burn, like mountain air, too cold too bright –*

VIRGINIA: *As if a tonic had been administered. So thrilled, my breath is panting, every nerve springs forward at attention, a burning sensation throughout my limbs, a barking sensation in my mouth –* She is like a man –

ALICE: Prosperous.

VIRGINIA: And like a man. Resolving –

ALICE: Acting, planning, ordering people about.

VIRGINIA: We'll go for Monica.

ALICE: For Monica.

SCENE 4: BUDDING MORSEL

Sunday in a city park. Bright sunshine, ducks in a pond. EVERARD and MONICA walk together.

MONICA: This is my one free day. I often come to the park to enjoy the sun. You must know that I never go out with gentlemen I don't know. But as I am not acquainted with any gentlemen, my sisters know none, there are none in the streets, none in the shops …

EVERARD: So if you are to have any male company at all, you must take a risk.

MONICA: You seem safe.

EVERARD: *As safe as I can be around a budding young morsel.*

MONICA: *Be contained and virtuous, do not allow the flutterings down below – the fit of his fine wool trousers stretched over well-nourished thighs – no, stop –* I work in a shop.

EVERARD: How lovely.

MONICA: I am endlessly in between – caught, you see. My sisters made me half a lady and half a shopgirl. *I want to lie with him while he licks fine wine off my belly, no, can't stop thinking about it, always thinking about it –*

EVERARD: What a delightful little metamorpho you are. I should put you on exhibit: "Ladies and Gentlemen, here you see a hermaphroditus. Half-lady! Half-shopgirl!" *And probably a virgin, about to be initiated / by someone –*

MONICA: *My eyes drop, of course they drop, to his marriage finger, that singular finger –*

EVERARD: *Ripe, needing to be plucked, breasts like / great round apples –*

MONICA: *And there is no ring –*

EVERARD: *Let me suck the cranberries of your nipples / suck the juice –*

MONICA: *Handsome, educated, a waistcoat that would cost / me a year's wages –*

EVERARD: *Let it dribble down my chin onto your tight little …*

MONICA: *Is he crippled in mind or body, / has he detestable vices?*

EVERARD: *Teach you mysteries –*

MONICA: *No ring on his finger, no ring –* You're not married?

EVERARD: I can't afford to be married.

MONICA: But you're rich.

EVERARD: I'm not. I did work.

MONICA: But now you don't?

EVERARD: Now I'm a man of leisure with a small inheritance.

MONICA: *Monica is pretty, Monica must marry.*

EVERARD: Meet me here next Sunday. I want to see the sunlight glitter on your throat, I want to hear you prattle.

MONICA: My sisters are withered old maids. The sight of them makes me want to off myself. I'm bad, aren't I?

EVERARD: I too saw my family and thought, "I will never be like them," and so I became nothing. *She'll come next Sunday, I see it in her eyes.*

MONICA: *I've been immodest, I've been desperate. I am so weary.*

EVERARD: Yes, I believe you are. *I am striving to be a good man, yet a virile man, to search for my happiness without hurting others, to take pleasure in women because not to do so is to repress one of life's great joys, and so I do dally but often do not taste, I am not at the mercy of my staff, I have practised the breathing methods of India to control my urges – yet when I see a woman of a certain shape, a certain smell, all the husbands I know are in a state of abject misery, this bargain is impossible to make, and yet I see a woman at my hearth, no not a hearth, in Venice, in Paris, a salon with a woman presiding, giving as good as she gets – could this odd girl become a real woman, a New Woman? I want to embrace my age, the machines and the women, I want to measure and to annotate, perhaps I might even work again if a* *woman were there to do what they do, to encourage and support, I would let her be free, I am no barbarian to lock a woman up, forbid her to walk alone, yet we would walk together.* Next Sunday then?

MONICA: Perhaps.

SCENE 5: THE REMINGTONS

MARY BARFOOT's sitting room. VIRGINIA, ALICE, and MONICA arrive. MARY and RHODA receive them.

ALICE: Our deepest apologies, we are so / behind our time, we had to dress, of course, but then Virginia –

VIRGINIA: Such difficulties, Miss Barfoot, we were quite lost, the streets seemed to alter themselves / as we walked –

MONICA: It's a splendid house, real velvet curtains ... ohhh, lovely touch –

MARY: And you must be pretty Monica –

VIRGINIA: *Does she look a little tarty? She does, she looks a little tarty.*

ALICE: *It is her chance, all our chances, hold fast, smile, dear girl, no don't smile, be serious, but not excessively serious –* They work her half to death for a pittance in that shop, Miss Barfoot.

MARY: Mary.

ALICE: Mary.

VIRGINIA: Thirteen hours on her feet, six days of a week.

MARY: Monica, do you wish to change your situation?

MONICA: No, I wish to sludge away in the dung-heap of reputable slavery till I die a joyless old maid. Oh, forgive me, I didn't mean to, sisters, you know I love you, am grateful to you –

ALICE: I prefer "spinster" to "old maid." "Spinster" has dignity. A word from seventeenth-century France. A woman who spins fibre into thread at a spinning wheel, a woman who earns her keep.

VIRGINIA: We don't want Monica to end up like us.

MARY: No one has ended up anywhere.

MONICA: Is it true you were a suffragette? Did you starve yourself, were you beaten? *Flirting, can't stop, can't stop flirting, my body does it all by itself –*

MARY: *Fascinating, one of those girls who exudes sex scents from the cradle –*

MONICA: Have you heard the music hall song, (*speaking*) "She's not a lady, she's a la-di-da for the vote"?

MARY: (*singing*) "She won't have a sweetheart, she won't have a child or a coat, she'll only have a la-di-da vote!"

MONICA: Are all the women you teach spinsters?

ALICE: / Monica!

RHODA: Odd women.

MONICA: *Oh God, don't let it happen to me, alone alone, dry as a bone, wrinkled and hopeless and poor, never kissed, never lain with –*

RHODA: Odd or "redundant" women. We prefer to be odd.

VIRGINIA: I feel redundant.

ALICE: I have heard that "odd woman" means abnormal. A deviant / person –

RHODA: It is a privilege to be an odd woman.

MARY: It is as if the birth rate is on the side of women's rights. There are over four hundred thousand more women than men in this land. A flood, a torrent, a statistical bomb of women.

ALICE: Yes, Rhoda did mention the / population imbalance.

RHODA: Men downed by wars and sex disease, by drink and drug, women eating their vegetables, staying at home –

MARY: Female molecules forming together, ovaries creating more ovaries, wombs more wombs –

VIRGINIA: We did hear / from Rhoda that there is –

RHODA: One out of four women will never be able to marry. Without the burden of children and a husband, they have the leisure to contemplate their circumstances and the need to enter forbidden areas of employment.

ALICE: *We should never have come, our mended skirts, boots with holes, stomachs empty, let us lie down and expire on the carpet.*

MARY: Rhoda, dear, see to luncheon.

RHODA: Yes, Mary. (*exits*)

MONICA: You are against marriage, then?

VIRGINIA: Of course she's not.

ALICE: Monica, you are too bold.

MARY: We are not against marriage. However, every happily unmarried woman is a silent reproach to the conditions of marriage. In this contract, a woman sells herself for her livelihood. She becomes the legal property of her husband, relinquishing all power over her wealth, her children, and her own body. It is legal prostitution. The woman becomes an unpaid breeding machine, with fewer rights than any spinster in this room.

Mini-pause.

VIRGINIA: Miss Barfoot, have you ever flung a bomb or offered a bomb, or however it's said –

ALICE: It is "flung," I believe. Yes, you must have many humorous stories of your exploits as a suffragette.

MONICA: Then you are against marriage.

MARY: Not in its essence. There are many married women in the movement, others are attempting free unions –

MONICA: Free unions?

VIRGINIA: Offering or flinging bombs and such –

MARY: My militancy was limited. I merely committed arson, window smashing, and flooded men's putting greens with a thousand signs saying, "No Vote. No Golf."

RHODA re-enters.

RHODA: Luncheon is ready.

MARY: I ordered a substantial meal, I hope it's not too heavy for you.

RHODA: We'll do this in the new style, as a buffet. Each person serves themselves.

VIRGINIA: Meat?

ALICE: Virginia became a vegetarian when she lost her employment.

VIRGINIA: But perhaps today, in honour of our hostess –

ALICE: Monica, make certain you eat. I am not very hungry, but perhaps a small selection –

VIRGINIA, ALICE, and MONICA begin to load their plates and eat during the rest of the scene.

VIRGINIA: *Goose stuffed with candied ginger, beef tongue with pear dressing –*

ALICE: *Capon with sliced oranges, roast Wellington with chives, I want to tear the flesh with my hands –*

MONICA: *Great plates of steaming oysters / slippery with butter, pimento, sprinkled with parmesan – hungry, so hungry –*

VIRGINIA: *Curried chicken with raisins and pistachios / so hungry hungry –*

ALICE: *Sweet vinegar and / beetroot, sage, and watercress, ohh blessed saliva, hungry so hungry hungry –*

VIRGINIA: *Brandy, brandy in the plum sauce, brandy on the pears / brandy in the custard, lick the brandy, lick it up –*

MONICA: *Roast potatoes with rosemary, creamed parsnips / with parsley and salt –*

ALICE: *Delicious little carrots sprinkled with / cinnamon, nutmeg –*

VIRGINIA: *Sweet strawberries, chocolate rosettes, marzipan hearts –*

ALICE: *Turkish delight –*

MONICA: *This is a trap, it's in all the penny stories, the women ply you with food but it's filled with drug and when you wake, they ravish you.*

RHODA: Have you given any thought to your plans for the future?

ALICE: *(eating)* Plans?

VIRGINIA: *(eating)* Future?

MONICA: *(eating)* I'm getting married.

ALICE: Monica!

MONICA: In the future.

ALICE: Oh yes –

MARY: But until then –

VIRGINIA: Our father brought us up to be ladies. Teaching, governessing –

RHODA: Starving.

MARY: Rhoda.

RHODA and MARY draw apart. MONICA, VIRGINIA, and ALICE continue eating.

RHODA: I can't bear these moping, mawkish creatures, and now this cheap miss –

MARY: Who must be protected. Why do you balk at these sisters? You've helped women like this all over London –

RHODA: I shouldn't have invited them. Suddenly I hate them –

MARY: Then you hate women, then our struggle is for nothing.

RHODA: So sick of prompting and praising, only to have them put the shackles back on their own wrists.

MARY: Oh, don't be so daft.

MARY addresses the room.

Rhoda and I will now give a demonstration of our secret weapon in the battle for equal opportunity.

Magical sound cue. MARY draws aside a curtain and reveals three Remington type machines, circa 1885, splendidly lit.

Behold the Remingtons!

ALICE: Remingtons! I have heard of them.

MONICA: Machines for the future –

VIRGINIA: Glorious, yet appalling. When I look at them I feel I am disappearing into thin air. Where is the beauty of the handwritten note which tells so much? The handwritten note is personal, physical, of the body, of mortal flesh –

ALICE: Virginia. You are not quite yourself.

VIRGINIA: It must be the meat. I murdered that beef.

MARY: And, to show off, yes women may show off, we will perform blindfolded. Alice, may I have your scarf?

MARY and RHODA sit behind the Remingtons, blindfold themselves, and begin to type like virtuoso pianists. What follows is a thrilling percussive duet played on the typewriter keys. The rhythms are complex and gutsy, reminiscent of tap dancing. They build to a crescendo. RHODA and MARY end with a flourish and remove their blindfolds, amid clapping.

VIRGINIA: Thrilling! Spellbinding!

MONICA: A perfectly printed page –

ALICE: And this is what you teach?

MARY: We teach typewriting, shorthand, book-keeping, and correspondence.

VIRGINIA: Oh, I could never do that.

RHODA: Which?

VIRGINIA: Any of it.

RHODA: Why not?

MARY: We enter the closed monolith of business humbly, as assistants and secretaries. But once our pointed boot is in the door, we may involve ourselves in commerce, investment, trade –

VIRGINIA: And you would accept us? The three of us?

RHODA: Well, we would need to discuss / all aspects –

MARY: Yes, we'll accept you.

ALICE: How lovely, so you help needy women.

MARY: No, this is a business, not a charity. Those who can't afford tuition take a loan, which is paid off when they find employment.

MONICA: And if they don't?

RHODA: They're indentured for life, like white slaves.

ALICE: We would live here?

MARY: There are rooms available, at an extra cost.

MONICA: You would own us.

RHODA: We would teach you.

ALICE: But men are secretaries.

MONICA: I've heard wives don't want female secretaries about, tempting their husbands –

RHODA: The girls we teach can be around a man without jumping into his lap over dictation.

MARY: Well, most of them can.

VIRGINIA: I don't know, I don't know – Alice?

RHODA: You may wish to think it over.

ALICE: No. *I want to plant a garden, I want to chance death by childbirth, I want to manage my own home, scrub till my hands crack, I want to shop for food, service a husband, whisper with women about my genitals, I want to burn and sweat through the change of life in quiet seclusion and yet I am denied, I am denied –* Your offer is very kind. We accept. We will be enormously in your debt.

MARY: I imagine a world where we might rage and cry, give birth, weep for a kitten, then oversee a transaction worth millions.

MONICA: *Too many women, they'll pollute my thoughts, make me ashamed of my desires, I have to find a man, a hundred men, before it happens to me –*

RHODA: *They will drag us down, we have larger dreams, remaking a society / a world, we should choose the best, only the best, why serve everyone –*

MARY: *Love the prodigal, the dull, the narrow, help them –*

VIRGINIA: *Give us small comforts, a glass of gin, the liquid burning my throat, feeding my fancies, a drink / a drink a drink a drink, my liver is burning, thirsty thirsty a drink a drink a drink a drink a drink –*

MONICA: *Men balance the world, men as Darwin sees them, achieving, / succeeding, and winning, their deep calm voices, their feet planted in the ground –*

RHODA: *Women with intelligence and ambition to succeed, achieve, and win / willing to climb forbidden mountains –*

MARY: *Encourage and praise and prod and love, never give up, all worthy, all full of hidden treasure –*

ALICE: *We must get out –*

VIRGINIA: *We'll never get out –*

MARY: *The younger one is pretty and the older ones will love me.*

SCENE 6: GYNECOLOGIST

A medical examination room with an examination table, one chair, and a stool. A small utility table holds medical instruments, a wash basin, and towel. MARY sits on the examining table. RHODA sits near her. EVERARD appears.

EVERARD: Cousin Mary, you look exactly the same as when I left.

MARY: You look older. It's all that exotic travelling.

EVERARD: You took over three weeks to answer my note. I was looking forward to dining with you again, arguing till the wee hours –

MARY: My pardon. The school is a very large endeavour.

EVERARD: Dear Mary, I have no idea why you insisted on my examining you. London is full of doctors.

MARY: Sadists. My last doctor was in the habit of performing clitoridectomies as a cure for excessive nerves.

EVERARD: Not on you, I presume.

MARY: Dr. Elizabeth Garrett is overwhelmed and three other physicians have refused to treat me. All I ask is that you give me fair warning when it is time for the speculum. There's a reckless use of that instrument among your profession.

EVERARD: It isn't my profession. I haven't practised for years. I was always more of a dilettante scientist, and now I've given up even that. Now sit still while I listen to your heart ... pray relax yourself.

MARY: Impossible.

EVERARD: *(listening through his stethoscope)* Strong and even.

MARY: I tell women to be examined once yearly and I must be an example.

EVERARD: After returning from my travels, I hoped to visit you for a good meal, not to examine your nether regions.

MARY: Reproductive system. And you will visit, Everard. Soon.

EVERARD: Miss Nunn, do you also wish to be examined?

MARY: She has already had her appointment.

RHODA: I've already had my appointment.

EVERARD: Ah.

EVERARD returns the stethoscope to the table.

MARY: Do you still believe that women in menopause automatically become nymphomaniacs?

EVERARD: I no longer believe in automatic ovario-uterine excitement.

MARY: Good.

EVERARD: Or in the wandering-uterus theory.

EVERARD covers MARY's lower body with a sheet.

MARY: Even better.

EVERARD: But there are indications that child-bearing capacities are compromised by too much thinking. Now, lie down.

MARY lies down on the examining table, facing away from the audience.

As vital energy is drawn away to support the intellect, the ovaries wither.

MARY: Yes, I am nature, of the body, while you are culture, of the intellect. This creates, for women, a diabolical collapsing of physical function and social creation.

EVERARD begins palpating MARY's lower abdomen.

EVERARD: To challenge these distinctions is to go against our inherent sex natures.

MARY: I've been unsexing myself for years – be careful down there.

EVERARD: *(feeling her, completely professional)* Mmhuhh, ahhh ... yes, against our inherent natures, which involve all qualities of behaviour. The manner in which we smell a rose. Now breasts.

EVERARD checks MARY's breasts, feeling them in a circular motion.

And as women's nerve centres are in a greater state of instability, they are more easily deranged.

RHODA: I've heard that everything is allied – our brains, nerves, muscles, organs.

EVERARD: She speaks.

RHODA: I draw my brain away from my womb and I am free to reason.

EVERARD: And how do you accomplish that?

RHODA: By concentrating my thoughts.

EVERARD: Ah.

MARY: These breasts have been palpated enough.

EVERARD moves to a utility table to retrieve his speculum.

EVERARD: But you are built to bear children.

RHODA: And you are built to hunt bison.

EVERARD: Fair warning, Mary. Now the speculum.

EVERARD sits at the end of the table on a small stool, facing the audience.

 Move down. Farther …

MARY moves her bottom down towards EVERARD. Her knees are apart, the sheet covers her.

Farther …

MARY: Oh God.

EVERARD ducks underneath the sheet, covering his head. He peeks out at times to speak.

EVERARD: Good. You see, the cervix is comparable to the tonsils, the womb has a neck and a throat.

EVERARD inserts the speculum.

RHODA: Then you might as well look down her mouth.

MARY: Couldn't the instrument be warmed?

EVERARD: Then visit a real physician.

MARY: Real physicians place it in ice.

EVERARD: Huhmmh … ahha (*pulling out the speculum*) Gently, gently … Mary, you are a paragon of health.

MARY: I need a glass of wine.

EVERARD: I could do with a whole bottle. This is a borrowed office, but there is always some port for the fainters. I'll wash up and then we'll celebrate our reunion. Wine calms the nerves even better than a hysterectomy. Ladies, a joke – *Why has she done this, why act out doctor and patient, I feel as if I had been examined, as if she wanted to test me before her protégé* – Cousin Mary, you've chosen an odd way to introduce me to your protégée.

EVERARD wheels the small table away as he exits.

RHODA: *Utterly odd.*

MARY: (*calling after EVERARD*) This is not an introduction, it is a business appointment – *If she was going to meet my comely cousin, better in a borrowed office, an instrument of torture in his hand –*

RHODA: He's not a monster.

MARY: I never said he was.

RHODA: You did.

MARY: You see a handsome man, intelligent, well-spoken, one who's suffered in the mysterious fashion that travelling brings on. But he has been a rogue and may remain one.

RHODA: Rogues are immoral.

MARY: Men are immoral. Perhaps I feel some guilt. Everard's father objected to his roguish behaviour and changed his will. Everard received enough to live fairly well, but most of the inheritance came to me.

RHODA: That's how you got the school. I didn't know. Do you feel you owe him something?

MARY: I owe him nothing.

EVERARD enters with wine and glasses in hand. He pours for the ladies.

EVERARD: Miss Nunn, you know that I am in sympathy with your cause.

MARY: Bollocks.

EVERARD: Mary went to jail so often that, as a youth, I was unable to shock our family.

MARY: You managed to shock.

EVERARD: And paid for it.

MARY: You did.

EVERARD: To the New Woman.

They drink.

You see, you ladies are actually working for the betterment of men. The majority of women are poor creatures, dependent, wracked with nerves. They want to trap men into marriage, then nag them to the grave. What's an intelligent man to do? Where can he find a mate? In the New Woman, who can converse intelligently and who doesn't rely on love to provide all inner resolve. You are creating better wives for my future.

MARY: It's a buyer's market in wives right now.

EVERARD: Oh, I'll never marry. I've seen too many hounded men.

RHODA: I too will never marry.

EVERARD: You might still be asked.

RHODA: I am not waiting to be asked.

MARY: Rhoda is truly a New Woman.

EVERARD: She hates men.

RHODA: She sees men for what they are.

EVERARD: Selfish, dominating –

RHODA: Beings that need to be woken up.

EVERARD: Then wake us up.

RHODA: I am in the business of waking up the women, you should wake up the men.

EVERARD: But I need help.

RHODA: I need none.

MARY: I don't approve of the way you approve of us. Everard, we must go. You may be a man of leisure but we are working women.

EVERARD: *My doodle is stirred again, that pretty girl in the park was very sweet, but women like this, old and young, hawkish and proud, the thought of lifting their skirts and seeking out the moist folds beneath, of bringing brilliant heady women to their knees moaning, grasping at me –*

RHODA: *A comely man of thirty-five, the sight of him, the fact he is large, that I would feel small, that I could sink into him tiny and kept, protected and loved, I am spinning, spinning towards him –*

MARY: *Refuse him entry, tell him he's not allowed, no comely young men allowed here –*

EVERARD: Now that I've proven myself by playing the doctor, may I visit if I am very good? I do admire you. I didn't need heroes when I was growing up, I had glorious Mary.

MARY: You are welcome to visit, Everard. *Why, why do I say it?*

EVERARD: Thank you, cousin. I'll expect an invitation to dinner. Miss Nunn. Until we meet again.

SCENE 7: THE INSTRUCTION

MARY BARFOOT's sitting room. The Remingtons are lined up, shining metallic in the light. RHODA, VIRGINIA, and ALICE stand in front of them.

ALICE: They seem rather ferocious.

VIRGINIA: Violent, yet lonely.

RHODA: They're not lonely. They feel nothing. They are machines.

ALICE: Lonely.

VIRGINIA: Definitely.

ALICE: Evil?

VIRGINIA: Perhaps.

RHODA: Then the first step will be to become familiar with them. We will merely look at the Remingtons.

VIRGINIA turns away. We see her pull a mickey from her pocket and take a slug of brandy.

ALICE: Look, as in regard? Regard an instrument of torture, a cold clattering mechanism? It will pinch my fingers, make me feel stupid. We are beset with constant new devices and inventions –

VIRGINIA: So exciting. I am so invigorated by this ... by ... the keys which seem to be moving by themselves, weaving like stiff fingers pointing out of a shallow grave.

RHODA: I'm teaching you separately so that you can catch up with the other girls.

ALICE: Girls? Are they all girls?

RHODA: Women, the other women.

ALICE: But we are older than the others.

RHODA: Monica isn't older, and after she settles into her room, she'll join us.

ALICE: It is the new, you see, Miss Nunn –

RHODA: Rhoda, please.

ALICE: We are always behind, unsuited and unfit, those who are able to keep up and those who cannot. I want to shout, "Stop, this quickness will kill us all!" But no one listens, and I don't shout or speak. Ohh, ohhh – *I'm burning, bones melting, molten lava, drenched in sweat –*

RHODA: What is it? You're perspiring / so profusely.

VIRGINIA: Is it the –

ALICE: Twice this morning already, and all last night.

RHODA: A fever?

ALICE: My younger self is being burned out of me ... it's passing.

RHODA: But what is it? Malaria? The flux? Should we call a doctor?

ALICE: Women change, it will happen to you.

VIRGINIA: We bleed, and then we burn.

ALICE: And burn and burn.

RHODA: Oh. I see. We should start working.

ALICE: *It'll happen to her one day, one day she'll start to burn, her womb will burn, her heart and limbs, her nerves shrivelling in the flame –*

VIRGINIA: I wish to train my mind and heart to be independent and strong, like you, Rhoda. I can feel a change already. Do you see it in my countenance?

ALICE: We have always worked hard, but it is the fear, you see. Instinctive female fear.

VIRGINIA: Inbred tremulousness, inbred nervous agonies.

RHODA: Enough gazing. Now you will touch the Remingtons.

They touch them.

VIRGINIA: Oh God.

RHODA: What?

VIRGINIA: Metal.

ALICE: *Conducting heat and cold, / malleable and ductile –*

VIRGINIA: *Coursing through me, chemical combinations –*

RHODA: Now the basic keys. Have you ever had piano lessons?

ALICE: A few, but Father felt it was too much for Virginia.

RHODA: Think of the type machine as a literary piano. Begin by pressing the keys at random, to get the feel of them.

They do.

VIRGINIA: It makes no impression.

RHODA: Press harder. (*showing her*)

VIRGINIA: My fingers pain me. You see, still nothing.

RHODA: Harder. Alice, keep your wrists even.

VIRGINIA: Alice's wrists aren't even.

ALICE: My fingers bend in an odd way, you see, at the ends? It makes pressing firmly very difficult. Our father used to say I was born for a life of ease.

RHODA: Like this –

ALICE: Oh yes, that's a little better.

RHODA: You will memorize this chart, which refers to the position of the keys.

VIRGINIA: Memorize the chart.

RHODA: Then we'll add shorthand, dictation, and / correspondence –

VIRGINIA: Good, of course, shorthand and dictation and more, I hope there is more. Much more.

ALICE: And we'll learn all this in just six months?

RHODA: Perhaps a little longer. We'll start with the basic position of the hands. Hold your hands just above the keys ... without pressing the keys, merely hold them –

ALICE and VIRGINIA continue to play with the keys.

RHODA: If you could refrain from pressing the keys for a moment.

ALICE and VIRGINIA continue to play with the keys.

RHODA: Stop pressing the ...! Thank you. Settle yourselves. Now look at the first diagram. Extend your fingers –

VIRGINIA: I've slipped again.

RHODA: Then try again. Press each finger in succession from left to right –

ALICE: *We're very bad, you should punish us –*

VIRGINIA: *Father used to spank us when we were naughty –*

ALICE: *We were always the better for it –*

VIRGINIA: *It / hurt him more than it hurt us –*

ALICE: *He made us work harder –*

VIRGINIA: *We were always slow –*

RHODA: *You want me to dominate the room, dominate the teaching, dominate you poor excuses for women, who remind me of every lacklustre female relative –*

VIRGINIA: I cannot learn, I do not understand. (*She begins to cry.*) It is hopeless, hopeless. How can I imagine myself working in an office, a boss of a man watching over me, telling me I do it wrong, criticizing constantly and buzzing around me, like bees with quick fingers, well-dressed ambitious young people, bred of machines, born of machines, who is that faded old maid, she can't keep up, she can't keep up!

RHODA: We'll proceed more slowly.

ALICE: Dear, you've exerted yourself too much. Miss Nunn, perhaps we could rest a while?

RHODA: I understand that both of you are in poor health but –

ALICE: Poor health? Our muscles ache, our energy is sapped, our nerves are raw strips of flesh, our self-respect rots in an old hope chest as beetles and worms eat our girlish dreams.

VIRGINIA: Why didn't Father see to it that we were fit for something!

ALICE: Father? What has Father to do with learning / to use a type machine –

VIRGINIA: We can't even teach school properly. Did he think our great beauty and brilliant conversation would buy us husbands?

ALICE: You are desecrating our father's memory!

RHODA: Fathers want their daughters to be compliant / feminine in the sense of –

ALICE: What do you know?

RHODA: I know how to typewrite.

RHODA begins typing under.

VIRGINIA: Where are they? Where are the men? Why now, of all the ages of the world, are women left so alone? We are slaves, ignorant and fearful, degraded, raped, and pillaged –

ALICE: You don't even understand the ideas you are parroting, / they're making you hysterical.

VIRGINIA: Humiliated! Forsaken! / Battered! Beaten!

ALICE: Hysterical mania!

RHODA: Type, damn you. Type! It's the way to liberty!

VIRGINIA: I cannot live. I can't earn enough to keep from starving! Why shouldn't I be / hysterical?

RHODA: Now I am hysterical!

ALICE: You have murdered our peace!

VIRGINIA runs out of the room.

ALICE: Virginia!

ALICE runs after VIRGINIA.

RHODA: *An odd woman cries out to God that she's been robbed of children, robbed of a husband's love, robbed of the joys of amorous union. God answers that she has been abandoned in order to rise up and challenge all that has ever been. Is that what I believe? What do I believe?*

SCENE 8: SEXOLOGISTS

EVERARD's apartment. He stands gazing out a window, naked except for a silk kimono, speaking to someone in the next room.

EVERARD: Traditional society regarded women as sexually treacherous and insatiable. Modern society regards them as sexually pure and passionless. Now

we have the science of sexology to discover the sex truth. But they have barely begun to enlighten us. There should be a Sexologist Exhibition, a circumstance for people to match with each other – large signs proclaim the categories of desire. A brightly coloured sign proclaims "Sex Act but No Love" – a like-minded crowd gathers. Sexologists scurry after them to make notations.

MONICA enters in bloomers and chemise – she snuggles into EVERARD.

EVERARD: Another large coloured sign: "Love but no Sex Act." How many would gather, I wonder?

MONICA: One would say "Spanking and Worse."

EVERARD: "Touching and Holding Only."

MONICA: One would say "Frig Me into the Ground."

EVERARD: Once a shrinking virgin, now a wild woman.

MONICA: Oh God, what would my sisters say if they heard me? If they saw me?

EVERARD: *I couldn't help myself, such a luscious creature, about to be initiated by someone, and after a few encounters, a true participant –*

MONICA: *There is still time to save yourself, leap out the window, run through the streets in your bloomers, confess to a priest – dear Father, I am at the mercy of my flesh, it speaks to me at night, I cannot tame it, even though hell waits for me – Why aren't you married?*

EVERARD: I love freedom.

MONICA: So do I, but at the shop I saw girls who were free but common. I don't wish to be common even if I am free.

EVERARD: Don't bother your uncommon little brain. Just rest, while this great strong man holds you in his arms. Next Sunday then?

MONICA: Next Sunday I will drain your coffers dry.

SCENE 9: THE FIGHT

MARY BARFOOT's sitting room. RHODA paces. MARY takes her hand, begins to massage her shoulders.

MARY: You're restless again.

RHODA: It's the three sisters.

MARY: You've been fighting with them. You've been rude.

RHODA: Yes, Mary. Forgive me, Mary.

MARY: You must apologize.

RHODA: I will not.

MARY: They will find work, especially Monica. These women are no worse than many we've taught.

RHODA: Why send out hopeless cases who will do the school's reputation terrible harm?

MARY: Hopeless? You taught the girl who couldn't speak above a whisper, you taught Sarah – remember Sarah with syphilis? When did you become so hard?

RHODA: *How to explain what happened when I met him, how my mind swirled, how my body thrummed, how the three sisters felt part of it all, the icy breath of change –* The school is a political and social experiment with great consequences for the movement. We must be consistent.

MARY: In a pig's arse. When has anything alive, breathing, and farting ever been consistent? We must open our arms to contradiction. Find the human path.

RHODA: If you love me, get rid of them.

MARY: Throw them out to starve? You are a changeling – the Rhoda I love will return. Beware of losing your compassion.

RHODA: I feel no compassion.

MARY: In that case I will take the decision independently and allow the sisters to stay.

RHODA: Then I have no say as to what happens? Perhaps I should no longer be employed here.

MARY: You are not "employed."

RHODA: No, our friendship keeps it from being that, but if we were no longer friends –

MARY: No longer friends?

RHODA: I could no longer live here.

MARY: If you do not wish to be friends any longer –

RHODA: Then would I still have employment?

MARY: Of course / but –

RHODA: But it wouldn't be the same if we weren't friends. You and I are not partners –

MARY: If we use business language, yes, we are like partners –

RHODA: Not officially, not legally –

MARY: You are in my will.

RHODA: And so you have power over me, to go above my wishes for the school –

MARY: Yes, I have power, it is my school.

RHODA: Then what am I?

MARY: You are my ... you are my –

RHODA: I see, I see it all clearly. If I have a different opinion than yours, I am hard and inhuman.

MARY: Yes, inhuman – I look for a shred of womanly grace –

RHODA: But you are weak. Giving in to "womanly" sentiment and weeping emotions. Weak, weak, weak.

MARY: How dare you / call me weak?

RHODA: Perhaps you are correct in your self-criticism, perhaps you are a coward.

MARY: I have withstood torture, / I have –

RHODA: Deserting the true cause, afraid / of real struggle. A coward.

MARY: I could tear your hair out / for that.

RHODA: Tear away. Or I'll pack my bags first.

MONICA enters and stands watching, unseen.

MARY: Pack 'em quickly or I'll show you what I learned in prison!

RHODA: Go ahead, / I said do your worst.

MARY: I must get out before I do something horrific.

MARY storms out. MONICA comes fully into the room.

MONICA: I am ready for my lesson. But perhaps you are occupied with something horrific.

RHODA: Why did you come here?

MONICA: To sit on the lap of my employer, to blackmail him to his wife, to gain entry into a forbidden world, and suck it for all I can. Isn't that what you think?

RHODA: Please be seated at the type machine.

MONICA: You're not really all that plain, you know.

RHODA: *Plain from Mary, plain from this flirty cow –*

MONICA: And you laugh more than I thought, I caught you laughing with Mary.

RHODA: *Laughing with Mary –*

MONICA: *She'll soon see that I'm not wicked, or, if I am wicked, she will punish me, punish the part of me that will meet him to fuse breaths, tongues, skins, to share that piercing joy, that suddenly cares nothing of what anyone thinks* – My sisters ruined me. They made me half a / lady and –

RHODA: So you keep saying. I only see the shop-girl – *So appallingly ripe, while I am rotting on the vine.*

MONICA: Bluestockings are supposed to be virtuous and kind – *at night I touch and rub myself even if it will make me blind, I am being driven to madness –*

RHODA: *She's exuding an animal scent, feral and fecund and fertile* – Sit down at the type machine.

MONICA: You are against marriage, but what do you think of a girl marrying to help not only her own situation but that of others?

RHODA: Press the keys in order left to right. The third finger on the left hand is the most difficult to strengthen.

MONICA: The marriage finger.

RHODA: Then marry. Give over to servitude, ravishment, and theft. Become a sex slave.

MONICA: What if I wish to be a sex slave? Women seek it, they must want it –

RHODA: In the future, it will be possible to exist with a man as an equal.

MONICA: When in the future?

RHODA: In thirty years. By 1915.

MONICA: Thirty years ... I'll be fifty!

RHODA: Pray excuse me, the lesson is finished. We will make it up at another time.

MONICA: You're protected by Miss Barfoot – she is the husband and you are the wife.

RHODA: I told her she shouldn't let you in.

MONICA: She was bored. She needed new blood.

As RHODA exits.

Don't go. You wouldn't use a man to escape a life of drudgery? You would, I know you would!

VIRGINIA staggers in, very drunk.

MONICA: Virgie.

VIRGINIA: I must have fallen ... I haven't been well, just risen from a nap, the schooling here is very rigorous. I must practise, the Remington seems / to be broken ...

MONICA: Virgie, are you ...?

VIRGINIA: You notice a smell perhaps? I had to ask Miss Barfoot for a little medicine, I felt rather faint –

MONICA: It's brandy.

VIRGINIA crawls underneath the Remington looking for a hidden mickey.

VIRGINIA: Yes, I told you. The machine is broken, Rhoda fixes them with a great wrench – *Lord, I've got a head on me like a forty-shilling piss-pot –*

MONICA: *None of us will say it, that my sister reeks of drink, that my sister's mind is sodden –*

VIRGINIA: *Poor little slut, dear little angel –*

VIRGINIA finds her bottle.

MONICA: Virgie, you've had a terrible time, really.

VIRGINIA: Not at all. There is sometimes a feeling of emptiness, a desire for ... a kind of laughter.

MONICA: I used to make you laugh.

VIRGINIA: You were a laughing child – *A little girl jumps up and down, she pokes at us, lifting her skirts, laughing and laughing –*

MONICA: *My sister's hands, lifting me carefully, pressing their palms against my mouth, quiet, dear, shshhhhhh, smelling of lye and lavender –*

VIRGINIA: (*begins to cry*) Alice dislikes me now. All our lives we've been like two peas in a pod and now we're barely speaking. She resists the new theories while I have become very revolutionary ... Sometimes I think I should go to Berlin and learn to smoke and wear trousers.

MONICA: Wherever did you get that idea?

VIRGINIA: In a house of New Women there are always lots of pamphlets.

MONICA: I will repay you for all your sacrifices – *for the papery caresses, the feeling that I'll owe you forever as you sink lower and lower –*

VIRGINIA: I'll sleep a bit. Perhaps right here. *Dear little tart, dear little grubbian –*

VIRGINIA lies down on the floor, her head in MONICA's lap. MONICA strokes her hair.

VIRGINIA: ... Cash out my share of the principal and take ... the night train ... to Berlin ...

SCENE 10: WEEPING WOMAN AND HANDKERCHIEF

A park bench. A dull day. RHODA sits miserably. She's been crying. EVERARD enters.

EVERARD: Miss Nunn. I've just called at the house. Mary was unable to see me. Is she ill?

RHODA: A headache perhaps.

EVERARD: Your eyes look quite red.

RHODA: It's the fog.

EVERARD: It makes your eyes weep.

RHODA: No one is weeping!

EVERARD: Of course not – *For God's sake be calm, I'm not here to steal your virtue.*

RHODA: Mr. Barfoot, I wish to be alone.

EVERARD: Of course.

He sits down beside RHODA.

It seemed Mary was upset.

RHODA: I am upset.

EVERARD: Then you admit it.

RHODA: Mary is the more upset.

EVERARD: You and my cousin are much more than mistress and employee, you are …

RHODA: What? What are we?

EVERARD: Friends. Good women friends.

RHODA: *What is his idea of women friends, girlish talks with tea and biscuits? Can he imagine breast against breast in the night?*

EVERARD: *She seems less plain than before, a glow of intelligent unhappiness, so different from unintelligent unhappiness* – Miss Nunn, I am a bit of an occultist, I detect frequencies about you. There has been a disturbance between you and Mary.

RHODA: I'm afraid we may have to part.

EVERARD: You and I?

RHODA: Mary and I.

EVERARD: Surely not.

RHODA: I've grown hard, she thinks me hard … *(begins sobbing)*

EVERARD: *(offering handkerchief)* Allow me.

RHODA: *The horrible banality, weeping woman and handkerchief, stop, I cannot stop, I said malicious things and now she doesn't love me* – She doesn't love me.

EVERARD: Of course she loves you. You and Mary aren't ordinary women who tear each other's hair and have snits and gossip evil about each other – *I know how to comfort her, the warmth is pouring out of me, I am aroused by a bluestocking with a red nose* –

RHODA: Everything we've built is at risk if unsuitable or immoral girls, women, are sent out.

EVERARD: I agree, throw out the chaff, teach the wheat dictation.

RHODA: Why do you assume I am in the right? *His hands are long and white.*

EVERARD: Because I admire you.

RHODA: There's no logic in that –

EVERARD: *The swell of her breasts* –

RHODA: *The bulge in his trousers* –

EVERARD: I wish to see your cause succeed.

RHODA: Mary understands our cause better than any woman alive – *Mary, who I betray in my thoughts* –

EVERARD: I only meant … that the cause shouldn't be served only by unmarried women – *That doesn't follow, why did I say it?*

RHODA: Of course not – *That doesn't follow, why did he say it?*

EVERARD: I understand that you want the fair sex to control their own purses, even when they're married. I need – *An heiress with a swollen, bulging purse* –

RHODA: What do you need?

EVERARD: Stimulation.

RHODA: I have a stimulating life.

EVERARD: And yet you are unfulfilled. Scientifically unfulfilled.

RHODA: Scientifically?

EVERARD: Physically.

RHODA: What if I said that I was physically fulfilled? *Why suddenly does it seem untrue? Far down in me a swelling, an arching* –

EVERARD: You are an odd woman, so I assume that … I presume that – *that she is hymen intacta at the very least, yet she has the smell, the look of, no, not quite, not quite a virgin* – Forgive me, I am a mere mortal gazing at a warrior maid. Artemis of the type machines.

RHODA: Women have travelled a great way, our lives are nobler and richer than they were, but they are also fiendishly difficult. We are cruelly bruised as we reach for the light.

EVERARD: How beautifully you speak your ideas, / how beautifully –

RHODA: And now, if you please, I will take my leave. Your handkerchief will be returned –

EVERARD takes RHODA's hand.

RHODA: *I will not sleep with it under my pillow, hold it to my heart, rub it between my, between my legs –*

EVERARD: Miss Nunn, if I have offended you in any way –

RHODA: Pray release my hand –

EVERARD: A strong hand. You make no attempt to attract male attention and that in itself is attractive.

RHODA: I don't expect or desire male admiration. *True, completely true, almost true, true till this moment …*

EVERARD: *She will desire me, I'll make her twitch and buck –*

He releases her hand.

RHODA: Mr. Barfoot.

EVERARD: Always a pleasure, Miss Nunn.

SCENE 11: REHEARSING AND FAINTING

MARY BARFOOT's sitting room. MARY reads from a typewritten speech. ALICE, MONICA, and VIRGINIA sit expectantly. RHODA stands in the shadows.

MARY: Last night I slept not at all. I awoke from a fantasy. I realized we have been utterly wrong in everything we have fought for. We must abandon all reforms for women before we do irreparable harm. We are creating abominations. The financial dependence of women stems from our reproductive capacities. It is of the natural order. We are weaker! Our minds buckle, our nerves fray, our friendships wither when put to the test. When we enter men's realm of ambition we become hard and uncaring. While a man may be his natural self as he competes for power, we lose our very souls. Instead of altering the fabric of business as we enter it, we imitate its worst transgressions, trampling our poorer sisters for a few extra pence. Aye, we unsex ourselves and disrupt the balance of the world in the name of many freedoms which do not lead to liberation but are dangerous indulgences with consequences beyond knowing. The way ahead is full of shame, of tears and terror, of wild love and losses so deep they have no name. We will watch society crack with our freedom. Go back to your homes, you stupid women. It is over.

Pause. Uncomprehending applause from VIRGINIA and ALICE. MONICA claps with less enthusiasm. RHODA still watches in the shadows.

VIRGINIA: I am speechless, I am stirred. I want to, I don't know what I want to do. Alice?

ALICE: I feel as if I have walked upside down or swallowed a large building. Monica, what do you think?

MONICA: Is that the speech you're going to give at the rally?

MARY: Why ever not? *So tired of mouthing the same old arguments, don't give a rat's arse anymore, blah blah blah –*

MONICA: How could you mean it? You challenge us with negation.

MARY: Do I?

MONICA: Was it done for effect?

MARY: Let women lie down and be tramped on for all I care – *Still mouthing, still, blah blah –*

MONICA: But you cannot believe that women should abandon / all that has been –

VIRGINIA: Yes, we are challenged to counter your assumptions which are, which are –

ALICE: I am experiencing a shortness of breath –

MONICA: I see what has happened. Your cause has ignored inconvenient truths. Now you see the effect of your revolution and you pale.

MARY: In my darkest hours I do pale –

MONICA: Deny marriage and stir up women –

MARY: We do not deny the importance of family –

MONICA: The balance of the world is already upset and these "dangerous indulgences" are erotical freedoms which naturally result from what you have set in motion –

MARY: You've been reading the books I suggested.

MONICA: One or two.

MARY: We have ignored some aspects of – provocative girl –

MONICA: Erotical freedoms are historically inseparable from the discourse of liberation.

MARY: True, often true. Devious minx. But the real danger is our own weakness – we must speak more –

RHODA joins the group.

RHODA: My congratulations, Mary. The speech is brilliant, shocking, horrifying even.

MARY: I don't even know what I said. *I know exactly what I said, anger fuels the brain –*

RHODA: *I could never leave you –*

MARY: *Liar –*

MONICA: Pardon me, Mary and I were conversing.

RHODA: And now Mary and I are conversing.

MONICA: *Is something moist going on? Is it possible they're smashed on each other?*

ALICE: I believe they're setting up the buffet. Let us freshen up. No one will miss us.

VIRGINIA: *You will miss me, dear mouldy old Alice, I am taking destiny in my hand and booking the night train to Berlin –*

ALICE and VIRGINIA exit.

MONICA: I've met a man.

RHODA: Of course you have.

MONICA: If I were a New Woman, would I have to marry him in order to explore my bodily desires?

MARY: There is no unified doctrine –

RHODA: You must think. That is what we're trying to teach women to do –

MARY: If you are to act upon your appetites, at least use a cundum.

MONICA: A what?

RHODA: A cundum. Available at the druggists.

MARY: A French letter, a Spanish bull cup.

RHODA: A Russian pot holder.

MARY: They're made of sheep intestines and the man pulls it over his member, with some difficulty / and there it sits, protecting –

MONICA: No man would do any such thing –

ALICE runs in, a train schedule in her hand. VIRGINIA follows.

VIRGINIA: Alice!

ALICE: Miss Barfoot, what did you know of this? Virginia says she is going to Berlin of all places on God's earth.

MARY: Berlin, why Berlin?

MONICA: Are you really going?

ALICE: You knew? Did everyone know?

VIRGINIA: No one knew.

MONICA: She said something when she was in the drink. Oh Virgie, I didn't mean to –

MARY: Yes, the drink. Alice, did you hear what Monica said?

ALICE: She has broken into the principal! Stolen money from the principal!

VIRGINIA: Stolen my own third!

RHODA: Alice, the medicine your sister has been taking is brandy and gin.

VIRGINIA: How can you suggest such unladylike behaviour? I have been ill, very ill –

MARY: Do you deny it?

ALICE: Is this true? Virginia?

VIRGINIA: I'm cronked most of the time, I slather for it. I sneak to the bar at the train station and drink with prostitutes and sailors, I drink in our room, on the street, I lie beneath the Remingtons and lap it up like a mangy dog. It makes me feel that my life is grand / and exuberant, that my life isn't wasted –

ALICE: She starved herself to buy liquor and now she is running away.

VIRGINIA: I have tried to stop, you don't know how I have tried, but I am in its grip.

ALICE: You will get on a train by yourself? Go off to a foreign place by yourself?

VIRGINIA: I must do something radical!

MARY: Berlin can be a dangerous place –

ALICE: You are incapable of any such action.

VIRGINIA: Yes, the schedules and timetables will be wearying and difficult / perhaps …

ALICE: You'd leave me alone? – *I will tear your hair out first, I will go to lawyers and leave you destitute, I will bite you in the stomach, I will watch your spleen and liver spill to the ground and devour them, I will devour you, burp you out* – I know you, sister, I know the melancholia that drives you to deaden your senses. Do you think you won't meet the same feelings even if you travel to the ends of the earth?

MARY: Perhaps you should stop the drink first, then go on a small holiday, / perhaps the seaside –

VIRGINIA: But I must be large, a small holiday / would be meaningless–

RHODA: Virginia, if you wish to alter your habits –

VIRGINIA: I am being hounded by feminist persons! Help! / Someone, help!

ALICE: Years together, helping you find employment, supporting you mentally while you were drinking like a navvy, I have had opportunities –

VIRGINIA: With men? Ha! Not a single … cock has ever come near you.

ALICE: With you around, what … cock would dare?

VIRGINIA: I feel faint –

ALICE: Faint, then.

VIRGINIA: I am going to faint.

ALICE: Do you think I cannot faint? I will faint first. Observe. I pant with shame and betrayal, and then ... ahhhh ...

ALICE faints.

VIRGINIA: Shame and betrayal? I faint from the weighty chains of sisterly love! Ahhhhhhh!

VIRGINIA faints.

MONICA: Chains? Pretty Monica, what would she know of chains? I'll faint – wait. Why faint at all if there's no man to catch you? *Am I a nymphomaniac?*

RHODA: We faint because our corsets are too tight, we faint because we're encouraged to take no exercise –

MARY: I'd love to faint.

RHODA: No, not you.

MARY: To sink, to flutter, to be caught. Then, if the faint is real, to vomit in someone's hat.

RHODA: Women feign weakness to barter for security which creates loneliness – oh, go ahead.

MARY: It isn't easy to fall to the ground, I'll have to do it in stages ... ahh ... ahh ... ahhhhh ...

MARY faints.

So voluptuous to be feeble –

MONICA: I will faint better than any of you. I pale delightfully, I waver, but recover, then slip gracefully ... ahhhh.

MONICA faints.

ALICE: (*from the floor*) I feel ridiculous.

VIRGINIA: I feel sublime.

MONICA: Rhoda, you must faint, too.

RHODA: But what am I fainting from?

MARY: The sheer weight of the Woman Question.

RHODA: Oh yes, it is a weight, a boulder of mammoth proportions ... I wobble –

MONICA: Not so stiff.

RHODA: I surrender, I allow a desperate yet pleasantly overwhelming / giddiness to ... yes ... almost ... almost ... ah ... ah.

VIRGINIA: Yes! / Keep it up!

MARY: Yes! More / surrendering!

MONICA: You can do it!

RHODA: Ah ah ahhhhhh –

RHODA faints. All the women lie fetchingly on the floor. Enter EVERARD.

EVERARD: No one answered the door. Rhoda? Monica? What is happening here?

MARY: We have all fainted.

He regards the women.

EVERARD: Men aren't afraid of women, really, only of women in groups.

ACT TWO

SCENE 12: IMPRESSIONISTS

The first Impressionist exhibition in London. The characters are shocked, yet exhilarated by the paintings. They move in pools of light, hanging on to their programs for dear life.

EVERARD alone but near MONICA. MARY, ALICE, and RHODA form a group.

EVERARD: *Impressionism! Impressions of objects, impressions of figures, impressions of impressions – vulgar mockery or painterly inspiration? –*

ALICE: *Scrawls and splatters, indecipherable chaos, my eyes lose focus, the floor tilts, there is no ground under my feet, unfinished, completely unfinished –*

MONICA: *Rough and bold, vibrant and free, a leap into the unknown, / freedom from form, freedom from construction –*

MARY: *Subversion, emancipation from rigid structures, / the abandoning of all tradition –*

RHODA: *Blotches of water, a twist of parasol, no clear lines, / no depth or projection, the flaming of light and dust, a level of enchantment –*

ALICE: *Smear a panel with grey, plonk some black and yellow lines, dot it with red and blue blobs, / violent, loud, clumsy, naked brush strokes, tortured nature, great gaps of nothingness, subverting all sense of delicacy, of beauty –*

EVERARD: *Imperfect, deliberately imperfect, shadowy ness, / transience, nothing fixed, nothing certain –*

RHODA: *All is movement, combustion and flux, / flickering and insubstantial –*

MONICA: *Seething, wavering, waving, ravishing shimmerings of light and shade, bursting forth with colour –*

MARY: *The world is now divided into two, those who can stand these wild impressions and those who cannot bear to see the shapes within.*

EVERARD notices MONICA.

EVERARD: Miss Monica, I never thought to see you here.

MONICA: The exhibition of the century and you think me too simple to know it?

EVERARD: No, not at all, I / merely –

MONICA: An astounding eruption of new vision and yet these artists are called primitive.

EVERARD: You've changed since I last saw you, and not merely in your dress. Are you here alone?

MONICA: I came with a friend. A gentleman. There, by the ballerina with the heavy legs.

EVERARD: And there is mysterious Rhoda Nunn.

MONICA: Mysterious as a plank.

EVERARD: He looks very posh. Who is he?

MONICA: Keep your eyes on the paintings or my friend will interrupt us.

RHODA: *(to MARY)* There's Monica. With Everard. *Monica with Everard, Monica with Everard, he leans towards her as if ready to pluck her breasts and bite –*

MARY: Monica seems to have lost interest in the school.

RHODA: She rarely attends class, comes and goes as she pleases, and gives out that she's engaged, although to whom is unclear.

ALICE: In just four months she has had at least two fiancés. I won't join her yet, she's speaking with Everard. He is a good influence on her, so steady, so remote. Her present fiancé seems more impressionable –

MARY: Who is this fiancé?

ALICE: Monica is much admired –

RHODA: But where does she go?

ALICE: An engaged woman has many duties and responsibilities – *The pain is blinding, why can no one see it, my heart shrieks with loneliness, it is eating my soul like a scabrous disease –*

EVERARD: *(to MONICA)* I have every respect for what you are, or have become, but since spending time with Rhoda and Mary, I've become aware that some aspects of male behaviour are not ... are quite ... I am ashamed of my behaviour towards you.

MONICA: Ashamed? *Ashamed of our lusty afternoons, of the curve of my flank, the soft hair of my feather, you'll not see me weep –* Those women have unsexed you, you're soft as a girl, you weren't like that when we sneaked into your rooms, when you licked me like a cat –

EVERARD: The instinct of the female is resistance, then if she is won, surrender. This keeps a balance in nature –

MONICA: You poor booby. As you speak, the world explores free lovism.

EVERARD: Free lovism? Are you practising free lovism? I've heard there is a colony of them outside London –

MONICA: Physical liberty is the personal expression of revolutionary change – *I know the glory of my quim –*

MONICA moves away from EVERARD.

ALICE and MARY together.

ALICE: In spite of your philosophies, Mary, you must resent these artists rending the world asunder.

MARY: Oh yes, I resent it, even as I adore them. *Dining with Rhoda and Everard night after night, she getting sharper and sharper and he beginning to burn like the sun.*

MARY moves to RHODA.

RHODA: Nut-brown women on yellow horses in forests of blue trees –

EVERARD and MONICA.

EVERARD: *(to MONICA)* I suddenly realize how alone I am, I weep easily, look, here's a tear – I can no longer speak to my male friends, the married ones are miserable, the unmarried speak about women in a fashion that now seems despicable. My head aches, I have pains in my stomach, in my liver –

MONICA: *Piss on his liver, he is like me, hot-arsed, lewd, and lubricious – but a coward.*

EVERARD: But are you practising free lovism?

MONICA moves to the next painting.

MARY and RHODA.

MARY: Why do you ignore Everard?

RHODA: I'm not ignoring him. From a distance the patterns are clear but go closer and all that is recognizable disappears.

MARY: These artists have been vilified yet their ardour has not been dampened.

MONICA and EVERARD.

MONICA: I believe our true natures to be multi-amorous – I have a few good friends, like that very learned gentleman, who support this view. I've been true to each, each I've loved, yet still I hope for –

EVERARD: For ...?

MONICA: *For an end to my desires, for a housewife's cares, tiny hands clasping, a husband waiting –*

EVERARD: It is so close here, the intense coloura-tion / the vibrating brush strokes –

RHODA alone.

RHODA: Not a landscape but the sensation pro-duced by a landscape –

MONICA and EVERARD.

MONICA: You keep gazing at Rhoda – you may join her if you wish.

EVERARD: I don't know what I wish. Rhoda has ideals.

MONICA: She'd trade them all for a good match. There, my friend is getting truly impatient ...

EVERARD again looks at RHODA.

MONICA: ... and your confusion is ebbing away –

ALICE crosses to MONICA.

ALICE: Monica dear, I am shaken to the core, yes, here is sunlight, here is water, but it wavers so. Virginia would adore this anarchy, but she has dis-appeared into meagre postcards marked "Berlin."

MONICA: She has not disappeared. And neither have I.

ALICE: Is that your fiancé? He's quite changed from when I last met him, but then my eyes aren't what they used to be. Since Virginia has gone, only extremes penetrate them now.

MONICA: *I am progressive, but no whore – now I see that I am alone, completely alone.* We must go or we shall be late for an engagement. Good day, dear Alice. Mary. Rhoda. Everard. (*exits*)

EVERARD: An unsettling exhibit.

RHODA: I find it invigorating.

MARY: *I always suspected she was a dilettante – is she an odd woman or will she be paired like any gaggle of gloves in a drawer – he is almost her match,*

almost – Alice, I am determined that you recognize the rapture of this Renoir.

ALICE: (*as she exits*) Rapturous ...

MARY and ALICE exit.

EVERARD: You've been avoiding me. I've been visiting for over six months, but lately I dine only with Mary, you are always out with elusive friends.

RHODA: *Keep your distance or I'll scream like a stuck pig.*

EVERARD: You have spoken once or twice as if you were not quite happy with your life.

RHODA: Of course I'm not happy. What woman above the level of a petted pussycat is happy?

EVERARD: *I would like to pet your pussycat.*

RHODA: *Rub me, scratch me, dig your fingers into my pubis.*

EVERARD: If I'd married when I was young, I would have chosen, as the average man does, some simpleton.

RHODA: Any woman who reads the marriage contract and still gets married deserves what she gets – *Why do I find his condescension so arousing?*

EVERARD: *She is unaware of the delights of physical union, except I suspect something vaguely Greek is going on with Mary* – I will never marry in the legal sense, my companion must be as independent of these forms as I am. A free union, however, is possible –

RHODA: *A quivering, a quickening in my loins* – In a free union, the man and woman live as one, but there is no contract, legal or religious?

EVERARD: Freedom for both. Equality for both.

RHODA: *So the woman ends up with a passel of brats and no securities, while the man is free?*

EVERARD: I believe you to be my equal – do you realize the enormity of that admission?

RHODA: We fight for more than equality, we fight to endow our differences with dignity and prestige.

EVERARD: *I've got a boner so hard it's going to burst through my trousers –*

RHODA: *He's got a boner so hard it's going to burst through his trousers* – I'll see the Pissarro again, he has thrown out reality, like yourself.

EVERARD's handkerchief, which has been nestled in RHODA's bosom, flutters to the ground.

RHODA: Oh!

EVERARD: Allow me.

RHODA: No, I will –

EVERARD: My handkerchief.

RHODA: Oh God.

EVERARD: It gives me hope.

EVERARD and RHODA move to a garden area of the exhibition, a gently lit place of colour and possibility.

EVERARD: I have an income – not a large one, but sufficient for us to live, to travel, to study freely.

RHODA: *Never to work again, to see the world with a man on my arm – no, I would be on his arm –*

EVERARD: At first I didn't think of you as a woman – you were interesting because of your mind. Plain, proud, prickly as a briar. Then what was plain began to glow and the pride became delicious, I began to experience your very barbs with a physical thrill. Now your face is lit with a beauty I have rarely seen. It is the one face in all the world I wish to see.

RHODA: *Is it possible? A man, not any man, but an intelligent, well-spoken, well-endowed man with an income loves me – not for beauty or money or position but for myself, for my poor plain soul. Oh, damnable throbbing –*

EVERARD: Rhoda / Rhoda, Rhoda, Rhoda –

EVERARD crushes RHODA to him.

RHODA: *His manhood pressing against me, the first I've ever felt, I want to sink, swoon, scream!* No! *(She tries to pull away.)* Release me.

EVERARD: Release you? Do you mean it? *(still holding her)* Love brings out the savage.

RHODA: Do not use your strength over me!

EVERARD: Women love the feeling of men's strength.

RHODA: Their strength is tyranny!

EVERARD: It is ardour!

RHODA: Domination! *(She breaks away.)* All our talk, and you understand nothing of who I am. I am dedicated to a great work.

EVERARD: A free union needn't interfere with your work!

RHODA: Impossible. My work involves not just teaching but *being* an odd woman –

EVERARD: Let someone else sacrifice their life –

RHODA: Showing by example that an unpaired life needn't be a misery, that it can be full of purpose, friends, laughter. Mary is a leader – through my endeavours, so am I. Do you not see the power, the rare power I have found, how it fuels my very being?

EVERARD: Ay. You would be a traitor.

RHODA: I would lose my soul.

EVERARD: Yet it is because you are dedicated to a cause beyond yourself that I admire you the most.

RHODA: *We are lost.*

SCENE 13: THREE VIRGINS AND THE MOON

MARY BARFOOT's sitting room. Late at night. ALICE and MARY have been drinking. ALICE is pounding the type machine ecstatically.

ALICE: I love this machine. I love this machine.

MARY: Thirty words to the minute! Incredible!

ALICE: The precision of it, the sound of it!

MARY: The exultation of the teacher – I haven't felt it in so long. Go on, Alice! Go on! Have some more gin.

ALICE: *I am linked to these keys, to the miraculous pounding, the strength of them opening my mind, I can go more and more quickly and yet not lose the clarity of the print –*

MARY: A spontaneous combustion of learning!

ALICE: *(still typing)* I am beginning to understand the glory of chastity – it isn't the result of not being chosen, a void of negativity, but is part of nature's plan – *If I am happy, I say the unthinkable, that the sex act is not a necessity for everyone, not a necessity for me, I have never yearned as Monica has yearned, but I won't think of Monica, I have been ashamed of the ease of my chastity and now the strength of it pours through me like clear water, like a river in spring!*

MARY: For many women, chastity is more than comfortable –

ALICE: Are you chaste?

MARY: By the letter of the law.

ALICE: Chaste women are the backbone of your movement, yet now these female energies must move towards the earning of money, is that what you believe?

MARY: It is the great flaw in our movement. Women are endlessly, boringly poor.

ALICE: But the world is fuelled by the certain fact that women give. Forgive me, I am on the brink of a thought and it is making all my limbs itch, my arms and my ankles – no, keep the thought – I want tea, cake, gin, itching, I am cold, tired, keep the thought –

MARY: Breathe from the stomach, control your mind –

ALICE: You want to stop us giving and loving for no profit, put a price on caring for a sick animal or a sick parent or the poor –

MARY: Prosperity will bring us freedom.

ALICE: But this returns to love. My constancy, my natural devotion – I am losing it again –

MARY: Your constancy is –

ALICE: Is part of giving with no reward ... devotion, love, the idea is coming ... yes! I am capable of fearsome feats of devotion, I love objects like this locket, I loved my cat with a gut-wrenching passion, I loved the house we lived in so deeply I felt it part of my skin, I loved my father even though he treated me like an imbecile, Monica, Virginia, I love as I could never love myself. It seems to be in me, in many of us, to love with no reward, and if physical love is a reward, many of the creatures we love longest and most deeply are those we have never even touched. Boundless love, undaunted by ill treatment, abandonment, or death. I am showing you love now, by discussing, arguing with you.

MARY: You are making me sing with love.

ALICE: And yet I'm not young and beautiful, like Rhoda.

MARY: I tell her she isn't beautiful.

ALICE: You are wrong.

MARY: Have I ignored you?

ALICE: Yes, but I am old and slow.

MARY: And I am addicted to the young and quick. Forgive me.

ALICE: I was born forgiving people, I forgive curtains and outhouses, slugs and flies, ottomans / and needles –

As a bright moon throws light into the room, RHODA enters, dressed in a shimmering white nightgown.

RHODA: Ohh, I cannot sleep. I cannot even begin to sleep. Why is no one asleep?

MARY: It's a moony night.

ALICE: She is so enormously full, almost blinding –

RHODA: Why is the moon always "she"?

ALICE: Three virgins and the moon.

RHODA: Have you been drinking? You have, you're both soused.

ALICE: Here's some of poor Virginia's poison.

RHODA takes a glass of gin.

ALICE: Rhoda? There is a flush on you. Has he spoken?

RHODA: No one has spoken.

MARY: Alice is your confidante?

ALICE: Love, hopeless, unflinching love. The gorgeousness of it –

RHODA: I'm thirty-five years old and I've never had words of love spoken to me by a man.

MARY: Are their words so different?

ALICE: Why aren't you happy for her? If I was a woman who yearned, I'd want Everard. Handsome, manly, a bit of a cad –

RHODA: Pass the gin –

MARY: You have had love.

RHODA: A wonderful love.

MARY: Passion.

RHODA: But not –

MARY: Penetration?

ALICE: Mary, I do not believe you are using your intellect –

MARY: Obviously you should accept him.

RHODA: He has not proposed.

MARY: Ha.

RHODA: If he were to propose, which he hasn't, I would not accept him.

ALICE: Not accept him?

RHODA: Of course I wouldn't, but to know that it were possible –

ALICE: If you married you could have children.

RHODA: I could.

MARY: I always wanted a child.

RHODA: You?

MARY: I've seen women driven mad with the lack, but for me, it remains a small but not overpowering anguish.

ALICE: If only it were possible without the sex act. Perhaps one day –

RHODA: *All I know is that a man held me and I felt a quiver of such exquisite pleasure –*

ALICE: *I ill-wish women who have children. I wish them horrible trials, babies with club feet or born with huge bulbous ears, I wish to crush the complacency out of them, the way they say "my" child – "my," "my," "my"!*

MARY: Of course, there would be a financial cost to marrying. The loss of the school, its business, your job, and three fine Remingtons.

RHODA: You would disown me?

MARY: Why should I will the school to someone who cannot live up to our principles?

RHODA: Being unmarried is not a principle and never was.

MARY: Fidelity, loyalty are principles.

ALICE: Important principles.

RHODA: But not bondage.

MARY: Bondage! Have I kept / you against your will?

RHODA: No, forgive me, Mary, I am confused, / I spoke hastily, never, no, I was confused, I am confused, no, no chains –

MARY: Have I kept you from your separate friends, your own entertainments, locked you in chains? Suddenly I am a great spider, trapping you with filigrees of half-truths. Our conversation has been a god's nectar to us both. Our bodies have known each other, I have licked the crux of you, and I have heard you moan my name. Do not let my age wither your reason.

ALICE: Whenever I hold a baby, I fear I'll break into great roaring, howling, gaping sobs, I want to snatch it up, run through the filth of the streets, shrieking, "I am the real mother!"

MARY: Alice, you are overwrought.

ALICE: Shall we typewrite?

RHODA: We must.

Their passions must find release in the keys. ALICE, RHODA, and MARY move quickly to the Remingtons.

ALICE: *I am alone and the pain is burning, I am alone and the pain is sublime, goading me to new heights, / all props are gone, even love, even family –*

MARY: *I am alone and the pain is burning, I am alone and the pain is sublime, goading me to new heights, / all props are gone, even love, even family –*

RHODA: *I am alone and the pain is burning, I am alone and the pain is sublime, goading me to new heights, / all props are gone, even love, even family –*

ALICE: *Now I soar in my mind, transform myself, though I backslide a thousand times, / I will wander in darkness and disarm the light –*

RHODA: *Now I soar in my mind, transform myself, though I backslide a thousand times, / I will wander in darkness and disarm the light –*

MARY: *Now I soar in my mind, transform myself, though I backslide a thousand times, I will wander in darkness and disarm the light –*

All typing stops.

RHODA: Mary, I desire you no more.

SCENE 14: BERLIN

Days later. MARY's sitting room. ALICE and MARY are typewriting. VIRGINIA enters and stands in the shadows. She is bloodied, dressed in a man's suit, which is ripped and torn.

MARY: Yes? Did you ring the bell?

VIRGINIA: No, I didn't ring. Don't you recognize me?

VIRGINIA sways and almost falls.

MARY: Pardon, I don't … you're bleeding … Virginia?

ALICE: No, it can't be Virginia. *It's someone else, some other poor, wrecked creature who's been beaten by navvies, some paltry, pinched creature who's stolen men's clothes.*

VIRGINIA: *Alice, Alice forgive me, Alice I've changed, Alice I have been so far, I am altered to the core, yet not altered at all –*

ALICE: *Beast! What have you done with my sister?*

MARY: I'll get bandages. Do we need a doctor? Virginia?

VIRGINIA: No doctor.

MARY exits.

VIRGINIA: When I arrived after crossing the Channel, there were large men, very large. My attire offended them. They kicked me as if I was a man, but they knew I was a woman – Alice?

ALICE: I'll get you brandy.

VIRGINIA: No. No brandy, that is over.

ALICE: I assume you have a story.

VIRGINIA: I never thought to arrive like this.

ALICE: *Go back, go back to where you came from.*

VIRGINIA: Alice –

ALICE: Here, I can at least wipe your face. (*She wipes blood away with her handkerchief.*) I would do that for a stranger, which is what you are.

VIRGINIA: I wrote.

ALICE: Your cards were very informative: "Berlin very gloomy, everyone speaks German." Why not add, "Dressing like a man. Learning to shave"?

VIRGINIA: I found such freedom. I learned to whistle. Think of it. Your sister, batty Virginia, walking down the street – no, strolling, swaggering ... ahhhh, my rib is slightly crushed.

ALICE: Swaggering, whistling. Prancing and hopping even.

VIRGINIA: I was very lonely when I first arrived. I lived in a little room not different from our old room, except that you weren't there.

ALICE: No, I was here.

MARY enters with a basin of water and bandages. MARY and eventually ALICE bandage one of VIRGINIA's wrists and one hand.

VIRGINIA: I am no longer a drunk, does that have no meaning? You liked me when I was dependent, a ditherer, a sodden lump of a brain-soaked body, a body-soaked brain / a great –

MARY: The point is taken. Give me your face.

VIRGINIA: Owww ...

MARY: Sit still. *She'll bring attention to us all, parading around in men's duds, who is she to be so brazen?*

ALICE: *My sister is hurt, my sister is bleeding, don't let her be in pain, let me be cut, let me be bruised –*

VIRGINIA: I am healed.

MARY: You are to be congratulated.

ALICE: Bollocks.

VIRGINIA: You have changed.

ALICE: Not as much as you.

VIRGINIA: It's just a suit of clothes.

MARY: *Desire is gone, I am desired no more.*

VIRGINIA: For weeks I stayed alone in that room, a prisoner of nameless terrors, until I realized I had a purse stuffed full of pound notes.

MARY: Of course. You were freed by having money. / It buoyed up your inner resolve.

ALICE: The principal, the principal –

VIRGINIA: I ventured into the city, spending as I went, and began to notice a group of men about the town – they leaned against walls with such panache. One day, I staggered up to them and saw that they were women. They became my friends. They distracted me from my craving, they held me when I shook, they laughed like men but cried like women –

MARY: Did you seek them out because you felt of their kind?

VIRGINIA: May I smoke?

ALICE: I don't care if you set your bum on fire.

MARY: But did you –

VIRGINIA: Did I what?

MARY: *Did you learn what love was, as I learned long ago, before Rhoda, before apprentices and causes.*

VIRGINIA fishes out a package of tobacco and rolling papers from her pocket. As she speaks, she rolls a cigarette but doesn't light it.

VIRGINIA: In no time I had a suit of men's clothes and my hair was shorn. We all went about. Little wants and desires began creeping out of me, like mice seeking the air. To sit in a café, to cross my legs in public, to expound on a topic even though I knew nothing – oh, the wonder of pockets, my hands, being confined, felt freed.

ALICE: But what did you do with these persons?

VIRGINIA: Do?

ALICE: They were deviants.

VIRGINIA: Not at all. The younger ones had beaus, two had children, the others ...

MARY: The others?

VIRGINIA: These were passionate friendships, but friendships they were.

ALICE: Then why did you leave?

MARY: You felt desire.

VIRGINIA: Desire? I'm not certain I would recognize it if I felt it.

MARY: But something frightened you.

VIRGINIA: One night I shared a bed with one of them, which we often did for sisterly economy, but this night she reached for me, I do not know what I felt, will never know, for I began to gasp. I looked down at the locket with Mother and Father's hair intertwined and saw the hair was growing out of the locket 'round my heart, then around my throat, pulling tight, strangling me, Mother and

Father and yes, you Alice and Monica were above me calling to me that I had betrayed you and as I lay there I knew it was so. I found myself beating my friend, my hands squeezing, throttling her neck, I nearly killed her. I left on the next train. I return changed but not altered, I have known pockets and cigars, but I am your sister, and our father's daughter still.

ALICE: Are you unnatural or not?

MARY: *She's not unnatural, I am unnatural, shriek it to the skies.*

VIRGINIA: I may never know what I am. But I have been to Berlin. I wish to be a woman, yet dress as a man. Is that so much to ask?

ALICE: Mary, could you allow Virginia to come and go as she is?

MARY: I can be no such rebel. She would draw dangerous attention to the school.

VIRGINIA: Alice, forgive me.

ALICE: Don't you dare! How I wept in despair, how I tore my breast, I don't need you now, blood of my blood –

VIRGINIA: In the name of our dead sisters, of Martha and Isabel –

ALICE: The bonds between women are laughable to the world, but they are marriages in a sense, and they may be betrayed.

MARY: "Boundless love, undaunted by ill treatment, abandonment, or death." Forgive her, Alice, and take her to your room.

ALICE: Monica said you would own us.

VIRGINIA: Where is Monica?

ALICE: In hell. Come upstairs, Virginia.

VIRGINIA: Thank you, Mary.

ALICE: Mary be damned. Mary always finds a way to win.

ALICE exits. VIRGINIA hangs back, lights her cigarette, and has one long, satisfying puff before following ALICE to their room.

SCENE 15: WOMEN FRIENDS

MARY's sitting room. RHODA is fixing a type machine with a great wrench. MONICA enters and watches for a moment.

RHODA: Monica. We see you so rarely now, it seems you come to the house only to change your attire.

MONICA: (*showing her dress*) What do you think?

RHODA: I notice you're wearing a ring. Which "fiancé" is it now?

MONICA: Let us say I am involved in a free union.

RHODA: Pardon?

MONICA: As a New Woman you should approve.

RHODA: Suddenly, free unions seem common as dirt.

MONICA: *Whip me with your disdain, Rhoda Nunn, and I will gnash my teeth with pleasure.* I was hoping we could have a lesson.

RHODA: A lesson. Why not? Be seated. *She's learned to dress, even though her titties are showing.* Place your hands in position.

MONICA: What position would you like? I can suggest several.

RHODA: One with some dignity.

MONICA: If free unions are undignified and there are no men to marry, then are odd women never to experience passions?

RHODA: I will dictate from this book.

MONICA: We must speak openly of these matters. Erotical silence keeps us all in chains –

RHODA: A demented view of our political ideas.

MONICA: Physically awakened women are a force to be reckoned with – I am beginning to see this power, to know its strength, its reality –

RHODA isn't listening.

MONICA: Why have you never liked me? Why?

RHODA: Why should all women be friends with each other? Smiling and cooing and exchanging confidences – *Because the hierarchy of beauty offends me, offends the cause, let us scratch our faces so no woman is more beautiful than the other, receives advantages over the other through an accident of birth, pretty, pretty, born pretty, all your life pretty –*

MONICA: *Let us argue and discuss as you and Mary do, let our minds be kindled –*

RHODA: *She flaunts it, uses it like poppy, like fog.*

MONICA: *The floodgates are open, there is an erotical revolution –*

RHODA: *Everyone assumes you're an old maid because no one wants you and then when they do want you, when they do, you can't believe them –*

MONICA: Some women blaze, we pulse and boil – are you one of us and don't know it? You and I are fertile, soon the time will be gone. I feel myself to be so dreadfully fertile, let me frighten you with what I know. The rubbing and the rocking, then the liquid, filled with babies, boys and girls, dark and fair, running down my legs, some sticking deep inside –

RHODA: Stop, this is a frenzy, a sickness –

MONICA is dizzy.

MONICA: *Help me, my body is strange, it feels full of water.*

RHODA: Have you been drinking?

MONICA: A touch of stomach distress.

RHODA: Not the clap?

The two women stare at each other. The tension is palpable. MONICA breaks the bond and exits.

SCENE 16: PACKING

MARY's sitting room. A spring evening. EVERARD and MARY.

EVERARD: I've never resented the inheritance. Well, not really.

MARY: Then why mention it?

EVERARD: It may be between us.

MARY: That is not what is between us. Do you believe I owe you something?

EVERARD: Not at all.

MARY: Good.

EVERARD: Be sensible, Mary. Give her up.

MARY: And who am I to say yea or nay?

EVERARD: Don't you see me trembling with the effort of not taking what I choose, of conforming to the ideal of a man who resists the pounding of his own blood? As I resist, my whole body shakes. I was born to be unfair, science tells me that I'm unnatural if I am not savage when I need to be.

MARY: *All my life I have preached the glory of contradiction, yet now my contradictions are repulsive to me, I am caught between waving her farewell or binding her to me with dastardly skills.* You speak of a free union to test her, to see if she's willing to become an outcast for you.

EVERARD: Why shouldn't I test her? She has spoken against love, against marriage, against men – do you think there's no price for those words, that men do not hear them, that we do not wonder and quake?

MARY: I don't give a tinker's damn what she's said. Marry her. Trust her.

EVERARD: I must know her true feelings. If she truly is a New Woman, she must find marriage abhorrent and accept a free union. If she accepts the free union, she proves both her politics and her love for me. Then I will, of course, marry her.

MARY: Why men call women's logic impaired, I will never know.

RHODA enters.

RHODA: Everard.

EVERARD: Rhoda. I hear you're taking your holidays.

RHODA: I leave tomorrow for the Lake Country.

EVERARD: I'll be in the area myself. We could meet, have a day's ramble together.

RHODA: The Lake Country is free to you.

EVERARD: I'll stay in Seascale, at a small inn called the Traveller.

RHODA: I can't promise to be at any one particular spot – we may meet, by chance. By merely walking about, as we'll be in the same area, at the same time, as the lush spring unfolds, as the animals are pawing and mating. I must go. Pack.

EVERARD: I will hope to meet up with you. Until then –

RHODA: Until then –

EVERARD: (*as he exits*) Mary.

RHODA: *I am softer now, I feel that I am softer. Can you see it?*

MARY: *I am blind at the moment.*

RHODA: *My shoulders melt instead of stiffen in a crisis, my breastbone yields. Tell me you see it –*

MARY: *Forgive me. I wanted to keep you as a talisman against death.*

RHODA: *You let him into our lives, you handed him to me –*

MARY: *Perhaps I did, but you didn't have to take him.*

RHODA: *A test? A trick? Be sweet, Mary –*

MARY: *Why sweet? Mary Barfoot who has spit and smashed is now meek and humble?*

RHODA: *Smash me and make me whole again. I am so afraid.*

MARY touches RHODA on the cheek.

MARY: Never be afraid. May these holidays be all that you wish them to be. (*exits*)

SCENE 17: SEASCALE

A grassy hilltop overlooking the sea. Bright sunshine. Birds twitter. EVERARD and RHODA loll on a picnic blanket.

EVERARD: *A perfect day, yet everything is in the balance –*

RHODA: *If I'm about to burst into flower, then let it happen –*

EVERARD: I think we should live in that cottage for six months, then take the Orient Express to the Bosporus, winter in Florence –

RHODA: We'd be so tired of each other by then.

EVERARD: Shhh, the day is perfect. We'd be end-lessly enchanted and inspired. Tomorrow we go to Coniston.

RHODA: We?

EVERARD: We. Yes. Rhoda –

RHODA and EVERARD lunge at each other's mouths, fall backward onto the blanket, thrashing, running their hands over each other's bodies. In a moment of true heroism EVERARD drags himself away.

EVERARD: We must speak. Mary / is ...

RHODA: Is a wise woman.

EVERARD and RHODA resume kissing, touching, panting, exploring passionately.

EVERARD: I have longed to speak freely of my love.

RHODA: But what is your love worth?

EVERARD: In pounds? Four hundred a year. In constancy ...

RHODA drags herself away.

RHODA: Wait! *Bargain, I must bargain for my life –*

EVERARD: *And so it begins, with my balls aching and my strength rising, how not to be a barbarian?*

RHODA: Is there any woman living who has a claim on you?

EVERARD: No promise of love exists between myself and any woman.

RHODA: I would deeply resent unfaithfulness.

EVERARD: That is the understanding between man and wife.

EVERARD and RHODA lunge together again. RHODA pulls away quickly.

RHODA: But what do you mean by "man and wife"?

EVERARD: I mean we would be "as" man and wife.

RHODA: But not?

EVERARD: You have often said, "Any woman who reads the marriage contract and still gets married ..." However it goes –

RHODA: Don't trap me with my own words – *I announce that I have refused marriage, live openly with a man, how noble, how emancipated –*

EVERARD: Your ideals will be protected. Even if you teach no more.

RHODA: *Teach no more – but without a public promise, I could be abandoned without a thought –*

EVERARD: *Prove your love, Rhoda, prove your love –*

RHODA: It's no small thing to be an outcast – are you prepared to lose family, friends, all but the few who would accept us?

EVERARD: If we think of ourselves as married, we are married. I don't need to convert the world.

RHODA and EVERARD kiss and grope with even greater urgency. EVERARD puts his hand up RHODA's skirt. We see a flash of lace.

RHODA: Then we would merely say that we are married? That is not an ideal, it's deception.

EVERARD pulls away.

EVERARD: Do you doubt your own love?

RHODA: I do not doubt it. In spite of all my efforts, I love you, Everard Barfoot. I love the struggle I see in you, I love your intellect, I love your physical self.

EVERARD: Then give me your left hand.

EVERARD slips a ring on RHODA's marriage finger.

RHODA: What –

EVERARD: We'd wear rings for certain circum-stances, / they can be bought readily and ...

RHODA: No! Horrible, take it off, it's burning me, it's a lie, we would be liars, neither heroic nor con-ventional, / this proves to me I cannot pretend. Take it back or I'll drop it in the sand!

EVERARD: We would use it merely for convention, if we were travelling for instance, for hotels and trains, for relatives abroad – it's merely a ring.

RHODA: More than a ring. Dearest, Everard dearest –

EVERARD: *Oh God, the iron fist in the velvet glove.* Say it once more.

RHODA: Dearest – *See how well I do it, like any woman, / like an ordinary woman with all her wretched wiles –*

EVERARD: *She's like an ordinary woman asking for ordinary things –* You want that old idle form?

RHODA: I find that I do.

EVERARD: *Who is she?* We can get a licence from the registrar and be married in that little … church.

RHODA: Church?

EVERARD: Grove? Mud hut? Pub?

RHODA: If it must be a church –

EVERARD: Then I am resigned.

RHODA: Resigned?

EVERARD: Ecstatic.

RHODA: *He is disappointed, he has changed –* Do you love me any the less? *Weak, simpering girl –*

EVERARD: Come here. *Do I love her less?* Let me dominate you in this at least.

They kiss, but less passionately than before.

EVERARD: I have been weak.

RHODA: Yielding in the one point that didn't matter to you at all?

EVERARD: Yielding at the very beginning of the war.

RHODA: There's someone coming.

EVERARD: It's the boy from the hotel. He's waving a letter.

RHODA: I feel faint.

RHODA and EVERARD remain onstage during the next scene.

SCENE 18: INFIDELITY

MARY's sitting room. ALICE has called a meeting. MARY, VIRGINIA, ALICE, and MONICA. VIRGINIA is dressed in women's clothing.

ALICE: Monica is pregnant and we believe the father is Everard Barfoot.

MARY: What? / No, oh no –

ALICE: He used Monica to sate his desire while he waited patiently for Rhoda.

MARY: You've been intimate with him? Monica?

ALICE: This is the future, emancipated women claiming their bodies in order to frig as many men as they possibly can.

MARY: That is not what emancipation / signifies.

ALICE: Monica told me she was engaged.

VIRGINIA: Fanciful manias – that she was engaged, yet every man she introduced you to was different? You closed your eyes, sister.

MARY: Monica needs your pity and your help.

VIRGINIA: What does it matter? Our dear little girl will give us a child. Forget marriage, let us care for it –

ALICE: A bastard. What life would it have?

MONICA: Stupid Everard and stupid, stupid Rhoda!

MARY: What do you know about Rhoda?

MONICA: He talked to me about her, how he was going to get her to bed without marriage just to prove she was like any other woman – *She is free and I am trapped, as all women are trapped by the very nature of our bodies, I hate my body, I hate it!*

MARY: She is in the country now, with Everard.

ALICE: You must warn her.

MARY: But is the child Everard's? Monica, do you hear me? A woman's future is at stake.

MONICA: I used a reproductive pamphlet I found in this house, counted the days – the pamphlets are wrong, we are ignorant, left to the mercy of creation which damns all our hopes!

ALICE: Mary, you must write Rhoda. She is about to marry the man who must now marry Monica.

MARY: Monica? Is it that you don't know who the father is?

ALICE: / Oh God.

MARY: Do you know? Then who is it?

VIRGINIA: Why won't you speak?

ALICE: It is Everard's.

MARY: Rhoda will hate me forever if I am the one to tell her.

ALICE: She'll hate you more if she knows you didn't warn her. You must write her now, before she accepts him.

MARY: Monica, is this true? Monica? I swear to heaven, if I were a man, I'd beat it out of you!

ALICE: You / will do no such thing.

VIRGINIA: Touch one hair on her head –

MONICA: Go to hell. All of you, be cursed as I am cursed!

MONICA runs out of the room.

MARY: It is all ruined. Why did I let you in? Why did I let any of you in? (*exits*)

ALICE opens a notebook.

ALICE: (*writing*) "Dear Rhoda, I must inform you of a matter of a desperate and urgent nature ..."

The grassy hilltop. RHODA holds ALICE's letter in her hand.

EVERARD: I have told you it isn't true! Why won't you believe me?

RHODA: Then what is the explanation?

EVERARD: I have none.

RHODA: You refuse to explain?

EVERARD: I will not. You must trust me.

RHODA: I cannot offer blind trust!

EVERARD: When you are prepared to take my word, you know where to find me.

SCENE 19: ALONE

Five months later. A dull afternoon. MARY's sitting room. RHODA and MONICA. MONICA is seven months pregnant.

MONICA: It's taken me many months to find the courage to see you.

RHODA: Five. Five months to be exact.

MONICA: I am going to die.

RHODA: Such a loss.

MONICA: When he heard what was said, how did Everard respond?

RHODA: You know that he denied it. He was above explanations. We haven't spoken since that day.

MONICA: Not a word in five months? No wonder you look so drawn and liverish.

RHODA: And you look like a wraith who's swallowed a balloon.

MONICA: It wasn't him. It wasn't Everard.

RHODA: Why should I believe anything you say?

MONICA: We did explore the amatory act on a number of pleasant occasions, but long before. The man whose child this is abandoned me. You saw him at the exhibition. He's wealthy and a shite.

RHODA: So you did lie with Everard.

MONICA: It's not Everard's. You ruined everything. You couldn't just love him, you couldn't just trust him.

RHODA: Then why didn't you speak at the time? Do you hate me that much?

MONICA: You were about to leave us all behind.

RHODA: Why are you speaking now?

MONICA: I felt it move.

RHODA: Felt it move?

MONICA: And I needed money from the real father. I've hated it all this time, and / now –

RHODA: And now you love it. You felt it move.

MONICA: I feel nothing for it. But it is moving, like a fish in its watery bowl. Before I die, it deserves the truth.

RHODA: All new mothers believe they're going to die.

MONICA: My sisters are taking care of me and the man has sent money so he isn't even a complete villain. But I am so weary. I can feel the child wanting hope, sucking, searching for it, and I have none. It is as if all I believed in was a lie.

RHODA: No. It isn't.

MONICA: I always felt that you had something to give me, that you could help –

RHODA: Are you shaming me? I should be ashamed. I have always been a jealous person.

MONICA: And I've been green with envy – I'll get out my whip and flay us both. Tell me about the future.

RHODA: The future? That tired old horse? Oh God, but I'm weary, too.

MONICA: But you believe.

RHODA: Yes. We live for the future. You must live for the future.

MONICA: I cannot. I fear I will die with this newness inside me, struggling to be born.

RHODA: This is defeat. And I won't have it. I am able to stop these thoughts with my will, can you feel my will?

MONICA: It's like a ray of cold steel.

RHODA: Then I'll warm the metal. Think. Feel. Every breath you take, you are breathing the future. The reddest blood must flow to it, the strongest muscle, your heart, must pound for the child. Hear its rhythm, feel its pulse. Let it be a drum that drowns out weakness, that dwells on life, as we must. As we must.

MONICA: As we must. Yes. We could have been friends.

RHODA: Yes.

MONICA: Goodbye, Rhoda.

RHODA: Not goodbye.

MONICA: It is a shame that sex matters are so ... untidy.

MONICA exits. EVERARD rushes in.

EVERARD: *You stubborn cow –*

RHODA: *You could have told me –*

EVERARD: *You look older and your dress is out of style –*

RHODA: *I didn't quite believe you –*

EVERARD: *I've been travelling for months –*

RHODA: *There have been casualties for the cause –*

EVERARD: *Paris, Florence, the beauty of the frescoes –*

RHODA: *Two suicides, one genteel starvation –*

EVERARD: *It wasn't true, I wasn't pure, but I wasn't –*

RHODA: *I know, I know –*

EVERARD: *I am a magician, I wave my wand and take us back to that day in Seascale, the sun sparkles, the grass is green, I ask you to marry me –*

RHODA: *That is not what you asked –*

EVERARD: *It was a good offer, an excellent offer –*

RHODA: *Neither of us was happy –*

EVERARD: DO NOT TOY WITH ME! I ask for the last time, will you marry me?

RHODA: *This is the man for me, made and unmade for me –* I am not a very rapid typist. If you type-write at high speeds, there comes a time when you can't comprehend the words, you must surrender to the physical movement and become an automaton. When this occurs, I always become afraid. I deliberately stop, even stumble, so that my brain will catch up and I am able to understand. There is wonder in the surrender and pain in the stopping, but only then am I fully conscious. I will always remember that day.

EVERARD: Rhoda. Even now ...

RHODA: Even now, I have just enough courage left to send you on your way.

EVERARD bows his head to RHODA and exits.

SCENE 20: THE GARDEN

Three months later. Bright sunlight floods a garden outside a country house. ALICE is holding a baby. MARY sits beside her. VIRGINIA behind them, dashingly dressed in men's clothing.

MARY: Alice, I have never seen you looking so well.

ALICE: Yes, she definitely agrees with me. (*to baby*) Don't you, little Monica? Yes, yes you do.

VIRGINIA: She is always hungry.

ALICE: I love to watch her eyes as she drinks. They stare at me with such an expression.

VIRGINIA: Greed.

ALICE: Stop it.

VIRGINIA: It is a greed for life.

MARY: Rather than greed, call it lust.

ALICE: Lust? This poor little creature?

VIRGINIA: I've got such a lust for a pint of gin. The only way I can keep off the bottle is to dress like a man. It fortifies me in a very deep and superficial way.

ALICE: But only within the home.

VIRGINIA: My rebellion is contained but not obliterated. I long to see Berlin again –

ALICE: Not yet, dear.

VIRGINIA: No dear, not yet.

RHODA enters.

RHODA: The house is lovely.

ALICE: Paid for by little Monica's father. He's been very good, really. It's the old kind of commerce. I give you a baby, die, and you support it and my two sisters. Once she's older, we'll finally become business women and open a school for young children. We'll call it Day Time Care.

MARY: Brilliant.

VIRGINIA: Let me take her.

ALICE: I would prefer to hold her.

VIRGINIA: You must be tired.

ALICE: I'm not tired.

VIRGINIA: She's about to cry.

ALICE: She is smiling.

MARY: May I hold her?

ALICE: She's very heavy.

MARY: I have muscles of iron.

ALICE: If you insist.

MARY: Yes, yes, little one. Sqoodgy woodgy woodgy ... she is smiling.

RHODA: I enjoy watching other people hold babies.

ALICE: Do you see Everard? I mean, as friends?

RHODA: Not often.

VIRGINIA: Is it true he's married?

RHODA: Her father is quite wealthy, but I hear she's an intelligent girl. For a trollop.

MARY: She has her mother's light bright eyes. Monica's funeral was the saddest I've ever attended.

RHODA: It was gut-wrenching.

ALICE: I thought some of the men she serviced could have come.

VIRGINIA: There were a few. Now I will hold her.

MARY: Very well.

MARY passes the baby to VIRGINIA.

ALICE: Our poor dear had a terrible time. At the end, it seemed the baby would never be born, but then Monica rallied, swore like a sailor, gave a great push, and little Monica was born.

VIRGINIA: She was very brave.

RHODA: More than brave.

MARY: A casualty of the war.

Pause.

RHODA: (*leaning over the baby*) It's as if she's thinking of something astonishing.

VIRGINIA: She's soiling her nappy.

ALICE: I wonder if she'll learn to typewrite.

MARY: She won't have to typewrite.

RHODA: Now I would like to hold her.

VIRGINIA passes the baby to RHODA.

VIRGINIA: Mind her neck.

RHODA: I am minding her neck.

VIRGINIA: And her little foot.

ALICE: You look a little stiff.

RHODA: I am capable of holding an infant.

ALICE: Does your heart melt?

RHODA: Not quite.

VIRGINIA: And your work?

MARY: Flourishing. Of course, Rhoda's taken over a great deal of the daily duties while I travel the world giving speeches.

ALICE: So you won. You have your apprentice after all.

MARY: Rhoda is no longer an apprentice but a business partner. She now owns half of our enterprise.

VIRGINIA: Equals?

RHODA: Perhaps.

VIRGINIA: *Lovers?*

RHODA: *No longer.* We're doing so well, we have to purchase a larger building. And we are beginning a women's publishing house.

MARY: The first in London.

RHODA: People keep suggesting martyred titles like Crucible Press. But I think it should say something about freedom.

ALICE: She looks irritable.

RHODA: She's very happy at the moment.

ALICE: I will hold her.

RHODA: Soon.

VIRGINIA: Is she asleep?

RHODA: Not yet.

ALICE: I'm so glad it was a girl.

VIRGINIA: Are you?

RHODA: The fire has been lit, it is burning through society with ferocious speed, no household is safe, the world is moving. (*to baby*) In thirty years it will all be accomplished.

They form a loose tableau.

The lights dim very slowly ...

Until finally ...

The women disappear.

END

THEATRE REPLACEMENT

(est. 2003)

"*BIOBOXES* unsettled me like no other performance I have ever attended. I felt unhinged somehow, turned over" (Solga). "It actually feels like hypnosis, with their eyes connecting with yours from less than a metre away" (Nestruck). "Outside the box, released from the performance, I find that I am a little giddy – and I am not the only one" (Stephenson). "Not even lap dancing gets as intimate ..." (Thomas). "*BIOBOXES* blew my brain wide open." That last comment is mine, from my review of Theatre Replacement's *BIOBOXES: Artifacting Human Experience* in 2007. *BIOBOXES* fundamentally altered my sense of how theatre works, my understanding of the relationship between audience and play. As the above sampling indicates, the experience is visceral.

Each in this series of six intimate playlets is seen by only one audience member at a time. Each actor performs a short piece, sitting in a chair with his or her head inside a small cardboard box that serves as the stage. Performer and audience sit very close, face to face, knees touching. The actor, I was self-consciously aware, could smell my breath. The contents of the playlets are extremely varied. They derive from the experiences of people who have immigrated to Canada, but the immigrant experience itself – whatever that might mean – appears the primary subject of only one or two of them. Collectively, they speak of ethnic and linguistic diversity. Each playlet is bilingual, the actor performing in English and a second language (French, Japanese, Cantonese, German, Italian, Serbo-Croatian). In both form and content, *BIOBOXES* reflects the commitment of Theatre Replacement and its principals to experimental, collaborative, intercultural theatre.

Theatre Replacement grew out of the ferment in mid-1990s Vancouver that gave rise to a vibrant community of alternative companies experimenting with collective, site-specific work: Electric Company, Neworld, Radix, Rumble, The Only Animal, Leaky Heaven Circus, and more. In 1997 a group of Simon Fraser University theatre grads formed Boca del Lupo, whose trademark became its free, highly physical, summer spectacles among the big trees in Stanley Park. Two of its founding members, Maiko Bae Yamamoto and James Long, formed Theatre Replacement in 2003. Their process involves collaboration with artists of diverse backgrounds and disciplines, often using biographical material to "artifact" human experience.

Many of their major projects have shared parts of the theatrical agenda that produced *BIOBOXES*. *Sexual Practices of the Japanese* (2006) put Theatre Replacement on the map, playing to strong reviews in Vancouver, Ottawa, and Seattle. Written and performed by Yamamoto, Hiro Kanagawa, and Manami Hara, and directed by Long and Yamamoto, it provides a feminist critique of Japanese patriarchal culture while having playful, sexy fun with ethnic stereotypes. Yamamoto wrote *Train* (2008) about her father, Kofu Yamamoto (who constructed the boxes for *BIOBOXES*), and performed it with him. *Clark and I Somewhere in Connecticut* (2008) was created by a collective that included *BIOBOXES* actor and writer Anita Rochon and videographer Candelario Andrade. Its stories are based on information and speculation about people in a photo album that Long found discarded in an alley. He performed the play across Canada. That same fertile year, 2008, produced Long and Yamamoto's *WeeTube*, in which they manipulate and respond to publically posted comments on YouTube videos. *WeeTube* has travelled to numerous national and international festivals.

Yamamoto and Long directed *The Greatest Cities in the World* (2010), a large-scale collective about community and ethnicity. Its text derived from company members' interviews with people from Tennessee towns named Athens, Paris, and London. Winner of the Rio Tinto Alcan Performing Arts Award in Vancouver, it also played at Montreal's Festival TransAmériques. A similar creative structure produced *Dress Me Up in Your Love* (2011), which combines biography and song in commentary about clothing from around the world. The ensemble included writer and performers Rochon, Cindy Mochizuki, and Donna Soares from *BIOBOXES*, plus co-directors Long and Yamamoto. *100% Vancouver* (2011) put one hundred non-actors onstage to tell their own stories about being Vancouverites. *Winners and Losers* (2012), written and performed by Long and Neworld's Marcus Youssef, explores autobiography, competition, and economics. It has toured widely since its Vancouver premiere, which won the Critics' Choice Innovation Award.

BIOBOXES developed from Theatre Replacement's *Box Theatre*, produced at Vancouver's Powell Street Festival in 2005. Six people, including Long and Yamamoto, wrote short scripts based on their own experiences, designed the boxes that fit over their heads, and performed their mini-shows for one-person audiences. Yamamoto and Long subsequently commissioned Vancouver actors Rochon, Mochizuki, Soares, Una Memisevic, Marco Soriano, and Paul Ternes to interview first-generation Canadians of their own linguistic background, and write and perform a verbatim script gleaned from the interview. Each playwright-performer designed their own box, which had to include three actual artifacts belonging to the interviewee. *BIOBOXES* premiered in 2007 at Calgary's High Performance Rodeo and Vancouver's PuSh International Performing Arts Festival, with subsequent performances in Regina, Ottawa, Toronto, Montreal, Calgary, and the PAZZ Festival in Germany.

Audience members pay to see anywhere from one to all six of the mini-shows, which are played simultaneously in a single open space, each performer and his or her solo audience concealed from the others by a curtain. Between each playlet, while waiting to be called and seated by a performer, audience members watch and listen to video of the original interviews. The boxes themselves are filled with tiny props and dollhouse-size sets, complemented by lighting, sound, and an array of low-tech special effects, all manipulated by the performer, who may also invite the audience member to get involved: write in a notebook, light incense, hold a flashlight, pose for a photo. At the front of each box an arrow points to English or the alternate language. The audience can move the arrow back and forth at any time as many times as they want, causing the performer to switch languages.

The title suggests the dual nature of this theatrical experience. *Bio* may refer to the *biographical* content of each playlet contained in the text, embodied in the onstage artifacts of the immigrant subject, narrated and enacted by the performer in the subject's own languages. It may also reference the *biology* of the actor, his or her physical presence. The primary object contained in each box is the actor's head and sometimes hand or hands. With the actor's face and body so close to one's own, the audience intensely experiences the *liveness* of live theatre. A thematic effect of this may be the sense that ethnic difference is trumped by human similarity. Another effect may be the awareness of one's own performance as audience member. You become intensely aware of where you're looking, whether you're laughing, whether your mind is drifting; you know the actor can see it in your eyes. Maybe the reception of ethnicity is as performative as ethnicity itself. In a fascinating *Canadian Theatre Review* article, five theatre scholars excitedly compare their own responses after just having come from a performance of *BIOBOXES* (see Levin et al.).

But how do we *read* this multi-text? What sense does it make on the page without the stage? First, be aware that the verbatim text, the words of each interview subject, has been "artifacted," reorganized into theatrical art by each playwright. Next, know that the order of the playlets is somewhat arbitrary. An audience member would see all six in random order. (I saw the Italian box first, for example.) Each tells its own story but together they invite us to consider certain broader ideas. Opening as it does with the French box, this version of *BIOBOXES* might appear to emphasize dissatisfaction. If you were to read or see the French, Cantonese, and Italian boxes back to back, family and gender issues might loom large. The French and Italian boxes foreground Canadian and European cultural difference, an idea also suggested obliquely in the Serbo-Croatian box. The Japanese and German boxes, through photography and video, bring audience and immigrant subject into a common frame within stories that suggest the potentially divisive nature of language and national histories. (For a compelling reading of the Japanese box by someone who never saw *BIOBOXES*, see Kim.)

Disease is a common denominator in the Japanese, Cantonese, and Serbo-Croatian boxes, although more figurative than literal in the first. We should be careful about reading disease as a metaphor but the notion of dis-ease may be a primary thread tying together all six parts: immigration-as-trauma, the uneasiness and anxiety brought about by changing one's language and homeland. On the other hand, the Serbo-Croatian box that concludes this version of *BIOBOXES* focuses on changes to the brain that have nothing to do with linguistic or national boundaries. Its final line suggests that we might, "if we tried," find a human commonality transcending difference. Similarity-in-diversity may be the primary "human experience" of the subtitle, artifacted in this remarkable work.

BIOBOXES

Theatre Replacement

Artifacting Human Experience

BIOBOXES: Artifacting Human Experience
premiered at High Performance Rodeo, Calgary,
January 3, 2007, co-produced by Theatre
Replacement and the High Performance Rodeo,
with the following creators and performers:

ANITA ROCHON
CINDY MOCHIZUKI
DONNA SOARES
PAUL TERNES
MARCO SORIANO
UNA MEMISEVIC

Directed by James Long and Maiko Bae
Yamamoto
Boxes Constructed by Kofu Yamamoto
Dramaturgy by Kris Nelson
Video by Candelario Andrade

CHARACTERS

AT HOME WITH JEANNE-PIERRE
APPLE
RÉMY MARTIN
EGG (JEAN-PHILIPPE)

FLIGHT
PILOT

MY BROTHER, MY HERO
GIRL

A MODERNIST NIGHTMARE
CHILD
MAMA
COW
KING OTTO
NARRATOR
REPORTER

LA STORIA DI ANNA
ANNA
MAN

HYPOCHONDRIAC
WOMAN

PRODUCTION NOTE

BIOBOXES: Artifacting Human Experience is a collection of short one-person shows for one-person
audiences that take place in a very intimate theatre:
a box worn on the actor's shoulders. The boxes are
modelled after your standard cardboard box; they
are just twenty-four inches wide by sixteen inches
high by sixteen inches deep.

Through an interview process with first-generation Canadians, six artists created tiny shows
that are performed in both English and another
language. The audience members choose when
they would like to change languages, switching
back and forth at any time. All of the texts used in
BIOBOXES are verbatim, meaning the words are
taken directly from transcripts of the interviews.

The languages and cultures represented in
BIOBOXES are Cantonese, French, German, Italian,
Japanese, and Serbo-Croatian.

French / English box and Anita Rochon. Photo by Shannon Mendes courtesy Theatre Replacement

AT HOME WITH JEANNE-PIERRE

(*FRENCH / ENGLISH BOX*)

BY ANITA ROCHON

In front of a red velvet curtain that is drawn closed, a sign appears: "Amuse-gueule." A light shines on it, like a searchlight. Downstage left another light comes on. We see an apple.

APPLE: (*sings*)

> *And I try*
>
> *And I try*
>
> *And I try*
>
> *Ooh I try …*

APPLE inhales, exhales. Beat. A light turns on to reveal a small bottle of Rémy Martin cognac.

RÉMY MARTIN: My wife.

APPLE: (*sings*) *I can't get no.*

RÉMY MARTIN: My second wife.

APPLE: (*sings*) *Satisfaction.*

RÉMY MARTIN: Not happy.

APPLE: (*sings*) *Hey hey hey* … Yeah, I guess I've always been an emotional person.

RÉMY MARTIN: Not happy.

RÉMY MARTIN crosses over to APPLE.

I've been married twice, yeah, and one relationship. There's one thing I always told my mom: "You know, when I grow up I'm going to marry a woman with blonde hair and blue eyes."

RÉMY MARTIN kisses APPLE. Another light comes on.

And I did!

APPLE: I had a kid in the relationship when I was not married.

Another voice is heard behind the curtain. It is the voice of EGG, a.k.a. Jean-Philippe.

EGG: And we don't talk!

APPLE: Jean-Philippe!

The bottom part of the curtain begins to rise, revealing the performer's face. She looks at an egg.

EGG: We don't. Talk.

APPLE: We talk. My son, Jean-Philippe.

EGG: First of all, I wasn't wanted –

RÉMY MARTIN: Oh, here we go with that again …

RÉMY MARTIN scuttles away. Another sign is revealed: "Hors d'oeuvre."

EGG: In those days they were struggling for everything, and my mom didn't want a kid. And she was pregnant with twins and she managed to get them – you know – aborted.

APPLE: Jean-Philippe!

EGG: And so when I came, she tried everything that she could to get rid of me. But I hanged in there. I almost died.

EGG smiles big.

APPLE: I like Cuban music, I like opera, rock and roll, I love the Rolling Stones, I like …

EGG: This ring? This ring is the last thing my dad left me.

A ring appears and is placed onstage. EGG sits on the ring.

And I didn't have time to really know my dad. I know he was a fabulous dancer …

APPLE: We used to go out dancing every night in France. It's always been music that has made a lot of sense to me. In those days we used to work so hard, long hours, split shifts. Then we got the chance to move to Canada.

EGG: He died around Christmas. Yeah. The twenty-third. The twenty-third of December he died and I never could say bye-bye but whatever, that was a long mourning. Here, you can hold his ring.

EGG floats up. The performer gives the audience member the ring to hold. EGG floats back onto the table where he was standing before.

RÉMY MARTIN: Okay!

The curtains open even wider to reveal RÉMY MARTIN taking a tour of his restaurant. He scuttles around the stage.

A regular day for me would be running a restaurant. So I would get up in the morning, take a shower, have a coffee, and go to work. I go pick up some food for the restaurant, cook lunch. After lunch if I have somebody, I would go home and in a better word I would "play" for a little bit …

He kisses APPLE and she laughs.

And come back to the restaurant around four-thirty, five o'clock, and start cooking again. That's it, that's my life.

Sad times? Oh yes I've had sad times.

He moves downstage, emoting.

I've always been emotional. But I'm just like a cat. I land on my feet.

I like cooking lamb. Maybe because I'm good at it. I have a feeling for it. I can feel it. I like it, too.

He crosses downstage right.

EGG: (*sitting on the table as it moves forward, inching closer to the audience*) I like eggplant and I like goat's cheese. My favourite dish is a combination of eggplant … goat's cheese … and other things.

APPLE: You know, I never could remember the alphabet? I lived for fifty years before finding out I was completely dyslexic.

Another sign is shown, "Entrée."

And now people tell me there might be a better way of doing things, reading, writing …

APPLE floats up to peruse the bookshelf, reading all the different titles.

It's not that easy. Because of the comfort zone, I have ways to remember things. Tricks. And I don't want to do this … I don't want to do that.

Can you do something for me? Write a letter for me? For my son, Jean-Philippe.

A big red notebook and a pencil appear and are offered to the audience member. APPLE dictates.

After the rain comes the sun. And where there is life, there is hope.

She takes back the notebook.

Jean-Philippe, look …

She brings the notebook up to EGG and holds it open for him to read.

I don't know that I've ever been really happy in my life.

RÉMY MARTIN: Too emotional.

APPLE: And the way I'm working these days, I don't know how long I'll be around for.

RÉMY MARTIN: Non, non, non.

RÉMY MARTIN bumps into APPLE. The red notebook that EGG has been reading closes with a snap.

Japanese / English box and Cindy Mochizuki. Photo by Shannon Mendes courtesy Theatre Replacement

EGG: I think it's possible. Happiness. And I'm going to find it. I am going to find my happiness.

Come on, everyone. Dinner.

*A sign appears, "Dessert," as a chocolate is placed on the table. It is offered to the audience member. As the curtains close, **APPLE** sings "(I Can't Get No) Satisfaction" again.*

APPLE:

> *And I try*
> *And I try*
> *And I try*
> *Ooh I try.*

*Just before the curtains close completely, the performer bites into **APPLE**.*

END

FLIGHT

(*JAPANESE / ENGLISH BOX*)

BY CINDY MOCHIZUKI

*A red light beams through the back of the box. A head pops up slowly. A **PILOT** appears. She is wearing a camera around her neck and aviator headgear with goggles à la Amelia Earhart. She pushes the goggles up on to her head.*

Images of the city are all around. The soundscape of a city can be heard.

PILOT: I don't want to be a bird but I want to be *like* a bird. "Ko" ... a dove.

*The city begins to recede as more of the **PILOT**'s face is revealed.*

A yellow beak, pure white feathers. Like this size, a little smaller than a seagull.

She flashes a light onto a white bird above. She holds a mini battery-powered fan, which she uses to blow air on the bird and the audience member.

Yes, that's right. I don't need to fly that fast. Slowly flying "Ko" ... looking down ... "Ko" ... but looking over and around ...

She holds up her camera, gestures to ask if she can take a photo.

Usually people ask to make, uh, to make a posture or faces. But I don't like such a picture. Usually when I ask people to make a face, the people like to be a handsome guy. Like this way.

She shows the audience member the picture she has just taken of them.

This is not a natural face. I try to say it this way. There is no mistake. I ask for a natural look.

A pile of photos and a small flashlight are handed to the audience.

Whatever I ask, the expression is ghastly. Same face. Same pattern. I don't like it ... The expression on their face. Only that person holds the expression I want to take.

About one thousand pictures. In one's mind there are memories, but if you don't take photos you will forget ...

The sound of birds chirping can be heard.

Yeah ... I got the "I don't want to speak English" disease three to four months ago.

A box is lifted to reveal many bright yellow beaks inside.

The reason why I got this was – is ... I was scared to say English to people who say English. A little bit, my feeling ... I don't know, my speech is a little bit fragile. So maybe if people say, "Huh?" or "Pardon?" or "Sorry?" or "What did you say?" I feel so sorry, so bad, so freaked out, so yeah ...

Still. But it's much better now.

It helped but I took a one-month break in my school and I stayed home for two weeks and I travelled to eastern Canada, to Montreal, Toronto, Ottawa.

Three small paper buses with the PILOT in each move past the audience's eyes.

A bus package tour. I signed up alone. I went there with no one.

But it worked. Yeah, kind of. No. I didn't get confidence, but I learned I don't have to speak English perfectly ...

The PILOT asks the audience to take a Japanese good-luck charm and pull it. Temple flags rise up and music can be heard.

There is a Japanese history. Used to be this guy, Sugawara Michizane – the emperor's right-hand man. But there were two. The other guy didn't like Sugawara. So he put, he sent him to this area. This area was not a good place because it was close to other countries. Sometimes war happens and people came to conquer the area. So ... he died there. Because of a disease. And after that the Sugawara ghost appears as a head.

A ghost flies down and hovers overhead.

The head hangs around the street. The ghost appears to the guy, so after that they built the Sugawara Shrine, where, yes, I got this charm.

The PILOT asks the audience if they would like to light some incense in memory of Sugawara. She hands them a stick of incense and lights a match. She asks them to place the incense in a holder. The box fills with the scent of burning incense. A part of the floor opens up to reveal glowing white feathers.

I want to be *like* a bird. "Ko" ... a dove. A yellow beak, pure white feathers.

The PILOT flashes a light on many people below, casting their shadows. She places onto the landscape a figurine of a PILOT and his camera.

Thinking that there can be such a world flying ahead and occasionally looking down and thinking of places where it might be fun or places I haven't seen before or wondering what people are doing, and if I'm curious, I fly down and see things I don't know and learn ...

A glowing egg appears and opens up. A good-luck charm is offered to the audience member to take with them.

In one's mind there are memories, and if you don't take ... you will forget.

END

Cantonese / English box and Donna Soares. Photo by Shannon Mendes courtesy Theatre Replacement

MY BROTHER, MY HERO

(*CANTONESE / ENGLISH BOX*)

BY DONNA SOARES

We hear the plucking of delicate strings, an eerie music. Suddenly someone begins coughing uncontrollably. Lights come up on GIRL, holding a handkerchief over her mouth.

GIRL: He will never call me again. Not being able to talk to him makes it hard. He looks like me. Slightly taller. I think he's about your height. How tall are you again?

The audience member responds.

Yeah, he's about that height. He's very, very skinny, though. Like if I compare my arm with his, I'm actually more fat than he is. He actually quite resembles Andy Lau, the Hong Kong pop star.

She reveals pin-up posters of Andy Lau on the wall with a flashlight. She sings a few lines from an Andy Lau song. She coughs.

My brother is Joon Yeen, "Jenkin." His middle character means handsome.

I would definitely say my brother is cute. My mom always says that because she's the prettier one, like, compared to my dad, my brother is the more handsome one, so he looks like my mom, whereas I'm more ugly so I look more like my dad, which is true because I have my dad's facial structure.

She lights her face with the flashlight. She lights the walls again.

Maybe because he's older than me, but my brother's so cool, cooks really well, really takes care of his family. My brother is perfect.

She blows Andy Lau a kiss.

Two, three years after he graduated high school, he really wanted to find something to do. My dad's cousin's a barrister in Hong Kong, and my brother went back to do work experience for three months. He came back and said that he would pursue that dream. About three years ago, he went back to Hong Kong.

My parents are absolutely very lucky, but me being in the world kind of brings them bad luck. My mom and dad have both been sick. Sometimes I kind of blame my –

I don't know, I just … I was a surprise baby to them. They never planned me, and all of a sudden they got pregnant.

A tiny, plastic baby falls from the ceiling. GIRL picks it up and sticks it to the wall.

So I just felt like … I did not bring them happiness 'cause I was a fussy girl. My brother was such a perfect child, and then they had me.

I found this guy unexpectedly in a math lab. It was really magical. I was picking a seat, you know how sometimes girls will see cute guys and sit by them to see if anything happens? One of my classmates came in and sat next to me and it just so happens that she knows this guy. They started talking and I cut in. After the lab closed, I didn't want to leave.

"So where are you going now?"

"I'm going somewhere and do more math."

"Can I come with you?"

"Sure, let's go do math together."

We stayed for an hour and talked some more. We exchanged phone numbers. I've never known a guy that I had so much spark and chemistry with right at the first moment. His first voice mail is still in my mailbox. I just don't want to delete it, it's filled with memories.

She coughs.

Going back to Hong Kong was really dangerous because of SARS.

She places her hand on the audience member's knee.

He went back all by himself, so of course my mom and dad were very worried.

She retracts her hand. A string of surgical masks begins to pass in front of the GIRL's face. She speaks from behind the masks.

Bad luck. I was shocked. Heartbroken. Close to death? My heart fell and shattered like glass. I tried to hold back my tears. He's leaving us. Our family is coming apart. I don't want that to happen. I always want … My safest moment is when everyone's home at night. Just to have everyone home. What if mom and dad leave one day?

I already felt like I was an only child. My brother's eight years older than I am. The only time that I see him is basically at dinnertime. So his leaving is just a matter of not being able to see him. My brother was such a perfect child, and then they had me.

A curtain of teardrops emerges.

The first few nights, I couldn't do anything.

"Leave me alone, I don't want to see you guys."

I am so tired of it. I've cried way too many times.

That morning, when he called me, I made sure to sound as cheerful as I could. He said, "Jenine, I just want you to know that I really, really care about you."

The string of surgical masks is lowered.

He calls every night. Just to check up on mom and dad. Superhero. I love him very much. Even though I don't say it to him, but he knows. To Chinese people, it's too –

She grimaces and shakes her head.

I'm just happy to have him.

An Andy Lau song plays. A teddy bear emerges and waves.

This reminded me of you. I wanna see you.

There's so little memory of him somehow, thinking about it.

Lights begin flashing, creating a somewhat ghastly look on GIRL's face.

I'm pretty lonely. There's always something about him that I miss. Even if I cry these days, it's about him. Sometimes I think that other people will think that my EQ is very low, because I can for one minute be laughing like crazy, then the next minute I'll be crying like crazy, then the next minute I'll be laughing like crazy again.

She laughs until she coughs. Music fades out.

END

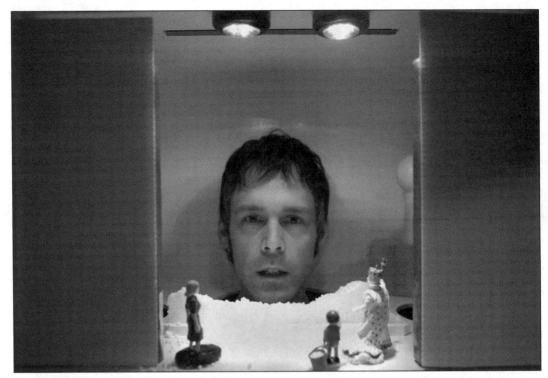

German / English box and Paul Ternes. Photo by Shannon Mendes courtesy Theatre Replacement

A MODERNIST NIGHTMARE

(*GERMAN / ENGLISH BOX*)

BY PAUL TERNES

*A Styrofoam wall separates the **NARRATOR** and the audience. A Bavarian folk song is heard, and the **NARRATOR** begins to dance an Alpine schuhplattler (shoe-slapping) dance. As the song and dance ends, a small figurine of a woman appears from behind the wall and moves to centre stage.*

MAMA: Büchenbach –

NARRATOR: Büchenbach –

You have heard of Büchenbach? There's not much there. It's about a thousand years old and it hasn't changed much except for the last forty years.

I remember things fit together in a way that I thought they ought to. And it was pretty.

*A figurine of a **CHILD** carrying a red bucket enters from behind the wall.*

CHILD: There was a lake nearby that would freeze in the winter and you could go skating on it. There were always places to go.

MAMA: Yes, when we were six we would disappear for the afternoon after school was out.

CHILD exits. MAMA exits after CHILD.

NARRATOR: This is something children don't do anymore. They tend to be supervised all the time. Büchenbach had one of everything. A school, a baker, a post office, a gas station. And the gas station in those days was a Caltex gas station.

CHILD enters again on top of a toy Volkswagen Beetle.

CHILD: (*sings*)

California, California Texan Oil

California, California Texan Oil ...

NARRATOR: Rounded corners with glass brick and everything arrayed to reflect the Caltex insignia. So the people ran around in white coveralls, and they had little white oil cans.

CHILD exits.

MAMA: (*offstage*) And this to my mind was no different than any other part of this world in the sense that it, too, was a naturally occurring gas station in the same way that cows were a naturally occurring feature of this landscape.

Figurine of a COW enters.

COW: In Bavarian, there is a term for anyone who lives north of the Main River: *Saupreiss*. Pig-Prussian.

MAMA enters.

MAMA: Whereas northerners tend to look at anyone south of the Main as being, well, agrarian.

They face off.

COW: They roundly loathe one another.

CHILD re-enters without the car, followed by a figurine of KING OTTO.

CHILD: Ladies and gentlemen: Otto the First, first king of the German nation!

KING OTTO steps forward.

KING OTTO: Thank you very much. That reminds me of the time that Charlemagne went into Saxony, and massacred about three thousand people in an afternoon because they wouldn't become Christian. So he put them to the sword.

COW quickly exits, followed by KING OTTO.

MAMA: One day all German Caltex stations were rebranded as Texacos. And this meant that everything was now dark brown and orange and there was the star.

We hear the sound of a power drill as it begins drilling through the Styrofoam wall.

And for the first time in my life, I realized that some part of the world was arrayed by different forces other than just natural evolution.

A finger pokes a hole through the Styrofoam. The NARRATOR's mouth appears.

And I never quite forgot this moment, because it seemed to mean that the world was capable of lying. And there was someone somewhere who owned the world that I couldn't sense.

The NARRATOR's eye appears in the hole.

NARRATOR: They went for a walk every evening and said, "We are the people." No one shot at anyone. This was the only bloodless revolution in Europe.

The powers that be called the Russian commanders and asked them to send the tanks in. The Russian commanders said no, and Gorbachev said sort this out on your own.

I was there when the wall came down.

The NARRATOR's hands appear on either side of the wall and begin tearing it apart. Pieces fall forward onto the audience member's lap. The NARRATOR and the audience member are face to face for the first time.

It was extraordinary.

The NARRATOR softly blows away the last pieces of wall debris. Behind his head, stage left, is a small brick wall with barbed wire placed in front of a tower that holds up a white sphere the size of a tennis ball.

Back in Canada, I had a dinner party around the time that Germany unified. A number of people who had known me since I had come here started to talk about the changes in Germany that had occurred after the wall came down.

The NARRATOR places a tiny video monitor in front of his face and begins speaking as a TV news REPORTER. The MAMA and CHILD figurines face the screen, which is blank.

REPORTER: The neo-Nazis were suddenly having a field day, especially in the eastern parts that were economically depressed. People were attacked. People were killed. For about six months, there was an attack every day.

The NARRATOR peers out from behind the monitor..

NARRATOR: And at that dinner party, somebody asked me whether I could understand the sentiment of the people who were now sort of asserting their German-ness. And well, I could make it known if I felt that, now that the situation had been changed, felt maybe not approval of that particular activity, but that I would embrace my nationality.

The people sat around the table and looked at me, interested to see what I would now say. They were just wondering how I would field this one.

The sphere on top of the tower begins to turn and an embedded camera lens points at the NARRATOR, who is now also visible on the video monitor.

Crypto-Nazi.

He turns to speak directly into the camera.

I felt utterly alone. And in some strange way I became German after that. And it was painful.

The KING OTTO figurine pops up in front of the camera lens – a close-up of his face appears on the monitor.

Italian / English box and Marco Soriano. Photo by Shannon Mendes courtesy Theatre Replacement

KING OTTO: The situation has changed. There is nothing to be gained from another fascist Germany. The corporations, which, after all, got Hitler into power, currently have no interest in repeating this. Now the corporations are international conglomerates that see the nation-state as an impediment to the free flow of money. I mean, it is sufficient for 20 per cent of the population to bully the remainder, and clearly you can coerce people.

MAMA exits, leaving behind CHILD, who turns toward audience while onscreen KING OTTO exits off camera.

CHILD: Um, I used to do the Rommels' lawn. They lived just down the street. And they had, um, a hovercraft lawnmower. There was a company called Flymo, which made hovercraft lawnmowers that didn't run on wheels.

A small windup toy of a pair of lederhosen with feet are placed next to CHILD and begins to hop about.

And for mountainous areas, these were very useful.

The camera lens turns to face out toward the audience member who now appears on the monitor. CHILD turns to face the screen, and then exits after MAMA.

END

LA STORIA DI ANNA (ANNA'S STORY)

(ITALIAN / ENGLISH BOX)

BY MARCO SORIANO

A paper screen separates the performer and audience member. Throughout the piece, only parts of the performer's face will be seen in cut-out boxes in the screen. The screen scrolls in both directions, revealing various images on two rotating pillars sandwiching the performer's head. The back wall is painted with a magnificent sunset, which is only partially visible behind the performer's head.

The words "La Storia di Anna" (Anna's Story) are the first thing revealed on the screen. The performer is hidden behind the screen.

A tarantella plays and the screen scrolls to reveal the performer's eyes, made up with blue eyeshadow. ANNA speaks with an Italian accent.

ANNA: Well, many years ago, when I was a young girl, it was in to have a lace dress for the evening and a mink collar. So my mother gave me this wild, Canadian mink ...

She touches and reveals a mink wrapped around her neck.

The mink became very nostalgic so I brought it back home to Canada.

The scroll moves to reveal a map of Italy with inset of Turin. It continues to move, showing a pretty watercolour of Turin.

I was born right in the middle of the city of Torino in northwestern Italy – in the shadow of the Mole Antonelliana. I remember I would travel, I would play bridge and tennis, I would ski, and I would work, of course, and I always worked very hard. But at the time there was no way you would leave home. And so I had a very, very easy, pleasant life.

The scroll moves quickly back to reveal the MAN's mouth. He speaks with no accent.

MAN: She didn't even know what Canada was at the time. She didn't want to come to Canada. It was the man she married who didn't want to live in Italy anymore.

ANNA: Vincent went to Libya in the spring. In the fall he came back with an engagement ring. Then he went off to London, to find work, and we had decided to not even think of getting married 'til September. So he calls me the sixth of July, 1966, and says, "Anna, we have to get married by the end of the month because I've got this job at the beginning of August and they want me here." What? "I'll be there tomorrow." Because he loved challenges, right … My mother was all excited – she wanted grandchildren. Plus Vincent was … wonderful. He could imitate anyone, he had a wonderful bass voice …

An engagement ring with a green stone is revealed. "Lauretta Mia" plays, an Italian ballad that is traditionally the first dance at a wedding reception, where fathers dance with their daughters as a farewell of sorts.

MAN: She said:

ANNA: "Mother, I don't have a dowry, I have nothing, I don't even have a piece of a towel."

MAN: So she started laughing and walked to this enormous closet like they have in Italy, to the ceiling, and she starts throwing at me towels and sheets.

The scroll moves quickly back to reveal the engagement ring again.

They were married in the mountains two hours from town, and it was truly one of the best weddings she was ever at.

"Lauretta Mia" stops. The Union Jack is revealed.

ANNA: I had been to England a few years before to study and they said they could only give me six months, but I think the immigration officer liked me because he gave me a year. So I thought they were all nice and sweet. This time, there were three entrances, British, Commonwealth, and aliens. Vincent was Commonwealth and I was an alien …

A passport with a red X on it appears.

I go with my passport and he says, "Where is your visa?" "I don't have a visa. I just got married and my husband is inside." Well, he said, "All right," put a big red cross, got Vincent back, put another big red cross and said, "All right, for two years you can't come back and you have to stay here tonight because you missed the last ferry."

The scroll moves and the screen becomes prison bars. There is a pause, and then the scroll continues to reveal a little box cut in the screen just a bit higher than the performer's eyes.

We went to the consul general in Milan and he said, "You both speak English, you must go to my city." So he opens the map, and says this is Vancouver. Vincent looks at all of this water, the mountains – well … that's how it happened. When we decided we would come to Canada, my father, he loved to research, to read, so he found out that Canada was the second-largest country in the world, it had one-third of the fresh water of the world. He never told me that Vancouver was nine thousand kilometres from Torino.

We see an airplane in a cloudy sky and hear the sound of an airplane taking off.

I was twenty-nine. The sixteenth of October. It was a time when everybody was coming to Canada. I hated it. First of all, it was a long, long trip. I'm not a good traveller. It was foggy and there was already tension between me and Vincent. So we stopped in Montreal for a night and then came to Vancouver, where it rained and it rained and rained … 'til February!

The incessant sound of rain plays through the next section of text. A motel Vacancy sign is revealed, then a miniature mop and bucket.

Serbo-Croatian / English box and Una Memisevic. Photo by Shannon Mendes courtesy Theatre Replacement

MAN: Vincent had decided that Anna was spoiled, and that she deserved to be punished. So he didn't even look for an apartment. They lived in motels and she hated it. She washed the floor every day. She's not very domesticated, but what does one do in a motel? All of a sudden she found that she had to please a person in a manner that she did not understand.

An image of miniature bread and a rolling pin is revealed.

She couldn't cook, she still can't cook ... she hates cooking, but she had to cook for him. The moment she began being able to cook something, he wanted something else – he wanted to change.

The scroll moves quickly across to reveal a miniature bible.

ANNA: I made friends with some Jehovah's Witnesses who came around every week, a mother and a son. I always confronted them of course with my own ideas, but they were company. It was very nice to have someone to visit me.

Through the following section of text, images of eight motel rooms are shown on the screen. The sound of rain continues.

Thank God we got away from there. For someone like me, who comes from a city like Torino – they call us "bougianais," which means we do not move. So for someone like me, you know, who is born in the Abougino ... I lived in three apartments in Italy, and here I was moving eight apartments in four years.

The screen stops. A larger square hole reveals more of ANNA's face.

Torino ... I remember in Torino we used to go walking. To the theatre or a restaurant. One night in Vancouver we went to Granville Street – not a soul! There were no restaurants! Eventually I found this restaurant called Torna Sorrento. We walked in and I said, "Pizza!" I looked at the menu and thought, "Wow, these pizzas are expensive, but, well, it's Canada." We were really hungry. I ordered a medium, Vincent ordered a large. When the pizzas came, they wouldn't even fit on the table. We only ate two slices! So they said okay, it's fine, you can take it home. "Doggy bags?!"

We see miniature pink boots.

I couldn't find shoes because I used to wear a size thirty-four.

A drawing of a foot on the performer's left palm is revealed. He traces the image with the index finger of his right hand as he speaks.

So I had to design my foot on the paper, and I would send it to my mother and she would have shoes made for me. When the Chinese started arriving, then I could find shoes, because Chinese women have smaller feet, and I keep telling them, "Thank you for coming, otherwise I would be going barefoot!"

The scroll moves back to reveal ANNA's eyes, but the hole is too high. She stands on tiptoe to make eye contact. The sound of typing can be heard.

I couldn't stand being at home, I'm not a home person. But I had no Canadian experience. So I looked in the Yellow Pages and I found Catholic Immigration Services, and that's where I worked for the first year.

The image of a baby boy is revealed.

David was born in '67, and for a year and a half I stayed at home with him. Then for a year and a half I worked part time at this credit union and went back and forth, back and forth. I took five buses! With the child things became a bit ... difficult.

Typing sound out. Another airplane can be heard. We see a plane.

I didn't go back to Italy until '73. I could've stayed; they offered me two tremendous jobs. All my friends would call and were saying, "Stay, Anna, stay." And they didn't even know about my problems at home.

The performer violently grabs the audience member's knee. The scroll moves to reveal the biggest cut-out yet. An Italian song, "Che Sarà," plays.

When I flew back to Vancouver, the weather was beautiful. You could see everything: Greenland, the mountains ...

The plane landed at nine o'clock on a Saturday night, and I knew that at home was going to be troubles, but I looked around me and there was this enormous sky. This magnificent sunset ...

The performer slowly drops his head out of the box, so as to reveal the magnificent sunset painted on the back wall. His bald head becomes the setting sun. After a moment he raises his head back into the box.

So here I am.

The scroll moves so that the screen is partially covering the performer's head. Only half his face is visible.

MAN: Anna and Vincent split in '75.

He leans his head to the side and becomes ANNA.

ANNA: But this is just *one* of my stories.

The tarantella plays. The scroll moves quickly to reveal the word "Fine."

END

HYPOCHONDRIAC

(*SERBO-CROATIAN / ENGLISH BOX*)

BY UNA MEMISEVIC

A flashlight moves in the darkness to reveal images of brain X-rays on a transparent screen that separates the performer and the audience member. A voice can be heard.

WOMAN: (*reciting*)

Frustration

Slashed blood pressure

Split consciousness

Bruising of the head

Small little concussion

Flexing out

Pseudo seizures

Loose centre of attention

Extreme anger

Collapsed bilirubin and liver enzymes

Embarrassed kidneys and stomach

Embarrassed breast electricity

Embarrassed chest X-ray

Chest trauma

Inability to fall asleep or stay asleep

Aggressive control

Personality concussion

Stretched brain tumour

Scraping out of proportion

Unusual, hurtful, inappropriate, aggressive socializing

Positive fears and traumas and

Hypochondria

The screen lifts. The sound of a heartbeat being tapped out on the outside of the box is heard. The WOMAN's head appears. A green light, like an MRI scan, moves across her face.

Code Blue is medical emergency, cardiac arrest. Code Red is fire. Code Yellow is missing patient. Code White is aggressive patient. Code Brown is a chemical emergency, like biohazard. Code Orange is ...

I don't remember what Code Orange is.

I wonder if this machine is going to make me lose my memory.

A red light begins flashing on WOMAN's face.

I can't believe I turned the ambulance away.

A bright light turns on.

I started experiencing on-and-off headaches ... and I was in Home Depot and I collapsed ... I had a seizure ... I collapsed ... I rolled my eyes back and twitched and ... I peed myself ... I collapsed ... I completely lost control over my bladder ... I collapsed.

I don't remember the whole forty-five seconds of the event; I maybe remember the last five and that was my fiancé's hand in my mouth trying to get my tongue out, which is something you don't do anymore.

The person twitching and seizing is trying to bite, so what happens is: they bite their tongue off and blurpblurpblurpblurp! They will be tongue-less. Imagine the world without a tongue, it would be terrible! So many pleasures cut out ...

Bright light cuts out and the red flashing light comes back on.

Why did I turn the ambulance away?

The lights shift back again to bright light.

Working in neuromedicine, and surgery, I see a lot of people coming in with a history of head-aches for weeks, and not going to the doctor. On the other hand, you have people who just collapse and they come to the Emergency. And that's how the system gets clogged up! Go to your GP so that you can get worked up properly, blood work, chest X-ray, instead of coming to the Emergency, wait-ing here for five hours just to be seen.

People who shouldn't be worried are, and those who should be worried aren't.

Not going to the doctor, not going and then going to the doctor, getting a CAT scan, and there would be a tumour there, or a blood vessel would be thickening, or there is a buildup on a blood vessel so there is no blood flow to the head. And if they came on time, everything would have been fine!

Bright light goes out. The green MRI light moves across her face.

I know this is my fifth opinion!

I just ... I want to be sure.

That I don't –

Lights shift. Bright light comes on again. WOMAN is looking up at the ceiling, where we now see a collage of black-and-white images of people: family members, old lovers, etc., held together by thread and chewing gum.

I come from that part of the world, where people speak the truth.

I jump on people's chests, give them medication, use electricity to jump-start their heart – blood splashing everywhere ...

And they speak as they feel it.

You look at the person and you think, "Okay, how does he look?" People tell it like it is. Does he look clean or like he's living on the street? Does he look like a drug user, does he have HIV, hepatitis? Don't get anything into your eyes, anybody have goggles? Need goggles, mask, face shield –

Bright light goes out. Green MRI light comes back on.

The adrenaline is unbelievable when you are working on somebody.

Lights shift again. Bright light comes back on.

This twenty-seven-year-old guy had a lump on his left testicle. Way too embarrassed to tell anyone. Pain for months and months. It got to that point when he couldn't get off the bed. His father forced him to go to the Emergency.

The tests showed cancer that started from the little knot, the lump in his left testicle.

His stomach had a fist-sized tumour by that point. Tumours on his spine. Each vertebra had a tumour and he had a small nodule on his head. He came in weighing seventy kilos. Last time I saw him, he looked like a person from a concentration camp.

He was twenty-seven at the time. I was twenty-nine. I shaved his head after his first chemo.

I shaved his head.

People are very box-like and very close-minded. You really have to drill some serious holes in order for some air to move and some understanding to happen.

> *Suddenly, salt begins to pour from a hole in the ceiling. **WOMAN** looks around, takes the gum that she's been chewing out of her mouth, and uses it to plug the hole.*

> *Bright light out. Green MRI light comes back on.*

Oh ... I am dying.

When I had these headaches, I already had cancer.

"Yes, you do have a condition."

And already chemotherapy – my head was shaved – I was already wearing a wig and I said my last goodbyes to my fiancé.

"But you will live with it for the rest of your life, because you lived with it probably since your birth."

I was born; I died in chemotherapy. I created everything with these headaches.

"You are not dying. And no, you won't have surgery. And no, you are not going to have a long-term disability leave. You are going back to work."

I am sure if we tried we could find a little bit of everything in everybody.

> *Lights out.*

END

MARIE CLEMENTS

(b. 1962)

Métis/Dene playwright, actor, director, and producer Marie Clements has become one of contemporary Canada's most compelling Aboriginal artists – and one of its most dynamic theatre artists, period. She is among the few First Nations playwrights, since Tomson Highway broke through to mainstream success in the 1980s, to amass a major body of work and be regularly produced in professional theatres. Her artistically complex, often oblique, and always political plays have attracted significant scholarly attention, including a special issue of *Theatre Research in Canada* (Fall 2010). As founding artistic director of urban ink productions, Clements turned to producing her own work and that of other artists of colour in collaborative ways, and she learned to direct by co-directing her own plays. With her new company, red diva projects, she has begun making short films and music videos as an extension of her artistic practice. Among her subjects: residential-school survivors, Aboriginal women in prison, and those gone missing or murdered.

Written and staged in conjunction with a photography exhibition by Rita Leistner, *The Edward Curtis Project* investigates different ways of seeing, of experiencing (mis)representation, and of understanding "the vanishing Indian." The play extends Clements's ongoing project of dramatizing contemporary North American aboriginality through intense close-up portraits of individuals framed within a variety of historical contexts, both Western and indigenous.

Born in Vancouver, Clements earned a diploma in broadcast journalism from Calgary's Mount Royal College. Returning to Vancouver to work in radio, she found herself getting more work as a stage actor with small, independent companies. The first play she wrote, *Age of Iron* (1993), premiered at the Firehall Arts Centre in Vancouver's Downtown Eastside, Canada's poorest neighbourhood and home to many Aboriginal people. An adaptation of Euripides's *Trojan Women, Age of Iron* conflates Greek tragedy and modern Canada, ancient Troy and the urban Aboriginal ghetto. Clements herself played Cassandra. Two one-acts followed in 1995, *Now Look What You Made Me Do*, a play about violence against women, and *The Girl Who Swam Forever*, about a pregnant First Nations girl in the 1960s who runs away from residential school.

Clements first came to wide public attention with *Urban Tattoo* (1999), a solo show she wrote and performed. The multi-media story of an Aboriginal woman from the Northwest Territories who leaves home with dreams of being a movie star but finds herself on the mean streets of

Edmonton instead, *Urban Tattoo* was developed through years of workshops in Canada, the United States, and the United Kingdom, then played venues across North America. *The Unnatural and Accidental Women* (2000) cemented Clements's reputation as a brave new talent. It premiered at Vancouver's Firehall, in the neighbourhood where the notorious central events of the play took place. Between 1965 and 1988, dozens of mostly Aboriginal women had died of alcohol poisoning from drinks administered by a local barber, who was ultimately convicted of manslaughter despite coroners' reports declaring the deaths "unnatural and accidental." The surreal and surprisingly comical play centres on a young woman looking for her mother, whose ghost and those of the other murdered women hunt their killer. Clements wrote the screenplay for director Carl Bessai's film, *Unnatural and Accidental* (2006), which opened at New York's Museum of Modern Art.

Burning Vision* (2002) also premiered at the Firehall. A complex play about the connection between radium mining by Dene in the Northwest Territories and the atomic bomb dropped on Hiroshima in 1945, *Burning Vision* was nominated for the Governor General's Literary Award, won the Canada-Japan Literary Award, and toured Canada with stops at Montreal's Festival des Amériques and Magnetic North in Ottawa. In 2001, Clements founded urban ink productions to "celebrate and bring together different cultural and artistic perspectives and inter-racial experiences." One of its first projects was *Women in Fish* (2004), a multimedia series of installations and live radio plays, co-written and co-directed by Clements, bringing together Aboriginal and non-Aboriginal professionals and community women to tell the story of a 1960s fisheries disaster.

Copper Thunderbird* (2007), a play about Ojibwa painter Norval Morrisseau, was co-produced by urban ink at Ottawa's National Arts Centre, directed by NAC English Theatre's artistic director Peter Hinton. *The Edward Curtis Project* premiered as part of the 2010 Cultural Olympiad and PuSh International Performing Arts Festival at North Vancouver's Presentation House Theatre. Co-directed by Clements and Brenda Leadlay, it received Jessie Richardson Award nominations as Best New Play and Best Production. Talonbooks published the play along with Rita Leistner's photographs in a volume titled *The Edward Curtis Project: A Modern Picture Story* (2010). Clements alone directed a 2013 National Arts Centre / Great Canadian Theatre Company remount in Ottawa. The script published here is a revised version based on that Ottawa production. Clements's *Tombs of the Vanishing Indian* (2011) takes up the *Curtis Project*'s vanishing Indian theme, following the lives of three Native American children sent to separate foster homes after their mother is killed by police. Commissioned by the Autry National Centre and Southwest Museum of the American Indian in Los Angeles, where it received several workshops and staged readings, it premiered at Toronto's Buddies in Bad Times Theatre, co-produced by Native Earth Performing Arts and Clements's red diva projects.

Clements, who lives in Vancouver, has been playwright-in-residence at the National Theatre School, Banff Centre for the Arts, National Arts Centre, Firehall Arts Centre, Rumble Productions in Vancouver, and

Playwrights Workshop Montreal. In 2013, she was writer-in-residence at Simon Fraser University.

The Edward Curtis Project tells the story of Angeline, a contemporary Aboriginal journalist undergoing a severe emotional crisis precipitated by her having witnessed the tragic deaths of three Aboriginal children accidentally left by their drunken father to freeze in the snow on a northern reserve (based on an actual incident in 2008). When her psychiatrist sister, Clara, gives her Edward Curtis's book of photographs, *The North American Indian*, to try to help ease her depression, Curtis himself appears in a series of hallucinations to Angeline – and, in Clements's characteristically surreal style, to her boyfriend Yiska as well. Curtis's story intersects hers, revolving around his troubled relationship with his wife, Clara (played by the same actress who plays Angeline's sister Clara), and his 1911 lectures on "The Vanishing Indian" (quoted verbatim in the play), illustrated with his brilliant pseudo-documentary photographs. Curtis likes to call himself "Chief," and he too seems on the verge of a breakdown – partly, he suggests, as a result of immersing himself in the lives of starving Aboriginal people. Despite Angeline's resistance and Yiska's outright hostility, Curtis (whose first photo was of a Duwamish woman named Angeline) takes a folksy interest in Angeline, even cooking meals for her in her kitchen, and Angeline reciprocates. At some psychological level she sees him as her double.

The historical Edward Curtis (1868–1952) gained fame as the foremost chronicler of North America's Aboriginal people, whose images he wanted to capture on film before they died out or became fully assimilated, as he and many of his contemporaries assumed they would. He took more than forty thousand striking photos, most carefully staged to show the exotically dressed Native subject in a primitive, romanticized state. He even shot an extraordinary silent film on the British Columbia coast (*In the Land of the Headhunters*, 1914), using local Kwakwaka'wakw non-actors. Curtis's magnum opus, *The North American Indian*, was published in twenty illustrated volumes between 1907 and 1930, many of its gorgeous sepia images becoming iconic. Celebrated for the artistry of his photographs, Curtis has been criticized for what Rita Leistner, in the published volume, calls "the havoc Curtis and his colonial contemporaries had wrought" (71): the historical distortions and racist misconceptions of Aboriginal people that his artistry helped publicize. In the play, Yiska accuses Curtis of being a thief, just another white man coming through and appropriating everything he could. Both he and Angeline accuse Curtis of mistaking his idea of the Indian, his perceptions, for the reality. But for Angeline, Curtis's presence is more complicated and even more troubling, because she sees in him reflections of her own guilt, her own crimes.

As a journalist doing stories on Aboriginal life, as a chronicler of Native people "frozen in time" and dying before her eyes, as a responsible witness, Angeline feels as complicit as Curtis in the suffering that both failed to accurately depict. "I didn't write the whole story ... the real story," she tells Yiska in anguish over her failure to interpret in a productive way the story of the dead children, their father ("so young, so poor"), and the conditions that produced the tragedy. "Maybe we should all own a little piece of it," she wonders, framing the key ethical issue of the play. Meanwhile, she struggles, taking out her frustrations on Clara and Yiska, trying desperately to "get out of all the lies that have framed me." In the ambiguous ending, Curtis may be a catalyst that helps her reframe her life and makes her "ready to see everything" again.

The references to framing, photography, and visualization are made concrete in the script and vivid in production through photos projected onto the set. During the production Curtis's photos, in large format, appear on the cyclorama at the back of the stage. But we also see Angeline's family portraits (created by Rita Leistner) magically floating in space on a downstage scrim around the actors, out in front of Curtis's images. The visual dialogue, or dialectic, created by that juxtaposition has been further extended in both productions to date by Leistner's exhibition of photographs, also titled *The Edward Curtis Project*, in an adjoining gallery. Leistner travelled North America, photographing Native people, creating what she calls "diptychs": pairs of photos showing an Aboriginal person in his or her everyday dress alongside the same person dressed up in some authentic regalia. Her work ironically echoes Curtis's exotic, nostalgic portraits while reporting the recovery of proud traditions and heritage among a resilient living people who refuse to vanish.

The Edward Curtis Project

Marie Clements

The *Edward Curtis Project* premiered January 21, 2010, at Presentation House Theatre, North Vancouver, with the following cast:

ANGELINE / PRINCESS ANGELINE	Tamara Podemski
EDWARD CURTIS / CHIEF / FATHER	Stephen E. Miller
CLARA CURTIS / DR. CLARA	Kathleen Duborg
YISKA / ALEXANDER UPSHAW / HUNGER CHIEF	Kevin Loring

Directed by Marie Clements and Brenda Leadlay
Photography by Rita Leistner
Costume Design by Barbara Clayden
Set and Props Design by Andreas Kahre
Lighting Design by John Webber
Projections Design and Photography by Tim Matheson
Music and Sound Design by Bruce Ruddell
Songs Written and Performed by Leela Gilday
Stage Managed by Jan Hodgson

CHARACTERS

EDWARD CURTIS, *1900s. American. Forty-three to sixty-three years old. Photographer, businessman, filmmaker, explorer. At the prime of his life and career.*

ANGELINE, *Present. Dene / Russian-Canadian. Early forties. Journalist.*

PRINCESS ANGELINE, *1903. Duwamish. Seventy years old. Daughter of Chief Sealth (Seattle), clam-digger.*

YISKA *("After the Dark"), Present. N'lakap'mux / Canadian. Late thirties. Angeline's boyfriend.*

ALEXANDER UPSHAW, *1904. Crow translator. Educated at the Carlisle School. In Edward Curtis's words: "The most remarkable man I ever met – perfectly educated and absolutely uncivilized."*

THE HUNGER CHIEF, *Timeless. A bear-like leader of all peoples and all nations. A shaper of storms and clear skies.*

DR. CLARA, *Present. Russian-Canadian. Early forties. Shrink. Feminist.*

CLARA, *1900s. American. Early forties. Edward Curtis's wife and business partner.*

FATHER, *Present. Angeline's and Dr. Clara's father.*

MUSIC

Traditional and contemporary Native music and orchestrations inspired by the Indianist Music Movement led by Arthur Farwell and played with nostalgia, as well as wax cylinder recordings and adaptations.

SET

Extremely bare except for walls of light and dark that are able to transform space and time.

LIGHTING

Carved and sculpted light that reveals and vanishes.

COSTUMES

Period clothing for both traditional Euro and Aboriginal scenes. Modern clothing for periods in between.

MEDIA

Photography, archival film, film, video, archival writing, Euro-Aboriginal and Aboriginal-Euro orchestral scores, wax cylinders, magic lanterns.

FRAME SHIFT

A focus and perspective, both using physical choreography and photo-manipulation, incorporating closeup, long shot, wide shot, studio, landscape, and cultural ranges of seeing.

THE PICTURE STORY SEQUENCES

In the winter of 1911–12, Edward Curtis toured the continent with his "musicale" or "picture opera," *A Vanishing Race*. It combined photographs, motion pictures, and Henry Gilbert's music. The Carnegie Hall premiere in New York was a resounding success.

THE NORTH AMERICAN INDIAN PROJECT

Edward Sheriff Curtis began his career as a professional photographer in 1891. His first picture of a North American native was an 1895 portrait of "Princess Angeline" (Kickisomlo), the daughter of Chief Sealth of Seattle. In 1904, J.P. Morgan's daughter-in-law purchased some Curtis photographs at an exhibit in New York. Two years later, Morgan provided Curtis with funding to conduct fieldwork for a planned twenty-volume illustrated text originally called *American Indians*.

The first volume of this monumental work appeared in 1907 under the title *The North American Indian*, with an introduction by Theodore Roosevelt. Curtis himself described the importance and urgency of his work in that first volume: "The information that is to be gathered ... respecting the mode of life of one of the great races of mankind, must be collected at once or the opportunity will be lost."

Though Curtis has often been criticized for staging his photos to recreate an idealized image of American Aboriginal peoples before contact with the colonial culture that was already irrevocably changing their lives, there can be no doubt as to the dedication and commitment Curtis brought to his tireless effort to document what he and his contemporaries considered to be the "vanishing Indian."

In addition to finally completing the twentieth volume of his epic publication project in 1930, featuring many of his forty thousand images taken among more than eighty native tribes, Edward Curtis made films and recorded more than ten thousand wax cylinders of Indian language and music containing tribal stories and history, wrote short biographies of tribal leaders, and described traditional foods, housing, clothing, games, and ceremonial and funeral customs.

Despite the criticisms that his work was at times staged and therefore inaccurate, Curtis's ethnographic material remains, in most cases, the only recorded history of the "North American Indian."

THE SUN DANCE

According to ethnographic, archaeological, and oral histories, the annual Sun Dance ceremony held at the time of the summer solstice has been the most important religious ritual among the many Aboriginal peoples of the Great Plains of North America for millennia. At the centre of the circular Sun Dance lodge, a sacred tree is erected from which families and individual members of the tribe hang sacrificial tokens; in earlier times young men often pierced their bodies to suspend themselves from it as a rite of passage into adulthood; and the dancers, separated within the lodge by barriers or "hedges" into a men's and women's side, to this day embark on vision quests brought about by up to three days of dancing without rest, food, or water. The Sun Dance tree, with its base planted on the ground by a buffalo skull and its topmost branch singed by a ritual fire symbolizing the sun, though unique to the North American prairie, has many close analogues among the so-called "shaman's trees" central to ancient rituals stretching from Northern Europe to Siberia.

The ceremony is used to honour the cycle of the four seasons, to give thanks for the yearly return of the great buffalo migrations, to recite the individual and family stories of power that create and maintain the relations among members of the community, to celebrate the sacred interdependence of all living beings, and to offer totems and make sacrifices to the creator. It is said that Sitting Bull, too old to participate as a warrior, sacrificed forty pieces of his own flesh at the Sun Dance ceremony at the time of the battle of the Little Big Horn.

ACT ONE

SUBTITLE SLIDE: *"Prelude"*

*Lights fade up on **ANGELINE**'s fingers as her body lies almost suspended on an empty floor. Her fingers begin to move as if she were playing a piano. She hits a note. Then another. The notes gather oddly into music under.*

MUSIC: "A Snow Lullaby" – Leela Gilday

*The notes build clearly and beautifully as the light exposes more of **ANGELINE**, wrapped in a blanket on the floor. Her eyes open as she wakes from a deep sleep. Family photographs begin to develop on the dark walls surrounding her.*

ANGELINE: My mother's walls were filled with pictures ... evidence of our success as a family ... unit. Smiling children. Two girls. One older. Clara. One younger. Me. A handsome mother. A beautiful father. Mixed-race marriage. Contemporary.

She looks around, peering at the photographs.

ANGELINE: We posed like all families pose. Arranging ourselves ... until we began to understand with age ... our poses had always been pre-arranged.

A photograph of her mother smiling.

ANGELINE: Lee Anne, my mother ... smiling. She died last year ... Isn't she beautiful?

As she speaks, she writes on the floor a caption for her mother's photograph.

SLIDE CAPTION: "Lee Anne, mother, Dene-Saulteaux"

A photograph of her father, hunting rifle in hand, standing beside an upside-down deer.

ANGELINE: Steve, my father, hunting defenceless animals.

As she speaks, she writes on the floor a caption for her father's photograph.

SLIDE CAPTION: "Steve, father, Russian descent"

A photograph of her psychiatrist sister, sitting in her professional office, appears. She gets up and walks toward it.

ANGELINE: My sister Clara ... a doctor ... a shrink, that is ... trying to look above normal.

As she speaks, she writes on the wall a caption for her sister's photograph.

SLIDE CAPTION: "Dr. Clara, daughter of mixed marriage ..."

She looks intently at her sister's photograph and then continues to write.

SLIDE CAPTION: "Rather white-looking"

SFX: The sound of the Arctic begins to seep in under.

She looks over at a photograph of herself that is beginning to develop on the wall beside her. In the photograph, she is wearing the same dress but is holding an award. She walks toward the developing portrait, inserting herself into the picture.

ANGELINE: Myself ... accepting an award today ... For a story ... a story I was the first to break. I was up north covering the Arctic Games ... I was up north.

SFX: The sound of her newscast builds under.

ANGELINE: This was supposed to have been a great night. A perfect picture.

She tries to get out of her award photograph as the newscast begins to encase her. Finally disengaging herself from the frame, she backs away, hardly able to breathe as the sound rises.

SFX: The sound of a family celebration dinner becomes louder.

Her sister approaches her carrying a large gift-wrapped book.

DR. CLARA: Look who's up ... We thought you were going to sleep the night away.

ANGELINE: Why didn't you wake me?

DR. CLARA: You fell asleep ... you seemed so tired we thought it was better you get your beauty rest ...

ANGELINE: You think I need it?

DR. CLARA gives her a hug and kiss.

DR. CLARA: Supper's almost ready ... oh ... you're freezing.

DR. CLARA grabs ANGELINE's hand to take her to the table and ANGELINE drops it. DR. CLARA continues to move toward the dinner table, where her FATHER and YISKA sit.

ANGELINE: I don't feel cold …

DR. CLARA stops and looks back at her. Her FATHER and YISKA look up. They barely move.

ANGELINE: I don't feel … anything.

SFX: The sounds of the Arctic wind increase.

ANGELINE: I was standing there, my skin beginning to burn, burn, with a cold beginning … frozen, I could see the details without the distraction of caring.

A shutter and flash. ANGELINE looks back at the table that begins to stutter. She looks intently at her FATHER.

ANGELINE: My father's handsome face … he has always been so charming, so charming it can hurt.

A shutter and flash. ANGELINE looks at her sister.

ANGELINE: My sister's flawless porcelain skin.

A shutter and flash. ANGELINE looks at her boyfriend.

ANGELINE: My boyfriend Yiska, a translator, the linguist …

YISKA looks up at her, catching her eye.

ANGELINE: His dark eyes see everything.

They hold a moment with their eyes. A shutter and flash. She writes his caption.

SLIDE CAPTION: "Yiska, my boyfriend, N'lakap'mux"

A shutter and flash begins to stutter in a choreography of family-dinner poses that are surreal, stuttering in reality and still frames.

Shutter. Flash. Frame.

ANGELINE: I looked at them – and all I wanted to do was get out. Get out of the picture that was made for me – get out of the picture I had made for myself. Get out of all the lies that have framed me.

Shutter. Flash. Frame.

YISKA: Ange?

YISKA moves toward her, she sees him dressed in a parka. Then –

FATHER: Angeline?

She turns toward her father's voice, confused.

ANGELINE: I'm just going to /

SFX: The sound of young children's voices.

Startled, ANGELINE turns to the sound. DR. CLARA gets up and moves toward her.

DR. CLARA: Angie?

ANGELINE steps back.

FATHER: For God's sake Angeline, come sit down and join us … we've been waiting for hours … I'm starving /

ANGELINE looks at her FATHER.

ANGELINE: / Are you?

Pause. Her FATHER looks at DR. CLARA and YISKA.

ANGELINE begins to back away from their eyes.

ANGELINE: I'm not feeling well … I think I need to lie down …

YISKA grabs her hand and tries to pull her to him.

ANGELINE: Let me go.

YISKA: You don't need to lie down … you need to / stay with us.

She looks directly at him, defiant.

ANGELINE: / You don't know what I need.

DR. CLARA touches her shoulder.

DR. CLARA: Angie?

ANGELINE moves from her touch and, backing away from them, takes off her shoe.

ANGELINE: I took my shoe off. Just one. I took the heel … the heel of my shoe, the heel … like a pointer really pointed to get a point across to a blunt world …

DR. CLARA: Angie … it's all right …

ANGELINE: No, it's not … nothing's all right … Nothing is *all* right.

ANGELINE freezes, her hand gripping the shoe like a weapon. She moves toward them, raising her heel, then takes aim at their image and hits, shattering the photograph.

SFX: The sound of glass breaking and falling like crystals.

Shards of glass fall to the ground.

ANGELINE: I think when they really think about it … they will be relieved I released them from me. I know I felt better. I feel better. (*She smiles for a moment.*) I felt better ...

> *Blackout. A long beam of light drives down, lighting a sliver of ANGELINE's face.*

ANGELINE: It's beautiful, don't you think? ... How the light hits you so purposefully just before you will never be seen again ...

> *She smiles.*

ANGELINE: My sister thinks I am having a breakdown but she doesn't know everything ... I am having a ... break ... through ... I am breaking through ...

> *Hands move into the light. Her FATHER hands her a crucifix, YISKA a rock, DR. CLARA the large gift-wrapped book. She begins to unwrap the book. She looks down at it, then laughs as she holds it up.*

ANGELINE: My family has been showing up, leaving ... odd ... things out of nowhere.

> *She smiles.*

ANGELINE: My sister gave me this book by Edward Curtis. It is heavy. *The North American Indian.*

> *She flips through the pages.*

ANGELINE: It didn't make me feel better.

> *She opens to a page and looks in.*

ANGELINE: But at least I found a caption in the darkness I can identify with.

> *MUSIC: Orchestra Prelude: "By the Arrow," String Intro. – Henry Gilbert*

> *She writes a caption for herself that appears below her.*

> *SLIDE CAPTION: "The Vanishing Indian"*

ANGELINE: *The Vanishing Indian.*

> *She opens the cover of the book and begins to read as the lighting changes to light her like a beautiful Edward Curtis photograph.*

ANGELINE: "Age upon age, generation upon generation, they have slowly eroded their social structure. The Crucible of time has developed their primitive laws to a protection against their own weakness."

> *SLIDE: Portrait of a young, dashing Edward Curtis.*

> *SLIDE CAPTION: "E.S. Curtis, 1899, self-portrait"*

> *She looks over as a portrait develops in its full glory, almost coming alive as EDWARD CURTIS begins to speak.*

EDWARD CURTIS: Proud, arrogant in their imagined superiority, disdainful of civilization's strength, which they cannot comprehend. Fools! They knew not with what they reckoned. Advancing civilization has crushed all before it; primitive man can but snap and snarl like a brute cur at the giant which has been his destructor. (*He walks toward her in the dark.*) The buffalo are gone; the human brother is but a human fragment, robbed of his primitive strength, stripped of his pagan dress, going into the darkness of the unknown future ...

> *ANGELINE looks up in the light as his dark hands touch her face softly.*

EDWARD CURTIS: So said E.S. Curtis ...

> *His hands covering her face with gentleness, romantically the lights slowly fade to darkness.*

ANGELINE: (*from the darkness*) Finally, a darkness that has my name on it.

> *An unknown darkness takes over the space. It is entirely dark.*

> *End of prelude.*

FRAME SHIFT.

> *MUSIC: "By the Arrow" cont. – Henry Gilbert*

> *SUBTITLE SLIDE: "Picture Story I: Carnegie Hall, New York, 1911"*

> *A stereoptical illusion comes into focus, highlighting a now-standing EDWARD CURTIS, age forty-three, as he appears in his prime, ready to engage his audience.*

> *The rich backdrop of Carnegie Hall fades up: dark-gold and auburn Greek pillars and grandeur.*

> *SUBTITLE SLIDE: "The Vanishing Indian"*

> *SUBTITLE SLIDE: "by Edward Curtis" joins the title.*

> *SLIDE: An Edward Curtis photograph of horses and Indians going into the darkness.*

> *SLIDE CAPTION: "The Vanishing Race, Navaho, 1904"*

> *SFX: The sound of thunderous applause.*

EDWARD CURTIS stops and then looks out into the audience. He poses, adjusting his face in the light for effect.

EDWARD CURTIS: Thank you. Thank you indeed ... it is a fine evening, a fine introduction. (*He lights a cigarette*) My greatest desire tonight is that each and every person here enter into the spirit of our evening with the Indians. We cannot weigh, measure, or judge their culture with our philosophy. From our analytical and materialistic viewpoint theirs is a strange world. Deity is not alone in a world of universal voice, universal spirit. I want you to see this beautiful, poetic, mysterious, yet simple life, as I have grown to see it through the long years with the many tribes. Toward that end let us close our eyes for an instant, and in a flash of time span the gulf between today's turmoil and the far away enchanted realm of primitive man. We have entered what is to us a strange land. Man and nature are one and a-tune. All about us are the mysteries of the Infinite.

FRAME SHIFT.

SUBTITLE SLIDE: *Rita Leistner's "Field Work I: The West, 2013"*

MUSIC: *"Let the Rest of the World Go By" – Words and Music by J. Keirn Brennan and Ernest R. Ball*

SFX: *The sound of soft rain.*

SFX: *The sound of a pill bottle falling to the floor and pills rolling.*

Lights up on ANGELINE as she sits on the floor, reaching for the pill bottle and spilled pills in the darkness. The hand of EDWARD CURTIS reaches inside her light and offers her the pill bottle, then the spilled pills. He stands just outside her light, looking down.

ANGELINE: I'm having a bad day ... or maybe it's a bad night. A bad year maybe? One day. One night. One year. All the same really.

EDWARD CURTIS: Do the pills help?

ANGELINE: (*shrugs*) Pills do what they are supposed to do ...

She shakes the pills out of the bottle and into her palm.

ANGELINE: ... they take the edge off reality, putting me in control of my own numbness.

EDWARD CURTIS: (*hands her a glass of water*) A small consolation, I suppose.

She swallows the pills and as she looks down, the light expands to include the room with CURTIS in it. She watches as he looks at her home.

ANGELINE: You're ... the photographer?

EDWARD CURTIS: I've retired actually.

ANGELINE: Believe me, nobody retires from who they are ... It's admirable to try but not worth the effort.

EDWARD CURTIS: Is that right?

ANGELINE: That's the way I've come to understand it.

EDWARD CURTIS: That seems so ominous ... no wonder you look so down.

ANGELINE: They call it depression. It makes me want to lay my head down but the angle doesn't stop me from thinking ... Have you ever been depressed?

EDWARD CURTIS: Off and on /

ANGELINE: For how long?

EDWARD CURTIS: My whole life.

ANGELINE: Reassuring.

He offers his hand and pulls her up. They sit at a table and chairs where a bottle of Scotch and two glasses have been left.

EDWARD CURTIS: I was in Seattle one time, in a deep black fog barely able to get out of bed. But I said to myself get up and go for a walk, that will clear your head. So off I went, walking in the streets. Suddenly I heard birds, and a beautiful light just happened from the clouds and then there was music. Music? I turned toward the music but it had no face. I looked down and looking up was the face of a cripple strapped to a wooden board on wheels. I looked at him playing the accordion. Playing the accordion? I figured if that man could put his soul in his music from down there, I would not give up either.

He offers her a smoke.

ANGELINE: I don't smoke.

But she takes it anyway. He lights her cigarette and then his own.

EDWARD CURTIS: Me either.

ANGELINE: What should I call you?

They sit and smoke.

EDWARD CURTIS: People close to me call me Chief.

ANGELINE: Seriously?

He nods and takes out a journal from his inside coat pocket. He begins to write.

EDWARD CURTIS: I'm going to call you /

SLIDE CAPTION: "Primitive Indian Wo- …"

ANGELINE: / Aren't you going ask me what I call myself?

EDWARD CURTIS: I wasn't going to … but if you think it's important.

ANGELINE: I do … I do.

She takes his journal and pen and crosses out the "Primitive Indian Wo- …" and writes.

REVISED SLIDE CAPTION: "Most Beautiful Woman You've Ever Met"

ANGELINE: I call myself "Most Beautiful Woman You've Ever Met."

EDWARD CURTIS: Please …

ANGELINE: It only seems fair if I have to call you Chief …

She motions to pour him a drink.

EDWARD CURTIS: Fair enough … I don't drink.

She pours him a drink anyway. She pours herself a drink. They do "cheers."

ANGELINE: Me neither.

They drink in silence.

ANGELINE: On second thought, just call me Angeline … "Most Beautiful Woman You've Ever Met" is a lot to live up to … And if I were you I would reconsider "Chief" … for the same reasons …

The SLIDE CAPTION disappears. He looks at her.

EDWARD CURTIS: Are you married?

ANGELINE: Living together … Trying.

His face screws up slightly.

EDWARD CURTIS: Yes … there is always trying.

ANGELINE: Did your break-up hurt?

EDWARD CURTIS: Why do you think my marriage broke up?

ANGELINE: Because you look pained.

He doesn't answer.

ANGELINE: Or constipated.

EDWARD CURTIS: Pardon me?

ANGELINE: You look pained … as in your marriage caused you pain … or you look like you are having a hard time passing something … constipated.

EDWARD CURTIS: Thank you for the clarification. Let's talk about something else …

ANGELINE: Fine.

He lights another smoke.

EDWARD CURTIS: Are you hungry?

ANGELINE: I'm always hungry.

EDWARD CURTIS: Would you like me to fix you something? I'm an excellent cook.

ANGELINE: Seriously? How humble.

He gets up and takes out a portable stove from his bag.

EDWARD CURTIS: Don't be a wise head …

ANGELINE: All right … How attractive …

EDWARD CURTIS: Better.

He assembles cooking utensils from the darkness.

ANGELINE: I have some buffalo in the freezer. I've been keeping it for a special occasion.

EDWARD CURTIS: It *is* a special occasion … to meet a writer.

ANGELINE: How did you know I was a writer?

EDWARD CURTIS: Anybody who wants to rewrite something I wrote is usually a writer.

ANGELINE: Or an Indian.

Pause.

EDWARD CURTIS: What did you say?

She doesn't respond. He smiles.

EDWARD CURTIS: I forgot how good it feels to cook for someone.

He turns his back toward the stove.

FRAME SHIFT.

SLIDE: Prairie field.

ANGELINE looks up as a round yellow sun glares down around her. Gradually a yellow prairie takes over the space, rolling as far as the eye can see. From far away YISKA appears, drumming. He begins to sing a traditional song on the open prairie.

MUSIC: Traditional song – YISKA sings.

ANGELINE looks at him and then stands on the chair, raising her body up to get closer to the sky. YISKA turns around and looks at her.

YISKA: I'm praying for you.

They look at each other.

FRAME SHIFT.

DR. CLARA: (*offstage*) What are you doing?

ANGELINE turns her head to the sound of her sister's voice as the prairie disappears suddenly and she is left standing on a chair. DR. CLARA enters her office as framed university degrees begin to appear on the walls.

ANGELINE: Who's asking?

DR. CLARA: Who do you think?

ANGELINE smiles.

DR. CLARA: I asked you to wait in my office ... I thought you might be climbing the walls but I didn't think you'd be climbing the chairs ... get down ...

ANGELINE: No ... I like the view.

DR. CLARA looks around and sees only darkness.

DR. CLARA: That's an expensive chair ...

ANGELINE: Would it be all right if it was a cheap chair?

DR. CLARA: Get down ...

ANGELINE: No.

DR. CLARA: I think it's only fair ... if you're in someone else's room you play by their house rules.

ANGELINE shrugs.

ANGELINE: Stupid people follow stupid rules ...

DR. CLARA: Get down.

ANGELINE: No.

They just look at each other. ANGELINE stretches herself toward the sky.

ANGELINE: Do you ever wonder what it would feel like to stretch yourself so fully to the sky you become a part of it? Just raise yourself above the petty shit of perfectly placed furniture, and all the things that look so right but are so fucked ... Detach yourself from all the things you can't fix. All the things that don't make sense but should.

She breathes into the sky.

ANGELINE: Standing here like this above yourself ... you see land so flat it's hard to know where the sky ends and the land begins, where you begin and end. You see everything because you are a part of everything and there is nothing you don't know ...

EDWARD CURTIS turns around from carving the buffalo into steaks. His hands bloody, he stops and looks at her.

FRAME SHIFT.

EDWARD CURTIS: You're right. You're right.

ANGELINE sees him. They smile.

ANGELINE: You understand?

EDWARD CURTIS: Yes, I understand.

FRAME SHIFT.

DR. CLARA: Angie?

ANGELINE keeps looking at EDWARD CURTIS. He finally turns toward his cooking.

DR. CLARA: Angie ...

ANGELINE finally looks at her.

DR. CLARA: What did you do today?

ANGELINE gets down from the chair, deflated.

ANGELINE: I came here to "do" lunch.

DR. CLARA: I wanted to talk to you /

ANGELINE: / Talk.

DR. CLARA: / to you because I want you to see a colleague of mine /

DR. CLARA hands her a business card.

ANGELINE: / Very tricky.

DR. CLARA: / Dr. Wilson. I set up an appointment /

ANGELINE: / I didn't agree to this ...

DR. CLARA: How unusual ...

ANGELINE: (*hands back the card*) I'm fine.

DR. CLARA: You're a mess.

ANGELINE: Is that a professional opinion, or a personal one?

No answer.

DR. CLARA: Both.

They look at each other.

ANGELINE: Thanks.

DR. CLARA: (*looks down*) I'm sorry ... I'm just worried about you ...

ANGELINE: You make me tired. I think I'm just going to lie down on your couch ...

DR. CLARA: ... Angie?

ANGELINE: I'm o-kay ... people need to lie down after they've been standing on a chair for a long time ... it's normal.

DR. CLARA: Normal.

DR. CLARA covers her sister with a blanket. ANGELINE looks up as a framed family portrait begins to fade up on the wall.

SLIDE: Sears Studio portrait of Dr. Clara, her husband, two daughters and a son, circa 1996.

SLIDE CAPTION: "Big C, Ted, and kids"

ANGELINE: You still have that photo up.

No answer.

DR. CLARA: Ancient history.

ANGELINE: Is it?

DR. CLARA: It's 1996, for Godsakes, look how heavy I was.

Pause. DR. CLARA walks toward her family portrait. She touches her husband, adjusting his jacket lapel. She looks right at him.

DR. CLARA: I'm finally going to ask him for a divorce.

ANGELINE: I'm sorry ...

She backs away slightly and looks at her children.

DR. CLARA: It's time ... we haven't lived together in years ...

ANGELINE: You still love him? ... Or just the idea of him?

DR. CLARA: (*looks at ANGELINE*) Maybe I still love the idea of *us*.

Pause. They both look out into the darkness.

MUSIC: "The Night Scout" – Henry Gilbert

SUBTITLE SLIDE: "Picture Story II: Carnegie Hall, New York"

A stereoptical illusion comes into focus. The rich backdrop of the theatre fades up in dark-gold and auburn, in Greek pillars and grandeur surrounding EDWARD CURTIS as he continues his lecture series.

Dissolving flickering SLIDE SEQUENCES I–VI: I, "The Vanishing Race, Navaho, 1904"; II, "The Hunkalowanpi 'Offering the Skull'"; III, "The Indians of the Palm Canyons and Cactus Plains"; IV, "The Apaches"; V, "The Hopi and Snake Dance"; VI, "Evening in Hopi Land."

EDWARD CURTIS: Tonight we go to the land of the Indian, and as in other travels, let us glance at the scope of the project. First, what is an Indian? The American Indian is one of the five races of man, and of this race there are yet to exceed fifty linguistic stocks in North America. When I say that – I mean just that – languages fundamentally differing. Of dialects there were at one time – at the time of discovery – fully one thousand in North America. Passing through the linguistic groups, let us glance at the life and manners. We have natives of the subtropics dwelling beneath the waving palms in the land of perpetual warmth and, to the contrary, natives of the Arctic directing their frail skin crafts among the dangerous icebergs. And between these extremes are countless tribes, all, according to habitat, differing in cultures.

MUSIC: "The Night Scout" – Henry Gilbert, adapted by Leela Gilday

SLIDE: An Edward Curtis photograph of a man standing on the open land in a buffalo robe.

SLIDE CAPTION: "For Strength and Vision, 1904"

YISKA, dressed in a large buffalo robe, turns from the photograph. He looks at CURTIS. They stare at each other for a long time not moving, barely breathing.

YISKA: (*in Peigan*) I am not for your eyes ... lower your need to see what is not for you. I am not for your eyes. Step backward and I will erase your footprints on my spirit. Step backward one clumsy foot at a time, backward toward your own knowing. I am not for your eyes. Stay where I cannot see you and you cannot see me. Let us stand that way, our eyes lowered for the good of all men and all gods.

CURTIS steps back slowly, slowly, slowly.

FRAME SHIFT.

MUSIC: "Let the Rest of the World Go By" – words and music by J. Keirn Brennan and Ernest R. Ball.

SUBTITLE SLIDE: Rita Leistner's "Field Work II: The West, 2013, continued"

SFX: The sound of rain.

EDWARD CURTIS turns and appears. He lights a cigarette.

EDWARD CURTIS: Did I tell you I saw the Sun Dance back in 1900 on the Plains with the Peigans? I saw it and it changed me so entirely it remapped the course of my life.

ANGELINE: You saw it?

EDWARD CURTIS: I saw it. I wasn't supposed to ... You don't believe me?

ANGELINE: I believe you believe it.

EDWARD CURTIS: Do you believe that in that instant – a chance encounter changed my past and my future? ... Does that sound odd?

ANGELINE: No. Chance encounters can do that.

He sets down a pot of buffalo stew and brings a salad to the table, setting it for two with ease. He smells the stew.

EDWARD CURTIS: I wrote about it ... the Sun Dance ... Like many things I have seen I was the first white man to write about it. To take a picture so no one would ever forget they were here ...

ANGELINE: Amazing ... This is really good stew /

EDWARD CURTIS: / Thank you ... The Snake Dance, Hopi. The Yeibachai Dance, Navaho, etcetera, etcetera ... They thanked me for taking it ... for preserving it forever ...

ANGELINE: Did they ... Did they really?

EDWARD CURTIS: Do you want to know why? Because pictures are ... realities.

ANGELINE: Are they? Or are they just perceptions? And if so, of whom? Those who take the picture or those who pose for them?

He pauses and takes a bit of meat.

EDWARD CURTIS: If I'm not mistaken the same could be said for a writer ...

ANGELINE: The difference is I don't write pretty words ... I don't write words people want to dress in ... You do.

EDWARD CURTIS: People don't see me as a writer.

ANGELINE: But you did write. You wrote word pictures and your pictures became word.

EDWARD CURTIS: I saw it. I photographed it. I wrote about it. It's not that complicated.

SLIDE: Lights fade up on a portrait of Clara Curtis. They both watch as CLARA fades up and breathes into herself.

SLIDE CAPTION: "Clara Curtis, 1914"

ANGELINE: No, it's not ... It's beautiful.

He looks at the photo and then reaches down and lights another smoke.

CLARA: Edward?

He doesn't address her as she moves into the space and toward blue developing solution in a basin. She immerses her hands in the water as a beautiful Edward Curtis photograph develops up.

FRAME SHIFT.

MUSIC: "Kutenai Country" – Henry Gilbert

SLIDE: An Edward Curtis photograph of a Kutenai canoe on a lakeshore dissolves up, surrounding CLARA.

SLIDE CAPTION: "Kutenai Girls, 1910"

CLARA smiles as she looks at the photograph.

CLARA: Edward, it is so picture-perfect I can almost hear the bottom of the canoe as it hits the mouth of the water ... the oar as it touches the glass surface ...

She looks over and then turns into the darkness, almost shyly toward him.

EDWARD CURTIS: A crackerjack picture to be sure.

CLARA: (*smiles*) Edward, you did hear me.

He hesitates, not looking at her, and then exits. She hears his footsteps trail off.

CLARA: Perhaps not.

FILM: She watches as the Kutenai canoe animates and moves across the water in frames.

CLARA: Where did poor Clara go? She went on a canoe across a great lake.

She laughs and then looks down.

CLARA: I wish to lower my hands off the sides of the canoe and let my fingers touch the bulrushes that reach up to me, touching my hands so lightly, so right ... if only to interrupt my sad story for a moment ...

MUSIC: "Kutenai Country" – Henry Gilbert, adapted by Leela Gilday

SLIDE: The eyes of a Kutenai girl fade up under the dark surface of the water in the basin. Her hair fades up in long black strands.

CLARA looks down into the basin of dark water and watches as ANGELINE takes over the image. CLARA cups the water with her hands, pouring it over ANGELINE's hair, affectionately. She whispers closer to ANGELINE's ear.

CLARA: Your dark eyes look back into me for days on end ... and I wish to tell you everything that is left unsaid. Undone. Unloved. Maybe secrets can exist between us ...

She looks out.

CLARA: Secrets can exist between those who are only seen for convenience.

CLARA looks down again, changed. She talks softly but her hands become tense, as do her words as she chokes them out.

CLARA: But here there is only one secret worth saving ... do you hear me? I will always be his wife ... the mother of his children ... his partner ... but you ... you in the end will be nothing but the memory of an Indian.

CLARA takes her hand and covers ANGELINE's mouth and pushes her face back into the water. ANGELINE struggles against her force and then submerges under the water. There is a long silence as CLARA backs away from the basin, wiping her hands on her white apron, backing away into the darkness as the music rises.

MUSIC: "Kutenai Country" – Henry Gilbert

ANGELINE suddenly gasps up from the wet darkness.

ANGELINE: I wish to rise from the roots of bulrushes ... I wish to rise from the roots of bulrushes ... I wish to feel the water ... feel the water ... feel the water ...

YISKA appears from the darkness, reaching her across space, calling out to her, his words getting closer.

YISKA: Open your eyes, Ange ... open your arms ... look at me ...

ANGELINE: I can't.

YISKA: You can.

He appears, finally taking her in his arms.

YISKA: (*in Kutenai*) I wish to rise from the roots of bulrushes ... take my clothes off, every stitch ... feel the water like ice on my skin and rise to the shock of being touched by a god that has many names ... I wish to be free of all things I am not and will never be ...

She opens her eyes.

YISKA: Sleeping in water ... What were you thinking?

ANGELINE: I just closed my eyes for a minute ... do we have to do this right now?

YISKA: No.

ANGELINE: Perfect.

Pause.

YISKA: Do you wanna talk about it?

ANGELINE: I have an appointment to talk with someone professional ... Clara's arranging it /

YISKA: / Just like she's arranged the drugs ...

She gives him the look.

YISKA: Fine.

She picks up a pack of smokes and takes a cigarette out. He gives her the stop-smoking look.

ANGELINE: Stop looking at me.

He approaches her.

YISKA: You're smoking again ...

He takes the cigarette from her hand.

ANGELINE: I don't smoke.

YISKA: Right. (*He looks at her.*)

ANGELINE: Really ... I feel better ... I'm on a plan ... everything is looking up.

YISKA: Really?

She smiles. He touches her face.

YISKA: Liar.

A long pause. She stares at him and turns from him coldly.

ANGELINE: I wish you'd just leave ... How long you going to hang in there? You're fucking everything up ... I'll smoke if I want to ... Why can't a person smoke if they want to? ... Why can't a person die if they want to? ... Why can't they just lay down and die if they want to without having to fucking explain every fuck-ing detail ... I just want to die ... all right ... there ...

YISKA: (*moves toward her*) You can't say that ... don't you dare say that ... don't you ever say that to me again ...

ANGELINE: (*begins to cry*) I'm sorry ...

YISKA: You can't keep doing this ... do you understand me? You can't ...

ANGELINE: I'm sorry ... I'm sorry for everything ...

He looks at her.

ANGELINE: I'm sorry.

YISKA: You're safe with me, Ange ...

ANGELINE: Am I? You say I am but when you get tired of dealing with it you will look away and I won't be able to find your face.

YISKA: (*bends to her*) My face is right here. My face is here, Ange ... you just have to look.

ANGELINE: What do you want me to say? What do you want me to do? Tell me.

He reaches out to her and touches her face, her lips. He places his hand on her eyes.

YISKA: You don't have to say anything. You don't have to do anything. You just have to be ... here. You just have to be here.

They kiss and begin to make love.

CURTIS stands from a distance and watches, taking out his lens. He looks at the scene and then, taking the lens away from his eye, looks on.

EDWARD CURTIS: I wish to rise from the roots of bulrushes ... take my clothes off, every stitch ... feel the water like ice on my skin and rise to the shock of being touched by a god that has many names ... I wish to be free of all things I am not and will never be ...

FRAME SHIFT.

MUSIC: *Haida war song – Haida Chief Guujaaw*

SLIDE: *An Edward Curtis photograph of whaling fades up.*

CAPTION: *"The Captured Whale, 1915"*

FILM: *Fades up in full greys. Whales begin to appear throughout the grey, appearing and submerging, appearing and submerging ...*

SFX: *The sound of whales.*

EDWARD CURTIS closes his eyes and shifts, shifts, like a man hearing something below himself that is large. CLARA approaches him softly as he talks. He doesn't acknowledge her but allows himself to be undressed through his monologue. She takes off his boots, places them together on the floor. She removes his pants, careful of his bad hip, then removes his shirt. He is left wearing only his long johns.

EDWARD CURTIS: Did I ever tell you the time I was hunting whales with the Haida? An extraordinary field trip ... great big swells the size of mountains ... taking the boat up and down, climbing and then crashing and then right beside you like a monster from a different world – a whale ... crashing down on the boat ... unbelievable strength and grace ... coming down on you, coming down on you like a hammer, spraying you with air and water, coming up and then again crashing down on the boat, crashing down on the men, crashing down on me, on this hip, trying to break me ... break me in two.

She looks right at him.

CLARA: I miss you.

He looks down at his journal.

EDWARD CURTIS: I miss you too, Clara ... I miss you ...

He continues to write as she stands and then leaves the space.

EDWARD CURTIS: Love to you and the children, kindest regards, I am ... sincerely yours, E.S.C.

EDWARD CURTIS gets up and looks over at ANGELINE, sleeping. He takes a lens out of his pocket and looks at her intently, framing her.

FRAME SHIFT.

MUSIC: *"Let the Rest of the World Go By" – words and music by J. Keirn Brennan and Ernest R. Ball, adapted by Bruce Ruddell*

SUBTITLE SLIDE: *Rita Leistner's "Field Work III: The West, 2013, continued"*

SFX: *The sound of rain.*

Suddenly ANGELINE looks up at EDWARD CURTIS. He smiles and puts the lens back in his pocket. She smells the air. It smells like coffee.

EDWARD CURTIS: I made some coffee. Do you want a cup?

ANGELINE nods. He stands with a coffee pot and cups. He pours them coffee and lights another cigarette.

ANGELINE: It smells good ... (*She looks at the coffee pot.*) I don't recognize the coffee pot ...

EDWARD CURTIS: Oh, it's mine. I travel with it everywhere. I don't like taking chances with my coffee. It's important if you travel a great deal to ... put out the little things that make you feel at home ... Smoke?

He lights a cigarette and passes it to her. They smoke.

EDWARD CURTIS: My father was a Baptist minister, did I tell you that?

ANGELINE: I read it somewhere ...

EDWARD CURTIS: I travelled with him out West, preaching the word of God.

ANGELINE: Did you believe any of it?

EDWARD CURTIS: It was enough that he did. He believed it with a wondrous zeal that consumed him ... I think perhaps I inherited the zeal.

ANGELINE: Not the light of God.

EDWARD CURTIS: No ... just the belief in light ... but I suppose the belief in darkness, too. That intense darkness transforms what your naked eye sees into what it could only imagine holding. If light is the basis of photography ... maybe darkness is the basis of humanity.

She smokes.

ANGELINE: Hmmm ... The small circle, the glass, you carry ... in your pocket ...

EDWARD CURTIS: My father gave it to me when I was a boy ... a stereoscopic lens from a camera he brought back from the Civil War.

ANGELINE: You carry it everywhere with you?

EDWARD CURTIS: Yes ... A reminder to see everything as if it is for the first time.

EDWARD CURTIS gets up and cracks a few eggs in the frying pan.

EDWARD CURTIS: Are you hungry?

ANGELINE: No, thank you. I have to get dressed today. I have an appointment, which means I should do something with my hair.

EDWARD CURTIS: I might be able to help with that.

CURTIS opens his bag and pulls out a few long black wigs. He places one on her head.

ANGELINE: I'm not going there alone.

He puts a black wig on. They laugh. YISKA appears in his underwear, looking at them. CURTIS continues laughing but extends his hand.

EDWARD CURTIS: People that know me call me Ch- ...

YISKA just looks at him, giving him the eye.

EDWARD CURTIS: ... I mean Edward ... Ed, if you like.

YISKA: I don't like.

He looks at ANGELINE.

YISKA: Who's this?

ANGELINE: You can call him Ed if you like.

YISKA: I don't want to call him anything ...

ANGELINE gives him the look. CURTIS approaches.

EDWARD CURTIS: Can I ask you your name?

YISKA: No.

ANGELINE: People call him Chief too.

EDWARD CURTIS: A pet name?

YISKA glares at him.

ANGELINE: No, because he is one ...

EDWARD CURTIS: I see ...

YISKA: Do you?

EDWARD CURTIS looks at him. YISKA looks back.

EDWARD CURTIS: You remind me of someone ...

CURTIS looks confused for a minute.

YISKA: We all look the same ... don't worry about it ...

EDWARD CURTIS: I had a friend a long time ago, a translator I worked with whose name was Alexander ... Upshaw.

YISKA: Let me guess ... he was Indian.

CURTIS goes about cooking eggs and bacon.

EDWARD CURTIS: An educated Indian. Crow. He had gone to the Carlisle School. He graduated and went on to become a leader of his people. An educated Indian /

YISKA: You said that /

EDWARD CURTIS: loved by his own people, hated by whites. He died young ... a tragic death ... he died before his promise.

He dumps a couple of eggs on a plate and hands it to YISKA.

YISKA: Tragic. Do you have any bacon with that sunny side up?

EDWARD CURTIS: Yes I do ... Yes I do ...

CURTIS scoops a couple of strips, happily serving them to YISKA.

EDWARD CURTIS: You from around here?

YISKA puts the bacon in his mouth and nods with a full mouth.

EDWARD CURTIS: What do you do?

YISKA: I'm a translator of Aboriginal languages at the university.

CURTIS watches him, then takes out his lens and begins to frame him and ANGELINE.

EDWARD CURTIS: What kind of chief are you?

YISKA: The real kind. You?

EDWARD CURTIS: It's a name of affection given to me because I worked and lived with so many Indians ... over many /

YISKA: / How touching ...

CURTIS lowers his lens briefly.

EDWARD CURTIS: Are you upset?

YISKA: No, do I look upset? ... I feel crowded. You ask too many questions.

EDWARD CURTIS: Occupational hazard. Sorry. I guess it is hard to separate what you do from who you are.

YISKA: Listen ... I don't like waking up to strange men ... on my own land, if you get what I am saying ... especially those who talk too much and get things from my fridge.

He pauses.

EDWARD CURTIS: I'm just passing through.

YISKA looks at all of him.

YISKA: Nobody who looks like you passes through without taking everything he can.

LIVE PICTURE PORTRAIT: YISKA freezes in his pose.

FRAME SHIFT.

SLIDE: An Edward Curtis photograph of ALEXANDER UPSHAW in a bone breastplate fades up as YISKA breathes into it.

SLIDE CAPTION: "Alexander Upshaw, Crow"

EDWARD CURTIS: I'm sorry, I didn't mean /

EDWARD CURTIS watches the transformation.

ALEXANDER UPSHAW: / He's asking you why you are here. He doesn't trust you ... just so that you know ... he doesn't trust no white man, no how, no way, and no bacon and egg is going to change that. Some things a frying pan can't fix. Sometimes a translator has to speak even when two men are speaking the same language.

EDWARD CURTIS: I am a patient man. Good things come to those that are patient. He'll like me sooner or later.

ALEXANDER UPSHAW: You are a stubborn man. A gun comes to those that are stubborn. Or a knife maybe in the small of the back. Trust me ... you always gotta watch the curve of a dark road ... it can go either way.

EDWARD CURTIS lights another cigarette and smiles.

EDWARD CURTIS: I always said you were perfectly educated and absolutely uncivilized.

UPSHAW laughs. CURTIS smiles and then looks intently at the photo of YISKA. He moves slightly this way and that, uncomfortable.

ALEXANDER UPSHAW: You are worried. Then worry. A man should worry ... I should have worried more. I married a white woman because I had the taste of her tongue on my voice. I was walking as any man has a right. I was walking home and then there, just a movement in the darkness that you know is no good, then no good comes into me like a knife ... bleeding then, dying then. There.

EDWARD CURTIS: He's looking at me. His eyes are following me.

ALEXANDER UPSHAW: Get used to it. An Indian has to have eyes on their back.

CURTIS looks deeply into the eyes of YISKA in the photograph.

FRAME SHIFT.

*He looks as the portrait of **ALEXANDER UPSHAW** fades and then vanishes, leaving **YISKA**.*

*YISKA looks over at **CLARA** as she stands crying, her hands wiping up blue water that has fallen on the floor.*

YISKA: Shouldn't you be with your own people? Your own family?

FRAME SHIFT.

MUSIC: "Clara's Song" – Bruce Ruddell

EDWARD CURTIS walks toward her.

EDWARD CURTIS: Clara, are you all right?

She doesn't respond immediately. She wipes her eyes with her wrists and looks up, pretending she hasn't been crying.

CLARA: Yes. Yes. I am fine. My hands are deep in Indians, as yours, and getting deeper. (*She grabs a towel and wipes her hands.*) I'm surprised ... Why the sudden concern?

EDWARD CURTIS: Don't be like a cross child, Clara. I've missed you ... I know you feel there is something wrong /

CLARA: / You haven't been home for months.

He tries again softly.

EDWARD CURTIS: We've had this conversation /

CLARA: / Then start a new one.

He just looks at her.

EDWARD CURTIS: Clara ... I don't want to deal with this drama every single time I come home ... I want /

CLARA: / I want.

He stops.

CLARA: I want. It sounds strange to say it out loud. I want. (*She smiles, clipped.*) Did you ever ask me what I wanted. Did you ever ask? "Clara, my love, my wife, mother of my children, my partner ... What is it that you want?"

EDWARD CURTIS: You knew from the beginning what it was going to be like.

CLARA: Did I? With all the lies of the future untold how does anybody know what it is going to be like ...

CURTIS doesn't say anything.

CLARA: I want ... more ... I need more. In case you were going to ask now. I want more. Abstinence from existing makes a person hungry. (*She looks at him.*) And I am so hungry. I could eat you ...

EDWARD CURTIS: I don't know what you want me to say?

She turns away.

CLARA: Then by all means cook an omelette and pat yourself on the back ...

EDWARD CURTIS: What would make you happy, Clara? God forbid you take any happiness from our success.

She turns to him.

CLARA: You mean "your" success.

EDWARD CURTIS: Don't put words in my mouth. I didn't come back to argue.

CLARA: Why did you come back, Edward? Why? When clearly you would rather be somewhere else with someone else.

Pause.

EDWARD CURTIS: (*gathering his words*) I don't know ... I thought we could ... I could make things better ... (*finally, embarrassed*) I don't have time for this, Clara ...

She gathers her words.

CLARA: I can wait for you, but you don't have time ... Yet you have time to gallop around the country doing your Indian lectures, dining with presidents and society women, raising money – raising your hand under some dress ... for what? One more book. One more field trip ... One more ... One more / ... One more ... (*She looks at him directly.*)

EDWARD CURTIS: / What exactly are you accusing me of?!

CLARA: The women!! You think I don't see the women, Edward? ... Am I to pretend it's all just rumour? ... What strange bedfellows will you lie with next?

It is incredibly still as his eyes turn hateful.

EDWARD CURTIS: You ... you have offended me with such allegations. You have offended my very cause, my work, my very being.

CLARA sits down slowly, suddenly weighted.

CLARA: Lay down with them all for all I care, Edward. Lay down … What does any woman know of her husband's passions? … All she needs to understand is that they don't include her.

She turns cold.

EDWARD CURTIS: Are you finished?

Pause.

CLARA: Yes, I believe I am. I am. I want a divorce. (*She looks up at him.*) Who would have thought I could say it?

CURTIS sits down heavily in a chair, stunned.

FRAME SHIFT.

CLARA looks up and walks toward a beautiful life-size image of a young Edward Curtis.

SLIDE: *Edward Curtis portrait.*

SLIDE CAPTION: *"Edward Curtis, 1899"*

She takes her hand and strokes his face and leans in to kiss his lips. The photograph doesn't respond.

FRAME SHIFT.

ANGELINE continues looking at all the framed degrees as they appear on the wall. DR. CLARA turns.

DR. CLARA: What are you doing here?

ANGELINE: You took the picture down. Good for you.

DR. CLARA: Thanks … you're supposed to be at your appointment.

ANGELINE: I got all dressed up but couldn't make myself go.

DR. CLARA: Then you should have called me and I could have cancelled.

ANGELINE: Why did you give me the book?

DR. CLARA: It just makes me look bad.

ANGELINE: Always worried about appearances.

ANGELINE picks up a framed certificate.

DR. CLARA: What book? Put that down.

ANGELINE: Scared I'm going to break it?

DR. CLARA: No … Yes.

ANGELINE plays with the frame, moving it from hand to hand.

ANGELINE: Let's try again … Why did you buy me the book?

DR. CLARA: I'm not in the mood … All right …

She looks at ANGELINE, who isn't budging.

DR. CLARA: Because I thought you would enjoy it.

ANGELINE: I'm trying to get my head together and you thought I would enjoy looking at beautiful pictures of "vanishing Indians."

DR. CLARA: It was just a gift to show you I cared. Edward Curtis was a photojournalist of sorts and you're a journalist … It's a coffee-table … book. You put it on your coffee table … if you had one.

ANGELINE: This is how you care … because this is how you think.

She looks at the framed certificate with its golden seal.

ANGELINE: Wow, you've adopted a starving black kid from Africa for what – thirty dollars a month – and put it on your wall. Impressive … I mean, maybe I should donate some money to Africa … or at least fuck Bono /

DR. CLARA: (*turns away*) / Maybe I shouldn't have framed it …

Pause.

ANGELINE: I thought for a minute you were going to say, "Maybe I shouldn't have fucked Bono."

ANGELINE smiles. Long pause.

ANGELINE: You know what would be really impressive framed on your wall? A golden certificate saying you donated money to starving kids in your own country.

Pause. ANGELINE doesn't say anything.

DR. CLARA: Point taken.

DR. CLARA moves toward ANGELINE and takes the framed certificate from her.

DR. CLARA: Is it the photographs that have gotten to you?

ANGELINE: The photos are so beautiful I am barely able to breathe.

DR. CLARA: Have you been able to write?

ANGELINE shakes her head.

DR. CLARA: It must be hard … You're not just any writer, are you? You're a foreign correspondent … an Aboriginal foreign correspondent … in your own country ... hired by the biggest national newspaper to cover Aboriginal issues ... in your own country ...

ANGELINE: Stop saying "in your own country" ... it's freaking me out.

Almost crying, ANGELINE looks away.

DR. CLARA: Look at me ... What's wrong?

ANGELINE: Everything.

DR. CLARA: Can you be more specific?

ANGELINE: No.

SFX: The faint sound of children playing in the snow.

ANGELINE: Everything is not the way it should be. It's like I'm still laying in the snow and everything looks so beautiful. (*She looks up.*) I can hear them ... you know? I can hear them ... Sometimes when I put my hand out I can touch them. If I leave they will be so alone, Clara, so alone ... and it's so cold ...

She closes her eyes and begins to hum and then sing. DR. CLARA covers her with a blanket and they both sing.

MUSIC: "Snow Lullaby"

FRAME SHIFT.

MUSIC: "Snow Lullaby" – YISKA sings.

YISKA appears from the darkness and puts his arms around ANGELINE. She opens her eyes.

ANGELINE: I didn't write the whole story.

YISKA: You wrote the facts. You wrote what you were expected to write.

ANGELINE pauses.

ANGELINE: Did I? I didn't write the real story ...

She doesn't wait for his response.

YISKA: Ange ...

ANGELINE: I wrote that an Indian father was drunk and dropped his three kids in the snow ...

YISKA: He did ...

ANGELINE: Did he? Or did we drop him a long time ago? I should have written that the father of those children was so young, so poor ... living in a house that was so contaminated it should have been torn down ... living between cardboard walls with no food, no clean water, no phone, no heat, and the only reason he decided to go out into minus thirty-eight weather was because one of his kids was sick ... He went out to get help ... Do you think it was all his fault? Or maybe we all should own a little piece of it?

YISKA: We do Ange, because we've survived, but most people don't want to hear the whole truth ... they don't want to see it, they just want us to disappear.

She gets small.

YISKA: You have to find a way to keep going.

ANGELINE: Are you scared I will die?

YISKA: (*in Salish*) I am afraid I would die without you. I am afraid I would die.

ANGELINE: (*looks at him*) I am afraid to live.

YISKA: If we stand here like this just the two of us ... then we balance the whole world out.

ANGELINE: Say it in my language.

YISKA: (*in Dene*) If we stand here like this just the two of us then we balance the whole world out.

They stand, not moving.

FRAME SHIFT.

MUSIC: "Signal Fire to the Mountain God" – Henry Gilbert

SUBTITLE SLIDE: "Picture Story III: Carnegie Hall, New York, 1911"

A stereoptical illusion comes into focus. The rich backdrop of the theatre fades up in dark-gold and auburn, in Greek pillars and grandeur.

Dissolving, flickering SLIDE SEQUENCES VII–XII: VII, "The North West Plains Life"; VIII, "North Pacific Coast Tribes"; IX, "The Kutenai of the Lakes"; X, "Invocation to the Buffalo"; XI, "The Mountain Camp"; XII, "On the Shores of the Pacific."

EDWARD CURTIS: The first and greatest problem before all human beings is that of food, and naturally the culture of any group is largely determined by this. Students of primitive religion will tell you that the question of food is the first thought in a majority of religious systems. This admitted, let us look at it in relation to the Indian. We pass from the proud buffalo-hunting Indian to the less favoured ... I have asked you to take this broad glimpse at the Indian subject that you have firmly in mind that we cannot refer to the Indian as a unit, as is often done, but rather we must in a measure consider each group as a ... nation ... a project unto itself.

He watches as the photograph of a Yeibachai Dancer projects up. EDWARD CURTIS watches as the ribs of the Yeibachai Dancer seem to move as if breathing. He places his hands on the photograph and then backs away.

EDWARD CURTIS: There is an erroneous impression perhaps fathered by our own presumption in considering our reaching out to the Infinite to be religion, and the Indian's like act to be heathenism.

CURTIS bends down to the photograph of an Indian bending down to the water. As he bends, CURTIS places his hand in the imagined water. The face of the Indian suddenly turns to look at him.

EDWARD CURTIS: They are looking at me ... Stop looking at me ...

He gathers himself and launches into his lecture again.

EDWARD CURTIS: Rather than being without religion, every act of his life was according to divine prompting. True, the gods bore strange names, but the need was as great, the appeal as devout ... the appeal as ...

He stands as a number of Edward Curtis Indians now seem to move in a blur around him.

SFX: The sound of breathing begins to fill the room.

SFX: The sound of oars in water.

He looks for the sound and then moves toward the developing tray with caution. Bending down, his hands in water, he pulls out a plate of glass. He looks at it as a small canoe develops up and then the image of a woman. The canoe makes its way across the glass and then is projected onto the wall.

FILM: CLARA sits inside the canoe, looking into the water.

Relieved, CURTIS recognizes her.

EDWARD CURTIS: Clara ...

FILM: CLARA drops her hand into the lake and leans in toward the water, as if touching the other side.

EDWARD CURTIS: (*confused, rattled*) Clara, it is you ... What are you doing?

A small light on ANGELINE.

CLARA: I had a dream I was moving across the lake like I'd done a million times before. I stopped just then by chance almost, my reflection perfect. Strong.

EDWARD CURTIS: Clara ... please answer me ...

CLARA: The thought clear ... I truly am invisible.

ANGELINE: From what I could see she was quite beautiful. Auburn hair. Fair skin. She was wearing a white blouse and a long skirt.

CLARA: I was wearing a beautiful hat ...

ANGELINE: She was waiting ... A kind of waiting that made me sad because she was looking into the water seeing everything she had lost ... and not looking away.

CURTIS reaches out his hand to her.

FILM: CLARA reaches her hand deeper into the water.

EDWARD CURTIS: Clara ...

FILM: CLARA releases herself into the deep water and falls into its depth as long reeds of bulrushes rise up and over her.

EDWARD CURTIS: She is gone ... my wife is gone ... my partner ... the mother of my children ...

CURTIS looks around at the suddenly empty dark space.

EDWARD CURTIS: It is dark.

He locks eyes with ANGELINE.

EDWARD CURTIS: I am ... / alone

ANGELINE: / Alone ... I know.

From the darkness.

FRAME SHIFT.

YISKA watches EDWARD CURTIS as he rummages madly through his stuff, looking for his journal as YISKA begins to circle him.

YISKA: Leaving so soon.

EDWARD CURTIS: I was just getting my things together.

YISKA: Your things?

EDWARD CURTIS: Yes, my belongings.

YISKA: You missing anything?

EDWARD CURTIS: Yes ... I seem to have misplaced my journal and some photographs I have taken on this trip.

YISKA: (approaches) You mean these?

YISKA has the journal in his hand. He takes the photos from the middle of the journal and passes the journal to EDWARD CURTIS.

EDWARD CURTIS: Yes ... I would like my photos back.

YISKA: Even if they are of us ... they are still yours.

EDWARD CURTIS: Please ... my photos ...

YISKA turns deadly cold. He rips the photos in half and the pieces fall to the ground.

YISKA: I want you to get out before I kill you ... I want you out. I want you gone.

EDWARD CURTIS: Is that right?

YISKA advances on CURTIS threateningly. CURTIS pulls out a gun and shakily points it at YISKA. YISKA stops.

YISKA: You fuckin' ... fuckin' ... I should wring your scrawny fuckin' ...

EDWARD CURTIS: This is no joke. No joke. A serious affair.

YISKA: No one's laughing here, Chief.

EDWARD CURTIS: You were going to scalp me and I had to take matters into my own hands.

YISKA: (looks at him) What are you talking about?

EDWARD CURTIS: I've been in this situation before. When I was living with the Sioux – a Sioux warrior pulled a knife on me because he didn't want me to take any more pictures. I knew I'd seen you before.

YISKA: I'm not Sioux. Put the gun down.

EDWARD CURTIS: Not until you put your knife down.

YISKA: (shrugs) I don't have a knife.

EDWARD CURTIS: Indians always have a knife.

YISKA: I don't have a knife.

EDWARD CURTIS: Have it your way ... just don't get close to me or so help me God, I will shoot you.

CURTIS waves his gun and motions for the journal and pieces of torn photographs. YISKA steps closer and leaves them on the table. CURTIS waves YISKA back. He looks over his stuff and tries to piece the photographs together.

YISKA: Do you think that the Indians you took pictures of thought you were actually taking pictures of them?

EDWARD CURTIS: What are you talking about?

YISKA: You were taking pictures of your idea of them. Big difference.

EDWARD CURTIS: They understood the power of art, so they understood me, and I understood them.

YISKA: Did they understand the ramifications of being frozen in time without the possibility of seeing what survival looks like?

EDWARD CURTIS: Academic babble.

CURTIS puts the journal in his jacket. YISKA moves toward him. CURTIS motions with the gun for YISKA to stay where he is.

EDWARD CURTIS: I don't like you.

YISKA: I've never liked you.

Pause.

EDWARD CURTIS: I don't get it. I've been nothing but cordial to you since I arrived, and from the very beginning you looked at me like I'm one of them.

YISKA: (begins to get closer) You are one of them.

EDWARD CURTIS: I held high views of the North American Indian ...

YISKA: Get off the pedestal ...

EDWARD CURTIS: I dedicated my life ... over thirty years of my life documenting the North American Indian, my health, any money I made, any hope of lasting happiness.

YISKA: And we are grateful ...

EDWARD CURTIS: I stood up for them ...

YISKA: (gets closer) When it suited you ... when everything suited you ...

EDWARD CURTIS: I asked you to step back and put the knife down! I warned you ...

CURTIS raises his gun.

YISKA: Spoken like a true Custer.

EDWARD CURTIS: Don't you dare ... don't you dare compare me to that longhair! Put the knife down!

YISKA looks at him and mimes putting a big knife down.

YISKA: I am putting the almighty scalping knife down! Chief ! (Pause.) What are you going to do now Chief, shoot me?

EDWARD CURTIS begins to crumble. YISKA approaches him.

YISKA: Shoot me Chief, and get it over with.

They stare into each other.

YISKA: What, you think you can cook a pair of eggs and everything is fine?

EDWARD CURTIS lowers his gun, ready to explode.

EDWARD CURTIS: Yes ... yes I do ... I do ... because it has to be! I cooked for them, and I cooked for them, and I cooked for them ... do you want to know why? Because I couldn't stand watching them starve to death over and over and over ... everywhere I went ... starvation, death, incarceration, hunger ... They were so hungry I would cook for them every chance I got ... every goddamn chance I got ... Goddamn it! Goddamn, goddamn it to hell!

He stops and looks at YISKA, trying to reel himself in, barely breathing, almost crying. He suddenly stops, catching the air.

EDWARD CURTIS: I smell peaches.

FRAME SHIFT.

DR. CLARA appears from just outside the darkness.

DR. CLARA: Let me help you ... I can help you ... you look so sad.

ANGELINE: I hate sad people ... it's so privileged.

DR. CLARA: Privileged?

ANGELINE turns toward her sister.

ANGELINE: Maybe we're so privileged it has made us sad.

DR. CLARA just looks at her.

ANGELINE: If we were all sinking in a boat right now ... who do you think would get out first?

DR. CLARA: I don't know ... you're acting weird.

ANGELINE: Seriously ... who do you think would get out first? ... You've seen the movie – a big fuckin' indestructible boat filled with rich people filling their gaps, a drunk captain, an iceberg ... the music plays – If both of us were on the same boat, but different levels, who do you think would get out first? You or me?

DR. CLARA: It would depend on chance. Life depends on chance and circumstance /

ANGELINE: Chance? /

DR. CLARA: / Circumstance. Survival /

ANGELINE: / And survival depends on the chance of your skin being white or brown?

DR. CLARA: You're twisting things ...

ANGELINE: Because they are twisted ... Aboriginal people are at the bottom of the boat ... and everyone else is in first class fighting to get on a life raft while the music plays. I'm not saying they don't feel sorry for taking all the life rafts ... that's what the music is for ... I'm just saying ... the movie never changes ... When is the movie going to change?

DR. CLARA: I don't know what you are talking about?

ANGELINE: Sure you do. You do, because you would be in the first dingy wouldn't you? ... First dingy, Clara.

DR. CLARA: We have the same blood. The same history ...

ANGELINE: But not the same colour of skin so not the same reality. You are an onlooker that has the ability to feel sorry for someone while remaining tight-fisted.

DR. CLARA: And what are you?

ANGELINE looks at her wall of degrees.

ANGELINE: So many degrees and yet you have so little depth. You are dimensionless.

She looks at DR. CLARA.

DR. CLARA: What are you? What are you in all this? Please clarify it for me ... so complicated, so complex, so brown? /

ANGELINE: / Say it /

DR. CLARA: / So fucked up.

DR. CLARA looks down, about to apologize.

ANGELINE: At least I never left my children to a white man to raise.

DR. CLARA ices.

DR. CLARA: What did you say?

Pause.

ANGELINE closes her eyes.

DR. CLARA: You think that because you are fucked in the head ... you can say anything you want ...

ANGELINE: I'm sorry ... I'm sorry, Clara ... I didn't mean to /

DR. CLARA: / They wanted to stay with him. So ... they stayed with him.

ANGELINE moves toward her. DR. CLARA moves from her.

DR. CLARA: No ... no.

ANGELINE stops and catches the wind.

ANGELINE: I can smell peaches. Can you smell them? I can smell the wind and it smells like peaches.

DR. CLARA stares at her sister.

DR. CLARA: Do you want to know the thing I miss the most? I miss putting them to bed. Having the blankets pulled up to their little chests. They are so warm and small. You bend down into their little necks, just below their ears, and your cheek touches theirs, and you kiss them then ... hesitating before you rise because what you wanted, what you really wanted all along was to smell them. To smell them because it smells like ...

ANGELINE: Peaches.

DR. CLARA: Like peaches ...

DR. CLARA closes her eyes. ANGELINE closes her eyes.

FRAME SHIFT.

EDWARD CURTIS closes his eyes. YISKA closes his eyes. They all stand in a pose as Canyon de Chelly fades up, leaving them in a peach grove.

SLIDE: Across the backdrop, an Edward Curtis photograph of the beautiful Canyon de Chelly fades up in oranges.

SLIDE CAPTION: "Canyon de Chelly – Navaho, 1904"

YISKA: Like peaches planted in the most unexpected of places ...

YISKA closes his eyes and begins to sing.

MUSIC: YISKA sings.

EDWARD CURTIS: Across the worlds I went. I was only frightened when I was scared. In the deep red canyon down where green peach trees grow despite themselves, just before dawn, a baby is trying to be born. I camped there in the valley not yet understanding that my very presence was a curse. A curse once spelled to the wind can never be taken back. A baby was trying to be born, stuck, they said because of me. Stuck between flesh and

spirit, between surviving and vanishing. Because of me they said. Because of me just being somewhere a white man had never been. Were they right? Does it matter? Were they wrong? It doesn't matter. Was it real? It was real ... real as that baby's cry finally lifting into a wind that smelled of ripe peaches ... reaching me telling me ... its first day will allow me to live another. Telling me to never forget ... never forget ... the balance between being killed or saved is but a child's struggle to breathe and the belief of one man over another.

YISKA: (*in Dene*) If we stand here like this we balance the whole world out.

They all stand, not moving, breathing in the moment.

The sand of the desert begins to rise under the following scenes, swirling.

CURTIS begins to move. YISKA looks at him and whispers a warning.

YISKA: Don't move.

CURTIS takes his lens out and raises it to his eye.

YISKA: One day. One night. One year.

FRAME SHIFT.

CURTIS turns and looks over.

SLIDE: Desert sand swirls and settles, forming the West Coast shore, fog rising through.

SLIDE: An Edward Curtis portrait of Princess Angeline fades up as she bends down on the shore, collecting clams.

SLIDE CAPTION: "Princess Angeline, 1902"

PRINCESS ANGELINE: (*in Salish*) It's hard to believe in another day when you are hungry.

SFX: The sound of the tide grows louder.

CURTIS looks over at the portrait.

FRAME SHIFT.

ANGELINE bends up from the portrait as PRINCESS ANGELINE, age seventy. CURTIS moves toward her, relieved to see an old friend.

EDWARD CURTIS: Is that you Princess? Is that you? I can hear you like I can hear the sea ... a tide coming in like a whisper leaving behind nothing and everything ... cold at my feet with the shock of a clock that is wet ... I saw you there bending down, putting your hands in the deep sand, reaching down in, and pulling up spitting clams. And then later on the side of the street, crouched down, head up staring into a horizon that was us white and moving forward. I said then ... Are you Princess Angeline, daughter of Chief Seattle?

He looks over. PRINCESS ANGELINE does not look at him.

EDWARD CURTIS: You said nothing ... such is the state of any princess. (*He walks closer to her.*) I walked closer and again I said ... are you Princess Angeline, daughter of the great Chief Seattle?

She smiles slowly.

EDWARD CURTIS: You didn't look up but smiled. I was man enough to know ... a smile is at least a door. (*He bends down to her level.*) Can I take your picture? A picture. It meant nothing to you. A picture.

He brings his lens to his eye.

FRAME SHIFT.

SLIDE: An Edward Curtis portrait of Alexander Upshaw.

SLIDE CAPTION: "Alexander Upshaw, Crow"

YISKA appears as ALEXANDER UPSHAW.

ALEXANDER UPSHAW: (*in Salish*) He wants to take your picture?

She turns and looks at the translator.

PRINCESS ANGELINE: (*in Salish*) Why?

ALEXANDER UPSHAW: (*in Salish*) That is what he does.

PRINCESS ANGELINE: (*in Salish*) That is what he does with his pretty white hands. Me, my hands like crow's feet are bent and salted. Me, my hands are old and smell like the bottom of a great water. Tell him yes ... if he has any food to spare.

She looks down at her rusted and salted hands.

PRINCESS ANGELINE: (*in Salish*) Me, my hands are tired of being hungry ... diggin' ... diggin' ... diggin' even in my sleep, diggin' for food that is nothing more than a hard shell.

EDWARD CURTIS: What does she want?

UPSHAW looks at her for a long time.

EDWARD CURTIS: Alexander, what does the squaw want?

He looks back at CURTIS and, making a decision, stands in a formal stance.

ALEXANDER UPSHAW: Money. The daughter of the great Chief Sealth wants one dollar a picture. The daughter of the great Chief Sealth will not pose for less than one dollar a picture.

CURTIS looks at her, amazed by the request.

EDWARD CURTIS: Tell her that is too much. What does she think I am made of?

UPSHAW looks into the eyes of the old princess. She puts out her hand.

PRINCESS ANGELINE: (*in Salish*) Food.

He hesitates and then bends to her with honour and a soft voice.

ALEXANDER UPSHAW: (*in Salish*) You will make him a great man by letting him take your picture and for this great honour he is going to give you a dollar a picture.

He looks over at a puzzled CURTIS and makes his play.

ALEXANDER UPSHAW: She thinks that you must be a great man to be able to capture the very image of her soul.

CURTIS puffs up ever so slightly.

ALEXANDER UPSHAW: For this she agrees that a dollar would be an equitable trade between artists. So it is done.

CURTIS extends his hand toward the princess hesitantly. They shake.

ALEXANDER UPSHAW: Congratulations sir, you have made your first transaction with an Indian ... your first picture.

CURTIS reaches inside his pockets.

EDWARD CURTIS: Yes ... I have ... Yes, I did ...

CURTIS lays a silver dollar in her weathered hand. He goes to draw away and she grabs his hand suddenly and looks right into him.

PRINCESS ANGELINE: Did you capture my soul? Or did I capture yours? It was never about the money ... It was about food ... We are still hungry ...

She takes the silver dollar and wraps his fingers around the coin.

PRINCESS ANGELINE: Our people are still starving still digging ... digging ... digging ... for food that used to be a feast and now is nothing more than leftovers ...

FRAME SHIFT.

SLIDE: Edward Curtis studio portrait of Princess Angeline.

SLIDE CAPTION: "Princess Angeline, Seattle Studio, 18"

Stunned, EDWARD CURTIS stands looking at her for a long time. The coin drops from his hand and rolls.

SFX: The sound of a coin rolling.

FRAME SHIFT.

SFX: The sound of a wax cylinder rolls under.

SFX: The sound of being under a great lake.

EDWARD CURTIS looks over at the bending form of the HUNGER CHIEF, who stands before the water. Bending down, he takes water into his hands, wiping his face and hair until they are wet. He looks up and into CURTIS. He moves toward him. The world carves a circular motion backwards.

EDWARD CURTIS: What do you want from me? I've nothing left.

HUNGER CHIEF: Then you are finally one of us. The only way a white man can become an Indian is to starve. You want to come inside ... You want to live with the Indians, then you must die with us ... Come inside ... come inside our belly ... Come inside ... come inside my belly ...

EDWARD CURTIS: I am afraid ... I am afraid ...

The HUNGER CHIEF moves toward him slow and staggered.

HUNGER CHIEF: I am going to put you into the water, midnight, an oar, black clouds, salt, something bad, something different, one night, one day, one year ...

FRAME SHIFT.

From across the space under the lake CLARA sits bent over. EDWARD CURTIS moves slowly toward her, careful not to walk on pieces of broken glass. Careful of the sound of her hand breaking glass plates.

EDWARD CURTIS: You don't have to wait for me anymore, Clara ... I am here ...

He takes the rock from her hands and moves the wet strands of hair from her face until he takes her face in his hands and they lock eyes.

He leans in to kiss her.

HUNGER CHIEF: We eat together. I am going to put you into the water, midnight, an oar, black clouds, salt, something bad, something different, one night, one day, one year ... We eat together.

They freeze as the HUNGER CHIEF turns and transforms the world forward.

FRAME SHIFT.

SFX: A blinding snow storm builds.

ANGELINE appears, stops and listens to the drum and song, recognizes the voice and then sees YISKA.

MUSIC: YISKA sings.

YISKA: I'm praying for you.

He moves toward her but she backs away.

YISKA: We are and remain thin. We want to eat. We don't want to be sick. We want to get well.

ANGELINE: We are and remain thin. We want to eat. We don't want to be sick. We want to get well.

YISKA: You want them to be warm. You want them to be well. You want them to live ...

ANGELINE: I want them to drink clean water. I want to be safe. I want them to live. I want them to love. I think of them.

YISKA: I'm praying for you.

ANGELINE: I don't want them to be frozen. I don't want them to be frozen ...

YISKA: We eat together. I am going to put you into the storm, one day, a light, bright sun, tears, something bad, something different, one day, one night, one year. We eat together.

FRAME SHIFT.

SLIDE CAPTION: "Arctic, 2013"

EDWARD CURTIS and DR. CLARA stand wrapped in blankets. YISKA in his parka. They stand in the snow.

YISKA: There was a call around four in the morning ...

DR. CLARA: There was a call ...

EDWARD CURTIS: A call that rang throughout the village ...

DR. CLARA: A call you don't want to hear because you know it's not good.

YISKA: I picked up ... probably every house in the village picked up and set out into the night that is day /

EDWARD CURTIS: / Day that is night.

ANGELINE looks around at the stark beautiful village landscape.

ANGELINE: I set out like everyone else blankets in hand ... The sun was just coming up or down ... it was beautiful. Like nothing could touch the way it looked ... I walked through the snow ... slower ... less able to walk in deep snow ... less able to keep up with those that have been doing it all their lives ... they passed in front of me like a wave of bodies and breath that clung to the air. I was behind but I was also able to see things for the first time. Seeing so clearly I could hear ...

YISKA: A young father had been found in the snow ... almost frozen ...

EDWARD CURTIS: Almost frozen ...

YISKA: Drunk ... and then thawing ... asking where his three kids were.

"Where are my kids?"

DR. CLARA: "Where are my children?"

YISKA: They weren't in his house. They weren't in any home.

EDWARD CURTIS: They weren't in any home. They weren't in any house.

SFX: The faint sound of children's voices singing.

ANGELINE: But there was a sound ... A kind of a beautiful sound that found me, and I looked down ...

YISKA: They were outside.

SLIDE: A baby impression in the snow.

ANGELINE freezes and stumbles toward the baby's impression.

ANGELINE: Frozen. She froze in minus thirty-eight degrees. In a small sweater. A small pink sweater. I kept thinking ... Jesus Christ ... Jesus Christ ...

She stumbles forward.

SLIDE: Another larger impression of a boy in the snow appears.

ANGELINE: I stepped forward ... and there ... five steps in the snow ... another child, age four, frozen ... these beautiful rosy chubby cheeks ... Jesus Jesus Christ ... I stepped back.

EDWARD CURTIS: One day. One night. One year.

She falls back.

SLIDE: A larger impression of a girl in the snow appears.

ANGELINE: I stumbled back ... when my hand landed ... landed on something solid but soft ... Jesus no ... no ... I looked back and her hand was reaching out as if she had seen something ... a possibility, age eight. She reached out and froze in that possibility ...

DR. CLARA: One day. One night. One year.

ANGELINE shakily takes out her notepad and pen and tries to write.

ANGELINE: I knew it was too late because they were so beautiful. Perfect. Frozen in time. Dead ... I begin to write ... "Three children were found in the snow ..." And that's as far as I got ... Three children were found sleeping ...

She begins to take her outer clothing off and lays it on the snow.

ANGELINE: I began to sing a song my mother used to sing to me when I was a child.

YISKA: One day. One night. One year.

MUSIC: "Snow Lullaby" – Leela Gilday

ANGELINE: As I sang ... I began to take my coat off ... the layers I had put on ... I took off and I put them on their little bodies ... It was so cold ... and they were so alone ... I laid down with them, covering them with a blanket the best I could ... I rocked them into their sleep, tucking them in ... into their sleep ... shhhh ... baby ... I'm here ... I'm sorry, I'm sorry, I'm so ... so sorry this happened to you ... I became so tired ... I could barely keep my eyes open ... because I was so sorry so tired ... so I shut my eyes ... I shut them ... so I shut my eyes ... because I could no longer see what I could no longer know.

ANGELINE looks up, covered in a blanket of snow. She looks directly at CURTIS.

ANGELINE: Aren't you going to take the picture? ... take the picture ... if vanishing is so beautiful ...

take the picture ... take the picture ... if vanishing is so ... beautiful ...

> *CURTIS pauses and looks at her.*

EDWARD CURTIS: I can't take the picture ... I can't take the picture, Angeline ... because I am not alive. You are.

> *CURTIS begins to freeze in his pose.*

> *SLIDE CAPTION "Edward Curtis, 1868–1952"*

> *CURTIS fades and vanishes.*

> *FADE OUT.*

> *MUSIC: "A Snow Lullaby" – Leela Gilday*

> *SUBTITLE SLIDE: "EPILOGUE"*

> *Lights fade up on ANGELINE's fingers as her body lies almost suspended on an Arctic landscape. Her fingers begin to move as though she were playing a piano. She hits a note. Then another.*

> *SFX: In the distance sled dogs bark.*

> *From a distance YISKA moves toward her.*

ANGELINE: I hear the sound of dogs barking and the sled scraping the surface, snowshoes on this world made of ice. I heard. I hear voices and finally a shadow above me all tall-limbed into the sky.

YISKA: Ange ...

> *He reaches her and extends his hand. She grabs his hand and he begins to raise her.*

ANGELINE: I have to stand ... I know.

YISKA: One day. One night. One year ...

> *She stands with him tall to the sky.*

ANGELINE: We have to stand.

> *Rita Leistner's Field Work photographs begin to develop up on the dark walls surrounding them.*

> *Blackout.*

END

INS
CHOI

(b. 1974)

Kim's Convenience is a phenomenon, a play so popular that it sold out every performance at its Toronto Fringe Festival premiere in 2011, as well as every performance of its subsequent Soulpepper run in 2012, leading to a remount four months later that also sold out. In 2013, the play was revived for a third time in less than two years by Soulpepper, followed by a Canadian tour, and then – who knows what? This is all the more remarkable considering that *Kim's Convenience* is Ins Choi's first play and the first new Canadian play produced by Soulpepper, Toronto's premier theatre company. A realist drama about the immigrant experience, leavened with terrific comedy, it invites comparison with David French's *Leaving Home* (see *Modern Canadian Plays*, vol. 1), another first play about immigrant parents and their Canadian children in Toronto; another play that held up a mirror to its Canadian audiences and brought them en masse to their feet.

Both *Leaving Home* and *Kim's Convenience* have broad appeal as emotionally powerful family plays about situations that transcend their particular cultural orientation (Newfoundland-Canadian in one, Korean-Canadian in the other), and both feature at their centre a funny, theatrically dynamic father bordering on ethnic stereotype. But much has changed in Canada in the four decades separating the appearance of these two plays. Asian immigration has transformed Toronto and other Canadian cities into some of the world's most ethnically diverse metropolises, and Canada's new demographics have made "Asian-Canadian" an important, if somewhat ambiguous and even contested, category. The spectacular emergence of *Kim's Convenience* attests not only to Choi's substantial talents but to an evolving Asian-Canadian theatre culture that increasingly provides infrastructure, support, and opportunities for playwrights like Choi.

Born in Seoul, Korea, In-Surp Choi came to Canada with his family as an infant in 1975, growing up in the Toronto suburb of Scarborough. His father, a pastor, worked in his uncle's convenience store while establishing his own Korean church in Toronto. Choi studied acting at York University (BFA Theatre, 1998) and soon became involved in Toronto's burgeoning Asian-Canadian theatre scene. In 2004, he joined The Kitchen, the playwrights unit of fu-GEN Asian Canadian Theatre Company (est. 2002) for its first annual Potluck Festival, where new scripts get staged readings. He was also a cast member of fu-GEN's first full production, Leon Aureus's *Banana Boys*, a play about young Asian-Canadian men and the stereotypes associated with them. Choi received a Dora Mavor Moore Award nomination as part of the ensemble. Aureus would later join him as co-producer of *Kim's Convenience* at the Toronto Fringe.

Choi was admitted to the Stratford Festival's Birmingham Conservatory for Classical Theatre in 2006 and spent two seasons performing Shakespeare at Stratford. In 2009 he was back with fu-GEN, earning a Dora nomination as best actor for his lead role in the premiere of David Yee's noir thriller about Chinese-Canadian history and redress, *lady in the red dress*. That year he also became a member of the Soulpepper Academy, deepening his acting experience in the modern classics (*The Cherry Orchard, Death of a Salesman*) and co-creating new work: *(re)Birth: E.E. Cummings in Song, Window on Toronto,* and *Alligator Pie*. As part of the *Alligator Pie* ensemble, Choi received three more Dora nominations (as performer, creator, and director) in 2013.

At the prompting of fu-GEN artistic director Nina Lee Aquino, Choi rejoined fu-GEN's playwriting unit while performing in *Banana Boys* in 2005–06, and *Kim's Convenience* had its genesis there. As the play developed over the next five years, receiving readings at fu-GEN Potluck festivals, Choi tried unsuccessfully to shop it to local companies. He finally decided to self-produce (and direct and perform in it) at the 2011 Toronto Fringe, where *Kim's Convenience* won the New Play Contest and Patrons Pick Award, proving so popular at the Best of the Fringe Uptown festival that it generated a bidding war. Soulpepper won, and its 2012 productions garnered a Dora nomination for *Kim's Convenience* as best new play, and Toronto Theatre Critics' Awards for best Canadian play and best actor (Paul Sun-Hyung Lee as Appa). In 2013, Choi continued performing in *Kim's Convenience* as an associate artist with Soulpepper. He also developed a postmodern solo work about a homeless man, *Subway Stations of the Cross*, which he performed in churches and subway stations across Toronto.

Choi has one foot in a Canadian theatrical subculture that has existed for barely three decades but is becoming more prominent by the day. Nina Lee Aquino's two volumes of Asian-Canadian plays, *Love and Relasianships* (2009), and a collection of critical essays, *Asian Canadian Theatre*, edited by Aquino and Ric Knowles (2011), reveal that only since 1983, with R.A. (Rick) Shiomi's *Yellow Fever*, have Asian-Canadian plays been professionally produced in Canada. They argue that Asian-Canadian is a fraught term, eliding differences between cultures and ethnicities, fusing Chinese-, Japanese-, Korean-, Filipino-, and other specific Asian-Canadian categories, while excluding South Asia and the Middle East. Still, the very existence of these books, and the plays and arguments they contain, indicates the growing vibrancy of contemporary Asian-Canadian playwriting, playmaking, and performance, however defined. Since the 1990s, when Canada's stages first began reflecting the cultural diversity on its streets, companies like Toronto's fu-GEN, Loud Mouth Asian Babes (founded by Jean Yoon, the original Umma in *Kim's Convenience*), Cahoots Theatre, and Carlos Bulosan Theatre; Teesri Duniya Theatre in Montreal; Theatre Replacement, Neworld, and Vancouver Asian Canadian Theatre on the West Coast; and Halifax's Onelight Theatre have helped ensure that Asian-Canadian theatre artists play a prominent part.

Kim's Convenience is firmly rooted in the specifics of Korean immigrant experience, even to the extent that Korean-language dialogue in the play is not translated in production (although it is, helpfully, in Choi's script). The importance of the church in Appa and Umma's lives, Appa's anti-Japanese sentiments, and the evocation of a Korean immigrant community with shared mercantile values and widespread convenience store ownership further ground the play in the culture in which Choi grew up. In a program note, however, he calls Kim's Convenience "my love letter to my parents and to *all* first-generation immigrants who call Canada their home" (my emphasis). Experiences like Appa's and Umma's are common to more than just first-generation *Korean* Canadians – and Janet and Jung's to more than just the children of that particular community. Similarly, the Kim family's relationships with the various black men in the play may be specific to Toronto's Regent Park but could stand in for the intercultural tensions and possibilities dividing and connecting various ethnic groups across Canada. The anxieties about gentrification and Walmartization also resonate beyond the play's specific geography. Kim's Convenience derives its widespread popularity as well from the broadly human experiences of love, fear, ambition, rebellion, regret, and hope that it chronicles with such keen perception and great humour.

Kim's Convenience

Ins Choi

Kim's Convenience was first performed at the Toronto Fringe Festival on July 6, 2011, at the Bathurst Street Theatre, with the following cast:

APPA	Paul Sun-Hyung Lee
UMMA	Jean Yoon
JUNG	Ins Choi
JANET	Esther Jun
RICH, **MR. LEE**, **MIKE**, **ALEX**	Andre Sills

Directed and Produced by Ins Choi
Co-Produced by Leon Aureus
Design by Ken Mackenzie
Stage Managed by Kat Chin

CHARACTERS

APPA, *fifty-nine-year-old first-generation Korean-Canadian man, owner of Kim's Convenience store. Speaks with a thick Korean-Canadian accent*

UMMA, *fifty-six-year-old first-generation Korean-Canadian woman. APPA's wife. Speaks with a thick Korean-Canadian accent*

JUNG, *thirty-two-year-old second-generation Korean-Canadian man. APPA and UMMA's son*

JANET, *thirty-year-old second-generation Korean-Canadian woman. APPA and UMMA's daughter*

RICH, *a young black man*

MR. LEE, *a successful black real estate agent and friend of APPA*

MIKE, *a black man with a thick Jamaican accent*

ALEX, *thirty-two-year-old black police officer and childhood friend of JUNG*

SETTING

The present. A convenience store in Toronto's Regent Park, a low- to middle-income neighbourhood made up mainly of recent immigrants.

1. OPEN

Autumn. Morning. Inside a convenience store.

APPA is heard humming a medley of hymns as he enters from the back of the store with a pocketful of money, scratch-and-win card trays, and a mug of coffee in hand. He puts the coffee mug on the counter, sorts the money into the drawer of the cash register, and slides in the scratch-and-win trays. He turns on the lights, then goes to the window and flips the Closed sign to Open. He unlocks the front door. He returns to the counter, pours sugar in his coffee, and stirs. As he looks out the window, he sips. He sighs. He turns on the radio, picks up a price gun, and begins pricing a case of cans.

2. I AM KOREAN

Early afternoon. Bell. RICH enters.

APPA: Hi.

RICH: Hey, wassup?

APPA: Nice day.

RICH: Yeah. Hook me up with a scratch-and-win card, please? (*APPA pulls out the tray and RICH chooses a card.*) Thanks.

APPA: Is that one you car?

RICH: Sorry?

APPA: (*pointing to a car outside*) Is that one you car?

RICH: Is that one my car?

APPA: Yah.

RICH: Which one?

APPA: White Honda in no-parking zone. Is that one you car?

RICH: No, man, I don't even have a car.

APPA: Oh.

RICH: And a du Maurier Balanced, please.

APPA: Large or small?

RICH: Small.

APPA: King size or regular?

RICH: King size.

APPA: If you don't have car, why you ask, "Which one?" when I ask, "Is that one you car?"

RICH: I don't know. Didn't know what you were talking about.

APPA: (*indicating the case of cans on the counter*) Insam energy beverage?

RICH: What?

APPA: It's insam energy beverage. It's new one, very good from Korea. Made from –

RICH: Ginseng.

APPA: No, insam.

RICH: No, like what it's made from, looks like ginseng.

APPA: No, looks like insam. That's why it's call –

RICH: You're not hearing me. (*picking up a can*) The picture, right here, it's ginseng.

APPA: No, picture is insam.

RICH: Yo – forget it, it's no big deal. (*puts the can back*)

APPA: Yo, it's very big deal. Look same, not same thing. 1904. You know what happen 1904? Japan attack Korea.

RICH: Japan attacked Korea?

APPA: Yah.

RICH: In 1904?

APPA: Yah.

RICH: Are you Japanese?

APPA: No.

RICH: You look Japanese.

APPA: No.

RICH: Yo, you look like that guy in *The Last Samurai*.

APPA: Who, Tom Cruise?

RICH: No, the Japanese guy.

APPA: Look same, not same thing. You look like you is from Kenya.

RICH: I am from Kenya. I was born there. How'd you know that?

APPA: I can tell.

RICH: Really?

APPA: Yeah. Really.

RICH: Yo, that is cool.

APPA: I know. I am.

RICH: Why were we talking about Japan attacking Korea?

APPA: Japan attack Korea 1904, make slave of Korean. I am Korean. Ginseng is Japanese name. Insam is Korean name. (*beat*) Look same –

APPA & RICH: – not same thing.

APPA: You understand.

RICH: Yeah, I gotcha. Hook me up.

APPA: Okay. I hook up. Anything else?

RICH: No, that's it.

APPA: (*tallies up the total on the cash register*) $12.52.

    RICH gives APPA a twenty.

RICH: Thanks.

    APPA gives RICH his change.

APPA: Okay. See you.

    RICH remains at the counter and plays the scratch-and-win card. He loses.

APPA: You win?

RICH: Nah.

APPA: You choose bad one. Okay, see you.

RICH: Yeah, have a good one.

    RICH exits. Bell.

3. CALL POLICE

    JANET enters from the back of the store with her camera bag. She goes to the side closet for her jacket and fills up on candy throughout the scene.

APPA: Janet.

JANET: Bye Appa.

APPA: Call police.

JANET: (*startled*) What happened?

APPA: Car is no-parking zone. (*offers her the cordless phone*) Call police.

JANET: I gotta go.

APPA: (*slowly dialing*) Nine ... one –

JANET: Stop being so nosy.

APPA: YOU nosy! Talk to police.

JANET: I'm not talking to the police.

APPA: I'm push last one.

JANET: I don't care if you push last one. I'm not talking to the police.

APPA: I don't care if you don't care, I'm push last one.

JANET: Mind your own business, Appa.

APPA: This is my business. Talk to police.

JANET: What, it's a Toyota?

APPA: No.

JANET: Mitsubishi?

APPA: No. (beat) Okay, it's Honda, but still –

JANET: How many times do I have to tell you, Appa, Japanese people aren't the only ones driving Japanese cars.

APPA: You buy Japanese, you is guilty by associationship.

JANET: What about your Canon SLR camera, made in Japan?

APPA: Appa get half-price.

JANET: Your money still went to Japan.

APPA: Half-price, I rip off Japan.

JANET: Still Japanese.

APPA: I scratch name. Nobody can tell. Talk to police.

JANET: What about Mr. Shin? He's a salesman for Honda.

APPA: Mr. Shin is Mr. Shit.

JANET: I thought you guys were best friends?

APPA: No, he is pimping the Jesus now.

JANET: What?

APPA: He is pimping the Jesus.

JANET: He's doing what to Jesus?

APPA: Pimping.

JANET: Peemping?

APPA: Not peemping, pimping.

JANET: Pimping.

APPA: Yah. He is using church to selling Honda. Different church every Sunday, selling Honda. That's pimping the Jesus.

JANET: How'd you learn about a word like "pimping"?

APPA: Janet, I am cool, what you talking?

JANET: Okay, what about Mr. Park? He sets up cheap sushi restaurants in the Annex. He's promoting Japanese cuisine. He's guilty by asso-ciationship, and since you're his best friend, so are you.

APPA: No.

JANET: Yes.

APPA: No.

JANET: Yes.

APPA: No. That's different. He is pimping Japan. Pimping Japan is okay. He is make money selling Japan food, but he is Korean. White people can't tell difference. Kind of look same. Korean Grill House, run by Chinese. Chinese pimping Korea. That's no good. Appa boycott. Talk to police.

JANET: Talk to them yourself.

APPA: Police hear accent, they don't take serious.

JANET: Appa –

APPA: Janet! 1904 Japan attack Korea –

Bell. **MR. LEE**, a successful real estate agent, enters.

JANET: Okay, fine! I'll call the police.

APPA: 그래! 아이씨 참! [That's right!]

JANET takes out her cellphone.

4. THE OFFER

LEE: Mr. Kim.

APPA: Oh, Mr. Lee! My black friend with Korean last name!

LEE: Hi, Janet.

JANET: Hey, Mr. Lee.

JANET exits. Bell.

APPA: Long time now see.

LEE: Yeah, it's been a while.

APPA: Wah, look at you, nice jacket, pants. Turn around. Turn around. (LEE does a flashy Michael Jackson turn.) Wah, looks very good.

LEE: You like this? I can get you one.

APPA: Oh no, no thank you. Not my style. How's Mommy, Daddy?

LEE: They're doing very well, thank you.

APPA: And how's you business?

LEE: Business is good. Business is very good. (*beat; gazes out the window*) Lotta condos going up in the area, eh, Mr. Kim?

APPA: Yah, very fast. They is working hard.

LEE: Did you hear about Walmart?

APPA: Walmart? What's Walmart?

LEE: Apparently once those condos are up and ready, Walmart's moving in.

APPA: Why Walmart wants to moving to Regent Park?

LEE: 'Cuz once those condos are up and ready, Regent Park isn't gonna be Regent Park anymore. (*hands APPA his card*) Here.

APPA: I already have you card.

LEE: This is a new one. Flip it over.

APPA: What flip?

LEE: The card. Flip the card over, Mr. Kim.

APPA turns the card upside down.

LEE: That's not a flip, that's a turn.

APPA: Oh, flip, okay.

APPA flips the card over twice.

LEE: You're back on the same – just – I'm serious, Mr. Kim!

LEE grabs APPA's hands, showing him the back of the card.

There. See?

APPA: No, I can't see. Light is no good here. (*going back behind the counter*) What is?

LEE: That's my offer for your store, Mr. Kim.

APPA: Offer?

LEE: Mr. Kim, I want to purchase your store.

APPA: You want to buy my store?

LEE: Yes, I want to buy your store for that amount.

APPA: Oh, Mr. Lee, this is lots of money.

LEE: I wouldn't dare insult you with anything less.

Beat.

APPA: This is very generous, Mr. Lee, but, no. This community need me. Even if Walmart moving in, people in neighbourhood need this store.

LEE: I understand that, Mr. Kim, but once Walmart moves in, I'm sorry to say, but that's it. No one can compete with that kinda buying power. Dufferin Mall, Jane and St. Clair –

APPA: Mr. Lee, my answer is no! Thank you.

APPA offers the card. LEE takes the card and resolves to leave.

LEE: Mr. Kim, do you have an exit plan?

APPA: Exit plan?

LEE: What's your exit plan, Mr. Kim? What's your exit plan from this life? You plan on working at the store till you die? That's not a good exit plan. You've had a rough life, especially with your son. Don't think for a minute that I don't remember the kind of trouble Jung put you through. Now if Jung were here, he'd take over the store. But he's not here and he's not coming back. (*offering his card*) This is your only opportunity to enjoy life a little, Mr. Kim, before there's only a little life left to enjoy.

APPA doesn't take the card. LEE puts it on the counter.

LEE: Well, think it over. Give me a call tonight. I gotta go. I'm parked in a no-parking zone.

Bell. JANET enters.

JANET: Appa, did you see my Day-Timer?

APPA: Mr. Lee!

JANET puts her bags on the counter and rushes into the side closet.

APPA: White Honda is you car?

LEE: Yeah. Mr. Shin gave me an offer I couldn't refuse. Give me a call.

Bell. LEE exits. APPA takes out a printing calculator and adds up some figures. He tears off the receipt and looks at it close up. It's impressive. He puts LEE's card on the cash register and begins making a list of things to pick up at the wholesaler.

5. I AM SERIOUS

JANET is in the side closet looking for her Day-Timer.

APPA: Janet?

JANET: What?

APPA: Did you call police?

JANET: Yeah.

APPA: Good. Now, call police again and cancel order.

JANET: What?

APPA: Cancel order, we don't need.

JANET: Forget it. You cancel the order.

APPA: I am serious, Janet.

JANET: Seriously?

APPA: Yah, seriously.

JANET: No kidding?

APPA: No kidding.

JANET: You serious?

APPA: Yah, I am serious.

JANET: No foolin'?

APPA: Who is fooling?

JANET: You.

APPA: No. What you talking?

JANET: (appearing) I'm talking serious.

APPA: Me too.

JANET: You don't look serious.

APPA: My face is serious.

JANET: That's your serious face?

APPA: This is my serious face!

JANET: Seriously?

APPA: Seriously!!

UMMA enters with her jacket on, carrying her purse and a covered tray of food.

UMMA: (to APPA) 그만해 아이씨참!! [Will you two quit it!!]

JANET, with a mischievous smile, exits to the back of the store.

APPA restocks the gum shelf as UMMA puts the tray of food behind the counter.

6. I'M GOING

UMMA: 내가 이따가 와서 치울께요. [Just leave it, I'll clean it up when I get back.]

APPA: 주일날 최집사님이 저녁 같이 하자네. 시간돼? [This Sunday Mr. Chae wants to get together for dinner. How's your schedule?]

UMMA: (picking up LEE's card) 이게뭐에요? [What's this?]

APPA: 어 ... 그거 ... 그러니까 그게 ... Mr. Lee 가 오퍼 넌거야 ... 우리가게. [Oh ... that's, uh ... Mr. Lee's offer ... for the store.]

UMMA: 오퍼요? 가게 판다는 얘기 안했잖아요. [I didn't know you were selling the store.]

APPA: 팔려고 하는게 아니라 ... Mr. Lee 방금 오퍼를 상의 도 없이 주고 갔데니까. [I wasn't ... Mr. Lee just made an offer. Just now.]

UMMA: 가격은 꽤 괜찮네. [It's a generous offer.]

APPA: 그러게 ... [I know ...]

UMMA: 은퇴할 수 있겠네. [You could retire.]

APPA: 그러게. [I know.]

UMMA: (beat; gets herself together) Janet, I'm going. Janet, I'm going to church. Janet? Janet!

JANET: (appearing) What?!

UMMA: 엄마 갔다올께. [I'm going to church.]

JANET: Then 가 [go] already.

UMMA: (under her breath as she leaves) 아휴, 이 기집애 때매 내가 죽겠다, 죽겠어. [Ugh, I swear, she's gonna be the death of me, the death of me.]

UMMA exits. Bell.

7. WHAT'S YOUR PLAN?

APPA resumes pricing the cans. JANET is organizing her camera lenses and lens-cleaning materials at the counter.

APPA: Janet.

JANET: What, Appa, she drives me crazy!

APPA: Do you have exit plan?

JANET: What?

APPA: Do you have exit plan?

JANET: Do I have a what?

APPA stops pricing.

APPA: Exit plan. You having?

JANET: An exit plan? For what?

APPA: No, like what's you life plan?

JANET: What are you talking about?

APPA: You is thirty years old now. Have to think what is plan you future. What you think, take over store?

JANET: I don't want to work at the store.

APPA: What's wrong with store?

JANET: How can I work at the store, Appa? I'm busy.

APPA: Not work at store. I am talking take over store. Make Kim's Convenience dynasty.

JANET: Take over the store?

APPA: Yah.

JANET: Don't you want me to succeed in life? Look, Appa, you did what you had to do, right? And I appreciate that. I do. But didn't you do what you had to do so I wouldn't have to do what I had to do but could choose what I wanted to do?

APPA: What?

JANET: I'm a photographer, Appa. This is what I've chosen to do.

APPA: Yah, you can do weekend. Hobby, like me. But you don't make money take picture. Store make money. Take over store: money. Picture: hobby. It's good deal for you.

JANET: I don't want to take over the store. I don't even know how to run the store.

JANET goes back into the closet.

8. JAMAICAN

Bell. MIKE enters. He speaks with a thick Jamaican accent.

MIKE: Hey, man, wa gwan? D'ya have a tub o' Vaseline fa me? A tub o' Vaseline?

Beat.

APPA: What?

MIKE: D'ya have a tub o' Vaseline?

APPA: Seen? Sorry, I don't – I can't catch fast what you talking.

Beat.

MIKE: What?

APPA: I can't catch hearing you speak mouth too fast.

MIKE: What ya talking about?

APPA: No, uh, what you talking?

MIKE: About what?

APPA: What?

MIKE: What what?

APPA: No, you ask me –

MIKE: Y'aks me what I talking, what ya referring to?

APPA: Why you talking like you want to fight me?

MIKE: Me not speaking like me want to fight ya. Me not want to fight. Me just need a tub o' Vaseline, see, and dis how me speak, take it or leave it.

APPA: Okay, I take.

MIKE: Ladda mercy, me look for it me damn self. Cha! (*as he walks down an aisle*) Chinaman wan run business in Canada and him can't even speak da language proply.

9. STEAL OR NO STEAL

JANET appears and APPA ushers her behind the counter at the window.

APPA: Janet, Janet, you see?

JANET: See what?

APPA: That guy.

JANET: Which guy?

APPA: Not front of store, back of store. See? Don't look! See, but don't look.

JANET: The black guy?

APPA: Janet, don't be racist.

JANET: What?

APPA: You see?

JANET: Yeah, I saw the guy. So?

APPA: He is steal.

JANET: What?

APPA: He is steal.

JANET: You saw him take something?

APPA: No, he is going to steal.

JANET: How can you tell?

APPA: He is black guy, jean jacket. That combo is steal combo. You don't know how to run store, I teach you. This is training day. Lesson number one, steal or no steal. Every customer, have to know. Steal or no steal. (*beat; pointing to a girl outside*) See that girl? She is no steal. She is black girl, fat. Fat black girl is no steal. (*pointing to a guy outside*) Fat white guy, that's steal. Fat guy is black, brown shoes, that's no steal. That's cancel-out combo.

JANET: That is so awkwardly racist.

APPA: Not racist ... survival skill. Look. Secret survival skill. (*closes his eyes and looks around*) Make eyes very small. Then nobody know you even looking. (*reopens his eyes*) Okay, brown guy, that's steal. Brown girl, that's no steal. Asian guy, that's no steal. Asian girl, that's steal. If you is the gay, that's no steal. Easy. The gay is never steal. If you is the lesbian – that is girl who is the gay – that's steal, 100 per cent guarantee they is steal. But two lesbian, that's no steal, cancel-out combo.

JANET: What about a black lesbian with long straight hair and a fat Asian gay man with short hair together? Steal or no steal?

APPA: That's impossible.

JANET: What's impossible?

APPA: The gay, Asian, fat?

JANET: Appa, there are Asians who are gay, y'know?

APPA: I know, but the gay Asian is never fat. Only skinny Asian is the gay. That's rule. Shhh.

10. HAPKIDO

MIKE: Me find it in da back.

MIKE comes to the counter with a tub of Vaseline.

APPA: Oh, Vaseline. You using for feet? I using for feet. My heel get hard and cracking. Vaseline make smooth.

MIKE: Right.

APPA: (*tallies up the total on the cash register*) $4.65.

MIKE gives APPA a twenty.

APPA: Thank you. Okay, I give to you change.

APPA closes the cash register and comes around to the other side of the counter, standing between MIKE and the door.

MIKE: Wa gwan?

APPA: I have you change here my hand. I give to you change, you give to me what you steal.

JANET: Appa!

MIKE: What?!

APPA: Give to me what you steal, I give to you change.

JANET: Appa!

MIKE: 'Cuz me black, y'accusing me of teefin'?

JANET: No! I'm sorry, sir –

APPA: (*to JANET*) Janet, stay back. (*to MIKE*) No, I'm not accuse you. I'm tell you, you is steal.

JANET: (*coming forward*) Appa, stop it! (*to MIKE*) Sorry, he's got a weird sense of –

APPA: Janet! (*JANET moves.*) Give to me what you steal from back of store and I give to you change.

MIKE: Excuse me, but –

APPA: No, I don't excuse you. You have no excuse. You living in Canada, you is healthy, you is smart, you is good boy, you have no excuse to steal.

MIKE: Ya making big mistake –

JANET picks up the phone.

APPA: No, you making big mistake. I know hapkido. You know hapkido? It's Korean fighting style. That's big mistake for you. Now, you want something, you pay. You can pay cash or you can pay I kick you ass.

MIKE attempts to run. APPA grabs his arm, twisting it, sending MIKE to the floor in a submission hold.

MIKE: AH!

APPA: Empty pocket. Empty pocket!

APPA applies pressure to MIKE's arm.

MIKE: AH!

MIKE takes a pack of razors out of his pocket.

Please don't hand me over.

APPA: You didn't pay for this.

MIKE: Please, me sorry. (*APPA applies pressure to MIKE's arm.*) AH! Please don't hand me over.

MIKE takes a pack of toothpaste out of his pocket.

APPA: You didn't pay for that.

MIKE: Please.

APPA: "I am steal from you store, Mr. Kim." Repeat. "I am steal from you store, Mr. Kim. Please forgive me." Repeat!

MIKE: I am steal from ya store, Mr. Kim. Please fahgive me.

APPA: "Dear Jesus."

MIKE: What? (*APPA applies pressure to his arm.*) AH!

APPA: Repeat. "Dear Jesus."

MIKE: Dear Jesus.

APPA: "Please forgive me I am steal from Mr. Kim."

MIKE: Please fahgive me I am steal from Mr. Kim.

APPA: "Help me be good example to black kid."

MIKE: Help me be a good example to the black kids them.

APPA: "I accept you in my heart."

MIKE: What? (*APPA applies pressure to his arm.*) AH!

APPA: Repeat!

MIKE: I accept ya in a me heart.

APPA: "Amen."

MIKE: Amen.

APPA: Walk out slow. And if I ever see you, I shit kick you fuck ass, you understand?

MIKE: Ya, man.

APPA lets go. MIKE makes to leave.

APPA: (*getting his attention*) Ya.

MIKE turns around. APPA tosses him the tub of Vaseline. MIKE catches it.

MIKE: Thank you, Mr. Kim.

MIKE walks out. Bell.

APPA: You not welcome.

11. YOU STUPID

APPA: See, I tell you he is steal. (*picks up the stolen items, putting them on the counter*) That is lesson number one. Steal or no steal. Have to know. Okay, lesson number two –

JANET: That was the most idiotic, insanely stupid thing I've ever seen you do, and you've done a lot of stupid things, Appa.

APPA: YOU stupid.

JANET: Appa!

APPA: He is stupid too.

JANET: Of course he's stupid! Why else would he be stealing unless he's stupid!

APPA: David Chen, Lucky Moose in Chinatown, do same thing. He is hero. I am hero.

JANET: Kenny Kim, Queen and Sherbourne, did the same thing and it cost him his life.

APPA: Kenny Kim is die because cigarette company and government is so greedy. They make cigarette so expensive, people can't afford and have to steal. Then convenience store owner is victim. That's why Kenny Kim is die. Don't get mix up, Janet.

JANET: Appa, that guy could've had a gun.

APPA: I know hapkido.

JANET: (*picking up the stolen items and placing them behind the counter*) Is it worth it? Is it really worth it? Grow up, Appa!

APPA: YOU grow up.

JANET: Did you even think about –

APPA: YOU think.

JANET: What?

APPA: YOU what.

JANET: Stop doing that!

APPA: YOU stop.

JANET: I'm not doing anything.

APPA: YOU doing.

JANET: I'm just talking.

APPA: YOU talking.

JANET: Appa, that doesn't even make any –

APPA: YOU doesn't.

JANET: You're just repeating –

APPA: YOU.

JANET: All right!

APPA: YOU all right.

JANET: Fine.

APPA: YOU fine.

JANET: Forget it.

APPA: YOU forget.

Beat.

JANET: Turn.

APPA: YOU turn.

JANET: Niverse.

APPA: YOU niverse.

JANET: Tube.

APPA: YOU tube.

JANET: Calyptus!

Bell. Police officer ALEX enters.

APPA: YOU calyptus!

JANET: Thanasia!

APPA: YOU thanasia!!

JANET: Kulele!!!

APPA: YOU kulele!!!!!

12. POLICE

ALEX: Excuse me, sir, did someone here call 9-1-1?

APPA: Yah.

ALEX: Who called 9-1-1?

APPA: I do.

ALEX: Is there an emergency? Sir!

APPA: Yah, used be emergency. You take so long time not emergency now.

ALEX: What was the emergency, sir?

APPA: White Honda is parking no-parking zone. Then drive off. You take too long.

ALEX: Sir, 9-1-1 is reserved for emergency situations. Please don't abuse it with trivial matters like illegally parked cars. There are severe consequences –

APPA: Actual, I don't call 9-1-1, Janet is.

JANET: Appa!

ALEX: Is this true, miss?

JANET: Well, yes, officer, technically –

ALEX: Janet?

JANET: Yes?

ALEX: Planet Janet?

JANET: Alex?

ALEX: Look at you.

JANET: Oh my God, you're a cop.

ALEX: And you're ... all grown up.

Beat.

APPA: What's happen?

JANET: Appa, this is Alex. He ... he was a friend of Jung.

ALEX: Hi, Mr. Kim.

APPA: Oh, yah, I remember you, yah. Hi, Alex. (*beat*) You is now police?

ALEX: Yeah.

APPA: Real police?

ALEX: What can I say, Mr. Kim. People change. (*shows APPA his badge*)

APPA clears his throat and gestures for the badge. ALEX gives it to APPA. APPA checks to see if it's real and then returns it.

APPA: You daddy must be very proud of you.

ALEX: Yeah, he was. He passed away two years ago, but he was very proud.

APPA: I'm sorry.

ALEX: That's okay.

APPA: How's you mommy?

ALEX: She's good, very busy at church, as usual. Wow, can't believe you guys are still here. Is Jung here?

Beat.

APPA: Alex, you want something drink? Janet, take to back, give him something drink.

ALEX: No, it's okay.

APPA: Not okay.

ALEX: No, I'm fine.

APPA: Not fine.

ALEX: Please –

APPA: Please take something.

ALEX: No, it's really okay, Mr. Kim –

APPA: Not really okay, Alex.

ALEX: Mr. Kim –

APPA: Alex! You in my store, you is my business! (*giving him an insam drink*) Take drink, give to you energy. Janet, take to back, give him snack. Police is hungry job, need energy.

JANET and ALEX go to the back of the store.

APPA: Peanuts. Take peanuts. Peanuts is good snack. Janet, give to him peanuts. Salty peanuts. Honey-roasted peanuts. Chocolate-cover peanuts, that's good taste. (*JANET and ALEX are chuckling.*) It's true.

JANET: Okay, Planters cocktail peanuts. How about a Clif Bar?

APPA: Yah, okay.

JANET: You like Crispers?

APPA: Good.

JANET: Gotta be ranch. Oh, and Pringles, pizza-flavoured. Definitely a couple of Combos Cheddar Cheese Pretzels. That's for sure.

APPA: Okay, that's good enough.

JANET: Peek Freans Shortcake. Gatorade Cool Blue.

APPA: Okay, that's last one.

JANET: Hubba Bubba Strawberry –

APPA: Janet!

JANET comes to the front. ALEX has his arms full of stuff.

JANET: What?

APPA: What you doing? He is back to working time is now.

JANET gets ALEX a plastic bag for the snacks.

ALEX: He's right, I gotta go, Janet. This is more than enough. Hey, could I get Jung's number? I'd really like to hook up with him.

APPA: What? Oh sorry, no, we don't having that kind.

Okay, bye, Alex.

ALEX: Yeah. Okay. Bye, Mr. Kim. It was really good seeing you, Janet.

JANET: Yeah, same here.

ALEX: Yeah, me too.

JANET: Yeah.

Beat.

APPA: Okay, bye, Alex, see you.

ALEX exits. Bell. JANET watches ALEX exit.

APPA: (*checking his watch*) Okay, Janet, I have to take big *ddong* now. We continue training after. Watch store.

APPA takes the cordless phone and exits to the back. JANET resumes looking for her Day-Timer behind the counter.

13. WHERE'S YOUR BROTHER?

Bell. ALEX enters the store.

ALEX: Hi.

JANET: Hi. Did you forget something?

ALEX: No.

JANET: You need more peanuts?

ALEX: (*chuckles*) Wow. No, I have enough. I just wanted to leave my number for Jung. What? What is it?

Beat.

JANET: Guess you guys haven't kept in touch, eh? (*beat*) He left ... a long time ago.

ALEX: He left?

JANET: Yeah. He left home when he was sixteen.

ALEX: Didn't know that.

JANET: You remember Jung's temper? My dad was the same. Even worse.

ALEX: What happened?

JANET: Uh, well, during one of their arguments, Jung said that Appa was a horrible husband, that he was treating my mom like a slave. And Appa hit him. Hard. Jung was hospitalized for a few days. After he was released, everything seemed to be back to normal. Then, one day, my dad went to get the money from the safe and it was empty. So was Jung's room.

ALEX: Wow.

JANET: Once in a while, I catch my dad looking out the window. Most of the time he's looking for

illegally parked Japanese cars, but sometimes I think he's looking for Jung.

ALEX: Where is he now?

JANET: I don't know. Heard he was in rehab for a while. He meets my mom at church sometimes.

Beat.

ALEX: Sorry to hear that.

JANET: That's okay.

Beat.

ALEX: That your camera bag?

JANET: Yup.

Beat.

ALEX: Are you a photographer?

JANET: Yup.

ALEX: How'd you become a photographer?

JANET: OCAD [Ontario College of Art and Design]. How'd you become a cop?

ALEX: Cop school. (*JANET chuckles.*) No, my life changed a lot after I moved out of this neighbourhood. I forgot how much you used to follow us around.

JANET: Can I take your picture?

ALEX: Uh, sure, okay.

JANET gets her camera. ALEX does a "hot cops" pose. JANET chuckles.

ALEX: Just playin'.

JANET: What did you have for breakfast?

ALEX: For breakfast?

JANET: Yeah.

ALEX: Cereal, some fruit, coffee.

JANET begins shooting.

JANET: What kind of cereal did you have?

ALEX: Mini-Wheats.

JANET: Have you always had Mini-Wheats?

ALEX: No, used to be Frosted Flakes – when I was a kid. My dad liked Frosted Flakes. We'd eat it together. We had this routine, this tiger thing we'd do. "They're gr-r-reat!" Yeah, Frosted Flakes.

JANET: What about Cheerios?

ALEX: Nah.

JANET: What's wrong with Cheerios?

ALEX: For me, it had to do with what the cereal did to the milk. That bowlful of sweetened milk right at the end was what breakfast was all about.

JANET: Like the chocolate tip at the bottom of an ice cream Drumstick?

ALEX: Exactly.

Beat.

JANET: Wanna see?

ALEX: Sure. (*JANET shows ALEX his picture on the LCD screen.*) Wow. I look so ... artsy. (*JANET giggles.*) What?

JANET: I was actually on my way to check out a site for a wedding I got tomorrow –

ALEX: When I came in?

JANET: When you came in.

ALEX: Where you shooting?

JANET: The Distillery. Where you shooting? That was a joke.

ALEX: Need a lift?

JANET: I gotta cover for my dad.

ALEX: Till when?

JANET: Another ten minutes? (*beat*) You married?

ALEX: Yeah, no – used to be. Divorced. You married?

JANET: No. Any kids?

ALEX: No. You?

JANET: No. But I want kids. Like, if I met the right guy and got married to him, then yeah, of course, no question, absolutely.

JANET ducks down behind the counter.

ALEX: What kind of guy you looking for, maybe I can keep an eye out for you. (*beat*) Did you eat lunch?

JANET: No. You?

JANET rises with her hair undone, all sexy-like, and proceeds to move in front of the counter.

ALEX: No.

JANET: We could eat.

ALEX: We could. What do you want to eat?

JANET: I don't know. What do you want to eat?

ALEX: Anything's good.

JANET: Yeah, anything's good for me too.

ALEX: I'm not feeling anything in particular.

JANET: Me neither.

ALEX: Could do just about anything.

JANET: Yup, me too.

ALEX: You allergic to anything?

JANET: Melons.

ALEX: Melons? Really?

JANET: Yeah. Kinda developed it.

ALEX: Didn't know you could develop melons – allergies.

JANET: I used to not be allergic to melons, now I am.

ALEX: That's too bad. I love melons.

Beat.

JANET: Korean or Indian?

ALEX: Who?

JANET: Food. You. Choose. Korean or Indian?

ALEX: Korean.

JANET: Now it's your turn. Offer me a choice.

ALEX: Oh okay, uh ... Christie and Bloor ... or Yonge and Finch?

JANET: Christie and Bloor. Rice or noodles?

ALEX: Rice. Meat or vegetarian?

JANET: Meat. Pork or beef?

ALEX: Pork. Hot and spicy or extremely hot and spicy?

JANET: Extremely hot and spicy. In a stone bowl or in a stainless steel bowl?

ALEX: Stone bowl. Gamjatang or pork mandu soondubu?

JANET: Gamjatang. KaChi or Booungee?

ALEX: Han Kuk Kwan.

14. TAKE OVER THE STORE

APPA: (*offstage, returning from the back of the store, talking on the phone*) No, it's Christie –

ALEX: I'll pick you up in ten minutes.

ALEX exits. Bell. JANET returns behind the counter and begins to put on some makeup.

APPA: – then Bathurst, then Spadina, St. George, Bay, Yonge, Sherbourne, then is Castle Frank. Yah, 100 per cent guarantee. Yah, okay. (*hangs up the phone*) 아이씨 바보. [Idiot.]

APPA pulls out JANET's Day-Timer and reads from it.

Okay, Janet, lesson number two: "Old is cold, new out of view." Old can is cold can, put in front. New can is not cold can, put out of view. "Old is cold, new out of view."

JANET: Appa, where'd you find that?

APPA: Upstair washroom.

JANET: I've been looking for that. Give it to me.

APPA: Wait, lesson number three is –

JANET: Appa, I gotta go.

APPA: Wait, we have to finish training, I make list –

JANET: Appa, I'm not taking over the store.

APPA: Janet, you is thirty years old now and still single. You have to understand, now is desperation time for you. Sudden death, overtime, penalty kick shootout. Expiration date is over. Take over store is only choice you having.

JANET: I can't believe –

APPA: Me and Umma is struggle whole life make life for you. We do what we have to do, hope you can be doctor, lawyer, big success, but what you do? Take picture. We don't have to come to Canada for you take picture. Even you can take picture in North Korea.

JANET: Appa –

APPA: Janet, I am dying … one day in future and before I dying, I –

JANET: You want to retire.

APPA: What is my story? Hmm? What is story of me, Mr. Kim? My whole life is this store. Everybody know this store, they know me. This store is my story. And if I just sell store, then my story is over. Who is Mr. Kim? Nobody know that. You take over store, my story keep going.

JANET: But Appa, that's life. Whether you choose it or get thrown into it, you make it what it is. And if you're not happy with your life, I'm sorry, but you can't expect me to make your life – I don't know – meaningful.

APPA: But I give my life, my story for you.

JANET: But you're the parent. You're supposed to.

APPA: Why is that supposed to? I don't have to give to you my life. I could throw you away as baby. I don't have to love you as baby, but I do. That is choosing. I choose like that. So, you have to be thank you and give to me you life. Second half. Fifty-fifty. That's fair. Yah, lookit, I am work at store, what you do, you don't work at store and

still you eat, sleep upstair, yah? You whole life, that's how we doing. Thirty years. So, just switch side now, like soccer. Second half, you work at store and I don't work at store and still I eat, sleep upstair. Understand? (*beat*) I'm not live more than ten years, it's good deal for you.

JANET: That's a messed-up idea, Appa.

APPA: What you talking?

JANET: That's a seriously messed-up idea.

APPA: YOU seriously messed up –

JANET: No, Appa, that's –

APPA: YOU no.

JANET: No, Appa, really –

APPA: YOU really.

JANET: Stop doing that!

APPA: YOU stop.

JANET: Give me my Day-Timer, Appa!

APPA: Take out garbage and I give to you.

JANET ties the garbage bag to take it out.

APPA: What you doing? (*He unties what JANET has done and ties it his way.*) Have to roll like this. Push out air. Make tight. Small package. Then tie round back. That's best way.

APPA offers it to JANET. JANET takes it and unties what APPA has done and reties it.

JANET: That's your way. And if it matters that much to you, then do it yourself.

APPA: Janet, that's you job.

JANET: My job? I haven't taken out the garbage in sixteen years. All of a sudden it's my job again? Fine. But it wasn't even my job back then, 'cuz if it were my job, then I would've gotten paid. So, what in fact I did back then and am doing right now is a favour for you. I wish you would at least appreciate this favour I'm doing for you, Appa.

JANET leaves with the garbage bag. Bell.

APPA: You pay rent? You pay for food? (*following JANET*) What you talking? Take picture. Take picture! What's that?! Waste!!!

JANET returns with the garbage bag. Bell.

JANET: For my whole life I've worked at least four hours a day covering for you guys, and I've never asked you for anything in return. I've never complained about it and never bitched about not getting paid. I've been here for you for my whole life, Appa. When Jung left, I was here. When Umma was sick, I was here. What would be nice is a simple thank-you. A little appreciation, that's all I need. To hear you say "thank you." Just once.

APPA remains silent. JANET drops the garbage bag.

JANET: Okay, fine. (*She goes behind the counter, takes out the printing calculator, and punches in the numbers.*) Four hours a day, six days a week, fifty-two weeks a year, for the past twenty years, eight dollars an hour – subtract room and board … You owe me a grand total of $102,720! Give me my money, Appa!

Beat.

APPA: Piano lesson. Piano lesson. $20 every lesson. Once a week. Every week. Five years. I pay.

JANET tallies it up.

APPA: Golf lesson. $500. I invest in you.

JANET tallies it up.

APPA: Summer art camp. Material fee. $200. Every year.

JANET tallies it up.

APPA: Winter church camp. $100. Blue Mountain ski pass –

JANET: Wait.

APPA: Blue Mountain ski pass. $50. Grade 8 semi-formal dress –

JANET: Wait.

APPA: Prom dress –

JANET: Wait!

APPA: Diet program. Dating program. Orthodontist. (*JANET stops tallying the numbers.*) Computer. Camera. Hand phone. Tuition fee. Trip to Korea. TTC Metropass. Weight-losing program. Internet. Shoes. Clothes. Haircut. Everything you have, Appa give to you. All Appa having, Appa invest to you and what you doing? Waste time. Waste money. Waste hope. What I still owe to you? Tell to me, Janet. I give to you my whole life, what fucking I still owe to you?!

Beat.

JANET: My Day-Timer.

APPA hurls the Day-Timer at the front door.

APPA: Ahhhhhh!

JANET slowly gets the Day-Timer and walks out. Bell.

Beat.

Bell. UMMA returns.

UMMA: 아이고, 내 정신 좀 봐. 맨날 이래, 맨날. [Oh my goodness, look at me, always forgetting things, always.]

UMMA takes an envelope from underneath the tray in the cash register. Beat.

왜 그래요? 뭔일 있어요? [What's wrong? What is it?]

APPA: 아니야. [Never mind.]

UMMA: 여보? 여보? [Honey? Honey?]

APPA exits to the back.

15. HI JUNG

UMMA sees the garbage bag and puts it in the closet. UMMA begins to sing as she gets her things together to leave.

UMMA:

천사의 말을 하는 사람도
사랑 없으면 소용이 없고

[If I speak in the language of heaven,
but speak it without love, it means nothing.]

JUNG enters wearing a knapsack. He sings in harmony with UMMA.

UMMA & JUNG:

심오한 진리 깨달은 자도
울리는 징과 같네

[If I understand all mysteries,
but understand them without love,
it means nothing.]

하나님 말씀 전한다 해도
그 무슨 소용있나
사랑 없으면 소용이 없고
아무것도 아닙니다

[What meaning is there even in sharing
the message of God
if it is shared without love?
Anything, without love,
amounts to nothing.]

[*Based on 1 Corinthians 13:1–2*]

UMMA's church sanctuary at night.

UMMA: You remember church family singing contest? You was eight years old. Janet was six. We is stand up here in church. You, me, Appa, Janet, all together, hold hands. We win first place. That is my most happy memory.

JUNG: What about the time when I was born, Umma?

UMMA: That is my most painful memory. You work today?

JUNG: Yeah. What's with all the decorations?

UMMA: This Sunday is last day. Last day for our church.

JUNG: The condo thing? They bought it?

UMMA: Yah.

JUNG: 3.2?

UMMA: $3.9 million.

JUNG: Wow. Now you guys can move to North York. Buy a church with a parking lot.

UMMA: Our church is not moving.

JUNG: What, you guys gonna be at the bottom of the condo?

UMMA: They is closing our church.

JUNG: Who? The condo company?

UMMA: Church head office think waste of money to build new church. Not enough people. So, they closing our church and using money for mission work in North Korea. Bible say time to start, time to finish. Now is time to finish. When *Moksanim* [pastor] first start church, only six Korean church in Toronto. All downtown, small, no money. Now, over two hundred Korean church, all move out of downtown, big building, lots of money. We is last Korean downtown church.

> *Beat.*

JUNG: Here, I got something for you.

> *JUNG gives UMMA a photo.*

UMMA: Wah! Sonam. He is get so big. Two months?

JUNG: Yeah.

UMMA: Looks like six months old.

JUNG: Yeah, people say he's really big for his age.

UMMA: Looks just like Janet when she was baby.

> *UMMA offers the photo back.*

JUNG: Keep it. It's yours.

UMMA: Appa should know he is *halabujee* [grandfather] now.

JUNG: How's Janet doing?

UMMA: She is still single, ready to mingle.

JUNG: Hey, Umma, you ever think Janet might be "the gay"?

UMMA: The gay? If Janet is lesbian, that's okay because then at least I know reason why she has no boyfriend. (*UMMA gives JUNG the envelope.*) For baby.

JUNG: Thanks, Umma.

> *JUNG kisses UMMA on the cheek.*

UMMA: What's wrong, Jung?

JUNG: I'm not happy.

UMMA: Can't always be happy, Jung.

JUNG: I don't like my life, Umma. I was at work today – do you know what Facebook is, Umma?

UMMA: Facebook?

JUNG: It's a website on the Internet. It's kinda like email, but it connects more people. And friends can find other friends and there's lots of photos – you remember Mike from church, long time ago, he was on the soccer team?

UMMA: 깍두기 아줌마 아들? [The son of that woman who makes that radish kimchee?]

JUNG: Yeah, right. He found me on Facebook today and soon the whole crew found me, the old church soccer team. We're all chatting away, checking out photos, like a reunion. Suyoung put up an old picture of the team, and he starts writing this play-by-play. Centennial Park, Etobicoke. The Toronto Korean inter-church annual soccer tournament. Under-sixteen division. Game one, Haninjangno Church: (*explosion sound*) conquered. Game two, Dong Bu Church: (*explosion sound*) conquered. Game three, Bethel Church: tied. Quarter-finals, United Church: (*explosion sound*). Semi-finals, Young Nak Church: (*explosion sound*). Final championship game, the Catholic church: tied. Extra time: tied. Extra extra time: tied. Penalty kick shootout. (*UMMA joins in on making the explosion sound.*) So glorious, right? Mike lives in Richmond Hill. He drives a Beemer. 5-Series. He's got great-looking kids, a sexy cute wife, family vacations all around the world every year. I've seen all his photos. Jason, Rich, Tech, Tom, Henry, Mike, Jong, Young, Young Jong, Suyoung.

All of them. They're all successful. They start asking about me. What I do, where I been. I start making stuff up, trying desperately hard to sound impressive, but just sounding desperate. I was their captain.

I was their captain, Umma. I was smarter than all of them, faster, stronger. I didn't dream I'd end up renting cars to people. Nine to five. Checking for dents and scratches. Living in a shithole in Parkdale. Apartment's a constant mess. Fight all the time, his mom and me. She thinks I'm a loser – I don't even know why I'm with her anymore. And all he ever does is cry and cry and cry and cry and cry. Just wanna leave, y'know? Just go. Start over. Somewhere else. Calgary, Vancouver – doesn't matter where. It'd be so easy too. Bay and Dundas, hop on a bus and leave. I rent cars to people, then take the streetcar home. What is that? That's a joke.

Beat.

UMMA: You Appa was teacher in Korea. He was very good teacher. Student all love him. He have lots of friend. We have very good life in Korea. Then we coming to Canada. But he can't be teacher here. His English is very ... no good. We get store. And he work every day. No weekend, no time off, no vacation, always have to be open, no retirement. Why? Why he doing like that? For you. For you and Janet. He is choosing like that for you. (*offers the photo*) You choosing like that for him. (*JUNG takes the photo.*)

JUNG: How's Appa doing, anyway?

UMMA: Appa is getting old. You remember Mr. Lee?

JUNG: Black man with the Korean last name?

UMMA: Yah. He is make offer to buy store.

JUNG: Appa selling the store?

UMMA: No, Mr. Lee just make offer.

JUNG: How much?

UMMA: Enough to retire.

JUNG: What's Appa gonna do?

UMMA: I don't know. Go home, Jung. Go home.

JUNG exits.

16. NAMING

A memory of APPA and UMMA. Underscored.

APPA: What you think, Kim's Variety Store?

UMMA: Kim's Variety Store?

APPA: Yah. Kim's Variety Store. What you think?

UMMA: Mr. Kim has already.

APPA: Who Mr. Kim?

UMMA: Yonge and Finch Mr. Kim.

APPA: Mr. Kim, Yonge and Finch, has Kim's Variety Store? Then just Kim's Variety. Take out "store." What you think?

UMMA: Kim's Variety?

APPA: Yah.

UMMA: St. George Mr. Kim has already.

APPA: St. who?

UMMA: St. George.

APPA: Who is St. George?

UMMA: St. George is St. George.

APPA: St. George? Sound like St. Jajee.

UMMA: Not St. Jajee, St. George.

APPA: Kim Cheese. Like Mac's Milk, but Kim and cheese.

UMMA: We don't only sell cheese.

APPA: Mac's don't only sell milk. (*beat*) 7-Twelve. Like 7-Eleven but ... (*beat*) KFC. Kim's First Convenience. No, people think we is Kentucky Fries Chicken. Then we have to sell chicken, fries, and turkey. (*beat*) Kim Hortons.

UMMA: (*rubbing her belly*) What you think of name is Jung? (*pause*) If baby is boy, Jung Kim. What you think?

17. WHAT IS IT?

Store. Night.

APPA: 언제 왔어? [When did you get in?]

UMMA: 조금 전에요. 내가 해논거 다 먹었어요? [Just got here. Did you eat?]

APPA: 먹었어. 왜 그래? [Yeah. What is it?]

UMMA: 아니에요 ... Janet 은요? [Nothing ... Where's Janet?]

APPA: 나갔겠지. 주일날 최집사님이 저녁 같이 하자네. 듣고있어? 왜 그러냐까? [Out. Mr. Chae wants to have us over for dinner this Sunday. Did you hear me? What's wrong?]

UMMA: 아니에요. 당신이 알아서 해요. 저 먼저 올라가요. [Nothing. Yeah, it's fine. I'm going up.]

APPA: 뭐냐까? 여보? 여보? 여보? 아이씨 참! [What is it? Honey? Honey?]

UMMA takes the tray of food and exits to the back. APPA looks at Mr. Lee's offer and picks up the phone.

18. WHO YOU GO OUT WITH?

JANET enters. Bell.

JANET: Closing?

APPA: Soon.

JANET: Want some help?

APPA: It's okay.

JANET: How's business?

APPA: Same same. (*JANET begins to exit to the back.*) You go out?

JANET: Yeah.

APPA: Who you go out with?

JANET: Alex.

APPA: Alex? Black police Alex?

JANET: (*coming forward*) Yes.

APPA: You used to have crush on him. You have fun time?

JANET: Yeah.

Beat.

APPA: You remember Mr. Chae?

JANET: Ingoo's Appa?

APPA: Yah. He is having store in South Central L.A., California. Lots of black people is living there too. One day black lady is come and ask five-dollar loan. So, he give loan five dollar. Next week, she come and pay back. No interest. Then she ask loan ten dollar. And he give and she pay back. And continue. They have good friendship. She tell all her friend, and they come and ask loan too. He is help all of them. Then 1992. Rodney King L.A. riot happen. All Korean convenience store is on fire and black people stealing. So he take shotgun and go to store. When he gets out of car, he see fire and smoke, people screaming, running, crazy, and he look at store. He see all black people in front of store. So, he get gun, ready to shoot, then he stop. What he see is that black woman who he give to loan and all his black customer hold hand, make big wall, stop other people stealing his store.

Beat.

JANET: What are you trying to say, Appa?

APPA: Alex is not Korean, but if you want to marry him, that's okay with me.

JANET: We went out on one date. I don't even know if he had a good time.

19. LET'S TALK

Bell.

ALEX: Hi.

APPA: Alex.

ALEX: (*to JANET*) Can I talk to you?

APPA: Yah, okay, talk.

ALEX: Uh, I didn't –

APPA: No, it's okay.

ALEX: No, Mr. Kim, I didn't mean –

APPA: Alex, it's okay, take easy, nice and slow. We is here for you. Talk. (*beat*) We closing soon. Hurry up.

ALEX: Uh, okay. I have this, uh, friend, this girl, who's just a friend.

APPA: Okay.

ALEX: She recently met an old friend of hers, uh, this guy.

APPA: Okay.

ALEX: They used to know each other when they were kids. I mean, he was best friends with her brother and she'd always be around and he never thought much of her, growing up – see, the thing is, he was a bad kid.

APPA: Oh.

ALEX: And she knows all about the stuff he used to do, like really stupid stuff. Anyway, so they meet and they go out … on this date, I guess, and, well, it wasn't like an official date per se, but … uh … Sorry, this was a bad idea. (*He makes to leave.*)

APPA: Alex! Do you think she like him?

ALEX: Who?

APPA: You friend.

ALEX: Oh, uh, I don't know. I'm not sure.

APPA: Janet, do you think she like him?

JANET: Uh –

APPA: Okay, Alex, do you think he like her?

ALEX: Um, that's a good question, Mr. Kim. Well, uh, see, ever since his divorce … uh … see, the thing about it is, he went through this phase where –

APPA: Okay, that's enough! Alex, do you believing in the Jesus?

ALEX: What?

JANET sighs.

APPA: Do you believing in the Jesus?

ALEX: Yes, I believing in the Jesus.

APPA: You have job?

JANET: Appa –

ALEX: I'm a cop.

APPA: Do you think my Janet is the sexy?

JANET: Appa!

ALEX: What?

APPA: Do you think my Janet is the sexy?

JANET: Appa!

ALEX: Mr. Kim – AH!

APPA twists ALEX's hand, forcing ALEX to his knees, writhing in pain.

ALEX: – AH!

JANET: Appa! What the hell are you doing?

APPA: You want to know answer? Alex, do you think my Janet is the sexy? Yes or no?

ALEX: Yes!

APPA: (*lets him go*) Good. (*beat*) Then give to her popo.

JANET: Appa, stop it!

ALEX: What? You want me to give her a popo?

APPA: Yah.

ALEX: What's a popo? (*APPA kisses the air twice.*) You want me to kiss your daughter?

APPA: Yah.

ALEX: Now?

APPA: Yah.

ALEX: In front of you?

APPA: My store, my business.

ALEX slowly, awkwardly kisses JANET. Then she kisses him. Then he goes in for another kiss and APPA grabs his arm in such a way that ALEX is up on his toes, writhing in pain.

APPA: What's you problem, Alex?

ALEX: What? You told me to give her a popo.

APPA: Do I tell you popo two times?

ALEX: She popo me.

APPA: I know she popo you, I see she is popo you, I was here, I was supervise. But then you try popo her one more time after she popo you. Two popo, too many popo.

ALEX: Sorry.

APPA: (*lets him go*) Okay. Now, step two. Do step two.

Beat.

ALEX: You're gonna have to give me some clarification on what step two is, Mr. Kim.

APPA: 아이씨 참! [Good grief!] Step two is, ask Janet marry you.

ALEX & JANET: What?

APPA: Ask Janet marry you.

ALEX: Mr. Kim –

APPA twists ALEX's hand, forcing ALEX to his knees, writhing in pain.

ALEX: Ah!

JANET: Appa, just stop –

JANET tries to pull APPA's hand off ALEX. APPA then twists JANET's hand, forcing her to her knees, writhing in pain.

JANET: Ah!

APPA has both of them on either side of him, on their knees, writhing in pain.

APPA: Alex, do step two.

ALEX: Mr. Kim –

JANET: Appa –

APPA: Alex, do step two.

ALEX: Ah! Janet, will you marry me?

JANET: Ah! Appa, this is ridiculous!

APPA: Ask again!

ALEX: Janet, will you marry me?

APPA: Janet, say yes.

JANET: Stop! Ow!

APPA: Ask again!

ALEX: (*simultaneously*) Ah! Janet will you marry me?! Ahhhhh!

JANET: (*simultaneously*) Ah! Appa, you're ruining everything!

APPA: (*simultaneously*) Janet, say yes! This is last chance for you – AH! (*ALEX does a reversal and has APPA in a hold.*)

ALEX: I'm sorry, Mr. Kim. I'm sorry. I just need to talk – I came here to talk to your daughter.

APPA: Okay, hurry up, talk.

ALEX: Uh, okay. Um. Janet, I've always thought of you as a younger sister, following us around like a chubby little puppy dog. Wait, but when

I saw you today, like, now – you're so beautiful. You're smart, talented, you make me laugh – I don't understand why you're still single. The only way I can figure it is God must love me so much that he's kept you single for all these years to bless me with you.

JANET: I've had a crush on you since I was ten years old, Alex. Still do.

ALEX: Seriously?

JANET: Seriously.

ALEX: I'm off tomorrow, you wanna do something?

JANET: I got a wedding to shoot.

ALEX: Need a helper?

JANET: You wanna be my assistant?

ALEX: I do.

JANET: Pick me up at seven a.m.?

ALEX: I'll be here.

ALEX and JANET go in for a kiss, inadvertently putting pressure on APPA's hand.

APPA: AH!

JANET: What about him?

ALEX: Come here. Apply pressure right here.

They transfer holding APPA.

APPA: AH!

ALEX: Bye, Janet.

JANET: Bye.

ALEX: Please don't hold this against me, Mr. Kim. I just needed to talk to your daughter.

APPA: Okay, see you.

ALEX exits. Bell.

APPA: Okay, Janet, enough is enough, let go.

JANET: Thank you.

APPA: You welcome. Now let go.

JANET: "Thank you … Janet." (*beat*) Repeat. After. Me.

APPA: What? Ah!

JANET: Repeat after me. "Thank you, Janet."

APPA: AH!

JANET: Repeat after me. "Thank you – "

APPA: You welcome.

JANET: Repeat after me! "Thank you, Janet!"

APPA: Ah! Ah! Okay, okay, okay. Thank you, Janet. Okay, enough is enough, let go.

JANET: "I'm sorry."

APPA: That's okay. Ah!

JANET: Repeat after me. "I'm sorry."

APPA: Ah! Okay, okay, I'm sorry.

JANET: "I love you, Janet. I love you, Janet." (*beat*) "I love you, Janet!"

APPA: Ah! Okay! I love you, Janet!

JANET releases APPA.

JANET: I love you too, Appa. (*with arms open*) And see, no one's twisting my arm to say it.

JANET slowly lowers her arms, picks up her bag, and walks to the back of the store.

APPA: You was fourteen years old. (*JANET stops.*) You was fourteen years old, school project: "What I am most proud of." You write story how we begin store. Then you take picture of me in front of store. That is my most happy memory, Janet. I don't want you take over store. I want you live life best way you choosing.

JANET takes the garbage bag from the closet and approaches the front door.

APPA: Yah. (*APPA takes it from her.*) Go upstair. Go. Sleep.

JANET embraces APPA.

APPA: Okay, okay, okay, that's good enough, let go, Janet.

JANET exits to the back and APPA takes the garbage out. Bell. APPA returns. Bell. Turns off the lights. Goes to the cash register.

20. HI APPA

Bell. JUNG enters wearing a knapsack, no tie, and shirt dishevelled.

APPA: Sorry, we is closing.

JUNG: Hi, Appa. (*beat*) How you been? (*beat*) You look good. I take it the store's doing well? (*beat*) Still smells the same. A good smell. Familiar.

APPA: You voice is change.

JUNG: Sorry?

APPA: You voice, you voice is … change.

JUNG: My voice. Right. Yeah, I guess it has. Your English got a lot better.

APPA: Umma is upstair. I go call her.

APPA makes to leave.

JUNG: That's, uh – that's all right. Um … (*beat*) What is that? What are those? Energy drinks? Insam energy drinks?

APPA: Yah. New one. From Korea.

JUNG: KBA?

APPA: Mr. Park bring in. (*beat; offering one*) You can have.

JUNG: That's okay. (*as APPA is about to put the can back*) Sure, yeah, okay.

JUNG walks to the counter and takes the can from APPA. He cracks it open and takes a sip.

APPA: What you think?

JUNG: It's good. Yeah, it's really good. Not too sweet. Not too mediciny. (*seeing the price*) A dollar fifty? You could sell this for two dollars to black people and two-fifty to white people. Rock Star, Red Bull, they go for, like, three in my neighbourhood.

APPA: Oh, yah?

JUNG: Yeah.

APPA: That's kind of rip-off.

JUNG: Yeah, it is. I was just … How's Janet?

APPA: Good.

JUNG: Still single, ready to mingle?

APPA: She has boyfriend now.

JUNG: She has a boyfriend now?

APPA: Yah.

JUNG: You sure?

APPA: Yah, I was supervise. (*beat*) She is upstair too.

JUNG: Lotta condos going up, eh? It'll be good for business. A good location is finally building itself around the store. (*beat*) Remember when I wanted to run the store all by myself? I was eleven. You told me I was too short, so I went to the back of the store, strapped milk crates onto my feet, and came out walking tall. (*steps up on a milk crate, then steps down*) You were so impressed you let me run it for twenty minutes, all by myself. Eight customers.

APPA: I let you run store all by you self because you pass my test.

JUNG: Right. Your Korean history test.

APPA: My proud moment Korea history test.

JUNG: Right.

APPA: (*beat*) 1592. 1592.

JUNG: 1592? Oh, uh, that's Admiral Yi-Soon Shin invents the Turtle Ship. The world's first ironclad battleship in 1592.

APPA: Sixty-six.

JUNG: 1966 World Cup soccer. North Korea beats Italy in the sixteens to advance to the quarter-finals.

APPA: Eighty-four.

JUNG: 1984. Hyundai's Pony arrives in Canada in 1984. Its initial five-thousand-unit projection totals at fifty thousand units sold, becoming Canada's bestselling car in '85.

APPA: Sea of Japan.

JUNG: Sea of Japan doesn't exist. The body of water between Korea and Japan is called the East Sea.

APPA: Kim Hyung-Soon.

JUNG: Kim Hyung-Soon. The Korean guy in America who crossed a peach and a plum, inventing the nectarine.

APPA: Ninety-eight.

JUNG: Ninety-eight? 1998. Uh … LPGA. Se Ri Pak becomes the first non-white woman to ever win the LPGA golf championship, which is still dominated by Korean women today.

APPA: O-two.

JUNG: 2002 World Cup soccer, hosted by South Korea and Japan. Korea placed fourth. Also, 2002 international breakdance champion is a Korean guy named Bruce Lee. He did this one move, Appa, oh, you gotta YouTube him.

APPA: Ten.

JUNG: 2010. Vancouver Olympics. Yuna Kim wins the gold medal in figure skating, beating out that Japanese girl.

APPA: Thirteen.

JUNG: Thirteen? Uh … Park Ji-Sung. His number. The captain of South Korea's national soccer team. And Manchester United's midfielder. Third Lung. They call him Third Lung 'cuz he's not a finesse player, but he never gives up.

APPA: Good. Very good.

JUNG: I have a son, Appa. He's two months old. That's right, you're a halabujee now. (*gives him the photo*) That's him. He's really big for his age. I was thinking maybe if I start him early enough, he could make the NHL. First Korean NHL superstar. What do you think?

APPA: What his name?

JUNG: Sonam. Sonam Kim. It's a Tibetan name. It means "The Fortunate One."

APPA: His mommy is Korean?

JUNG: No. She's Tibetan. She's from Tibet.

APPA: You married?

JUNG: Yeah. No. No, I'm not married.

APPA: What you doing job? Working?

JUNG: Yeah, I rent cars to people. I work at Discount Car and Truck Rentals in Parkdale.

APPA: You like working at Discount?

JUNG: I hate it. I can't stand working there. It's just, with my record, it's … um …

Beat.

APPA: I think of you, Jung. I think of you lots of time. Every day. You was very smart kid. Good looking. Natural leader. Lots of girl like you. Good at sports, music, lots of thing. You was so full of …

JUNG: Potential.

APPA: Yah, potential. Could be best, I always dream like that. Could be best. But that is my dream, not you dream. (*beat*) If Sonam don't become NHL superstar, don't get angry, it's okay. You can still be proud of him. You understand?

JUNG: Can I work here, Appa? What do you think of me working here? I could stock, clean, y'know, go to KBA, do the wholesale pickup, research all the best prices in town. You wouldn't have to pay me that much and you could always cash out. I don't have to handle the money. What do you say?

APPA: Take over store.

JUNG: What?

APPA: Take over store, Jung.

JUNG: What? You want me to take over the store?

APPA: Yah.

JUNG: You giving the store to me?

APPA: Yah.

JUNG: Seriously?

APPA: Seriously.

JUNG: No, Appa, seriously?

APPA turns to JUNG with tears streaking down his face.

APPA: This is my serious face.

JUNG: Store's probably worth a lot of money. You could sell it and retire. Why do you want to give it to me?

APPA: What is my story? What is story of Mr. Kim? My whole life I doing store. This store is my story? No. My story is not Kim's Convenience. My story is you. And Janet. And Umma. And Sonam. You understand?

JUNG nods his head yes. APPA gets the pricing gun and offers it to JUNG.

APPA: Change price. Make two dollar. That's good idea.

JUNG takes the pricing gun with both of his hands. APPA exits to the back. JUNG goes behind the counter, adjusts the numbers on the pricing gun, and begins repricing the cans.

Lights slowly fade to the sound of the pricing gun.

END

A SELECTIVE BIBLIOGRAPHY OF SOURCE MATERIAL

I. Selected Websites and Journals

A huge amount of material on Canadian theatre is available online, though the rapidly changing nature of the digital world means that what you may be able to find on the Web today may be gone tomorrow. Googling a play, playwright, actor, or director will give you immediate access to a good deal of online information, often including their own website. Ditto for YouTube, a valuable resource for accessing scenes from productions and playwright interviews. But not everything can easily be found via the common search engines. The websites listed here provide important information about Canadian theatre, and many have links to other excellent sites. All were active as of July 2013.

Atlantic Canada Theatre Site:
www.lib.unb.ca/Texts/Theatre/index.html

Canadian Adaptations of Shakespeare Project:
www.canadianshakespeares.ca

Canadian Association for Theatre Research:
www.catr-acrt.ca

Canadian Theatre Critics Association:
www.canadiantheatrecritics.ca

Canadian Theatre Encyclopedia:
www.canadiantheatre.com

Canadian Theatre Record:
http://canadiantheatrerecord.torontopubliclibrary.ca

Chalmers Public Theatre Resource Collection:
www.stratford.library.on.ca/chalmers2.htm

L.W. Conolly Theatre Archives at University of Guelph:
www.lib.uoguelph.ca/resources/archival_&_special_collections/the_collections/digital_collections/theatre

Theatre Museum Canada:
www.theatremuseumcanada.ca

The primary journals in the field of Canadian theatre studies are *Canadian Theatre Review*, which began publication in 1974; *Theatre Research in Canada* (formerly *Theatre History in Canada*), published since 1980; and *alt.theatre*, in existence since 1998. The journal *Canadian Drama* ran from 1975 to 1990, and *Theatrum* lasted from 1985 to 1995.

II. Backgrounds, Surveys, and General Studies

Alvarez, Natalie, ed. Latina/o *Canadian Theatre and Performance*. New Essays on Canadian Theatre, vol. 3. Toronto: Playwrights Canada, 2013.

Anthony, Geraldine, ed. *Stage Voices: Twelve Canadian Playwrights Talk about Their Lives and Work*. Toronto: Doubleday, 1978.

Appleford, Rob, ed. *Aboriginal Drama and Theatre*. Critical Perspectives on Canadian Theatre in English, vol. 1. Toronto: Playwrights Canada, 2005.

Aquino, Nina Lee, and Ric Knowles, eds. *Asian Canadian Theatre: New Essays on Canadian Theatre*, vol. 1. Toronto: Playwrights Canada, 2011.

Astle, Robert. *Theatre without Borders*. Winnipeg: Signature, 2002.

Atkey, Mel. *Broadway North: The Dream of a Canadian Musical Theatre*. Toronto: Natural Heritage, 2006.

Barker, Roberta, and Kim Solga, eds. *New Canadian Realisms*. New Essays on Canadian Theatre, vol. 2. Toronto: Playwrights Canada, 2012.

Barton, Bruce, ed. *Collective Creation, Collaboration and Devising*. Critical Perspectives on Canadian Theatre in English, vol. 12. Toronto: Playwrights Canada, 2008.

———, ed. *Developing Nation: New Play Creation in English-Speaking Canada*. Toronto: Playwrights Canada, 2009.

Bennett, Susan, ed. *Feminist Theatre and Performance*. Critical Perspectives on Canadian Theatre in English, vol. 4. Toronto: Playwrights Canada, 2006.

Benson, Eugene, and L.W. Conolly. *English Canadian Theatre*. Toronto: Oxford UP, 1987.

———, eds. *The Oxford Companion to Canadian Theatre*. Toronto: Oxford UP, 1989.

Bessai, Diane. *Playwrights of Collective Creation*. Toronto: Simon & Pierre, 1992.

Brask, Per, ed. *Contemporary Issues in Canadian Drama*. Winnipeg: Blizzard, 1995.

Breaugh, Sean, and Patricia Flood. *Risking the Void: The Scenography of Cameron Porteous*. Toronto: Theatre Museum Canada, 2009.

Brenna, Dwayne. *Our Kind of Work: The Glory Days and Difficult Times of 25th Street Theatre*. Saskatoon: Thistledown, 2011.

Brisset, Annie. *A Sociocritique of Translation: Theatre and Alterity in Quebec, 1968–1988*. Trans. Rosalind Gill and Roger Gannon. Toronto: U of Toronto P, 1996.

Brockhouse, Robert. *The Royal Alexandra Theatre: A Celebration of 100 Years*. Toronto: McArthur, 2008.

Brookes, Chris. *A Public Nuisance: A History of the Mummers Troupe*. St. John's: Institute of Social and Economic Research, Memorial Univ. of Newfoundland, 1988.

Brydon, Diana, and Irena R. Makaryk, eds. *Shakespeare in Canada: "A World Elsewhere"?* Toronto: U of Toronto P, 2002.

Burnett, Linda, ed. *Theatre in Atlantic Canada*. Critical Perspectives on Canadian Theatre in English, vol. 16. Toronto: Playwrights Canada, 2010.

Carson, Neil. *Harlequin in Hogtown: George Luscombe and Toronto Workshop Productions*. Toronto: U of Toronto P, 1995.

Chapman, Vernon. *Who's in the Goose Tonight? An Anecdotal History of Canadian Theatre*. Toronto: ECW, 2001.

Clarke, George Elliot. *Directions Home: Approaches to African-Canadian Literature*. Toronto: U of Toronto P, 2012.

Conolly, L.W. *The Shaw Festival: The First Fifty Years*. Don Mills: Oxford UP, 2011.

————, ed. *Canadian Drama and the Critics*. Rev. ed. Vancouver: Talonbooks, 1995.

Cushman, Robert. *Fifty Seasons at Stratford*. Toronto: McClelland & Stewart, 2002.

Davis, William B. *Where There's Smoke: Musings of a Cigarette Smoking Man*. Toronto: ECW, 2011.

Däwes, Birgit. *Indigenous North American Drama: A Multivocal History*. Albany: State U of New York P, 2013.

Day, Moira, ed. *West-Worlds: Celebrating Western Canadian Theatre and Playwriting*. Regina: Canadian Plains Research Centre, 2011.

Diamond, David. *Theatre for Living: The Art and Science of Community-Based Dialogue*. Victoria: Trafford, 2007.

Donohoe, Joseph I. Jr. and Jonathan M. Weiss, eds. *Essays on Modern Quebec Theatre*. East Lansing: Michigan State UP, 1995.

Dudeck, Theresa Robbins. *Keith Johnstone: A Critical Biography*. NY: Bloomsbury Methuen, 2013.

Filewod, Alan. *Collective Encounters: Documentary Theatre in English Canada*. Toronto: U of Toronto P, 1987.

————. *Committing Theatre: Theatre Radicalism and Political Intervention in Canada*. Toronto: Between the Lines, 2011.

————. *Performing Canada: The Nation Enacted in the Imagined Theatre*. Kamloops, BC: Univ. College of the Cariboo, 2002.

————, ed. *Theatre Histories*. Critical Perspectives on Canadian Theatre in English, vol. 13. Toronto: Playwrights Canada, 2009.

Gallagher, Kathleen, and David Booth, eds. *How Theatre Educates: Convergences and Counterpoints with Artists, Scholars and Advocates*. Toronto: U of Toronto P, 2003.

Garebian, Keith. *A Well-Bred Muse: Selected Theatre Writings, 1978–1988*. Oakville, ON: Mosaic, 1991.

————, ed. *William Hutt: Masks and Faces*. Oakville, ON: Mosaic, 1995.

Gilbert, Helen, and Joanne Tompkins. *Post-Colonial Drama: Theory, Practice, Politics*. London: Routledge, 1996.

Glaap, Albert-Reiner, with Rolf Althorp, ed. *On-Stage and Off-Stage: English Canadian Drama in Discourse*. St. John's: Breakwater, 1996.

Glaap, Albert-Reiner, and Michael Heinze. *Contemporary Canadian Plays: Overviews and Close Encounters*. Trier: Wissenschaftlicher Verlag, 2005.

Glaap, Albert-Reiner, Michael Heinze, and Neil Johnstone. *Jewish Facets of Contemporary Canadian Drama*. Trier: Wissenschaftlicher Verlag, 2008.

Grace, Sherrill, and Albert-Reiner Glaap, eds. *Performing National Identities: International Perspectives on Contemporary Canadian Theatre*. Vancouver: Talonbooks, 2003.

Grace, Sherrill, and Jerry Wasserman, eds. *Theatre and AutoBiography: Writing and Performing Lives in Theory and Practice*. Vancouver: Talonbooks, 2006.

Green, Lynda Mason, and Tedde Moore, eds. *Standing Naked in the Wings: Anecdotes from Canadian Actors*. Toronto: Oxford UP, 1997.

Hadfield, D.A. *Re: Producing Women's Dramatic History: The Politics of Playing in Toronto*. Vancouver: Talonbooks, 2007.

Hengen, Shannon. *Where Stories Meet: An Oral History of De-ba-jeh-mu-jig Theatre*. Toronto: Playwrights Canada, 2007.

Hodkinson, Yvonne. *Female Parts: The Art and Politics of Female Playwrights*. Montreal: Black Rose, 1991.

Houston, Andrew, ed. *Environmental and Site-Specific Theatre*. Critical Perspectives on Canadian Theatre in English, vol. 8. Toronto: Playwrights Canada, 2007.

Hurley, Erin. *National Performance: Representing Quebec from Expo 67 to Céline Dion*. Toronto: U of Toronto P, 2011.

Jennings, Sarah. *Art and Politics: The History of the National Arts Centre*. Toronto: Dundurn, 2009.

Johnston, Denis. *Up the Mainstream: The Rise of Toronto's Alternative Theatres*. Toronto: U of Toronto P, 1991.

Johnston, Kirsty. *Stage Turns: Canadian Disability Theatre*. Montreal: McGill-Queen's UP, 2012.

Johnston, Sheila M.F. *Let's Go to the Grand! 100 Years of Entertainment at London's Grand Theatre*. Toronto: National Heritage, 2001.

Kennedy, Brian. *The Baron Bold and the Beauteous Maid: A Compact History of Canadian Theatre*. Toronto: Playwrights Canada, 2005.

Kerr, Rosalind, ed. *Queer Theatre in Canada*. Critical Perspectives on Canadian Theatre in English, vol. 7. Toronto: Playwrights Canada, 2007.

Knowles, Ric. *Reading the Material Theatre*. Cambridge: Cambridge UP, 2004.

————. *Shakespeare and Canada: Essays on Production, Translation, and Adaptation*. Brussels: P.I.E.-Peter Lang, 2004.

————. *The Theatre of Form and the Production of Meaning: Contemporary Canadian Dramaturgies*. Toronto: ECW, 1999.

Knowles, Ric, and Ingrid Mündel, eds. *"Ethnic," Multicultural, and Intercultural Theatre*. Critical Perspectives on Canadian Theatre in English, vol. 14. Toronto: Playwrights Canada, 2009.

Knutson, Susan, ed. *Canadian Shakespeare*. Critical Perspectives on Canadian Theatre in English, vol. 18. Toronto: Playwrights Canada, 2010.

Ladouceur, Louise. *Dramatic Licence: Translating Theatre from One Official Language to the Other in Canada*. Trans. Richard Lebeau. Edmonton: U of Alberta P, 2012.

Levin, Laura, ed. *Theatre and Performance in Toronto*. Critical Perspectives on Canadian Theatre in English, vol. 21. Toronto: Playwrights Canada, 2011.

Loiselle, André. *Stage-Bound: Feature Film Adaptations of Canadian and Québécois Drama*. Montreal: McGill-Queen's UP, 2003.

Longfield, Kevin. *From Fire to Flood: A History of Theatre in Manitoba*. Winnipeg: Signature, 2001.

McKinnie, Michael. *City Stages: Theatre and Urban Space in a Global City*. Toronto: U of Toronto P, 2007.

————, ed. *Space and the Geographies of Theatre*. Critical Perspectives on Canadian Theatre in English, vol. 9. Toronto: Playwrights Canada, 2007.

Martz, Fraidie, and Andrew Wilson. *A Fiery Soul: The Life and Theatrical Times of John Hirsch*. Montreal: Véhicule, 2011.

Maufort, Marc. *Transgressive Itineraries: Postcolonial Hybridizations of Dramatic Realism*. Brussels: P.I.E.-Peter Lang, 2003.

Maufort, Marc, and Franca Bellarsi, eds. *Crucible of Cultures: Anglophone Drama at the Dawn of a New Millennium*. Brussels: P.I.E.-Peter Lang, 2002.

————, eds. *Siting the Other: Re-visions of Marginality in Australian and English-Canadian Drama*. Brussels: P.I.E.-Peter Lang, 2001.

————, eds. *Signatures of the Past: Cultural Memory in Contemporary North American Anglophone Drama*. Brussels: P.I.E.-Peter Lang, 2008.

Miller, Mary Jane. *Turn Up the Contrast: CBC Television Drama Since 1952*. Vancouver: UBC Press, 1987.

Moore, Mavor. *Reinventing Myself: Memoirs*. Toronto: Stoddart, 1994.

Morrow, Martin. *Wild Theatre: The History of One Yellow Rabbit*. Banff: Banff Centre, 2003.

Moynagh, Maureen. *African-Canadian Theatre*. Critical Perspectives on Canadian Theatre in English, vol. 2. Toronto: Playwrights Canada, 2005.

Much, Rita, ed. *Women on the Canadian Stage: The Legacy of Hrotsvit*. Winnipeg: Blizzard, 1992.

Nardocchio, Elaine. *Theatre and Politics in Modern Quebec*. Edmonton: U of Alberta P, 1986.

New, William H., ed. *Dramatists in Canada: Selected Essays*. Vancouver: UBC Press, 1972.

Nothof, Anne, ed. *Theatre in Alberta*. Critical Perspectives on Canadian Theatre in English, vol. 11. Toronto: Playwrights Canada, 2008.

O'Donnell, Darrin. *Social Acupuncture: A Guide to Suicide, Performance and Utopia*. Toronto: Coach House, 2006.

Perkyns, Richard. *The Neptune Story: Twenty-Five Years in the Life of a Leading Canadian Theatre*. Hantsport, NS: Lancelot, 1989.

Pettigrew, John, and Jamie Portman. *Stratford: The First Thirty Years*. 2 vols. Toronto: Macmillan, 1985.

Plummer, Christopher. *In Spite of Myself: A Memoir*. NY: Alfred A. Knopf, 2008.

Podbrey, Maurice. *Half Man, Half Beast: Making a Life in Canadian Theatre*. Montreal: Véhicule, 1997.

Prentki, Tim, and Jan Selman. *Popular Theatre in Political Culture: Britain and Canada in Focus*. Portland: Intellect, 2000.

Ratsoy, Ginny, ed. *Theatre in British Columbia*. Critical Perspectives on Canadian Theatre in English, vol. 6. Toronto: Playwrights Canada, 2006.

Rewa, Natalie. *Scenography in Canada: Selected Designers*. Toronto: U of Toronto P, 2004.

————, ed. *Design and Scenography*. Critical Perspectives on Canadian Theatre in English, vol. 15. Toronto: Playwrights Canada, 2009.

Rubin, Don, ed. *Canada on Stage: Canadian Theatre Review Yearbook*. Toronto: CTR Publications, 1974–88.

————, ed. *Canadian Theatre History: Selected Readings*. Toronto: Playwrights Canada, 2004.

Rudakoff, Judith, ed. *Questionable Activities: Canadian Theatre Artists Interviewed by Canadian Theatre Students*. 2 vols. Toronto: Playwrights Union of Canada, 1997.

————, ed. *TRANS(per)FORMING Nina Arsenault: An Unreasonable Body of Work*. Bristol: Intellect, 2012.

Rudakoff, Judith, and Rita Much. *Fair Play: 12 Women Speak: Conversations with Canadian Playwrights*. Toronto: Simon & Pierre, 1990.

Ruffo, Armand Garnet, ed. *(Ad)dressing Our Words: Aboriginal Perspectives on Aboriginal Literatures*. Penticton, BC: Theytus, 2001.

Saddlemyer, Ann, and Richard Plant, eds. *Later Stages: Essays in Ontario Theatre from the First World War to the 1970s*. Toronto: U of Toronto P, 1997.

Salverson, Julie, ed. *Community Engaged Theatre and Performance*. Critical Perspectives on Canadian Theatre in English, vol. 19. Toronto: Playwrights Canada, 2011.

————, ed. *Popular Political Theatre and Performance*. Critical Perspectives on Canadian Theatre in English, vol. 17. Toronto: Playwrights Canada, 2010.

Scott, Shelley. *Nightwood Theatre: A Woman's Work Is Always Done*. Edmonton: AU Press, 2010.

Stephenson, Jenn. *Performing Autobiography: Contemporary Canadian Drama*. Toronto: U of Toronto P, 2013.

————, ed. *Solo Performance*. Critical Perspectives on Canadian Theatre in English, vol. 20. Toronto: Playwrights Canada, 2010.

Stuart, E. Ross. *The History of Prairie Theatre: The Development of Theatre in Alberta, Manitoba, and Saskatchewan, 1833–1820*. Toronto: Simon & Pierre, 1984.

Theatre Memoirs: On the Occasion of the Canadian Theatre Conference. Toronto: Playwrights Union of Canada, 1998.

Tompkins, Joanne, ed. "*Theatre and the Canadian Imaginary*." *Australasian Drama Studies* 29 (Oct. 1996).

Usmiani, Renate. *Second Stage: The Alternative Theatre Movement in Canada*. Vancouver: UBC Press, 1983.

Vogt, Gordon. *Critical Stages: Canadian Theatre in Crisis*. Ottawa: Oberon, 1998.

Wagner, Anton, ed. *Contemporary Canadian Theatre: New World Visions*. Toronto: Simon & Pierre, 1985.

————, ed. *Establishing Our Boundaries: English-Canadian Theatre Criticism*. Toronto: U of Toronto P, 1999.

Walker, Craig Stewart. *The Buried Astrolabe: Canadian Dramatic Imagination and Western Tradition*. Montreal: McGill-Queen's UP, 2001.

Wallace, Robert. *Producing Marginality: Theatre and Criticism in Canada*. Saskatoon: Fifth House, 1990.

Wallace, Robert, and Cynthia Zimmerman, eds *The Work: Conversations with English-Canadian Playwrights*. Toronto: Coach House, 1982.

Weiss, Jonathan M. *French-Canadian Theater*. Boston: Twayne, 1986.

Whittaker, Herbert. *Whittaker's Theatre: A Critic Looks at Stages in Canada and Thereabouts, 1944–1975*. Ed. Ronald Bryden with Boyd Neil. Greenbank, ON: The Whittaker Project, 1985.

Wilmer, S.E., ed *Native American Performance and Representation*. Tucson: U of Arizona P, 2009.

Zimmerman, Cynthia. *Playwriting Women: Female Voices in English Canada*. Toronto: Simon & Pierre, 1994.

III. Individual Playwrights and Plays

Note: Wherever a book in this section has already appeared as an entry in Part II, I have used a short form here. *Canadian Theatre Review* is abbreviated *CTR*.

ROBERT LEPAGE, MARIE BRASSARD and *Polygraph*

Ackerman, Marianne. "The Hectic Career of Robert Lepage." *Imperial Oil Review* 74 (Winter 1990): 14–17.

Beauchamp, Hélène. "The Repère Cycles: From Basic to Continuous Education." *CTR* 78 (Spring 1994): 26–31.

Bunzli, James. "The Geography of Creation: Décalage as Impulse, Process, and Outcome in the Theatre of Robert Lepage." *TDR* 43.1 (Spring 1999): 79–103.

Campbell, James. "The Lie of the Body." *Times Literary Supplement* (London), 3 Mar. 1989. 222.

Carson, Christie. "Collaboration, Translation, Interpretation: Robert Lepage Interviewed." *New Theatre Quarterly* 9.33 (Feb. 1993): 31–36.

Caux, Patrick, and Bernard Gilbert. *EX MACHINA: Creating for the Stage*. Trans. Neil Kroetsch. Vancouver: Talonbooks, 2009.

Charest, Rémy. *Robert Lepage: Connecting Flights*. Trans. Wanda Romer Taylor. London: Methuen, 1997.

Conlogue, Ray. "Lepage's Evocative Polygraph Possesses a Disquieting Beauty." *Globe and Mail*, 23 Feb. 1990. C6.

Crew, Robert. "Quebec Maestro in Top Form." *Toronto Star*, 21 Feb. 1990. F4.

Dault, Gary Michael. "*Le Confessionnal* & *Le Polygraphe*: A Rumination." *Take One* 5.15 (Spring 1997): 17–21.

Delgado, Maria M., and Paul Heritage, eds. *In Contact with the Gods? Directors Talk Theatre*. NY: Manchester UP, 1996.

Dickinson, Peter. *Screening Gender, Framing Genre: Canadian Literature into Film*. Toronto: U of Toronto P, 2007. Ch. 5.

Donnelly, Pat. "Enigmatic Lepage Play Disappoints." *Montreal Gazette*, 18 Nov. 1988. C5.

————. "Lepage's *Polygraph* Improves with Age." *Montreal Gazette*, 21 Mar. 1991. D10.

Donohoe, Joseph I., Jr., and Jane M. Koustas, eds. *Theater sans frontières: Essays on the Dramatic Universe of Robert Lepage*. East Lansing: Michigan State UP, 2000.

Dundjerovic, Aleksandar. *The Theatricality of Robert Lepage*. Montreal: McGill-Queen's UP, 2007.

Dykk, Lloyd. "Stunning Stagecraft Saves this Unlikely Tale." *Vancouver Sun*, 24 Oct. 1992. C20.

Fouquet, Ludovic. *The Visual Laboratory of Robert Lepage*. Trans. Rhonda Mullins. Vancouver: Talonbooks, 2013.

Gardner, Lyn. "Polygraph." *Guardian* (London), 17 Nov. 2001. 21.

Garner, Stanton B., Jr. *Bodied Spaces: Phenomenology and Performance in Contemporary Drama*. Ithaca, NY: Cornell UP, 1994. 225–30.

Gibson, K. Jane. "Seeing Double: The Map-Making Process of Robert Lepage." *CTR* 97 (Winter 1998): 18–23.

Gibson, Margaret. "The Truth Machine: Polygraphs, Popular Culture, and the Confessing Body." *Social Semiotics* 11.1 (Apr. 2001): 61–73.

Godfrey, Stephen. "A Riveting Exploration of Memory and Survival." *Globe and Mail*, 18 Nov. 1988. D9.

Harvie, Jennifer, and Erin Hurley. "States of Play: Locating Québec in the Performances of Robert Lepage, Ex Machina, and the Cirque du Soleil." *Theatre Journal* 51.3 (Oct. 1999): 299–315.

Hobson, Louis. "*Polygraph* Draws Viewers in with Twisted Plot and Dazzling Effects." *Calgary Sun*, 25 Mar. 2013.

Holden, Stephen. "Metaphysics and Crime." *New York Times*, 27 Oct. 1990. I12.

Hunt, Nigel. "The Global Voyage of Robert Lepage." *TDR* 122 (Summer 1989): 104–18.

Hunt, Stephen. "Able Cast Breathes Life into Thriller." *Calgary Herald*, 26 Mar. 2013. C8.

Innes, Christopher. "Puppets and Machines of the Mind: Robert Lepage and the Modernist Heritage." *Theatre Research International* 30.2 (July 2005): 124–38.

Jacobson, Lynn. "Tectonic States." *American Theatre* 8.8 (Nov. 1991): 16–22.

Kingston, Jeremy. "Polygraph." *Times* (London), 16 Nov. 2001. Times.2.

Knowles, Ric. "From Dream to Machine: Peter Brook, Robert Lepage, and the Contemporary Shakespearean Director as (Post)Modernist." *Theatre Journal* 50 (May 1998): 189–206. Rpt. Knowles, *Shakespeare and Canada*. Ch. 4.

Lacey, Liam. "*Polygraph*'s Evolving X-Ray." *Globe and Mail*, 23 Feb. 1990. C6.

Lavender, Andy. *Hamlet in Pieces: Shakespeare Reworked by Peter Brook, Robert Lepage, Robert Wilson*. NY: Continuum, 2001.

Lefebvre, Paul. "Robert Lepage: New Filters for Creation." *CTR* 52 (Fall 1987): 30–35.

Loiselle, André. *Stage-Bound: Feature Film Adaptations of Canadian and Québécois Drama*. Montreal: McGill-Queen's UP, 2003.

Manguel, Alberto. "Theatre of the Miraculous." *Saturday Night* 104 (Jan. 1989): 32–39, 42.

Nicholls, Liz. "Brilliant Multi-Layered Fantasia on Truth, Fiction, and Memory." *Edmonton Journal*, 7 Apr. 1991. D2.

O'Mahoney, John. "Aerial Views: The Guardian Profile: Robert Lepage." *Guardian* (London), 23 June 2001. 6.

Rewa, Natalie. "Clichés of Ethnicity Subverted: Robert Lepage's *La Trilogie des dragons*." *Theatre History in Canada* 11.2 (Fall 1990): 148–61.

Salter, Denis. "A State of Becoming." *Books in Canada* 20.2 (Mar. 1991): 26–29.

———. "Borderlines: An Interview with Robert Lepage and Le Théâtre Repère." *Theater* 24.3 (1993): 71–79.

Shevtsova, Maria, and Christopher Innes, eds. *Directors/Directing: Conversations on Theatre*. NY: Cambridge UP, 2009. Ch. 5.

Sidnell, Michael J. "*Polygraph*: Somatic Truth and an Art of Presence." *CTR* 64 (Fall 1990): 45–48.

Spencer, Charles. "Brilliant Tale of Life, Death, and Lie-Detectors." *Telegraph* (London), 14 Nov. 2001. 25.

Winston, Iris. "*Polygraph*: A Riveting, Powerful Whodunnit with a Difference." *Ottawa Citizen*, 13 Mar. 1991. C7.

Ziraldo, Cristiana. "Lepage's *Polygraphe* in Italy." *CTR* 105 (Winter 2001): 16–19.

MORRIS PANYCH and *7 Stories*

Ajzenstadt, Michael. "The Unfinished Morris Panych." *Theatrum* 22 (Feb.–Mar. 1991): 29–30.

Anderson, Doug. "Man on the Ledge of a Breakdown." *Sydney Morning Herald*, 4 Feb. 2000. 13.

Chamberlain, Adrian. "A Deranged Look at What We Are." *Times-Colonist* (Victoria), 8 June 1997. 1.

Christianson, Richard. "Eccentric Characters Leap Out from Red Orchid's '7 Stories.'" *Chicago Tribune*, 23 Dec. 1994.

Citron, Cynthia. "Suicidus Interruptus at Theatre 40." *Santa Monica Daily Press*, 20 Feb. 2013.

Clark, Bob. "Hilarious Leap into Laughter." *Calgary Herald*, 17 Oct. 2009. D8.

———. "On the Edge of Surrealism." *Calgary Herald*, 15 Oct. 2009. E2.

Conlogue, Ray. "Many Worlds on a Narrow Ledge." *Globe and Mail*, 1 Mar. 1991. C9.

Coulbourn, John. "Still Falling for '7 Stories.'" *Toronto Sun*, 14 Nov. 2009.

Cushman, Robert. "Survival of the Fittest." *National Post*, 17 Nov. 2009. AL4.

Donnelly, Pat. "Style and Substance." *Montreal Gazette*, 17 Aug. 1992. C6.

Dykk, Lloyd. "Opening Windows on Lives in Chaos." *Vancouver Sun*, 13 May 1989. E8.

———. "Triple-Threat Panych Fans the Stage Fires." *Vancouver Sun*, 14 June 1989. C5.

Fuller, Cam. "There's Plenty of Reasons to Enjoy Greystone Offering." *Star-Phoenix* (Saskatoon), 7 Feb. 2005. D2.

Genzlinger, Neil. "Man on a Ledge, Interrupted by Neighboring Oddballs." *New York Times*, 12 Aug. 2008. E2.

Gilbert, Reid. " 'And Then We Saw You Fly Over Here and Land!': Metadramatic Design in the Stage Work of Morris Panych and Ken MacDonald." *Theatre History in Canada* 11.2 (Fall 1990): 134–47.

—. "The Theatrical Stories of Morris Panych." *CTR* 67 (Summer 1991): 5–11.

Hindle, Alan. "20th Anniversary Brings Out the Best of Panych." *Vancouver Sun*, 23 Apr. 2004. D9.

Kaplan, Ben. "Sage of Majority." *National Post*, 26 Nov. 2009. AL1.

Lederman, Marsha. "Still Out on the Ledge." *Globe and Mail*, 17 Oct. 2009. R6.

Leiren-Young, Mark. "7 Stories." *Theatrum* 15 (Sept.–Oct. 1989): 50.

Linden, Audrey. "Flight of Fancy in '7 Stories.'" *Los Angeles Examiner*, 27 Jan. 2013.

Miliokas, Nick. " '7 Stories' the Perfect Vehicle for Students." *Leader-Post* (Regina), 1 Apr. 2000. D8.

Morrow, Martin. "Muted Metaphysical Fluff Doesn't Fly." *Calgary Herald*, 21 Sept. 1991. F8.

Nestruck, J. Kelly. "A Window into the Beginnings of Panych." *Globe and Mail*, 16 Nov. 2009. R5.

Ouzounian, Richard. "Stories Well Told." *Toronto Star*, 13 Nov. 2009. E2.

Page, Malcolm. "7 Stories." *CTR* 72 (Fall 1992): 81.

Panych, Morris. "Contradictions." *CTR* 76 (Fall 1993): 58–59.

Ryan, Denise. "The Panych Button." *Vancouver Magazine* 30 (Apr. 1997): 20–21.

Sumi, Glenn. "Surreal Stories." *Now* 29.12 (17–24 Nov. 2009).

Szaffkó, Péter. "The Story of Morris Panych's *7 Stories* in Hungary: A Documentary Production Analysis." *Performing National Identities*, ed. Grace and Glaap. 198–210.

Tattrie, John. "7 Stories." *Halifax Magazine*, 1 Nov. 2010.

Thomas, Colin. "7 Stories." *Georgia Straight*, 29 Apr. 2004.

Wagner, Vit. "First-Rate Cast Binds Play Together." *Toronto Star*, 27 Feb. 1991. F3.

Weiss, Heidi. "7 Stories Has Many Levels." *Chicago Sun-Times*, 18 Dec. 1994. 74.

Wicks, Heidi. " 'Seven Stories': A Feast of Existentialism?" *Telegram* (St. John's), 26 Nov. 2009.

Wood, Chris. "Body – and Soul – Language." *Maclean's* 113.6 (7 Feb. 2000): 60–62.

DANIEL MacIVOR and *Never Swim Alone*

Berson, Misha. "What's Below Surface of Macho Posturing – 'Never Swim Alone' " *Seattle Times*, 8 Dec. 2006. J4.

Bolt, Carol. "Introduction." *Never Swim Alone & This Is a Play* by Daniel MacIvor. Toronto: Playwrights Canada, 1993. 7–9.

Brooks, Daniel. "Some Thoughts about Directing *Here Lies Henry*." *CTR* 92 (Fall 1997): 42–45.

Chapman, Geoff. "Furious Word-Duels Convey Male Idiocy." *Toronto Star*, 21 Jan. 1994. D12.

Clark, Bob. "Bitterness Evident in Short Play." *Calgary Herald*, 10 Feb. 2000. B13.

Donnelly, Pat. "Odd Strokes from Cult Dramatist." *Montreal Gazette*, 24 Oct. 1997. D5.

Dupuis, Chris. "Theatre Artist Daniel MacIvor." *Xtra!*, 14 Sept. 2006.

Halferty, Paul. "Interview with Daniel MacIvor." *Questionable Activities*, ed. Rudakoff, vol. 2. 6–11.

Hall, Lynda. "*Never Swim Alone & This Is a Play*." *CTR* 82 (Spring 1995): 95–96.

Hallett, Bryce. "Beware the Undertow as Friends Become Foes." *Sydney Morning Herald*, 2 June 2007. 23.

Hampton, Wilborn. "13 Corporate Rounds, Mano a Mano." *New York Times*, 20 July 2000. E3.

Hood, Sarah B. "*Never Swim Alone*, A Cruel Comedy." *Theatrum* 23 (Apr.–May 1991): 38.

Kirchhoff, H.J. "*Never Swim Alone*." *Globe and Mail*, 25 Jan. 1994. C4.

Knowles, Ric. *The Theatre of Form and the Production of Meaning*. 72–73, 198–202.

Livingstone, David. "Jump Starter." *Flare* 14 (Sept. 1992): 76, 180.

MacIvor, Daniel. "This Is an Article." *Theatrum* 30 (Sept.–Oct. 1992): 15–17.

Posner, Michael. "Avant–garde Duo Creates a Monster." *Globe and Mail*, 21 Apr. 1998. C1.

Prosser, David. "Looking Past the Print." *Books in Canada* 23.6 (Sept. 1994): 31.

Stephenson, Jenn. *Performing Autobiography*. Ch. 6.

Vaughan, R.M. "A Gay Man's Everyhomo." *Books in Canada* 24.9 (Dec. 1995): 10–11.

Wagner, Vit. "MacIvor Dives Deep into Stylish Oneupman-ship." *Toronto Star*, 1 Mar. 1991. D9.

—. "Playwright Daniel MacIvor: Down the Road and Back Again." *ARTSatlantic* 14 (Fall 1995): 34–36.

Wallace, Robert. "The Victor(y) of the Subject." *House Humans* by Daniel MacIvor. Toronto: Coach House, 1992. 7–14.

Wilson, Ann. "Lying and Dying: Theatricality in *Here Lies Henry*." *CTR* 92 (Fall 1997): 39–41.

Zinoman, Jason. "Somewhere under the Radar, a Discovery Awaits." *New York Times*, 23 Aug. 2006.9 E1.

WENDY LILL and *The Glace Bay Miners' Museum*

Barton, Bruce. "Introduction to *The Glace Bay Miners' Museum*." *Marigraph: Gauging the Tides of Drama from New Brunswick, Nova Scotia, Prince Edward Island*. Ed. Bruce Barton. Toronto: Playwrights Canada, 2004. 194–95.

Belliveau, George. "Glace Bay to Hollywood: A Political Journey." *Theatre Research in Canada* 22.1 (Spring 2001): 46–57.

Bennett, Susan. "The Occupation of Wendy Lill: Canadian Women's Voices." *Women on the Canadian Stage*, ed. Much. 69–80.

Bergman, Brian. "Enter Stage Left." *Maclean's* 111.7 (16 Feb. 1998): 61.

Birnie, Peter. "Actors Find Gold in Coal-Miners' Story." *Vancouver Sun*, 8 May 2001. B9.

Carley, Dave. "Wendy Lill: Passionate Witness." *CanPlay* 22.3 (Spring 2006): 15–17.

Chamberlain, Adrian. "Glace Bay Miners' Play Well Worth Digging Into." *Times-Colonist* (Victoria), 20 Nov. 1999. D13.

Clark, Bob. "King Coal Rules Their Lives." *Calgary Herald*, 16 Apr. 2000. F5.

Currie, Sheldon. "The Glace Bay Miners' Museum." *Antigonish Review* 24 (Winter 1975): 35–53.

————. *The Glace Bay Miners' Museum*. Wreck Cove, NS: Breton Books, 1995.

Cushman, Robert. "Warning: Includes Bagpipes." *National Post*, 23 Nov. 1999. B6.

Donnelly, Pat. "Glace Bay Miners' Museum Has the Familiarity of Kitchen Sink." *Montreal Gazette*, 28 Sept. 1996. E7.

Enright, Robert. "The Explorer of Human Emotions: An Interview with Wendy Lill." *Border Crossings* 10 (Jan. 1991): 12–17.

Everett-Green, Robert. "Political Playwright Turns Theatrical Politico." *Globe and Mail*, 14 Feb. 1998. C7.

Friedlander, Mira. "*The Glace Bay Miners' Museum*." *Variety* 377.4A (6–12 Dec. 1999): 94.

Gilodo, Karen. "Interview with Wendy Lill." *The Glace Bay Miners' Museum* Study Guide. Ottawa: NAC English Theatre, 2012. http://nac-cna.ca/en/englishtheatre/studyguide/the-glace-bay-miners-museum/extras.

Golfman, Noreen. "Mining Margaret's Museum." *Canadian Forum* 75 (Apr. 1996): 28–31.

Grace, Sherrill. "Gendering Northern Narrative." *Echoing Silence: Essays on Arctic Narrative*. Ed. John Moss. Ottawa: U of Ottawa P, 1997. 163–81.

Grace, Sherrill, and Shelley Newman. "Lill in Review: A Working Bibliography." *Theatre Research in Canada* 21.1 (Spring 2000): 49–58.

Heald, Susan. "Wendy Lill and the Politics of Memory." *Canadian Dimension* 29.2 (Apr.–May 1995): 54–56.

Hubbard, Sarah. "Conversation with Wendy Lill." *CTR* 128 (Fall 2006): 37–40.

Kennedy, Janice. "*Glace Bay Miners' Museum* Strong, Stirring – Right On!" *Ottawa Citizen*, 27 Feb. 1998. E5.

Langston, Patrick. "Bravery, Defiance, and Death." *Ottawa Citizen*, 13 Oct. 2012. D1.

Lill, Wendy. "Playwrighting Politician." *Theatre Memoirs: On the Occasion of the Canadian Theatre Conference*. Toronto: Playwrights Union, 1998. 66–68.

MacDonald, Reg Foley. "Lill's Stage Museum a Triumph." *Halifax Daily News*, 22 Sept. 1995. 31.

McNulty, Jim. "The Curious Career of Wendy Lill." *Province* (Vancouver), 19 July 1998. A47.

Metcalfe, Robin. "Profile: Letters Out." *Books in Canada* 19.2 (Mar. 1990): 21–24.

Miliokas, Nick. "*Glace Bay Miners' Museum* an Absorbing Tale." *Leader-Post* (Regina), 18 Mar. 2000. D7.

Mitchell, Nick. "A Feeling for Our History: An Interview with Wendy Lill." *Prairie Fire* (Fall–Winter 1985): 16–19.

Moore, Michael Scott. "Working in a Coal Mine." *SF Weekly* (San Francisco), 7 July 1999.

Nemetz, Andrea. "Miners' Museum Well Worth Revisiting." *Chronicle Herald* (Halifax), 2 Mar. 2013.

Nicholls, Liz. "Thick Layer of Coal Dust Covers *Miners' Museum*." *Edmonton Journal*, 26 Jan. 2003. B7.

O'Flanagan, Rob. "STC Production Deeply Moving, Accomplished Theatre." *Sudbury Star*, 7 Nov. 2000. B10.

Pederson, Stephen. "Lill's Play Digs Deep into Miners' Lives." *Chronicle Herald* (Halifax), 11 Aug. 1995. A9.

Rudakoff, Judith. "Wendy Lill Interview." *Fair Play*, ed. Rudakoff and Much. 37–48.

Smith, Doug. "Writer in Non-Residence." *NeWest Review* 14 (Apr.–May 1989): 52–54.

Stewart, Jesse. "The Politics and Business of Playwriting." Ed. Ric Knowles. *CTR* 115 (Summer 2003): 43–46.

Urquhart, Peter. "Whose Museum Is It, Anyway? Discourses of Resistance in the Adaptation of *The Glace Bay Miners' Museum* into *Margaret's Museum*." *Working on Screen: Representations of the Working Class in Canadian Cinema*. Ed. Malek Khouri and Darrell Varga. Toronto: U of Toronto P, 2006. 148–57.

Walton, Glenn. "Lill Women, Lill Men: Glenn Walton Interviews Playwright/MP Wendy Lill." *ARTSatlantic* 16 (Fall 1998–Winter 1999): 41–43.

Wasserman, Jerry. " 'God of the Whiteman! God of the Indian! God Al-fucking-mighty!': The Residential School Legacy in Two Canadian Plays." *Journal of Canadian Studies* 39.1 (Winter 2005): 23–48. Rpt. *Theatre in Atlantic Canada*, ed. Burnett. 135–45.

RAHUL VARMA and *Counter Offence*

Babarik, Sylvie. "A Counter Offence against Racism and Violence against Women." *McGill Tribune*, 19 Mar. 1996. 17.

Birnie, Peter. "Play's Power Lost behind Sound and Fury." *Vancouver Sun*, 15 Feb. 2000. F4.

Charlebois, Gaëtan. "Backlashing the Backlash." *Montreal Mirror*, 21–28 Mar. 1996. 26.

—————. "Subversive Shtick." *Montreal Gazette*, 10 Mar. 2005. D5.

Delean, Paul. "Counter Offence Has Topicality, Guts." *Montreal Gazette*, 16 Mar. 1996. E7.

Dharwadker, Aparna. "Diaspora and the Theatre of the Nation." *Theatre Research International* 28.3 (Oct. 2003): 303–25.

Donnelly, Pat. "Counter Offence Tackles Family Violence." *Montreal Gazette*, 26 Sept. 1997. D5.

—————. "La Nouvelle vague?" *Montreal Gazette*, 27 Feb. 1999. D1.

—————. "Play Gets Its Day – in French." *Montreal Gazette*, 18 Feb. 1999. C11.

Fine, Philip. "Directors Combine Politics, Theatre in a Smooth Mix." *Globe and Mail*, 11 May 2000. R7.

Nothof, Anne. "Canadian 'Ethnic' Theatre: Fracturing the Mosaic." *Siting the Other*, ed. Maufort and Bellarsi. 193–215.

Owens, Jolene. "Rahul Varma – Playwright." http://inspiringinterviews.wordpress.com/2011/12/02/rahul-varma-playwright/

Parameswaran, Uma. "Rahul Varma and Teesri Duniya." *Toronto Review* 13.1 (1994): 7–14.

Peerbaye, Soraya. "A Subtle Politic." *CTR* 94 (Spring 1998): 5–9.

Radz, Matt. "Struggle with Ethnic Adversity." *Montreal Gazette*, 26 Feb. 2005. H3.

Salter, Denis. "Change the World, One Play at a Time: Teesri Duniya Theatre and the Aesthetics of Social Action." *CTR* 125 (Winter 2006): 69–74.

Stewart, Jesse. "Politics and Plays: Playwrights Discuss the Nature, Social Role and Reception of Political Theatre." Ed. Ric Knowles. *CTR* 115 (Summer 2003): 52–56.

Sutton, Winston. "Playwright Comes of Age with *Counter Offence*." *CTR* 94 (Spring 1998): 23–24.

Varma, Rahul. "Contributing to Canadian Theatre." *CTR* 94 (Spring 1998): 25–27.

—————. "Playing for a Just World: The Work of Theatre Teesri Duniya." *CTR* 117 (Winter 2004): 38–41.

—————. "Playwright's Foreword." *Counter Offence* by Rahul Varma. Toronto: Playwrights Canada, 1997. 7–8.

—————. "Teesri Duniya Theatre: Diversifying Diversity with Relevant Works of Theatre." *South Asian Popular Culture* 7.3 (Oct. 2009): 179–94.

Wasserman, Jerry. "Where Is Here Now? Living the Border in the New Canadian Drama." *Crucible of Cultures*, ed. Maufort and Bellarsi. 163–73. Rpt. *"Ethnic," Multicultural, and Intercultural Theatre*, ed. Knowles. 83–93.

GEORGE F. WALKER and *Problem Child*

Barnard, Elissa. "Bizarre Action Drives Wacky Problem Child." *Chronicle Herald* (Halifax), 8 Nov. 1998. B5.

Bemrose, John. "Heartbreak Motel." *Maclean's* 110.48 (1 Dec. 1997): 85.

Birnie, Peter. "Motel Plays Get Mixed Reception." *Vancouver Sun*, 9 Mar. 1999. C5.

Borkowski, Andrew. "Theatre of the Improbable: George F. Walker." *Canadian Forum* 70 (Sept. 1991): 16–19.

Bruckner, D.J.R. "Down and Out but Dead Set on Recovering Their Baby." *New York Times*, 26 May 1997. 16.

Burliuk, Greg. "One Problem Theatre Goers Are Lucky to Have." *Kingston Whig-Standard*, 15 Mar. 2003. 35.

Chamberlain, Adrian. "Growing Pains: George F. Walker's *Problem Child* Poses Challenges for Theatre Companies." *Times-Colonist* (Victoria), 20 Feb. 2010. C6.

Chapman, Geoff. "Walker's Dramatic Return." *Toronto Star*, 27 Oct. 1997. E5.

Clark, Bob. "There's a Problem with this Child." *Calgary Herald*, 29 Oct. 2000. D5.

Conolly, L.W., ed. *Canadian Drama and the Critics*. 207–16, 297–301.

Corbeil, Carol. "A Conversation with George Walker." *Brick* 58 (Winter 1998): 59–67. Rpt. *George F. Walker*, ed. Lane. 114–26.

Coulbourn, John. "Room with a Super, Sordid View." *Toronto Sun*, 26 Oct. 1997.

De Raey, Daniel. "Introduction." *Suburban Motel* by George F. Walker. Rev. ed. Vancouver: Talonbooks, 1999. 4–6.

Donnelly, Pat. "Pas de Problème Here." *Montreal Gazette*, 16 Oct. 1998. D7.

Foley, F. Kathleen. " 'Problem,' 'Risk' Present Winning Mix of Loser Characters." *Los Angeles Times*, 19 Feb. 1999.

Gardner, Lyn. "Problem Child." *Guardian* (London), 28 Oct. 2003. 26.

Gass, Ken. "Introduction." *Three Plays* by George F. Walker. Toronto: Coach House, 1978. 9–15. Rpt. *George F. Walker*, ed. Lane. 1–7.

"George F. Walker." *Contemporary Literary Criticism: Yearbook 1989*, vol. 61. Ed. Roger Matuz. Detroit: Gale, 1990. 422–34.

Gilbert, Reid. "Escaping the 'Savage Slot': Interpellation and Transgression in George F. Walker's *Suburban Motel*." *Siting the Other*, ed. Maufort and Bellarsi. 325–45. Rpt. *George F. Walker*, ed. Lane. 138–54.

Hadfield, Dorothy. "The Role Power Plays in George F. Walker's Detective Trilogy." *Essays in Theatre* 16 (Nov. 1997): 67–84. Rpt. *George F. Walker*, ed. Lane. 95–113.

Haff, Stephen. "Slashing the Pleasantly Vague: George F. Walker and the Word." *Essays in Theatre* 10 (Nov. 1991): 59–69. Rpt. *George F. Walker*, ed. Lane. 75–84.

Johnson, Chris. *Essays on George F. Walker: Playing with Anxiety.* Winnipeg: Blizzard, 1999.

————. "George F. Walker: B-Movies Beyond the Absurd." *Canadian Literature* 85 (Summer 1980): 87–103. Rpt. *George F. Walker*, ed. Lane. 8–23.

————. "George F. Walker Directs George F. Walker." *Theatre History in Canada* 9.2 (Fall 1988): 157–72.

Johns, Ian. "*Problem Child / Last Train to Nibroc.*" *Times* (London), 3 Nov. 2003. 17.

Johnston, Denis W. "George F. Walker: Liberal Idealism and the Power Plays." *Canadian Drama* 10.2 (1984): 195–206. Rpt. *George F. Walker*, ed. Lane. 37–50.

Knowles, Ric. "The Dramaturgy of the Perverse." *Theatre Research International* 17.3 (Autumn 1992): 226–35.

Lane, Harry, ed. George F. Walker. *Critical Perspectives on Canadian Theatre in English*, vol. 5. Toronto: Playwrights Canada, 2006.

Lane, William. "Introduction." *The Power Plays* by George F. Walker. Toronto: Coach House, 1984. 9–14

————. "Introduction." *Zastrozzi: The Master of Discipline* by George F. Walker. Toronto: Playwrights Co-op, 1979. 3–6.

Maufort, Marc. "A Passage to Belgium: George F. Walker's 'Problem Child' in Brussels." *CTR* 105 (Winter 2001): 20–23.

Mazey, Steven. "Memorable Performances Shine in Shabby Motel." *Ottawa Citizen*, 28 Feb. 2003. E5.

Nicholls, Liz. "Rage Checks in at *Suburban Motel.*" *Edmonton Journal*, 21 Nov. 1999. C6.

Parisien, Aurèle. "Taking a Walker on the French Side." *CTR* 102 (Spring 2000): 28–32.

Posner, Michael. "Strange Voices from a Motel." *Globe and Mail*, 23 Oct. 1997. D1.

Pressley, Nelson. "Disturbing, Funny 'Problem Child.'" *Washington Post*, 12 Sept. 2001. C9.

Radz, Matt. "Pillars of the Canadian Stage: Playwright George F. Walker and Director Ken Gass Have Redefined Our National Theatre." *Montreal Gazette*, 23 Feb. 2002. D7.

————. "Two Tales of Troubled Youth." *Montreal Gazette*, 6 Dec. 2002. D8.

Smith, Gary. "A Riveting Look at Down-and-Out Reality." *Spectator* (Hamilton), 22 Feb. 2006. G12.

Taylor, Kate. "*Problem Child.*" *Globe and Mail*, 27 Oct. 1997. C3.

Thomas, Colin. "A Darkly Comic Double Bill." *Georgia Straight*, 11 Mar. 1999. 73.

Wagner, Vit. "Drawing Us All into One Flea-Bag Room." *Toronto Star*, 20 June 1998. M3.

————. "Playwright Walker Takes Audience for Wild Ride." *Toronto Star*, 11 Oct. 1998. B3.

Walker, Craig. *The Buried Astrolabe*. Ch. 5. Rpt. *George F. Walker*, ed. Lane. 155–76.

Wallace, Robert. "Looking for the Light: A Conversation with George F. Walker." *Canadian Drama* 14.1 (1988): 22–33. Rpt. *George F. Walker*, ed. Lane. 51–60.

Wallace, Robert, and Cynthia Zimmerman, eds. *The Work*. 212–25. Rpt. *George F. Walker*, ed. Lane. 24–32.

Wasserman, Jerry. " 'It's the Do-Gooders Burn My Ass': Modern Canadian Drama and the Crisis of Liberalism." *Modern Drama* 43 (Spring 2000): 32–47.

Wicks, Heidi. "George Walker's 'Problem Child' a Commendable Debut." *Telegram* (St. John's), 23 Apr. 2010.

Wynne-Jones, Tim. "Acts of Darkness." *Books in Canada* 14 (Apr. 1985): 11–14.

DJANET SEARS and *Harlem Duet*

Al-Solaylee, Kamal. "Baring the Burden of Race." *Globe and Mail*, 3 July 2006. R3.

Bennett, Susan. "Text as Performance: Reading and Viewing Djanet Sears's *Afrika Solo.*" *Contemporary Issues in Canadian Drama*, ed. Brask. 15–25.

Breon, Robin. "Carte Blanche. Blackface: Thoughts on Racial Masquerade." *CTR* 98 (Spring 1999): 60–62.

Brown-Guillory, Elizabeth. "Place and Displacement in Djanet Sears' *Harlem Duet* and *The Adventures of a Black Girl in Search of God.*" *Middle Passages and the Healing Place of History: Migration and Identity in Black Women's Literature*. Ed. Elizabeth Brown-Guillory. Columbus: Ohio State UP, 2006. 155–70.

Bruckner, D.J.R. "A Tortured Duet with History." *New York Times*, 21 Nov. 2002. E3.

Buntin, Matt. "An Interview with Djanet Sears." Canadian Adaptations of Shakespeare Project. http://www.canadianshakespeares.ca/i_dsears.cfm.

Burnett, Linda. " 'Redescribing a World': Towards a Theory of Shakespearean Adaptation in Canada." *CTR* 111 (Summer 2002): 5–9. Rpt. *Canadian Shakespeare*, ed. Knutson. 77–84.

Chapman, Geoff. "A Brittle Celebration of Race and Gender." *Toronto Star*, 2 Nov. 1997. C6.

Coulbourn, John. "Harlem Rendered in Vivid Colour." *Toronto Sun*, 26 Apr. 1997.

————. " 'Harlem Duet' a Powerful Piece." *Toronto Sun*, 4 July 2006.

Cushman, Robert. "Playing the Race Bard." *National Post*, 10 July 2006. AL4.

Dickinson, Peter. "Duets, Duologues, and Black Diasporic Theatre: Djanet Sears, William Shakespeare, and Others." *Modern Drama* 45.2 (Summer 2002): 188–208. Rpt. *Canadian Shakespeare*, ed. Knutson. 101–16.

Donnelly, Pat. "Race, Jealousy, and a Standout Script." *Montreal Gazette*, 27 Oct. 2012. E9.

Elam, Harry J., Jr. "Remembering Africa, Performing Cultural Memory: Lorraine Hansberry, Suzan-Lori Parks and Djanet Sears." *Signatures of the Past*, ed. Maufort and De Wagter. 31–48.

Erickson, Peter. *Citing Shakespeare: The Reinterpretation of Race in Contemporary Literature and Art*. NY: Palgrave Macmillan, 2007. Ch. 6.

Fischlin, Daniel. "Nation and/as Adaptation: Shakespeare, Canada, and Authenticity." *Shakespeare in Canada*, ed. Brydon and Makaryk. 313–38.

Friedman, Sharon. "The Feminist Playwright as Critic: Paula Vogel, Ann-Marie MacDonald, and Djanet Sears Interpret *Othello*." *Feminist Theatrical Revisions of Classic Works: Critical Essays*. Ed. Sharon Friedman. Jefferson, NC: McFarland, 2009. 113–31.

Gruber, Elizabeth. "Practical Magic: Empathy and Alienation in *Harlem Duet*." *LIT: Literature Interpretation Theory* 19.4 (2008): 346–66.

Hannaham, James. "Defiance and the Boogie-Woogie: The State of Black Theater in New York." *The Village Voice*, 8 Jan. 2003. 58–59.

Harrington, Louise. " 'Excuse Me While I Turn This Upside-Down': Three Canadian Adaptations of Shakespeare." *British Journal of Canadian Studies* 20.1 (May 2007): 123–42.

Hood, Sarah B. "Adventures of a Black Playwright in Search of Community." *CanPlay* 21 (Spring 2004): 15–17.

Kaplan, Jon. "A Riveting Duet." *Now*, 31 Aug.–7 Sept. 2006.

Kidnie, Margaret Jane. "There's Magic in the Web of It: Seeing Beyond Tragedy in *Harlem Duet*." *Journal of Commonwealth Literature* 36.2 (2001): 29–44. Rpt. *African-Canadian Theatre*, ed. Moynagh. 40–55.

————. *Shakespeare and the Problem of Adaptation*. NY: Routledge, 2009. Ch. 3.

Knowles, Ric. "*Othello* in Three Times." *Shakespeare in Canada*, ed. Brydon and Makaryk. 371–94. Rpt. Knowles, *Shakespeare and Canada*. Ch. 6.

MacDonald, Ron Foley. "Exquisite Theatre in *Harlem Duet*." *Halifax Daily News*, 9 Apr. 2000. 27.

Moser, Marlene. "From Performing Wholeness to Providing Choices: Situated Knowledges in *Afrika Solo* and *Harlem Duet*." *Theatre Research in Canada* 29.2 (2008): 239–57.

Newmark, Judith. "Tale of Lost Love Has Political Overtones." *St. Louis Post-Dispatch*, 27 Apr. 2008. F7.

Nolan, Yvette. "*Harlem Duet*." *Prairie Fire* 19 (Summer 1998): 199–200.

Nurse, Donna Bailey. "Black in Print." *Globe and Mail*, 21 Feb. 2004. D15.

————. "An *Othello* Built for the Nineties." *Globe and Mail*, 18 Nov. 1997. C5.

Ouzounian, Richard. "Playwright Takes NY by Storm." *Toronto Star*, 24 Nov. 2002. D2.

————. "Woman in Pain Lifts *Harlem Duet*." *Toronto Star*, 30 June 2006. C9.

Petropoulos, Jacqueline. "Performing African Canadian Identity: Diasporic Reinvention in *Afrika Solo*." *Feminist Review* 84 (2006): 104–23.

Sanders, Leslie. "*Othello* Deconstructed: Djanet Sears' *Harlem Duet*." *Testifyin': Contemporary African Canadian Drama*, vol. 1. Ed. Djanet Sears. Toronto: Playwrights Canada, 2000. 557–59.

Scott, Shelley. *Nightwood Theatre: A Woman's Work Is Always Done*. Edmonton: AU Press, 2010.

Sears, Djanet. "Afterword." *Afrika Solo* by Djanet Sears. Toronto: Sister Vision, 1990. 95–101.

————. "The AfriCanadian Playwrights' Festival." *CTR* 118 (Spring 2004): 3–5.

————. "Introduction." *Testifyin': Contemporary African Canadian Drama*, vol. 1, ed. Sears. Toronto: Playwrights Canada, 2000. i–xiii.

————. "Naming Names: Black Women Playwrights in Canada." *Women on the Canadian Stage*, ed. Much. 92–103.

————. "nOTES oF a cOLOURED gIRL: 32 sHORT rEASONS wHY i wRITE fOR tHE tHEATRE." *Harlem Duet* by Djanet Sears. Winnipeg: Scirocco, 1997. 11–16.

Sears, Djanet, and Alison Sealy Smith. "The Nike Method." *CTR* 97 (Winter 1998): 24–30.

Smith, Gary. "Stratford's *Harlem Duet* Deserves to Be Seen." *Spectator* (Hamilton), 26 Aug. 2006. D18.

Taylor, Kate. "*Harlem Duet*." *Globe and Mail*, 28 Apr. 1997. C3.

Thieme, John. "A Different 'Othello Music': Djanet Sears's *Harlem Duet*." *Performing National Identities*, ed. Grace and Glaap. 81–91.

Tompkins, Joanne. "Infinitely Rehearsing Performance and Identity: *Afrika Solo* and *The Book of Jessica*." *CTR* 74 (Spring 1993): 35–39.

————. "The Politics of Location in *Othello*, Djanet Sears's *Harlem Duet*, and Ong Keng Sen's *Desdemona*." *Contemporary Theatre Review* 19.3 (2009): 269–78.

Wagner, Vit. "Theatre as It Should Be." *Toronto Star*, 27 Apr. 1997. B3.

Wasserman, Jerry. "Where Is Here Now? Living the Border in the New Canadian Drama." *Crucible of Cultures*, ed. Maufort and Bellarsi. 83–93. Rpt. *"Ethnic," Multicultural, and Intercultural Theatre*, ed. Knowles and Mündel. 83–93.

————. "Whose Blues? AfriCanadian Theatre and the Blues Aesthetic." *Theatre Research in Canada* 30.1–2 (2009): 37–57.

Yhap, Beverly. "On Their Own Terms." *CTR* 56 (Fall 1988): 25–30.

RONNIE BURKETT and *Street of Blood*

Anthony, Vincent. "A Snapshot of Puppeteers of the United States and Canada." *American Puppetry: Collections, History, and Performance.* Ed. Phyllis T. Dircks. Jefferson, NC: McFarland, 2004. 9–21.

Astle, Robert. *Theatre Without Borders.* Winnipeg: Signature, 2002. 106–22.

Blumenthal, Eileen. *Puppetry: A World History.* NY: Harry N. Abrams, 2005.

Brantley, Ben. "Jesus May Pull the Strings in this Town, but this Marionette Has Other Ideas." *New York Times*, 8 Sept. 2000. E3.

Brennan, Brian. "No Fairy-Tale Ending on an AIDS Deathbed." *Edmonton Journal*, 7 Mar. 1992. B6.

Brown, Mark. "Pulling Strings." *Scotland on Sunday*, 9 June 2002.

Burkett, Ronnie. "The Mentored Path." *CTR* 84 (Fall 1995): 16–21.

————. "On Puppetry Organizations and Whether We Even Need Them." *Puppetry Journal* 58.4 (Summer 2007): 23–29.

Coffey, David. "Pandemonium Prairie." *Xtra!*, 7 Oct. 1999.

Cushman, Robert. "Compelling Characters with Strings Attached." *National Post*, 24 Sept. 1999. B12.

Feingold, Michael. "Puppet States." *The Village Voice*, 22 Sept. 1998. 153.

Friedlander, Mira. "Street of Blood." *Variety*, 3–9 Jan. 2000. 89.

Gardner, Lyn. " 'Puppetry is Ridiculous – I Wouldn't Pay to See It.' " *Guardian* (London), 27 Apr. 2004. 14.

————. "Love among the Puppets: *Street of Blood*." *Guardian* (London), 17 May 2002. 16.

Giltz, Michael. "Gay Strings Attached." *The Advocate* 823 (24 Oct. 2000): 87.

Hutchinson, Alex. "The Puppet Master and the Apprentice." *Walrus* 7.3 (Apr. 2010): 64–68.

Isherwood, Charles. "Street of Blood." *Variety*, 11–17 Sept. 2000. 32–33.

Kennedy, Janice. "Dear Mr. Burkett: You're a Fabulous Puppeteer, but You Do Go On." *Ottawa Citizen*, 7 May 1998. H8.

Lacy, Liam. "This Man Pulls His Own Strings." *Globe and Mail*, 2 Nov. 1991. C10.

Mansfield, Susan. "That String Thing." *The Scotsman* (Glasgow), 29 May 2002.

Morrow, Martin. "Jesus Spotted in Turnip Corners." *National Post*, 16 Nov. 1998. D4.

————. "Homophobia to Jellied Salad: Ronnie Burkett Covers It All." *Calgary Herald*, 19 Nov. 1998. B12.

Nicholls, Liz. "Marionettes Linked by Blood." *Edmonton Journal*, 9 Jan. 1999. C2.

————. "More Marionette Madness." *Edmonton Journal*, 7 Jan. 1999. C1.

————. "Puppet Love." *Edmonton Journal*, 25 Sept. 1997. D1.

————. "Puppet State: Alberta – Home of the New Puppet Radicalism." *Alberta Views* (July–Aug. 2003): 37–42.

————. "World on a String." *CTR* 95 (Summer 1998): 31–37.

Nunns, Stephen. "Holiday for Strings." *American Theatre* 17.7 (Sept. 2000): 32–35, 89–91.

O'Connor, C.J. "Blood on the Boards." *Eye Weekly*, 23 Sept. 1999.

O'Connor, Jennifer. "Pulling Strings, Making Trouble." *This* 41.3 (Nov.–Dec. 2007): 18–21.

Periale, Andrew. "Breaking the Boundaries." *Puppetry Journal* 52 (2000): 2.

Scott, Alec. "Guys 'n' Dolls." *Toronto Life* 40 (Apr. 2006): 33–36.

Stephenson, Jenn. *Performing Autobiography.* Ch. 5.

Taylor, Kate. "A Flawed but Seminal Work from Risk-Taker Burkett." *Globe and Mail*, 24 Sept. 1999. C9.

————. "Puppeteer Tugs at Heartstrings." *Globe and Mail*, 10 Apr. 1998. C2.

JOAN MacLEOD and *The Shape of a Girl*

Adcock, Joe. "Thought Provoking but Tough to Watch." *Seattle Post-Intelligencer*, 2 Mar. 2004. E6.

Belliveau, George. "Investigating British Columbia's Past: *The Komagata Maru Incident* and *The Hope Slide* as Historiographic Metadrama." *BC Studies* 137 (Spring 2003): 93–106.

Birnie, Peter. "Youth's Trials and Joys in Good Shape." *Vancouver Sun*, 12 Oct. 2001. F5.

Byers, Michele. "Putting on Reena Virk: Celebrity, Authorship, and Identity." *Reena Virk: Critical Perspectives on a Canadian Murder.* Ed. Mythili Rajiva and Sheila Batacharya. Toronto: Canadian Scholars' / Women's, 2010. 199–234.

————. "The Stuff of Legend: T/Selling the Story of Reena Virk." *Canadian Ethnic Studies* 41.3 (2010): 27–48.

Chamberlain, Adrian. "Bullying, in *The Shape of a Girl*." *Times-Colonist* (Victoria), 21 Feb. 2002. D7.

Coulbourn, John. "Bully for this Shape." *Toronto Sun*, 13 May 2011.

————. "Girl Has Many Shapes." *Toronto Sun*, 30 Mar. 2002.

Cushman, Robert. "An 'Emotional Truth' in Play about Girls Who Bully." *National Post*, 30 Mar. 2002. T08.

Derksen, Céleste. "B.C. Oddities: Interpellation and/in Joan MacLeod's *The Hope Slide*." *CTR* 101 (Winter 2000): 49–52.

Gabruch, Jenny. "Terrible Teens: Youth Play Examines Bullying." *Saskatoon Sun*, 3 Feb. 2002. 27.

Gallagher, Kathleen. "Interrogating Talk about 'Not Fitting In': Using Drama to Work through Gendered Issues of Education [*The Shape of a Girl* workshop]." *Orbit* 34.1 (2004): 12–15.

Glaap, Albert-Reiner, and Michael Heinze. "Tackling the Bully: Joan MacLeod's *The Shape of a Girl*." *Contemporary Canadian Plays*. 133–41.

Godfrey, Rebecca. *Under the Bridge: The True Story of the Murder of Reena Virk*. Toronto: HarperCollins, 2005.

Heylin, Liam. "*The Shape of a Girl*." *Irish Theatre Magazine*, 27 Oct. 2010.

Jones, Chris. "Pegasus Players' 'The Shape of a Girl' Gets Lost in Emotional Crisis." *Chicago Tribune*, 5 Mar. 2009.

Kirchhoff, H.J. "The Reincarnation of Joan MacLeod." *Globe and Mail*, 28 Mar. 1992. C6.

Leiren-Young, Mark. "Joan MacLeod: The Shape of a Playwright." *CanPlay* 22.4 (Fall 2004): 16–17.

MacLeod, Joan. "Dreaming Scout." *CTR* 133 (Winter 2008): 17–20.

———. "Interview with Joan MacLeod." *Capilano Review* 2.12 (1994): 68–90.

Mazey, Steven. "A 'Bully' Deftly Explores Her Crisis of Conscience." *Ottawa Citizen*, 14 Feb. 2003. E8.

Miliokas, Nick. " 'Shape of a Girl' Carries a Valuable Message." *Leader-Post* (Regina) 11 Jan. 2003. A9.

Morrow, Fiona. "My Plays Are All about Family." *Globe and Mail*, 14 Mar. 2009. R12.

Much, Rita. "Joan MacLeod Interview." *Fair Play*, ed. Rudakoff and Much. 190–207.

Nevius, C.W. "Girl Bullies' Quiet Style of Brutality." *San Francisco Chronicle*, 1 Mar. 2005. B1.

Nicholls, Liz. "Taut Production Shines Its Light into Shadows Where Evil Breeds." *Edmonton Journal*, 2 Feb. 2002. E6.

———. "Trail of Guilt Doesn't End with Perpetrator." *Edmonton Journal*, 26 Nov. 2002. C2.

Nothof, Anne. "The Construction and Deconstruction of Border Zones in *Fronteras Americanas* by Guillermo Verdecchia and *Amigo's Blue Guitar* by Joan MacLeod." *Theatre Research in Canada* 20.1 (Spring 1999): 3–15.

Radz, Matt. "*Cette fille-là* Inspired, Superbly Executed." *Montreal Gazette*, 28 Mar. 2004. B4.

Ratsoy, Ginny. "Dramatizing Alterity: Relational Characterization in Postcolonial British Columbia Plays." *Embracing the Other: Addressing Xenophobia in the New Literatures in English*. Ed. Dunja M. Mohr. Amsterdam: Rodopi, 2008. 295–306.

Scott, Shelley. "Hell Is Other Girls: Joan MacLeod's *The Shape of a Girl*." *Modern Drama* 45.2 (2002): 270–81.

———. *The Violent Woman as a New Theatrical Character Type: Cases from Canadian Drama*. Lewiston, NY: Edwin Mellen, 2007.

Stewart, Jesse. "Politics and Plays: Playwrights Discuss the Nature Social Role, and Reception of Political Theatre." Ed. Ric Knowles. *CTR* 115 (Summer 2003): 52–56.

Taylor, Kate. "Girl Fights." *Globe and Mail*, 29 Mar. 2002. R2.

Tompkins, Joanne. "The Shape of a Life: Constructing the 'Self' and 'Other' in Joan MacLeod's *The Shape of a Girl* and Guillermo Verdecchia and Marcus Youssef's *A Line in the Sand*." *Theatre and AutoBiography*, ed. Grace and Wasserman. 124–36.

Wasserman, Jerry. "Introduction." *The Shape of a Girl / Jewel* by Joan MacLeod. Vancouver: Talonbooks, 2002. 7–11.

———. "Joan MacLeod and the Geography of the Imagination." *Performing National Identities*, ed. Grace and Glapp. 92–103. Rpt. *Theatre in British Columbia*, ed. Ratsoy. 153–64.

Youds, Mike. "Play Explores Vulnerability and Violence." *Kamloops Daily News*, 20 Sept. 2001. A12.

Zinoman, Jason. "When Mean Girls Are Not Stopped." *New York Times*, 26 Jan. 2005. E5.

ROBERT CHAFE and *Tempting Providence*

Birnie, Peter. "Exquisite Piece of Stagecraft at PuSh." *Vancouver Sun*, 12 Jan. 2006. D7.

Chamberlain, Adrian. "Stalwart Newfoundland Nurse Inspires Actress." *Times-Colonist* (Victoria), 2 Mar. 2006. D7.

Citron, Paula. "An Eventful Life, Simply Presented." *Globe and Mail*, 7 Apr. 2007. R16.

Clark, Bob. "Tempting Production a Visual Treat." *Calgary Herald*, 17 Mar. 2007. D3.

Cushman, Robert. "Our Town Revisited, a Nurse Discovered." *National Post*, 14 Apr. 2007. TO20.

DeMara, Bruce. "Nursing the Rock to Life." *Toronto Star*, 6 Apr. 2007. C11.

Devine, Michael. "Keileydography: The Symphonic Theatre of Jillian Keiley." *CTR* 128 (Fall 2006): 31–36.

Glaap, Albert-Reiner, and Michael Heinze. *Contemporary Canadian Plays*. 117–32.

Green, H. Gordon. *Don't Have Your Baby in the Dory: A Biography of Myra Bennett*. Eugene, OR: Harvest House, 1974.

Keiley, Jillian. "Igniting Imaginations with Actor-Manipulated Design." *CTR* 150 (Spring 2012): 53–55.

———. "Theatre Unplugged: The Technology of a Performer-Centred Theatre." *CTR* 131 (Summer 2007): 99–101.

Keiley, Jillian, and Robert Chafe. "An Introduction to Artistic Fraud of Newfoundland." *Theatre Research in Canada* 26.1–2 (2005): 105–13.

Langston, Patrick. "A Striking Portrait of a Nurse's Heroism." *Ottawa Citizen*, 10 Jan. 2009. F4.

Lawson, Catherine. "Story of Heroic Nurse a Compelling Portrait." *Ottawa Citizen*, 24 Apr. 2003. E2.

Lynde, Denyse. "Introduction." *Robert Chafe: Two Plays*. Toronto: Playwrights Canada, 2004. iii–ix.

————. "Robert Chafe: The Last Two Years in Review." *CTR* 128 (Fall 2006): 58–62.

McMillan, Joyce. "Fringe Reviews: *Tempting Providence*." *The Scotsman*, 14 Aug. 2004. 10.

Posner, Michael. "Toronto Catches Up to Cow Head." *Globe and Mail*, 14 Apr. 2007. R9.

Prokosh, Kevin. "Cast, Director Spin Dramatic Gold from Historical Yarn." *Winnipeg Free Press*, 16 Nov. 2007. D4.

Rigler, Michael. "Nurse Myra Bennett Captured Playwright's Passion." *Telegram* (St. John's) 10 June 2002. B4.

Smillie, Ruth. "Magic Happens behind the Scenes." *Leader-Post* (Regina), 12 Oct. 2006. D1.

Spencer, Charles. "A Tempting Tale of Old-Fashioned Heroism." *Telegraph* (London), 9 Aug. 2004. 15.

Stacey, Jean Edwards. "Writer Loves Acting." *Telegram* (St. John's), 1 Dec. 2002. B3.

Todkill, Anne Marie. "Extreme Nursing." *Canadian Medical Association Journal* 171 (26 Oct. 2004): 1079–80.

Wasserman, Jerry. "Understated but Spectacular." *Province* (Vancouver), 12 Jan. 2006. B2.

WAJDI MOUAWAD and *Scorched*

Al-Solaylee, Kamal. "Mouawad Works in Many Languages." *Globe and Mail*, 11 Nov. 2005. R29.

————. "White-Hot Epic Is a Tour de Force." *Globe and Mail*, 1 Mar. 2007. R4.

Arseneault, Michel. "Solidarity of the Shaken: Wajdi Mouawad's Theatre of War." *Walrus* 10.3 (Dec. 2006–Jan. 2007): 88–90.

Bickis, Heidi. "Shared Histories and Collective Stories." *CTR* 129 (Winter 2007): 95–96.

Charlebois, Gaetan L. "Doubt and Faith." *Montreal Gazette*, 26 May 2003. D5.

Choplin, Olivia. "Où placer les bombes? Art and Violence in Wajdi Mouawad's *Le sang des promesses*." *Quebec Studies* 54 (Fall–Winter 2012): 77–87.

Clark, Bob. "Sage's *Scorched* Proves More of a Slow Burn." *Calgary Herald*, 21 Nov. 2009. D5.

Coveney, Michael. "*Scorched*." *Independent* (London), 18 Sept. 2010. 24.

Cushman, Robert. "Devastation All Around." *National Post*, 3 Mar. 2007. TO21.

Dahab, Elizabeth. *Voices of Exile in Contemporary Canadian Francophone Literature*. Lanham, MD: Lexington Books, 2009. Ch. 5.

Donnelly, Pat. "The Play at Home." *Montreal Gazette*, 6 Oct. 2008. A3.

————. "Silent Heirs Are Saddled with Bizarre Conditions." *Montreal Gazette*, 11 Oct. 2008. E3.

Evans, Everett. "*Scorched* Reveals One Family's Tragedy." *Houston Chronicle*, 12 Aug. 2009. 4.

Fisk, Robert. "Torture in Lebanon via a Toronto Stage." *Independent* (London), 10 Mar. 2007. 46.

Furey, Anthony. "Haunted Legacy: Striking New Theatre Explores the Wreckage of a War-Torn Century." *Literary Review of Canada* 17.10 (Dec. 2009): 16–17.

Gaboriau, Linda. "Finding Just '*le Mot Juste*': *Scorched* Dramaturg Beatrice Basso Interviews Translator Linda Gaboriau." *Scorched: Words on Plays* 18.4 (San Francisco: American Conservatory Theatre, 2012): 11–19.

Gana, Nouri. "Everyday Arabness: The Poethics of Arab Canadian Literature and Film." *New Centennial Review* 9.2 (Fall 2009): 21–44.

Gardner, Lyn. "*Scorched*." *Guardian* (London), 10 Sept. 2010. 40.

Gauthier, Natasha. "Hope Emerges out of Despair." *Ottawa Citizen*, 16 Oct. 2003. E3.

————. "*Scorched* Suffers a Little in English Translation." *Ottawa Citizen*, 7 Apr. 2007. H10.

Hallett, Bryce. "Step by Step into a Tragic Heritage." *Sydney Morning Herald*, 25 July 2008. 16.

Hemming, Sarah. "*Scorched*." *Financial Times* (London), 10 Sept. 2010. 11.

Hurley, Erin. "What Consolation? *Incendies* on Stage and Screen." *alt.theatre* 8.3 (Mar. 2011): 23–28.

Isherwood, Charles. "Bearing Witness to the Chaos of War." *New York Times*, 22 Mar. 2009. AR9.

Jennings, Sarah. *Art and Politics: The History of the National Arts Centre*. Toronto: Dundurn, 2009.

Marlowe, Sam. "*Scorched*." *Times* (London), 8 Sept. 2010. 55.

McCallum, John. "Letters Stir the Plot in Distant War Zone." *Australian* (Sydney), 28 July 2008. 16.

Meerzon, Yana. "The Exilic Teens: On the Intracultural Encounters in Wajdi Mouawad's Theatre." *Theatre Research in Canada* 30.1–2 (2009): 82–110.

————. *Performing Exile, Performing Self: Drama, Theatre, Film*. NY: Palgrave Macmillan, 2012. Ch. 5.

————. "Searching for Poetry: On Collective Collaboration in Wajdi Mouawad's Theatre." *CTR* 143 (Summer 2010): 29–34.

―――. "Staging Memory in Wajdi Mouawad's *Incendies*: Archeological Site or Poetic Venue?" *Theatre Research in Canada* 34.1 (Spring 2013): 12–36.

Moss, Jane. "The Drama of Survival: Staging Post-Traumatic Memory in Plays by Lebanese-Québécois Dramatists." *Theatre Research in Canada* 22.2 (2001): 173–89.

Nestruck, J. Kelly. "A Haunting Look into Humanity's Dark Corners." *Globe and Mail*, 8 Sept. 2008. R3.

Nicholls, Liz. "Director Liked What He 'Saw.' " *Edmonton Journal*, 10 Jan. 2009. D1.

―――. "Racing in Circles through Time and Space." *Edmonton Journal*, 17 Jan. 2009. D6.

Ouzounian, Richard. "Pain Scented with Poetry." *Toronto Star*, 28 Feb. 2007. B4.

Pressley, Nelson. "*Scorched*: A Searing Tale of Love and War." *Washington Post*, 7 Oct. 2010. C2.

Preston, Virginia. "Imag/ing Theatre in Wajdi Mouawad's *Seuls*." *TheatreForum* 35 (Summer–Fall 2009): 17–25.

Prokosh, Kevin. "A Literally Breathtaking Tragedy." *Winnipeg Free Press*, 14 Nov. 2008. D3.

Radz, Matt. "*Incendies* Walks Tall in Trenches." *Montreal Gazette*, 8 Nov. 2006. D7.

Rubin, Dan. "Wajdi Mouawad: At Home with Words." *Scorched: Words on Plays* 18.4 (San Francisco: American Conservatory Theatre, 2012): 4–10.

Telmissany, May. "Wajdi Mouawad in Cinema: Origins, Wars, and Fate." *CineAction!* 88 (Summer 2012): 48–57.

Wilson, Calvin. "Siblings' Search of Their Mother's Past Is Provocative and Challenging." *St. Louis Post-Dispatch*, 14 Sept. 2008. F8.

MARCUS YOUSSEF, GUILLERMO VERDECCHIA, CAMYAR CHAI and *The Adventures of Ali & Ali and the aXes of Evil*

Adams, Rachel. *Continental Divides: Remapping the Cultures of North America*. Chicago: U of Chicago P, 2009.

Adcock, Joe. "Diabolically Funny, 'Ali and Ali' Takes Aim at Bush & Co." *Seattle Post-Intelligencer*, 18 May 2007. 27.

Al-Solaylee, Kamal. "The World According to Ali and Ali." *Globe and Mail*, 23 Feb. 2004. R8.

Barton, Bruce. "Communicating across '*Fronteras*': Wideload on the Wide Screen." *Essays in Theatre* 20.2 (May 2002): 113–36.

Berson, Misha. "Political Satire with an Extra Bite." *Seattle Times*, 18 May 2007. E1.

Birnie, Peter "How to Skewer Liberal Smugness." *Vancouver Sun*, 12 Feb. 2004. C7.

Chamberlain, Adrian. "Score One for Appendicitis." *Times-Colonist* (Victoria), 9 May 2007. C11.

Coady, Lynn. "Irony Is Alive and Wearing a Pair of Boot Cut Jeans." *Globe and Mail*, 17 Feb. 2004. R1.

Corey, Paul. "Canadian Theatre and the Tragic Experience of Evil." *Theatre Research in Canada* 27.2 (Fall 2006): 289–314.

Coulbourn, John. "*Ali & Ali* Not the Greatest." *Toronto Sun*, 23 Feb. 2004.

Coulthard, Lisa. " 'The Line's Getting Mighty Blurry': Politics, Polemics and Performance in *The Noam Chomsky Lectures*." *Studies in Canadian Literature* 20.2 (Summer 1995): 44–56.

Cushman, Robert. "Brought to You by Osama." *National Post*, 24 Feb. 2004. AL2.

Gomez, Mayte. "Healing the Border Wound: *Fronteras Americanas* and the Future of Canadian Multiculturalism." *Theatre Research in Canada* 16.1–2 (1995): 26–39.

Harvie, Jennifer. "The Nth Degree: An Interview with Guillermo Verdecchia." *CTR* 92 (Fall 1997): 46–49.

Hoekstra, Matthew. "Balancing Tragedy with Comedy." *Review* (Richmond, BC), 23 Feb. 2006. 16.

Kaplan, Jon. "Axes' Satiric Spin." *Now* 23.25, 19–26 Feb. 2004.

Kareda, Urjo. "Foreword." *Fronteras Americanas / American Borders* by Guillermo Verdecchia. Vancouver: Talonbooks, 1997. 9–12.

Kerr, Rosalind. "Theatre as a Weapon against Mass Delusion." *CTR* 120 (Fall 2004): 91–93.

Ledingham, Jo. "Mad, Mad World of *Ali and Ali* Goes into Chaotic Overdrive." *Vancouver Courier*, 15 Feb. 2004. 36.

Nicholls, Liz. "Mideast Vaudeville Full of Charm, Cheese." *Edmonton Journal*, 13 June 2004. B5.

Nothof, Anne. "The Construction and Deconstruction of Border Zones in *Fronteras Americanas* by Guillermo Verdecchia and *Amigo's Blue Guitar* by Joan MacLeod." *Theatre Research in Canada* 20.1 (Spring 1999): 3–15.

Ouzounian, Richard. "Give these Guys the Axes." *Toronto Star*, 23 Feb. 2004. E3.

Posner, Michael. "Actor-Playwright Has Always Taken the Challenging Road." *Globe and Mail*, 14 June 1999. C4.

Radz, Matt. "Political Theatre Fails Yet Again." *Montreal Gazette*, 14 Mar. 2004. B4.

Sadowski-Smith, Claudia. *Border Fictions: Globalization, Empire, and Writing at the Boundaries of the United States*. Charlottesville: U of Virginia P, 2008.

Sherman, Jason. "The Daniel Brooks Lectures." *CTR* 67 (Summer 1991): 17–21.

Stewart, Jesse. "The Politics and Business of Playwriting." Ed. Ric Knowles. *CTR* 115 (Summer 2003): 43–46.

Taylor, Kate. "Enter Gomery, to Keep Our Theatre Alive." *Globe and Mail*, 28 May 2005. R2.

Thomas, Colin. "*The Adventures of Ali & Ali and the aXes of Evil*." *Georgia Straight*, 19 Feb. 2004.

Verdecchia, Guillermo. "Blahblahblahblah Memememememe Theatreschmeatre." *Theatre and AutoBiography*, ed. Grace and Wasserman. 332–35.

————. "*Léo* at the Tarragon: Naturalizing the Coup." *Theatre Research in Canada* 30.1–2 (2009): 111–28.

————. "Politics in Playwriting." *Betty Lambert Society Newsletter* (Sept. 1992): 2–4.

Verdecchia, Guillermo, et al. "Culture Inc." *This* 32.2 (Sept.–Oct. 1998): 14–17.

Wasserman, Jerry. "Bombing (on) the Border: *Ali & Ali and the aXes of Evil* as Transnational Agitprop." *Modern Drama* 51.1 (Spring 2008): 126–44.

————. "Remembering Agraba: Canadian Political Theatre and the Construction of Cultural Memory." *Signatures of the Past*, ed. Maufort and De Wagter. 101–14.

————. " 'We Know You're not Somalia': Radical Performance and Canadian-American Exile in *Ali & Ali and the aXes of Evil*." *Performance, Exile, and "America."* Ed. Silvija Jestrovic and Yana Meerzon. NY: Palgrave Macmillan, 2009. 220–43.

Youssef, Marcus. "On the Beauty of Our Perpetual Marginality, and Why it Might Be Time for All of Us to Figure Out Our Position on Social Housing." *CTR* 150 (Spring 2012): 34–35.

LINDA GRIFFITHS and *Age of Arousal*

Al-Solaylee, Kamal. "Busting Out of Corsets and Genres." *Globe and Mail*, 27 Nov. 2007. R4.

Bateman, David. "*Age of Arousal*: We Are Amused." *Xtra!*, 6 Dec. 2007.

Bennett, Susan. "Performing Lives: Linda Griffiths and Other Famous Women." *Performing National Identities*, ed. Grace and Glaap. 25–37.

Bessai, Diane. *Playwrights of Collective Creation*. Ch. 5.

Brown, Mark. "Poetic Script Captures Early Age of Feminism." *Sunday Herald* (Glasgow), 6 Mar. 2011. 59.

Burnside, Anna. "*Age of Arousal*, Tron Theatre, Glasgow." *Independent* (London), 21 Mar. 2011. 24.

Clark, Bob. "Griffiths Arouses Greatness." *Calgary Herald*, 17 Feb. 2007. D3.

Cooper, Neil. "Linda Griffiths – *Age of Arousal*." *Herald* (Glasgow), 15 Mar. 2011.

Cushman, Robert. "Get Thee behind a Typewriter." *National Post*, 1 Dec. 2007. TO22.

Donnelly, Pat. "Wonderful Cast, Clever Exchanges Highlight Griffiths's *Age of Arousal*." *Montreal Gazette*, 28 Mar. 2009. E6.

Fisher, Mark. "Age of Arousal." *Guardian* (London), 26 Feb. 2011. 42.

Gissing, George. *The Odd Women* (1893). NY: Penguin, 1994.

Griffiths, Linda. *Age of Arousal*. Toronto: Coach House, 2007.

————. "I Am a Thief … Not Necessarily Honourable Either." *Theatre and AutoBiography*, ed. Grace and Wasserman. 301–05.

Griffiths, Linda, and Maria Campbell. *The Book of Jessica: A Theatrical Transformation*. Toronto: Coach House, 1989.

Kelly, Katherine E. "Making the Bones Sing: The Feminist History Play, 1976–2010." *Theatre Journal* 62.4 (Dec. 2010): 645–60.

Kerr, Don. "*Paper Wheat*: Epic Theatre in Saskatchewan." *Paper Wheat: The Book by 25th Street Theatre*. Saskatoon: Western Producer Prairie Books, 1982. 17–30.

McLeod, Katherine. "(Un)Covering the Mirror: Performative Reflections in Linda Griffiths's *Alien Creature: A Visitation from Gwendolyn MacEwen* and Wendy Lill's *The Occupation of Heather Rose*." *Theatre and AutoBiography*, ed. Grace and Wasserman. 89–104.

Miller, Melinda. "Great 'Age': Feminist Satire Is Both Poignant and Hilarious." *Buffalo News*, 20 Aug. 2010. G15.

Moss, Jennifer. "Inner Monologue Buoys Arousal." *Vancouver Sun*, 24 Apr. 2009. D2.

Nestruck, J. Kelly. "Women, Sex and Clashing Ideas." *Globe and Mail*, 18 Aug. 2010. R3.

Ouzounian, Richard. "She's Arousing Interest." *Toronto Star*, 17 Nov. 2007. E3.

Portman, Jamie. "*Age of Arousal* Not a Turn-On." *Ottawa Citizen*, 26 Aug. 2010. E6.

Prokosh, Kevin. "Play Wins Arousing Round of Applause." *Winnipeg Free Press*, 21 Mar. 2009. C3.

Rudakoff, Judith. "Linda Griffiths Interview." *Fair Play*, ed. Rudakoff and Much. 13–36.

Scott, Dawson. "A Hard Lesson in Suffrage at the Secretarial School." *Times* (London), 22 Feb. 2011. 18.

Scott, Shelley. *Nightwood Theatre: A Woman's Work Is Always Done*. Edmonton: AU Press, 2010.

————. "Sickness and Sexuality: Feminism and the Female Body in *Age of Arousal* and *Chronic*." *Theatre Research in Canada* 31.1 (Spring 2010): 37–56.

Shapiro, Howard. "Meaty Subject of Suffragism Suffers in the Telling." *Philadelphia Inquirer*, 14 Dec. 2007. W28.

Syam, Avimaan. "Age of Arousal." *Austin Chronicle*, 1 May 2009.

Thomas, Colin. "*Age of Arousal* Playfully Explores Dilemma between Feminism and Heterosexuality." *Georgia Straight*, 23 Apr. 2009.

Wasserman, Jerry. "Alien Creatures and the Ecology of Illness: Linda Griffiths' *Chronic*." *Chronic* by Linda Griffiths. Toronto: Playwrights Canada, 2003. i–iv.

THEATRE REPLACEMENT and *BIOBOXES*

Hansen, Pil. "Private Acts: Devising *Clark and I* from Found Memories." *CTR* 142 (Spring 2010): 24–29.

Kim, Christine. "Performing Asian-Canadian Intimacy: Theatre Replacement's *BIOBOXES* and Awkward Multiculturalisms." *Asian Canadian Theatre*, ed. Aquino and Knowles. 183–94.

Langston, Patrick. "From the Theatre of the Left Coast." *Ottawa Citizen*, 20 Apr. 2009. C5.

Ledingham, Jo. "*BIOBOXES* Gets in Your Face: Trippy Show Is a One-on-One Performance with an Actor." *Vancouver Courier*, 31 Jan. 2007. 31.

Levin, Laura, et al. "Performing Outside of the Box." *CTR* 137 (Winter 2009): 61–67.

Long, James. "*Clark and I Somewhere in Connecticut*: Family Albums Lost and Found." *Geist* 67 (Winter 2007): 38–43.

———. "Dear Citizens of Tennessee." *CTR* 145 (Winter 2011): 56–59.

Long, James, and Maiko Bae Yamamoto. "Manifesto." Vancouver: PuSh International Performing Arts Festival, Feb. 2009. http://www.theatrereplacement.org/media/files/manifesto-tr.pdf.

Miliokas, Nick. " 'BioBoxes' Real In-Your-Face Theatre." *Leader-Post* (Regina), 18 Sept. 2008. B3.

Nestruck, J. Kelly. "One-at-a-Time Show Is Brilliant Dramatic Thinking inside the Box." *Globe and Mail*, 30 Apr. 2009. R3.

Scott, Michael. "One-on-One Theatre 'a Real Trip' for Performers." *Vancouver Sun*, 1 Feb. 2007. B5.

Solga, Kim. "Arifacting an Intercultural Nation: Theatre Replacement's *BIOBOXES*." *TDR* 54.1 (Spring 2010): 161–66.

Stephenson, Jenn. "BioBoxes: Artifacting Human Experience." *New Canadian Realisms: Eight Plays*. Ed. Roberta Barker and Kim Solga. Toronto: Playwrights Canada, 2012. 128–33.

Thomas, Colin. "*Bioboxes: Artifacting Human Experience*." *Georgia Straight*, 31 Jan. 2007.

Wasserman, Jerry. "*BIOBOXES: Artifacting Human Experience*." Vancouverplays.com, Jan. 2007. http://www.vancouverplays.com/theatre/reviews_theatre/review_bioboxes.shtml.

———. "Collective Creation on the West Coast." *CTR* 135 (Summer 2008): 52–54.

———. "The View beyond the Stage: Collective, Collaborative, and Site-Specific Performance in Vancouver." *Collective Creation, Collaboration and Devising*, ed. Barton. 242–52.

Yamamoto, Maiko Bae. "All That Remains." *CTR* 135 (Summer 2008): 82–84.

———. "Undressing." *CTR* 145 (Winter 2011): 40–42.

MARIE CLEMENTS and *The Edward Curtis Project*

Bamford, Karen. "Romance, Recognition and Revenge in Marie Clements's *The Unnatural and Accidental Women*." *Theatre Research in Canada* 31.2 (Fall 2010): 143–63.

Banting, Sarah. "Being There: Stage Presence and *The Unnatural and Accidental Women*." *West Coast Line* 41.1 (Spring 2007): 80–85, 126.

Clements, Marie. "In the End You Are Made Accountable." *Theatre and AutoBiography*, ed. Grace and Wasserman. 329–31.

Clements, Marie, and Rita Leistner. *The Edward Curtis Project: A Modern Picture Story*. Vancouver: Talonbooks, 2010.

Couture, Selena. "Frames of Mind: *Beyond Eden* and *The Edward Curtis Project*." *alt.theatre* 8.2 (Dec. 2010): 10–17.

———. "Women's Auto/biographical Theatre: Affirmation, Preservation, and Intercultural Communication." *CTR* 139 (Summer 2009): 36–42.

Curtis, Edward S. *Sacred Legacy: Edward S. Curtis and the North American Indian*. Ed. Christopher Cardozo. NY: Simon & Schuster, 2000.

Däwes, Birgit. *Indigenous North American Drama: A Multivocal History*. Albany: State U of New York P, 2013.

Gilbert, Reid. "Introduction: Marie Clements." *Theatre Research in Canada* 31.2 (Fall 2010): v–xv.

———. "Marie Clements's *The Unnatural and Accidental Women*: 'Denaturalizing' Genre." *Theatre Research in Canada* 24.1–2 (2003): 125–46.

Gray, Nelson. "The Murmuring-In-Between: Eco-centric Politics in *The Girl Who Swam Forever*." *Theatre Research in Canada* 31.2 (Fall 2010): 193–207.

———. " 'Yes to Everything' – A Conversation on Theatre and Ecology: with Daniel Brooks, Marie Clements, Kendra Fanconi, and Karen Hines." *CTR* 144 (Fall 2010): 20–28.

Hargreaves, Allison. "A Precise Instrument for Seeing: Remembrance in *Burning Vision* and the Activist Classroom." *CTR* 147 (Winter 2011): 49–54.

Harris, Michael. "An Intervention into Native Identity Leads to More Questions." *Globe and Mail*, 25 Jan. 2010. R5.

La Flamme, Michelle. "Theatrical Medicine: Aboriginal Performance, Ritual, and Commemoration (for Vanessa Lee Buckner)." *Theatre Research in Canada* 31.2 (Fall 2010): 107–17.

Langston, Patrick. "Falsehoods and Photographs." *Ottawa Citizen*, 1 Apr. 2013. D1.

———. "Race, Identity, and Survival: Richly Imagined Multimedia Production Explores Complex Themes." *Ottawa Citizen*, 6 Apr. 2013. D4.

May, Theresa J. "Kneading Marie Clements' *Burning Vision*." *CTR* 144 (Fall 2010): 5–12.

McFee, Erin. "New Project Revisits Cultural Classic." *North Shore News* (North Vancouver), 15 Jan. 2010. 24.

Nanibush, Wanda. "The Frozen Bodies of Edward S. Curtis." *Literary Review of Canada*, Apr. 2011.

Perry, Mia. " 'Women in Fish': Collaborating with History." *CTR* 121 (Winter 2005): 78–81.

Rabillard, Sheila. "*Age of Iron*: Adaptation and the Matter of Troy in Clements's Indigenous Urban Drama." *Theatre Research in Canada* 31.2 (Fall 2010): 118–42.

Read, Jennifer. "Marie Clements's Monstrous Visions." *CTR* 120 (Fall 2004): 19–23.

Ruprecht, Alvina. "Journeys with a Shaman: Marie Clements Talks about *Copper Thunderbird*." *alt.theatre* 5.3 (Feb. 2008): 16–21.

Schaefer, Glen. "Keeping Native Cultures in the Picture." *Province* (Vancouver), 21 Jan. 2010, B5.

Severini, Giorgia. " 'You Do Not Understand ME': Hybridity and Third Space in *Age of Iron*." *Theatre Research in Canada* 31.2 (Fall 2010): 182–92.

Smith, Annie. "Atomies of Desire: Directing Burning Vision in Northern Alberta." *CTR* 144 (Fall 2010): 54–59.

Smith, Janet. "*The Edward Curtis Project* Is Wildly Ambitious." *Georgia Straight*, 25 Jan. 2010.

Wasserman, Jerry. "*The Edward Curtis Project*." Vancouverplays.com, Jan. 2010. http://www.vancouverplays.com/theatre/reviews/review_edward_curtis_project_10.shtml.

Whittaker, Robin C. "Fusing the Nuclear Community: Intercultural Memory, Hiroshima 1945 and the Chronotopic Dramaturgy of Marie Clements's *Burning Vision*." *Theatre Research in Canada* 30.1–2 (2009): 129–51.

Wunker, Erin. "The. Women. The Subject(s) of *The Unnatural and Accidental Women* and *Unnatural and Accidental*." *Theatre Research in Canada* 31.2 (Fall 2010): 164–81.

Yhap, Beverly. "Unclassified and Controvertible: *The Edward Curtis Project* and *Beyond Eden* in Vancouver, 2010." *CTR* 147 (Summer 2011): 105–09.

INS CHOI and *Kim's Convenience*

Arya, Sumedha. "Kim Much More than Just Convenient." *Gazette* (London, ON.), 20 Jan. 2013.

Baccari, Eva. "As Store or Play, *Kim's Convenience* Is Canonically Canadian." *Toronto Review of Books*, 1 Feb. 2012.

Baker, Kelley Tish. "*Kim's Convenience*." *Prism International* 51. (Spring 2013).

Belanger, Joe. "Brilliant Performances Served with a Life Lesson – Worth Seeing." *London Free Press*, 18 Jan. 2013.

Choi, Ins. "Author's Note and Introduction." *Kim's Convenience* by Ins Choi. Toronto: Playwrights Canada, 2012. v, xi–xvii.

Coulbourn, John. "Plenty of Joy in Store." *Toronto Sun*, 20 Jan. 2012.

Cushman, Robert. "Depth of a Salesman." *National Post*, 24 Jan. 2012. AL4.

Lee, Esther Kim. " 'Patient Zero': Jean Yoon and Korean Canadian Theatre." *Asian Canadian Theatre*, ed. Aquino and Knowles. 62–78.

Michel, Jen Pollock. "How a Korean Prodigal Son Landed on Toronto's Stage." *Christianity Today*, 5 Dec. 2012.

Nestruck, J. Kelly. "Over the Counter." *Globe and Mail*, 21 Jan. 2012. R2.

Ouzounian, Richard. "The Big Interview: Ins Choi: Over the Counter Culture." *Toronto Star*, 14 Jan. 2012. E3.

———. "Ins Choi: Playwright, Actor: People to Watch 2012." *Toronto Star*, 1 Jan. 2012. E6.

———. "*Kim's Convenience* Distills Them All." *Toronto Star*, 20 Jan. 2012. E9.

Sumi, Glenn. "Actor-Writer Sells Some Hard-Hitting Immigrant Truths in *Kim's Convenience*." *Now* 30, 7–14 July 2011.

COPYRIGHT AND PERMISSIONS

JERRY
WASSERMAN

Professor of English and theatre at the University of British Columbia, Jerry Wasserman has written and lectured widely on Canadian theatre. Books include *Spectacle of Empire: Marc Lescarbot's Theatre of Neptune in New France* and *Theatre and AutoBiography* (with Sherrill Grace). He has more than two hundred professional acting credits on stage and screen, and has reviewed more than fifteen hundred plays for CBC Radio, the *Province* newspaper, and his website, Vancouverplays.com. Wasserman is a recipient of the Killam Teaching Prize (1998), the Dorothy Somerset Award (2005), and the Sam Payne Award (2012), honouring a lifetime of achievement in the performing arts.